GNVQ Advanced
Business

2nd Edition

Stephen Danks

Stephen Danks has wide experience of industry, commerce and teaching. Formerly a Head of Business Studies in a large Further Education College, he has also taught in schools. He is a successful author of business studies texts at both introductory and advanced level.

He is currently NVQ Chief Verifier for Pitman Examinations Institute and Senior Verifier for Business Administration. He is also a former BTEC examiner, RSA examiner and City and Guilds Assessor.

DP Publications Ltd
Aldine Place
London
W12 8AW

1995

Acknowledgements

I am grateful to the following for permission to reproduce copyright material in the text.

ASDA
AT&T
Barclays Bank
Bolton College
Burtonwood Brewery
Daewoo Cars Ltd
D.T.I.
Caroline Horrigan
Commission for Racial Equality
Crown Copyright
Daily Mail
Department of Trade and Industry
Employment Department
Ford Motor Company
Foreign and Commonwealth Office
Further Education Unit
Girobank plc
G. Mex
Godfrey Hill
The Guardian
Health and Safety Executive
Pieda plc, Manchester
Proctor & Gamble plc
Marketing Magazine
Safeways
Sainsbury's
Sunday Times

I also wish to thank all the organisations and newspapers for the use of other materials (despite every effort, I have failed to trace the copyright holders for some of the material used).

I am indebted to Jo Kemp, Catherine Tilley and Dick Chapman of DP Publications for their valuable assistance and advice, and to all the lecturers who kindly completed the market research survey.

A CIP catalogue record for this book is available from the British Library

ISBN 1 858051 52 5

Typeset by DPP and Elizabeth Elwin, London

Printed by WM Print, Walsall, West Midlands

Contents

(handwritten: ✗ - tests P - Passed)

Preface

Aim

The aim of this text is to provide comprehensive coverage of the 1995 specification for GNVQ Advanced Business mandatory units. Together with its lecturers' supplement it provides complete course material for schools and colleges.

Need

This text answers the need for material that:

- ❑ has a lively and clear approach to business studies, providing the knowledge base for **coursework** and **external** testing
- ❑ includes a wide **variety** of tasks and assignments to assist the gathering of **valid evidence** for the students' coursework portfolio
- ❑ presents business studies in a way that develops **core skills and techniques** such as numeracy, communication, information technology and the selection and use of relevant information
- ❑ includes material to help students **self assess** progress
- ❑ is supported by a free lecturers' supplement to help plan and control students' progress.

Approach

The text has been written in a structured form, with numbered paragraphs, summaries, self review questions and many different assessment means. It is organised in the **sequence** of the **eight mandatory units**, and takes account of the constructive comments made by business studies lecturers in a survey of their requirements. Each chapter contains the following question types:

- ❑ **student-centred tasks** (answers in Lecturers' Supplement)
- ❑ **review questions** (with paragraph references to the answers in the text)
- ❑ **assignments** (answers in Lecturers' Supplement)

How to Use this Book

The book is designed to be used as a course text to support either courses with a high proportion of lecturer contact time or those that allow for less contact time and more directed self-study. In either case, the **text** will provide practical help in both understanding and completing coursework. The end of chapter review questions provide confirmation that the students have understood the topic covered.

The chapters can be tackled in any order, although Elements 8.1 and 8.2 assume a knowledge of some principles covered earlier.

No previous knowledge of business studies is required to use this text, but students may find it useful to refer to *A First Course in Business Studies* (S Danks, DP Publications) for additional background information.

The element(s) of the mandatory units covered in a chapter are indicated on the Contents pages and also clearly marked at the beginning of the chapter. Performance criteria covered by each task are indicated in the top right-hand corner of the task box. Many of the tasks also cover elements of the **core skills** units, and these are indicated in brackets in the task box.

GNVQ Information for the Student

Advanced GNVQ Business is a work-related qualification that gives a broad introduction to anyone wishing to follow a career in one of the many areas of business. It also provides a route into Higher Education.

The programme of study consists of eight **Mandatory Units** (all covered in this book), plus four **Optional Units**. Specialist **Additional Units** can also be added to your existing units to increase the value of your GNVQ (e.g. to help with entry into Higher Education). You will also be assessed on the **first three** of the six **Core Skills** Units – Communication, Application of Number, Information Technology, Working with Others, Problem Solving and Improving your Learning and Performance.

Key terms

It is not easy to get to grips with all the different terms used in the GNVQ specification, but the key terms that you should be familiar with are as follows:

Unit – an area of study e.g. *Unit 3 Marketing*. You will be tested on at least 12 units in order to achieve your Advanced GNVQ Business, i.e. 8 **mandatory** plus 4 **optional** (see above).

Element – a particular **topic** of study within a Unit e.g. *Element 3.1 Investigate the principles and functions of marketing in organisations*. Most units are divided into three or four elements.

Performance criteria (PC) – the essential knowledge or skills that you are expected to gain and understand for each element e.g. *3.1.4 Analyse marketing activities in business organisations*. Each element consists of between three and seven PCs.

Range – the area or extent of knowledge specified by the PCs e.g. *assessing market needs, satisfying customer requirements*, etc.

Evidence indicators – the proof needed that you have covered the full range of the PCs.

Assessment

Seven of the eight Mandatory Units are assessed with an **externally set** test (so are not under the control of your school or college). All units are also assessed by your college or school using the work that you produce **throughout the course**. (You may also be given credit for relevant previous achievement e.g work done for your GCSEs.) The Mandatory Unit tests check that you have (or have not!) understood the required material for each unit. Your coursework (projects/assignments for these units) will contribute to a final grade (pass, merit or distinction) for the whole your GNVQ course. This book provides you with the knowledge base to be successful in your coursework/external testing.

You will also find that tackling the many tasks provides an exciting way to learn/confirm understanding. The ones that you need to do for your course assessment will be decided by your teacher/lecturer. You must keep all your assessment material carefully in a **portfolio of evidence** file.

Lecturers' Supplement

A free supplement is available to lecturers on application to the Publishers in writing (on your school/college headed paper) stating the course on which the book is to be recommended, the number of students on the course, the probable number of books to be purchased by them and where they will buy them.

The Supplement contains

i)   **seven GNVQ-style question papers** which cover the mandatory units which can be photocopied and used for testing students.

ii) **outline answers** to

     the 350 plus in-text tasks

     the 28 end of chapter assignments

     and to the seven GNVQ-style question papers.

iii) **planning tables**. These link tasks to performance criteria and core skills and help the lecturer to decide which to recommend to students for their portfolio evidence-gathering and which to use for assessment purposes.

Suggestions and Criticisms

The author would welcome, via the publishers, any comments on the book. This will enable subsequent editions to be amended, if necessary, and made even more useful to students and teachers alike.

Discrimination between the Sexes

For reasons of textual fluency, you will find the words 'he/him/her' have been used throughout this book. However in most cases the person referred to could be of either sex.

Additional Notes for Students

Tasks and assignments

You will find that this book contains several different types of tasks and assignments including case studies, projects and practical exercises. These are designed to encourage you to take an active part in the process of learning.

A number of the tasks require you to work outside the classroom and can be carried out either as an individual or as a member of a group. Some assignments will also require you to make oral presentations. Where possible, you are advised to make use of information technology in your studies.

You will be asked to obtain a variety of information which will require you to use library reference books or other sources such as newspapers and journals. You will also need to contact various organisations, including local companies, to obtain information.

Presentation and Assessment

Your work should always be well organised and neatly presented. This is particularly important if it is to form part of your coursework portfolio.

A suitable structure for research reports might be as follows:

- ❏ Title and purpose of report
- ❏ Summary of findings, including any key recommendations
- ❏ Introduction
- ❏ Body of report, that is, presentation and analysis of data collected
- ❏ Conclusions or results

As you will see in Element 3.2, graphs, pie charts, pictographs and bar charts are particular good methods of presenting any numerical information.

Research projects are usually assessed on the quality and depth of the research, analysis of the data collected, evaluation of the findings and final presentation.

I hope that you will enjoy using this text and wish you every success in your coursework and in obtaining your qualification.

Stephen Danks
August 1995

1 The Business Environment

This Chapter provides a **general introduction to the subject of business studies** and is intended to provide a framework for future studies since many of the topics outlined are discussed in later chapters. Because of the integrated nature of business, many terms and concepts will recur throughout this text.

- ❏ What is Business
- ❏ Development of Economic Activity
- ❏ Needs and Wants
- ❏ Demand and Supply
- ❏ Scarcity and Choice
- ❏ Key Definitions
- ❏ The Resources of Business
- ❏ Profit
- ❏ Production
- ❏ The Economic System
- ❏ Organisations
- ❏ Business Objectives
- ❏ Objectives of Other Organisations
- ❏ Business Organisation
- ❏ Business Functions
- ❏ Management
- ❏ Decision Making
- ❏ Constraints on Business
- ❏ Measurement of Performance

What is Business?

1. The term business is used to describe all the commercial activities undertaken by the various organisations which produce and supply goods and services. Business affects nearly every part of our daily lives. Not only by supplying the food we eat, the clothes we wear and the transport we use to school, college or work, but also most of the jobs and wages which enable us to buy these goods and services.

Development of Economic Activity

2. ❏ In primitive societies, people were **self-sufficient**, hunting, growing and making what they needed for themselves.

   ❏ Later people began to specialise in doing what they were good at which enabled them to produce more than they needed for themselves.

   ❏ This **division of labour** led to the development of **trade** as surplus goods were exchanged for other goods.

   ❏ This earliest form of trade was called **barter.**

   ❏ As the population, specialisation and technical developments increased, **money** was introduced to make the process of exchange easier.

   ❏ This led to an increase in the quantity of goods produced and the rapid growth of trade both at home and overseas.

Needs and Wants

3. Goods and services are produced because people need or want them. In order to survive in life, we all **need** food, clothing and shelter. These are the basic needs which must be satisfied. **Wants** on the other hand are goods and services which people seek to obtain in order to improve their standard of living, i.e. quality of life.

Demand and Supply

4. When people talk about the **demand** for something, it means not just wanting it, but also being able to pay for it. Demand is discussed fully in Element 1.1, but it is important here to note the following:

    ❒ Generally speaking the **lower the price** the **greater** will be **the demand**.

    ❒ The **elasticity of demand** measures the extent to which demand changes in response to the changes in price or income.

    ❒ **Demand** is only **effective** if it is backed up by money.

    ❒ The term **aggregate demand** is used to describe the total expenditure of all the buyers of goods and services within the economy as a whole.

5. **Supply**, on the other hand, is the quantity of goods or services which producers are prepared to offer for sale at any given price. Supply is discussed fully in Chapter 4, but here we need to note the following:

    ❒ Generally speaking the **higher the price** the **greater** will be **the supply**.

    ❒ The **elasticity of supply** measures the extent to which supply changes in response to supply.

    ❒ The term **aggregate supply** is used to describe the total supply of all goods and services within the economy as a whole.

Scarcity and Choice

6. We would all like to have more or better possessions than we have now – clothes, houses, furniture, holidays etc. Our wants are unlimited, i.e. there is always something which we would like. However, our resources are **scarce** or limited. We only have a certain amount of money and therefore must make a **choice** of how best to spend it.

7. The problems of scarcity and choice also apply to businesses and countries. A business must decide how to make the best use of its limited resources. Likewise a country cannot produce unlimited amounts of goods and services if its resources are limited.

8. One way of looking at this problem is to say that the cost of any choice is the next best alternative which we decide to do without. This is what economists call **opportunity cost.** For example, the cost to a teenager of going to the cinema is the compact disc which could have been bought instead; a farmer may keep cattle instead of sheep; governments may spend money on roads instead of schools or pensions.

Task 1   **1.1.1, 1.1.2 (C3.2)**

1. Give 3 examples of your own 'needs' and 'wants'.

2. Think about the problem of scarcity and choice as it affects you. List 3 goods and 3 services which you have purchased in the last week and the opportunity cost of each of those items.

3. Three college students are faced with the following situations:

    a) Tony loses his Business Studies textbook which cost the College £9.95. He is asked to pay £5 towards the cost of replacing it.

    b) Peter earns £24 for working Saturdays on a market stall. He is picked for the College cricket team which only plays on Saturdays. He believes that a new bat will improve his play and purchases one for £20.

continued...

Task 1 continued   **1.1.1, 1.1.2**

c)   Jasmin wants to go on a College trip to Italy which will cost £285. Her parents say she can go and they are prepared to pay.

What is the opportunity cost:

i)   to Tony of losing his textbook?

ii)   to the local community?

iii) to Peter of playing cricket?

iv)   to Jasmin's parents of her trip to Italy?

v)   to Jasmin?

Some Key Definitions

9.   ❐ The provision of goods and services is called **production.** The people who buy them are **consumers**, who spend their **income** to satisfy their needs and wants.

❐ **Goods** are tangible items which we can see and touch, e.g. food, drinks, make-up, motor cycles, cars and washing machines. The first three examples are called **consumption goods** because because they are quickly consumed, The last 3 are **durable goods** because they last much longer.

❐ **Services** are not goods but things which we use like the telephone, buses, education and entertainment.

❐ The **environment** refers to the surroundings and circumstances which affect the way in which an organisation operates.

❐ A **system** can be defined as a collection of inter-dependent parts organised to achieve a particular objective. The change or removal of any of these parts will affect the way in which the system operates.

❐ **Objectives** are the aims or goals which a business seeks to achieve. In order to check whether or not they have been achieved, they must be measurable. For example, to increase sales by 10%.

❐ **Management** refers to a group of people who are appointed by the owners of a company to run a business on their behalf. Their role includes determining the distribution of profits to shareholders. Managers are expected to direct the efforts of their staff towards achieving the desired objectives. That is, to get things done through people.

❐ **Competition** refers to the amount of rivalry between organisations and their products or services or market. This may affect individual businesses in many ways, but in particular in terms of the prices which they can charge and quality of goods or services which they must supply in order to be competitive.

10.

Some goods and services

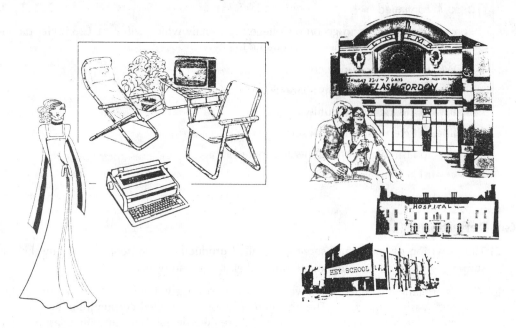

The Resources of Business

11.   In order to produce the goods and services needed to satisfy human wants, four essential resources are needed. These are also referred to as **factors of production** or **inputs**.

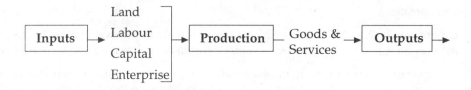

12.   ❐ **Land** consists of all natural resources and includes minerals, water, fish in the sea and land itself. Examples include Coal, Wood, North Sea Oil and Gas.

❐ **Labour** refers to the physical and mental skills of people who work. It is the human resource in production whether a labourer, teacher or office worker.

❐ **Capital** in its broadest sense means anything which is owned by a business and used to make production easier and more efficient. This includes buildings, machinery, equipment and vehicles.

❐ **Enterprise** or the entrepreneur is someone who organises the other inputs to initiate the process of production. They risk a loss if the business fails but if successful, are rewarded by making a **profit**. Very successful examples include Tesco, ICI and Boots.

13.   Clearly not all inputs are of the same quality. For example, barren hillsides will not grow crops, a clumsy person will not have the skills to produce jewellery; capital equipment may be new or worn, whilst some entrepreneurs will have more ability than others. The type and quality of inputs used will depend on the goods and services (call OUTPUTS) being produced.

Profit

14.   The difference between the total cost of running a business and the total income received by the business is the profit. The cost of the inputs include rent for land, wages for labour and interest on

capital. Income comes from sales to consumers. Owners or managers will try to increase sales through good marketing (see Chapters 10 and 11) and operate the business efficiently in order to reduce costs and therefore increase profits.

Task 2   5.1.1, 8.1.5 (C3.4)

A manufacturer of clothing has a large number of inputs.

1. Consider the following list and group them into Land, Labour, Capital and Enterprise.

LABOURER	FACTORY	COMPUTER	SECRETARY
WOOL	MANAGER	PHOTOCOPIER	PENCILS
SCISSORS	COTTON	MACHINISTS	WATER

2. Now draw up a similar list of resources for a service business such as an insurance company, transport firm or holiday tour operator or one of your own choice.

Production

15. We all consume a wide range of goods and services in life. Therefore, people work both to produce them and also to earn the money needed to buy them. Production can be considered under three main headings – primary, secondary and tertiary industries.

    ❑ **Primary**

    This consists of all the **extractive** industries, for example coal mining, quarrying, fishing, forestry and farming. Many of these primary products form the raw materials for secondary production.

    ❑ **Secondary**

    These are the **manufacturing** and **construction** industries which change the raw materials into finished products. Example include the manufacture of chemicals, textiles and shoes, and the building of roads, houses and bridges.

    ❑ **Tertiary**

    These industries do not produce goods, but provide **services**. Tertiary production is often referred to as Commerce and Direct Services. The latter are personal services, not directly related to trade but needed to increase production by looking after people's health and welfare.

16.   **Types of Production**

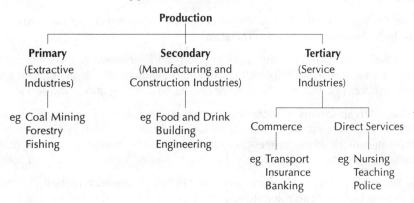

Primary	Secondary	Tertiary
Tree Felling	Car Manufacture	Oil Delivery

Task 3   **5.2.2 (C3.4)**

Consider the area in which you live or work. Identify by name the organisations concerned with the following types of production. List and briefly describe the products or services which they supply.

1)   2 examples of primary production.

2)   At least 5 examples of secondary production.

3)   Finally, at least 6 examples of tertiary production including 3 each of commercial and direct services.

4)   Are any organisations involved in more than one type of production?

State which they are and in what way they are involved.

The Economic System

17. There are 3 groups which make up what can be called the economic system of a country – individuals, business organisations and the State.

18. **Individuals –** We are all consumers of goods and services whatever our age, race or sex, free to spend our income as we choose. In addition, individuals are also important providers of capital and many also form part of the labour force needed to produce goods and services.

19. **Business Organisations** – These are the various suppliers of goods and services for consumption whether they be importers, manufacturers, processors or involved in the chain of distribution as wholesalers or retailers. Business organisations are also consumers of raw materials and/or finished goods and services and importantly they are also employers of labour and users of capital.

20. **The State** – A variety of roles are performed by the State which includes both local and central government as well as State run industries such as the coal mines and railways. The State is also an important consumer of goods and services and a major employer.

21. But importantly, the State is also the regulating body in our society. It has the key role of devising laws which both protect individuals and organisations and also help to resolve any conflict which may take place between them. Examples include laws on Health and Safety, Consumer Protection, Employment Protection, Environmental Protection and Sunday Trading.

Organisations

22. An **organisation** is a group of people who co-operate together for a common purpose. Organisations are of all types and sizes, exist everywhere and most of us belong to many of them during life as the following examples illustrate. Families, hospitals, churches, youth clubs, sports clubs, schools, colleges, libraries charities, trade unions, political parties and businesses are all organisations. In this text we are considering the wide range of business organisations which exist today and the environment in which they operate to achieve their objectives.

23. Business organisations range in size and structure from small sole proprietors owned and run by one person, to huge national and multi-national organisations run by managers and owned by many thousands of shareholders, to industries owned and controlled by the State. The **private sector** is the term used to describe all businesses owned by individuals or groups that are run essentially from profit. Businesses that are owned and controlled by the Government or local authorities and run for the benefit of the community operate in the **public sector**.

| **Task 4** | **2.1.1 (C3.2)** |

1. Make a list of all the organisations to which you belong.

2. Identify what you feel is the 'common purpose' of each organisation.

3. Now identify the 'purpose' of two organisations in the private sector and two in the public sector.

24. The specific components of a business organisation can be summarised as

❑ **A name** that gives it an identity, e.g. ICI, Boots, Asda.

❑ **People** who consist of the management and workforce and provide a range of skills, knowledge, commitment and drive.

❑ **A mission and set of objectives** which are needed to define the purpose of the organisation and what it is trying to achieve.

❑ **A hierarchy** with an organisational structure through which power can be exercised.

❑ **A culture** and set of values which give the organisation an ethos and spirit.

❑ **Communication** and information flows to enable decisions to be taken and implemented.

❑ **Systems and procedures** for undertaking defined tasks.

❑ **Recording systems** for reference, evidence, control and accounting purposes.

❑ **A control system** to audit and influence management decisions.

❑ **Specialist functions** through which tasks can be carried out.

❑ **Rewards and punishments** to provide motivation and ensure compliance with objectives.

❑ **A boundary** which defines the limits of the organisation.

❑ **Linking mechanisms** needed to relate to other organisations.

25. All these components need to be assessed and matched together to try to achieve a harmonious whole. Complete harmonisation is, however, unlikely to be achieved because the components are always subject to change as, for example, when staff leave or new staff are appointed. In this text, we shall be considering each of these components in more detail, including the importance of each for an organisation.

Task 5	**2.1.2 (C3.2)**

Choose any business organisation which you know well or can find out about and try to identify with examples, its specific components.

Business Objectives

26. Business organisations are established for the purpose of achieving specific objectives and it is against these objectives that the success or failure of the organisation can be judged. The key points about objectives are that they should be quantifiable, measurable and time specific, for example, to increase profits by 5% per annum.

27. There are four questions at the root of setting objectives.

   ❏ **What is the organisation trying to achieve?** What is important, for example, increasing the return on investment (capital employed), increasing market share or reducing bad debts?

   ❏ **How can this be done?** What methods or policies are needed, for example, increasing profit margins, improving the rate of sales growth, tighter credit control.

   ❏ **When must it be done by?** A time period should be set, for example, by the end of the next financial year.

   ❏ **How will it know that it has succeeded?** Thus a unit of measurement is required, e.g. 10%. This question also implies the need to monitor progress and take corrective action as necessary.

28.   **Example: Setting and Achieving a Business Objective**

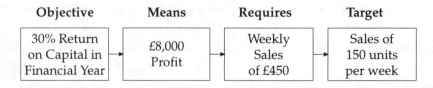

Objective	Means	Requires	Target
30% Return on Capital in Financial Year	£8,000 Profit	Weekly Sales of £450	Sales of 150 units per week

Why Objectives are Needed

29. Objectives are needed in an organisation for a number of reasons in particular because:
   ❏ they clarify for everyone what the business is working to achieve.
   ❏ they aid the decision-making process and the choice of alternative strategies (courses of action).
   ❏ they enable checks on progress and decisions on what needs to be done next.
   ❏ they provide the means by which performance can be measured and actions controlled.
   ❏ they provide a focus for individual roles in the organisation.
   ❏ they can be broken down to provide targets for each part of the organisation.
   ❏ they can be used to analyse the performance of the business and its employees.

30. It is important that an organisation's objectives are realistic in the light of market research and also achievable, particularly in relation to production. It is pointless, for example, if sales targets are 80 units daily, if production can only produce 55. It is also important that objectives are regularly reviewed to ensure that they are still relevant or realistic as circumstances change.

31. The specific objectives of an organisation will depend upon whether it is established in the **public** or **private sector**. However, in order for both sectors to be successful, the prime objective must always be to meet the needs of their customers or clients.

Objectives of Private Sector Organisations

32. Organisations in the private sector are usually created to earn **maximum profits** for their owners, i.e. to achieve the best possible return on the money which they have invested in the business.

33. However, whilst this will certainly be the main aim of most businesses, some may have other objectives which they pursue, particularly in the short-term. For example, a new business may see **survival** as its main objective in its early years i.e. ensuring that it makes sufficient **profit** to enable it to be in a position to continue trading. This could then be followed by **consolidation** and it may be some years before it reaches a position of high profit.

34. for a short time in order to achieve the objectives of **increasing sales and market share** i.e. selling more of the total sales of a product or service than their competitors. In the longer term, if successful, this may enable the firm to expand its output or product range and enter a period of **growth** which will enable it to benefit from **economies of scale.**

Objectives of Public Sector Organisations

35. Public sector organisations are created not to maximise profit but to achieve the maximum **benefit for the nation**. In order to achieve their objectives they may be involved in operating unprofitable services because it is in the public's interest to do so. For example, the provision of rail services to country areas. Another example would be keeping an uneconomic coal mine open in an area of high unemployment to prevent the loss of further jobs.

36. However, the government still expects public corporations to aim to at least 'break even' over a period of years and if possible to make sufficient profit to enable investment in new equipment to take place. Each one is set a profit target just like a commercial firm.

Task 6	**2.1.1, 8.1.2 (C3.2)**

Consider your place of study, work or any organisation which you know well. Find out and list its main objectives.

37. We have seen so far that people demand goods and services and that they are supplied by both the private and public sector organisations. In order to pay for these goods and services, individuals work for and invest money in these organisations. This is illustrated in the following diagram.

38.

The Economic System

Objectives of Other Organisations

39. So far we have discussed the objectives of business organisations in the public and private sector. We now need briefly to consider the objectives of some other organisations, including charities, quangos, economic interest and mutual help organisations.

Charities

40. Charities are normally formed by groups of caring people to provide goods and services for the needy. Examples of charities are Oxfam, National Society for the Prevention of Cruelty to Children (NSPCC) and the World Wildlife Fund. Although they are not formed to make a profit, they must, nonetheless, remain solvent in order to survive. Income is usually received from public donations and fund raising activities, and them distributed to achieve the charities' objectives.The objectives of the NSPCC, for example, include helping to prevent children from being mistreated.

41. Some organisations, however, such as public schools, take on the legal form and status of a charity in order to gain tax advantages. To help prevent unscrupulous people using them simply to make money for themselves, all charities must be approved by the Registrar of Charities.

Quangos (quasi-autonomous non-governmental organisations)

42. These are organisations set up by the government but run independently by nominated boards of directors. Examples include: the Welsh Development Agency, the purpose of which is to promote and encourage investment in Wales; Training and Enterprise Councils; and the Civil Aviation Authority. Almost any public body that is not elected could be called a quango.

Economic interest groups

43. Sometimes people or organisations with common objectives may join together to act as a pressure group to promote their interests. Examples include: the Confederation of British Industry (CBI) which represents employers; the Trade Unions Congress (TUC) which represents trade unions; the Consumers Association which promotes the interests of consumers; and trade unions which represent employees.

Mutual help organisations

44. Some organisations, such as co-operatives, are set up with the main objective of helping members rather than making a profit.

Other types of organisation

45. These include:

☐ **Political parties** such as Labour, Conservative and the National Front, each of which has its own manifesto which sets out its policies and objectives.

☐ **Legal organisations** that exist to administer justice, e.g. magistrates courts, county courts, industrial tribunals, the Monopolies Commission.

☐ **International organisations** such as the International Monetary Fund (IMF), and the European Union which promotes the common interests of member countries.

☐ **Multinational organisations** which are business organisations that have operations in many countries. Examples of multinationals include Unilever, BP and ICI.

☐ **Building societies and friendly societies** which are two examples of organisations which strictly speaking do not have a profit motive. They do, however, seek to make a cash surplus.

| **Task 7** | **1.1.5 (C3.3)** |

1. Find out about the organisation and purposes of your local Training and Enterprise Council.

2. Try to identify at least one local example of each of the types of organisation described in paragraphs 39–45. If you are unable to give an example, briefly explain why.

Building Societies

46. Building societies are mutual institutions owned by their savers and borrowers. They raise mainly short-term deposits from savers who are usually able to withdraw their money on demand or at short notice. The societies specialise in using these deposits to provide long-term loans for house purchase (mortgages). The rate of interest usually varies and the loan is secured against the property.

47. **Well-known Building Societies**

48. The Building Societies Act 1986 allows societies to:

i) **diversify and offer additional services.** These include the provision of current account facilities such as cheque books, personal loans, insurance broking, estate agency and property surveys;

ii) **convert to public limited companies,** discarding their mutual status, if their savers and borrowers agree. Abbey National was the first to do this in 1989. In this event the society becomes an authorised institution under the Banking Act 1987 and is supervised by the Bank of England;

iii) **operate in other countries of the European Union.**

49. The three largest societies (Halifax, Nationwide and Woolwich) account for nearly 50% of the total assets of the movement and the twenty largest for some 90%. Building societies are supervised under the 1986 Act by the Building Societies Commission.

Friendly Societies

50. Traditionally these have been unincorporated societies of individuals which offered a limited range of financial services to their members, in particular provision for retirement and against loss of income through unemployment and sickness.

51. The Friendly Societies Act 1992 gave them new powers to incorporate and offer a broader range of services. They are supervised by the Registrar of Friendly Societies.

Business Organisation

52. Organisational structures and job roles are discussed more fully in Element 2.1. It is useful here, however, to consider their impact on decision-taking in organisations.

53. In order to achieve its objectives a businesses resources must be organised and how this is done will depend upon a number of factors including the type of goods or services it supplies, the size of the market, the level of technology which it uses and the attitude and type of management which run it, all of which are discussed in this text.

54. The firms themselves also vary considerably in size and this is true even in the same industry or area of activity, for example building, retailing and farming. Hence the internal structure of a business will also vary according to its size.

Small Firms

55. Whilst an organisation is small, one man can often control it. He is able to do all of the important jobs himself, e.g. ordering, accounts, VAT returns and marketing, and is very closely involved in its day-to-day running.

56. However, as a business grows, one man may be too busy to perform all the jobs which he once did and he may therefore need to take in a partner or arrange for people who work for him to take on some specialist jobs, e.g. accounts and ordering.

57. If a firm continues to grow, additional skills may be required and as more staff are employed further specialisation can take place.

Larger Organisations

58. This process of growth and specialisation may continue as a firm develops into a private or public limited company. When this happens the shareholders will elect a Board of Directors to make the policy decisions on how the business should be organised and run in order to achieve its objectives (see Element 2.1).

59. **Organisation Chart**

    A typical organisation chart showing departments and their main functions. Businesses often use this form of diagram to illustrate positions of staff in their organisation.

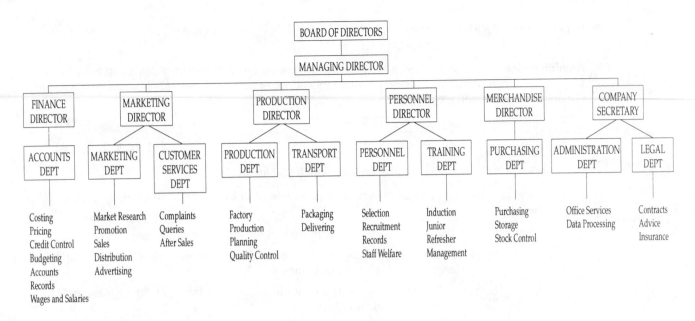

Specialist Departments

60. As shown in the organisation chart, the board will usually appoint a managing director or chief executive as head of a business. Specialist departments are often established, the actual number depending on the size of the firm, with a director in charge of each function, for example finance, production, marketing. The overall management and administration of the company involves the co-ordination of these different departments or functions of the business.

Business Functions

61. Whatever its size, there are a number of functional areas common in all business organisations. These are personnel (or human resource management), production, purchasing, accounting and finance, marketing and administration.

62. Each department or functional area will then contribute to the success of the organisation by having its own specific objectives and targets based on the general objectives which have been established.

63. **Personnel.** This activity is concerned with the management of people in an organisation including recruitment, selection, training, pay, welfare, conditions of employment and negotiations with trade unions (see Element 4.1).

64. **Production.** This function deals with the making of goods or services. It includes matters relating to location of the business, the planning, co-ordination and techniques of production and quality control. It may also include product research and development.

65. **Purchasing.** The acquisition of raw materials and other resources is the function of purchasing. It involves finding the best sources of supply, at the right price, the right quality and other factors which may be important in the organisation, like delivery times. Stock control may also be the responsibility of purchasing.

66. **Accounting and Finance.** All businesses need finance in order to start up and operate. Accountancy techniques are used to provide managers with financial control information which involves the collection, recording, presentation and analysis of data as a basis for forecasting and decision-making.

67. Other financial functions include the preparation of budgets, payment of suppliers, dealing with the payroll, calculating selling prices, credit control and the preparation of final accounts. (See Units 6 and 7.)

68. **Marketing.** This function is concerned with a whole group of business activities (known as the **marketing mix**) which are concerned with obtaining and keeping customers. It includes market research

to find out about a firm's customers, product design, pricing, sales promotion, advertising and distribution to the final customer. (See Unit 3.)

69. **Administration.** Many organisations have an administration office which provides a support service to the other functional areas. This may include reception, switchboard, typing, photocopying, secretarial and computer services.

Task 8   **3.1.1 (C3.2, C3.4)**

In Task 6 you selected an organisation with which you are familiar.

1. Now identify its functional departments or sections and list the main services which each provides.

2. Identify the functional area associated with each of the following activities:

   a) To maintain customer goodwill, encourage existing customers to purchase more and find new customers and sales opportunities.

   b) To obtain and control supplies from various sources, at the right time, in the right quality, and at the most favourable prices.

   c) To improve relationships between the organisation and its employees at all levels.

   d) To make a better product, find improved ways of making the product, and develop new products.

   e) To record all financial transactions in order to protect assets, maintain profitability and forecast future policy from past performance.

---

70. In practice, functional areas cannot operate in isolation because the input of one function is often the output of another. Sales, for example, cannot operate without production, whilst production cannot operate without purchasing. They are very much linked together and must co-operate with each other to enable the organisation to achieve its objectives, hence the importance of effective management.

Management

71. The business functions outlined above must be properly co-ordinated and managed if the organisation is to be successful. In a small business it may be the owner who is the manager, whilst in a large company, it will be the **Board of Directors.**

72. The primary task of management is to use the resources of the business efficiently and to make the right decisions in order to achieve its defined objectives.

73. Management involves 6 key tasks: planning, co-ordinating, motivating, controlling, problem solving and responding to change.

   ❏ **Planning** to set clear business objectives and make decisions on the best use of resources to achieve them.

   ❏ **Co-ordinating** and directing activities to ensure that everyone knows what is expected of them and are working towards the agreed objectives.

   ❏ **Motivating**, delegating to and communicating with staff to encourage them to give of their best and carry out their tasks efficiently and effectively.

   ❏ **Controlling** operations and checking on progress to ensure that objectives are being achieved. Also to modify objectives if circumstances change.

   ❏ **Problem solving** so that decisions are taken which help to resolve difficulties and enable tasks to be completed. This may involve choosing between different courses of action.

❐ **Responding to change(s)** in the environment to ensure that the organisation prospers. Good management must be dynamic and forward-looking to detect both threats to the business and opportunities for further development and respond accordingly.

Task 9   **4.2.1 (C3.4)**

NO ONE WANTS TO BE A BOSS!

Many junior executives are no longer reaching for the top because the incentives are not big enough, according to a recent survey.

It reveals that most companies have trouble filling senior posts, especially from inside their organisations.

This management malaise is not just in Britain but throughout Europe, according to the survey of 500 chief executives of top companies in ten European countries.

Their answers indicate that because of the demands of business life and the lack of incentives, tomorrow's executives may not be able to meet the demands of industry.

The quality of managers is improving but their jobs are getting harder and the incentive to reach the top is less than it was ten years ago.

A grim report on the survey, says: 'There is little sign of the situation improving and in the years ahead industry may well suffer from a shortage of really effective leaders.'

Chief executives in all ten countries believe the pressures on management have drastically increased in the past decade.

And there is widespread belief that the status of managers in the eyes of the community has declined.

Most top men say school-leavers are not as good as they used to be and that schools are not preparing pupils for careers in industry.

The answer, most executives believe, lies in closer liaison with educational authorities.

Read the above article and answer the following questions which are based on it.

1. Why are people no longer interested in becoming managers?

2. What consequences could this have for industry in the future?

3. If you were the Chief Executive of an organisation, what action would you consider taking to prevent your own firm suffering?

Decision Making and Constraints

74. Each of us is involved in making decisions. Daily we have to decide what to eat, what to wear and how to organise our time. Essentially, we are faced with having to choose between alternatives. Similarly there is a decision-making process in organisations. It involves using the information available in order to make a choice between the various alternative ways of achieving objectives.

75. Decision making is essential to determine the future direction of an organisation. We said earlier that the prime function of management is to make the right decisions. Some of the decision making techniques available to assist managers are covered in Units 6 and 7.

The types of decision making can broadly be classified into strategic, tactical and operational.

Strategic or Long-Term

76. These are decisions made by top-level management and are concerned with an organisation's overall objectives. Such corporate decisions include major capital investments, sources of finance and product and market choices.

Tactical or Medium-Term

77. These are concerned with the best use of an organisation's resources and the management of change to achieve the agreed objectives. Such decisions are made by senior managers and would include minor capital investment, product modification and changes to marketing plans.

Operational or Short-Term

78. These are decisions taken by departmental managers or lower level supervisors in order to put tactical plans into effect and control activities. Examples could include credit control, re-ordering of stocks and determination of delivery routes.

Process of Decision-Making

79. The process of decision making can be summarised as follows:

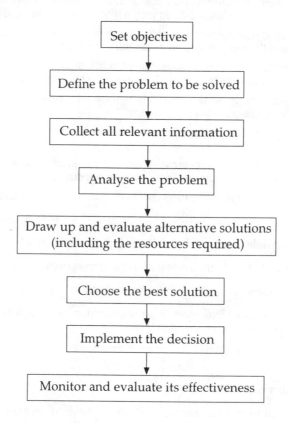

80. Not all of these processes will be needed at operational level but may be essential for tactical and strategic decision making.

Constraints on Business

81. Throughout this text we will be considering the environmental factors or constraints which influence decision making in a business. A constraint is something which prevents or makes it difficult for a business to achieve 'its' objectives and therefore influences decision making.

82. Broadly, these fall into constraints within the organisation itself **(internal)** and those from the environment in which it operates **(external)**.

83. **The Business in its Environment**

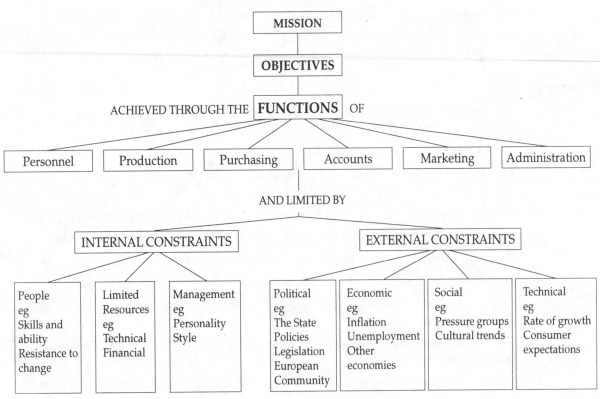

MISSION

OBJECTIVES

ACHIEVED THROUGH THE **FUNCTIONS** OF

| Personnel | Production | Purchasing | Accounts | Marketing | Administration |

AND LIMITED BY

INTERNAL CONSTRAINTS

| People eg Skills and ability Resistance to change | Limited Resources eg Technical Financial | Management eg Personality Style |

EXTERNAL CONSTRAINTS

| Political eg The State Policies Legislation European Community | Economic eg Inflation Unemployment Other economies | Social eg Pressure groups Cultural trends | Technical eg Rate of growth Consumer expectations |

Task 10 **1.2.4, 5.2.1, 7.1.2 (C3.2, C3.4)**

Refer back to the information which you obtained in Tasks 6 and 8. Try to identify what might be considered as internal and external constraints and discuss how these might affect the organisation and prevent it from achieving its objectives.

If you have difficulty in understanding any of the terms used on the diagram above, check the index and read about them elsewhere in the text.

Measurement of Performance

84. Traditionally an organisation can be seen in terms of a control loop which uses a range of inputs (such as labour and materials) to produce a range of outputs (goods or services). In order to achieve its objectives the management of an organisation must plan, monitor and control this process and recognise deviations from its plans in order to take corrective action as necessary. This is referred to as **Management By Objectives** (MBO).

85. **Control Loop**

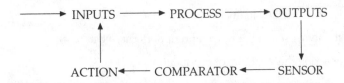

86. Control implies some form of quantitative measurement against which progress can be checked. The 3 fundamental aspects of performance which can and must be measured are:

❏ **efficiency** which is concerned with measuring the output from given resources.

❑ **economy** which involves obtaining the 'right' resources at the least cost.

❑ **effectiveness** which is about producing the right outputs in the right quantities.

87. There may also be other factors which are equally important but which cannot be easily quantified. Examples might be customer satisfaction, industrial relations and staff morale.

Summary

88. a) The term business is used to describe all the various commercial activities undertaken by organisations which produce and supply goods and services.

   b) The earliest form of trade was called barter.

   c) The division of labour or specialisation resulted in a big increase in the number of goods and services produced leading to the need for money.

   d) We all face the problem of scarcity and choice because our resources are limited.

   e) Land, labour, capital and enterprise are the 4 factors or inputs required for production.

   f) Production involves primary, secondary and tertiary industries.

   g) Economic systems are made up of individuals, business organisations and the State.

   h) Organisations exist in all walks of life and consist of groups of people co-operating together to achieve a common purpose.

   i) Business organisations set themselves specific objectives to achieve against which their success or failure can be measured.

   j) The main objective of private sector organisations is usually to achieve maximum profits.

   k) Public sector organisations also seek to make profits but their first concern is to operate for the benefit of the nation.

   l) In order to achieve its objectives, the successful running of any business, no matter how large or small, involves the co-ordination of many different functions including personnel, production, purchasing, accounts and finance, marketing and administration.

   m) Whereas in a large organisation a different department may exist to carry out each of these functions, in a small business they may all be performed by the owner or just a few people.

   n) Management involves planning, co-ordinating, motivation, control, problem-solving and responding to change.

   o) Decision making by managers to achieve objectives is influenced by both internal and external constraints.

   p) Performance must be measured to ensure that objectives are being met.

Review questions *(Answers can be found in the paragraphs indicated)*

   1. Using 2 examples, explain the meaning of barter. (2)

   2. Why does the division of labour lead to an increase in trade? (2)

   3. Briefly describe the key features of demand and supply. (4–5)

   4. Explain the terms scarcity, choice and opportunity-cost. (6–8)

   5. Briefly, describe the 4 factors of production. (11–13)

   6. Distinguish between primary, secondary and tertiary production. (15)

   7. Explain, with examples, what you understand by an organisation. (22–23)

   8. Explain what you understand by an economic system. (9, 17–21)

   9. Outline the main features of business organisations. (24)

10. Why do business organisations need objectives? (26–29)

11. Outline the main objectives of private sector and public sector organisations? (31–36)

12. Give 6 examples of other types of organisation and their main objective(s). (39–51)

13. Why are businesses organised in different ways? (53–58)

14. Describe the main functional areas in a business. (62–70)

15. Why is management needed in an organisation? (71–73)

16. Explain the difference between strategic, tactical and operational decision-making. (76–78)

17. Use examples to illustrate the difference between internal and external constraints on decision-making. (81–83)

18. How can performance be measured and controlled? (84–87)

Assignment – Information Profile

This assignment is designed to recap some of the key introductory concepts in this Chapter. It will be possible to use and develop the information collected in later tasks and assignments if required.

Choose two local business organisations, one public sector, the other in the private sector. If possible, select one which provides a service and one which is involved in manufacturing. Contact each by telephone, personal visit and/or correspondence. Use the information obtained to complete the following profile for each plus any other details which you feel are important.

1. Describe the type of organisation, its location and the type of products or services which it sells and where the demand comes from.

2. Identify the factors of production used and if possible the sources of supply.

3. State whether it is involved in primary, secondary or tertiary production.

4. Try to identify the organisational structure and functional areas in the business.

5. Identify its mission and objectives and how this is met through the organisational structure.

6. Describe the environment in which it operates and identify any internal and external constraints.

7. Finally, suggest ways in which you feel its performance could be measured.

2 Supply, Demand and Markets

This chapter introduces some important economic concepts including the significance of the market mechanism of supply and demand and theory of the firm. It covers:

Element 1.1

☐ Economics and Business

☐ Markets

☑ Types of Markets

☐ Market Prices

☐ Demand

☐ Changes in Demand

☐ Elasticity of Demand

☐ Exceptional Demand Curves

☐ Supply

☐ Changes in Supply

☐ Determinants of Supply

☐ Elasticity of Supply

☐ Interaction of Supply and Demand

Element 1.2

☐ Theory of the Firm

☐ Market Conditions

☐ Perfect Competition

☐ Monopoly

☐ Imperfect Competition

☐ Oligopoly

☐ Pricing

☐ Pricing Policies

☐ Cost-Benefit Analysis

☐ Environmental Change

☐ Environmental Strategies

Economics and Business

1. In Chapters 1 and 3 we consider how organisations can be affected by the economic environment in which they operate. Decisions taken may be influenced by economic factors such as the level of unemployment, inflation, interest rates and taxes. Since Economics and Business Studies are very closely linked it is important to have a general understanding of some of the main principles of economic theory and how these may influence the behaviour of organisations.

2. The most widely accepted definition of economics is that of Lord Robbins 'the science which studies human behaviour as a relationship between ends and scarce means which have alternative uses.' Essentially peoples' wants (ie demands) are almost infinite but the resources needed to satisfy them are very limited. Consequently, choices must be made about how to allocate (supply) resources. Economics is the discipline which analyses these decisions and the alternatives available. In this Chapter, we shall consider a number of key aspects of economic theory.

Task 1	**1.1.1, 1.2.1 (C3.2)**

1. List all the choices which you can remember having to make in the past week or month.

2. What type of factors influenced your final decision?

3. How, if at all, does this help your understanding of the definition of economics?

Markets

3. A **market** is defined as any situation where buyers and sellers are brought together. It may be located in a specific place or building or merely involve the use of the telephone, fax or some other means of communication. There are many types of markets ranging from

❏ you selling something to one of your friends

❏ to local street markets

❏ press or TV advertisements followed by telephone or postal transactions

❏ highly complex financial markets dealing in millions of pounds worth of goods and services, to

❏ international markets where demand can be worldwide.

4. We talk in terms of markets in, for example, tea, videos, sports cars, houses and insurance but it is not always easy to identify the limits of each. The market for cars, for example, ranges from three wheel Robin Reliants to Rolls Royces which are clearly very different. Therefore, a market is essentially what consumers see as offering the same goods or services even though different firms' products may vary slightly in terms of their design and specification.

Types of Markets

5. The main types of market can be summarised as:

❏ **Retailers** who sell goods and services direct to the final consumer, mainly through shops.

❏ **Wholesalers** who buy goods from manufacturers for sale to retailers.

❏ **Wholesale produce** markets which exist in most large towns to supply perishable goods to organisations such as shops, hotels, restaurants and schools.

❏ **Commodity Exchanges** or markets where manufacturers throughout the world can buy their raw materials. London is the centre for many of these important markets including metal, diamonds and furs.

❏ **Shipping and Insurance** markets. Britain is a world centre for both of these which are based on Lloyd's of London. Shipping freight services are also sold in the Baltic Exchange.

❏ **Financial markets**. London again is a national and international centre for these markets, including:

♦ **The Money Market** consisting of organisations like banks, discount houses and finance houses which borrow and lend money for short periods, usually up to 30 days.

♦ **The Capital Market** which provides longer-term finance for the Government, businesses and individuals. It includes Institutional Investors, the Stock Exchange and Issuing Houses.

♦ **The Foreign Exchange Market** which is essential for the import and export trade.

Task 2   1.2.1 (C3.4)

1 From the markets discussed above, identify those which supply the essential resources needed for production.

2 Name another factor market which is required for production.

Market Prices

6. In a free economy, market prices are determined by the interaction of demand and supply. It is the market mechanism which essentially determines how resources are allocated because:

❏ it enables individuals to maximise their satisfaction (utility) by choosing how they spend their income,

❏ it indicates consumer demand so that producers supply what goods and services are required,

❏ it encourages competition between producers leading to increasing efficiency and

❏ it increases the returns to the factors of production, such as higher wages for labour and profits for entrepreneurs.

Demand

7. This is the total amount of a particular product which consumers wish to buy at a given price, over a period of time. For example, the demand for commodity x at a price of £2 is 5,000 units per month. It is important that demand is **effective**, that is, wants are supported by peoples' ability to pay for them.

Types of Demand

8. When products are wanted for their own sake there is a **primary demand**, eg a video or carpet. Some products, however, have a **derived demand** due to their use as a factor of production. That is, they are wanted not for themselves, but what they go into making, eg sugar for jam, chickens for eggs, machinery and equipment to produce tins or packets. Other products are complementary, and in **joint demand** in that they are needed together. For example, petrol and cars, knives and forks, tennis balls and tennis racquets.

9. An important feature of demand is that for the great majority of products,

    ❏ if the price falls, consumers will buy more of it;

    ❏ if it rises then they will buy less.

    ❏ Hence, the demand curve slopes downwards from left to right.

10. This is explained by the:

    ❏ **Income effect,** essentially when prices fall, in effect real income increases and thus consumers are able to afford more; and the

    ❏ **Substitution effect**, as prices rise, other competitive products become relatively cheaper and therefore are substituted for it.

11. The market demand for any particular product is the sum of all the individual demands. This can be shown on a **demand curve** which represents the quantity of products demanded at various price levels. Hence, the demand curve slopes downwards from left to right as shown below.

Example of a Demand Schedule

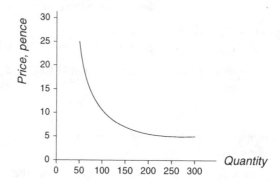

Changes in Demand

12. However, in addition to price, shifts (change) in demand are influenced by many other factors including:

    ❏ **Changes in the size and composition of the population** – for example whether it is increasing or decreasing which will affect overall demand or if it is getting younger or older, which will affect the demand for particular goods or services.

    ❏ **Consumer income** – if people have more money to spend then this is likely to increase demand.

    ❏ **Advertising and promotions** campaigns – these often increase the demand for a product, at least in the short term.

    ❏ **Consumer tastes and preferences** – changes brought about by such factors as advertising or climate. For example, the latest fashion is often a reason for purchasing new clothes.

- ❏ **Prices of complementary products** – for example to run a car you need petrol and oil and must also pay tax and insurance. A rise in the price of any of these therefore might reduce the demand for cars.

- ❏ **New improved products** – for example the introduction of colour television led to a big fall in the demand for black and white models.

- ❏ **Prices of substitute products** – for example an increase in the price of butter often leads to higher sales of margarine and vice versa.

- ❏ **Taxation** – the Government can influence demand by altering either the price of goods (for example VAT) or the level of people's income (for example income tax and allowances).

- ❏ **Legal requirements** such as the wearing of seatbelts in cars has dramatically increased the demand for them.

13. The demand curve in 11 above shows the relationship between demand and price assuming that the conditions of demand remain constant. Each time these conditions change, we get a new demand curve:

14.

Changes in Demand

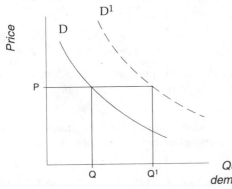

D^1 shows the **increase** in demand due to changes in demand conditions as a result of an increase in consumer income. More is now demanded at each and every price.

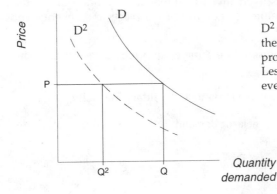

D^2 shows the **fall** in demand due to the reduction in price of a substitute product.
Less is now demanded at each and every price.

Task 3   **1.1.1 (N3.3)**

1. Draw the demand curves and describe the changes in each of the following situations.

   a) the records of a pop group which is no longer fashionable.

   b) the sales of Levi jeans, following the introduction of new, lower priced Wrangler jeans.

   c) the reduction in the price of electricity on electrical appliances.

2. Now illustrate what would happen to demand in the following situations:

   a) an increase in the price of apples.

   b) a government subsidy on rail travel.

Elasticity of Demand

15. The degree of responsiveness of demand to changes in demand conditions is called elasticity. There are three common forms:

   ❐ **price elasticity** which is the effect on demand of a change in price.

   ❐ **income elasticity** which is the effect on demand of a change in income levels and

   ❐ **cross elasticity** which is the effect on demand of a change in the price of other goods or services.

Price Elasticity of Demand (PED)

16. PED measures the responsiveness of demand to changes in price. It is calculated as:

$$PED = \frac{\% \text{ change in quantity demanded}}{\% \text{ change in price}}$$

17. If PED is greater than one, that is a small change in price causes a relatively large change in the quantity demanded, it is **elastic**. For example, if a 5% change in price causes an 8% change in demand.

18. If PED is less than one, that is a small change in price causes a relatively small change in the quantity demanded, it is **inelastic**. For example, if a 5% change in price causes a 2% change in demand.

19. If PED is equal to one, elasticity is **unitary.** That is, the proportionate change in quantity demanded is exactly the same as the proportionate change in price. Thus, for example, a 5% change in price causes a 5% change in demand.

20. Since elasticity links price and quantity demanded, it also shows the effect of changes in price and income on total revenue. This is particularly important to both businesses and government.

21. If demand is relatively elastic, a reduction in price causes total revenue to increase, whilst a price rise causes total revenue to fall. Thus price and revenue move in opposite directions.

22. If, on the other hand, demand is relatively inelastic, a reduction in price causes total revenue to fall and a price rise causes total revenue to increase. Thus price and revenue move in the same direction.

23. With unitary elasticity, total revenue stays the same at all prices. These relationships can be shown graphically as follows:

24. **Elastic Demand, Inelastic Demand and Unitary Elasticity**

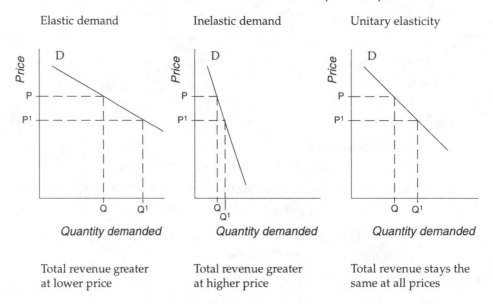

Task 4   **1.1.1 (N3.3)**

Demand price a	Schedule quantity b	Percentage change in D c	Percentage change in price d	Elasticity c ÷ d	Total revenue a x b
30p	200lb	$\frac{400-200}{200} \times 100 = 100\%$	$\frac{30-25}{25} \times 100 = 20\%$	5	60
25p	400lb				
20p	600lb				
15p	800lb				
10p	1,000lb				
5p	1,200lb				

1. Complete the above table which illustrates the relationship between PED and total revenue.

2. Indicate the prices at which demand is elastic, inelastic and unitary.

3. Present this information graphically.

25. Although in reality elasticity is difficult to calculate, what is important is that businesses have an awareness of the likely effect on demand, and therefore total revenue, when proposing to alter the price of their goods or services. A misjudgment of the price sensitivity could result in both falling sales and profits.

Factors Determining the Degree of Elasticity

26. The elasticity of any product in response to a change in price will depend upon a number of factors.

   ❑ **The availability of substitutes**. Glass, for example has no perfect replacement and is therefore very inelastic. Likewise, cars, cigarettes and newspapers are relatively inelastic but the demand for any particular brand could be elastic.

   ❑ **The proportion of income spent on a product**. Matches and salt, for example, are cheap to buy and therefore relatively inelastic in demand.

   ❑ **Necessities** such as bread, milk, potatoes and clothing are inelastic, whereas **luxuries** like foreign holidays, satellite television and computers are elastic. Although you might argue that these are necessities because, where incomes are steadily rising, the luxuries of one generation become the necessities of the next.

   ❑ **Habit forming products** such as tobacco and alcohol have a relatively inelastic demand.

Task 5   **1.1.1 (N3.3, C3.2)**

1. Suggest how the following might react to a 5% rise in the price of electricity.

   A family live in a 4 bedroomed house with electric central heating. They also have an electric oven and hob. Their bills average £450 in each winter quarter and £250 in each summer quarter. Their gross income is £18,000 pa.

2. Explain, with reasons, whether you think that the demand for electricity is relatively elastic or inelastic.

3. Draw a diagram which illustrates your views.

Income Elasticity of Demand (YED)

27. YED measures the responsiveness of demand to change in levels of income. It is calculated as:

$$YED = \frac{\% \text{ change in quantity demanded}}{\% \text{ change in income}}$$

28. As seen earlier, a change in income changes the demand conditions so that we get a new demand curve. if income is increased, the demand for necessities will probably not change much but the demand for luxuries is likely to increase.

29. If an increase in income produces a fall in demand, YED is negative. This is because people switch from 'inferior' to 'better' products. Examples would be, consumers buying less sausage and relatively cheap cuts of meat because they can now afford steak; or buying a car rather than using public transport.

Task 6   1.1.1 (N3.3, C3.3)

When John Smith had an income of £10,000 pa, he bought 4 bottles of beer per week. Following a rise in income to £12,000 pa, he now buys 5 bottles per week.

1. Calculate the elasticity of demand in this situation.

2. State whether or not demand is elastic.

3. Draw a diagram to illustrate your answer.

Cross Elasticity of Demand (XED)

30. XED measures the responsiveness of demand to changes in the price of other products. It is calculated as:

$$XED = \frac{\% \text{ change in demand for A}}{\% \text{ change in price of B}}$$

31. If XED is positive, the products are said to be **substitutes** for each other, for example, coffee and tea, butter and margarine.

32. If XED is negative, the products are said to be **complementary** (dependent), for example, golf clubs and golf balls, cars and petrol, video recorders and video tapes.

33. If XED is zero, the products are said to be independent, and therefore have no effect on each other. The demand for food and holidays, for example, are independent.

Task 7   1.1.1 (N3.3, C3.3)

An increase in the price of apples from 24p to 32p caused Nina Patel to buy more pears, 3lb instead of 2lb.

1. Calculate the cross elasticity of demand in the above situation.

2. Is demand elastic or inelastic?

Exceptional Demand Curves

34. There are some situations where the demand curve does not slope downwards from left to right. Examples include:

☐ **price movements linked to expectations**. For example, shares bought and sold on the Stock Exchange.

❏ **ostentatious products** such as diamonds, mink coats and Rolls-Royce cars, which are bought for 'snob appeal' and

❏ **inferior products** (known as 'Giffen' goods) which are bought when income is very low. As income rises (or prices fall) less is bought as consumers switch to 'better' products. This is true of basic foodstuffs in underdeveloped countries.

Supply

35. This is the total amount of a particular product which suppliers are able and prepared to offer for sale, at a given price, over a period of time. For example, the supply of commodity X at a price of £2 is 4,000 units per week.

36. This can be shown on a **supply curve** which represents the quantity of products which would be supplied at various price levels. The market supply for any particular product is the sum of all the individual suppliers.

37. The key features of supply are that normally,

❏ the higher the price, the greater the amount supplied because it is more profitable to producers.

❏ the lower the price, the less the supply,

❏ hence the supply curve slopes upwards to the right.

38. **Example of a supply schedule.**

Price Per Unit (pence)	Quantity Supplied (000's per week)
25	250
20	200
15	140
10	100
5	40

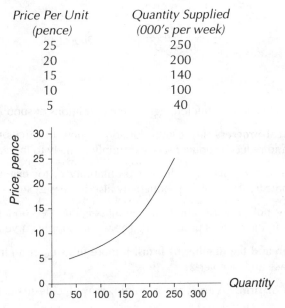

Changes in Supply

39. The supply curve above shows the relationship between supply and the quantity supplied assuming that the conditions of supply remain constant. If the price of products changes, this is shown as a shift along the supply curve. Each time the condition of supply changes, we get a new supply curve.

40.   **Changes in Supply**

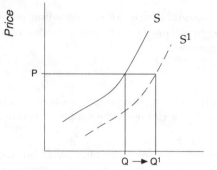

S¹ represents an **increase** in supply. More is now supplied at each and every price.

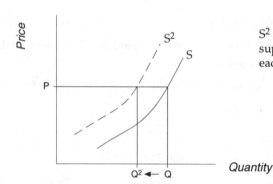

S² represents an **decrease** in supply. Less is now supplied at each and every price.

Determinants of Supply

41. Factors which will cause a shift (change) in the conditions of supply include:

☐ **Technological progress.** If the introduction of new materials, methods or equipment improve efficiency and reduce production costs, supply is likely to increase.

☐ **Changes in factor prices** which alter profitability if, for example, wages increase in a labour intensive industry then unless productivity also increases, supply may be reduced.

☐ **Government policy.** For example, when a tax is imposed on a product, it has the same effect as an increase in the costs of production. The whole supply curve moves upwards and to the left.

☐ **Competition and the number of firms.** If more firms enter an industry, supply would be expected to increase and vice versa.

☐ **Objectives of firms**. A firm, for example, may decide to increase market share by lowering prices.

☐ **Legal changes**. Government legislation may increase the costs of production for manufacturers. Examples being the introduction of safety or environmental measures.

☐ **Changes in demand.** The amount supplied will vary with the amount customers are prepared to buy at the market price.

Task 8

1.1.2 (N3.3, C3.3)

1. XYZ is a manufacturer of confectionery. Illustrate what would happen to the supply curve in each of the following situations.

   a) An increased volume of sales.

   b) A fall in the price of sugar.

   c) An increase in the price of sweets.

   d) An agreement with unions to increase wage rates.

   e) An increase in Uniform Business Rates.

2. Comment on your diagrams and what they reveal about the relationship between price and supply.

Elasticity of Supply (PES)

42. This measures the degree of responsiveness of supply to changes in price. It is calculated as:

$$PES = \frac{\% \text{ change in quantity supplied}}{\% \text{ change in price}}$$

43. If PES is greater than one, that is a small change in price causes a relatively large change in the quantity supplied, it is **elastic**. For example, if a 2% change in price causes a 5% change in supply.

44. If PES is less than one, that is a small change in price causes a relatively small change in the quantity supplied, it is **inelastic**. For example, if a 2% change in price causes a 1% change in demand.

45. If PES is equal to one, elasticity is **unitary.** That is, the proportionate change in quantity supplied is exactly the same as the proportionate change in price. Thus, for example, a 2% change in price causes a 2% change in supply.

46.   **This can be illustrated graphically as follows:**

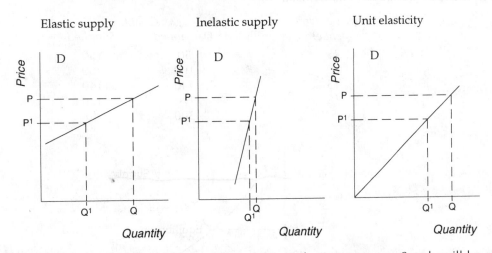

47. PES will depend upon the cost and flexibility of the productive resources. Supply will be elastic if production with existing capacity, can be quickly and easily expanded in response to changes in demand. Thus, for example, by overtime, employing more workers, using spare capacity or stocks. This may be possible in mass production industries such as cars, footwear and many services such as foreign holidays.

48. On the other hand, the supply of many products is inelastic. For example, it would take several years for a significant increase in the size of beef and dairy herds. Likewise, rubber trees take 5–7

years to grow, whilst the supply of many foodstuffs is governed by the acreage planted and the growing time involved. Supply will also be inelastic where the cost of entering a market are high.

Task 9   1.1.2 (N3.3, C3.3)

The following are the weekly supply schedules of 2 wheelbarrow manufacturers.

Laurel Ltd		Hardy Ltd	
Price, £	**Quantity**	**Price, £**	**Quantity**
10	5	10	0
20	10	20	0
30	15	30	20
40	20	40	25
50	25	50	30
60	30	60	35

1. What is the elasticity of supply of Laurel Ltd?

2. What is the elasticity of supply between £30 & £40 of Hardy Ltd

3. What is the total supply per week of wheelbarrows at a price of £40?

4. If prices rose to £50 what would be the increase in supply?

5. Give 3 situations which would cause the supply curve for wheelbarrows to move to the right.

Interaction of Supply and Demand

49. As shown in the following diagram, the **equilibrium price** is given by the interaction of the supply and demand curves ie 15p. At this price, the amount brought to the market by suppliers exactly matches the amount demanded by the buyers.

50. **Interaction of Supply and Demand**

Price per Unit (pence)	Quantity Demanded	Supplied
25	50	250
20	100	200
15	140	140
10	170	100
5	300	40

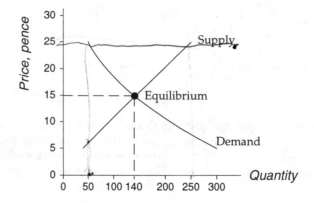

51. Above the equilibrium price, supply is greater than demand. Therefore the price must be reduced to attract more buyers. Below this price, demand is greater than supply. This will result in an increase in price. Further examples are shown below.

Task 10 **1.1.3 (N3.3, C3.3)**

Study the following data and answer the questions which follow:

Price, p	Quantity demanded	Quantity supplied
25	350	40
30	300	80
35	200	120
40	150	150
45	120	300
50	100	400

1. What is the equilibrium price?

2. If the government fixes a statutory maximum price of 35p, what will be the effect?

3. In what price range is demand inelastic?

52.

Fall in demand

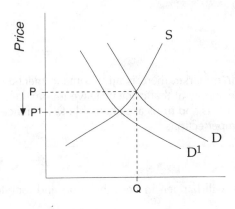

In the **short-run** price falls from P to P^1 because suppliers are unable to react to the fall in demand.

53.

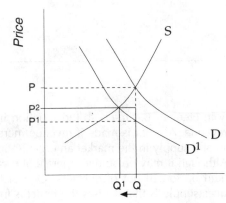

In the **long-run** the fall in demand forces many suppliers out of business. Therefore supply is reduced and a new equilibrium is reached at P^2Q^1.

54.

Fall in supply

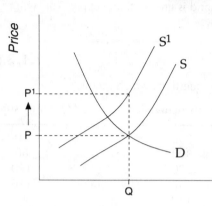

In the **short-run** a fall in supply causes the price to rise from P to P¹ as customers continue to buy the product.

55.

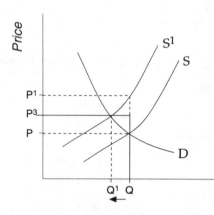

In the **long-run** many buyers will not pay the higher price which causes demand to fall until a new equilibrium is reached at P³Q¹.

56. This illustrates that, in theory, given a free market there is an automatic mechanism which determines price. Firms must either choose to supply at that price or leave the market. In practice, however, there are very few perfectly free markets and firms are often able to influence price because of their monopoly power or other market imperfections.

Task 11	**1.1.3 (N3.3)**

Draw the diagrams to illustrate what will happen in both the short and long-term in the following situations

1) An increase in demand

2) An increase in supply

Demand, Supply and Break-even

57. Break-even which is discussed more fully in Element 6.4 refers to the situation in an organisation where its total costs equal its total sales revenue. A profit is made if revenue increases beyond this point. In responding to changes in demand and supply in the market an organisation must be aware of the impact of its break-even position. Although it may be able to operate at less than break-even in the short-run, in the longer term it could be forced out of business. One of the problems, for example, which it might foresee if it reduces supply is that it loses the benefits from economies of scale. That is, the earnings which it can make by operating on a larger scale, for example bulk buying, which helps to reduce production costs.

Assignment – Supply and Demand   **Element 1.1**

You are asked to prepare a report based on primary or secondary data from the local or national economy. From this data construct supply and demand curves to analyse 2 products to explain:

1. the causes of change in demand and supply for your chosen products. The report should also analyse how the interaction of demand and supply has influenced decision making about the 2 products;

2. the importance to business of the relationship between price, demand and quantity supplied and the relationship between price, profit and quantity supplied;

3. the importance of customers and competitors in terms of their effect on demand, prices, supply and the consequences of shifts in demand and supply in terms of output and sales.

The report should also:

4. indicate that the equilibrium between demand and supply will determine both the price and sales of a particular product and indicate the effects on price and sales of changes in demand and supply;

5. suggest possible future changes in demand and supply for the 2 products and how these could affect decisions made by the 2 businesses.

Your report can use any medium e.g. oral, audio-visual, word processed or written.

Theory of the Firm

58. The purpose of the theory of the firm is to predict the prices which firms will charge for their products and the quantity they will produce in a given period. It is useful to briefly consider this aspect of economics because it helps to provide an understanding of the importance of the market environment and how it influences the way in which firms behave. In economic theory, a firm will maximise its profit where its **marginal costs (MC)**, ie the additional cost of producing one more unit, equals the **marginal revenue (MR)**, ie the extra revenue from the sale of one more unit. **Average revenue (AR)** is the amount which a firm receives for each unit of output sold, in other words, the price. The AR and demand curve are the same thing.

Market Conditions

59. The way in which the laws of supply and demand operate in any particular market will depend upon the conditions which prevail at the time.

    The most important conditions being the:

    ❑ **number of buyers and sellers. The** higher the number, the greater the competition and therefore the more difficult it is for any one buyer or seller to influence the price.

    ❑ **independence of buyers or sellers.** If either group are able to collude, they may collectively be able to influence the market price.

    ❑ **degree of product differentiation. An** important point in marketing is that a differentiated product can be sold at a price which may be slightly higher than the rest of the market.

    ❑ **external constraints.** Prices in any market may be influenced by factors which prevent the free operation of supply and demand, for example Government intervention, such as rationing or price control; consumer preferences, to save rather than spend perhaps because of high interest rates or fear of redundancy.

60. Therefore, it is possible to identify from these market conditions a number of different competitive situations which determine how firms behave. These are usually classified as:

    ❑ perfect competition

    ❑ monopoly

❐ imperfect competition

❐ oligopoly

Perfect Competition

61. In a perfectly competitive market:

❐ each firm supplies only a small fraction of the total supply

❐ each product has only one price which is determined by market forces of supply and demand and

❐ each individual firm has a perfectly elastic demand curve because no matter how many units it sells it cannot change the price.

62.

Individual Firm Under Perfect Competition

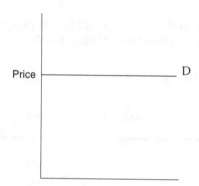

At a higher price, no demand exists and there is no incentive to sell at any lower price.

Output

63. For this 'ideal' situation of perfect competition to exist several specific conditions are necessary:

❐ **homogeneous products**, that is all sellers are offering the same product and thus there is no preference for any particular seller.

❐ **many buyers and sellers** so that no individual can influence price.

❐ **perfect knowledge** so that all buyers and sellers are fully aware of market conditions.

❐ **freedom of entry** which requires perfect mobility of factors of production and consumers. Entrepreneurs will seek to maximise profits and must be able to move resources freely to do this.

64. Perfect competition, therefore, encourages efficient production and keeps prices lower for consumers. In practice, however, these conditions are somewhat unrealistic and difficult to achieve. The nearest examples probably being the financial and commodity markets.

Task 12   **1.2.1 (C3.4)**

To what extent do the following markets meet the conditions of perfect competition?

    1.   Beef   2.   Envelopes   3.   Scissors

    4.   Furniture   5.   Beer

---

65. **Output Under Perfect Competition**

In paragraph 58 said that a firm's most profitable output is where MC=MR. The industry will be in equilibrium where all firms are producing the optimum output and earning what is called '**normal profits**'.

66. **This can be shown graphically as follows:**

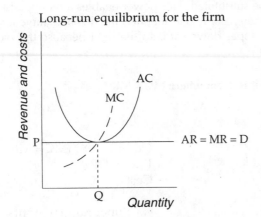

Long-run equilibrium for the firm

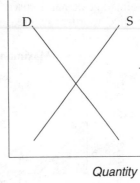

Equilibrium in the industry

67. If a firm is producing at a price which exceeds AC then '**super-normal profits**' will be made as shown by the shaded area in the diagram below.

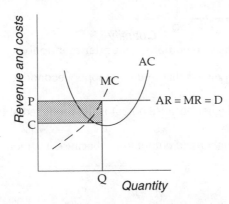

68. But, under perfect competition, new firms will be attracted into the industry and total supply will therefore be increased. This will cause the price to fall until all firms are only earning normal profit.

Task 13   **1.2.1 (N3.3)**

Draw the diagram and explain what would happen to a firm whose AC exceeds the price under perfect competition.

Monopoly

69. At the other extreme we have what is called a pure monopoly. In economic theory, this refers to a single supplier dominating a market but in practice this rarely exists. British Gas, for example, still competes with electricity and coal as a source of fuel.

70. Under UK law, a monopoly exists if either:

  ❏ one firm accounts for 25% or more of the total supply of given goods or service or

  ❏ two or more firms accounting for more than a 25% share of the market prevent, restrict or distort competition.

Output Under Monopoly

71. A firm under monopoly can either determine the **price** at which its product will be sold or the quantity of **output** it is prepared to supply. It is not possible to control both because it cannot control demand.

72. For monopoly power to exist, a firm must be able to both restrict the entry of competitors and also have a product which cannot easily be substituted. This power enables a monopolist to earn super-normal profits in the long-run. Since there is only one supplier, the demand curve for the product is also the market demand curve. This slopes downwards to the right because the monopolist must reduce price in order to increase sales.

73.

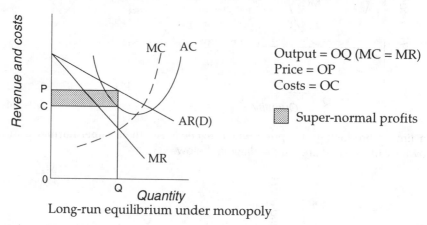

Maximum profit is again where MC = MR

Output = OQ (MC = MR)
Price = OP
Costs = OC

Super-normal profits

Long-run equilibrium under monopoly

74. Lack of competition means that under monopoly economic efficiency may be affected in two main ways:

  ❑ Costs could be higher because output is not produced at the lowest average cost. Excess capacity therefore exists and

  ❑ Price could be higher and output lower because it is more profitable for the firm.

Task 14   1.2.1 (C3.4)

'A monopolist sometimes finds it profitable to split a market into segments charging different prices in each for the same commodity. This is only possible where the elasticity of demand is different in each, there are no close substitutes and the market can be kept separate to prevent the product being bought only in the cheaper market. Telephone charges, for example, vary according to the time of day, whilst the railways, gas and electricity industries also discriminate in a similar way.' The above passage explains what is referred to as a discriminating monopolist.

1. Describe a discriminating monopolist in your own words.

2. Why do monopolists discriminate like this?

3. Why must the elasticity of demand be different in each market segment?

4. Which market would command the higher market price?

Imperfect Competition

75. The more usual situation is that of imperfect, sometimes called monopolistic competition, where a large number of firms each have a small share of the market. This may be due to one of several factors which help to differentiate products including:

  ❑ branding and trade marks

  ❑ packaging

  ❑ convenience of sellers' location

  ❑ patents

76. In effect, these give each firm a small monopoly but with many close substitutes. This is very important for marketing which is discussed in detail in Unit 3.

Output under Imperfect Competition

77. Under imperfect competition, a firm can charge a price which is different from its competitors. Sales therefore will depend on the price charged and thus the demand (AR) curve will slope downwards to the right. Output will also increase as the price falls and therefore MR is always less than AR. Maximum profit is again where MR = MC.

78.

Short-run equilibrium in imperfect competition

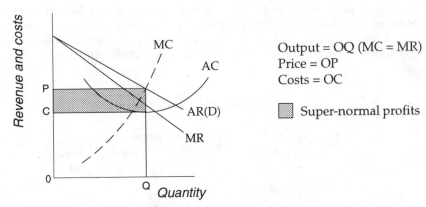

Output = OQ (MC = MR)
Price = OP
Costs = OC

Super-normal profits

79. In the short-run, the number of firms is fixed and therefore individual firms can make 'super-normal' profits of PC per unit. The firm is not producing at the lowest AC because it is more profitable. Thus spare capacity exists. This will continue until more firms are attracted into the industry.

80. As new firms enter, demand will be less for individual firms at each and every price, therefore the AR curve will shift to the left. Normal profits will now be earned.

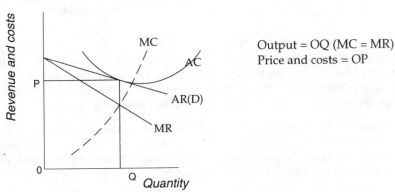

Output = OQ (MC = MR)
Price and costs = OP

Long-run equilibrium under imperfect competition

Task 15   1.2.1 (C3.2)

Study the market of a consumer product or service which you regularly use, such as soft drinks, bread or buses.

1. Identify the main 'brands' available locally and consider in what way(s) they are 'differentiated' from their competitors.

2. Consider also what possible substitutes exist and the extent to which this affects the price which you pay.

3. Comment on whether or not your study has affected your attitude towards the product or service which you use.

Oligopoly

81. A particular type of imperfect competition common in the UK is that of oligopoly which refers to markets dominated by just a few large firms. Examples include cars, cigarettes, soap powders, cement, petrol and banking. These usually develop from mergers and takeovers which result in economies of scale but give monopoly power. There are usually barriers to small firms wishing to enter or grow in such a market either due to the capital investment involved or because existing firms quickly increase promotional expenditure to 'kill-off ' any attempts.

82. Decisions on price and output in an oligopolistic market will depend upon the reactions of competitors who are likely to retaliate. Reduced prices, for example, are likely to be followed rather than risk losing business. On the other hand, where prices are increased, competitors are likely to prefer to try to increase market share rather than follow. This can be illustrated by the 'Kinked Demand Curve'.

83.

The Kinked Demand Curve

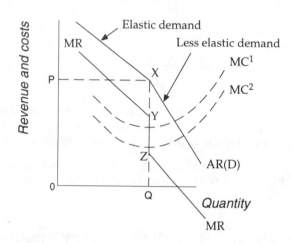

An oligopolist believes rivals will match price cuts but not price rises. Thus the demand curve is kinked at X. Price rises lead to a large loss of market share, but price cuts increase quantity only by increasing industry sales. MR is continuous at OQ. YZ = region of indeterminacy due to the sudden change in elasticity of demand. Thus MC can vary without altering price.

84. Consequently, oligopolists usually prefer **non-price competition** involving either **actual differences** between products such as quality, styling, reliability and after sales service; or **apparent differences** created by, for example, brand image, advertising and promotion which can influence customer perceptions of a product (see Unit 3 Marketing).

85. In practice therefore, prices set by oligopolists are often very similar, particularly where products are close substitutes, as price stability is preferred to price competition. Each firm realises that any attempt to maximise its own market share may result in a price war which will only reduce total profits in the industry as a whole and thus may leave all firms worse off.

86. The pressures towards price stability can often be recognised (implicitly or explicitly) in some form of collective pricing strategy or collusion as follows:

❏ **Price leadership** often occurs where firms follow that of the market leader. This form of tacit collusion is a common feature of oligopolistic markets.

❏ **Cartels** are agreements between firms to regulate prices and/or output, thereby effectively creating a monopoly. The best known example being the Organisation of Petroleum Exporting Countries (OPEC) which operates an oil cartel. Another example is where contracts are open to tender. Firms may agree to reduce competition by taking turns at offering the 'lowest' price in order to secure a regular flow of profitable work.

❏ **Exclusive dealing** involves a manufacturer preventing retailers from selling competitors' products as a condition of supply. For example Wall's and Mars ice-cream.

❏ **Full-line forcing** takes place when manufacturers will only supply retailers if they will sell the firms complete range of products. The costs involved thus limiting the number of suppliers a retailer can deal with.

87. All these forms of collusion are illegal in the UK under the Restrictive Practices Law because they are considered to be against the public interest. As such, they would need to be registered with the Office of Fair Trading for investigation. Most such agreements, however, are difficult to detect or prove and thus not easily prevented or controlled by legislation.

Task 16   **1.2.1, 1.2.2, 1.2.3 (C3.4)**

EU PROBE INTO STEEL CARTEL

British Steel has been accused by EU competition authorities of joining in an illegal Europe- wide cartel in steel beams for the construction industry. The UK steel-maker and at least five of its European competitors in France, Luxembourg, Spain and Germany could face fines of up to ten per cent of their annual turnover after Brussels competition authorities formally accused them of rigging markets and prices.

GLASS PRICE CARTEL IS UNCOVERED

A 'nationwide web of cartels on glass prices' has been uncovered, Sir Gordon Borrie, director general of fair trading said. It was a 'most serious breach of the law' and included price-fixing on window glass. The Office of Fair Trading began investigating after a building firm reported that it was 'tired of being ripped off'.

Action is expected in the Restrictive Practices Court.

SOAP GIANTS FACE MONOPOLY PROBE

The multi-billion pound detergent industry faces its biggest probe for more than 25 years.

A Monopolies and Mergers Commission inquiry is expected to examine the control Lever Brothers and Procter & Gamble have over the soap powders and washing-up liquids bought by every household in Britain.

The last Commission inquiry into the industry, in 1966, resulted in prices being capped for two years and cheaper 'square deal' packs. But it is felt in Whitehall that the industry continues to operate under a virtual monopoly, keeping prices artificially high, giving consumers a raw deal.

The new inquiry will examine whether Lever Brothers and Procter & Gamble prevent new competitors entering the lucrative market.

Lever Brothers spends millions promoting key brands such as Persil, Surf, Lux, Radion and Comfort. Procter & Gamble does the same for Ariel, Bold, Daz, Dreft and the newly launched Fairy Excel washing-up liquid.

From the above articles:

1. Identify the examples of potential restrictive practices.

2. Explain why the Government is concerned about them.

3. Describe the action being or likely to be taken to control them.

Pricing

88. Pricing is one of the most difficult areas in a business which is dependent upon a number of factors in addition to cost. To maximise sales and profits, a firm will seek to fix a price which suits the market so that it is judged by customers to be reasonable and offering value in the circumstances prevailing at the time. This will be based on a combination of factors including the firm's objectives, the market in which it is operating, the type of product and the expected life span of the product.

Thus, for example,

❏ with **new products,** consumers are often initially prepared to pay a higher price;

❏ likewise, **quality products** must be sold at a price which reflects that quality;

❏ the prices of commodities such as gold, sugar and wheat move up and down in response to changes in **supply and demand**;

❏ whilst a market trader selling fresh fruit and vegetables will often lower prices at the end of the day to **clear stock**;

❏ insurance premium are calculated from the **risk involved**;

❏ products **differentiated by branding** such as Heinz baked beans may well sell at a price higher than that of rivals. These examples merely serve to illustrate the vast diversity of markets and products and the importance of pricing in the marketing mix (see Element 3.1).

Task 17   **1.2.3 (C3.4)**

PRUDENTIAL CUSTOMERS PAY THE PRICE

Around 30,000 motorists have deserted the Pru and gone elsewhere. Following rises in motor premiums of 8% in January, 6% in March and 5% in August with further increases expected.

The increase in premiums meant that the company was getting roughly the same income from policies despite having fewer policyholders but this demonstrates the difficult balance which the company faces between providing profits for its shareholders without upsetting its policyholders.

So far, shareholders are winning hands down. Shares in the Prudential jumped 6p to 236p yesterday after a 46pc jump in half time pre-tax profits to £249m. The dividend is lifted 7.9pc to 4.1p. But the profit increases owed much to large rises in premiums on motor and household insurance policies, turning a loss of £23m last time into a profit of £3m.

Some city experts believe that the Pru only stays in the car insurance business to allow its sales force the chance to sell savings plans to customers. Profits from its life operation rose 5pc to almost £200m, helped by a 6pc rise in new annual premiums and a 56pc jump in single premiums which the company says reflects the benefit of reorganising its direct sales force.

Nonetheless, policyholders face the prospect of a cut in bonus rates for the third year running.

---

1.   What is the difficult balance which the Prudential faces?

2.   Why did the company need to put up its prices and what effects did it have?

3.   Explain the statement that 'so far the shareholders are winning hands down'.

4.   What type of pricing policy do you think the Company has adopted?

---

89. **Pricing Policies**

There are a number of different pricing policies or strategies which a firm amy adopt in order to achieve its pricing objectives. These include: skim, penetration, mixed, differential, absorption, promotional, marginal-cost, negotiable, single and market pricing.

90. **Skim Pricing** uses high prices to obtain a high profit and quick recovery of the research and development costs in the early stages of a product's life before competition intensifies. This is useful for products with a short life cycle such as 'pop' records and fashion items. Computers, videos, toys and compact discs provide other examples of 'new' products where consumers are often prepared to pay a high price. As competition increases price may be reduced to strengthen the market share.

91. **Penetration Pricing** is the use of lower than normal prices to increase market share. It is also used to establish a new product in a market which is expected to have a long-life and potential for growth. Consumer products are often introduced in this way. A price increase will usually take place once the product has successfully entered the market.

92. **Mixed Pricing** is a policy which initially uses skim pricing and then, as competition increases, price cutting, sometimes even below cost, to penetrate the market, increase market share and eliminate competition.

93. **Destructive pricing** involves reducing the price of an existing product or selling a new product at an artificially low price in order to destroy competitors' sales.

Skim, Penetration and Mixed Pricing

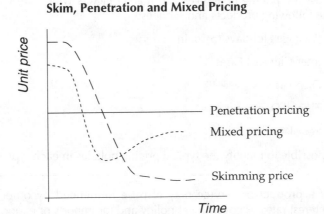

94. **Differential Pricing** is the use of different prices for the same product when it is sold in different locations or market segments. Large buyers for example, often receive quantity discounts, whilst small buyers or those located in remote areas may be charged a higher price to cover the additional distribution costs. Telephone, gas and electricity are sold at different prices to domestic and industrial consumers and the price charged also depends on the time of day used.

95. **Absorption (cost-plus or full-cost) Pricing** involves calculating the cost of producing each unit of output and then adding a fixed percentage profit mark-up to give the price e.g. cost per unit £10, percentage mark-up 20%, price £10 + 2 = £12. Relatively slow selling items such as furniture are usually given a high mark-up whilst fast turnover items like foodstuffs in supermarkets are given a lower mark-up.

96. **Promotional Pricing** involves the use of lower than normal prices either to launch a new product or to periodically boost the sales of existing products. Supermarkets for example, have regular special offers and sometimes use **'loss leaders'** where everyday goods like tea and sugar are sold at less than cost to attract customers into the store.

97. **Marginal Cost (or contribution) Pricing** is sometimes used when a firm has some spare capacity which it wishes to use without diverting away from its regular business. Essentially, a firm incurs fixed costs such as rent, light and heat whether or not it is operating at full capacity. These costs are covered by the firm's regular products. Therefore sometimes a firm is prepared to accept additional business provided that the marginal (i.e. additional) revenue covers the marginal costs (i.e. materials and labour) involved and makes at least some contribution to the fixed costs which represents the profit. Market traders, for example, use this method when clearing fresh produce at the end of the day. Another example is the 'last minute' holiday bargains offered by package tour operators.

98. **Negotiable (or Variable) Pricing** is common in industrial markets and the building trade. The price is individually calculated to take account of costs, demand and any specific customer requirements. Customers may obtain estimates from a number of suppliers before placing an order, although factors other than price, such as quality and delivery may also be important.

99. **Single (or range) Pricing** involves a policy of charging one price to everyone. Examples include standard fares on bus or tube routes and publishers who often have a range of books at one price.

100. **Market Pricing**. In paragraphs 49–56 we considered how prices can be determined by the interaction of demand and supply. The seller has little control over the price in this situation which is likely to fluctuate daily. Examples include commodity markets such as gold, silver, wheat and wool, and the Stock Exchange.

101. **Expansion pricing** involves setting a price which seems to maximise sales enabling the benefits of economies of scale to be gained. These savings help to sustain a lower price which helps to maintain or develop market share.

Task 18   **1.2.3 (C3.2)**

1. Discuss the pricing objectives and market factors which are likely to influence the price of the following products and services:

   a)   Package Holidays to Spain

   b)   Inter-City Rail Fares

   c)   Dishwashers

   d)   Tinned Dog Food

   e)   Petrol

2. Is it possible to identify the typical pricing policies in each type of market?

---

102. The price of a product or service may also be influenced by other factors. Examples include changes in interest rates or government policy and for imports or exports trading agreements, tariffs, barriers and customs duties. Also, non-pricing strategies may be used particularly in oligopolistic markets where advertising, promotion and public relations are used to develop consumers' perceptions of a product rather than price competition (see Unit 3).

Task 19   **1.2.3 (N3.3)**

1. Design a table/chart which summarises the key features of the different market structures under the following headings:

   • Number of firms.

   • Ability to influence price.

   • Barriers to entry.

   • Example(s).

2. Grabville, a small town in the West Country has 2 garages, Charlie Blacks and PRT. Both are selling petrol at the same price: unleaded at 55p per litre and leaded at 65p per litre. Charlie Black reckons that if he reduces prices, PRT will follow and between them, they will not generate much extra business. If he puts his price up, PRT would do nothing, so he would lose customers. Charlie estimates his demand schedule to be as follow:

Leaded price	Sales (litres per day)	Unleaded price	Sales (litres per day)
75	50	75	100
70	150	70	250
65	250	65	450
60	300	60	550
55	350	55	600
50	400	50	650

   a)   Draw the demand curves for Charlie's business.

continued...

Task 19 continued

b) Calculate his total revenue if he charged the following prices:

	1	2	3
leaded	65	70	75
unleaded	55	60	65

c) In what circumstances might Charlie consider increasing or reducing his prices?

d) Charlie knows the PRT manager well and is thinking about meeting to discuss an agreement on pricing to increase profits. He is considering 70p for leaded and 60p for unleaded. What advice would you give to Charlie?

e) Suggest ways in which Charlie could compete with PRT without getting involved in a price war.

Cost-Benefit Analysis

103. When the Government is considering a major item of public expenditure, for example, developing a new motorway or coal mine, it may decide to carry out a cost-benefit analysis. Such studies attempt to evaluate all the costs and benefits which are expected to affect the community. These costs can be both private and social.

104. The **private cost** of something is essentially the price which an individual or organisation pays for it, for example, buying a car for £8,000. The **private benefits** of this purchase are difficult to estimate but will include the convenience, flexibility and saving from not using other forms of transport.

105. However, there will also be wider social costs and social benefits from this decision to buy a car. **Social costs** are those which affect the community and will include the extra traffic congestion, noise, loss of business to public or other transport, pollution from exhaust fumes and the increased wear and tear of the roads. **Social benefits** which will occur include a more flexible, mobile work-force, additional employment – in garages for parts and servicing, or road maintenance, and more Government revenue from the tax on petrol sales.

106. Although cost-benefit analysis is usually associated with the public sector all decisions to supply a market will result in a similar mixture of costs and benefits. Any investment whether in new business, developments such as new offices, factories or extensions or the infrastructure of roads, railways, schools or hospitals can produce social benefits such as an increase in employment, income and job security leading to greater economic activity in the area concerned.

107. But such developments are also likely to have some adverse effects on the local environment in terms of air pollution, noise pollution, waste disposal and depletion of natural resources. For example, trees or countryside being 'lost', fishing or water sports destroyed by toxic waste, open views blocked by buildings and roads congested by extra traffic, all of which can affect people's health, leisure and lifestyle.

108.   **Social Costs and Benefits of Mining**

109. It is important in considering social costs and benefits to remember that what some people may see as benefits others may see as costs. For example, groups such as employers and the unemployed may see the building of an airport or motorway to support economic activity as a benefit which could lead to extra business and a growth in jobs. On the other hand, environmentalists may see it as destruction of the land, bringing pollution and congestion.

Task 20   1.2.3, 1.2.4 (C3.4)

1. Consider the potential costs and benefits of building either a major new car park, super-store or other development in a town or city near to where you live and work.

2. What difficulties can you foresee in putting a monetary value on the factors which you have identified?

---

110. In recent years organisations are facing increasing pressure to take account of social costs. This is partly due to the growth in the 1980's and 1990's of

   ❏ organised **pressure groups** with interests in areas like consumer protection, women's rights, ethnic minorities and health education. Such groups can range in size and permanency from well established international organisations like Greenpeace, to just a few local people getting together to campaign for a few days or weeks hoping to prevent a housing or factory development taking place, or the closure of a school or railway line.

   ❏ concern about **environmental issues** such as conservation and pollution has not only been supported by pressure groups but also recent government legislation. This has led to a demand for environmentally friendly, often called 'green', products and the development of recycled products, particularly paper, toilet rolls, paper bags and other forms of packaging. Whilst firms like ICI now publish environmental objectives with its Annual Report.

Environmental change

111. Concern about the environment has become an increasingly important issue in recent years to such an extent that both the Government and European Union have introduced important strategies covering protection, preservation and pollution. These measures are of major importance to business organisations because they must alter their trading practices in order to meet them. BS.7750 is an official British Standard against which environmental management systems can now be assessed. Recycling – the recovery and re-use of materials such as paper, metals and glass – has become increasingly important.

Environmental strategies

112. The **Environmental Protection Acts 1990 and 1995** are significant legislative measures which set out a wide range of powers and duties for central and local government including the control over litter and waste, air pollution, noise and emissions to water outlined below:

   ❏ **Litter and waste**. Local authorities how have a duty to control litter and make plans for the recycling of waste. The dumping of litter can result in fines up to £1,000.

   ❏ **Air quality and pollution**. Local authorities are given powers to deal with statutory nuisances including smoke, dust and smells. The 3 main air pollutants are ozone, nitrogen dioxide and sulphur dioxide which must now be controlled in both existing and new industrial plants.

   ❏ **Water.** In general it is against the law to allow any polluting matter to enter water in Britain without legal authorisation. Businesses who break the law face fines of up to £20,000.

   ❏ **Noise.** Local authorities have a duty to inspect their areas for noise nuisance and to investigate complaints about it.

Task 21   **1.2.4, 1.2.5 (C3.4)**

SHETLAND OIL DISASTER

The oil boom of the 1970's and 1980's brought great wealth to the Shetland Isles. But in January 1993, the area was hit by a major disaster when the engines of the oil tanker Braer failed in a fierce storm. It broke up spilling up to 80,000 gallons of crude oil into the sea and killing thousands of birds, otters and seals. It also caused extensive pollution to the environment as oil blown by the gales contaminated land affecting sheep and cattle farming. Crops were condemned as unfit for human or animal use.

Salmon farming, the island's second largest industry was affected by toxic chemicals used to disperse the oil. Marks and Spencer and other retailers quickly decided to stop buying fish from the area.

Many people faced financial ruin with the economic, environmental and social effects expected to last for years.

Much concern was expressed that the area had no radar to give early warning when ships were in trouble. Also, the tanker was sailing under a flag of convenience and therefore not subject to any stringent UK or other government safety standards. 60% of losses at sea are accounted for by such merchant vessels which are often poorly maintained. The Braer itself was 17 years old, in good condition for its age but with some leaking pipes which the owner could not afford to replace.

Complete the following which are based on the Braer disaster.

1. Identify the main industries of the area.

2. Who, if anybody, was to blame for the disaster?

3. What were the main economic, social and environmental consequences of the disaster?

4. What do you feel could be done to prevent such a disaster in the future and who should be responsible for it?

5. In June 95 environmental pressure groups cauesd the international oil company Shell to withdraw plans to dump an oil platform in the North Sea. Find out more about it and the potential social costs and benefits involved.

Other Environmental Strategies

113. Other government strategies include those covering land use, the countryside, conservation, wildlife and global warming.

   ❑ **The regulation of land use** and planning restrictions include the protection of 'green belts' which are areas intended to be left open and free to prevent the sprawl of large build-up areas.

   ❑ **Encouraging open-air recreation** takes place through the provision and improvement of country parks and picnic sites. This role is the responsibility of the Countryside Commission.

   ❑ **Heritage conservation** covers the protection of historic buildings, ancient monuments and areas of special interest.

   ❑ **Protection of wildlife** includes, for example, banning the import of seal pup skins, whale products and ivory from the African elephant.

114. **Global warming.** The so-called 'greenhouse effect' is a natural phenomenon which keeps the earth at a temperature which can sustain life. In recent years, there has been considerable concern about the emission of man-made gases which are leading to additional warming of the earth and could cause serious changes in the world's climate.

To help combat this problem, in 1991 the government introduced a number of measures, including:

   ❑ a pledge to achieve a 15% improvement in the efficiency of its buildings over the next 5 years.

❑ a major three-year publicity campaign on the greenhouse effect and use of energy in the home.

❑ tighter building regulations to promote energy efficiency in new houses.

❑ a commitment to phase out all ozone-damaging substances by the year 2000, including CFCs (Chlorofluorcarbons) which are artificial gases used in the manufacture of foams, as solvents, in refrigeration and as aerosol propellants.

❑ to reduce exhaust pollution from the 24 million vehicles on Britain's roads. Strict European Community standards for all new cars are now in force including the requirement to run on unleaded petrol which by May 1994 accounted for well over half of all sales.

Recycling

115. Sometimes called material salvage, recycling is the recovery and re-use of materials from spent products. It has become an important issue in recent years for two main reasons:

❑ On the one hand, the increasing scarcity and cost of natural resources such as oil, gas, coal, mineral ores and trees,

❑ whilst on the other hand, the increasing pollution of air, water and land by waste materials such as plastics and chemicals, many of which do not decompose and/or can emit harmful gases.

116. There are two basic types of recycling.

❑ **Internal salvage** is the re-use in a manufacturing process of materials which are a waste of that process. For example, re-melting and re-casting metal cuttings such as iron, copper or steel.

❑ **External salvage** is the reclaiming of materials from a product which is worn out or obsolete. For example, the collection of old newspapers for the manufacture of new paper products; bottles for glass; drink cans for aluminium or electric storage batteries for lead. Whilst bark, wood chippings and lignin from wood and paper mills are often used as animal bedding or returned to the soil as fertiliser.

117. The importance of recycling, whether internal or external, is that it helps to save scarce economic resources. To make this worthwhile, however, the cost of reprocessing must be less than the costs involved in processing new materials.

118. The Government encourages the reclamation of recycling of waste materials wherever this is practicable and has set a target that by 2000 half of all recyclable household waste will be re-used. To collect materials for recycling, there are currently some 5,000 'bottle banks' in Britain as well as 'can banks', 'paper banks' and in some places 'plastics' or 'textile banks'.

Task 22   **1.2.4, 1.2.5 (C3.4)**

MONEY FROM RUBBISH

Plans to increase recycled household rubbish by the turn of the century have been announced by Derbyshire county council.

The scheme will boost the amount of recycled domestic waste from the present 2.5 per cent to 25 per cent – or 1,000,000 tonnes – by the year 2000.

Recent changes in the law mean that the council can now pay a subsidy to rubbish collectors, provided the materials are to be recycled.

It has agreed to pay £6.40 per tonne to all waste collectors – including district councils and voluntary or non-profit making organisations – who will still be able to claim the full salvage value of the materials from the recycler. Among the items that could be reclaimed are glass, paper, metal cans, oil, textiles and scrap metal.

continued...

Task 22 continued

RECYCLED CARDS

A full circle will be completed with the launch of a Christmas card recycling scheme by the Countryside Commission in conjunction with Boots.

The money raised will be ploughed back into the development of the country's twelve community forests which are a joint initiative between the Countryside Commission and Forestry Commission in partnership with local authorities and communities. They will create wooded landscapes for wildlife, employment, recreation and education. Local schools have been invited to take part in the scheme.

A recycling point will be made available at Boots stores where customers will be able to return unwanted Christmas and other greetings cards.

In another scheme, some local councils have been shredding Christmas trees.

CANNY CASH

A new recycling service, aimed at schools and voluntary groups and organised by Alcan Aluminium Can Recycling enables people to trade aluminium drink cans for cash at the rate of 45p a kilo. Alcan reckon that millions of cans are thrown away every year. The cans are taken to a £28 million recycling plant in Warrington, Europe's largest, where they are melted down to use again.

Articles like those above regularly appear in local and national media. From these and others which you can collect yourselves, complete the following:

1. Identify, with the use of examples, at least 5 benefits from recycling.

2. Are there any potential drawbacks?

3. Who and why do you think stand to gain most from recycling – consumers, local authorities, businesses, other groups?

4. Suggest ways in which the organisation in which you work or study could benefit from introducing a recycling campaign.

5. Finally, draw up outline plans for a recycling campaign and include in it how you would address the following issues:

    ❑   how to encourage people to sort their waste for recycling.

    ❑   where the nearest 'banks' are or could be located.

    ❑   how to inform people about the campaign and where to find the banks, which may involve carrying out research before and after the campaign.

    ❑   how to evaluate the success of the campaign which may involve carrying out research before and after the campaign.

Summary

119. a)   Economics is the study of how limited resources (supply) are allocated to satisfy human wants (demand).

   b)   A market is any situation where buyers and sellers come together.

   c)   The main types of markets are retail, wholesale, produce, commodity, shipping, insurance, financial and foreign exchange.

   d)   Markets with many buyers and sellers operate according to the laws of supply and demand.

   e)   The 2 main laws of demand are

        ❑   the lower the price the greater the quantity demanded

❐ the higher the price the lower the quantity demanded

f) Price, income and cross elasticity can be used to measure degrees of responsiveness of demand, to changes in demand conditions.

g) Exceptional demand curves are those which do not slope downwards from left to right.

h) The 2 main laws of supply are

❐ the higher the price the greater the quantity supplied

❐ the lower the price the lower the quantity supplied

i) The elasticity of supply measures the degree of responsiveness of supply to changes in price.

j) In a completely free market, price is determined by the interaction of demand and supply.

k) The theory of the firm shows how price and output are determined under different market conditions.

l) In economic theory, the profit maximising output is where MC=MR

m) The 2 extremes of perfect competition and monopoly rarely exist in practice.

n) Imperfect competition is more usual as a result of product differentiation.

o) An oligopoly exists in a market dominated by just a few large firms.

p) Unfair trading practices such as cartels are controlled by legislation.

q) Pricing objectives may be related to a rate of return, growth, competition or market share.

r) Pricing policies include skim, penetration, mixed, destructive, differential, absorption, promotional, marginal-cost, negotiable, single, market and expansion.

s) Decisions by an organisation to supply a market will result in a mixture of social costs and benefits.

t) Increasing concern about the environment has lead to government legislation and strategies to protect it.

Review questions *(Answers can be found in the paragraphs indicated)*

1. Briefly describe and give examples of at least 4 different types of markets. (3–6)

2. What is demand and what determines the shape of the demand curve? (8–11, 34)

3. What factors change the conditions of demand and how is this shown graphically? (12–14)

4. Briefly explain price elasticity of demand and its importance to firms. (15–25)

5. Distinguish between income and cross elasticity of demand. (27–33)

6. What is supply and what determines the shape of the supply curve? (35–38)

7. What factors change the conditions of supply and how is this shown graphically? (39–41)

8. Briefly explain price elasticity of supply and its significance to firms. (42–48)

9. With the use of a simple diagram, explain how prices are determined by the interaction of supply and demand. (49–52)

10. Identify the 4 key factors which determine market conditions. (58–61)

11. Identify the conditions required for perfect competition. (61–64)

12. Explain how and why a firm with a monopoly can achieve super-normal profits. (69–74)

13. How is output determined under conditions of imperfect competition? (77–80)

14. Outline the distinguishing features of an oligopolistic market. (81–85)

15. Explain what you understand by collusion and why is it controlled by legislation. (86–87)

16. Distinguish between pricing objectives and pricing policies. (88–89)

17. Describe 4 pricing policies which an organisation may choose to adopt. (90–101)

18. Using examples distinguish between social costs and benefits and private costs and benefits. (103–109)

19. Outline the Government's strategy for protecting the environment (111–114)

20. Explain the 2 basic types of recycling. (115–116)

Assignment – Businesses and Markets   **Element 1.2**

You are asked to prepare a report which compares one competitive and one non-competitive market (e.g. computer software versus household gas or jeans versus domestic water supply) in terms of

1. the number of suppliers in the market (private or public sector monopolies or oligopolies);

2. the size of supplies and strength of demand in the market and

3. compares 2 businesses in one market showing shifts in demand curves and explains why the shifts have occurred.

The report should also describe how the competition affects:

4. consumer's choice and the quality of products;

5. pricing and non-pricing strategies to improve market position;

6. the costs and benefits to the wider community.

3 Effects of Government on Markets

In Chapter 1 we considered the many ways in which the government has an influence on all types of business organisations. In this Chapter, we are considering the intervention of the government in the economy in order to achieve its aims. It covers:

- ❏ Types of Economic Systems
- ❏ Government and the Economy
- ❏ National Income
- ❏ Use of National Income Statisticst
- ❏ Circular Flow of Income
- ❏ Keynes
- ❏ Aggregate Demand and the Multiplier
- ❏ Size of the Multiplier
- ❏ Inflationary and Deflationary Gaps
- ❏ Government Macro-Economic Aims
- ❏ Fiscal Policy
- ❏ Types of Taxes
- ❏ Tax and Business
- ❏ The Budget
- ❏ PSBR

- ❏ Public Expenditure
- ❏ Monetary Policy
- ❏ Monetary Sector
- ❏ Economic Growth
- ❏ Unemployment
- ❏ Inflation
- ❏ Government Influences on Business Location
- ❏ Urban Policy Initiatives
- ❏ European Union
- ❏ Consumer Protection Legislation
- ❏ Monopolies and Restrictive Practices
- ❏ European Competition Law
- ❏ Deregulation
- ❏ Economic Analysis

Micro-Economics

1. Much of what we consider in this text is called **micro-economics**. That is, it is concerned with the behaviour of individual consumers, firms or industries, including the allocation of scarce resources, determination of prices, supply and demand, perfect competition and monopoly and the theory of the firm. In each situation one individual, organisation or sector of the economy is considered in isolation from the rest of the economy.

Macro-Economics

2. In this Chapter we are considering the aggregate effects of individual behaviour, what is termed **macro-economics.** That is, how the economy as a whole works including the level of real income, the level of prices, the rate of interest, the rate of saving and investment, the rate of growth, the balance of payments and the level of unemployment.

Types of Economic System

3. All societies in the world face the basic economic problem of scarcity and choice. Because there are limited resources, it is necessary for each to decide what goods and services it is going to produce. How this decision is made will depend on the type of economic system which operates in the country.

Free Economy

4. At one extreme, all resources could be owned by individuals who organise them to produce what people want. There is no Government intervention. This is known as a 'Free Economy', sometimes called Market Economies, Capitalist Systems or Free Enterprises. What is produced and the price charged is determined by what is called the market mechanism of supply and demand. For

example, if there was no demand for wooden houses or bicycles, then an entrepreneur would not make any profit by supplying them. Therefore instead, he would use his resources to produce other goods. The USA, Canada and Japan are examples of free economies.

5. **Advantages of a Free Economy**
   - ❏ Consumers determine demand and therefore what is produced.
   - ❏ Increased competition which keeps prices down and improves efficiency and standards.
   - ❏ All members of the community are free to run businesses for profit.

6. **Disadvantages of a Free Economy**
   - ❏ Successful businesses may buy up smaller ones and control a larger share of the market. This can reduce competition and lead to higher prices.
   - ❏ Some goods and services required by the community as a whole may not be produced at all, for example, defence.
   - ❏ Pollution could increase because it may be difficult to control.

Controlled Economy

7. At the other extreme, all resources could be owned and organised by the State. In these economies, decisions on what to produce are taken collectively by the Government on behalf of its people. Bulgaria and Cuba are examples of controlled economies, often called centrally planned economies or Communist states.

8. **Advantages of a Controlled Economy**
   - ❏ Resources are used to produce what the community needs which eliminates wasteful competition.
   - ❏ More equal distribution of income and wealth
   - ❏ Prevents large firms controlling markets and putting up prices.

9. **Disadvantages of a Controlled Economy**
   - ❏ Lack of competition may reduce efficiency, enterprise and innovation.
   - ❏ Central control may make it difficult to respond quickly to changes in needs and conditions

Mixed Economy

10. Most countries in the world, including the UK, actually have what is called a mixed economy. This means that some resources and organisations are owned and controlled by the State (called the Public Sector) and others by private individuals or groups of individuals (Private Sector).

    This is more fully explained in Chapter 13.

Task 1   **1.3.1 (C3.2)**

Consider the following countries in terms of the characteristics of free, centrally planned and mixed economic systems. From what you know or can find out, place them in order from completely controlled to completely free.

UK	USA	FRANCE	ITALY	CANADA
GERMANY	CUBA	AUSTRALIA	BULGARIA	CHINA

Government and the Economy

11. The government intervenes in the running of the economy for a number of reasons and its policies and actions can and do have a major effect on business activities.

12. The main reasons for government intervention are summarised below:

- **To manage the economy** in order to control the level of economic activity, sometimes referred to as 'demand management'. This may range from formal planning of the economy to control of the balance of payments and inflation. It also includes measures to achieve economic growth, a higher standard of living and full employment.

- **To provide resources for social capital** such as roads, defence, schools, hospitals and amenities which are owned collectively by the nation.

- **To pay welfare benefits** to those who are unemployed, sick, on low incomes or retired.

- **To control monopolies and restrictive practices** in order to **increase competition** and encourage efficiency in the economy, particularly where natural monopolies exist such as water, gas and electricity.

- **To provide aid for industry** in order to tackle, for example, problems of regional unemployment or to protect firms from unfair foreign competition. It is usually given in the form of grants or other financial assistance.

- **To provide merit goods** and services for everyone's benefit such as education, libraries and art galleries which some individuals might not otherwise be able to afford to purchase.

- **To protect social and environmental interests** which can occur in a free economy. For example, the sale of harmful or dangerous items like drugs or pornography, or actions which result in pollution, congestion or noise.

- To **protect consumers** from unfair, dishonest and dangerous trading practices.

Task 2   1.3.1 (C3.2, C3.4)

1. Taking the reasons for government intervention above, identify what you feel are the most important economic and social issues and state why.

2. Are there any issues not mentioned which you would like to see included? Again give reasons.

National Income

13. In order to consider the government's macro-economic policies and how they affect businesses, it is important to understand how the government uses the national income to measure the level of economic activity in the economy.

14. The value of all goods and services produced by businesses in the UK each year is called the **Gross Domestic Product** (GDP). This can be expressed either:

- **in terms of market prices** that is, what people actually pay for goods and services, or

- **at factor cost** that it, the cost of producing goods and services, and ignoring any taxes or subsidies. This was £481,776 million in 1990.

15. GDP can also be expressed in

- **current prices**, that is, actual prices as they exist, or

- **constant prices**, that is, after removing the effects of inflation in order to measure the underlying growth in the economy.

16. GDP can be calculated in 3 different ways as the sum total of **income**, **expenditure or output**. Each method produces the same total in principle but there are slight differences. The definitive measure is therefore calculated as an average of these 3 methods. In 1990, the average of GDP at constant factor cost was 116.2 (1985 = 100) compared with 90.7 in 1980, an increase of 28% in 10 years.

17. **Table 1: Gross Domestic Product, Gross National Product and National Income**

	£ Million	
	1982	**1992**
Total final expenditure	347,343	745,801
less imports of goods and services	–67,762	–149,164
Gross domestic product at market prices	279,041	596,165
plus net property income from abroad	1,460	5,777
Gross national product at market prices	280,501	601,942
less factor cost adjustment (taxes less subsidies)	–40,656	–81,571
Gross domestic product at factor cost	238,385	514,594
Net property income from abroad	1,460	5,777
Gross national product at factor cost	239,845	520,371
less capital consumption	–33,653	–63,984
National income (net national product at factor cost)	206,192	456,387

Source: United Kingdom National Accounts 1993 Edition

Differences between totals and the sums of other components are due to rounding. See Monthly Digest of Statistics for most recent figures

18. Table 1 shows the average estimate of GDP at both current market prices and factor cost. It also shows the:

   ❑ **Gross National Product (GNP)** which is the total output of goods and services produced by UK businesses, plus net property income from abroad. In other words, GDP plus the output of UK owned businesses located overseas.

   ❑ **National Income**, that is, the net national product (NNP) at factor cost. Calculated as GNP minus capital consumption. That is, an allowance for depreciation of capital equipment.

19. **Table 2: Total Final Expenditure in 1992 at Market Prices**

	£ Million	per cent
Consumers' expenditure	382,696	51.3
General government final consumption	132,378	17.7
Gross domestic fixed capital formation	92.892	12.5
Value of physical increase in stocks and work in progress	–1,992	–0.3
Total domestic expenditure	605,974	81.3
Exports of goods and services	139,827	18.7
Total final expenditure	**745,801**	**100.0**

Source: United Kingdom National Accounts 1993 Edition

Differences between totals and the sums of other components are due to rounding. See Monthly Digest of Statistics for most recent figures

20. Table 2 shows the categories of final expenditure in 1992. As can be seen, consumers' expenditure accounted for 51% of total final expenditure, whilst exports of goods and services accounted for 19%.

Task 3   **1.3.1 (N3.1, N3.3)**

1. Find the latest figures available to update Table 1 paragraph 17 and Table 2 paragraph 19.

2. Compare the figures and comment on any major changes.

Problems of Measuring Economic Activity

21. These include:

   ❑ **Double counting**, that is, avoiding counting the same activity more than once. Components, for example, could be considered as the output of the firm selling them and the firm using them. Therefore only the value added to production by each firm is counted.

   ❑ **Transfer payments** of income from one group to another which are not in return for the provision of factor services need to be excluded to avoid double counting. Sickness, unemployment and pension benefits are examples.

   ❑ **Non-marketed output**. There is no allowance for work carried out at home, such as housework nor, for example, for voluntary or charity work.

   ❑ **'Black' or 'underground' economy.** This refers to unrecorded economic activity which is often carried out by people but not declared to avoid paying tax. This will produce some inaccuracies in the accounts and is considered to represent as much as 7.5% of national income.

   ❑ **Service industries.** Where no tangible product exists or what is produced is not sold, it is difficult to calculate 'value added'. The provision of health and education, for example. The output of these industries is therefore valued at cost.

Task 4   1.3.1 (N3.1)

A housewife decided to return to full-time work. Her job paid £10,000 per year having previously received a £5,000 housekeeping allowance from her husband. As a consequence, her teenage daughter agreed to give up her evening newspaper round because she was needed at home after school to look after her young brother. Her father offered to compensate her fully and increased her pocket money by £40 per month.

Calculate the increase in the family's contribution to the national income.

Use of National Income Statistics

22. The national income data is used by the government to assist it in formulating its economic strategy. It provides a useful measure of economic activity and by calculating income per head of population, is an indicator of standards of living both at home and for international comparisons.

23. The national income accounts are presented annually in what is commonly called the 'Blue Book'. It contains a detailed analysis of the components of national income and usually shows changes over a 10 year period. The range of detailed information available includes:

   ❑ **Trends in industrial production**
   ❑ **Trends in consumer expenditure**
   ❑ **Changes in the distribution of income**
   ❑ **Economic growth** and the standard of living
   ❑ **International comparisons**

Circular Flow of Income

24. The main principles behind the calculation of the level of national income in the economy can be illustrated in a simple circular flow of income.

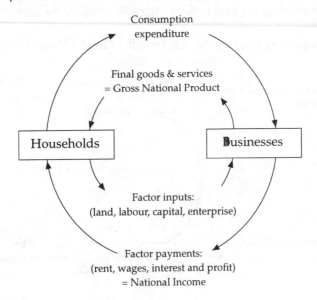

25. As shown above:

   ❑ Businesses produce goods and services which are consumed by households.

   ❑ Factor inputs are required for production and these are purchased by businesses from households in return for factor payments.

   ❑ everyone in the economy belongs to a household and therefore is a consumer,

   ❑ hence there is a circular flow of income as money flows from households to businesses and back again because all spending is someone else's income.

Injections and Withdrawals

26. The above explanation assumes a closed economy but in practice households do not spend all their earnings in this way on goods and services.

   ❑ part may be saved, for example in a building society or pension scheme.

   ❑ some goes in taxation, for example, income tax and VAT.

   ❑ part is spent on imported goods and services, for example, Japanese cars, foreign holidays.

   These are called **leakages** or **withdrawals** from the circular flow.

27. Likewise, not all income into a business comes from consumer spending. **Injections** into the circular flow come from:

   ❑ **government expenditure,** for example, on defence, education, or unemployment benefits.

   ❑ **exports,** for example, UK cars sold abroad and overseas visitors into the UK.

   ❑ **investment** which is expenditure on capital goods such as building new factories or buying new machines to increase future wealth.

28. Investment which requires an amount of current consumption to be foregone, (that is, saved to release the resources to finance it) can be divided into:

   ❑ **gross investment** which is the total amount of investment undertaken in an economy over a specified period of time, usually a year.

   ❑ **net investment** which is gross investment less capital consumption. That is, investment needed to replace capital which has depreciated or been used up.

29. The level of aggregate demand in the economy at any particular time depends upon the level of leakages and injections. If they are equal, the economy is said to be in equilibrium, although this may occur at a level that is less than full employment If leakages exceed injections, there is a net outflow of money from the circular flow which would reduce the level of demand. If, on the other hand, injections are greater than leakages, this will stimulate the economy and increase demand.

30.

Injections and Withdrawals from the Circular Flow of Income

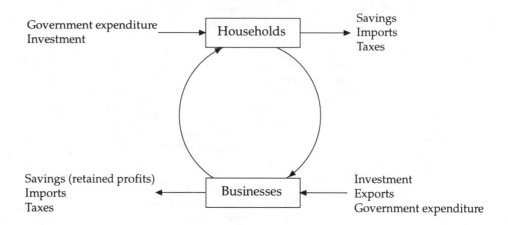

Task 5   **1.3.1, 1.3.2 (C3.4)**

In each of the following situations, state whether they are considered to be injections to, withdrawals from, or part of the circular flow of income

1. Widening of the M62 Motorway.

2. Insurance premiums paid by Greek ship owners to Lloyds of London.

3. Businesses retaining profits to increase their reserves.

4. The purchase of British machinery by a British manufacturer.

5. The purchase of British made consumer goods by British households.

Keynes

31. Macro-economic thinking developed very much from the work of **John Maynard Keynes** who in 1936 published 'The General Theory of Employment, Interest and Money'. His theory dominated government thinking from the post-war period until the 1970's.

32. Prior to Keynes, the so-called **classical economists**, such as Smith, Ricardo, Mills and Say, had stated that in a free economy, the laws of supply and demand would always automatically ensure the full employment of resources provided that all savings were invested. The pressure of accumulated savings would cause interest rates to fall, thereby encouraging businesses to borrow and invest more. Whilst falling wage rates and hence, reduced production costs would encourage the employment of more workers, hence solving the problems associated with recession.

33. This thinking, however, failed completely in the depression of the 1930's where mass unemployment existed. This led Keynes to look for other explanations. He was highly critical of the government at the time which not only failed to intervene in the economy but actually made matters worse by reducing public expenditure. Keynes concentrated on the economic aggregates of National Income, Consumption, Savings and Investment to produce a general theory to explain the level of economic activity.

34. Keynes argued that:

   ❏ the economy was not self-regulating.

❑ there is no assurance that savings would accumulate during a depression and reduce interest rates because savings depend on income and with high unemployment, income is low.

❑ households' consumption expenditure and savings plans are dependent on the level of national income,

❑ income depends on the volume of employment and the marginal propensity to consume determines the relationship between income and consumption. The term 'propensity' meaning a psychological inclination to consume or save.

❑ investment depends primarily on business confidence which would be low during a depression and therefore unlikely to increase even with low interest rates.

❑ wage rates were 'rigid' and therefore unlikely to fall much in a depression and if they did, it would add to the problem by reducing income and consumption.

❑ depression was caused by reduced aggregate demand and governments must intervene via fiscal policy to stimulate consumption. They should increase incomes through tax cuts or public expenditure in order to increase aggregate demand.

Task 6		**1.3.1 (N3.1)**

The following table shows consumption (C) and investment (I) at different levels of National Income (Y) in an economy.

Y	C	I
150	90	50
190	150	50
250	250	50
350	300	50
400	320	50

What is the equilibrium level of National Income?

Aggregate Demand and the Multiplier

35. We have seen that aggregate demand consists of all the money which is spent on goods and services by individuals, businesses and government in a specified period, usually a year. One of the important concepts developed by Keynes (although introduced by Kahn in 1931) was that of the **multiplier** which is concerned with the effects of changes in the level of injections or withdrawals on the equilibrium level of national income.

36. The multiplier is the number by which a change in any element of aggregate demand is multiplied to give the overall effect on the level of national income. The multiplier on the level of economic activity comes about because of the nature of the circular flow of income. Thus, for example, if the government increases expenditure on road building, incomes of firms building roads will increase. They in turn will employ more workers and buy more materials from suppliers whose income will also rise. Suppliers in turn will increase expenditure whilst all workers will spend more money in shops and other places and so on. Thus, the multiplier is a cumulative process involving successive rounds of additions to income.

Task 7	**1.3.2 (N3.3)**

Consider the likely multiplier effects of local councils deciding to reduce expenditure on house building.

Size of the Multiplier

37. The size of the multiplier will depend upon the proportion of any extra income which is spent on consumption, that is, the marginal propensity to consume (MPC) at each successive round. The marginal propensity to save (MPS) is the proportion of any extra income which is withdrawn from the circular flow. The greater the MPS the lower is the multiplier. MPS + MPC = I

Thus the multiplier (K) can be calculated as:

$$\frac{\text{change Y}}{\text{change I}} \quad \text{or} \quad \frac{I}{I - MPC} \quad \text{or} \quad \frac{I}{MPS}$$

38. For example, if an increase in government investment (I) from £40 billion to £60 billion produces a change in income (Y) of £80 billion then:

$$K = \frac{80}{20} = 4$$

Thus, every extra £1 of investment injected into the economy will eventually produce a £4 rise in national income.

If the MPC is $^3/_4$ then MPS = $^1/_4$ thus K = 1 ÷ $^1/_4$ = 4

39. This example pre-supposes a closed economy, in reality some of the consumption will take place on imported goods and services. Therefore any increase in government spending may not all go to assist the domestic economy unless there is also a corresponding increase in exports.

Task 8 1.3.1, 1.3.3 (N3.2)

1. It has been estimated that in the UK, on average, for every £1 increase in National Income, direct tax takes 24p, indirect tax 13p, personal savings 7p, 12p is spent on imports and businesses save 17p.

   On the basis of these figures, estimate the value of the multiplier in the economy.

2. If, for every extra pound of income received, people save 10p, spend 15p on imports and have to pay 30p in taxes.

   a) What is the marginal propensity to consume home produced goods and services?

   b) What is the marginal propensity to save?

   c) What is the value of the multiplier?

Inflationary and Deflationary Gaps

40. At any particular time, there is a level of national income which is sufficient to sustain full employment. If aggregate demand exceeds output at this level, we get an inflationary gap. That is, since output cannot be increased further, the excess demand will cause prices to rise unless the government intervenes to reduce it.

41. On the other hand, if the equilibrium level of national income is below the level that generates full employment, we get a deflationary gap which may lead to unemployment. To counteract these gaps, governments can use fiscal and monetary policies to reduce or expand aggregate demand accordingly.

42.

Inflationary Gap

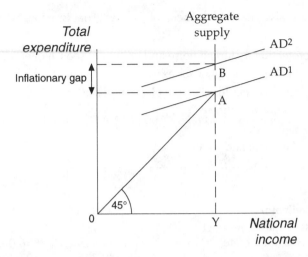

43. The full employment level of national income/output is reached at OY when the aggregate supply schedule becomes vertical. If aggregate demand was at the level indicated by AD^1, the economy would be operating at full employment without inflation (point A) However, if aggregate demand is at a higher level like AD^2, the excess demand would create an inflationary gap equal to AB.

44.

Deflationary Gap

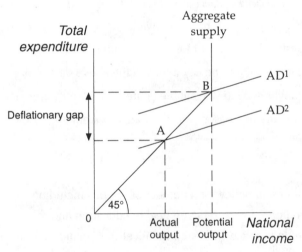

45. The full employment level of output/national income is reached at Point B on AD^1 when the aggregate supply schedule becomes vertical. If aggregate demand is at a lower level such as AD^2, then actual output will be at a where it intersects the aggregate supply schedule. At this point, there is a gap between actual and potential output.

Government Macro-Economic Aims

46. Since Keynes, the main aims of macro-economic policy have been to achieve:

❏ Economic growth and a higher standard of living. (see Paragraph 76)

❏ Full employment. (see Paragraph 80)

❏ Low inflation. (see Paragraph 95)

❏ Balance of payments stability. This is discussed in Element 5.3.

47. In seeking to achieve its economic aims, the Government makes use of both **Monetary Policy** (interest rates and credit controls) and **Fiscal Policy** (Taxation and Public Expenditure). Trying to achieve

these aims may cause certain conflicts. For example, a policy for growth may lead to balance of payments difficulties, whilst measures to reduce inflation may lead to unemployment.

48. The Government must also consider its social objectives. That is, issues which affect the community such as:

❑ Environmental protection including noise and pollution (see Chapter 9).

❑ The protection of individual's rights, for example, employment and consumer protection.

❑ Democratic decision making, for example election of MP's and local councillors.

❑ Freedom of opportunity and choice.

❑ Conservation.

❑ Fair distribution of income and wealth.

Task 9 **1.3.2 (N3.3)**

Economic Indicators	1980	1985	1990
Gross domestic product (average estimate)	323,419	356,083	416,888
Exports	88,726	102,208	123,642
Imports	80,781	98,866	139,123
Consumers' expenditure	195,825	217,618	273,304
Gross domestic fixed capital formation	53,416	60,353	79,893
Percentage increase in retail prices index	18.0	6.1	9.5
Workforce in employment (000s)	n.a	24,530	28,510
Percentage of workforce unemployed	n.a	10.9	5.8

Sources: United Kingdom National Accounts 1991 Edition; Economic Trends; Employment Gazette

£ million at 1985 market prices. n.a = not available.

See Monthly Digest of Statistics for most recent figures

1. Identify and comment on the key trends in the above data.

2. Update them with the latest available figures and identify any major changes.

3. If possible, identify the reasons for the changes identified.

Fiscal Policy

49. The Government uses fiscal policy for a number of reasons including:

❑ To finance expenditure, for example on health, education and roads.

❑ To control the economy and influence the level of demand, investment, inflation, employment and economic growth.

❑ To redistribute National Income and help the less well-off, for example, the unemployed.

❑ To give incentives to industry to influence location and encourage production and investment.

❑ To discourage smoking, drinking and gambling.

❑ To control the import of certain goods either for Balance of Payments or other reasons.

Types of Taxes

50. There are a number of different types of taxes which the Government can use including:

❑ **Progressive** – a tax which takes a higher proportion of income as income rises. Income tax (1995–96) has a lower rate of 20% on the first £3,200 then a basic rate of 25% with a higher rate of 40% for people who earn more than £24,300.

❑ **Regressive** – a tax which takes a higher proportion of income from the poor, for example, VAT and television licences.

❐ **Proportional** – a tax which takes a fixed proportion of someone's income. In 1995/96 income tax was proportional for the first £24,300 of taxable income because everyone paid 25% for each £ earned.

❐ **Poll Tax** – This is a tax levied equally on everyone. An example is the 'Community Charge' which was replaced by the Council Tax in 1993.

Direct and Indirect Taxes

51. Taxes are further classified as direct or indirect:

❐ **Direct taxes** are levied directly on the income or wealth of individuals and organisations. They are collected by the Department of Inland Revenue. The main direct taxes are income tax, corporation tax, petroleum revenue tax, inheritance tax and capital gains tax.

❐ **Indirect taxes** are levied on the expenditure on goods and services and therefore are paid indirectly to the tax authorities. These are collected by the Customs and Excise Department. They may be specific ie consisting of a fixed sum regardless of the value of the goods, for example, 90p per packet or pint on tobacco or alcohol or ad valorum ie a percentage of the value of the goods, for example, 10%. The main indirect taxes are Value Added Tax and Customs and Excise Duties.

52. **Direct Taxes**

❐ **Income Tax**. This is a progressive tax on people's income. A number of personal allowances reduce the amount of a person's taxable income. Most people pay their income tax under PAYE, whereby tax is deducted by their employer. The Government can alter the level of personal taxation by changing the rate of tax, for example, reducing the basic rate from 25% to 20% in the £ or by altering the allowances.

❐ **Corporation Tax**. This is a proportional tax on company profits. Companies are allowed to deduct certain expenditure as tax-free allowances from their gross profit. Tax must then be paid on the net profit remaining. The main rate is 33% with a reduced rate of 25% for small companies (those with profits below £300,000 pa). A high level of corporation tax could affect economic growth because it would leave firms with less money for investment.

❐ **Petroleum Revenue Tax (PRT)**. Companies like BP and Shell who make profits from the production of North Sea Oil and Gas are also charged PRT at 50% but only on profits from existing fields.

❐ **Capital Gains Tax.** When people sell assets such as shares, works of art or land, they are liable to pay 40% capital gains tax on any profits which they make in excess of £6,000. Exemptions are granted for the sale of certain assets, such as the sale of a person's home. Tax is charged at an individual's top rate i.e. 25% or 40%.

❐ **Inheritance Tax.** This tax applies to transfers of personal wealth from one person to another when they die or within seven years of their death. The rate of tax is nil below a certain threshold (£154,000 in 1995/96) and 40% on anything more. Some transfers are exempt, for example those between husband and wife or involving small businesses.

53. **Indirect Taxes**

❐ **Value Added Tax (VAT)**. VAT is levied at each stage in the production and distribution of goods and services. The final tax is paid by the consumer. The basic rate is $17\frac{1}{2}$% but some items are exempt (for example insurance, education and postal services) whilst others are zero rated, for example, most food, books, drugs and exports. For four years from 1993 the EU minimum standard VAT rate is 15%. The effect of VAT is to increase prices which generally reduces demand.

❐ **Customs and Excise Duties**. Customs duties are charged on all imported goods except those from the EU. They provide income for the Government and a measure of protection from foreign competition by increasing the price of imports. Excise duties are levied mainly on home produced goods and services including beer, wine, spirits, cigarettes, fuel and gambling.

Other Forms of Taxation

54. These include Stamp Duty, National Insurance, Licence Duties, Council Tax, air travel and insurance.

   ❑ **Stamp Duty**. This is charged at 1% on the total price of any property sold above a value of £60,000 (1995/96).

   ❑ **National Insurance**. This is a form of direct taxation collected specifically to help finance the National Health Service and to contribute to the funds needed to provide unemployment and sickness benefits. The rate paid varies with the size of a person's income, the higher the income, the bigger the deduction. Employers must also pay National Insurance for every person employed and they contribute over 50% of the total amount. Self employed people also pay National Insurance.

   ❑ **Licence Duties**. Television, driving and gun licences are all forms of taxation. A licence duty is also charged on all motor vehicles including cars, motor cycles, lorries and buses.

   ❑ **Council Tax**. This is the only major tax which is not paid to the central Government (see Element 2.1).

   ❑ **Air travel** tax was introduced in 1995/96 at a rate of £5 per person on all flights in the UK and Europe, and £10 on flights elsewhere.

   ❑ **Insurance**. There is a 2.5% levy on premiums for motor, home contents and building policies introduced October 1994

Task 10   **1.3.2 (N3.2)**

	£
Income Tax	60,000
VAT	24,000
Corporation Tax	20,000
Inheritance Tax	5,000
Capital Gains Tax	6,000
Motor Vehicle duties	4,000
Custom & Excise duties	7,000

From the above figures, calculate:

1. the total value of direct taxes.

2. the total value of indirect taxes

3. which tax would be most effective for redistributing incomes?

4. which tax would be used to control the import of goods or services?

Tax Implications for Business

55. Business organisations are affected by taxation in a number of ways including:

   ❑ **Economic activity** will be reduced unless the government ploughs back money from taxation. Consumer demand depends on disposable income which is reduced by direct taxation. Thus sales and profits will be affected.

   ❑ **Profits** are taxed thus reducing the amount available for reinvestment in the business or for distribution to shareholders.

   ❑ **Prices** are affected which can reduce demand.

   ❑ **Costs of Production** will increase if supplies of goods and services are taxed.

□ **Supply of labour** can be affected because high taxation can act as a disincentive to work for the low paid who may be better off on unemployment benefits, whilst those in work may not be motivated by overtime or bonuses.

□ **VAT registration** is a legal requirement for all firms whose turnover exceeds £46,000 (1994-5) thus involving them in extensive record-keeping and submission of VAT returns.

> **Task 11**   **1.3.2 (C3.2, C3.4)**
>
> Refer back to the taxes in Task 10.
>
> Comment on how each of these might affect a small business.

The Budget

56. Each year, the Chancellor of the Exchequer presents a Budget to Parliament. This is a Financial Statement which gives the Government's estimated revenue and expenditure of the last financial year, and forecasts for the next year. It also gives details of any proposed tax changes. Sometimes 'mini' budgets are used at other times of the year. The Budget which in 1993 was moved from March/April to November/December, has two main functions. It enables the Government to:

□ Regulate the economy by controlling the demand for goods and services.

□ Redistribute income and wealth among the various sections of the community.

Public Sector Borrowing Requirement (PSBR)

57. If the proposed revenue and expenditure are equal then the Budget is in balance. When revenue is greater than expenditure it is in **surplus**, if it is less than the Budget, it is in **deficit.** When the Budget is in deficit the Government must borrow in order to finance its expenditure. This is called the PSBR which in 1994/95 was £35.6 billion.

58.   **The PSBR and the Budget**

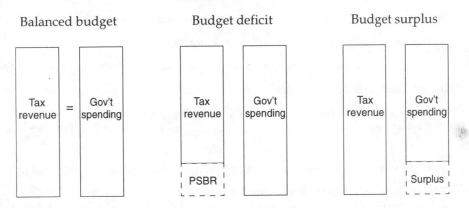

59. The Government borrows by issuing Treasury Bills, Gilt-edged stock and various kinds of savings certificates in return for the money lent to it. The accumulated PSBR owed by the Government, both to people in Britain and those abroad, is called the **National Debt**. In 1993 it stood at £135 billion.

Public Expenditure

60. This is the term used to describe the money which the Government spends for the benefit of the community as a whole. The Government uses the money which it collects in taxation to provide goods and services for the nation. Some of these are provided centrally whilst others are provided locally. As shown in the diagram below – total government spending in 1992-3 accounted for over 40% of the gross domestic product.

61. **Planned Receipts and Expenditure of Central Government 1992-93**

Where it comes from	Pence in every £	Where it goes[1]	Pence in every £
Income tax	22	Social security	$30\frac{1}{2}$
National Insurance contributions	14	Health	$13\frac{1}{2}$
Value-added tax	14	Education and science	$12\frac{1}{2}$
Local authority rates and community charge	9	Defence	9
Excise duties	9	Law, order and protective services	$5\frac{1}{2}$
Corporation tax[2]	6	Transport	4
Capital taxes	1	Other services	$17\frac{1}{2}$
Interest, dividends	2	Debt interest	7
Petroleum revenue tax and oil royalties	$\frac{1}{4}$	Other[3]	$\frac{1}{2}$
Other expenditure taxes	4		
Borrowing	14		
Other	5		
Total	**100**	**Total**	**100**

[1]   Figures are based on Table 2.5 of the Statistical Supplement to the 1992 Autumn Statement.

[2]   Including North Sea but excluding capital taxes on companies.

[3]   Other accounting adjustments, privatisation proceeds and adjustment.

Note: Differences between totals and the sum of their component parts are due to rounding.

Central Government Expenditure

62. The main items of Central Government expenditure are:

❏ Social Security and Personal Social Services – including pensions, benefits for the unemployed, sick and disabled and social security payments.

❏ Education and the Arts – grants to Universities, Colleges and Theatres.

❏ Defence – this includes the cost of keeping an army, navy and airforce at home and abroad.

❏ National Health Service – provision of doctors, dentists, hospitals etc.

❏ Debt Interest – the Government has to pay interest on the PSBR and National Debt.

❏ Nationalised Industries – loans to public corporations for capital expenditure.

❏ Trade Industry and Employment – this includes grants to industry and the cost of operating Job Centres, the Training, Education and Enterprise Directorate (TEED) and Training & Enterprise Councils (TECs).

❏ Environmental Services – including spending on roads, law and order, and housing.

❏ Grants to Local Authorities – the Government pays a 'revenue support grant' to help finance some of the services provided by local councils and also transitional relief for the new council tax.

Local Government Expenditure

63. The main items of Local Government expenditure are:

❏ Education – the provision of schools is the single most important item of local authority expenditure.

❏ Law and Order – police and fire services.

- ❏ Roads and transport – maintenance of minor local roads. Sometimes local transport services may be subsidised or free travel passes issued.

- ❏ Housing – provision of council houses and other accommodation.

- ❏ Social Services – for example children's homes, old people's homes, home helps and social workers for those who need help.

- ❏ Environmental services – including parks, cemeteries, refuse collection and toilets etc. Also sport centres, museums, libraries and other local facilities.

- ❏ Debt interest – local councils also borrow money to finance expenditure on which interest has to be paid.

Task 12   **1.3.2 (C3.4)**

SPENDING CUTS

The Government is to impose substantial public spending cuts to stop the budget deficit ballooning from the official forecast of £28 billion in the 1992/3 financial year to almost double that amount in 1993/4.

So far, the private sector has taken all the strain of the recession. Now, without cuts in public spending, we would either get tax increases or higher borrowing.

Tax increases would reduce the incentive for people to work. Many are already caught in the unemployment trap. They have little motivation to find work because their social security benefits are worth as much as their potential after-tax pay. Higher taxes would only increase the numbers of those caught in the trap who stay at home all day watching television - demoralising for them and disastrous for the economy. Increased borrowing would be just as bad. It would cause higher interest rates and thus discourage companies from investing again. Not the way to get the wealth-producing part of our economy going.

The spending cuts on the way include pay freezes for public sector employees and tighter conditions for social security payments.

There may be industrial unrest but the Government rightly wants to preserve as much as possible of the capital spending programme although some of this will also go.

Answer the following based on the above article:

1. Why does the government need to reduce public spending?

2. Why is it doing this in preference to using other policies?

3. How could this move affect the private sector?

Monetary Policy

64. The Government's monetary policy is operated by the Bank of England. Essentially, it involves the control of the supply of money circulating in the economy by altering interest rates, exchange rates and the availability of credit in order to control inflation and promote economic growth.

65. Monetary policy can be used to encourage or discourage spending which in turn affects investment, the demand for goods and services, prices, employment and foreign trade. For example, if people have more money to spend (from increased wages and extra credit) then unless output increases, prices are likely to rise, leading to inflation.

Money

66. Money which is anything generally acceptable as a means of payment, fulfils a number of important functions. It is a:

❑ **Medium of exchange** which allows goods and services to be easily bought and sold.

❑ **Measure of value** which is used to price goods and services.

❑ **Store of value** because money can be saved for future use.

❑ **Means of deferred payment**, for example, when goods are bought on credit, money is used to measure the amount owed.

67. The total supply or stock of money is currently measured in several different ways but which can be broadly defined as:

❑ **narrow measures** which concentrate on money as a medium of exchange.

❑ **broad measures** which include those assets which may be both a store of wealth and a potential medium of exchange.

68. **Definitions of Money**

❑ M0 the narrowest measure is the notes and coins in circulation, plus money actually held by banks (till money) and their deposits with the Bank of England.

❑ M2 is the money available for immediate use, that is, notes, coins and cash in banks and building society accounts.

❑ M4 comprises notes and coins in circulation together with all sterling deposits held with UK banks and building societies by the rest of the private sector.

❑ The Bank of England also publishes data for liquid assets outside M4.

Monetary Measures

69. **Interest Rates**. A link between the Bank of England and the commercial banks is provided by the **Discount Houses.** These are banks which specialise in buying Commercial and Treasury Bills at less than their face value (at a discount) and making a profit by keeping them until they mature. They obtain their funds mainly by short-term borrowing from the banks ie 'at call or short notice' which means that they can be asked for repayment at any time which is what happens if the banks need cash to meet their obligations to customers. When this happens, it leaves the Discount Houses short of funds which they are able to borrow from the Bank which acts as **'lender of last resort'.**

70. The Bank can choose the interest rate at which it provides these funds. When it changes its official dealing rate, the commercial banks promptly follow and change their own **base rates** for lending and borrowing. This in turn affects consumer demand, investment, output and ultimately prices.

71. **The Exchange Rate**. Interest rates also affect the value of sterling in terms of foreign currencies. Generally, higher interest rates attract foreign funds into the UK and this increases the rate of exchange whilst lower interest rates have the reverse effect. To control this, the Bank manages the UK's gold and foreign currency reserves through the **Exchange Equalisation Account**. This is a fund which is used by buy and sell sterling and foreign exchange in order to 'smooth out' fluctuations in the exchange rate, known as **intervention**.

72. **Other Policy Instruments**. Other techniques used in the past by the Bank to control the economy include:

❑ Ceilings on the amount of bank lending.

❑ Special Deposits ie cash reserves which banks had to deposit with the Bank.

❑ Guidance on bank lending aimed at discouraging loans to consumers and

❑ Open-market operations ie the buying and selling of Government Securities via the Stock Exchange to influence the money supply.

Task 13   **1.3.2 ,1.3.3 (C3.2, C3.4)**

Consider the likely impact on the domestic economy in each of the following situations.

1. The government increases the level of social security benefits.

2. VAT is raised from 17.5% to 25%.

3. Banks and building societies reduce the interest rates on savings accounts.

4. The value of the pound falls against other major currencies.

5. Businesses are expecting a boom in the economy.

The Monetary Sector

73. The 1979 and 1987 Banking Acts gave the Bank of England the powers to authorise and supervise all **deposit-taking institutions**. To become and remain authorised a 'bank' must have adequate capital; make provision against possible bad debts; have enough cash or liquidity to meet likely withdrawals and have fit and proper management. The aim of authorisation is to protect depositors against the risk of losing their money. If an authorised bank does fail, depositors are entitled to limited compensation from a **Deposit Protection Fund** set up under the 1987 Act and administered by the Bank but financed by contributions levied on the institutions.

74.

Monetary Sector

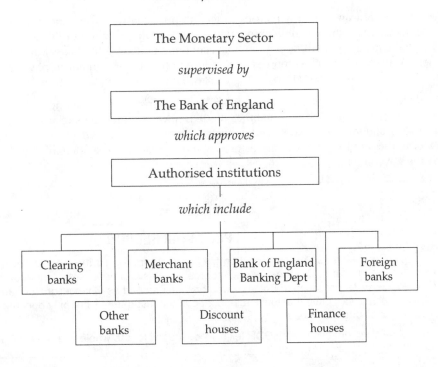

Authorised Institutions

75. There are some 550 institutions authorised to accept deposits by the Bank of England. These include:

- ❏ **Clearing Banks** and commercial banks which provide a wide range of services to personal and business customers.

- ❏ **Merchant Banks** and accepting houses which provide services almost exclusively for businesses. This includes accepting Bills of Exchange, acting as issuing houses for shares, providing loans and advising on business problems.

- ❏ **Banking Department of the Bank of England** which looks after the Bank's business with the exception of the issue of notes and coins.

- ❏ **Foreign Banks** – there are over 400 operating in the UK, the largest being American and Japanese.

- ❏ **Other Banks** – these include certain banks in the Channel Islands and the Isle of Man.

- ❏ **Discount Houses** – which borrow and invest short-term.

- ❏ **Finance Houses** – these make loans for hire purchase and general consumer expenditure, usually for two to three years. They also provide short-term finance for businesses.

Economic Growth

76. One of the main objectives of the government's macro-economic policy, economic growth is the term used for the annual rate of increase in the production of goods and services. It is measured by calculating the percentage increase in the national income.

77. Achieving economic growth depends upon a number of factors, including:

- ❏ **quantity and quality of the factors of production.** That is, national resources, skills of the workforce, capital investment and level of enterprise.

- ❏ **development and introduction of new technology** leading to new products, improved techniques and an increase in productivity.

- ❏ **level of education and training**. Knowledge and skills are essential for economic growth.

78. Whether or not an economy realises its growth potential will also depend upon the level of aggregate demand which must be high enough to ensure full utilisation of its resources. The government can influence the growth rate through its economic policies which affect the level of private investment. It can also switch resources from consumption to investment in physical capital which will reduce welfare today but allow for more growth and welfare in the future.

79. Economic growth enables a country to enjoy a higher standard of living with an increasing amount of goods and services. It is sometimes argued, however, that the **social costs** of economic growth such as pollution, congestion and a hectic lifestyle often outweigh the benefits. These so called **externalities** are likely to increase as production increases unless something is done to prevent them by the government.

Task 14   **1.3.2 (C3.4)**

POST WAR RECORD

Recession has now rumbled on for 2½ years, making it the longest downturn since World War II. But the 1992 fall in gross domestic product – the value of goods and services produced in Britain – was only half as bad as Chancellor Norman Lamont's prediction. Output actually rose 0.2 pc in the last quarter, but only because of a leap in oil and gas output.

Taking out such items GDP fell 0.1 pc. The fall for the whole year was 0.5 pc.

RECESSION CUTS DIVI

Anglo-French paper maker Arjo Wiggins Appleton is cutting its interim dividend from 3.3 pc to 2.65 pc after half-year profits fell from £135.5m to £99.1m.

Finance director Tony Issac says that 'Business and consumer confidence in the areas that affect our operations remain low', he adds, 'The outlook for the second half of the year is for a continuation, and possibly a weakening of the present difficult trading conditions.'

continued...

Task 14 continued

PROFITS WARNING

The recession has caught up with Body Shop, the high street retailer of natural skin and hair care products.

It warned today that lower than expected sales in the UK, particularly since June, have had an adverse affect on profits.

Answer the following based on the above articles.

1. What was the level of economic growth in 1992?

2. How does recession affect businesses?

3. Is there any evidence to suggest that the recession may be nearing its end? Study current media information and compare it in your answer with the articles above.

Unemployment

80. Since the depression of the 1930's and the work of Keynes, maintaining high and stable levels of employment has been an important government objective. In March 1993, Britain had over 3 million people unemployed which is 11% of the working population. The government must therefore be aware of the affects of its policies on the creation of jobs.

81.

Unemployment 1920-1993

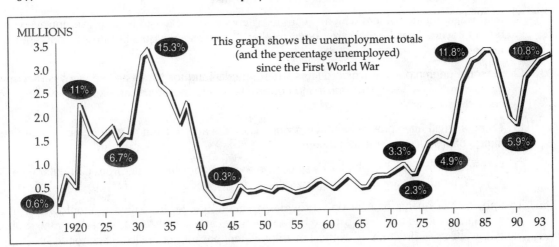

This graph shows the unemployment totals (and the percentage unemployed) since the First World War

Measuring the Level of Unemployment

82. Unemployment is a situation where people are actively seeking to obtain work but are unable to do so because there are insufficient jobs. It is officially measured by the Department of Employment as those people who are registered as unemployed and who are eligible for benefit.

83. It is believed that the official figures may well underestimate the true level of unemployment because some people

   ❑ do not register as unemployed because of pride or the nature of the benefits system.

   ❑ drop out of the jobs market when finding work is difficult. Students, for example, may decide to stay on at school or college, whilst women may stay at home.

   ❑ join government training schemes such as Modern Apprenticeships or Training to Work because no jobs are available.

   ❑ have to work short-time or part-time because full-time work is not available.

Types of Unemployment

84. Unemployment has a variety of causes and therefore a variety of possible cures. The three main types of unemployment are summarised below.

☐ **Frictional** unemployment occurs as individuals move from one job to another, incurring a temporary short period of unemployment (usually less than 3 months). A small amount of frictional unemployment is a permanent feature of any economy since even under conditions of 'full employment' a degree of this type of unemployment (at around 2-3%) will be present.

☐ **Cyclical** or 'demand deficient' unemployment which is caused by periodic downturns in the business cycle. Industrialised market economies tend to suffer regular booms and slumps. In a slump or severe recession, business activity is low and hence less labour is required leading to rising unemployment. In the 1930's, early 1980 and early 1990's the UK suffered badly from cyclical unemployment.

☐ **Structural** unemployment is the result of a mismatch between the skills of the workforce and the jobs available in a given local labour market. It is common, for example, where heavy manufacturing industries have entered a phase of long term decline and new service jobs require different skills to those possessed by displaced industrial workers. Thus, unless workers are geographically or occupationally mobile, and therefore able to move to areas of expansion, they are likely to become unemployed.

85. Other types of unemployment include:

☐ **Regional** unemployment which exists where the level of economic activity in certain areas is lower than the national average due to unfavourable location factors such as poor infrastructure or distance from markets. Where declining industries are concentrated in particular areas, structural and regional unemployment are closely interlinked.

☐ **Real wage** unemployment which is caused when wages are at too high a level for everyone to be employed. That is, they are above market clearing levels possibly due to powerful trade unions.

☐ **Seasonal** unemployment which occurs where the demand for goods and services is determined by the time of the year. The tourist and construction industries, for example, employ extra workers in the summer.

☐ **Technological** unemployment which occurs when the introduction of new equipment and techniques of production replaces workers.

☐ **Residual** unemployment which exists because some people who suffer from particular mental or physical handicaps are incapable of working.

86. This analysis of unemployment only provides a general guide. In reality, unemployment in any given area is likely to have not just one but a variety of causes whilst some areas are more vulnerable to the effects of structural or cyclical unemployment because of the local economic structure.

Task 15

1.3.3 (C3.2)

In each of the following situations, identify the type of unemployment concerned.

1. A disabled person unable to find suitable work.

2. Tourist guides unemployed in the winter months.

3. Car workers replaced by robots on the production line.

4. Young people unable to find a job at the end of their Youth Training programmes.

5. A fall in demand for cigarettes resulting in job losses at factories of the British American Tobacco company.

Reasons for Unemployment

87. In addition to the causes identified above, it is also important to realise that unemployment can be brought about by a number of other factors, in particular the

   ❑ **growth of the working population** that is those seeking work which has risen from 25.2 million in 1972 to 28 million in 1992.

   ❑ **foreign competition** which has caused the decline of many manufacturing industries such as textiles and motor vehicles. For example, the import penetration ratio of vehicles which was 23% in 1972 was nearly 60% in 1992.

   ❑ **poor industrial relations** which was a symptom of the 1980's and contributed to Britain's reputation for poor quality and unreliability thus providing opportunities for foreign competitors.

Policies for Reducing Unemployment

88. **Fiscal Policy**

   Since the Second World War governments have developed a number of standard fiscal economic policies to control unemployment based on the thinking of Keynes.

   ❑ **increased public spending** to create economic activity and expand employment via the multiplier effect.

   ❑ **reduced taxation** to increase disposable incomes in order to generate demand.

   ❑ **support for business** through investment incentives and export assistance.

89. **Monetary Policy**

   Since the 1970's the monetarist approach to managing the economy has prevailed whereby interest rates are used to control the money supply. Lower rates make saving less attractive and borrowing cheaper thereby encouraging consumers to spend and businesses to invest. The increased economic activity should help to reduce unemployment.

Direct measures

90. In addition to the main fiscal or monetary policies, governments have also introduced specific measures to combat unemployment. These are discussed more fully in Element 5.3, but examples include:

   ❑ **Enterprise schemes** offering financial and tax incentives to encourage the growth of new and small businesses.

   ❑ **Education and training** to provide the skills for future employment via the 80 Training and Enterprise Councils. They are responsible for a number of schemes, including Youth Training, Training for Work (aimed at long-term unemployed adults) and support for employers.

   ❑ **Reducing Social Security**. The government in 1993 announced that it intends to introduce a system of 'Workfare' whereby many unemployed people will only be paid benefits if they undertake community work or training schemes. This aims to 'force' people back to work.

   ❑ **Selective Regional Assistance**. Grants and tax relief are offered in areas of high unemployment to encourage firms to locate there.

   ❑ **Reducing Trade Union Power** and therefore excessively high wages which can distort the labour market. Legislation introduced in the 1980's and 1990's included removal of the 'closed shop' and measures to reduce picketing and therefore the effectiveness of strikes.

   ❑ **Information and advice** about job hunting and opportunities is available from, for example, Job Centres, Job Clubs and the Restart Programme.

Inflation

91. An increase in the general level of prices in an economy over a period of time is called inflation. It is measured by the Retail Price Index (RPI) which in June 1993 showed a 1.2% increase on the previous 12 months.

92.

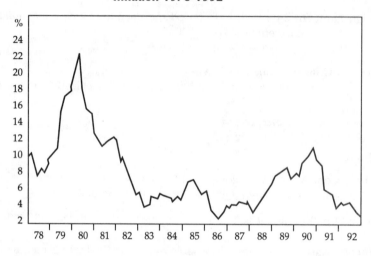

Inflation 1978-1992

93. The 2 extremes of inflation are:

❑ **Hyperinflation**. With severe inflation, prices rise rapidly and drastically. This happened, for example in 1923 in Germany and was so bad that in 1924, a completely new currency was issued.

❑ **Creeping inflation** is more common where the general price level rises gradually at an average rate of 2-3%. This is a situation achieved in the UK in the 1990's.

Task 16   **1.3.3 (C3.4)**

RUNAWAY TROUBLE

Inflation in Russia is running at 1,000 per cent as the price of everything from bread to vodka spirals out of control.

Some stores, especially those selling clothes and cigarettes imported from the West, now mark up prices daily rather than monthly.

And, like West Germany in the Twenties, when shoppers had to carry suitcases full of almost worthless paper money, Russians are now being forced to carry ever-larger bundles of notes to buy even basic goods.

Basic products became much more expensive after Russian President Boris Yeltsin freed price controls at the start of the year in an attempt to create an efficient, Western- style economy.

But the government is blaming the crisis on the semi-independent Central Bank for printing too much money. The average Russian now takes home around 3,500 roubles a month, which is worth less than £10 at current exchange rates. To cope with the problem of virtually worthless money, many factories have turned to giving workers food or goods instead of pay.

From the above article:

1. Identify the type of inflation which Russia is suffering from.

2. What has caused it?

3. What problems does it create for firms and individuals and how do they react?

Effects of inflation

94. The control of inflation has been a main objective of economic policy in the post-war period although the approach used varies according to the beliefs of the individual governments in power. Inflation is of concern because of the effects which it can have on individual businesses and the economy as a whole.

    The effects on individuals include:

    ❑ **fixed income recipients** suffer because their purchasing power is reduced, for example, shareholders of fixed interest securities, pensioners or those on benefit.
    ❑ **lenders lose** because the value of money repaid in the future is worth less than currently.
    ❑ **borrowers gain** because what they pay back is worth less.
    ❑ **'tax net'.** Inflated money wages bring more people to a taxable level of income making them worse off even though real income may actually have fallen.

95. The effects on business include:

    ❑ **resources are diverted** into non-productive items such as antiques or works of art as savers seek to hedge against inflation.
    ❑ **high interest rates** are needed to encourage people to save but they also add to the cost of borrowing, leading eventually to even higher prices.
    ❑ **investment** may be discouraged by a lack of business confidence and high interest rates making a profitable return more uncertain.
    ❑ **international trade competitiveness** is affected because exports become relatively more expensive and imports relatively cheaper. This may lead to Balance of Payments problems for the economy.
    ❑ **rising demand**. Inflation usually occurs when demand is buoyant which might produce rising sales and profits.

Effects on company accounts

96. In a period of rising prices, stock and fixed asset valuations based on historical cost are likely to overstate the real profit position of a firm. Therefore, in order to reflect the real progress in a business' company accounts must be adjusted to remove the effects of inflation.

97. Two common methods for overcoming this are:

    ❑ the **current purchasing power** method which uses the retail price index to adjust calculated profits and express them in real terms.
    ❑ the **current cost accounting** method is more detailed. Assets and depreciation are stated in the accounts at their current replacement cost values with adjustments for any specific, rather than general, price rises which have taken place in the financial year.

Causes of inflation

98. There are two main explanations of why inflation occurs – demand pull and cost push, although in practice there is a close interaction between the two and inflation is usually considered to be **multi-causal.**

    ❑ **Demand-pull** or 'too much money chasing too few goods'. Keynes argued that this results from excess demand when the economy is operating at full capacity which 'pulls-up' prices. Monetarists argue that demand-pull is caused by the government creating too much money in the economy making it easier for people to borrow funds which, unless supply increases, causes prices to rise.
    ❑ **Cost-Push** inflation is attributed to higher costs of production, in particular labour, which 'push-up' prices. Strong trade unions have often been blamed for this problem. Thus, for example, if a group of workers are given a 10% wage increase and produce exactly the same output as before then, usually prices must rise to prevent profits falling. Rising import prices and falls in the value of the exchange rate also contribute to cost-push inflation.

Expectations and inflation

99. The role of expectations can also be important in generating price rises. This is because wage claims are often excessive in anticipation of future rising prices, which then actually cause inflation as firms raise prices to cover the extra cost. This process can lead to what is called the **wage/price spiral.**

Task 17 1.3.3 (C3.4)

EXPECTATIONS ON INFLATION

In January 1993 the government announced that inflation had fallen to 1.7%. But does anyone really believe it? Especially if you exclude falling mortgage rates which were mainly responsible.

It means that on average, prices have gone up just under 2p in the pound since a year earlier.

That sounds unlikely; and you can produce dozens of examples of where it is not true. Except perhaps, wage packets which for one-third of the nation in the public sector, are now virtually frozen.

This is the rub. Inflation was when wages went up because prices had risen; deflation is when prices start to come down because wages have not risen. Most companies would like to put prices up. But if they try in the current recession, they cannot make the increases stick. So on items like furniture and white goods you now have 'negative inflation'. This is also seen in houses, land, property and even second-hand cars.

As for the future, what counts is 'expectations'. If you expect inflation, you will get it. People are not quite convinced that inflation is over as indeed it cannot be if the government, as suggested, puts VAT on food and newspapers, in line with other EU countries in the budget.

---

1. From you own experience, identify at least 6 examples of goods or services which have in the past 12 months risen in price faster than inflation.

2. What key factors are keeping prices lower?

3. How is the government controlling the cost-push element of inflation?

4. Why has 'negative inflation' come about in some markets?

5. In what ways can 'expectations' be said to influence inflation?

6. What effect, if any, does low inflation have on business decisions?

Policies to control inflation

100. There are a number of policies which governments may adopt to control the level of inflation which are summarised below: It is important to realise, however, that measures of control can sometimes cause bigger problems than the inflation itself.

101. **Monetary policies**

Higher interest rates can be used to reduce the money supply and therefore demand. However, this also raises the cost of borrowing to business which will particularly affect highly geared companies, that is, those with a high level of borrowed capital. Also, reduced demand will reduce sales and profits and thus can lead to unemployment. Higher interest rates also push up exchange rates which makes exports relatively dear.

102. Although, not favoured by the present government, it can if it chooses, issue instructions to banks to control credit by restricting the level and direction of lending for individuals and organisations. This, however, also reduces consumer demand and may affect the amount of funds available for investment.

103. **Fiscal Policy**

Higher taxes may be introduced to reduce demand because people have less to spend and/or goods and services cost more. This, however, does not help with cost-push inflation because it puts up prices. Government expenditure on, for example, health, education and roads may also be reduced to curb demand. However, both measures could cause unemployment.

104. Alternatively, additional public expenditure may be used to expand the economy and increase output in order to match demand. This however, will depend upon the multiplier effect and could also lead to further inflation.

Prices and incomes policies

105. Monetary and fiscal policies are indirect macro-economic policies. Alternatively the government may choose direct intervention to reduce wages and prices by 'freezing' them or restricting any rises to an agreed level, for example 3%, over a particular period of time or linking them to the Retail Price Index. Such policies may, however, be difficult to enforce, except in the public sector, other than on a voluntary basis (where unions, employers and the government agree) and may cause industrial unrest and confrontation. They may also only delay price rises and distort the market mechanism leading to factor or product shortages. Statutory policies were imposed in the mid 1960's, and late 1970's by the Labour government and in the early 1970's by the Conservatives.

106. **Price Control and Rationing**

As a last resort, a government could introduce statutory controls on prices but this is unlikely except in a short-term emergency.

Task 18 1.3.3 (C3.4)

INFLATION WORRY AS MONEY MISSES TARGET

Fears of a return to high inflation swept the City yesterday when a key money measure broke out of the Treasury's target range.

Some experts think the Government will have to postpone further cuts in interest rates until the outlook clears.

M0 – which measures the cash we all carry around with us – ended January up by 4.1 per cent compared with a year ago. The Treasury sees M0 as the most important barometer of money supply, and tries to keep it below 4 per cent.

Most economists believe a rise in money supply heralds inflationary pressure. But another measure – M4 which takes account of bank and building society deposits – seemed to be telling a different story.

In December, the latest figure available, it was rising so slowly that it fell below the Treasury's 4-8 per cent target to 3.7 per cent.

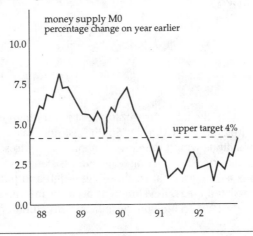

continued...

Task 18 continued

Answer the following, based on the above article.

1.   Why is a return of inflation feared?

2.   How can the government try to prevent this happening?

Deflation, reflation and disinflation

107. It is important to understand three other terms in relation to inflation.

❑   **Deflation** which is a situation where prices are falling because supply exceeds demand. It is characterised by falling output and unemployment and occurs when action is taken which lowers prices and output below the equilibrium level of full employment. This situation existed in the UK between 1920 and 1938 when the general price level fell by almost 50%.

❑   **Reflation** is a deliberate expansion of the money supply undertaken to stimulate demand and investment in an economy which is under employed.

❑   **Disinflation** is a milder form of monetary and fiscal action taken to control rising prices.

Government Influence on business location

108. Since the 1930's depression, Governments have played an important role in influencing the location of industry. This is because the concentration of industries like coal, textiles and shipbuilding in particular areas has brought with it various problems, such as:

❑   Traffic congestion, pollution, housing shortages and the strain on education, medical and social services.

❑   High unemployment as these industries have declined rapidly due to changes in demand, foreign competition and job losses from the introduction of new technology.

109.

How Unemployment Affects the Regions

Region	% of all employees				
	Jan '73	Nov '78	Jan '87	Jan '91	Jan '94
South East	2.0	3.9	8.5	5.0	9.6
East Anglia	2.6	4.7	9.3	4.8	7.8
South West	3.4	6.4	10.4	5.7	9.1
West Midlands	3.0	5.4	13.8	6.7	10.2
East Midlands	2.8	4.8	11.4	5.9	9.1
Yorks and Humberside	3.8	5.8	130.8	7.6	9.9
North West	4.6	7.2	14.3	8.1	10.2
North	6.0	8.6	16.9	9.2	11.8
Wales	4.9	8.3	14.3	7.3	10.0
Scotland	6.1	7.8	15.1	8.0	9.3
Northern Ireland	7.5	10.9	19.3	14.0	11.8
Average	4.1	6.7	13.4	7.5	10.0

As can be seen from the table, unemployment is very high in some regions of the UK, like the North and Northern Ireland. Whilst in the South East and East Anglia, it is considerably lower. It is this problem of imbalance which the Government is trying to solve through its **regional policies**. Hence governments have tried, by offering selective assistance, to attract new and expanding industries to so called depressed areas. That is, those with high and persistent unemployment which are classified as either **assisted areas**, **development areas** or **intermediate areas**. The Government reassessed these areas in July 1993 to include those facing structural unemployment following major coal mine closures.

110. Some of the measures used to influence the location of industry and attract new industry which are aimed at both UK and overseas firms include:

☐ **Financial incentives** to firms, for example grants for buildings and equipment, loans at special low rates of interest and special tax allowances.

☐ **Ready built factories** for sale or rent on favourable terms, for example rent free for twelve months.

☐ **Subsidies** to train workers taken on.

☐ **Prevention of industrial development** in other areas.

☐ **Building of New Towns**, for example Stevenage, Milton Keynes, Peterlee.

☐ **Government Departments** have been moved into assisted areas, eg DVLC (Driver and Vehicle Licensing Centre) is now located in Swansea and the DHSS (Department of Health & Social Security) in Newcastle.

Urban Policy Initiatives

111. The economic recovery of inner city areas is being encouraged by improving the environment, developing new and existing businesses and better training to improve job prospects. This is being achieved via a number of co-ordinated Government initiatives including:

☐ **Inner Urban Programme (IUP) Grants** – (Through 57 'target' local authorities eg Aberdeen, Newcastle, Nottingham and Leeds) to support capital investment projects for rebuilding. These are being phased out to end in 1995.

☐ **City Challenge** – Introduced in 1993 whereby local authorities were invited to bid, competitively, for £20m of resources previously allocated within IUP. Among those successful were Bolton, Blackburn, Wigan and Sefton.

☐ **Enterprise Initiative** – Which offers assistance towards the cost of between 5-15 days of consultancy for small firms (less than 500 employees) in key areas of marketing, design, quality, manufacturing systems, business planning and financial and management information systems.

☐ **Urban Development Corporations** – set up to use grants to reverse large scale urban decline, eg London Docklands, Merseyside and Cardiff Bay.

☐ **Enterprise Zones** – 26 set up offering tax incentives and easy planning permission for firms who locate there eg Belfast, Tyneside, Telford and Swansea Valley. Three new zones were added in 1994 in areas affected by recent colliery closures.

Task 19   **1.3.3, 5.2.4 (C3.4)**

FOREIGN FIRMS FLOCK TO THE VALLEYS

The Welsh Development Agency is delighted because despite the recession, overseas firms are descending on Wales after voting it the best place in Europe for a new factory. The legendary 'welcome in the valleys' helped to attract a record 71 new businesses over the last 12 months, official figures show. As a result 10,678 jobs were created or safeguarded, says the Department of Trade and Industry. Britain generally is attracting more foreign companies than anywhere else in the EU. In the 11 industrial development regions, including Wales, there were 332 new projects in 1991-92, bringing in 51,357 jobs. But Wales, with 30,000 steel and 28,000 coal mining jobs to replace after the decline of its traditional industries, is top of the league. It took 21 per cent of all foreign investment in the UK. Britain has proved more attractive than other EU countries because of a number of factors. One is the new era of industrial harmony, brought about by Government curbs on union power.

continued...

Task 19 continued

Another is the fact that craftsmen from the old smokestack industries can be readily trained in new skills. Whilst major investors like the Japanese prefer English-speaking countries because it is their main second language. Recent big developments in Wales include a decision by Japanese electronics giant Sony to build a £147 million television plant at Bridgend, Mid Glamorgan. US chemicals firm Dow Corning is setting up a £150 million methyl silicone factory at Barry, South Glamorgan, and the Dutch food packaging firm Tedeco has announced that it is to open a factory at Port Talbot, West Glamorgan, employing 55 people.

The following questions are based on the above article which is taken from newspaper reports.

1. Why are overseas companies descending on Wales?

2. Why has Britain proved to be more attractive to companies than other EU countries?

3. How important is the attraction of new industry to the UK economy?

European Union Aid

112. Whilst the principal responsibility for regional problems rests with the UK Government, the EU has a number of schemes which may be used to attract additional aid.

These are outlined in paragraph 126 and include the:

- ❏ **European Regional Development Fund (ERDF)**

- ❏ **European Investment Bank (EIB)**, and

- ❏ **European Social Fund (ESF)**

113.

The European Union

114. The European Union (EU) or Common Market was originally formed by the Treaty of Rome in 1957 by Belgium, France, Italy, Luxembourg, the Netherlands and West Germany. The UK, Eire and Denmark joined on 1 January 1973 followed by Greece in 1981 and Portugal and Spain in 1986. Austria, Finland and Sweden joined on 1st January 1995. The EU now has a total population of over 380 million.

115. The EU is a **customs union** in that it has:

☐ abolished virtually all tariffs between the member countries and

☐ established a common external tariff on all imported goods.

Britain applies the common customs tariff to all countries which do not belong to, or have any special arrangement with, the EU.

116. In addition to the removal of physical trade barriers the EU also aims to encourage the free movement of services, capital and people. The **Single European Act 1986** set an implementation date for this of 1st January 1993. Ultimately, European political and monetary union is planned with a single currency, a Federal Central Bank and one Central Parliament.

117. **European Monetary System (EMS)**

The EMS was set up in March 1979 with 3 aims:

☐ to stabilise currency fluctuations between EU countries

☐ to help keep down interest rates and

☐ to control inflation

118. The EMS consists of 4 main elements:

☐ **European Currency Unit (ECU)**

The ECU is a hypothetical exchange rate, based on a basket of EU currencies. It is used to value EU transactions, government bonds, travellers cheques and even mortgages.

☐ **Exchange Rate Mechanism (ERM)**

The ERM is a system of semi-fixed exchange rates within agreed bands. It limits how far member currencies can fluctuate against the ECU and between each other before intervention is demanded. Initially movements of 2.25% either way were allowed, although sterling and the peseta had a 6% band. In August 1993 the band was widened to 15% either way. If exchange rates look likely to break these guidelines, the 2 countries involved are obliged to buy or sell currency to push it up or down.

☐ **European Monetary Co-operation Fund (EMCF)**

The Co-operation Fund is used by EU Central Banks, including the Bank of England, for borrowing to balance their books after intervening in the foreign exchange markets to adjust supply and demand.

☐ **The Very-Short-Term Finance Facility (VSTF)**

The VSTF gives ERM members unlimited credit facilities in their own currency. This can be used to finance intervention when currencies reach their ERM margins.

Organisation of the European Union

119. As shown in the following diagram there are 5 main institutions responsible for the functioning of the European Community – the Council of Ministers, the European Commission, the European Parliament, the Court of Justice and the Court of Auditors.

120. **European Decision-Making**

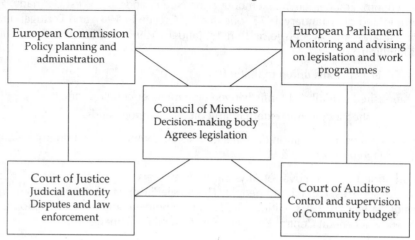

121. **The Council of Ministers** is the decision-making body with at least one Minister appointed by each member country. Decisions are made on proposals submitted to it by the Commission. On matters of major importance, the Council can only act on a unanimous vote. That is, all countries have a power of 'veto' which they can use to prevent a decision being taken. The Presidency of the Council, which rotates round member states every 6 months, was last held by the UK from July-December 1992.

122. **The European Commission**, based in Brussels, is the Union's planning and day-to-day administrative agency which proposes policies and legislation and executes decisions. It is led by 17 commissioners appointed by member states, to act in the interests of the whole Union, each with responsibility for a particular policy area. The Commission is divided into 23 administrative departments called Directorate Generals (DG's). Each DG is in charge of a specific policy area such as energy, agriculture, competition and transport.

123. **The European Parliament** meets once a month usually in Strasbourg (France). Member states elect representatives according to their population. Of the 518 Euro MP's, Britain has 81 (England 66, Scotland 8, Wales 4, Northern Ireland 3). The Parliament debates all major aspects of policy and influences the proposals made by the Commission. It also examines and approves the EU budget.

124. **The European Court of Justice** exists to ensure that EU laws are observed by member states and to deal with any disputes. It is based in Luxembourg. The Court consists of 13 judges whose decisions, which are made by majority vote, are binding on all Union institutions, governments, companies and individuals.

125. **The Court of Auditors** based in Luxembourg supervises the operation of the Union budget and is responsible for examining the accounts of all Union revenue and expenditure. It helps to counteract waste and fraud.

126. **Other EU Bodies** include:

   ❑ **European Investment Bank (EIB)**. Contributions from member states are used to make loans and help finance projects in the less developed areas of the Union or to support projects of common interest to several members such as the Channel Tunnel.

   ❑ **Economic and Social Committee** is an advisory body which must be consulted by the Commission on proposals relating to these matters.

   ❑ **European Regional Development Fund (ERDF)** . This is the largest of the EU's structural funds, which aims to help redress the principal regional imbalances by stimulating economic development in the least prosperous EU regions. Britain was allocated £571 million in 1993. ERDF is used to help finance initiatives such as environmental and infrastructure improvements, tourism and industry developments, R & D and vocational training.

   ❑ **European Social Fund (ESF)**, which provides money for re-training, is targeted at helping young people joining the labour market, the long-term unemployed, people with particular disadvantages in finding and keeping work and promoting equal opportunities at work. The UK is to receive £2.5 billion from ESF between 1994 and 1999.

❏ **European Agricultural Guidance and Guarantee Fund**. This operates the Common Agricultural Policy (CAP) which determines the price and distribution of food produce.

EU Budget

49. All members pay a contribution to a common fund to cover the costs of running the EU. The amounts paid by each member vary as does the amount of benefit which each receives.

Task 20   **1.3.2, 1.3.3 (C3.4)**

Read the following extract adapted from 'Britain in Europe' published by the Foreign and Commonwealth Office in 1992 and answer the questions which follow.

The Union's activities have to be financed by contributions from its member countries. In 1992 the Union plans to spend about £50 billion (about 3.5% of total central government expenditure in all EU member states). Some of this money (about £2.5 billion in 1992) is spent on aid to Eastern Europe and the developing world, but most of it is spent within the Union. At present, just over half goes on the Common Agricultral Policy (CAP) and about a quarter on aid to EU regions with particular problems.

All member states receive some money back from the Union budget as well as paying in. But the amount they get back varies. Countries with large farming sectors, or with many poorer regions, tend to receive more money than they pay in. Some countries, including the UK, Germany and France, are net contributors to the budget, paying in more than they receive. When we joined the Union we paid more than our fair share of the budget, but since 1984 we have received an annual rebate in which the Union pays some of our contribution back to us: we will retain this rebate in full in the future. Our net contribution for 1992, after all receipts from the Union, and after we have had our rebate, is expected to be around £1.7 billion. By comparison, the UK defence budget is £24.18 billion and the budget of the Scottish Office is £12.15 billion.

---

1.   What was the planned expenditure in the Union in 1992?

2.   Where is most of the budget spent, and which countries benefit most?

3.   How much did Britain contribute to the Union in 1992.

4.   In what ways, if any, could the extract be said to suggest that the cost of the Union is a good investment for the UK?

5.   Update the figures with the latest available, and comment on any significant changes.

Types of EU Legislation

128. Nearly 300 measures have been proposed within the Single European market programme. A basic knowledge of the different types of legislation is therefore useful for a broader understanding of the European business environment.

129. **Directives** are binding instructions to Member States to achieve a specified legislative result by a given deadline. Member States are allowed to determine how best to achieve this, taking into account its own circumstances, existing law, and enforcement methods. Directives can apply to all or only to specified Member States.

130. Three examples of directives follow:

❏ **The Directive for Minimum Health and Safety Requirements for the Workplace,** which came into effect on 1st January 1993, sets down general health and safety criteria for workplaces and covers specific issues such as emergency exists, fire detection, ventilation and stability of structures (see Element 4.1).

❏ **The General Product Safety Directive** which had to be implemented by Member States from June 1994. It aims to ensure that all products (new, used or reconditioned) marketed in the EU are safe for consumers. Manufacturers are made responsible for supplying safe products and ensuring that their products can be traced.

❑ **The Language Instruction Directive** implemented from 1st January 1993 requires companies exporting machinery in the Community to ensure that instruction manuals are available in the language of the country where it is to be used.

131. **Regulations** are laws which are directly applicable in **all** Member States, rather like an Act of Parliament. Regulations tend to be technical and used to deal with particular activities in areas such as agriculture and transport. Council Regulation 2137/85 introduced the European Economic Interest Grouping (EEIG) designed to facilitate cross-border collaboration and joint ventures between European Companies.

132. **Decisions** are addressed to particular parties – Member States, companies or individuals on whom they are binding. Many EU Decisions relate to cases of unfair competition.

133. In 1991, for example, the Commission decided that several leading European airlines were charging excessively high fares on European routes. The Decision was notified to the Member States concerned who were required to take steps to ensure a more balanced relationship between air fares and costs. As a consequence of this Decision, flights in Europe should be cheaper from 1993 onwards following agreement between Member States on a new formula for fixing fares on scheduled air routes.

134. **Recommendations and Opinions** merely state the view of the European institution that issues them and urge action for change. However, they are not legally binding.

Task 21   **1.3.3 (C3.4)**

CHICKEN CURRIE

Premier Poultry has been forced to close its plant at Ripon, with the loss of 400 jobs because of the cost of updating its processes and equipment to meet strict new EU standards. Concerned local councillors believe that Edwina Currie must share the blame because the firm never recovered from the chicken and egg salmonella scare which she started.

SCREEN TEST

The Intercare health products group was delighted on January 1, 1993 when a new Brussels directive required that anyone working at a VDU screen must have his or her eyes tested. Intercare's eyecare side now chips in with a quarter of group profits after two big recent purchases.

Read the articles and answer the questions which follow.

1. Why has Premier Poultry been forced to close?

2. Why was Intercare delighted about January 1st 1993?

3. What do these examples illustrate about EU directives?

4. What, if anything, can firms faced with EU directives do?

Benefits of EU Membership

135. As a result of the end to customs control and the many changes brought about by the UK's membership of the European Union, it is argued that it has and will continue to bring many benefits to us all including:

❑ Political stability thus lessening the risk of war.

❑ Prosperity from increased trade and investment

❑ Wider choice of goods and services.

❏ Higher quality food based on European Standards.

❏ Less lead pollution.

❏ A better protected ozone layer.

❏ More opportunities for living and working in Europe, with wider recognition of qualifications.

❏ More health benefits when travelling in Europe.

❏ More competition leading to lower prices, eg cheaper air fares.

❏ More jobs as business opportunities grow.

Impact of Membership on Business

136. In addition, businesses will **benefit** from:

❏ New market opportunities with all member states.

❏ Free movement of goods between member states.

❏ Economies of scale from increased output.

❏ Access to new sources of finance in European countries.

❏ Cheaper raw materials due to competition.

❏ Greater efficiency and innovation in response to competition.

137. Against this however, businesses also face some potential **disadvantages** including:

❏ Additional costs to implement EU directives such as those for Health & Safety and Product Standards and Labelling.

❏ Increased competition from EU firms.

❏ Complex VAT returns for registered businesses trading in the EU where imports/exports exceed £120,000 with penalties for non-compliance.

❏ Other VAT requirements such as the need to:

• Quote the customer's VAT number on each invoice.

• Provide a quarterly return showing the total sales to each registered customer.

• Be able to give a full description of the goods and their price.

Consumer Protection Legislation

138. The vast majority of businesses are run honestly. Their goods work properly and if problems arise they offer a service to put them right with the minimum of fuss and bother. However, unfortunately, some traders are dishonest. These people will often deliberately mislead consumers about the goods or services which they provide and some even sell faulty or dangerous products. Therefore, the government has introduced several laws to protect consumers against such trades.

139. The main legislation is briefly summarised below.

❏ **Trade Descriptions Acts 1968 and 1972** make it a criminal offense to give a false or misleading description to goods, services, accommodation and facilities. This includes sale prices where the Act stipulates that goods must only be marked as reduced if they have been sold at a higher price for at least 28 consecutive days during the previous 6 months.

❏ **Fair Trading Act 1973**. This set up the Office of Fair Trading (OFT) to look after consumer affairs and consumer credit. The OFT publishes information leaflets, prosecutes offenders, issues credit licences, encourages competition and fair trading, and recommends new laws.

❏ **Consumer Credit Act 1974** requires that all businesses offering credit (eg banks, retailers) must be licensed by the OFT; borrowers must be given a written statement of the total cost of interest on any loan, known as the annual percentage rate (APR), and makes firms supplying credit jointly responsible for faulty goods with the business who sold them.

❏ **Unfair Contract Terms Act 1977** prevents traders from refusing to accept responsibility for specific events by using 'small print' exclusion clauses or notices. It allows consumers to claim compensation for negligence or breach of contract, for example, if a garage scratches your car or a dry cleaner damages your clothing.

❏ **Sale of Goods Act 1979** states that goods sold must be of **merchantable quality** ie a new item should work properly; **as described**, thus plastic shoes should not be called leather; and **fit for** the **purpose** for which they are generally used. If glue is sold to mend shoes, it must do just that. Consumers are entitled to a refund or replacement if these conditions are not fulfiled.

- ❏ **Weights and Measures Act 1985.** This Act makes it an offense for traders to give short weight or measure. Inspectors visit trade premises such as shops, public houses and garages to check that the scales, beer or petrol pumps used are accurate.

- ❏ **Consumer Protection Act 1987**. This Act consolidated and enhanced previous legislation concerned with the sale of dangerous goods. Certain goods (eg bleach) must be marked with **warnings** (including symbols) and **safety advice** (eg first aid); many goods are covered by **safety regulations** including heaters, toys and nightwear and under an EC Directive on product liability, damages can be claimed against suppliers of defective products which cause death or injury. The Act also makes it an offense to give false or **misleading price indications.**

- ❏ **Food and Drink Acts 1955, 1976 and 1982.** These Acts are concerned with the **hygiene, composition and labelling of food** and make it an offense to sell food which is unfit to eat.

- ❏ **Food Safety Act 1990** requires all food handling businesses (eg manufacturers, restaurants, snack-bars, shops) to take all **reasonable precautions** in the manufacture, transport, storage, preparation and sale of food; introduce **appropriate hygiene controls** and **ensure that food is safe** both chemically and microbiologically.

- ❏ **Environmental Protection Act 1990** introduces controls on **pollution** to water/land/air covering **public nuisance** (from smoke, fumes, litter, odours, noise), **noise** where this is a risk to employees, and **waste disposal** where this can be potentially hazardous and damaging to the environment

Task 22   1.3.2 (C3.4)

CDs A RIP-OFF

Evidence is growing that compact disc prices are a 'rip-off' says the Consumers' Association.

It has found that every one of the 30 top-selling pop and classical CDs is more expensive in Britain than in the US. CDs cost just £1 to produce but are retailed at up to £12.99 – a third more in Britain than the US. But the alternative LP is becoming increasingly difficult to buy, and is soon likely to become obsolete.

There have long been rumblings about the high cost of CDs, and in 1993 a Parliamentary Select Committee strongly condemned the pricing practices of the major record companies and called for a reduction of at least £2 in the cost of full-price CDs.

The Office of Fair Trading decided to take no action after an investigation into claims of collusion between manufacturers and retailers to keep CD prices artificially high. They cost similar or less than an LP to produce, yet invariably they are more expensive in the shops. But a retail consultants report which agrees that CDs are expensive says it is because consumers are willing to pay more, not because of a price fixing conspiracy. About 85 million CDs are now sold in Britain every year, with sales peaking at Christmas.

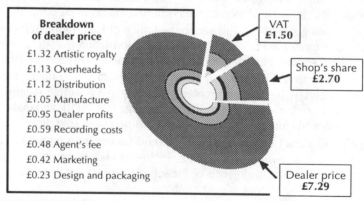

Breakdown of dealer price

£1.32 Artistic royalty
£1.13 Overheads
£1.12 Distribution
£1.05 Manufacture
£0.95 Dealer profits
£0.59 Recording costs
£0.48 Agent's fee
£0.42 Marketing
£0.23 Design and packaging

VAT **£1.50**

Shop's share **£2.70**

Dealer price **£7.29**

continued...

84

Task 22 continued

£31.6m mainly because of the old story of last minute discounting. Airtours is the third biggest operator after Owners Abroad and Thomson. It started its own airline in 1992. Owners owns Enterprise, Sovereign, SunMed and Falcon, and also has its own airline, Air 2000. It has about 19 per cent of the UK travel market, compared with Airtours' 17 per cent. Owners' immediate response to the bid was to urge shareholders to take no action and not to sell. Chairman of Owners, Howard Klein said:'Owners Abroad is seeking to create a group with a strong presence throughout the European market. 'This contrasts with the defensive proposal by Airtours, which is clearly designed to protect its position in the United Kingdom in a way which we believe will work against the interests of both the industry and the consumer,' he added. Profits of holiday companies are notoriously fickle. There would undoubtedly be big savings to come out of either deal but they are some way down the road. In the meantime it would be no surprise if Thomson tightened the screw while its two competitors slug it out.

The following are based on the above article.

1. Identify the facts in the article about the price of CDs.

2. Why is the OFT concerned about the price of CDs?

3. What evidence is there to suggest that CD prices are not a 'rip-off'?

4. What possible explanation is there for the high price of CDs?

5. What effect, if any, do you feel the OFT's investigation is likely to have on the industry and who are the potential winners and losers?

Monopolies and Restrictive Practices

140. The growth of firms can lead to monopoly situations. If monopolies are likely to operate against the public interest, then the Director General of Fair Trading can prevent them being formed (or break-up existing ones). For example, when a firm buys up other firms because this reduces competition it may lead to higher prices.

141. The **Monopolies and Mergers Act 1965** set up the Monopolies and Mergers Commission to investigate any mergers which might be against consumers interests. If a proposed merger would result in 25% or more of a market being controlled by one supplier (or the total assets from the merger would exceed £30 million), then it can be referred to the Commission which decides whether or not it can go ahead.

Task 23   1.3.3 (C3.4)

CONSUMER GROUP FIGHTS BID

The Consumers' Association declared its formal opposition to north-west based Airtours' hostile £237m bid for rival holiday company Owners Abroad. It wrote to the Office of Fair Trading urging for the bid to be referred to the Monopolies and Mergers Commission on the grounds that Airtours would have between 27 and 30 per cent of the holiday tour market if successful. This, it considers to be too high, particularly given the fact that Thomson, the Number One operator, has itself about 30 per cent of the market. Airtours and the Consumers' Association clashed earlier this week over the group's criticism of the holiday company's operating standards. Owners Abroad was also criticised.

continued...

Task 23 continued

AIRTOURS BIDS FOR RIVAL

In 1994, Airtours launched a hostile bid worth £237m for Owners Abroad, its big rival, in an attempt to wrestle dominance of the package holiday market from industry giant Thomson. A combined Owners and Airtours would have about 29% of the holiday market and could be referred to the Monopolies & Mergers Commission. But that market share, it is suggested, could be comfortably whittled down by selling some of the holiday operations. There were hopes that Thomson's takeover of Horizon in 1989, giving it over 35% of the market, would be accepted as a precedent. But how the authorities will react is uncertain. Airtours chairman David Crossland made it clear that the bid would be withdrawn if Owners Abroad went ahead with its proposed link with travel agent Thomas Cook, which is owned by the German holiday group LTU which bought 90% last year. Last month, Airtours reported a full-year 32 per cent increase in profit to a record £36.5m in 1993, and Mr Crossland made it clear then that he was planning to expand by buying more holiday companies in Britain and Europe. Three months earlier the company had bought Pickfords Travel from NFC. Owners profit for the year to last October was down from £2.5m to

Read the articles on the previous page, and answer the questions which are based on them.

1. Why was Airtours' bid considered 'hostile' and what does this mean?

2. What were the main reasons for the bid?

3. Why was the Consumers Association opposed to it?

4. If the bid had been referred to the Monopolies Commission, what factors would it need to investigate?

5. From the information available and your own knowledge, comment on whether or not you feel such a bid should be allowed to go ahead. Consider in your answer the interests of shareholders, consumers and the two companies.

142. **Arguments Against Monopoly**

The lack of competition and therefore potential abuse of the market power of monopolies often leads to a number of arguments being put forward against them including the following:

❐ **Slow innovation** because without competitive pressures, it is not essential to produce new goods or services in order to survive and prosper.

❐ **Reduced choice** because new firms can be prevented from entering a market.

❐ **Inefficiency** because without the incentive to compete, costs may rise which can result in increased prices and/or falling standards.

❐ **Reduced supply** resulting from a desire to create shortages in order to raise prices and profits, particularly where demand is inelastic.

143. **Collusion**

Sometimes instead of merging, firms may come to an agreement with each other to restrict competition. For example, two large bread manufacturers may agree to restrict production in order to create a shortage of bread and therefore keep prices at a high level. An extreme form of collusion would be a **cartel** such as OPEC. Such practices can be illegal in the UK. Under the **Restrictive Trade Practices Act 1976**, the Director General of Fair Trading can refer restrictive practices to the Restrictive Practices Court for investigation, whilst anti-competitive practices are controlled by the **Competition Act 1980.** In both situations firms can be ordered to discontinue practices found to be against the public interest.

European Competition Law

144. In addition to UK laws, the European Union also has legislation which deals with anti-competitive practices across the EU. This covers attempts to fix prices, restrict production or technical development, mergers, control of supplies and the use of unfair contracts.

Deregulation

145. In Element 2.1 we consider government measures to promote competition in marketing including privatisation, contracting-out and deregulation, a recent example of which is the relaxation of controls on shopping.

146. Until December 1994 most shops had to close at 8.00 pm under the **1950 Shops Act**, with an option to stay open until 9.00 pm on one day between Monday and Saturday. They are now allowed to stay open 24 hours a day as part of the Government's ongoing drive to cut business red tape. The Shops Act also stated that only certain goods could be sold on Sundays. However, many retailers used to break these laws which were considered to be out-dated. The **1994 Sunday Trading Act** changed all this and made Sunday trading legal. Big department stores and supermarkets may now open for 6 hours while small shops can open when they like. Restrictions on the sale of alcohol have also been removed.

Task 24	1.3.2, 1.3.3 (C3.2)

1. Discuss the current and potential impact of Sunday trading on consumers, employees, employers and other groups affected such as religious bodies, transport services and local residents.

2. Can you identify any other examples of deregulation and its affect on local organisations?

Economic Analysis

147 It is important therefore to realise that strategic decision taking in organisation is influenced by current government policy and legislation. Because of the impact they can have, for example, the general state of the economy can seriously affect the success or failure of a business because it affects **purchasing power.** This depends on **disposable income**, which is the amount left over after deductions such as tax and national insurance, in other words 'take-home pay', and **discretionary pay**, which is the amount left over after essential spending on food, clothing, housing etc. Changes in either of these can affect **consumer demand**.

148. In times of recession, many people are **unemployed,** many others face the threat of redundancy and even those in employment may have less money to spend or chose to save for fear of the future. **Consumer confidence** is affected which reduces spending. Thus, in these circumstances a firm may, for example, be forced to reduce prices, and therefore profit margins, or alter some other element of the marketing mix, just to survive which in turn business confidence and the willingness to invest. On the other hand, in times of **economic growth**, people spend more freely, business may boom and the potential for higher profits is greater.

Task 25   **1.3.2, 1.3.3 (C3.4)**

PIT LOSS

British Coal has closed 31 of its 50 deep mines with a loss of over 30,000 jobs. This leaves only 11,000 working miners. The closures are blamed on cheaper coal imports and the move from coal to gas by privatised electricity generating companies Powergen and National Power. The move could lead to dearer electricity because although gas fired power stations are cheaper, cleaner and quicker to build, production costs are higher. Potential knock-on effects include the consequent closure of 16 power stations, the loss of jobs at BR and Road Hauliers who transport the coal and in the mining equipment industry and a social and economic decline in many communities, particularly where coal mining is the main industry

The following questions are based on the above article which was written from media reports.

1.   Why are the pit closures taking place?

2.   What are the immediate effects of the closures?

3.   How is the economy as a whole likely to be affected?

149. Organisations may also be affected by factors such as

❑ the level of **inflation** which reduces consumer purchasing power, unless wages increase proportionately, and can affect an organisation's costs, prices and profits

❑ new **taxes** which can affect prices and/or the distribution of income and, therefore, patterns of demand

❑ the **rate of interest** which affects not just the cost of borrowing but also disposable income and therefore the level of consumer demand. For example, a rise in the cost of mortgages leaves consumers with less to spend

❑ where an organisation is involved in importing or exporting its raw materials or products, then **exchange rates** are important because they affect the relative cost of products and services both at home and overseas

❑ **financial assistance** available such as grants to locate in regions of high unemployment.

Summary

150. a)   Micro-economics is the study of individual behaviour whilst macro-economics is about the economy as a whole. The government's policies have an influence on both.

b)   Economic systems can be free, controlled or mixed.

c)   National income (Net National Product) measures the level of economic activity in the economy.

d)   The principles behind the National Income, including injections and withdrawals, can be illustrated in a circular flow of income diagram.

e)   Classical economists believed that the economy was self-regulating but this thinking failed completely in the 1930's depression.

f)   Keynes argued that unemployment was caused by reduced aggregate demand which governments could boost via fiscal policies and the multiplier.

g)   The size of the multiplier depends upon the proportion of any extra income which is spent on consumption.

h)   If aggregate demand exceeds output at the full employment level of national income, we have an inflationary gap. If national income is below the full employment level we get a deflationary gap.

i) The main aims of macro-economic policy are economic growth, full employment, low inflation and balance of payments stability.

j) To achieve these aims, the government uses fiscal policy (taxation and public expenditure) and monetary policy (interest rates and credit controls).

k) Taxes can be direct on individuals and organisations, such as income tax and corporation tax, or indirect on the expenditure of goods and services, for example VAT and Customs and Excise duties.

l) The Budget is a statement of how the Chancellor of the Exchequer intends to raise revenue to pay for the Government's planned public expenditure.

m) The main items of expenditure are on Social Security, Health, Defence, Education and National Debt interest.

n) Economic growth is important for raising the standard of living.

o) Unemployment can be frictional, cyclical, structural, regional, real wage, seasonal, technological and residual.

p) It has important economic, social and political effects and therefore the government may use fiscal, monetary or direct measures to control it.

q) An increase in the general level of prices is called inflation and it has important effects on both individuals and businesses.

r) Inflation can be demand-pull, cost-push or multicausal.

s) Policies to control inflation can include monetary and fiscal policies, or direct measures such as a prices and incomes policy.

t) The government influences the location of organisations by offering incentives to move into areas of high unemployment which can also benefit from European aid.

u) The Single Market EU is Britain's largest trading partner and through its directives, regulations, decisions and recommendations and opinions has a major impact on businesses and individuals.

v) Considerable UK and European legislation exists to protect consumers from unfair, unhealthy and dangerous trading practices.

Review questions *(Answers can be found in the paragraphs indicated)*

1. Why do governments intervene in the running of the economy? (3–12)

2. How is the national income measured? (13–20)

3. Explain the circular flow of income and injections to and withdrawals from it. (24–30)

4. How did the thinking of Keynes differ from that of the classical economists? (31–34)

5. Using an example, explain the concept of the multiplier. (35–39)

6. What is the difference between an inflationary and a deflationary gap? (40–45)

7. List the main aims of government economic policy. (46, 48)

8. Using examples of each, distinguish between direct and indirect taxes. (51–53)

9. In what ways are business organisations affected by taxation? (55)

10. What are the main functions of the Budget? (56)

11. Briefly explain what is meant by Public Expenditure? (60–62)

12. Describe the main measures of monetary policy. (64–72)

13. Why is economic growth important? (76–79)

14. What is unemployment and why might it be underestimated? (82–83)

15. Describe the main causes of unemployment. (84–87)

16. Distinguish between the economic, social and political effects of unemployment. (88–90)

17. How can unemployment be reduced? (92–94)

18. What is the difference between creeping and hyper-inflation? (95–97)

19. Describe the main causes and effects of inflation on individuals and businesses and the policies to control it. (99–110)

20. Give 4 examples of measures which the government has used to try to influence the location of industry (108–111)

21. Briefly describe 2 EU schemes which provide regional aid to business (112, 126)

22. How is the European Union organised? (113–123)

23. Briefly distinguish between the different types of EU legislation. (128–134)

24. With the use of examples, explain why legislation against unfair, unhealthy and dangerous trading practice is necessary. (138–143)

25. Briefly analyse the potential effects of government policies and legislation on business organisations. (144–148)

Assignment – Influencing the Market Economy   Element 1.3

The following data is based upon the Financial Statement and Treasury forecasts in the Budget Report 1993–4.

SHORT-TERM ECONOMIC PROSPECTS

% changes on previous year unless otherwise stated	1992	1993	1994 (H1)	Av'ge errors in past f/cast[1]
GDP and domestic demand at constant prices				
Domestic demand of which:	1/2	1¼	3	1¼
Consumers' expenditure[2]	¼	1¼	1¾	1¼
General govnmnt consumption[2]	−¼	¼	1¼	1¼
Fixed investment	−¾	1/2	2¾	2¾
Change in stock-building[3]	1/2	¼	1¼	¼
Exports of goods and services	2	5½	10¼	1¼
Imports of goods and services	5¼	4¾	9¼	2
GDP (average measure)	−½	1¼	3	1
Non-North Sea GDP	−½	1	2¼	1
Manufacturing output	−¾	1½	2¾	1
Balance of Payments				
£ billion	−12	−17½	[4] −18½	4¾
percent of GDP	−2	−2¾	−2¾	¾
Inflation				
Retail prices index (Q4)	3¾	3¾	3¾	¾
Producer output prices (Q4)[6]	2¼	4	[5] 3¼	¾
GDP deflator at mkt prices (fncl yr)	3¼	2¾	-	1
Money GDP at mkt prices (fncl yr)				
£ billion	599	628	-	-
percentage change	3¼	4¾	-	1½
PSBR (financial year)				
£ billion	35	50	-	6½
per cent of GDP	5¾	8	-	1

[1] Average errors regardless of sign over past 10 years (apply to forecasts for 1993 or 1993-4. [2] Expenditure adjustment. [3] Percent of GDP. [4] At annual rate. [5] Q2. [6] Excluding food, drink and tobacco.

MEDIUM-TERM TARGETS

PUBLIC SECTOR BORROWING

£ billion[1]	'91-2	'92-3	'93-4	'94-5	'95-6	'96-7	'97-8
General govmt expenditure	236.1	260	280	296	314	329	342
Genl govmt receipts	222.2	224	229	251	275	293	311
GGBR	**14.0**	**36**	**51**	**45**	**40**	**36**	**31**
Public corporations market and overseas borrowing	−0.2	−1	−1	−1	−1	−1	−1
PSBR	**13.8**	**35**	**50**	**44**	**39**	**35**	**30**
Money GDP	580.4	599	628	671	716	756	792
PSBR as % of money GDP	**2.4**	**5¾**	**8**	**6½**	**5½**	**4½**	**3¾**

Rounded to the nearest £1 billion from 1992-3 onwards

OUTPUT AND INFLATION

	1992-3	1993-4	1994-5	1995-6	1996-7	1997-8	
General govmt expenditure	236.1	260	280	296	314	329	342
Genl govmt receipts	222.2	224	229	251	275	293	311
GGBR	**14.0**	**36**	**51**	**45**	**40**	**36**	**31**
Public corporations market and overseas borrowing	−0.2	−1	−1	−1	−1	−1	−1
PSBR	**13.8**	**35**	**50**	**44**	**39**	**35**	**30**
Money GDP	580.4	599	628	671	716	756	792
PSBR as % of money GDP	**2.4**	**5³/₄**	**8**	**6¹/₂**	**5¹/₂**	**4¹/₂**	**3³/₄**

Rounded to the nearest £1 billion from 1992-3 onwards

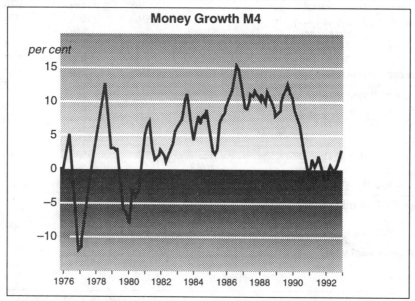

Money Growth M4

per cent

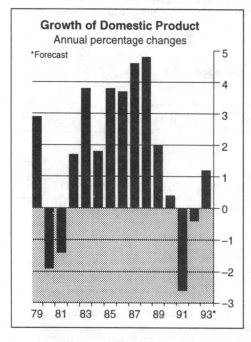

Growth of Domestic Product
Annual percentage changes

*Forecast

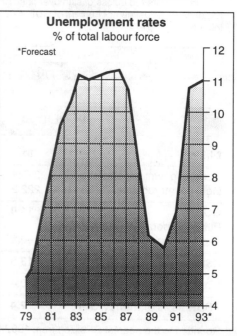

Unemployment rates
% of total labour force

*Forecast

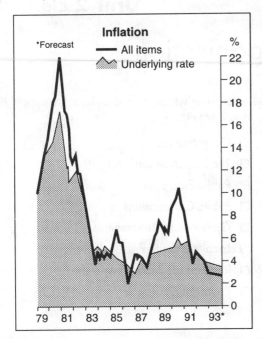

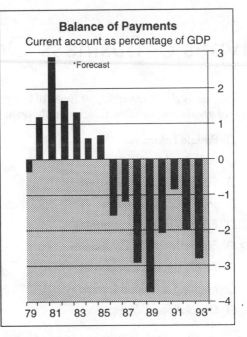

The Government's Medium Term Financial Strategy (MTFS) sets out its plans for achieving economic growth. This was based on low inflation within 1–4 %, interest rates dependent upon exchange rate movements and the growth of money supply confined within a monitoring range of 3–9% for M4 and a reducing PSBR. The Government believes there is no immediate prospect of unemployment falling below three million.

1. Update this information with the latest data available and identify any major changes or trends.

2. Using all the available information, devise a Budget which you think would be appropriate to our economy at the present time. List your proposals, give reasons for your decisions and outline the likely effects on the economy as a whole, in both the short and longer term.

3. Consider the likely impact of your Budget on the local economy. Use examples to illustrate the points which you make.

4. Develop this further by summarising the ways in which at least two government policies affect local or national markets.

5. Finally make notes on why governments need to intervene in markets.

4 Types of Business Organisation

This chapter is about the different types of business enterprises which have developed to supply the wide range of goods and services which people want to buy. It covers:

❒ Private Enterprise   ❒ Co-operatives

❒ Sole Traders   ❒ The Franchise Business

❒ Partnerships   ❒ Public Enterprise

❒ Joint Stock Companies   ❒ Public Corporations

❒ Private Limited Companies   ❒ Government Departments

❒ Single Member Companies   ❒ Local Authorities

❒ Public Limited Companies   ❒ Reasons for Public Ownership

❒ Forming a Limited Company   ❒ Privatisation

❒ Dissolution of Companies

Types of Business Organisation

1. We saw in Chapter 1 that Britain has what is known as a mixed economy where goods and services are supplied by both private and public sector organisations.

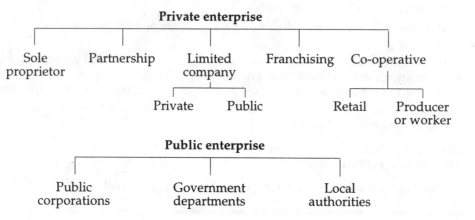

2. The private sector or **private enterprise** is the term used to describe all businesses which are owned by individuals or groups of individuals and run essentially for profit. About three-quarters of all trading in Britain is controlled by private sector organisations. The rest, known as the **public sector or public enterprise** are businesses which are owned and controlled by the Government or local authorities and run for the benefit of the country.

Types of Private Enterprise

3. There are six main forms of business ownership in the private sector of the economy:

❒ Sole Traders

❒ Partnerships   }   of which there are more than one million

❒ Private Limited Companies

❒ Public Limited Companies

❒ Co-operatives

❒ Franchising

Sole Traders (or Proprietors)

4. The oldest, simplest and therefore most common form of business unit is the sole trader or one-person concern. This is somebody who is self-employed and who usually starts a business with capital from their savings or by borrowing from friends or a bank. **Capital** is the money which every business needs to enable it to set up and operate, for example to buy premises, equipment, stock and pay wages.

    A sole trader is not necessarily a one-person business and may have many employees or branches. However, the business is owned by only one person and it is they who receive the profits.

5. If a business operates under a name other than that of its owner(s) then under the **Business Names Act 1985** it must:

    ❏ display in a prominent position the name of the owner(s) and a UK address where documents may be served.

    ❏ show this information on business stationery including letters, orders, receipts, invoices and demands for payment.

6. A large number of retail outlets are owned by sole traders, for example many shoe repairers, hairdressers, cafes, launderettes, 'corner' shops and newsagents. Other examples include many market traders, window cleaners, farmers, lorry drivers, building workers and small manufacturing concerns.

Task 1	**2.1.2 (C3.2)**

The Department of Trade and Industry, Companies Registration Office provides guidance notes and a specimen notice on business names. Suggest why you think it could be sensible for a sole trader to obtain this information.

7. **Advantages of Sole Traders**

    ❏ This type of business can be set up relatively easily with a small amount of capital and few legal formalities.

    ❏ The owner is the 'boss' and can make decisions quickly about how the business is run.

    ❏ Personal contact with customers, particularly where a business operates in a local area.

    ❏ All profits belong to the owner.

    ❏ Satisfaction and interest is gained from working for yourself.

    ❏ Business affairs can be kept private except for completing tax returns.

8. **Disadvantages of the Sole Trader**

    ❏ Unlimited Liability – this means that if the business fails and makes a loss, then the owner is responsible for all the debts incurred. Consequently, a sole trader takes the risk that they could lose all their personal possessions including their car, house and furniture.

    ❏ May be unable to benefit from buying in bulk (large quantities) and thus be unable to offer competitive prices.

    ❏ Expansion may be limited because the owner lacks capital and may have difficulty in borrowing.

    ❏ Division of labour may be difficult because of the small size of the business. In a small business, the owner must do most jobs themselves.

    ❏ Lack of continuity. If the owner dies or retires the business may go out of existence.

Task 2   **2.1.2 (C3.2)**

1. In the area in which you live, study or work, identify as many examples as possible of sole traders. Name them and state the type of business concerned.

2. Comment on any significant features or trends.

Partnerships

9. As the one-person business expands, it may overcome some of its disadvantages, such as lack of capital, by changing to a larger unit. For example, a plumber whose business is growing could invite one or more friends to join him to form a partnership.

10. Under the **1890 Partnership Act**, a partnership is defined as 2-20 people (10 in Banking) who agree to provide capital and work together in a business with the purpose of making a profit. More than 20 partners are allowed in the case of accountants, solicitors and members of the Stock Exchange.

11. **Advantages of Partnerships**

    ☐ Easy to set up.

    ☐ More capital can be brought into the business.

    ☐ Division of labour is possible as partners may have different skills. For example, in a firm of solicitors one partner may specialise in the buying and selling of houses, another in divorce and another in criminal offences.

    ☐ Responsibility for the control of the business is shared with more than one person. Therefore the problems of holidays, illness and long working hours are reduced.

12. **Disadvantages of Partnerships**

    ☐ Partners have unlimited liability and are therefore personally liable for the debts of the business.

    ☐ Disagreements among partners may cause problems.

    ☐ Lack of capital may limit expansion.

    ☐ There is no continuity of existence i.e. a partnership is dissolved (automatically ends) if one of the partners dies, resigns or becomes bankrupt.

13. People wanting to form a partnership normally draw up a legal document called a **Partnership Deed of Agreement**. This sets out the details of the partnership including the objects of the firm, how much capital each partner will provide and how profits or losses are to be shared. This Agreement is not necessary by law but is obviously very useful if a dispute arises over the terms of the partnership. If no Agreement exists then the rights and duties of the partners are determined by the **1890 Partnership Act** which states, for example, that any profits or losses must be shared equally.

14. Partnerships are usually found in the professions such as Estate Agents, Insurance Brokers, Dentists, Doctors and Accountants, although they are also found in other occupations including garage proprietors, taxi drivers, small factories and workshops, and painters and decorators. Sometimes a partner may put capital into a business but not take any active part in how it is run. In this situation they are known as sleeping partners.

15. Under the **1907 Partnership Act**, the **ordinary partnership** described above may be changed into a **limited partnership**. This involves at least one partner agreeing to accept unlimited liability. The number of such partnerships is quite small because limited partners are not allowed to take any active part in running a business.

Task 3   **2.1.2 (C3.2)**

K. Clayton, a successful sole proprietor in the retail trade is seeking to expand her business. She cannot decide whether or not to enter into partnership with J. Wilson. She seeks your opinion as to the potential problems and benefits of forming a partnership and asks you to advise her on what to do.

Outline your response.

Joint Stock or Limited Companies

16. As businesses wish to expand they need more capital and in order to obtain this, they frequently become limited companies. These are business units established under the regulations of the various **Companies Acts 1948 to 1989**. Limited companies are sometimes referred to as **joint-stock** companies because the capital of the business is jointly owned by the shareholders.

17. Companies differ from sole traders and partnerships in 5 main ways:

   ❏ **Share Capital**

   In order to raise capital, companies issue (sell) shares which means that many people are able to own a small part of the business, i.e. they become shareholders. This gives the company permanent capital. If a shareholder wishes to get their money back they can sell the shares but the company's capital does not change.

   ❏ **Companies have limited liability**

   This means that should the business fail, the people who have invested their money in it cannot lose any of their personal possessions i.e. their liability is limited to the amount invested. It is this important feature which gives people confidence to invest in companies without the risk of losing everything.

   ❏ **Companies are Corporate Bodies**

   That is, they have a separate legal identity from their owners (shareholders). This means that a company continues to exist in business even though the owners may change. Some may die, others may sell their shares but the legal existence of the company is not affected.

   ❏ **Separation of ownership and control**

   The formation of a limited company enables people who cannot or do not want to take part in its management to still contribute capital and share any profits.

   ❏ **Legal Control**

   Companies must by law present annual accounts to an annual general meeting to which all shareholders must be invited. The accounts must also be submitted to the Registrar of Companies.

18. As shown in the following diagram, shareholders provide the capital for the company and elect a Board of Directors to run it on their behalf. In return they are entitled to share any profits made by the firm, which is commonly called a **dividend**. The directors make the important policy decisions on how the company is to operate and may appoint managers to organise its day-to-day running.

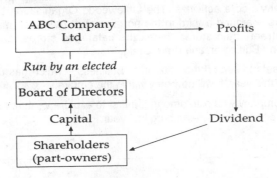

Private Limited Companies (Ltd)

19. There are two types of limited company – private and public. Both must have at least two share-holders but there is no maximum.

20. The most important features of private limited companies are:

   ❐ They are usually, but not always, small 'family' concerns.

   ❐ The name of the company must be registered with the Registrar of Companies and it must end with the word 'Limited' (or its abbreviation Ltd), for example Travis Builders Ltd.

   ❐ They are not allowed to offer shares to the general public.

   ❐ Shareholders may not be able to sell their shares without the agreement of the other shareholders.

21. There are about 500,000 private limited companies in Britain, one of the largest being Littlewoods, the stores, pools and mail order firm. Other well-known examples are Famous Army Stores, Pickfords Removals and J C Bamford who specialise in making plant hire equipment. Your local Yellow Pages will include many other examples.

22. **Advantages of Private Limited Companies (Ltd)**

   ❐ Limited liability for Shareholders.

   ❐ Continuity of existence

   ❐ Minimum number of shareholders is only two.

   ❐ Greater capital potential

   ❐ Benefits from operating on a larger scale for example bulk buying, employment of specialist staff, use of mass production techniques.

23. **Disadvantages of Private Limited Companies (Ltd)**

   ❐ Growth may be limited by lack of capital since shares cannot be offered to the general public.

   ❐ Transfer of shares may be limited to 'approved' new members.

   ❐ A copy of the audited accounts must be sent to the Registrar of Companies.

Task 4   **2.1.2 (C3.4)**

LITTLEWOODS UNCERTAIN FUTURE

New challenges and uncertainties face Littlewoods – Britain's second largest private company founded in 1923 as it moves into its 70th year, determined to remain private. The football pools business, on which the Moores empire was founded, could be badly hit by the government's national lottery plans.

On the High Street the longest recession in 60 years continues. And next Spring, Sir Desmond Pitcher departs after 14 years as chief executive, during which time the annual turnover has reached £2.5 billion and profits have risen tenfold to £97m. He has brought Liverpool-based Littlewoods up-to-date improving business in all the company's core activities. The Littlewoods Organisation Ltd employs over 30,000 workers – around a third in the north west. It has three main retailing operations – high street chain stores, Index the catalogue stores, and mail order operations including Burlington and Peter Craig.

Proposals to sell off the mail order business – which has 6.5m agents – foundered earlier this year. It will now stay within the empire.

The company was also among the first to explore ventures in Russia – including two shops opened in St Petersburg last year.

continued...

> **Task 4** continued
>
> Littlewoods other major interests include pools and competition partnerships operating the largest treble chance in the world. Over 5,000 people work in that pools operation, processing the eight million coupons filled in every week. But there is no doubt that for the future the company fears the competition from the national lottery.
>
> The company's concerns were justified. The lottery started in November 1994 and the competition caused the pools business to fall by 15%. Responding to pressure the government removed previous restrictions and allowed pools firms to advertise on television. Littlewoods responded immediately by launching a £5m campaign.
>
> Read the article and answer the following questions.
>
> 1. How can Littlewoods private status be identified?
>
> 2. Which family founded the company and when?
>
> 3. What are Littlewoods' core activities?
>
> 4. What are the challenges and uncertainties faced by the company?
>
> 5. What could be the potential impact on the Company's future of these challenges and uncertainties?
>
> 6. What was the actual impact and how did the company respond.

Single Member Companies

24. In 1992, new regulations came into force to allow the formation of private limited companies with only one shareholder, and to permit existing private limited companies to become single member companies. The Companies (Single Member Private Limited Companies) Regulations, which were made under the European Communities Act, implement the Twelfth Company Law Directive.

25. The regulations also provide certain safeguards. They require a single member company to ensure:

    ❑ That the terms of certain contracts with the single member are recorded in writing.

    ❑ That information concerning its status as a single member company is recorded in its register of members.

    ❑ That all decisions taken by the person who is the single member acting as the company in general meetings are recorded in writing.

    Criminal penalties exist for breach of these requirements.

Public Limited Companies (PLC)

26. Public limited companies must be registered with the Registrar of Companies, have limited liability, raise capital by issuing shares and are run by a Board of Directors elected by the shareholders. However, they are different from private companies in several important ways:

    ❑ They can advertise their shares to the general public to raise capital. To do this they must issue a **prospectus**. This is a printed document which gives details about the company (i.e. its history, profit record and future plans), the amount of capital it is raising and information about the share offer.

    ❑ Shares can be freely bought and sold on the Stock Exchange.

    ❑ The company must indicate its public status in its name by using the words 'Public Limited Company' (or its abbreviation PLC).

27. Usually a business will start as a private company and then goes 'public' at a later date in order to raise more capital to enable it to expand. To do this it must have a nominal or authorised share cap-

ital of at least £50,000 of which it must issue (i.e. sell) at least a quarter. The **nominal or authorised** capital is the value of the shares which the company is allowed to have. So for example, if its nominal capital is £100,000 it must issue at least £25,000 worth of shares if it wants to go public.

28. Public Limited Companies vary considerably in size from relatively small localised firms such as the world famous Caithness Glass Company based at Wick in Scotland, to very large national companies like Boots, British Telecom and Dixons, to international concerns like Shell, ICI, Ford and Unilever.

29. **Advantages of Public Limited Companies (PLC)**

   ❑ Limited liability for shareholders.

   ❑ Continuity of existence.

   ❑ Easier to raise large amounts of capital and expand.

   ❑ Shares freely transferable on the Stock Exchange.

   ❑ Easier to borrow money i.e. from banks.

   ❑ Benefits from economies of scale.

30. **Disadvantages of Public Limited Companies (PLC)**

   ❑ Their formation requires many legal documents and may be very costly.

   ❑ Can become very large and impersonal. People may not feel that they 'belong' to the organisation.

   ❑ Inefficiency may result if a firm becomes very large and difficult to manage.

   ❑ Annual accounts must be published.

   ❑ Risk of 'take-over' bids by other companies because shares can be easily bought on the Stock Exchange.

Forming a Limited Company

31. In Britain, certain legal requirements must be met before a company is allowed to begin trading and these are laid down in the various Companies Acts. Two documents must be drawn up, the **'Memorandum of Association'** and the **'Articles of Association'**.

32. The 'Memorandum of Association' gives important information about the company including:

   ❑ The name with 'Limited' (Ltd) or 'Public Limited' (PLC) as the last word according to its status.

   ❑ Its business address.

   ❑ The objects of the company, for example to manufacture baked beans.

   ❑ Details of the company's capital, for example, £250,000 divided into 250,000 Ordinary Shares of £1 each.

   ❑ That the shareholders liability is limited.

33. The 'Articles of Association' are the **internal rules** of the company which give details of such matters as the number of directors, the voting rights of the shareholders and how profits are to be shared. The 'Memorandum' and 'Articles' must be sent to the Registrar of Companies in London. When satisfied that the prospective company has met the legal requirements, he will issue a **Certificate of Incorporation** which allows it to begin trading.

Task 5   **2.1.2 (C3.4)**

CADBURY CODE OF PRACTICE

Tough new guidelines about the way public companies should run themselves were published in December 1992 by the Cadbury Committee on Corporate Governance.

It recommended that

❏ All UK quoted companies should follow a Code of Best Practice and be required by the Stock Exchange to say in their annual reports that they are complying, and if not why not.

The main proposals were:

❏ Boards to have a minimum of three non-executive directors.

❏ Directors' service contracts not to exceed three years without shareholders' approval.

❏ Full disclosure of directors' total pay and those of the chairman and highest paid director, including pension scheme and stock options.

❏ Executive directors' pay to be decided by a sub committee made up entirely or mainly of non-executive directors.

❏ Clearly accepted division of responsibilities at the head of a company to prevent any individual such as the Chief Executive having unfettered power of decision.

❏ The board should include high calibre non-executive directors so that their views carry a significant weight in board decisions.

❏ Most non-executive directors should be free of any management or other tie up with the company.

❏ The board should establish an audit committee of at least three non-executive directors with written terms of reference.

The Code aims to improve financial reporting by providing a checklist for company shareholders which will strengthen their influence thus helping to protect their investment and also prevent another 'Robert Maxwell affair'.

Little thought, however, was given to small companies for whom 3 non-executive directors may be costly.

From the information above and your own knowledge or research, answer the following:

1. Why was a Code of Best Practice for companies needed?

2. What is the most significant proposal of the Cadbury Committee?

3. What effect, if any, do you think it will have on companies?

Dissolution of Companies

34. As stated earlier, changes in a company's shareholders have no effect on the company or its capital. However, companies which fail to achieve their objectives and make successive losses may become insolvent (unable to pay their debts) and therefore be wound-up (liquidated). This is a legal process which can take 3 forms.

❏ **Compulsory liquidation.** When a firm is unable to pay its debts, a creditor may apply to Court for a winding-up order. This can also occur if the company does not meet its statutory requirements such as failing to begin trading within one year of incorporation or not holding shareholders meetings. In this situation, a liquidator is appointed to take control of the company. This may be the Official Receiver, which is an office of the DTI.

❏ **Voluntary liquidation**. Sometimes shareholders pass a 'special resolution' agreeing to dissolve a company. This may be because the company wants to merge with another or merely to discontinue trading.

❏ **Winding-up under supervision of the Court**. Where a company is voluntarily wound-up, the Court may still order that dissolution takes place under its supervision and in this instance may again appoint a liquidator to take control.

35. **Liquidator**. A liquidator therefore, can be appointed either by creditors, shareholders, or the Court. Their job is to sell any assets and distribute the proceeds to the Company's creditors. If there are insufficient funds to pay all creditors, then under the **Insolvency Act 1986**, preferential creditors such as the Inland Revenue, for tax due, are paid first; then ordinary creditors. Any surplus is then distributed to the shareholders.

Task 6   **2.1.2 (C3.4)**

DIRECTORS DISQUALIFIED

The DTI's Insolvency Service's network of Official Receivers are an important part of the regulatory framework protecting the public against delinquent company directors who abuse the privilege of limited liability. Over 1,000 incompetent, dishonest and negligent directors have been investigated and received disqualification orders, removing them from corporate activities.

---

1. Explain the 'privilege of limited liability'.

2. What does insolvency mean?

3. Why is a regulatory framework needed?

4. What does disqualification mean for a company director?

Co-operatives

36. A further form of business organisation is that of the co-operative. The basic idea is a large number of small separate units working together in their mutual interest to achieve economies of scale. For example, the saving from bulk buying of goods and equipment, joint advertising and the use of specialist staff. There are two basic types – retail (or consumer) co-operatives and producer (or worker) co-operatives.

37. The modern Co-operative movement began in 1844 when a group of 28 working men founded the Rochdale Equitable Pioneers Society. Its aims were to supply members with pure, wholesome food (adulteration was widespread at the time), at fair prices and return any profit as a 'dividend'. This proved so successful that the movement grew rapidly throughout the UK and abroad, gradually widening its range of products.

38. Societies do not operate under the same rules as limited companies. They are registered under the **Industrial and Provident Societies Acts 1965–1975** and are responsible to the Registrar of Friendly Societies to whom they submit an Annual Return and financial statements.

39. The main features of retail co-operatives are:

❏ They are owned by their customers who can become a member (or shareholder) by purchasing £1 shares.

❏ They are run by a Board of Directors elected by the members.

❏ Each member has only one vote regardless of how many shares they hold.

❏ Each society operates independently under its own name (e.g. Greater Nottingham, Ipswich, Leicestershire). They are linked together through the Co-operative Union.

❏ The concept of a 'dividend' i.e. sharing of profits with customers.

Producer or Worker Co-operatives

40. Producer co-operatives have been most successful in agriculture for example in Denmark, New Zealand and Spain where groups of small farmers have got together to share their marketing and production facilities. This enables them to gain the maximum benefit from economies of scale and therefore to operate more efficiently.

41. Except in farming, producer co-operatives were almost non-existent in Britain until the early 1970's. At this time, the Government was faced with the problem of rising unemployment. Therefore it began to offer financial help to firms which were likely to close down and make their employees redundant (dismiss them because they were no longer needed). Worker co-operatives were formed where each employee bought shares in the firm and shared the profits. Through Co-operative Development Agencies, they also became important for the growth of small businesses.

42. There are now over 1500 Worker Co-operatives. Examples include Suma (wholefood) wholesalers, Paper Back (paper recyclers), Scott Bader (Chemicals) and Soft Solution (Computer networks).

Task 7   2.1.2 (C3.4)

A STITCH IN TIME

When a clothing firm shut down one of its factories, nine workers decided to pool £1000 of their redundancy money ... And went back into business as a workers' co-operative. Now Topstitch, at Cradley Heath, West Midlands, have won £16,000 in grants and loans to help them expand. Their former employers are also lending a hand, supplying machinery and the promise of orders.

1. From the article, identify some of the advantages of forming a workers' co-operative.

2. Can you identify any potential disadvantages?

The Franchise Business

43. A comparatively new but growing form of business ownership in Britain is called **franchising**. Franchising involves an existing, usually well-known established company allowing someone the exclusive right to manufacture, service or sell its products in a particular area.

44. The franchise company also helps the person to set up and run the business by giving training, advice, supplying equipment and materials and assisting with the location of premises and marketing. The company charges a royalty (fee) for its services which is usually in the form of a lump sum (e.g. £10,000) and a share of the profits of the business (e.g. 10%). Cars, petrol, printing services, certain foods and restaurants are frequently sold like this. Examples of franchises in Britain include McDonalds, Sock Shop, Dyno Rod, Holland and Barratt, Kentucky Fried Chicken and Prontoprint.

Task 8   2.1.2 (C3.4)

1. Re-read the paragraphs about franchising. Identify the main advantages and disadvantages of a franchise business.

2. Why do you feel that this type of business ownership is growing rapidly?

Charities

45. There are currently 170,000 registered charities in Britain (see also Chapter 1). In the legal sense charities are trusts set up exclusively for either

   ❏ The relief of **poverty** e.g. Oxfam, Shelter, Christian Aid, Save the Children Fund.

   ❏ The advancement of **education** e.g. most public schools and examination boards.

❑ The advancement of **religion** e.g. York Mission Fabric Fund, Salvation Army.

❑ Other purposes beneficial to the **community** e.g. RNLI, NSPCC, RSPCA, Imperial Cancer Research Fund, Samaritans.

46. Although they operate in what is called the **voluntary sector** in order to help those in need many charities are run as business organisations often employing professional fund raising and public relations staff to generate income. They often use a range of activities to maximise funds which may include advertising and mail shots to encourage individuals and businesses to support them, as well as holding special events, selling merchandise, or even running shops.

47. Charities are usually run by a Board of Trustees who are responsible for managing the funds and ensuring that they are used properly. Although they may employ some administrative staff, many of the people who help are usually voluntary workers, while trustees are also often part-time and unpaid.

48. However, even though charities are voluntary organisations like any other business they must still keep accurate financial records which account for the use of funds and expenses. Indeed trustees could find themselves legally and financially liable if funds are misused. Whilst some charitable trusts are incorporated as limited companies, the majority are unincorporated organisations.

49. Most of the legislation relating to charities is now contained in the *Charities Acts 1960 and 1992*. Under these Acts **Charity Commissioners** are appointed by the Home Secretary to whom they make an annual report which is presented to Parliament.

50. The Commissioners have power to:

❑ give information and advice to Charity trustees on any matter which helps to make the charity more effective

❑ investigate misconduct and abuses of assets including taking or recommending remedial action and

❑ maintain a public register of charities.

Local Authorities keep a register of local charities.

Task 9   **2.1.2 (C3.2, C3.4, T3.2)**

Working either individually or in a small group identify any two local and any two national charitable or voluntary organisations.

Find out all you can about each organisation including

❑ its main purpose and legal status

❑ how it is managed and controlled

❑ its main sources of income and methods of fund raising

❑ how its funds are used.

Finally produce a word processed report including your ideas on how each organisation could generate more income and any other suggestions which might help it to achieve its objectives.

Public Enterprise

51. Public sector business organisations can be divided into 3 broad categories:

❑ Public Corporations or Nationalised Industries.

❑ Government Departments.

❑ Local Authority or Municipal Undertakings.

Public Corporations

52. Public corporations are industries which are owned and controlled by the Government and therefore have no shareholders. To raise capital they can:

    ☐ 'Plough' back profits.

    ☐ Borrow from the Government.

    ☐ Borrow from banks or

    ☐ Issue loan stock to the public

53. When an industry which was privately owned is taken over by the Government, it is said to have been 'nationalised'. When this happens the previous owners are paid compensation.

54. Although the names may be slightly confusing, whether they are called Boards, Commissions, Councils, Authorities or Corporations, all nationalised industries are in fact public corporations, set up by an Act of Parliament and run by the government on our behalf.

55. Some examples and the year when they were nationalised are as follows:

    1933 London Transport

    1946 British Coal*

    1946 Bank of England

    1947 Electricity Council*

    1948 British Gas Corporation*

    1948 British Rail†

    1948 National Water Council*

    1954 Atomic Energy Authority

    1967 British Steel Corporation*

    * Now privatised (see paragraph 66)
    † Split into 17 companies in April 1994 in preparation for privatisation.

56. Other public corporations were set up by the government in the first place. Examples of these include:

    1927 British Broadcasting Corporation

    1969 The Post Office

57. A Minister is put in charge of each industry to determine the general policy, and he appoints a Chairman and Board with responsibility for the day-to-day management. An annual report has to be prepared and submitted to the Minister who may be questioned on it by Members of Parliament. In this way, a public corporation is said to be made accountable (i.e. responsible) for its activities.

58. The chief aim of a public corporation is to provide an efficient public service at a price low enough to avoid making excessive profit but high enough to cover investment costs, although sometimes other priorities may be considered as being more important than making a profit. For example, some railway lines are kept open, despite the fact that they are making a loss, in order to supply some remote areas with a transport service. The Government however, believes that nationalised industries should act as commercial enterprises and has set policies accordingly.

59. Each industry is expected to achieve a **'required rate of return'** on its assets currently 6 per cent in real terms before tax. The financial target set by the Government is usually supported by a series of performance aims, covering costs and, where appropriate, standards of service. External financing limits, which control the amount of finance (grants and borrowing) that a nationalised industry can raise in any financial year, are an important operating control. They are set in the light of the industry's financial target and its expected performance and investment. Any losses are financed from taxation whilst profits are used to repay loans or finance the future development of the industry. In recent years, the proportion of investment financed from internally generated funds has increased.

Task 10   2.1.2 (C3.2)

External scrutiny of nationalised industry efficiency is conducted by the Monopolies and Mergers Commission and where appropriate, investigations may also be undertaken by management consultants. Whilst House of Commons Select Committees, such as the Treasury and Civil Service Committee and the Public Accounts Committee, also scrutinise the industries' performance.

1.   How can the efficiency of industries owned and controlled by the Government be measured?

2.   Why do you think that such industries require external scrutiny?

Government Departments

60.   As well as running many industries, the government also has departments which provide a variety of services. Examples of these include the Royal Mint which supplies the country's money, Her Majesty's Stationery Office (HMSO) dealing with Government publications, the Central Office of Information which prepares Government statistics, and the Forestry Commission which controls the production and supply of timber. The Post Office was once a government department but since 1969 has been a public corporation.

Local Authority or Municipal Undertakings

61.   There are also many important services which are operated by Local Authorities for the benefit of the local community. Local Councils use money collected from rents, the council tax, business rates, government grants (revenue support grant) and by borrowing to provide services for the town. Examples include schools and nurseries for education, health clinics and hospitals, police and fire services and recreational facilities such as parks and libraries. The local authority may also receive income from trading activities. That is, many councils provide services which you pay to use, for example sports centres, entertainment facilities, public baths and cafes.

62.   **Local Authorities** are managed by a combination of employed staff and councillors elected by the local people. The councillors make the policy decisions on how the town should be run and the employees implement these and carry out the day-to-day administration. The **Council Tax** which they collect, is based on the value of domestic property and the number of people living there. This was introduced in 1993 to replace the **Community Charge** (Poll Tax) which itself replaced domestic rates in 1990. The **Uniform Business Rate (UBR)** is based on the rateable values of business properties. The UBR figure is set by the government and in 1995/6 was 43.2p in the pound in England and 45.3p in Wales.

Task 11   2.1.2 (C3.4)

COUNCIL TAX INTRODUCED

Council Tax was introduced in 1993 to replace the ill-fated poll tax. The government contributes some of the cost of council spending through grants. The balance is raised largely through council tax and business rates. Local councils are given spending targets and are subject to `capping' if these are exceeded. The amount of council tax to be paid per property falls into one of eight bands which relates to its value, with the standard considered to be Band D. A transitional relief scheme was financed by the Government for 2 years to ensure no household paid more than £3.50 a week extra following the abolition of poll tax. The idea being that it would only be necessary to pay more if, for example, a council exceeded its spending ceiling or assumed a tax collection rate of less than 98%.

continued...

Task 10 continued

Final bills can vary widely between councils because some authorities have had to raise more cash to cover poll tax arrears and appeals against home valuations. Unlike poll tax, which was a personal tax, the council tax is a property tax and more difficult for people to avoid paying. But while many large households are better off, nearly every person who lives alone pays more. One in four households is made up of a single person. Under poll tax, they had to pay half as much as a couple sharing a house or a third as much as three adults sharing. Now they pay three-quarters of the full bill. Many people do not have to pay full council tax or are completely exempt. Students do not pay and people who have savings of under £6,000 and are on a low income may qualify for Council Tax Benefit.

There was a fear that the tax could trigger a fresh fall in house prices because owners would be reluctant to 'trade up' to houses in higher bands. This would be likely to depress the value of more expensive houses still further. Some prices in London and the South-East were considered to be likely to fall by more than 4 per cent. Many councils have made drastic cuts in services and jobs to avoid overspending and 'capping'. But the government has always said that there would be no need for job losses if local authorities manage their resources sensibly and adhere to the public sector pay policy guidelines which in recent years have ranged from 0–3 per cent.

Council Tax in England

	House Value	Transitional Relief (per wk)
BAND A	(less than £40,000)	£1.75
BAND B	(£40,000– £52,000)	£2.00
BAND C	(£52,000– £68,000)	£2.25
BAND D	(£68,000– £88,000)	£2.50
BAND E	(£88,000–£120,000)	£2.75
BAND F	(£120,000–£160,000)	£3.00
BAND G	(£160,000–£320,000)	£3.25
BAND H	(over £320,000)	£3.50

1. Outline the key features of the new Council Tax.

2. How does it differ from the former Poll Tax?

3. Explain, with examples, the transitional relief scheme.

4. Who, if anyone, is better-off or worse-off under the new tax?

5. What problems, if any, could the new tax lead to?

Reasons for Public Ownership

63. ❐ Political – to enable the nation to share the profits of industry.

   ❐ Control of vital industries and commercial activities for example central banking and railways

   ❐ Control of monopolies – many nationalised industries are 'natural' monopolies i.e. they have no real competition, for example post.

   ❐ Protection of national security – e.g. Atomic Energy

   ❐ Capital Costs – sometimes the capital costs of setting up or modernising an industry may be too great or unprofitable for private enterprise, for example coal and docks.

❑ Provision of social services – which private enterprise would not wish to provide because they are unprofitable, for example railways and postal services to remote rural areas.

❑ Survival of unprofitable industries – which might otherwise be forced to close down, creating problems of unemployment, for example steel in the 1970's and early 1980's.

64. Advantages of Public Ownership

❑ It enables the government to plan large sections of the economy in the public interest.

❑ Profits belong to the nation and are therefore for everyone's benefit not just a few shareholders or individuals.

❑ The benefits of economies of scale can be gained from operating as a large unit.

❑ Reduces unnecessary and wasteful duplication of resources. For example, imagine the problems from competition if a number of companies ran the railways.

❑ Ensures survival of important industries.

❑ Provides capital investment for modernisation.

❑ Operates in the public interest in the provision of goods and services.

65. Disadvantages of Public Ownership

❑ Lack of competition often makes it difficult to assess their efficiency. Greater possibility of waste, over-manning and poor quality service.

❑ Government may delay decision-making or pursue policies which are not in the best interests of the business.

❑ Government interference may make it difficult for them to operate efficiently i.e. control of prices, or investment decisions.

❑ Any losses must be paid for out of taxation

❑ May become impersonal with lots of 'red tape'.

❑ National decision-making does not always work in the best interests of a local community, e.g. regional unemployment in the coal industry if uneconomic pits are closed.

Privatisation

66. The reasons for the organisation and control of some industries may be based on political issues rather than just the business factors which affect it. A lot of government control of industry has taken place in periods when the Labour Party was running the country particularly from 1946-1951. However, the Conservative Party does not support public ownership to the same extent and indeed in the 1980's introduced a policy of **privatisation**. That is, it has been selling off some public corporations to the private sector as public limited companies. Recent examples of such privatisation include Cable and Wireless (1981), British Telecom (1986), British Gas (1986), British Airways (1987), Water (1989) and Electricity (1990). Plans to privatise the Post Office, however, were postponed in November 1994 in the face of opposition from many Conservative MPs.

67. Other forms of privatisation which the Government has introduced include:

❑ **Competitive Tendering or Contracting Out** whereby Private Sector firms are now invited to bid for contracts alongside local authority departments for refuse disposal, school catering and cleaning, security of council property and repairs and maintenance.

❑ **Deregulation** where 'traditional' state run activities are opened up to private sector competition as, for example, with long distance coaches (1980) and local bus services (1985). 'Big-bang' was another form of deregulation to promote competition among Stock Exchange members.

❑ **Substitution** of tax finance with a customer fee as for example, with charges for dental check-ups, eye tests and NHS prescriptions.

❏ **Domestic property** where over 1 million council houses were offered for sale to their occupiers at discounts of up to 60% of the 'market' price.

68. The main objectives of the privatisation programme are:

❏ **To increase efficiency** by creating greater competition which provides an incentive to reduce costs.

❏ **To reduce Government financin**g because losses and investment would no longer come from the Government. In addition, over £30 billion has been raised from the privatisation sales.

❏ **To increase customer satisfaction** because competition widens choice and company service. Waiting lists, for example, have virtually disappeared since BT's privatisation in 1984, whilst the choice of telephone products has increased.

❏ **To widen share ownership**. The government saw privatisation as an opportunity to introduce the concept of share ownership to 'ordinary' individuals. Since 1979, the number of shareholders has more than trebled to over 11 million.

69. **Criticisms of Privatisation**

❏ **Consumers are worse off** because in effect, they create private monopolies as with Gas, Water and Electricity. Also the removal of cross-subsidisation in some industries could mean some consumers will lose services completely or have to pay much higher charges. On the railway for example, profitable commuter routes are currently used to subsidise less busy lines.

❏ They **bring major job losses** in order to increase efficiency in industries often regarded as being heavily overmanned.

❏ **'Selling the Family Silver'.** Privatisation means selling the State's assets and placing them in the hands of the minority of people who can afford to purchase shares in them.

70. **Regulation of Privatised Industries**

The privatised public utilities have monopoly characteristics and therefore the government has set up specific industry watchdogs to manage the transition and protect consumers by monitoring prices, competition and quality of service. These are OFTEL (Telecommunications), OFGAS (Gas), OFWAT (Water) and OFFER (Electricity).

71. They relied on negotiation and the government claims that consumers get a better deal from privatised utilities than when they were in the public sector with no independent regulation at all. But the watchdogs have been accused of having 'no teeth', because despite a stringent pricing formulae, based on price rises not exceeding the 'Retail Prices Index plus or minus X%' the new companies have made 'excessive' profits and give massive pay awards to their chairmen and senior executives. There have also been many thousands of complaints to the watchdogs.

72. Therefore, to extend the powers of the watchdogs, the **Competition and Service (Utilities) Act 1992** was introduced. It gives the regulators legal power:

❏ to set guaranteed quality standards,

❏ to arrange compensation when things go wrong.

❏ to insist that consumers are kept informed about standards and performance against them.

❏ to intervene in disputes.

❏ to peg prices if performance targets are not met.

❏ to stop unreasonable costs being passed on to consumers e.g. huge pay rises for bosses.

Task 12   **2.1.2 (C3.4)**

THE PRICE OF PURITY

Consumers has been warned that even allowing for inflation, water bills could double by the year 2000 according to the industry's watchdog OFWAT. Most of the rise will reflect the enormous cost of obeying stringent EC directives on water quality and water disposal. The water companies, under fire for making huge profits and giving massive pay rises to their bosses, claim that it is not necessary to meet the new standards which are far higher than those for food. Britain, however, could face prosecution if it does not meet the regulations. It is also argued that since 12 million people receive drinking water which is contaminated at some time with pesticides, polluters not consumers should pay the cost of cleaning it up. There are other costs connected with water management, such as preventing the pollution of rivers, cleaning up beaches and treating sewage, where again the degree of cleanliness hugely affects the costs which industry and the public must bear. Environmentalists, like Friends of the Earth, believe that the acceptance of lower standards is pandering to shareholders and overpaid water company bosses. They argue that it ignores the public good at the expense of profit. Privatisation therefore has brought the clash of interests out into the open. It has shown that water quality should not be dictated by laboratory experts but a rational consumer choice determined by balancing the social costs and benefits of water of a supremely high standard and very high bills against accepting a small risk and lower bills.

Read the article and answer the following questions.

1. Why is OFWAT warning consumers?

2. How has the water industry been affected by Britain's membership of the European Community?

3. What disadvantages or criticisms of privatisation can you identify?

4. What are the problems and issues associated with water management?

5. In what sense has privatisation brought a clash of interests out into the open?

Methods of Privatisation

73. The government has used various methods to privatise enterprises including:

❏ **Stock Exchange Flotation**. The most common method is the sale of shares direct to the public, financial institutions and foreign buyers. e.g. British Gas, British Steel.

❏ **Sale to a single purchaser**. In some cases all the shares have been bought by a single company as for example with the Rover Group and Sealink Ferries.

❏ **Management or Employee Buyout**. In the case of the National Freight Corporation, the existing workforce was given the sole right to buy the shares and own the enterprise.

Summary

74. a) All businesses are either owned privately by individuals (or groups of individuals) or publicly by the Government.

b) Private enterprise includes sole traders (or one-person concerns), partnerships consisting of 2–20 people, private and public limited companies, co-operatives which can be either retail or producer and franchises where people set up in business using the trade name and with the help of existing companies.

c) All these different types of organisations need capital in order to pay for the costs of running the business. This capital is usually raised by sole traders and partnerships, from savings or borrowing from friends or a bank, whilst limited companies issue shares.

d) Shareholders own part of the business and in return for lending the capital they receive a dividend each year which is a share of any profits which the firm makes.

e) The ability of companies to raise large sums of capital has been very dependent upon limited liability. This means that if a firm is unprofitable and goes out of business then shareholders can only lose the amount of money which they have invested and not any of their personal possessions such as their house or furniture.

f) To form a limited company it is necessary for the firm to draw up a Memorandum of Association and Articles of Association giving details of the type of business and how it is to be run. These documents are sent to the Registrar of Companies who issues Certificates of Incorporation to companies who meet the legal requirements.

g) A company can be wound up either compulsorily or voluntarily. A liquidator is usually appointed.

h) The shares in a public limited company, are bought and sold on the Stock Exchange which is very important to the economy because it makes it possible for companies and the government to raise large sums of money.

i) Many charitable trusts are also run as business organisations using income from donations and fund raising to achieve their objectives.

j) Public sector businesses are those which are owned and controlled by the government on behalf of the nation and include: Public Corporations, Government Departments and Municipal Undertakings.

k) Public Corporations are formed by an Act of Parliament and can be set up directly by the government as with the BBC or be the result of nationalisation for example coal and railways.

l) Government Departments provide a variety of services examples of which are the Royal Mint and HMSO.

m) Municipal Undertakings are the services and trading activities provided by the local council for example schools, libraries, sports centres and entertainment facilities.

n) Reasons for public ownership include political arguments, to control vital industries, to control monopolies, protect national security, provide capital, provide social services and to ensure the survival of certain unprofitable industries.

o) In the 1980's and 1990's the Conservative Party has pursued a policy of privatisation by selling off nationalised industries.

p) Other forms of privatisation include competitive tendering, deregulation, substitutions and the sale of council houses.

Review questions *(Answers can be found in the paragraphs indicated)*

1. Draw a diagram to illustrate the different types of privately owned business organisations. (1)

2. Outline the main features of the Business Names Act 1985. (3)

3. Give 2 advantages and 2 disadvantages of being a sole proprietor. (7–8)

4. What are the advantages and disadvantages of forming a partnership? (11–12)

5. What is a Partnership Deed of Agreement? (12–13)

6. Explain the difference between limited and unlimited liability. (7,11,14,16)

7. Give 3 important features of private limited companies. (19–22)

8. Explain 3 features of public limited companies. (25–29)

9. Briefly explain the 2 legal documents which control the affairs of limited companies. (30–32)

10. In what ways can a company be 'wound-up'? (33)

11. How do producer or worker co-operatives differ from retail co-operatives? (36–42)

12. What is franchising? (43–44)

13. Why are charities formed and how do they operate? (45–50)

14. What are the aims of a public corporation? (58–59)

15. Outline the difference between a public corporation and a Government Department. (60)

16. How does the local council get the money to pay for the services which it provides? (61–62)

17. Give 4 reasons, with examples, for public ownership. (55, 63)

18. List 3 advantages and 3 disadvantages of the public ownership of industry (64–65)

19. Explain with examples the meaning of, and reasons for, privatisation. (66–67)

20. How are privatised utilities regulated? (70–72)

Assignment – Privatisation   *Elements 1.3.2, 2.1.2*

Study past and current quality newspapers and business studies magazines/journals and from them collect any articles which refer to privatisation. Use these to:

1. Illustrate the benefits or advantages and

2. the criticisms or disadvantages of privatisation.

3. Analyse one of the recent privatisations such as Gas, Water or Electricity and prepare a report stating, with reasons, whether you agree or disagree with it.

4. Prepare a report on the arguments for and against a proposed privatisation like the railways or coal.

5. Finally, prepare a 5 minute presentation on your views of the likely impact on privatisation policy if there was a change of government.

5 Organisational Structures

In Chapter 4 we considered the different types of public and private sector organisations which exist to supply goods and services. This chapter looks at the different ways in which business organisations may be structured in order to achieve their objectives and the factors which influence these structures.

It includes:

- Devising an Organisational Structure
- Grouping of Work
- Hierarchical Structures
- Advantages of Line Structures
- Disadvantages of Line Structures
- Span of Control
- Flat Structures
- Committee Organisations
- Matrix Organisations
- Centralisation and Decentralisation
- Formal and Informal Organisations

- Organisational Culture
- Organisational Management Theory
- Scientific Management
- Administrative Management
- Human Relations
- Expectancy Theory
- Contingency Approach
- Specialisation
- The Size of Organisations
- The Growth of Organisations
- Comparing Organisational Structures

Organisational Structures

1. Whether an organisation operates in the public or private sector it consists of two key groups:
   - people with skills and knowledge who work together in groups or teams, and
   - managers who work through people to achieve the organisation's objectives.

   The framework needed to enable these two groups to work together effectively is called an **organisational structure**. This shows the relationship between the role and/or function of individuals, usually in the form of an **organisation chart**. There is no such thing as the 'perfect' structure and therefore each organisation must develop one which best suits its particular needs.

Devising an Organisational Structure

2. Developing a new structure or reorganising an existing one involves at least three basic steps:

   - **determining the work to be done**

     This involves setting objectives and considering the workloads and procedures needed to achieve them to the required standard.

   - **dividing and allocating the work to positions**

     This involves analysing the work to be done, the co-ordination and decision-taking needed and the likely contribution of each manager to the process.

   - **classifying the positions into a suitable grouping**

     Logical groupings must be determined according to the type of work involved. The basic idea behind grouping is the principle of specialisation based on the division of labour. To increase efficiency, work is given to those best suited to perform it.

3. Other factors to consider include:

   - **size of the organisation** – the needs of large and small organisations are likely to require different structures

❏ **stratification** – the number of tiers of management required

❏ **formalisation** – how formal the communication systems and procedures need to be

❏ **centralisation** – the degree of delegation to be allowed

❏ **complexity** – simple line structures are usually easier to understand

❏ **organisational culture** – which determines how tasks are organised and controlled.

Grouping of Work

4. Work can be grouped in a number of different ways depending on the type and needs of the organisation concerned. In larger organisations more than one type of grouping may be used. The most common groupings used are by

❏ **function** i.e. by specialisation such as marketing, production, finance, personnel. Further groups may also exist within each function e.g. sales, advertising, promotion and public relations within marketing.

❏ **product/service**. This is often used in large organisations particularly those with a diverse range of products. Soap powder manufacturers, for example, operate with brand managers.

❏ **customer**. This is often used in service industries, e.g. account executives in an advertising agency; small business advisors in banks.

❏ **location or geographical basis**. This may be used when several functions or offices exist in different places or where sales teams operate across the whole country. Many large organisations operate like this on a regional basis, whilst multi-nationals may have divisions in several different countries.

Task 1	**2.1.3 (C3.2)**

Using the organisation selected in chapter one or the place where you work or study, identify, with examples, how work is grouped.

Hierarchical Structures

5. The simplest and most common form of organisation has a pyramid structure which involves what is called **line management** or a **'chain of command'**. This is commonly shown on an organisation chart which is used to indicate the formal position of each person in the structure. The number of levels in the management hierarchy varies considerably usually with the size of the organisation. Generally, the fewer the number of levels, the easier is communication, and the more responsible are particular jobs. Instructions in the organisation are passed along lines in the hierarchy (usually downwards) as shown in the diagram on the following page. It is through this formal communication network that decisions and instructions flow and feedback is received.

6. ❏ **First-line managers**, sometimes called supervisors or foremen (particularly in factories) have no subordinate managers and are directly concerned with getting the job done.

❏ **Middle or senior level managers** are less involved with operational details and more concerned with what jobs should be performed and how.

❏ Whilst at **top level management** the chief executive is concerned with setting long-term plans and policies and checking that managers carry these out. Chief executives usually delegate to functional specialists typically covering marketing, production, finance and personnel management.

These are discussed in more detail in Element 4.2.

7. A hierarchical organisation's structure generates the need for objectives to be established at each level of management. Only by this means is it possible to achieve the overall objectives of the business.

8. Within an organisation structure, there may also be specialist advisory or support services, such as legal advice or computer services, which are outside the line management structure. Frequently these service several departments and therefore are referred to as **staff function**s.

9.

An organisation chart

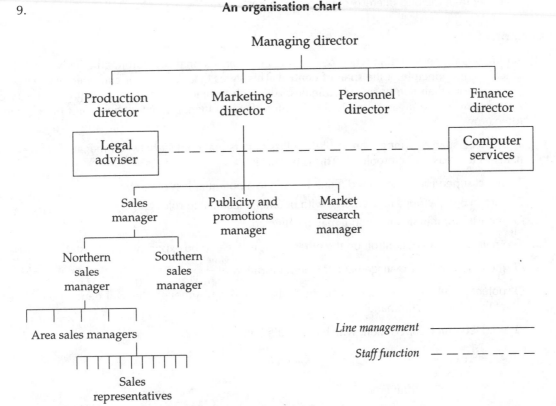

10. An organisation chart then shows clearly at a glance who staff are responsible to (the person immediately above them) and those over whom they have authority (those immediately below them).

Task 2	**2.1.3 (C3.3)**

From the organisation chart 9. above, identify examples of first-line, middle, senior and top level management.

Advantages of a Line Structure

11. There are a number of advantages relating to the use of line structures of organisation including:

- ❏ simple to understand and operate
- ❏ direct chain of command enabling quick decision-making
- ❏ clear division of responsibility and allocation of authority
- ❏ leads to a stable, more easily controlled organisation

Disadvantages of a Line Structure

12. With line structures each department/section is effectively an autonomous unit which relies heavily on the ability of the leader. This may reveal a number of disadvantages including:

- ❏ each member's experience across the organisation as a whole may be limited
- ❏ leaders may be autocratic and thus stifle the initiative of subordinates

❏ departments can become inflexible and slow to change which may restrict organisational growth

❏ problems of co-operation and co-ordination may come about if the department 'looks after itself' rather than the best interests of the organisation.

Span of Control

13. An important consideration when developing an organisational structure, particularly if it is hierarchical, is the principle of the **span of control**. This states that no superior can directly supervise the work of more than five or six subordinates. Although in practice the span of control will vary considerably from one organisation to another, for effective management it should not be too wide or too narrow.

14. Too wide a span of control can result in a loss of personal contact between managers and subordinates which may cause problems. This is because:

❏ direct supervision becomes difficult leading to a potential loss of control

❏ informal sub-groups may emerge with unofficial leadership roles and

❏ motivation, morale and output may be affected.

15. Too narrow a span of control, on the other hand, is likely to be expensive and wasteful because of

❏ increased costs of management and administration

❏ potential delays which may occur in decision-making. Although this will depend on the length of the 'chain of command',

❏ and too much supervision, which may stifle initiative.

16. **Example**

Narrow span of control   Broad span of control

Flat Structures

17. An organisation with just a few levels of management and a broad span of control has what is called a **flat structure**. Alternatively a **tall structure** indicates a narrow span of control which requires more levels of management.

18.

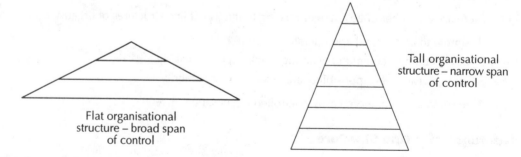

Flat organisational structure – broad span of control

Tall organisational structure – narrow span of control

Committee Organisations

19. Committees have always been used in non-profit organisations such as charities and local and central government. Many businesses also use committees to increase worker participation in decision-making, particularly to deal with issues such as pay, working conditions and other aspects

of industrial relations. The Board of Directors is, of course, the most important committee in any organisation.

20. A committee is a group of people brought together to deal with a specific area of activity. It may be a regular standing committee or one formed for a special purpose. It is important that the authority of committees is clearly defined. Many do not have any executive powers but exist essentially to provide advice and make recommendations to management.

21. Committees are useful to increase worker involvement and share news and expertise across an organisation. They are, however, time-consuming, rely heavily on the skills of the chair person and may be slow to reach decisions which are often a compromise and therefore not necessarily the best.

Task 3   **2.1.3 (C3.2)**

1. Identify at least six examples of local government committees in your area.

2. Now identify six committees in the place where you work or study. Comment briefly on how each fits into the overall decision-making structure of the organisation.

Matrix Organisations

22. Matrix organisation structures, which are growing in popularity, can take a number of different forms, although they are usually developed in conjunction with a traditional line structure.

23. A matrix is essentially a grid showing different relationships of authority which affect individuals. Each function e.g. production, personnel, finance has a functional manager. Whilst at the same time each person within each function is a member of an operating department with a line manager. Hence each member of staff reports to two people. The functional manager who is responsible for the technical performance and the operational manager responsible for all other aspects of their work such as welfare and discipline.

24. In a common variation to this a functional line management structure is the norm, but with a matrix used for special tasks or projects. In this situation the project manager concerned would select a suitably skilled team drawn from the functional areas. During the period of the project the staff 'on loan' would report to the project manager.

Matrix and semi-matrix structures are common in universities and further education colleges and are often used for research, development and problem-solving purposes in industry.

25. **Advantages of a matrix structure** include:

   ❑ useful for quickly tackling complex problems

   ❑ uses variety of skill and expertise

   ❑ saves time in communication

   ❑ facilitates cross-fertilisation of ideas between departments.

26. **Disadvantages of a matrix structure** include:

   ❑ may be difficult to understand

   ❑ no unity of command leading to

   ❑ risk of staff confusion and divided loyalties

   ❑ may lead to power struggles between managers with potential to usurp authority to detriment of organisation's efficiency.

27.

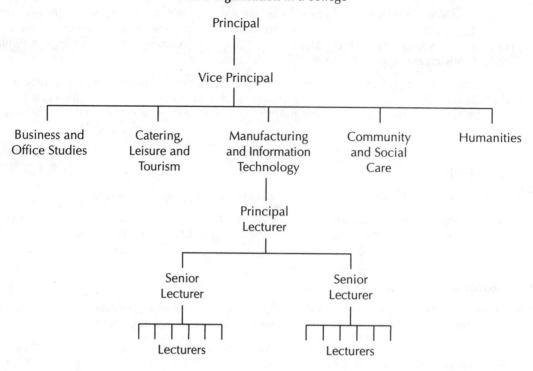

Examples of organisational structures
Line organisation in a college

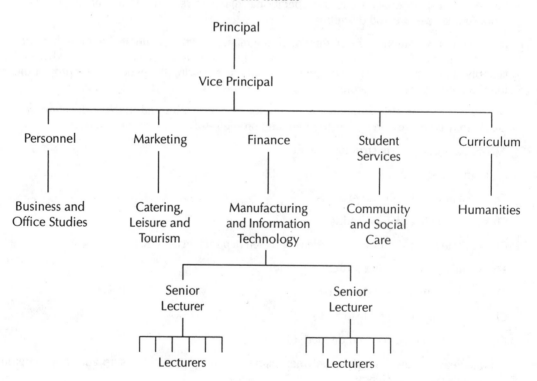

Semi-matrix

Task 4   **2.1.3 (C3.3)**

1. Prepare an organisation chart for the place where you work or study.

2. Briefly describe the type of structure and span of control.

3. Comment, from your own experience, on the main advantages and disadvantages of the organisational structure.

Centralisation and Decentralisation

28. Centralisation and decentralisation are other terms used when referring to the way in which businesses are organised. If a business is **centralised**, its activities are grouped together to enable it to operate more efficiently and effectively. Purchasing, advertising, personnel, typing and other functions are all carried out centrally rather than in different parts of the organisation. Management may also be centralised so that the business is run and controlled from one place.

29. Alternatively, a business may be **decentralised** whereby work is carried out in a number of different places. This may mean each department is managed separately, organising its own services such as typing, purchasing and advertising. Often firms with a number of branches or locations operate on a decentralised basis with managers in charge of each place. This enables decisions to be made faster and gives staff more responsibility.

30. In practice many firms often have some activities centralised and others decentralised. For example a supermarket chain may have its advertising centralised at Head Office whilst allowing each store manager to recruit their own staff.

31. **Centralisation has a number of advantages**. For example, it makes it easier for an organisation to have:

   ❑ standardised systems and procedures

   ❑ better co-ordination and control by a small number of decision-makers

   ❑ more efficient utilisation of resources – staff, equipment, premises

   ❑ reduced duplication of effort.

32. On the other hand, **the disadvantages of centralised management** are that is limits authority and delegation which can:

   ❑ slow down decision-making

   ❑ frustrate the initiative of junior managers

   ❑ increase bureaucracy and 'red tape' resulting in extra paperwork and record keeping

   ❑ lead to decisions being made by managers with limited knowledge of the actual work situation.

Formal and Informal Organisation

33. Formal relationships between people in any organisation are those shown on an **organisation chart**. However, most businesses also tend to have an informal organisation which operates at the same time. This results from the personal relationships which exist between individuals and groups of people in one department or several departments who have similar interests and ideas. These so called **primary groups** are important because through them, individuals develop attitudes, opinions, goals and ideals which can conflict with an organisation's objectives. If for example, a group does not agree with a particular policy, then it may deliberately try to obstruct it or make it difficult to implement.

Task 5   **2.1.3 (C3.2)**

1.   Refer back to Task 4. Try to identify any examples of informal organisation.

2.   Comment on how this affects the functioning of the organisation.

Co-operative Alliances

34. The growth of supermarkets and other large retailing outlets has made it increasingly difficult for small independent retailers to compete in terms of price and variety therefore they have joined together to form bulk-organised buying groups. That is, a wholesaler will gather round him a group of retailers who agree to pool their orders and buy a regular amount of goods from him.

35. This enables the wholesaler to buy in bulk from manufacturers and pass on the saving to the retailers who in turn can offer lower prices to their customers and/or improve profits.

     These **co-operative alliances or voluntary groups** are usually limited to a local area as few wholesalers operate nationally.

36. Voluntary chains are an extension of voluntary groups where a number of wholesalers join together throughout the country to pool their resources. In this way symbol chains such as VG, Spar, Nisa and Wavy Line have been able to compete with the larger supermarkets, and Numark with larger chemists.

37. Both voluntary groups and chains offer special services to their retail members. For example newspaper and television advertising, window posters, plus information and advice on layout and display to improve image and sales.

38. This type of organisation has become very successful and important in helping independent traders to survive. They enable the benefits and competitive prices of large organisations to be combined with the personal, friendly service of local family shops.

Task 6   **2.1.3 (C3.2)**

Identify 3 examples of co-operative alliances in the area where you live.

Comment on any similarities and differences between the organisations concerned.

Organisational Culture

39. Everyone in an organisation is affected by its 'culture'. That is the **basic assumptions, attitudes and standards** which determine the systems, structure and rules in an organisation and hence the way things are done.

40. 'Culture' is important because it influences patterns of behaviour, attitudes to change and the motivation, morale and performance of employees. It can also have a significant impact on both business development and staff recruitment because the 'cultural reputation' can attract people to, or deter them away from, an organisation.

41. An organisation's culture is affected by a number of factors including:

     ❐ The **environment** in which the organisation operates. Internally, this is often conveyed by its physical layout which can, for example, reflect warm friendliness or cold efficiency.

     ❐ The **beliefs, values and norms** of employees within the organisation, particularly those communicated by top management, eg the way customers and staff are treated, even the way people dress.

     ❐ The formal and informal **leaders** who personify the organisation's culture.

❐ The **procedures** that have to be followed and the behaviour expected of people within the organisation, eg the structure and reporting arrangements.

❐ The network of **communications** which disseminates the corporate image and culture. This might include, for example, high-profile publicity and advertising, staff magazines, social events, briefing meetings, pep-talks and employee participation in decision-making.

❐ **Other factors** could include the organisation's size, history, ownership and technology; all of which can influence the development of its culture.

42. It is important that management communicates and encourages all staff to follow the desired culture, even though many employees' attitudes will obviously come from outside the organisation. New employees are introduced to the culture either formally through induction and training or informally through the people they work with. This process of **socialisation** is important because it affects the individual's future attitudes, thoughts and behaviour.

43. Some people may not readily accept an organisation's culture. Where this **individualisation** takes place, it may be disruptive and lead to a lack of co-ordination and integration. This in turn may affect the corporate image, long-term objectives and ultimate success of the organisation.

Task 7   **2.1.3 (C3.2)**

Think about the culture of an organisation such as Marks and Spencer, Sainsburys, or any other in which you have worked or studied.

1.   How would you describe the culture?

2.   What affect(s) does it have on their staff and customers/clients? Use examples to illustrate your answer.

3.   How are you personally influenced by the culture?

4.   How is the culture communicated?

Organisational Management Theory

44. There have been many writers on the principles and practices of management each concerned with how to manage workers more efficiently and effectively.

45. Although you do not need to have a full understanding of different organisational theories it is useful nonetheless to have a general awareness of how thinking has developed and changed. The five major schools of thought and their recognised 'pioneers' are as follows:

❐ Scientific Management (Taylor, Gantt, Gilbreth)   ⎫ Together often referred to

❐ Administrative Management (Fayol)   ⎬ as the Classical School

❐ Human Relations (Maslow, Aldefer, McGregor, Mayo and Hertzberg) and Expectancy Theory (Vroom and Porter, Lawler)

❐ Systems Approach (Trist, Bamforth) (see Element 2.2)

❐ Contingency Approach (Woodward, Burns & Stalker)

45.

Development of Management Theory

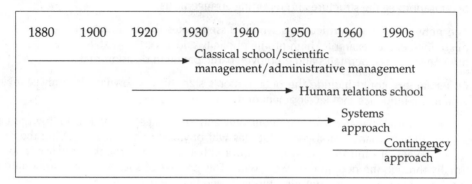

Scientific Management

46. Some of the earliest thinking on management theory was that of **Frederick W Taylor** (1856-1915). an American engineer who pioneered work study and spent years researching ways of increasing productivity in factories by making work easier to perform. He advocated the breaking down of jobs into small elements so that people could specialise and become very competent in particular tasks (see paragraph 51).

47. Taylor suggested that people worked simply to earn money and that nothing else was important. He therefore devised financial incentives offering large bonuses to workers if they increased output. The main problem he found was in devising a scheme which was seen as 'fair' by both workers and management. He also ignored the boredom from repetitive tasks, and peoples' psychological needs. Many incentive schemes today are nonetheless based on Taylor's work study techniques.

Task 8   2.1.3 (C3.4)

The first industrialist to link Taylor's principles to serve a mass market was Henry Ford in the early 1900's. He based standardised production of the famous Model T cars on the extensive use of the division of labour and specialist machinery which required minimum job-learning times. The major drawbacks were the costs of supervision and co-ordination as work becomes fragmented and workers get bored. It also requires specialist indirect labour such as quality inspectors and work study engineers.

1. Identify the main advantages and disadvantages of 'scientific management'.

2. Give at least 5 examples of other markets where these principles have been applied.

3. Can you suggest markets not suited to the principles?

Henry Gantt

48. Gantt, a colleague of Taylor, helped to humanise scientific management by replacing the piece-rate system of pay with a day-rate, with bonuses for each worker who met and exceeded their set targets. Workers were also given greater responsibility for the tasks which they were performing.

49. Gantt is probably best remembered for developing a bar chart to show the relationship between the sequence of events in the production process and how far a task had been achieved in comparison with the optimum targets set. A Gantt chart shows the planned amount, the actual amount achieved each week and the cumulative amount over successive weeks.

50.   **Example of a Gantt chart**

Operator		Week 1	Week 2	Week 3	Week 4
		Assembly shop output control			
		Four weeks commencing _1.9.19._			
B Read	Standard	300	300	300	300
	Actual	240	300	300	315
	%	80	100	100	105
S Tool	Standard	450	450	450	450
	Actual	338	450	360	450
	%	75	100	80	100
R Winter	Standard	400	400	400	400
	Actual	200	400	400	400
	%	50	100	100	100

KEY

—— Standard output to be achieved
– – Actual output produced
%   Percentage of actual to standard

This chart shows the performance of 3 shopfloor workers and, in particular, draws attention to exceptional circumstances. The low output of all three workers simultaneously in week 1 indicates some common problem which if not addressed would continue in future weeks.

51. **Frank and Lillian Gilbreth**

The Gilbreths made significant contributions in the fields of time and motion study. Frank Gilbreth (1917) divided work into fundamental elements which were then timed. Operations were studied and resources using **flow process charts** with symbols for

Operation	◯	When an activity takes place
Inspection	▢	To measure or test in some way
Storage	▽	An object kept before further use eg parts in stock
Transportation	⇨	Movement from one place to another
Delay	D	If something doesn't happen when it should

52. Motion Study was carried out to find the best way of doing jobs thereby improving production and reducing fatigue among workers. Using these symbols the number of times each particular type of function occurs in a process is recorded and used as a basis for analysing the process to try and improve it.

Administrative Management School

53. Parallelling the growth of scientific management thinking, which was concerned mainly with first-line management, was administrative management particularly the studies of **Henri Fayol** (1841-1925) who analysed the work of chief executives into the following 5 principal components:

   ❐ **Planning** – determining objectives and developing strategies to achieve them.

   ❐ **Organising** – determining the tasks which need to be performed, grouping them into jobs and delegating the authority to individuals to enable them to carry them out.

   ❐ **Commanding** – giving instructions to subordinates

   ❐ **Co-ordinating** the groups in the organisation so that they are all working towards the overall objectives.

   ❐ **Controlling** – monitoring and correcting the performance to ensure that it meets the requirements of the plan.

54. Fayol saw the task of management as being to steer the organisation to achieve its agreed objectives. He believed that if these 5 functions were applied, it would enable managers to run businesses positively and make clear decisions which they could then communicate to workers. Clear objectives for workers would then increase motivation and output.

55. **Fayol's Principles of Management**

   From the 5 functions, Fayol then developed the following 14 principles of management as a guide to management action. Subsequent writers including **Lyndall Urwick** have also developed very similar analyses of the job of management.

56. ❐ **Division of work** – that is the specialisation of tasks to increase efficiency and output.

   ❐ **Authority and responsibility** – managers with responsibility to carry out a task must be given the authority necessary to complete it.

   ❐ **Discipline** – to get things done which requires good managers at all levels in an organisation.

   ❐ **Unity of command** – this means that subordinates should report to and receive orders from one supervisor only.

   ❐ **Unity of direction** – each group of activities should have one plan and one manager so that everyone works towards the same objectives.

   ❐ **Subordination** – of the individual to the general interest of the organisation.

   ❐ **Remuneration** – and methods of payment should be fair and give satisfaction to both employees and employers.

   ❐ **Centralisation** – the extent to which authority is concentrated or dispersed which will vary with the organisation's circumstances.

   ❐ **Scalar chain** – an organisational hierarchy is necessary for unity of direction. Fayol suggested that the span of control should not normally exceed 7 or 8.

   ❐ **Order** – essentially this is a principle or organisation, requiring all resources, including people, to be properly structured and arranged.

   ❐ **Equity** – management should treat people fairly if they want loyalty and hard work.

   ❐ **Stability of tenure** – high labour turnover is a sign of bad management therefore workers need training and the opportunity to prove themselves to gain job satisfaction.

   ❐ **Initiative** – which managers should encourage to the full with all subordinates.

   ❐ **Esprit de corps** – the need to develop good team spirit and morale between workers and management.

| **Task 9** | **2.1.3 (C3.2)** |

In the organisation in which you work or study or any other organisation which you know well, try to identify an example of each of Fayol's principles of management.

Human Relations School

57. We are all different in the way that we think and behave and each of us is motivated by varying needs which change frequently. There have been many studies of human behaviour and motivation covering, in particular, the factors which influence people's performance at work. Some of the most influential writers on this include:

   ❑ **Maslow** – Hierarchy of needs
   ❑ **Alderfer** – Hierarchy of needs
   ❑ **McGregor** – Theory X and Theory Y
   ❑ **Mayo** – Hawthorne experiments and
   ❑ **Herzberg** – Motivators and Hygiene factors

Hierarchy of Needs

58. In 1968 **A Maslow**, an American psychologist, produced what he called a hierarchy of human needs using the 5 categories shown on the next page.

59.
Maslow's Hierarchy of Needs

Examples of needs		**Importance at work**
	Self actuali-sation needs	Using abilities to the full
Creativity Achievement Self-fulfilment		
Status, recognition, responsibility Feeling valued	Esteem or ego needs	Promotion opportunities Delegated tasks 'Thank you' from supervisors
Belonging, friendship Love Respect	Social needs	Liking colleagues Being liked by colleagues
Shelter Warmth Self-defence	Safety (or security) needs	Job security Pleasant environment
Food Clothing Sleep	Physiological (or basic) needs	Adequate wage

60. Maslow believed that people initially worked to satisfy their physiological needs which were met by employers paying an adequate wage. Once these were satisfied, individuals were motivated by safety needs, then social needs, esteem needs and if all these are satisfied, by self-actualisation needs. But, if while trying to satisfy a higher need a more basic need returns, an individual will turn his or her attention to the basic need until it is satisfied.

Task 10　　　　　　　　　　　　　　　　　　　　**2.1.3 (C3.2)**

As people progress in their career, they are more likely to seek to satisfy the higher needs in Maslow's hierarchy.

Suggest at least 3 reasons why this might happen.

61. **Alderfer (1972)** disagreed with Maslow and put forward a simpler model based on only 3 factors E.R.G. where:

    E = Existence – physiological and safety needs

    R = Relatedness – the need for social relationships

    G = Growth – the need to develop and fulfil personal potential

62. Whichever theory is preferred, it is important that managers recognise that employees basic needs must be met if they are to function effectively and concentrate on the job itself rather than worrying where the next meal is coming from.

Theory X and Theory Y

63. **D. McGregor** (1906–1964) in 1960 suggested that many managers adopt a particular style due to their basic beliefs concerning human nature.

64. **Theory X** – managers assume that:

    ❑ people dislike work and will avoid it.

    ❑ people must be coerced, controlled, directed and threatened in order to get them to work.

    ❑ the average person prefers to be directed, has little ambition, and avoids responsibility.

65. **Theory Y** managers assume that:

    ❑ work is as natural as play.

    ❑ people can exercise self-direction.

    ❑ people seek responsibility.

    ❑ the potential in people is not fully exploited by managers.

66. McGregor believed that people-centred management (Theory Y) was more effective for motivation than work-centred management (Theory X). In practice, management styles vary considerably between these two extremes.

Hawthorne Experiments

67. **Elton Mayo** conducted experiments into group behaviour between 1924 and 1932 at the Western Electric Company's (WEC) Hawthorne plant in Chicago, where over 30,000 employees assembled telephone equipment. WEC wanted to increase productivity and job satisfaction by improving working conditions.

68.. Mayo and his colleagues varied lighting levels and discovered that social pressure within formal groups at work could increase output even when the working environment was made worse. Conversely, output could be restricted by informal group attitudes even when individuals were offered financial incentives to increase it.

69. After the Hawthorne experiment it was clear that people are **social** animals who work better when they are organised into small groups, feel appreciated for their efforts, are consulted on decisions and enjoy the company of the people they work with.

70. It was also recognised that the beliefs, objectives and aspirations within informal groups at work frequently produce pressures which can exceed the strength of the formal rules and regulations and thus conflict with an organisation's objectives.

Task 11   **2.1.3 (C3.2)**

Discuss possible situations in any organisation well known to you where informal group pressures could influence decision taking and outweigh formal business arrangements.

Motivation and Hygiene Factors

71. Following Mayo, **Frederick Herzberg** (1966) developed the idea of **motivators** which lead to job satisfaction and **hygiene factors** which reduce job dissatisfaction.

72. **Motivators include:**
    - ❏ Recognition for work done
    - ❏ Promotion prospects
    - ❏ Sense of achievement
    - ❏ Responsibility for tasks
    - ❏ The job itself – when it is challenging and rewarding

73. **Hygiene (or maintenance) Factors include:**
    - ❏ Relationships within the organisation
    - ❏ Rules and regulations
    - ❏ Fringe benefits and social facilities
    - ❏ Wages and salaries
    - ❏ Working environment
    - ❏ Style of supervision and management control
    - ❏ Status
    - ❏ Job security

74. Herzberg argued that people do not work any harder if the hygiene factors are present at work, but that their output can decline if conditions deteriorate and poor hygiene factors can cause job dissatisfaction. Motivators on the other hand, which are all related to the intrinsic nature of the work itself, produce job satisfaction and higher output.

Task 12   **2.1.3 (C3.4)**

1. Consider what you feel are the most important ideas in the Human Relations School of thinking and why.

2. What factors do you think are or would be most important to you in terms of performance at work?

75. The work of the Human Relations School has lead to organisations adopting new, more 'democratic' or 'participative' management styles and methods of motivation including job enlargement, job enrichment, job rotation and group working.

76. **Job Enlargement**

    This involves giving workers a number of tasks to perform rather than just one simple task to increase job enrichment. It is commonly used in mass production environments.

77. **Job Enrichment**

    This is the process of making tasks more interesting and satisfying to workers. It involves giving individuals more responsibility and recognition for their own work.

78. **Job Rotation**

To overcome potential boredom a worker's tasks can be regularly changed so that they spend a certain amount of time on one task before being moved on to another.

79. **Group Working**

This involves workers completing a whole task in teams rather than just one small part of it, thus increasing motivation, job satisfaction and output.

Task 13   **2.1.3 (C3.4)**

So far we have considered the simplistic view that people at work are motivated merely by money, moving to the idea of people as social animals who work better in social groupings, to the view that they seek self-fulfilment benefiting from job enrichment. More recent research has developed the further idea of **complex man** who is motivated by a variety of factors depending on the circumstances prevailing at the time.

Using this outline and referring back to Tasks 1 and 5, give some examples from your own experience to support the idea of complex man. Indicate the significance of your answers for managers in terms of organising and motivating workers.

Expectancy Theory

80. The theories of motivation considered so far have been based on the **content** or features of jobs and how they affect individuals at work. There are, however, also **process** theories which are concerned with how motivation works.

81. An example is the **expectancy (or path-goal) theory** developed by **Vroom and Porter** and **Lawler.** In expectancy theory, effort and performance is seen as linked not just to the desire of individuals to achieve a particular goal but also by their expectation of achieving that goal. The problem with this theory is that the goal or satisfaction the individual is seeking may not necessarily be found within the organisation.

82. Other process theories are based on rewarding employees who work to achieve business objectives with prompt praise, or possibly pay increases or promotion. Employees are not rewarded if their behaviour does not contribute to the objectives of the organisation. Examples of the application of this theory are prisoners gaining remission for good behaviour and footballers receiving bonuses for winning matches.

Task 14   **2.1.3 (C3.2)**

Can you suggest other situations which you have experienced or are aware of where people are rewarded for good or bad performance or behaviour.

Contingency Approach

83. Developed during the 1950's and early 1960's by **Joan Woodward** and **Burns and Stalker** contingency theory is based on the belief that there is no one best method applicable to all situations. Instead, the most appropriate organisational structure and its effectiveness is seen as dependent upon a number of factors including the size, history, environment and level of technology in the organisation.

Specialisation

84. In the nineteenth and twentieth centuries people increasingly specialised in particular jobs, for example farmers, builders, bakers and carpenters. This resulted in a big increase in the number of goods produced and the rapid growth of trade.

This division of labour is now widely used in modern industry. Work is divided into a number of processes along a 'production' or 'assembly line' with each worker specialising in carrying out just one or two clearly defined tasks.

85. Specialisation enables **mass production** to take place. Large quantities of standardised (similar) goods can be made using automatic machines and relatively few workers to operate them. Car factories, for example, are organised in this way. The shell of a car begins at one end of the 'line'; and as it passes along a conveyor belt system, different parts of the car are added by each worker. By the end of the line the car is complete.

86. **Advantages of specialisation**

   ❐ Factors of production can be used more efficiently, e.g. people can specialise in what they can do best.
   ❐ More goods are produced at a lower cost.
   ❐ Special machinery and equipment can be used.
   ❐ Practice makes perfect so each person becomes better and faster at their job.
   ❐ Time is saved because workers do not have to move from one operation to another.
   ❐ Training is much quicker because jobs are easier to learn.

87. **Disadvantages of specialisation**

   ❐ Boredom – repeating the same task can make workers dissatisfied
   ❐ Standardised products – results in many households having similar taps, televisions, cars etc.
   ❐ Decline in crafts and skills – because work is now done by machines
   ❐ Dependence on other people – for example absent or slow workers could disrupt the production line
   ❐ Problems if workers lose their jobs – because they only have a few skills.

88. **Limits to specialisation**

   The mass production of goods is not suitable unless there is a large market in which to sell them. There would be no point in mass producing planes, ships and racing cars. However, soap powder, chocolate, toothpaste, family cars and telephones all have mass markets and therefore can be manufactured on a large scale.

89. Specialisation can now be seen not just by **product** or **process**, but in many other ways including by:

   ❐ **firm**, e.g. Burtons menswear, MacDonalds fast food, and Prudential insurance
   ❐ **industry**, e.g. coal, rail, engineering, telecommunications
   ❐ **area or region**, e.g. textiles – Yorkshire and Lancashire; engineering – West Midlands; footwear – East Midlands
   ❐ **nation**, e.g. UK cars and chemicals; Brazil – coffee; New Zealand – lamb and butter.

Task 15   **2.1.3 (C3.2)**

From your own knowledge and experience

1. Identify examples of specialisation in the place where you work or study.

2. Discuss the advantages and disadvantages which you are aware of.

3. Finally, identify examples in your area of each type of specialisation referred to in paragraph 89.

The Size of Organisations

90. Organisational structures will vary with the size of an organisation. This can be measured in a number of different ways, each of which could give different results including:

   - ❑ **The number of employees**. However, a firm can still be 'big' without employing many people, particularly if it uses a lot of computer technology.

   - ❑ **Profits.** Although small firms are unlikely to make very large profits, large firms can and do make losses.

   - ❑ **Number of places of business.** A firm with branches or factories throughout the UK and overseas will obviously be large. However, many large firms produce a lot in a small number of workplaces.

   - ❑ **Market Share.** This is the percentage of the total volume or value of sales which a firm has in a particular market. For example, IBM and Amstrad both have about 30% each of the business in micro-computer markets. However, this does not say how big the market is.

   - ❑ **Capital employed.** The more capital invested in a business, then the bigger it is likely to be. However, although this is a good measure of size, it is not always easy to calculate the value of a firm's assets.

   - ❑ **Turnover.** A firm doing a lot of business is likely to be larger than another doing very little. Therefore, measuring the value of a firm's sales probably gives the best indication of its size. This is particularly true if the number employed and capital are also considered.

The Growth of Organisations

91. There are many reasons why organisations wish to grow in size but at least three important ones should be noted:

   - ❑ To achieve economies of scale and reduce costs.

   - ❑ To increase market share, possibly to gain a monopoly position.

   - ❑ To reduce risks and obtain greater security by extending the range of products, or controlling supplies of raw materials or sales outlets.

92. **Methods of Growth**

   Growth can be achieved by three methods:

   - ❑ **Internal Growth** – that is by making more of existing products or extending the range by making new products. This may need extra capital which can be obtained by 'ploughing-back' profits, issuing further shares or by borrowing.

   - ❑ **Merger or Take-over** – expansion may also take place by:

     Merger – where two or more firms agree to amalgamate together, or

     Take-over – where one firm, not necessarily with the consent of the other, gains a controlling interest. This is possible because shares can be freely bought and sold on the stock market.

   - ❑ **Joint Ventures** – where firms agree to work together, eg Honda and Rover, Thorn-EMI and JVC. Other examples include Franchising, Licensing and Agency Agreements.

93. **Holding Companies**

   We noted above that one firm usually merges with or takes over another by buying all of the others' shares. However, sometimes a firm does not actually own another completely, but still controls it by buying over 50% of its shares. A **holding company** is a company specifically formed to take a controlling interest in other firms. The firms controlled are called **subsidiaries.**

94. **Conglomerates**

Many large companies also hold such controlling interests which enables them to diversify into a wide range of completely different product areas. Such companies are called **conglomerates**, examples of which include Great Universal Stores (which has a controlling interest in many companies including Kays, Lennards, Home Charm, Times Furnishing, Burberrys and Scotch House) and Sears (Freemans [mail order], Adams [childrens' wear]. Shoe Express, Shoe City, Hush Puppies, Miss Selfridge, Wallis, Richards, Olympus and Selfridges.)

Task 16   **21.2, 2.1.3 (C3.4)**

ICE CREAM YOGHURT

International food businesses BSN and Unilever have formed a joint venture to develop and market worldwide new yoghurt and ice cream combinations. BSN, with the Danone brand, and Unilever are the worlds leading producers of yoghurt and ice cream, respectively. Joining each partner's specific expertise offers the opportunity to develop products of unique quality they say.

Actual joint product development has reached such a stage that the joint venture can introduce its first yoghurt ice cream combination in France and Spain in the near future. Following this, extension to other countries will take place.

BSN and Unilever will each have a 50 per cent interest in the joint venture.

SWEET PROSPECTS

Cadbury Schweppes has won an important toehold in the huge German confectionery market by agreeing to buy 70% of Bavarian chocolate liqueurs and sugar products maker Piasten for about £20m. Piasten (sales £43m) has 2% of the market and its own sales force, which should help other Cadbury products. Germans eat 1m tonnes of confectionery a year and the total is growing as East Germans get their teeth into Western treats. Cadbury has an option on the remaining 30%.

BA BUYS GERMAN LINE

British Airways has bought a German airline in a first step towards establishing a Continental operating base. Delta Air, based in Frederikshaven, flies 19 routes in Germany and to several European cities. It will be renamed Deutsche BA. The takeover, for an undisclosed sum, comes after the Bonn government required BA to withdraw from domestic German flights in favour of home companies. BA joined forces with three German banks to buy Delta Air and now has a 49 per cent stake in the airline and its ten twin-prop commuter planes.

BREWER IN BID

Brewer Greene King launched a £101.3m takeover bid today for the small independent brewer Morland.

Greene King, based in Bury St Edmunds, Suffolk, said the deal would enhance its position as the largest regional brewer in the south of England. The bid is worth 477p a share.

SCHOLL GOES HERBAL

SCHOLL, the personal care products group best known for its comfort footwear, is moving into herbal medicines with the acquisition of Gerard House. Gerard markets 30 licenced herbal medicine products.

continued...

Task 16 continued

BISCUITS IN SPAIN

United Biscuits subsidiary McVitie's is to form a joint sales company with Spanish food group Royal Brands to distribute their products throughout Spain.

Read the above newspaper extracts and from them:

1. Identify with examples, the different methods of business expansion mentioned.

2. The reasons and/or benefits which they are expected to bring to the organisations concerned.

3. How could these changes influence the organisational structures?

Integration

95. When two or more firms combine together to form a larger unit it is called **integration**. This can be horizontal, vertical or lateral.

   ❑ **Horizontal Integration** takes place when firms at the same stage of production combine together under the same management. For example Dixons and Curry's, GEC and Ferranti, Ikea and Habitat.

   ❑ **Vertical Integration** is the amalgamation of firms in the same industry but at different stages of production. This may take place either **'backward'** towards the source of the raw materials, or **'forward'** towards the market. For example, hop farms and public houses are all concerned at different stages with the supply of beer. Thus a brewery which acquires its own hop farms is said to be integrating backward. If it acquires its own public houses it is integrating forward.

   ❑ **Lateral Integration** occurs when firms with similar, but not competing products, merge together. This enables firms to diversify and offer a wider range of related products, for example Cadbury-Schweppes (Food and Drink).

96.

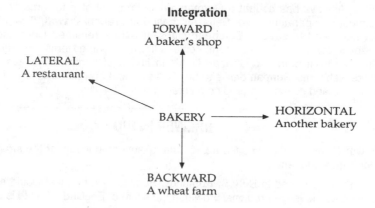

Comparing Organisational Structures

97. We have seen that there are many different factors which contribute to how an organisation is structured in order to achieve its objectives. As organisations change so structures are also likely to change.

98. Structural changes may be needed, if for example, an organisation changes either in terms of

   ❑ **size** – if it achieves growth or declines.

   ❑ **location** – it may need to move to a new or an additional location to accommodate growth or in order to operate more efficiently.

- **type of product** – new or modified products may be developed to replace existing ones.

- **functions** – new functions may be introduced as a result of management information systems or other new technology bringing about a reorganisation to meet future needs.

99. Changes like these have made organisational change a common feature in recent years as organisations strive to remain competitive by cutting costs and operating more efficiently. A number of key factors now influence thinking on the way in which organisations are now structured.

100. These include

- **Benchmarking** – judging management systems, such as employee communication, against those of other organisations and setting standards accordingly.

- **Delayering** – taking away levels of management hierarchy, thus flattening the structure to create leaner, fitter businesses.

- **Down-sizing** or **rationalising** – reducing the size of organisations by cutting the workforce to the 'rightsize' in order to create a more cost-effective organisation.

- **Empowerment** – enabling employees to reach their full potential by delegating decision-taking down to the individuals actually doing the job.

- **Outsourcing** – contracting with external organisations to perform some of the organisations functions where this can be done at less cost. (See Element 5.2)

- **Re-engineering** – radically redesigning business processes to achieve dramatic improvement in company performance.

Task 16   2.1.3 (C3.4)

HSS OPENING NEW HIRE SHOP

The HSS Hire Shop group plans to open shortly a 7,000 sq.ft. shop in Manchester's Ashton Old Road. It will replace two smaller units, one already on Ashton Old Road and the other in Pottery Lane.

STRIKE OVER OUTSIDE TENDERS PLAN

Passport offices, prisons and airport immigration desks were expected to be hit by a strike of Home Office staff in the two biggest Civil Service unions, the Civil and Public Services Association and the National Union of Civil and Public Servants.

The strike, approved by a two-to-one majority in a ballot, is over government plans to invite outside firms to tender for work now done by thousands of civil servants.

A Home Office spokeswoman said what it called 'market testing' of some sections was aimed at showing the feasibility of using outside firms to get greater value for money.

'Inside bids' were not ruled out.

JOB LOSS THREAT

Talks on possible job cuts at a Tretford engineering plant are set to get underway next week.

Bosses and unions at the Lumberger Road Factory – which has a workforce of just under 800 – are scheduled to meet on Monday.

Management have already indicated that some job losses are on the cards. No figure has been announced.

A spokesman at the firm's head office said: 'Because of the changing business and market requirements we are currently discussing the future with our employee representatives. We have no further comment.'

continued…

Task 16 continued

YATES TARGETS GROWTH

Despite the recession Bolton-based Yates Wine Lodges, the specialist retail and wholesale drinks group, have unveiled ambitious expansion plans for the 1990's. In all, 32 towns and cities have been highlighted and new sites are being targeted particularly in the north-west, north-east, Yorkshire, Midlands and Greater London areas. The company's property director, Tim Meggit says: 'Our wine lodges are traditional, stylish and fitted out to very high standards.'

He adds: 'We are highly selective in our acquisitions and carefully research locations, population and local tastes prior to our move into new areas.'

RHM UNWRAPS 3-WAY SPLIT

Facing a £ 780m takeover bid from Hanson, Baker Ranks Hovis McDougall announced proposals to break itself up into three sections:

– Milling and Baking: Hovis, Mother's Pride and Nimble, with a turnover of £ 682 million, the UK's second largest bread baker.

– Grocery and speciality products: McDougalls, Bisto, Paxo, Saxa, Atura, Chesswood, Robertsons, Keiller, Just Juice, De L'Ora and Sharwoods. This division would have a turnover of £ 673m.

– Cakes: Manor Bakeries, which makes the Mr Kipling range.

Headquarters staff could face job cuts as part of the proposals.

The demerger had the unanimous backing of the RHM Board which believed the plan would protect the true value of the companies many famous brands and enable the businesses to become more focused and better equipped to push ahead.

Similar splits have been used before by companies facing take-over threats such as Racal which floated off locks group Chubb and BAT which sold off Argos.

ICI also announced a break-up after it too faced a perceived take-over threat from Hanson.

The above articles are based on local and national media reports.

1. In each situation comment on the potential impact on the organisations structure.

2. Using local media identify 2 local business organisations undergoing change and comment on how it could affect the organisational structure of each.

Summary

101. a) An organisational structure provides a framework to enable managers and workers to achieve objectives.

b) Work can be grouped by function, product/service, customer or geographical location.

c) The most common form of structure is a hierarchical pyramid which indicates the formal line position of each person in an organisation.

d) The span of control is important for effective supervision.

e) Flat organisational structures have a narrow span whilst tall structures have a broad span.

f) Committees are often used to increase participation in decision-taking.

g) Matrix structures are essentially grids showing how different relationships of authority affect individuals.

h) An organisation can operate by grouping its activities and controlling them centrally or by decentralising so that work is carried out in a number of different places.

i) Co-operative alliances or voluntary groups have developed to help small retailers to compete with larger organisations.

j) Everyone in an organisation is affected by its 'culture' which influences employees patterns of behaviour and performance.

k) Organisational theory includes Scientific Management (Taylor) which is based on specialisation to increase output and assumes that individuals are motivated by money.

l) Administrative Management (Fayol) thinking saw the need for clear objectives and identified specific management functions and principles.

m) Human Relations thinking emphasises the needs of individuals and their social interaction in organisations.

n) Key contributors include Maslow – Hierarchy of Needs; McGregor – X & Y Theory; Mayo – Hawthorne Experiments and Herzberg – Motivators and Hygiene Factors.

o) The Contingency approach (Woodward, Burns and Stalker) suggests that there is no one single structure applicable to all organisations.

p) Specialisation, which can take many forms, has both advantages and disadvantages and is limited by the size of the market.

q) Firms can grow either internally by expansion or externally by integration, which can be horizontal, vertical or lateral.

r) Organisational structures may need to change if the organisations size, location, products or functions change.

Review Questions *(answers can be found in the paragraphs indicated)*

1. Why do organisations need a structure and how can one be developed? (1–3)

2. Identify, using examples, different ways in which work can be grouped. (4)

3. What are the main features of a hierarchical structure? (5–10)

4. Outline some of the advantages and disadvantages of line structures. (11–12)

5. Distinguish between a narrow and a broad span of control and the significance of each. (13–18)

6. Why are committees commonly used in organisations? (19–21)

7. Briefly describe how a matrix structure operates. (22–27)

8. Discuss the potential advantages and disadvantages of organising a business so that it centrally controlled. (28–32)

9. Briefly outline what you understand by a co-operative alliance. (34–38)

10. What do you understand by 'organisational culture'? (39–43)

11. List and briefly describe the 5 main schools of thinking on organisational management. (44–83)

12. Explain the advantages and disadvantages of specialisation and how it makes mass production possible (84–89)

13. In what ways can the size of a firm be measured? (90)

14. Give three reasons why firms may wish to expand, and three examples of how they might achieve it. (91–94)

15. With the use of a diagram, briefly explain the difference between horizontal, vertical and lateral integration. (95–96)

16. What factors could you compare when looking at organisational structures and how or why might they change? (97–100)

Assignment – Organisational Structures   Element 2.1

You are asked to illustrate the different structures of the 3 business organisations studied in Chapter 4 by comparing their organisational charts.

Produce notes to support the charts which comment on the differences between the structures and note any recent or planned changes to either structures, locations or functions.

---

6 Administration Systems

Chapter 1 contained a brief outline of the key functional areas in a business which are needed to achieve objectives. These included personnel, production, purchasing, finance, marketing and administration. This chapter focuses on the administration systems which support an organisation and includes:

- Systems Approach
- Administration
- Purposes of Administration Systems
- Support for Resources
- Routine and Non-Routine Functions
- Recording and Monitoring Business Performance
- Legal Requirements
- Fiscal Requirements
- Accounting Systems
- Sales Systems

- Distribution Systems
- Personnel Systems
- Services Systems
- Quality Control Systems
- Systems Design
- Organisation and Methods
- Suitability of Administration System
- Information Technology
- Key Computing Terms
- Administration and change
- Improving Administration Systems

Systems Approach

1. Since the Second World War, methods of structuring organisations so that they can be managed efficiently have been influenced by the development of the systems approach based on the work of, among others, **Galbraith and Likert**. This considers an organisation as a total system consisting of interconnected and interactive sub-systems, all mutually dependent upon each other. An organisation is structured to achieve its objectives through the system.

2. The systems approach is based on the processing or conversion of inputs from the environment (e.g. premises, labour, machinery, materials) by economic, technical and psychological forces in the organisation into outputs as illustrated below.

3.

A Simple Business System

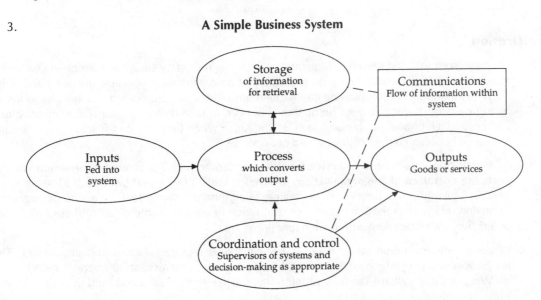

4. A business as a whole is a complete system structured on the basis of functions each of which can be classed as a sub-system. Each function operates within the framework of the corporate objectives. The functional activities are monitored and controlled by managers or directors and the Chief executive acts as the overall co-ordinator. Systems, therefore, should assist the co-ordination of activities, make work easier and ensure that it flows evenly. Without a system there is a risk of confusion caused by everyone doing their own thing.

5. The significance of the systems approach is that the failure of one sub-system affects the other subsystems dependent upon it and thus can prevent the organisation from achieving its basic objective of producing goods and/or providing services.

6. This was illustrated, for example, by the work of **Trist and Bamforth (1951)** who studied the relationship between technology and people in organisations. They found that new technology often led to absenteeism, disputes and low morale because it changed the previous social structure. They concluded that if new technical systems are introduced, they must be linked to social systems or the benefits may be lost or considerably reduced.

Task 1   2.2.1 (C3.2)

1. Identify the main inputs and outputs of any system with which you are familiar.

2. What other parts make up the system?

3. Can you identify any sub-systems.

4. Discuss the ways in which they are dependent upon each other.

5. Compare this with the interdependence between marketing and production in a business.

7. No one system can meet the needs of all organisations which vary considerably in terms of many factors such as size, location, history, structure, products or services, environment and level of technology. Therefore, each organisation must design a system to meet its own particular needs. The larger the organisation the more formal the structure and systems are likely to be, and vice-versa.

Task 2   2.2.1 (C3.2)

Identify and briefly describe any 3 specific systems or procedures in your place of work or study.

Specify each task in the process, why it is performed and how it inter-relates with other systems.

Administration

8. We have seen that a system is a sequence of activities necessary to achieve an objective. Administration is the activity concerned with ensuring that an organisation operates smoothly and efficiently. Without administration nothing can happen anywhere. For example, if you telephone a company to fit a burglar alarm in your home they will need to take details of your requirements plus your address and telephone number and then let you know when they can do the job. All this is administration without which the business could not operate.

9. Administration, therefore, is a **service function concerned with the flow of information which supports the operation of the organisation**. It covers a range of essential tasks such as reception, mail handling, telephones, typing/word processing, filing, photocopying, secretarial and management information. Many organisations have a central office to perform some or all of these tasks whilst in others they are undertaken within each functional area.

10. Wherever administration takes place, to be effective it requires systems and procedures. That is, methods of working which enable the various parts of the organisation to operate smoothly together. Without these systems the flow of information is likely to break down and the organisation will suffer accordingly.

Task 3   **2.2.1 (C3.4)**

MANAGING THE ADMIN CHORES

A large number of small businesses are often prevented from expanding because they cannot afford to take on staff to look after the administration.

While the owner or manager is away from the office the telephone has to be answered, mail shots to potential customers need sending out, invoices must be typed and despatched – the list goes on.

In the present economic climate few business people are willing to take on leases for office accommodation.

Too many instead continue to work from home long after their requirements have outgrown the facilities available. This is where a managed office can help. This can be hired on a weekly basis. Easy in, easy out terms mean there is no long-term commitment, and one payment covers rent, rates, heat, light, power, cleaning, telephone answering and reception facilities.

A full secretarial service is available, including typing, copying, fax, mailroom etc, on a 'pay as you go' basis, to avoid the necessity of employing a full-time admin person.

Each office is decorated and usually fully furnished, and separately locked for security.

1. How does the article illustrate the importance of administration in a business?

2. Why is it often referred to as being a chore?

3. What is a managed office?

4. In what situations might a business choose a managed office and what benefits could it gain?

Purposes of Administration Systems

11. The main purpose of administrative systems are to facilitate the flow of information necessary to enable an organisation to make decisions and operate on a day-to-day basis. An organisation needs information for its own internal purposes, but must also provide it externally to meet legal and statutory obligations and the needs of official bodies, business associates and potential investors.

12. Systems are required internally to support human, financial and physical resources, perform routine and non-routine functions and for recording and monitoring business performance.

Support for Human, Financial and Physical resources

13. The efficient administration of an organisation is the responsibility of its manager. In a company it is the Board of Directors who have the overall responsibility to 'administer' the business although in practice it is the responsibility of managers at all levels. It is they who must plan, organise, and control the resources in their functional operations to ensure that work gets done and objectives are achieved.

14. Having said this, every aspect of an organisation has to be supported by administration and every person is involved in some way.

   ❐ A factory worker, for example, may have to clock in or out so that his hours of work can be calculated by the wages department.

   ❐ An office holiday rota will be compiled from information supplied by each individual.

   ❐ A delivery driver will have to complete a form when filling his van

   ❐ Maintenance report forms will have to be completed and processed to ensure that premises problems are put right.

❏ Basic communication via internal and external mail and telephone are essential starting points in providing administrative support for an organisations resources.

Performing Routine and Non-Routine Functions

15. There are many administrative tasks which are carried out on a regular basis whether hourly, daily, weekly, monthly or annually.

16. For example, many organisations collate weekly sales figures for managers, regularly process orders, issue invoices and statements; internal and external mail is usually sorted and distributed at least once daily, whilst letters, minutes, memos and reports are frequently being processed as a matter of routine. Other examples include recruitment, filing, reprographics, petty cash, work rotas and stationary requisitions.

78. Most commercial organisations such as banks, travel agents, insurance companies and building societies now use computer systems to carry out most of their routine work.

18. Routine functions are usually handled by following the organisations established administrative systems and procedures. Not all activities, however, are routine and therefore a degree of flexibility is usually required in the systems in order to deal with them. An incomplete or unusual order, for example, may have to be taken out of the routine system and dealt with separately, such as when a credit check is needed for a new customer before the order can be processed.

Task 4   **2.2.1 (C3.2)**

We all have certain regular routines which we follow. They are carried out so automatically that we do not ever need to think about them because they do not cause us any difficulties.

1. Briefly describe a daily and a weekly routine which you have at home, college, school or work. Outline the sequences which you follow.

2. Now consider what happens to your routine when it gets broken, e.g. the alarm fails to go off in the morning.

3. Can you think of one or more non-routine activities which you have undertaken in the past few weeks? Briefly describe the situation and how you had to adapt to it.

4. How, if at all, does this help your understanding of routine and non-routine functions in a business?

Recording and Monitoring Business Performance

19. A major part of any administration system is concerned with record-keeping.

This is required to:

❏ keep **copies of any written work** which is **currently being processed**, e.g. letters, business documents and accounts.

❏ provide a **database for analysis and decision-taking**, e.g. listing overdue accounts, identifying areas of high expenditure, budgetary control, outstanding debts, breakdown of sales by area or product, costs and production figures.

❏ **store information** which is no longer current, i.e. filing for future reference.

❏ assist with **strategic planning** and enable future policy-making to be based on quantifiable data. For example, if an organisation sets itself a target of increasing profits it can decide whether this could be best achieved by either increasing prices or turnover, or by reducing unit costs and overheads or by a combination or both.

❏ **fulfil legal obligations** e.g. health and safety records, VAT, employer PAYE financial accounts, shareholders registered in a company

❏ to **provide documentary evidence** of transactions, e.g. invoices for sales or purchases.

❑ to **monitor business performance** – administration is essential to enable the organisation to review progress toward its objectives in a regular and systematic way. Business performance must be monitored and controlled to ensure that budgets and forecasts are being met so that adjustments can be made if necessary. Good management information systems are essential for this purpose.

Legal and Statutory Requirements

20. Administration systems are not just needed for an organisation's own purposes but also increasingly to enable it to fulfil certain legal requirements particularly in respect of health and safety, employment, company law, taxation and pensions.

21. An employer who breaks the law faces the risk of

   ❑ criminal prosecution leading to fines and or imprisonment plus
   ❑ possible closure,
   ❑ claims for compensation
   ❑ increased insurance premiums
   ❑ bad publicity
   ❑ problems with trade unions
   ❑ bad relations with employees and
   ❑ heavy legal costs

These risks are likely to increase as European harmonisation develops further and therefore good administration systems are essential.

Health and Safety

22. In Element 4.1 two important pieces of legislation which place great demands on employers are outlined. These are the Health and Safety at Work Act 1974 and the Health and Safety (General Regulations) 1992. In addition to having a safety policy, keeping records of accidents, providing safety training and equipment, and establishing safety committees, employers are now also required to carry out assessments of health and safety risks in the work place and to introduce control and monitoring procedures. Employers are also required to notify the Health and Safety Executive as soon as possible of any accident which results in the death of or serious injury of an employee and to report it in writing within seven days of its occurrence. Other examples of health and safety legislation which require the support of administrative systems are outlined below.

23. **Health and Safety (First Aid) Regulations 1981**

These require all organisations to have a first-aid box and, depending on the size of the organisation, to have a suitable number of staff trained in first-aid and a suitably equipped room.

24. **Electricity at Work Regulations 1989**

Most organisations use a wide diversity of portable electrical appliances and tools ranging from kettles to word processors to grass cutters to food mixers to power tools such as drills and saws. These are often distributed throughout virtually all departments within an organisation. This legislation requires organisations to regularly inspect and test all such appliances to ensure that they are safe to use and to keep appropriate records of the assessments.

Task 5	**2.2.1 (C3.2)**

1. Identify and list the main portable electrical appliances used in your place of work or study.

2. Outline what you feel are some of the potential dangers from using such appliances.

3. Try to discover what systems are in place for the inspection and testing of such equipment.

25. **Fire Precautions (Places of Work) Regulations 1994**

Under safety legislation employers are required to have effective means in place to reduce the risk of fire at work. This legislation specifically requires that regular Fire Risk Assessments are carried out at each workplace and records maintained.

26. **Control Of Substances Hazardous To Health (COSHH) Regulations 1988**

These cover virtually all substances capable of causing disease or adverse effects on health arising from work activities. This includes toxic substances e.g. chemicals, micro-organisms and excessive dust. Under COSHH employers must carry out a 'suitable and sufficient' assessment of the risk involved and have procedures in place to record, monitor and control any hazards by such methods as health surveillance and training. Measures such as ventilation and enclosure should be used to restrict employees exposure to hazards and personal protective equipment provided where necessary.

Task 6 2.2.1 (C3.4)

DRIVER SURVIVES 120FT FALL

The driver of a dumper truck survived a 120 ft plunge down a lift shaft. Amazingly, he was not hurt as he lay trapped by the leg. The lift shaft is part of the first phase of the new Paddington to Heathrow rail line.

PATIENT DIES IN FIRE.

An elderly patient died in a fire in a ward at Ruchill Hospital, Glasgow.

MAN BLOWN OFF HIS FEET

A man was blown off his feet when a propane gas cylinder exploded at the Fort Sterling paper mill in Mansell Way, Horwich. He suffered burns to his face, hands and legs.

FACTORY BLAST

Experts were today investigating a factory blast at Livingston, near Edinburgh, which killed one man and critically injured another.

The above news extracts illustrate the importance of health and safety at work.

1. Which health and safety legislation is likely to cover each situation?

2. What action would the employer need to take in each situation and how do they illustrate the need for proper systems?

Employment Law

27. In addition to Health and safety legislation there is also a lot of the important employment law which organisations must satisfy (see Elements 1.3 and 4.1).

28. Some examples of issues covered by legislation which create the need for administration systems include providing employees with

   ❏ written statements of terms and conditions of their employment, including hours of work and holiday entitlements.

   ❏ an itemised pay slip

   ❏ disciplinary and grievance procedures

☐ procedures for handling redundancies and

☐ equal opportunities

Companies Act

29. Limited companies are regulated by the Companies Act 1948 to 1989 and every company by law, must have a Company Secretary to ensure that statutory administrative requirements are met.

30. These include the need to:

☐ **maintain proper books of account**

☐ **hold annual general meetings** to which all shareholders must be invited and annual accounts presented

☐ **submit accounts to the Registrar of Companies** in Cardiff

☐ **maintain a register of directors and shareholders** in the company

☐ **minute shareholder and Board of Directors meetings**

Fiscal Requirements

31. Another important administrative burden on organisations of all sizes is that of collecting taxation.

This is discussed more fully in Element 1.3 but briefly the main requirements cover:

☐ **Inland Revenue** returns and payments in respect of

corporation tax which is an annual tax on company profits

income tax collected from employees under pay-as-you-earn (PAYE) which is paid to the Inland Revenue monthly.

national insurance contributions which, under the Social Security and Pensions Act 1975, must be paid by every employee and self-employed person based on the salary or income earned. Employers must also contribute over 50% of the total amount

☐ **Customs and Excise** returns for **value added tax** (VAT). Organisations liable for VAT must submit quarterly returns and payments.

Accounting Systems

32. Having considered some of the main purposes and legal requirements in respect of administration we can now identify some examples of administrative systems including accounting, sales, distribution, personnel and services.

33. **Accounting systems** are needed in order to monitor and control all the financial resources of the organisation. Such a system would cover, for example:

☐ recording all financial transactions in the books of account

☐ preparation of the annual trading and profit and loss account and balance sheet

☐ preparation of budgets and budgetary control

☐ costing and pricing

☐ security of all money received by the business including the bank account(s) and banking procedures.

☐ preparation and payment of wages and salaries

☐ national insurance and pensions

☐ handling of petty cash and other expense claims

☐ issuing of invoices and statements to customers

☐ collection of all debtor monies including credit control

- payment of supplies and other creditors
- possibly stock control
- internal auditing
- dealing with the organisation's tax liability, i.e. VAT and corporation tax

34. In a large organisation there may be separate sections or departments to handle these systems, whilst in smaller concerns they may be the responsibilities of just one or two people.

Sales Systems

35. **Sales systems** are needed in order to facilitate the efficient selling of an organisation's goods or services. Depending on the size and type of organisation, administrative systems are required which cover, for example:

- handling customer enquiries, e.g. by telephone, letter, advertisement reply coupon
- dealing with quotations and/or estimates
- processing orders
- recording enquiries and sales
- monitoring sales representative's reports and responding to them where necessary
- checking representative's expense claims before passing them to accounts for payment
- making arrangements for credit facilities where this is appropriate
- liaison with production, accounts, credit control and distribution
- customer care, e.g. in respect of after-sales service and handling complaints

36. In a smaller business it may be the owner or just one member of staff who handles the sales administration whilst larger organisations usually have a separate sales department for this purpose, or it may be part of the marketing department's function. A senior manager will be responsible and whilst many businesses will have a team of sales representatives visiting customers, others may well take orders by telephone or sell stock directly from vans where this is more cost-effective.

Task 7   2.2.1, 2.2.2 (C3.2)

In the place where you work or study describe the following administration systems and how they would operate for someone contacting the organisation for the first time.

Comment on their suitability and effectiveness.

1. A telephone caller asking to speak to the Principal or Chief Executive.
2. A personal caller wanting to make a complaint about a product or service.
3. An enquiry from a large organisation about a potential order for products or training for staff.
4. A sales representative offering a range of stationery products.
5. A personal caller looking for a job as a cleaner.

Distribution Systems

37. **Distribution systems** are essential to ensure that goods or services are available when they are required by customers. In industrial markets there is often a direct link between the manufacturer and customer. In consumer markets, however, distribution more commonly involves the use of wholesalers and retailers (see Element 3.4).

38. Distribution systems can therefore involve some or all of the following:

    ❑ material suppliers who distribute to manufacturers

    ❑ manufacturers who distribute finished products to consumers or wholesalers

    ❑ wholesalers who buy from different manufacturers in bulk and supply them to retailers in small quantities.

    ❑ retailers who buy direct from manufacturers and/or wholesalers and supply goods in quantities required by consumers.

39. From this it can be seen that distribution administration involves both the transport and storage of goods. Depending on the organisation concerned systems are needed which cover

    ❑ checking in of goods received

    ❑ appropriate storage – place, conditions, stock rotation

    ❑ checking goods out for delivery

    ❑ movement of goods within manufacturing plants, e.g. raw materials from stock to the factory for production

    ❑ movement of goods within retail outlets, e.g. from warehouse to shop floor

    ❑ stock control to ensure goods are always available when required

    ❑ delivery methods, e.g. road, rail, mail

    Increasingly information technology is being used to improve distribution administration making use of bar codes on products, computerised stock records, television and telephone shopping.

Personnel Systems

40. No organisation can function without people and therefore personnel administration systems are vital for efficient operation. Systems are needed to cover a range of activities including

    ❑ recruitment and selection (see Element 4.3)

    ❑ keeping staff records

    ❑ education and training

    ❑ industrial relations (see Element 4.1)

    ❑ working conditions including health and safety

    ❑ employee services and welfare

    ❑ dealing with grievances, discipline, promotions, transfers and appraisals

41. In all but the smallest organisations most of the systems needed will be the responsibility of the personnel department. Many large organisations have a separate training function.

Task 8   **2.2.1, 2.2.2 (C3.2, C3.4)**

1. Find out how the personnel system for recruitment and selection operates in your place of work or study.

2. Compare this with another organisation well known to you. Perhaps one of those chosen in the assignment in Chapter 1.

3. Comment, with reasons on any significant differences in the approach used and how each system meets the organisation's needs.

Services Systems

42. In addition to the main functional areas of accounts, sales, distribution and personnel there are a number of essential support services which an organisation needs to administer. All organisations will need to have systems for cleaning, maintenance of plant and equipment and stock control, whilst some will also provide catering services for employees. The importance of quality control systems is also being increasingly recognised in organisations.

Cleaning Systems

43. Cleaning would, for example, require systems which

   ❑ ensure that all areas are cleaned, e.g. offices, factories, shops
   ❑ provide cover for sickness and holidays
   ❑ avoid disruption to the business
   ❑ set standards of cleaning required, e.g. frequency
   ❑ ensure that standards are monitored and maintained.

Maintenance Systems

44. Systems for the maintenance of plant and equipment might include:

   ❑ regular inspections of buildings and machinery by staff or external specialists
   ❑ planned maintenance of buildings to prevent deterioration
   ❑ regular servicing of equipment to help reduce wear and tear and prevent potential breakdowns
   ❑ procedures for dealing with breakdowns when they occur, e.g. own maintenance team, regular contracts
   ❑ record-keeping of inspections and problems which require action
   ❑ record-keeping of maintenance activities and cost

Catering Systems

45. The provision of catering services would require systems which cover, for example:

   ❑ purchasing of supplies – food and equipment
   ❑ receiving deliveries
   ❑ storage
   ❑ stock control
   ❑ dealing with waste
   ❑ menu preparation
   ❑ handling money
   ❑ maintenance of equipment
   ❑ maintaining standards of hygiene

Task 9　　　　　　　　　　　　　　　**2.2.1, 2.2.2 (C3.2)**

Identify and write a brief report on at least 3 'service systems' in your place of work or study, operate.

Quality Control Systems

46. The object of quality control is to prevent faulty components or finished goods being produced, thereby reducing costs and helping to increase customer satisfaction. Most people will pay for quality and seek out a supplier who offers it. Thus, quality can give an organisation a competitive edge. The other value of quality control is that it actually reduces the costs of production. This usually involves both the systematic inspection of products during production and also the examination of any faulty goods returned so that corrective action can be taken and problems remedied. Quality control is also necessary because organisations have the legal responsibility of a duty of care towards their customers.

47. To be effective quality control must be maintained at all stages of production from the receipt of raw materials or components to the finished product. It also includes the need for regular training of employees, maintenance of plant and equipment and regular inspection of work as it is processed.

48. Quality systems are essential in all aspects of a business whether it sells products or services. Quality is about increasing customer satisfaction which helps to increase sales and profits. Therefore standards should be set in all areas of the business including administration and these must be monitored and controlled to ensure that they are being met.

49. Many organisations use the **British Standards Institute BS 5750** as a general standard against which its quality systems can be analysed and measured. This covers, for example, management responsibility, design control, document control, purchasing, production, inspection and testing, quality records, quality audits and training. BS 5750 can now be adapted by any type of organisation including those in the service sector. The BSI works closely with the International Standards Organisation (ISO) to promote internationally agreed terms, definitions and standards. BS5750 equates to ISO 9000 series.

50. The BS 5750 registration mark is not a product quality kitemark or specification but rather confirmation that an organisation has **quality systems** and procedures in place. This, however, is very important and nowadays many large organisations will only deal with suppliers who have achieved this standard.

51. Another approach, particularly in non-manufacturing organisations is what is known as **total quality management (TQM)** which originated in the USA and is now widely used both there and in Japan. TQM is the term used to describe the process and management of change in pursuit of quality. It involves an organisation's mission, culture and working practices being directed towards the continuous pursuit of improvement.

52. The basic philosophy behind TQM is that anything can be improved. To do this successfully requires:

   - ❒ **involvement and consultation with customers** in the pursuit of improvements – both internal and external customers.

   - ❒ **overcoming internal obstacles** and solving problems which prevent people from doing the best that they can.

   - ❒ **possible investment** in equipment, facilities and training to improve the skills of the workforce.

   - ❒ **management by targets** so that everyone knows clearly what is required and what progress is being made.

   - ❒ **people-based management** whereby participation in decision-making is encouraged and people work together to identify and solve problems in the pursuit of improvement. It is also important that people's efforts are recognised and acknowledged.

   - ❒ **implementation of systems and procedures** which regularly review and evaluate all aspects of the organisation's work.

53. TQM may take several years to achieve in an organisation because of a reluctance to change 'the way things have always been done', but once established, it provides a sound basis for continued quality and excellence. Many High Street banks, insurance companies, building societies and retail organisations have implemented TQM.

BS 5750 or TQM

54. BS 5750 and TQM are both methods available to managers seeking to implement quality assurance and control. BS 5750 is about systems and procedures which organisations should follow to achieve quality, whereas TQM is a process for managing and measuring the continuous quality improvement of everything that an organisation does. Some organisations have introduced one or the other whilst others have chosen to introduce both methods. The important issue is what best meets the needs of an organisation.

Task 10   **2.2.1, 2.2.2, 2.2.3 (C3.4)**

QUALITY CONTROL MANAGER

Competitive Salary + Car + Benefits

We are one of the country's leading 'Own Label' convertors of toilet rolls, kitchen rolls, facial tissues, cling film and aluminium foil. Our high speed, automated, rewinding and packaging lines are amongst the best in the industry, and represent our commitment to high quality, value for money products. As a prominent member of our management team, you will lead and motivate a small department responsible for quality assurance with 3 key tasks.

* Investigating and eliminating service quality failures

* Assessing and monitoring service quality to develop and enhance current levels

* Installing and maintaining BS 5750

The position carries overall control of quality systems company wide, and you will carry out systems audits and improvements, cost reduction programmes and supplier assessments. The role is vital to our company's continued progress, and will provide an exciting opportunity for a Quality specialist, who has a proven track record within a high volume production environment.

Qualified to degree level or equivalent, you will currently be providing a QA service through the implementation of TQM or BS 5750 in a small to medium size company. The successful applicant will be able to communicate at all levels within our company, and be confident in dealing with customers and suppliers.

Further details from _____

1. Explain the role of the quality control manager in the above post.

2. In what ways are TQM and BS 5750 important for quality control?

3. From your knowledge of quality control suggest ways in which the 3 key tasks can help to improve quality.

4. How might the introduction of new technology help to improve quality?

Systems Design

55. A system may be designed by the person responsible for its operation or alternatively by specialists from either inside or outside the organisation. A system can often be shown in the form of a Flow Chart as the following example illustrates.

56. Example

College Admissions Procedure for Full-Time Courses

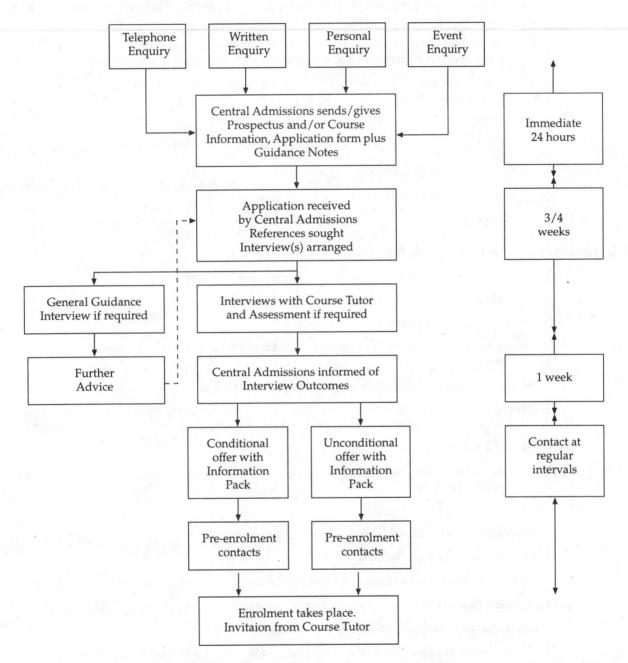

57. Sometimes existing administration systems have evolved over a number of years, often by trial and error, and therefore may not always be the most efficient and effective. Equally, the need for change brought about by reorganisation, existing inefficiency or the installation of new computerised technology may create the need for a new system to be designed. This involves a detailed appraisal of what currently takes place called a **systems analysis**.

Task 11   2.2.4, 2.2.5 (C3.2, C3.4)

Effective systems often depend on the use of documents which are logical and easy to read, understand, complete and process.

1. Collect four forms, two used in the place where you work or study and two from any other organisation, perhaps a bank, post office, insurance company or the local council.

2. Compare each of the four forms and comment, with reasons, on whether or not you think they are 'good' forms.

3. Suggest any ways in which you think each could be improved.

4. Redesign one or more of the forms to illustrate the improvements which you have suggested.

5. Finally comment on how, if at all, your ideas could affect the administrative systems of the organisations concerned.

Organisation & Methods (O & M)

58. One approach to systems analysis is the use of organisation and methods.

   The basic steps involved in O & M can be remembered by the mnemonic SREDIM.

   ☐ **Select** the job to be studied.

   ☐ **Record** the details of the job and method used. This is done systematically using a flow chart or similar technique.

   ☐ **Examine** the details critically to eliminate any duplicated effort.

   ☐ **Develop** a revised and improved method which might involve, for example, changes to the layout of a workplace, the sequence of operations or improvements in product or equipment design.

   ☐ **Install** the new method.

   ☐ **Maintain** the method by reviewing it on a regular basis to ensure that it is operating as planned and modify if necessary.

59. The benefits of using O&M include:

   ☐ **Identification and elimination** of problems and waste.

   ☐ **Cost reductions** from improved methods.

   ☐ **Improved employee performance**, particularly those engaged in repetitive tasks.

   ☐ **Improved flow of work** from more efficient procedures.

   ☐ **Better utilisation of space, equipment and materials**.

   ☐ **Closer control of operations** enabling easier access to information and a faster response rate to internal and external customers.

   ☐ **Improved security procedures**, for example, from better cash handling procedures or control of confidential documents.

   ☐ **An overall increase in efficiency and productivity** and therefore ultimately profit.

60. O&M It may also be used as the **basis of** a **job evaluation** exercise because jobs are systematically analysed and can be ranked in order of importance to determine their position in the pay structure.

Task 12   **2.2.4 (C3.2, C3.4)**

Consider an organisation well known to you such as your place of study or work.

1. Your task is to examine how organisation and methods techniques could be used change systems and to improve the efficiency of the organisation. Try to identify 3 different areas of its activities which you feel are in need of improvement and explain why this is needed.

2. Discuss any possible improvements which you feel could be made and what is required to bring them about.

3. If feasible, carry out some practical method study and write a brief report on your findings and recommendations.

Suitability of Administration Systems

61. We have seen that administration is concerned with the flow of information which supports the functional operations of an organisation. In Element 2.4 we discuss information processing systems and how these have and continue to be dramatically changed by developments in technology. Modern systems design is almost certain to include the use of computer technology in order to produce the most efficient system.

62. The suitability of any administration system can be assessed in terms of its

❑ **fitness for purpose**, that is, does the system appear to do the job for which it was intended considering the type, volume and speed of work required.

❑ **value for money**, that is, is it cost effective in improving efficiency? New technology involves both hardware and software costs, is relatively expensive to install and maintain and is likely to require regular updating.

❑ **security**, that is, can it only be used as intended? Can confidential data such as personnel records or payroll be restricted and kept secure with passwords or other encoding to prevent unauthorised access to it. Poor security could lead for example, to the risks of inputting to the system by unauthorised users who introduce viruses which may affect the accuracy and reliability of data, whilst in the case of the Internet and EDI theft of money or leaks of commercially sensitive information.

❑ **health and safety**, that is, what is the likely impact on the environment and on employees particularly in terms of their ability to cope with the systems change. The introduction of new technology can have both physical and psychological effects on people who may find it threatening and stressful which may offset the potential productivity gains.

Task 13   **2.2.2, 2.2.3 (C3.2, T3.3, N3.1)**

Consider the suitability of the information technology which you use in your GNVQ core skills in terms of the factors identified in paragraph 62.

Produce a word-processed report giving as much detail as possible, for example clearly identifying the hardware, software and any essential environmental conditions and the costs involved.

Comment on your findings.

Information Technology

63. **Computers** are simply electronic machines which are able to store, retrieve and sort data at great speed. Information can be retrieved either directly onto a screen, printing out a hard copy on paper or on microfilm. It can be stored on a hard disk in the computer itself, or on separate 'floppy disks', or on both. However it is stored, it is essential that an additional copy is made on a back-up disk.

64. The equipment used in a computerised system is called the **hardware**. It includes the Visual Display Unit (monitor), keyboard, printer and electronic components. The programs which tell the computer what to do are called the **software**.

65. Software programs which are discussed in Element 2.4 include commercial administration packages covering accounting, spreadsheets and databases. Packages are also available to provide administration support for other business functions, for example, personnel, purchasing, stock control and distribution. Whilst Microsoft's Word for Windows and MicroPro's Wordstar are examples of two of the most widely used word processing packages. There are also **integrated software programs** which allow a combination of different applications, for example, correspondence on a word processor, customer records in a database and budgets on a spreadsheet. Data can be easily transferred from one application to another. These packages are particularly useful to small businesses who have very few specialist computer staff.

66.

Networking

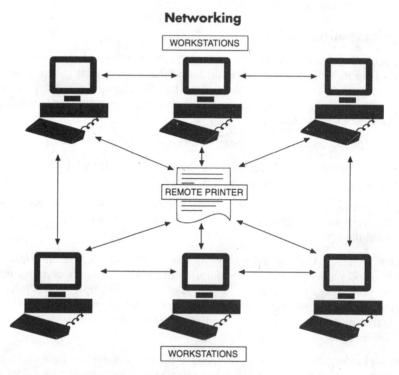

A feature of modern offices is the networking (linking) of free-standing computers to other machines within the same office or building. It is also possible to have a **wide area network** linking separate buildings on sites across the country via telephone modems.

Task 14   **2.2.3, 2.4.1 (C3.3)**

Carry out some research in your place of study or work.

1.   List as many different methods of storing data that you can find.

2.   Identify the different types of data stored, why and how long it is stored for.

3.   If possible, try to establish how much space, as a proportion of the total available, is used for storage.

4.   Suggest ways in which the amount of data stored could be reduced and comment on its potential impact on the organisation's administration.

5.   Present your answers in the form of a chart(s) or diagram(s) and comment on your findings.

Some key computer terms

67. As you will already have realised computers have a language of their own. To help you to understand this some key terms are explained below. The list is by no means exhaustive, so you may decide to add some further words of your own in the space provided.

Back-up: term used for making a copy of files held on disk. Important in case a disk crashes or becomes unreliable. Without it much information could be lost.

CD-ROM: stands for compact disk read only memory. Used to store masses of information such as large reference databases and multi-media software.

Central processing unit: the technical term for the 'brains' of a computer.

Computer aided design (CAD): can range from simple drawing programmes to very complex Desk Top Publishing packages. Allows the use and production of graphics on the computer e.g. plans of a building drawn by an architect.

Computer aided manufacturing (CAM): generally the automation of production lines.

Computer bug: unseen errors in a program which can cause computer malfunction.

Computer virus: a bug deliberately and unlawfully embedded into a program to corrupt data. It spreads when disks are copied.

Crash: when a computer stops working and will not respond to any instructions.

Cursor: marker on a computer screen which indicates where next character will appear.

Data: the term for information unputted into a computer.

Database: a collection of information or data which the computer can handle in different ways for searching, sorting etc.

Desk-top publishing (DTP): use of computers to produce high quality publications by combining text and graphics.

Disk: a memory device used for recording information (see Floppy disk and Hard disk).

Disk-drive: a piece of hardware used to record and recover information on a disk.

Disk-operating system (DOS): the programme which enables a user to operate a disk drive e.g. to tell the operating system to copy a file from one disk to another (see MS-DOS).

Down-time: the period when a computer is out of operation because of a technical fault.

Electronic mail: an alternative to sending letters by post, which involves the use of computer terminals linked via the telephone network. Subscribers who have a password to enter the system are able to send messages to a 'mailbox' where they are stored until 'opened' by the recipient. BT's Telecom Gold is a well-known example.

File: a collection of information usually stored on a disk.

Floppy disk: not actually floppy but small disks used in computers to store data. Standard size usually five and a quarter inches.

Hard-disk: a rigid magnetic disk used to store data.

Hardware: the equipment used in a computerised system.

Icon: a word or small picture displayed on a computer screen representing a function which is available.

Interface: used to enable a computer to communicate e.g. a keyboard interfaces between the computer and user and the Centronics interface between the computer and printer.

Menu: the range of options offered by a computer programme e.g. File, Edit, View, Help, etc.

Modem: a device used to connect computers through the telephone network.

Mouse: an electronic pointer used to operate computers without using the keyboard.

MS-DOS: Microsoft Disk Operating System which has become the industry standard operating system.

Multimedia: the integration of words, pictures, photographs, audio and video.

Network: the linking of computers using a cable or internal telephone line to enable machines to share information and resources.

Random Access Memory (RAM): the memory or working space in a software package, usually a minimum of 640k. It is usually possible to upgrade to a bigger memory at a later date.

Software: the programmes which tell the computer what to do.

Spreadsheet: a worksheet which allows data to be entered and calculations made easily and quickly. Changing any of the data causes all the results to be recalculated. Looks like a table of figures when presented on the screen.

Visual display unit (VDU): screen on which computer data is displayed.

Space for further computer terms

Multi-tasking

68. The power and speed of most Central Processing Units in computers is such that they can allow more than one task to be performed at a time. Most word processors, for example, as a minimum allow keying in at the same time as printing.

69. More advanced programs allow several applications at one time with different windows, for example housing a diary, note-book, word-processing and record-keeping facility at the same time with the ability to switch instantly from one to the other and import (copy) data or text created in one application to another. This **multi-tasking** is made even easier with the use of WIMP (Window-Icon-Mouse-Printer) software which provides a simple user interface which almost anyone can use with very little training.

Administration and Change

70. In Element 4.2 we consider in detail the reasons for change and how it can affect both systems in an organisation and the working conditions of its employees.

    For example, changed may be needed in order to

    ❑ **increase productivity and profitability** by reducing costs and for increasing output;

    ❑ **improve customer service** to give the organisation a competitive edge;

    ❑ **raise the quality** of both products and services to meet changing customer expectation;

    ❑ **produce new products or services** which may change the purpose of the organisation.

Task 15   2.2.4 (C3.4)

Identify three key areas, in the place where you work or study, with which you have regular contact. For example, the reception, library, flexible learning centre, general office, finance office or refectory. Write a brief comment on each in terms of

1. The main administration functions which it performs which affect you personally.

2. Any changes (including introducing new technology) in systems or procedures which have been made in the past 3–6 months and why.

3. The effect which you feel this has had, from your point of view, in terms of the factors identified in paragraph 70.

Improving Administration Systems

71. We have seen that the smooth running of an organisation depends very much upon its administration systems. **Systems which work well should**

    ❑ result in a more effective flow of work

    ❑ provide easier and more effective control over each stage

    ❑ help to clearly identify training needs for new staff and

    ❑ produce economies from more efficient operation

    Whilst **poor systems will result in**

    ❑ inefficiency

    ❑ ineffective control and consequently a

    ❑ potential loss of sales and profits

72. For example, consider what is likely to be the most efficient and effective method of administration in the following situations:

    ❑ A sales representative selling a limited range of goods could be asked to hand write a customers order. Alternatively a pre-printed form could be used listing all the products with boxes for the quantities to be entered into.

    ❑ 90% of a company's business relies on telephone ordering. Its present system involves writing orders down and forwarding them to the sales department for processing. It decides to input the data directly into a computer, where keying in the customers name or reference number produces all their current details including any credit limit. As the order and delivery instructions are inputted the customer can be informed of any out-of-stock products and potential delivery date. Sales data is immediately available for analysis and the invoice is automatically produced.

    ❑ A system which consists of several operations involving a number of departments, each with separate forms can be improved by using an initial master document which provides several copies for use at subsequent stages.

73. **Improvements** to administrations systems therefore are likely to result in:

    ❑ **new or modified procedures** which operate more efficiently

❑ **new equipment**, both hardware and software, more suited to the current and future needs of the organisation

❑ **training** in the changed procedures including any necessary up-dating of skills. Leading to

❑ **better service for customers** both internally and externally.

Task 16   **2.2.2, 2.2.5 (C3.1)**

Working in small groups discuss and then make written notes on each members experience(s) of business systems.

Consider systems which have operated successfully and those where things have gone wrong.

Possible experiences could cover many situations, for example, school, college or work, buying goods or services from shops or mail order, holidays, work experience, eating in a restaurant, applying for a job or place at a college or university.

Record as much information as possible about the systems and how they operated. Comment on the way each one affected individuals as 'customers' and their subsequent attitude to the organisation concerned.

Finally comment on how you feel the systems could have been improved and the role, if any, of new technology in making these improvements.

Summary

74. a)   A business as a whole is a complete system structured on the basis of functions, each of which can be classed as a sub-system.

b)   The administration system is concerned with ensuring that an organisation operates smoothly.

c)   Administration systems are needed internally to perform routine and non-routine functions, to provide support for the financial, human and physical resources and record and monitor business performance.

d)   They are also needed in order to meet legal and statutory requirements including health and safety, employment law, the Companies Act and fiscal and pensions payments.

e)   Systems are used to support all business functions including accounting, sales, distribution and personnel, and for the administration of services such as cleaning, catering and maintenance.

f)   Quality control systems can help to reduce the costs of production, increase customer satisfaction and therefore sales and profits.

g)   BS5750 and TQM are two commonly used quality systems.

h)   Systems can be designed by appropriate managers or specialists from inside or outside the organisation.

i)   Organisation and methods is often used for the purpose of systems analysis.

j)   The suitability of administration systems can be assessed against its fitness for purpose, value for money, security and effect on health and safety.

k)   Information technology is having a major impact on administration systems.

l)   Administration systems may need to change in order to increase productivity, improve customer service, raise quality or produce new products or services.

m)   Good administration systems will improve the efficiency, effectiveness and control of business functions.

Review questions *(Answers can be found in the paragraphs indicated)*

1. With the use of a diagram illustrate the components and significance of a simple business system. (1–6)

2. Explain, with examples, why different organisations require different business systems. (7)

3. Briefly explain what is called 'administration' in a business. (8–12)

4. In what sense is every aspect of an organisation supported by administration and every person involved in some way? (13–14)

5. Distinguish between a routine and a non-routine function in a business. (15–18)

6. Why is record-keeping a major part of any administrative system? (19)

7. Explain how the growth of health and safety legislation impacts on an organisations administrative systems? (20–21)

8. List four ways in which legislation puts an onus on companies to have administrative systems. (22–36)

9. With the use of examples explain why administrative systems are needed for the functions of accounting, sales, distribution and personnel. (37–46)

10. What services could an organisation use which create the need for administration? (47)

11. Why does an organisation need a system of quality control? (46–48)

12. Distinguish between BS5750 and TQM as systems of quality control. (49–54)

13. In what circumstances might a systems analysis be needed? (55–57)

14. Briefly outline how an organisation and methods study could take place and the benefits it might bring. (58–60)

15. How could the suitability of an administration system be assessed? (61–62)

16. LIst 10 key computer terms and explain briefly why you need to know them. (63–69)

17. Why might administration systems need to change? (70)

18. How, if at all, can an organisation's administration systems be evaluated and improved? (71–73)

Assignment – Investigating Administration Systems — Element 2.2

Study the administrative system of one of the organisations used for the assignment at the end of Chapter 1, or any other organisation which you know well such as your place of work or study.

1. Briefly describe the chosen organisation in terms of type, size, product/services, and functional areas.

2. Outline the administration system currently in place, including the procedures, processes and equipment.

3. Explain its suitability for the purpose of supporting one or more functions of the organisation.

4. Depending on the size of your chosen organisation study one or more function in detail, describing its systems and how they operate.

5. Explain how information technology is changing or has changed the administration system.

6. Explain one change in the organisation and how the administration system supports that change, customer service, productivity and quality.

7. Consider how the effectiveness of the systems in supporting the needs of the organisation can be measured, and comment on how the systems can be evaluated and improved. This could be presented orally and supported by notes.

7 Communication in Business Organisations

This Chapter looks at the need for effective communication in the business world. It gives details of the main methods of internal and external communications which are used today including the important impact of new computerised technology, and covers:

- Business Communication
- Types of Communication
- Objectives of Communication
- Internal Communication (Verbal)
- Business Meetings
- Internal Communication (Non-Verbal)
- Informal Communication
- Visual Methods of Communication
- External Communication
- Business Letters

- Telephone Answering
- Telephone Calls
- Postal Services
- Telecommunications Services
- Internal Communication Equipment
- Special Needs Communication
- Barriers to Effective Communication
- Electronic Technology
- Effective Communication
- Changes to Communication

Business Communication

1. The ways in which businesses communicate with each other have changed dramatically in recent years. The impact of new computer technology has greatly increased the speed of communications in the UK. The use of satellites has enabled communication, by both sound and vision, to be made throughout the world in a matter of minutes.

2. Nowadays we receive news almost as soon as it happens via television, radio and newspapers. Modern businesses therefore also expect their methods of communication to be fast and effective. The speed with which suppliers, customers, staff and other business providers, such as banks, are contacted is important to ensure that a firm operates efficiently. There are many different forms of communication which a business may choose and it is important to select the most effective in any particular situation.

Communication Defined

3. Communication is a two-way process to enable information to be passed from one person or organisation to another, or in the case of automatic systems, from one process to another. It involves the basic skills of listening, speaking, reading and writing in order to receive, interpret and understand messages and then respond to them accordingly.

4. The rapid growth in the use of computerised equipment makes the need to develop information technology skills increasingly important. To be effective, communication must be understood and acceptable by all parties, both those giving the information and those receiving it. Unfortunately, however, it is often very easy to misunderstand or misinterpret what is meant, as the cartoon illustrates.

Getting the Message

Types of Communication

5. Communication in a business may take place in many different ways. It may be:

    ❐ **Verbal** i.e. spoken by someone, for example face to face or on the telephone.

    ❐ **Non-verbal** i.e. written, for example letters, memos, reports and diagrams. Body language such as facial expressions, the use of the hands, and how people sit or stand can also represent an important form of non-verbal communication, often revealing a lot about how people feel or think.

    ❐ **Formal** i.e following correct laid down procedures of which records are usually kept, for example committees, recruitment interviews, safety notices.

    ❐ **Informal** i.e. as and when appropriate without the need to follow procedures or keep records, for example meeting or telephoning someone to discuss a particular problem as it arises.

    ❐ **Internal** i.e. takes place within a business organisation, for example between the sales and personnel departments.

    ❐ **External** i.e. outside an organisation or between organisations, for example with a customer or supplier.

Task 1	**2.3.1 (C3.2, C3.3)**

1. Outline, with reasons, the message which each of the following types of body language would give to you:

    a) a smile b) a frown c) folded arms d) clenched fists e) slouching in a chair.

2. Briefly describe the main forms of body language which you personally use.

3. Can you identify any situations where body language is, or might be, particularly important for communication in the place where you work or study?

Objectives of Communication

6. To be successful, a business needs to communicate effectively with a wide range of people both within the organisation (**internally**) and outside the organisation (**externally**). Imagine, for example, the chaos which could be caused if British Rail or your local bus company issued inaccurate

timetables. Think about what might happen if this type of communication problem occurred in your school, college or place of work.

7. **Effective communication** then, is important if an organisation is to achieve its objectives. Some of the reasons for this include the need to:

    ❐ **enable decisions to be taken** based on the best information available.

    ❐ **issue instructions to its staff** to tell them what to do and thus enable the business to operate. This is referred to as vertical communication.

    ❐ **enable people at the same level within the organisation to communicate with each other**. Different departments such as sales and production, for example, or employees who work in the same department. This is called horizontal communication.

    ❐ **communicate externally with its suppliers, customers, banks and other contacts** in carrying out its business. It must send information about its products, receive orders, supply goods, deal with documents and arrange payments.

    ❐ **keep staff up-to-date and informed of what is going on** so that they are able to perform their work better and enjoy what they are doing. It must transmit information about the firm's organisation, products, safety regulations and training. This is multi-directional communication.

    ❐ **provide essential information to staff** on pay, pensions, holidays, other benefits and general working conditions. This is also multi-directional communication.

Task 2   **2.3.1, 2.3.2 (C3.2)**

An urgent order has just been taken at the main branch of Exclusive Tailoring Ltd, a company which produces high quality made-to-measure suits.

1. List all the possible ways which you can think of to get the order to Head Office for processing.

2. What do you think might happen if the order does not reach Head Office quickly and accurately?

3. Which method of communication would you choose and why, in this situation?

---

8. Effective communication involves four elements:

    a) **The transmitter** i.e. the sender or source of the communication.

    b) **The message** or content of what is being communicated.

    c) **The channel** or method used to send the message for example, typed letter, fax, telephone call, leaflet, face-to-face conversation, non-verbal hand signals.

    d) **The receiver** i.e. the audience or people to whom the communication is being sent.

The Elements of Communication

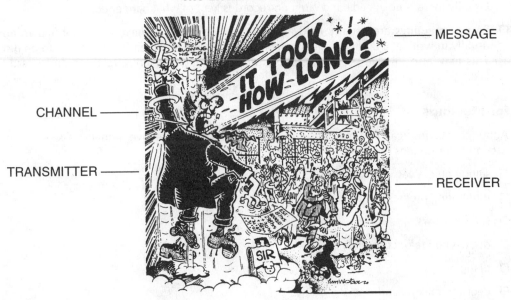

Most forms of communication require or produce a response known as **feedback**. It is this which indicates whether or not the message has been effectively communicated. That is, the message received is the one the sender intended.

9. **Channels of communication** may be:

☐ **Open** and accessible to anyone in an organisation, for example noticeboards, general memo's or newsletters and multi-user systems such as computer networks OR

☐ **Restricted** to a limited number of people because of the nature of the message. For example, Management Information Systems (MIS) are usually restricted so that confidential data only goes to specific people, whilst a memo or letter may only be sent to one person, a meeting might only involve 3 or 4 people.

☐ **Electronic**. In a modern business environment effective communication involves a vast number of different channels most of which are increasingly likely to be technology based.

Internal Communication – Verbal Methods

10. ☐ **Spoken** communications are the most common way of passing information within an organisation. This involves seeing people face to face, for example the holding of meetings or contacting them by telephone.

☐ **Telephone** extensions are frequently used in an organisation to enable communication to take place between various sections or departments. This saves time if it is not possible to meet someone to speak to them personally.

☐ **Interviews** or individual discussions with staff are common in all organisations. They are used not only to select staff but also, for example, to deal with particular problems or disciplinary matters or to assess staff performance.

☐ **Business meetings** may take place where a number of people need to be involved in discussions. These may be formal or informal.

Business Meetings

11. At any level in an organisation, employees may find themselves involved in attending meetings and as they move further up the promotional ladder, they are likely to find themselves attending an increasing number of them.

❑ **Informal meetings** may be called at short notice to discuss matters which arise suddenly. Usually there is no agenda and often no record is kept of what happened.

❑ **Formal meetings** are usually held after the people involved have been notified in advance, usually in writing and often with an accompanying **agenda** which lists the items to be discussed. This may also involve preparing reports or documents, speaking to them and possibly note taking.

Reasons for Meetings

12. Although meetings can be time-consuming and sometimes ineffective, nonetheless, they are widely used in organisations for

❑ setting objectives,

❑ monitoring progress,

❑ sharing views,

❑ discussing ideas, consultation,

❑ planning,

❑ decision-making and

❑ disseminating decisions.

13. **Example of an Agenda:**

ABC ELECTRICAL SUPPLIERS LTD

Meeting of Marketing Co-Ordination Committee

On Friday 14th January 1996 at 10am

To be held in the Boardroom

Agenda

1. Apologies for absence
2. Minutes of previous Meeting
3. Matters arising:

   Item 21 Sales Training

   Item 22 Promotion of New Products

   Item 25 Advertising Budget
4. Marketing Department staffing
5. Report on Sales Enquiry Forms
6. Exhibition Plan
7. Any other business
8. Date and time of next meeting

---

14. Most organisations, whether a Youth Club, School, College or Company have **committees** which meet to discuss and make policy decisions. Often these consist of people elected to represent the views of members. Formal bodies usually have an Annual General Meeting (AGM) held once a year to elect officials, receive reports and to give members an opportunity to speak; for example, a limited company will hold an Annual General Meeting to which all its shareholders are invited.

15. A formal meeting is controlled by a chairman and minutes are taken by a secretary. Minutes are a record of a meeting and serve as a reminder of the issues discussed and decisions taken. All members of the committee will receive a copy of the minutes and any matters arising will be discussed at the next meeting. The most important committee in a company is the Board of Directors which is discussed in Element 4.2.

Task 3   **2.3.1, 2.3.2, 2.3.3 (C3.1, C3.2)**

You are employed as one of 20 staff in the offices of a local insurance company. The office supervisor has been concerned for sometime about poor staff morale following the closure of a small nearby branch and redundancies in 2 others.

Reporting her concerns to the personnel manager, she is given assurances that your office will not suffer. He also recommends the setting up of a small committee to discuss the problems and come up with some positive suggestions for raising morale. He indicates that the company might also be able to find £200 from the personnel budget to assist in this matter.

1. As a group, form a committee(s) and decide on an appropriate chairperson, secretary and other positions which you feel are necessary.

2. Identify the reasons for each person being on the committee and the role they will be expected to undertake.

3. Decide when your meeting is to take place and draw up a suitable agenda.

4. Hold the meeting and from it, draw up a firm set of proposals, including the allocation of any expenditure. Ensure that minutes are taken.

5. Assuming you are the office supervisor, write a memo to the personnel manager, setting out the proposals. Include as much detail as possible and any potential benefits to the company.

Internal Communication – Non Verbal Methods

16. Earlier, we considered the main verbal methods of communication in an organisation. The non verbal (written) methods used include memos, minutes, letters, notices, house journals and reports.

   ❑ **Memorandum** (memos) are the method of written communication most commonly used within an organisation. They can be sent in a firm's internal post, are usually short and deal with only one or two specific points.

   ❑ **Minutes** are used to provide a summary of the main points which are discussed at a meeting and are filed for future reference.

   ❑ **Letters** are not normally used within a business. However, they are sent in some formal situations for example, to confirm the promotion of staff or to accept their resignation.

   ❑ **Notices** are often used to display matters of interest to staff. However, unfortunately there is no way of ensuring that these are either read or understood.

   ❑ **House Bulletins/House Journals**. In some organisations notices are circulated by means of a weekly or monthly staff bulletin. Some larger organisations also have a glossy house magazine or journal which includes information on a wide range of work-related and social topics, for example new products, new employees, births, deaths and marriages, or sports activities.

   ❑ **Reports** are formal written communications required to cover a certain business topic. They may be provided for a number of reasons. For example, many firms have a standard accident or sickness report form. Periodic reports may be needed to assess a firm's budget or sales performance. Technical reports may be prepared on new products and processes of production.

17. **Example of a report**

Report

To Mr C Houseman
Works Manager

From Conn McBride
Supervisor (Welding Section)
25th September 199-

Re: Accident to Julia Styles

As requested I have looked into the circumstances of the accident that happened to Julia. I understand the purpose of this report is to ascertain whether she can claim against Alpha Engineering (or its Insurance Company) for the injuries she received.

Cause of accident

It seems that when her gas canister ran dry Julia went to the reloading bay in compliance with the normal safety drill, but when she went back to her workstation she found the new canister malfunctioning. She then played with the fastening nut to tighten it, but instead loosened it. As a result, some of the liquid gas sprayed on to the flame of a workmate's gun.

Result of the accident

The blowback from the naked flame to the malfunctioning canister caused the casing to crack and release the rest of the gas. There was a massive explosion and, although Julia had thrust the canister away from herself just before it happened, her hair caught fire and the left hand side of her face was badly burned. A welding gun and some aluminium casings were completely destroyed.

Injuries incurred

I have visited Julia twice in hospital. The first time she was hardly able to speak, but when I saw her yesterday she was recovering. She was comforted by the news from the doctor that they would be able to repair all the damage with the aid of plastic surgery. Apparently, there will be no permanent scars.

Conclusion

I cannot see that Julia was in any way to blame for the accident, but on a strict interpretation of the rules applied in the Welding Section she should have gone to the reloading bay to adjust the gas canister.

Example of a Memorandum

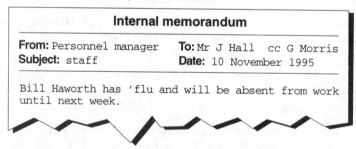

Internal memorandum

From: Personnel manager   **To:** Mr J Hall cc G Morris
Subject: staff   **Date:** 10 November 1995

Bill Haworth has 'flu and will be absent from work until next week.

Example of minutes

Burrage PLC Health and Safety Committee
20 September 1995

Present: J Drake, R Fisher, A Burnett, J Lock, P Street, M Fowler, C Cookson, F Arrowsmith.

Apologies: P Coin, R Eastham.

1   **Minutes of previous meeting**
The minutes of the previous meeting on 18 July 1995 were agreed a correct record.

2   **Matters arising from the minutes**
Mill works – inspection had been carried out and a report is being compiled with recommendations on storage problems for protective clothing.

3   **Appointment of Heath and Safety Officer**
Shortlisting due to take place on 1.10.95.

4   **First aid**
Some certificates expire in October 1995; AB to follow up. Mill works to be included.

5   **Crompton Road inspection.**
Temporary fire exit arrangements made whilst main entrance closed. Corridors with furniture have now been cleared.

6   **Fire practices**
MF indicated need for fire practices as soon as possible at Crompton Road and all other sites. Back staircase closed during installation of new goods lift. Short inspection arranged to check clarity of fire exits.

7   **Overcrowding**
Concern was expressed about utilisation of some rooms. PS indicated that sections had been asked to review requirements by the end of February. An overall accommodation strategy was being formed.

8   **Noise and dust**
JD requested that we pay attention to these problems when refurbishment works are being carried out.

9   **Site supervisors' room**
Room still requires work to ceiling. CC to follow up.

10   **Disabled access and facilities**
Concern was expressed about use of public lift, particularly whilst goods lift out of operation. MF and JD to investigate suitable signs. Disabled toilets will be installed on every floor as part of refurbishment. FA raised issue of skip blocking Silver Street access route.

11   **Toilets**
JL expressed concern about basement toilets. Problem with main sewer – being attended to. JD to follow up.

Any other business

a)   **Smoking**
Concern expressed about poor enforcement of No Smoking Policy.

b)   **Science laboratory inspection**
CC raised issue of new regulations coming into force.

c)   **Wolf Street**
RE indicated that some health and safety works were being carried out.

Date of next meeting: 10 November 1.30pm Mill works, inspection and full meeting.

Informal Communication

18. Communication may also take place in other ways in particular via the 'grapevine', over lunch and on social occasions.

   ❏ The **'grapevine'** or jungle telegraph is the term used to describe the rumours and general gossip which staff often use as a source of information in an organisation.

   ❏ Informal **lunchtime conversations** are often used for both internal and external communication. They may involve casual discussion between staff or be working lunches often with visitors to an organisation.

❑ **Social occasions** of all types provide a further opportunity for both internal and external communication to take place. Examples might include a Christmas Dinner, cricket match or annual outings where a number of staff will mix and talk together.

Visual Methods of Communication

19. Another important means of communication, both internal and external is the use of charts, graphs and diagrams. The use of visual presentation enables complicated information, particularly statistical data, to be more easily understood (see Element 3.2). The use of computer software packages and desk top publishing (DTP) have greatly improved the presentation of such materials (see Element 2.4).

Task 4   **2.3.1, 2.3.2 (C3.3)**

Consider the place where you work or study or any other organisation which you know well.

Give examples of situations where each of the following types of communication are used:

Spoken (face-to-face)
Telephone calls
Hand-written
Printed – forms
Electronic Transmission (other than telephones)
Social gatherings
Reports

External Communication

20. The most common forms of external communication are **letters** and **telephone**. In the UK the major suppliers of these and other external communication services are the Post Office and British Telecom (BT). These organisations provide a wide range of national and international communication systems which are becoming increasingly sophisticated with the introduction of new computerised technology.

21. Other external communication methods include

❑ **compliments slips** which are often used when a letter is not needed; for example when a firm sends out leaflets or other information which has been requested by potential customers whilst

❑ **advertising and sales promotion** are very important means by which a firm communicates with its customers and these are dealt with fully in Element 3.3.

❑ the **Annual Report and Accounts** which in a company, is issued to shareholders is another common form of external communication.

Task 5   **2.3.1, 2.3.2 (C3.2)**

1. Identify the external methods of communication in the following list: Newspaper advertisement, letter post, managers meeting, price list, memorandum.

2. State two methods of external communication and two methods of internal communication which a major soap powder manufacturer might use.

Business Letters

22. These are still by far the most important form of external communication and are used for a wide variety of purposes as the following examples illustrate:

- arranging meetings and/or confirming dates and times already agreed.

- letters of application from prospective employees.

- recruitment, e.g. invitations to interview, reference requests, offers of employment.

- advertising or sales letters to customers, e.g. to promote interest or advise of special offers.

- checking the credit worthiness of potential customers.

- complaints about faulty goods or other problems with suppliers, such as late or short deliveries, or queries about costs/prices.

- responding to customer complaints, possibly with letters of credit or some other form of compensation.

- providing estimates of costs or tenders for work.

- making enquiries or requesting additional information from suppliers about goods or services.

- placing orders (although actual order forms are often used).

23. The main reason for writing letters can therefore be summarised as to:

- provide or seek information.

- prompt action or a particular form of response.

- maintain or promote good relationships with customers and suppliers.

Writing a Business Letter

24. A letter, then, is used to get a written message across and therefore, to be effective, its tone and content are very important. A good letter, therefore, should be carefully planned and written so that it is:

- **clear and concise** – using simple, short sentences and paragraphs which get to the point, avoiding complicated technical terms or abbreviations wherever possible

- **specific to the reader** – providing the quantity and quality of information that the reader requires, e.g. when informing someone of an interview the letter should contain details of the day, date, time, location (might include a map) and any other important details relating to the interview

- **accurate and complete** – errors (particularly in spelling or punctuation) and omissions give a poor impression of an organisation and can also cause confusion and/or lead to a loss of business

- **polite and tactful** – so as to avoid giving the wrong impression or offending people. This is particularly important in order to avoid losing goodwill when dealing with complaints.

25. Business correspondence which provides the required information often requires a certain amount of **preparation**, for example reference to previous correspondence or consultation with other departments in the organisation. It is also important that in-coming correspondence should be dealt with promptly and efficiently.

26. Most organisations use headed paper for correspondence. Although the actual layout and style varies considerably, most will include certain basic information laid out in the corporate style to give a good and consistent impression of the organisation.

27.   **Example of a Business Letter**

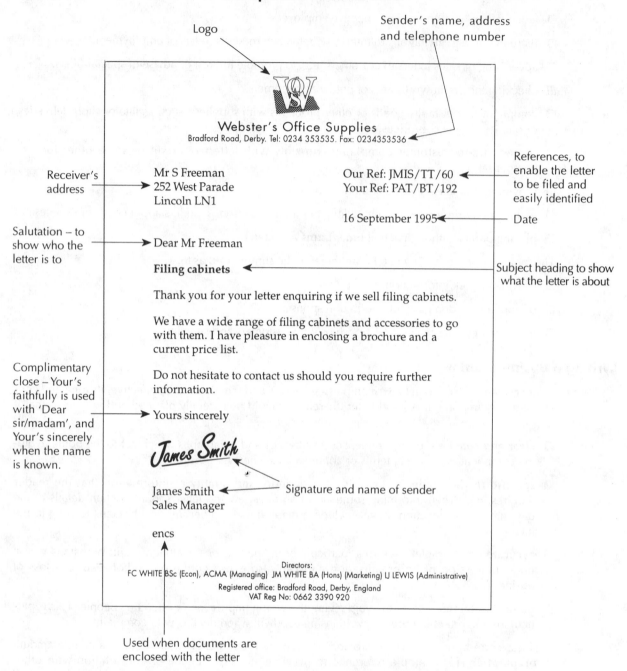

Logo

Sender's name, address and telephone number

Webster's Office Supplies
Bradford Road, Derby. Tel: 0234 353535. Fax: 0234353536

Receiver's address

Mr S Freeman
252 West Parade
Lincoln LN1

Our Ref: JMIS/TT/60
Your Ref: PAT/BT/192

References, to enable the letter to be filed and easily identified

16 September 1995

Date

Salutation – to show who the letter is to

Dear Mr Freeman

Filing cabinets

Subject heading to show what the letter is about

Thank you for your letter enquiring if we sell filing cabinets.

We have a wide range of filing cabinets and accessories to go with them. I have pleasure in enclosing a brochure and a current price list.

Do not hesitate to contact us should you require further information.

Complimentary close – Your's faithfully is used with 'Dear sir/madam', and Your's sincerely when the name is known.

Yours sincerely

James Smith

James Smith
Sales Manager

Signature and name of sender

encs

Directors:
FC WHITE BSc (Econ), ACMA (Managing) JM WHITE BA (Hons) (Marketing) LJ LEWIS (Administrative)
Registered office: Bradford Road, Derby, England
VAT Reg No: 0662 3390 920

Used when documents are enclosed with the letter

28.   Most business correspondence nowadays is typed on A4 size paper in a fully blocked, open punctuated style, as shown in the example. This means that there are no indentations – all typing, even headings, starts on the left-hand side – and there are no punctuation marks at the end of short, free-standing lines.

A letter of complaint

7 Greenmount Crescent
Harperley
Notts NG2 1YT

PLD Ltd
Albert Dock
Liverpool
L60 2AY

17/1/95

Dear Sirs

Re: Comfort Shoes R5267

I am writing to express my continuing concern about an order which was placed with you in July using my Visa card.

Having waited for over seven weeks for delivery of the shoes (you promised 28 days) I was obliged to buy elsewhere as they were needed for my holidays. I wrote to you accordingly on 10 September. Two weeks later the goods arrived — my letter ignored.

I wrote to you again on 1 November requesting a refund and reply paid label to return the goods. This letter was also ignored and I am now extremely annoyed about the matter.

I feel that I have given the company every opportunity to sort out the problem and therefore, unless I hear from you within 14 days I will have no alternative but to seek redress from the credit card company.

Yours faithfully

Mr J Smith
MR J SMITH

Task 6   **2.3.2 (C3.2, C3.4)**

1. Outline what action you could take in respect of the letter of complaint on page 169 which has been passed to you for attention.

2. Draft a reply on the assumption that the contents of the letter are accurate and the customer was fully justified in feeling annoyed.

29. Many business letters are, of course, routine or standard and therefore are often preprinted in order to save time and money. With the increasing use of **word processors** most standard letters can be stored on disk with names, addresses and any other details inserted as appropriate, giving the impression of a 'personal' letter. Some examples of this type of correspondence are quotations sent by insurance companies, banks promoting their services, *Which* and *Readers' Digest* offers and prize draws, acknowledgments of orders and requests/reminders for payment.

Task 7   **2.3.2 (C3.2, C3.3, C3.4)**

1. Collect at least three examples of standard letters, relevant to yourself, which are used in the place where you work or study, or which you have received at home.

2. Comment on each letter in relation to the factors in paragraph 24. Present your findings in the form of a table.

3   Now prepare a standard letter yourself which could be used by a local school or college to explain and promote, to parents, students or employers, the key features of GNVQ Advanced Business Studies.

Postal Services

30. Postal Services in the UK are provided by the Post Office which is a Public Corporation owned and controlled by the Government. Every working day it delivers over 50 million letters and 600,000 parcels.

31. Letter services include first and second class post, recorded delivery, registered post, freepost and the business reply service, whilst Overseas mail can be sent by ordinary post, Airmail or Swiftair if faster delivery is needed. A similar range of options are offered for parcel deliveries. Up-to-date information about all services can be found in the Post Office Guide which is published annually.

Telecommunications

32. The main telecommunications services which are summarised below are run in the UK by British Telecom (BT) which was government owned until 1986. It has now been privatised and operates in the private sector as a public limited company. In the 1990's, Mercury, run by Cable and Wireless plc, has developed as a competitor to BT. Another competitor, Ionica, is launching a service aimed at residential and small business customers in 1995, using low cost radio technology instead of expensive cabling.

33. When BT was privatised, the **Office of Telecommunications (OFTEL)** was set up. OFTEL is an independent body which monitors and regulates BT's prices, the services provided and gives advice and assistance to telecommunication users.

Telephones

34. The telephone is the main method of communication used by businesses today because it is very quick and relatively inexpensive. The cheapest time for calls is between 6.00pm and 8.00am and at weekends. Anyone who has a telephone is called a subscriber and they are able to make use of a wide variety of services offered by BT and Mercury. The Freephone facility for example, is used by many firms whereby they pay for the cost of calls made by customers, whilst **mobile radio phones**,

which enable calls to be made from anywhere in the UK, including cars and other vehicles are also increasingly being used in business.

Telephone Answering

35. The use of the telephone is now so important that many business organisations have a clear policy on how they expect calls to be answered. In addition they often set standards in terms of, for example, how long they expect phones to ring (e.g. six times) before being answered and, if the person required is not available at the time of the call, the return call time (e.g. within 24 hours).

36. A typical **answering policy** might be:

   ❑ always answer promptly.

   ❑ greet the caller with 'Good morning' or 'Good afternoon' as appropriate, and give the company name.

   ❑ be polite and courteous, saying 'How can I help you?' – remember that your tone of voice is a form of body language.

   ❑ speak clearly.

   ❑ try to deal with calls quickly, or pass them on to someone else if necessary/appropriate.

   ❑ keep a pen handy, and a company telephone message pad on which to record details if necessary.

Telephone Calls

37. Making telephone calls is, of course, also essential in business, and it is important that they are handled efficiently in order to be both effective and to keep the cost of the calls to a minimum.

38. Some things which will help to keep costs down and efficiency high are:

   ❑ preparing what you are going to say before you make a call.

   ❑ having all necessary information to hand.

   ❑ knowing who you need to speak to.

   ❑ speaking clearly and concisely.

   ❑ being prepared to leave a message if necessary.

Task 8   2.3.1, 2.3.3 (3.4)

You have recently started work in the offices of Software Products plc. During your first few weeks training you are asked to complete a number of tasks, including the following:

It is 0915 and you have just answered the telephone. 'Hello, my name is Tom Smith of Richard Ellis Computers Ltd. I would like to speak to Mr Whelan your Sales Director.'

You explain to the caller that Mr Whelan is out of the office at the moment, so he asks you to take a message. The following passage records the rest of the conversation:

'I had arranged to see him on Friday next. I was going to talk about the possibility of running a joint stand at the NEC Exhibition in five months time. I can still keep the appointment, but if it was delayed until next week I could show him our new model. I am away on business for the rest of the week, but will be in contact with the office for any messages. Could he let me know if it is convenient to change the date? At the moment I am free most of the following week. Perhaps he could ring my secretary on Derby 60791? If he wants to speak to me personally, my home number is 0161-797-6821, but I am not usually in before 6.30pm. Thank you.'

1   Underline or make a list of all the important details of the conversation.

2. Leave a message for Mr Whelan using the company's standard telephone message pad shown below

171

Telephone Message Pad

TO _____

DATE _____ TIME _____

WHILE YOU WERE OUT

M _____

OF _____

PHONE NO. _____

TELEPHONED ☐   PLEASE CALL BACK ☐

CALLED TO SEE YOU ☐   WILL CALL AGAIN ☐

MESSAGE _____

_____

_____

_____

_____

_____

_____

Other Telecommunication Services

39. There are a wide range of other important telecommunication services which you should be aware of, including telex, telemessages, electronic mail, voice messaging, fax, tele and video conferencing, teletext, prestel and datel.

40. **Telex**. This service uses a special teleprinter machine which can send and receive messages from similar machines in the UK and throughout the world. Providing the machine is switched on it will automatically receive messages at any time of the day or night. This is very useful when contacting businesses overseas where time differences exist, but is rapidly being replaced by fax.

41. The system is very similar to using the telephone except that the message is typed in and is then printed out at the other end. Each subscriber has a telex number and is issued with a UK Telex Directory. The cost of telex messages is based on the time it takes to transmit (send) the message and the distance involved.

42. **Telemessages**. These are accepted by telephone or telex and are delivered the next day by first class post. Telemessages replaced inland telegrams but **International telegrams** still exist. Again, these are becoming less important for businesses.

43. **Electronic mail**. This is an alternative to sending letters by post, which involves the use of computer terminals linked via the telephone network. Subscribers who have a password to enter the system are able to send messages to a 'mailbox' where they are stored until 'opened' by the recipient. BT's Telecom Gold is a well known example.

44. **Voice messaging**. Voicecom is BT's international voice messaging service. It provides a central number which can be dialled from anywhere in the world to leave and access messages. It is, in effect, a corporate communications network for smaller businesses and people on the move. Voicebank provides a message handling system which can be accessed from any telephone using a PIN number.

45. **Facsimile Transmission (FAX)**. A fax machine is rapidly becoming an essential piece of office equipment in business today.

   ❏ The Post Office's system for sending facsimile (exact) copies of letters, documents and other information is called **Intelpost**.

❏ British Telecom also has a facsimile service called **Bureaufax**. This enables firms with their own facsimile machine to send copies to other firms with similar machines either in the UK or overseas. The machines are linked by telephone and operate automatically once the contact is made. A **Freefax** service is available similar to Freephone.

46. **Tele and video conferencing**. This service links individuals or groups of people in different places by sound and vision. This can be quicker and cheaper than trying to get a group of people together. For example, sales staff throughout the country can be linked in this way for a conference thus saving travelling costs and hotel bills. Contravision links can now be made, via satellites, to many countries throughout the world. **Voice conferencing** can be used to link people by telephone only.

47. **An advertisement by the American company AT&T illustrating the use of contravision.**

Task 9   **2.3.5 (C3.4)**

OFFICES RUSH FOR FACSIMILE MACHINES AND MOBILE PHONES

More small companies are joining the communications revolution. About one in three now have facsimile machines, while 22% are equipped with mobile telephones, 13% have telex facilities and 11% have pagers. The new figures emerge from a recent small business survey which also underlines growing worries about high interest rates. The report says the biggest expansion in business telecommunications over the next year will be in facsimile. Only 3% of companies have electronic mail links and 5% on-line database services.

1. Briefly explain the following terms in the above article: 'communications revolution', 'telex', 'pagers', 'electronic mail', 'on-line database services'.

2. Discuss the potential for the use of new communication technology in small businesses.

3. What significance if any do the 'growing worries about high interest rates' have on small firms?

48. **Teletext** is used to describe any computerised information displayed on a television screen which is broadcast by a TV company. It includes Ceefax the teletex system provided by the BBC and Teletext (formerly Oracle) on the ITV channels. Over 4000 pages of information are available on what in effect is a very comprehensive electronic newspaper. Where telephone lines are used to transmit data it is called Viewdata, examples of which are British Telecom's Prestel and Datel Services.

49. **Prestel**. This is a computerised system which provides a database of both general and business information on a wide variety of topics, for example share prices, financial statistics and sports results. To use the system a specially adapted television set is needed which is connected to a telephone line linked to the Prestel computer.

    Prestel is what is referred to as an interactive or two-way system because as well as receiving information, users can also send messages both to each other and to information providers. The system can be used to order goods from a supermarket, book a holiday or hotel room or reserve a theatre seat.

50. **Datel**. This telecommunication service operates using the telephone lines and can link a computer in one place with computers in other parts of the country and in many overseas countries.

    This service is particularly useful, for example, where a firm has a number of branches but needs to process orders centrally. It can have its main computer at Head Office with links in each branch.

Task 10   **2.3.3 (C3.4)**

BT GOES GLOBAL

British Telecom is poised to launch a £500m worldwide telecommunications service for multinational companies. BT intends to build a network of computerised exchanges in major cities around the world dedicated to handling voice, data and video transmission services for large corporations. The first four will be installed in London, New York, Frankfurt and Sydney by the mid 1990's with 32 others in operation by 2002. The attraction for corporate customers would be cheaper bills. The new service could reduce existing charges by between 5% and 15%. BT is keen to get under way in the US before its rivals secure a foothold. There, the telecommunications market is worth more than $1bn a year. US analysts are understood to be impressed with BT's determination to press ahead with the network. One said: 'It is taking the most aggressive step towards becoming a global carrier. A UK analyst said: 'It seems a logical expansion for the company. BT wants to be a world player and this looks a way of doing that and generating more profits.'

---

1. From the article, identify the main reasons why BT is launching a worldwide telecommunications service.

2. Why is the service targeted at multinational companies?

3. How and why is the service being well received by analysts?

Internal Communication Equipment

51. We have already mentioned a range of typical equipment used in business today including the telephone, telex and fax. Other equipment in general use is summarised below.

    ☐ **Telephone Switchboard**. Most businesses have a telephone switchboard which, depending on the size of the firm, can vary from one main line with use of a few extensions to hundreds of lines and thousands of extensions.

    ☐ **Telephone Answering Machines**. These make it possible to leave messages for people when they are out. A tape recorder is attached to the telephone receiver which automatically switches itself on to receive incoming calls. This enables messages of all kinds to be left after business hours.

    ☐ **Intercom**. In addition to telephone extensions, many firms also use an intercom system. This is a small microphone and loudspeaker which enables two or more people to speak to each other.

For example, a manager may communicate with his secretary in this way or with staff in other offices or departments.

❏ **Paging**. The use of a pager enables businessmen to be contacted when they are out of the office. The pager bleeps to indicate when people are required who then go to the nearest telephone to take the call.

❏ **Public Address Systems (Tannoy)**. This is a loudspeaker system which is often used for calling people or playing music in factories and warehouses. They are also used at football matches and other sporting events.

Task 11   **2.3.3 (C3.2, C3.4)**

John Smith, a small local printer is considering various ways of developing his business. A friend has suggested that he should take a close look at the range of modern telecommunications services available which he says can be very profitable if used correctly. John obviously has a telephone but he is not keen on what he calls all this new complicated equipment.

1. From your own knowledge and with the help of a local Yellow Pages and Thomson Telephone Directory, suggest at least 6 services which might be of use to John in his business, giving reasons for your choice.

2. Is John right to consider any of the services suggested as being 'complicated'?

3. Compare a Yellow Pages and Thomson Directory. List the main features of each and state, with reasons, whether or not you feel that John should advertise in either or both of these publications.

Special Needs Communications

52. Some people may have problems which require special attention when it comes to communications. These could include people who are physically or mentally handicapped, the blind or partially sighted and those with hearing difficulties. It is important therefore to realise that specific methods of communication can be used to assist them. Examples include braille, sign language, audio-visual aids, minicom, typetalk and electronic voice.

53. **Braille**. This is a system of reading by touch using raised dots to create text. It is used by the blind all over the world. In the UK there are over 70 braille periodicals published.

54. **Sign Language**. This can be any means of communication using bodily movements, particularly the hands and arms, which is used wherever a language problem exists. For example, where someone is deaf or where a foreign language is involved which neither party understands. British Sign Language in its own right uses hand shapes, position and movement to create words. In the UK over 60,000 people use it as a first language instead of speech. To help them further many hearing impaired people also learn to lip read.

55. **Audio-visual aids**. It may be important to use a variety of both audio and visual methods when communicating. For example, written materials are of limited use to the partially sighted who need to be told what information they contain. Whilst, on the other hand, hearing impaired people need to see information written down. Television is an audio-visual media which increasingly is using sub-titles for this purpose. There are also a number of specific audio-visual aids which have been developed. Three examples of which are given below.

55. **Minicom** is a phone service which links the deaf via a special machine which sends and receives messages which are shown on a small visual display panel.

56. **Typetalk** is a phone service developed by BT and the Royal National Institute for the Deaf which allows deaf people to send typed or spoken messages. Specially trained operators (who can read British Sign Language) read the typed message to a hearing person as it is being typed in and then types the response back as it is being spoken.

57. **Electronic Voice**. This enables people with sight difficulties to access information using a computer linked to a voice synthesiser.

> ### Task 13   **2.3.1, 2.3.5 (C3.2)**
>
> Write a brief report on the special needs communication in the place where you work or study. Comment on how you feel it could be improved.

Barriers to Effective Communication

58. No matter how good the communication system in an organisation is, unfortunately barriers can and do often occur. This may be caused by a number of factors which can usually be summarised as being due to physical barriers, system design faults or attitudinal barriers.

59. **Physical barriers** are often due to the nature of the environment. Thus, for example, the natural barrier which exists, if staff are located in different buildings or on different sites. Likewise, poor or outdated equipment, particularly the failure of management to introduce new technology, may also cause problems. Staff shortages are another factor which frequently causes communication difficulties for an organisation. Whilst distractions like background noise, poor lighting or an environment which is too hot or cold can all affect people's morale and concentration, which in turn interfere with effective communication.

60. **System design faults** refer to problems with the structures or systems in place in an organisation. Examples might include an organisational structure which is unclear and therefore makes it confusing to know who to communicate with. Other examples could be inefficient or inappropriate information systems, a lack of supervision or training, and a lack of clarity in roles and responsibilities which can lead to staff being uncertain about what is expected of them.

61. **Attitudinal barriers** come about as a result of problems with staff in an organisation. These may be brought about, for example, by such factors as poor management, lack of consultation with employees, personality conflicts which can result in people delaying or refusing to communicate, the personal attitudes of individual employees which may be due to lack of motivation or dissatisfaction at work, brought about by insufficient training to enable them to carry out particular tasks, or just resistance to change due to entrenched attitudes and ideas.

62. Other common barriers to effective communication include:

    ❏ **psychological factors** such as people's state of mind. We all tend to feel happier and more receptive to information when the sun shines. Equally, if someone has personal problems like worries about their health or marriage, then this will probably affect them.

    ❏ **different languages and cultures** represent a national barrier which is particularly important for organisations involved in overseas business.

    ❏ **individual linguistic ability** is also important. The use of difficult or inappropriate words in communication can prevent people from understanding the message.

    ❏ **poorly explained or misunderstood messages** can also result in confusion. We can all think of situations where we have listened to something explained which we just could not grasp.

    ❏ **physiological barriers** may result from individuals' personal discomfort, caused, for example, by ill health, poor eye sight or hearing difficulties.

    ❏ **presentation of information** is also important to aid understanding as you will see in Element 3.2.

    ❏ **jumping to conclusions**. Sometimes people interpret communication as they expect or want it to be, and refuse to accept the actual message.

Task 12   2.3.3, 2.3.5 (C3.4)

1. Identify the main barriers to communication in your place of work or study.

2. Consider the type of problems which they cause and whether or not you feel they can be easily solved with minimum expenditure.

3. Read the following article and

    a) identify, with examples, some potential barriers to communication; and

    b) state what action you would advise a company to take to overcome these barriers.

WHAT'S IN A NAME?

A British household name can be an unknown quantity across the Channel; equally, would you buy an insurance policy from Munchener Lebensversicherung and what would German consumers make of the National Westminster Bank? As Europe opens its doors for business these questions become increasingly important.

For the consumer, a yet wider choice of broadly similar products is a daunting prospect and very often, selection is based on our perception of the organisation. For companies with a strong corporate identity, such as Body Shop or BMW, the company name is an essential part of this identity. However, many names which are strong and memorable in the home market may actually mislead, confuse or even alienate foreign audiences.

For example, a corporate name which is unique and distinctive in a national market may already be in use in another European country. Société Génerale, for instance, is Belgium's largest conglomerate. But how is the perception of its business affected by the French bank of exactly the same name? The situation is further confused by the Swiss Société Génerale and the Italian organisation Generali.

Initials

Using initials rather than names may seem like a good way to overcome some of the problems. Customers may, however, find meaningless letters equally confusing. Although a few notable exceptions like IBM, BMW and ICI have made a success of initials, this has been achieved only through heavy exposure over a very lengthy period.

It is difficult and expensive to build awareness for fabricated company names such as Matra or Cegelec as neither have any obvious meaning. By contrast, real words, or combinations of real words such as Eurotunnel and Aerospatiale, give a clear impression of the organisation's business activities.

The ideal name

The most effective European names are those which are easy to spell and pronounce and give an immediate impression of what the company does. Some companies have recognised and addressed the problem. Turkey's leading corporate bank was called Uluslararasi Interbank; with the pan-European audience in mind, it has rationalised its name to Interbank.

The new name has many of the features of the 'ideal', corporate name for a pan-European company. It is short, unique, memorable, free of national associations and pronounceable in all major European languages.

Reproduced from DTI's quality publication 'Single Market News', Autumn 1992.

Electronic Technology

63. Virtually every day new communications technology is being developed. The remarkable thing is just how rapidly it is being used in business organisations. **Word processing, E-mail, fax, DTP** and **computerised graphics** are as common today as the electronic typewriters and dictation machines were 20 years ago.

64. **Voice-messaging, tele and video conferencing** are also growing rapidly whilst developments in **digital** and **satellite** connections are continuing to improve the speed and clarity of communications throughout the world. Already most computers are relatively easy to use with **icons** (pictures) and a **mouse** but further advances in technology will eventually lead to even simpler **'touch screens'** with **'voice operated'** computers almost certain to replace key boards in the foreseeable future.

65. Voice operated systems already exist and are being used in Japan although they are by no means perfect yet. Also, computers exist which can **import** typed or printed images (e.g. graphics) or data by scanning them into a document reducing the need to key it in. In time computers will also be able to read hand-written information presented in a particular format.

66. Other major developments which are beginning to have a significant impact on business organisations involve networking and the growth of **Electronic Data Interchange (EDI)** discussed below and the **Internet** and **Superhighway** which are covered in Element 2.4.

67. EDI is an emerging technology which is growing rapidly throughout the world. EDI is just one component of electronic messaging which uses computer networks instead of paper based administration systems to communicate between businesses. The big users currently tend to be in the financial services, retail, distribution and computer manufacturing.

68. Initially EDI was often restricted to the use of E-mail to exchange orders, invoices and statements but ultimately it will be fully integrated into the IT systems of organisations world wide offering direct access for users. They will be able to access catalogues, select products, check stock levels, place orders and complete the whole transaction via computer including payment.

69. The following examples help to illustrate its likely future impact

   ❑ IBM wants 100% EDI for purchasing in Europe by 1997.

   ❑ Eagle Star, one of the UK's biggest insurance companies, has installed an EDI gateway as part of a new broker network.

   ❑ the European EDI market is predicted to grow 4-fold by the year 2000 driven initially by large companies.

   ❑ the 68 strong Local Authorities South East Region (LASER) consortium which spends over £ 50m annually on energy services has made EDI a mandatory requirement for its suppliers. Around 60% of LASER's estimated 80,000 energy bills involve EDI.

   ❑ Ford Motors has joined the Worldwide Integrated Purchasing System (WIPS) which by 1997 will handle all its purchasing activities worth nearly £ 25bn annually. WIPS has already been implemented in the United States where some 250 parts buyers are on the system.

70. Some of the **benefits** of EDI include

   ❑ quicker communication with and response to suppliers and customers

   ❑ improved cash flow and working capital – invoices delivered just one day earlier can have major effects on these

   ❑ reduced costs of buying products

   ❑ reduced manufacturing cycle times

   ❑ reduced stock levels

   ❑ a reduction in traditional business post

   ❑ increased productivity and profitability

   ❑ competitive edge.

71. Despite these benefits there is still a general lack of willingness among users to take up financial EDI. The reasons for this include

   ❑ not all banks offer EDI although they do all have electronic funds transfer (see EFTPOS Element 6.2)

   ❑ concerns about legal problems, audit and security of payments

   ❑ excessive bank charges for each transaction

   ❑ insufficient networking between banks and/or commercial EDI networks

   ❑ lack of awareness of the benefits.

Task 14　　　　　　　　　　　**2.3.1, 2.3.4, 6.2.4 (C3.2, C3.4)**

THE ELECTRONIC MARKET

At a conference in 1995 the speakers agreed that EDI is certain to be the way forward for business transactions. They also warned the public sector that if it does not quickly adopt this change it will fall too far behind to ever be able to compete with the private sector and will find it increasingly difficult to do business with organisations that do use it.

The EDI Association estimates that that, in 10 years, public-sector organisations will have about 200 EDI users in their day-to-day business contacts. Savings from introducing EDI to an organisation are estimated to be a minimum of five to 10 per cent. EDI systems also increase efficiency. A single transaction, from start to finish, is estimated to cost 14 or 15 pence, which includes wages, software and labour. It is also much faster to use EDI than it is to complete a task manually. Another benefit is reduced error levels as re-keying data is not necessary.

The cost of setting up an EDI system is between £2,000 and £4,000 which includes purchasing software and necessary peripherals, installation and staff training.

However, all speakers also stressed the importance of a detailed and thorough pilot system and involving suppliers at every stage during implementation.

The following questions are based on the article above plus the information in paragraphs 67–71.

1. Why is EDI considered to be the way forward for business transactions?

2. What are the implications for the public sector if it does not adopt ED1?

3. Why do some speakers stress the importance of a pilot system involving suppliers.

4. Why are some organisations unwilling to take up EDI?

72.

A Summary of the Main Methods of Business Communication

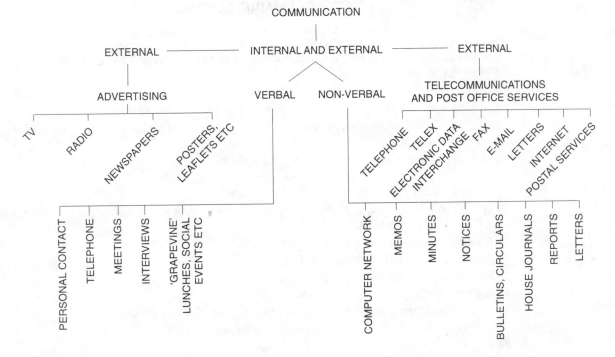

Effective Communication

73. In a modern business environment communication involves a large number of different channels most of which are increasingly likely to be technology based. Future information will be 'on-line' as information technology becomes an integral part of any business function. Effective communication therefore will depend upon a number of key factors which help to overcome the barriers identified in paragraphs 58-62. These factors discussed below include access, ease of use, user efficiency, interaction between people and organisations and control.

74. **Access** to information, particularly where it may be sensitive. User identification and passwords are commonly used which only give access to certain parts of a computer memory.

75. **Ease of use**. Is the system user friendly, that is, can anyone use it easily with some training, or does it depend very much upon the skill of the user.

76. **Efficiency of user**. In Element 2.4 we consider the effects of new technology on individuals in organisations. For example, it can cause stress if information cannot be easily recessed or is 'lost' instead of stored, whilst VDU's may be harmful to health. For skilled operators, however, it can lead to increased productivity and greater job satisfaction.

77. **Interaction between people**. Within an organisation this could be affected by factors such as the internal post, telephone or messenger systems, frequency of meetings and availability of notice-boards. Where technology is involved it will also depend on effective networking and the back-up system in case things go wrong.

78. **Interaction between organisations**. With the growth of E-mail, the Internet, and EDI networks this interaction will increasingly become more streamlined and efficient. Some traditional interaction such as telephone calls and personal meetings may still be needed but likely to decrease in importance.

79. **Controlling Communication**. In paragraph 9 we mentioned open and restricted channels of communication. Restrictions are needed both to make communications relevant to the receiver and also to control the **confidentiality and security** of information. This control is needed whether it is an internal or external network. EDI, for example, uses encoded data which can only be decoded by specific recognised formats to provide this control.

Task 15   **2.3.1, 2.3.3 (C3.2, C3.4)**

EFFECTIVE COMMUNICATION

The best choice of medium for any particular message will depend upon a number of factors, including the urgency; accuracy; security; who is to receive it; its length, complexity and confidentiality; the potential cost of sending it and whether or not a permanent record is required.

---

1. Discuss the view that effective communication is the key element in a successful business.
2. Suggest three possible methods of communication which could be appropriate in each of the following situations and
3. Decide on the best medium for each, giving reasons for your choice.

a) To invite a job applicant for an interview.
b) To give an official warning to an employee for persistent lateness.
c) To arrange an urgent internal meeting.
d) To organise the annual staff dinner/dance.
e) To present complicated statistical data to the Board of Directors.
f) To inform the staff that the hours of work are to be altered.
g) To confirm an offer of a job to a new employee.
h) To provide the Managing Director with technical details of a new product.
i) To respond to a letter of complaint from a potential new customer.
j) To request information from a potential new supplier.

Changes to Communication

80. The **positive effects** of changes to communication include:

☐ **Improved speed**. Information on virtually any aspect of an organisation can be sorted, analysed and retrieved almost instantly. Whilst externally, information can be sent to or received from thousands of organisations, just about anywhere in the world, in a matter of minutes.

☐ **Improved access**. Not only can information be obtained quickly but because vast amounts of data are stored on computer this provides easy access to a wealth of detail not readily available previously.

☐ **Potential to reach a wider audience** particularly through networks such as the Internet or satellite communication which operate worldwide.

81. The **negative effects** of changes to communications on the other hand, could include:

☐ **Incompatible equipment**. One of the biggest problems of information technology is the incompatibility of different manufacturers products, both hardware and software. (See Open Systems Element 2.4)

☐ **Cost**. Although improving communications is an investment in the future of an organisation nonetheless it can involve substantial initial and ongoing (updating and maintenance) hardware and software costs in order to retain a competitive edge.

☐ **Exclusion from communication**. The restricted access to some parts of the communication systems can result in a divided organisation where some people are in the 'know' whilst others are not.

☐ **Threat to security**. One of the main reasons given by many organisations not yet on the Internet or using EDI is concern about security. Just as access to information may be restricted and controlled internally to maintain confidentiality and reduce the risks of unauthorised persons using it, this becomes even more vital when external organisations are involved.

Task 16   **2.3.4, 2.3.5 (C3.2, C3.4)**

1. Reply, in detail, to the following memo from the Office Manager of a small manufacturing company

---

MEMO

To: R. Chapman   Date: 19/11/9-
From: J. Brown   Subject: Telecommunications

I have recently been reading an article on telecommunications which seemed to contain a lot of 'jargon'. Can you please find out the meaning of the following terms, and the potential benefits and drawbacks to the company.

E-mail, video conferencing, viewdata systems and facsimile transmission.

Do you think we should give serious consideration to introducing or using any of them?

---

2. It has been said that 'Information Technology is an integral part of business today, but frequently it fails to achieve the expected results'.

Explain what you understand by this statement and what a firm faced with this situation could do to improve matters.

Summary

82. a) Communication may be verbal, non-verbal, formal or informal, open or restricted and may take place inside an organisation (internal) or between organisations (external).

b) Effective communication is essential if a firm is to be successful. Staff need clear instructions whilst customers and other business contacts require a flow of information.

c) The main verbal (spoken) methods of communication are personal contact with people either face to face, in interviews, in meetings or by telephone. The 'grapevine', working lunches and social events are others.

d) The main non-verbal (written) methods of communication include memos, minutes, notices, staff bulletins, house journals and reports. Visual communication includes the use of charts and diagrams.

e) Letters are not usually sent within an organisation but are the main method of external communication. The telephone, other telecommunications and postal services are also important, as are the various forms of advertising and sales promotion.

f) The telephone is the main method of telecommunication. Other services include telex, telemessages, electronic mail, voice messaging, FAX and contravision.

g) To improve the efficient and effective use of the telephone, many organisations have policies on both answering and making calls.

h) Teletex is provided by Ceefax and Teletex whilst Prestel and Datel are other forms of viewdata.

i) Other internal communication equipment includes telephone switchboards and answering machines, intercoms, paging and public address systems.

j) Special needs communication may involve the use of braille, sign language, audio-visual aids or electronic voice as appropriate.

k) Physical barriers, attitudinal barriers and system design faults can all lead to breakdowns in communications.

l) The future of communication lies in electronic technology which already includes word processing, E-mail, FAX, DTP and computerised graphics as the norm.

m) In the near future EDI and the Internet are likely to have a major impact on communication between businesses.

n) To be effective technology based communication requires consideration of issues of access, ease of use, interaction between people and organisation and control.

o) Changes to communication can improve speed, access and the potential to reach a wider audience.

p) Associated problems could include incompatible equipment, cost, exclusion from communication and threats to security.

Review questions *(Answers can be found in the paragraphs indicated)*

1. Briefly define 'communication'. (3)

2. Explain the need for effective communication in business. (6–7)

3. List the main verbal and non-verbal methods of internal communication. (5,10–19)

4. What information is given in an Agenda and why are minutes taken in a meeting? (11,13,15–16)

5. Give two examples of visual means of communication. (19)

6. List four main methods of external business communication. (20–30)

7. Identify at least six situations where a business might need to send a letter. (22–23)

8. How can a business letter be made more effective? (24–29)

9. What could a firm do to improve its telephone communications? (34–38)

10. Briefly describe three other forms of telecommunication. (39–47)

11. Briefly describe why a facsimile transmission service is important in business. (45)

12. How might contravision help an international company? (46–47)

13. What are Ceefax and Teletext examples of? (49)

14. Explain why Prestel is described as 'inter-active'. (49)

15. How can a telephone answering machine assist a business? (51)

16. Identify some special needs communication problems and how they might be reduced or overcome. (52–57)

17. Outline the main barriers to communication in an organisation. (58–62)

18. In what sense is electronic technology dominating communications in business organisations and how is it likely to develop in the future? (63–71)

19. What factors need to be considered if technology based communication is to be effective in an organisation? (73–79)

20. In what sense could changes in communication be considered as both a good and a bad thing in organisations? (80–81)

Assignment – Communication in Business   *Element 2.3*

You are asked to prepare a report which

1. Investigates at least 2 examples of internal and 2 examples of external communication in a business organisation of your choice.

2. Explain how the business organisation uses its communications to achieve its objectives.

3. Analyse at least one internal and one external electronic method of communication for its effectiveness in enabling access to information and interaction between people.

4. Includes 2 proposals for changes to communications in the businesses organisation, justified in terms of their possible beneficial effects on the organisation.

5. Includes notes which explain at least 2 positive and 2 negative effects of change to communications in the business organisation.

---

8 Information Processing

This Chapter looks at the information processing systems in organisations, including the increasing impact of new technology on the collections, storage and use of data. It covers:

❏ Purposes of Information Processing

❏ Advantages of Information Technology

❏ Applications of Information Processing

❏ Use of Business Systems

❏ Office Technology

❏ Multi-media

❏ Analysing Information Processing Systems

❏ Data Protection Act

❏ Effects of the Data Protection Act

❏ Impact of IT on Business

❏ Organisational Benefits from IT

❏ Effects of IT on Individuals

❏ Future Developments

❏ Non-standardised Systems

Information Processing

1. We saw in Element 2.2, Chapter 6 that administration is concerned with the flow of information, whilst communication is about transmitting information and data, whether written, spoken, printed or electronic. Sound administration and effective communication are essential in order to provide the information necessary for managers to make decisions, to assist them in planning, monitoring and controlling, in order that the organisation can achieve its objectives.

2. In order for the information collected to be used, however, it has to be sorted and analysed and put into a form that is meaningful to those who need it. This is known as information processing, and is increasingly being carried out with the use of computerised systems, that is, information Technology (IT).

    The basic elements of information processing can be summarised as:

communicating	calculating	researching
copying	summarising	storing (filing)
retrieving	classifying	comparing
sorting	checking	analysing

3. Once information has been processed to be of value, it must be distributed and used. Examples of uses of information might include:

    ❏ recent sales figures used to enable the Sales Manager to compare the actual sales against the forecast sales.

    ❏ financial data used to enable the Accounts Department to prepare invoices and statements.

    ❏ cost and output data used to enable the Production Department to assess its performance.

    ❏ details of hours worked used to enable the Personnel Department to prepare data for the payroll.

    ❏ advertising and promotional expenditure data used to enable the Marketing Department to plan and control its budget.

4. **The purposes of information processing**

In the table below some traditional methods of information processing are compared with modern electronic computerised methods.

Information processing function	Traditional method(s)	Electronic processing
Receiving and distributing	Internal and external post; telephone	Computer terminals in departmental and branch locations transmit internal information to a central computer. Examples: banks, building societies, retail outlets, hotels and restaurants. Facsimile transmissions.
Sorting	Clerical operation	Coded information can be sorted by computer at considerable speed and with accuracy.
Analysing (to assist in decision making)	Analysing is often done by managers and technical experts and can be laborious and time-consuming	Computers can perform standard statistical analyses at high speed, and with great accuracy. Examples: financial ratios, budget variances, orders received, sales records. Forecasting is possible with variables quickly changed to produce 'what if' scenarios.
Filing (storage)	Filing by hand into filing cabinets and card-index trays	The memory in a computer can store large amounts of information, or it can be stored on small 'floppy' disks or magnetic tape cassettes
Retrieving	Clerical operation subject to human error	Information is readily available in visual (i.e. on a computer screen) or printed form, although print is only used when necessary. Examples: stock levels, daily sales, cross references, accounts overdue.
Communicating	Labour intensive operation often done by secretaries and typists	Electronic mail and work processing mean that communication with 'first rate copy' is available. Examples: invoices, letters to customers and suppliers, internal memos.

Task 1   2.4.1 (C3.3)

Draw up a similar chart to that shown in 4 above to indicate how, in the place where you work or study, each of the above information processing functions is carried out.

The Advantages of Information Technology

5.   These can be summarised as follows:

❑   **Speed**. Information on almost any aspect of an organisation's system can be sorted, analysed and retrieved almost instantly. Complex calculations can be carried out quickly and accurately.

❑   **Accuracy**. Employees' mistakes are the main cause of errors in information handling. There is far less human involvement in electronic information-processing, and consequently errors are reduced. For example, in word processing, standard letters need only be typed once and then stored for future usage, and spell checks can be used to correct errors before documents are printed out.

❐ **Reliability**. Micro-electronic equipment is more reliable than humans and mechanical equipment. People at work become tired and distracted and often make mistakes, while mechanical equipment has many moving parts, any one of which can fail or become damaged, causing the machine to break down.

❐ **Flexibility**. Electronic information processing means that the analysis of information is both accurate and sophisticated. Microprocessors can be programmed to perform many operations which would have previously been too complicated or too time consuming to do manually. For example, decision-making techniques such as operational research, investment appraisal and network analysis can all be carried out by computer programs.

❐ **Improved quality**. The presentation of the finished copy of written communication is greatly improved by word processing, desk top publishing and laser printing. In addition, the content can be improved, for example financial and other statistical information can be easily updated in reports, and information thus becomes less historical and therefore more useful.

Storage and Retrieval of Information

6. All businesses need a system whereby records, letters, documents and other information can be filed or stored. It is important for good communication that this data is kept clean and safe and can be quickly and easily retrieved when required. However, there is no one correct method of filing and consequently each firm must set up a system most suited to its own needs. Traditionally, **manual systems** with various types of filing cabinets have been used, but nowadays an increasing number of organisations use computerised systems.

7. Many firms need a lot of space for filing and this problem is reduced by **microfilming**, which involves taking miniature photographs of data. A special 'microfiche' viewer or reader is then used which enlarges the film so that it can be read easily. An example of the use of microfilm or microfiche can probably be seen in your local library which may store book lists or telephone directories in this way. **Optical disk systems** may also be used which can store vast amounts of data on a 'compact' disc.

Applications of Information Processing

8. Software programs can be linked together to create packages which can handle a range of needs. Typical business uses include databases, spreadsheets, desk top publishing, accounting and personnel packages.

❐ **Databases** are a store of information which has been inputted into a computer so that it is ready to be processed and made available as required. They may be used for a wide variety of purposes and store vast amounts of data, e.g. names, addresses, receipts, payments and other records.

❐ **Spreadsheets**. provide a matrix on which calculations can be performed. They show data in an easy to read format and can be used to answer 'what if' questions. Changes can be made to the data and the overall effects can be seen on the spreadsheet. This type of package is often used for budgeting, forecasting, project management, production planning, statistical analysis of data such as market research and financial planning. Spreadsheets also offer graphics facilities such as pie and bar charts.

❐ **Desk Top Publishing** packages allow text, computer aided design and graphics to be merged together to produce high quality documents. This has revolutionised the publicity and promotional material produced by many organisations because it is now possible to produce them quickly, cheaply and to an excellent quality in-house.

❐ **Accountancy packages** are now available which can carry out a wide range of functions including book-keeping, invoicing, customer accounts, VAT, stock control, payroll and for producing final accounts.

❐ **Personnel packages** can be used to keep a variety of employee records, including training, sickness and absenteeism, holidays and pensions.

Examples of Spreadsheets

A Basic Spreadsheet Layout

	J	F	M	A	M	J	J	A	S	O	N	D	TOTAL
WAGES													
RENT													
ELECTRICITY													
GAS													
TOTAL													

This simple spreadsheet to illustrate a firm's expenditure could also be developed to include anticipated income. The impact of potential changes such as a rent or wage rise can be entered into the computer, which will automatically calculate the effect of the change on total costs and profits.

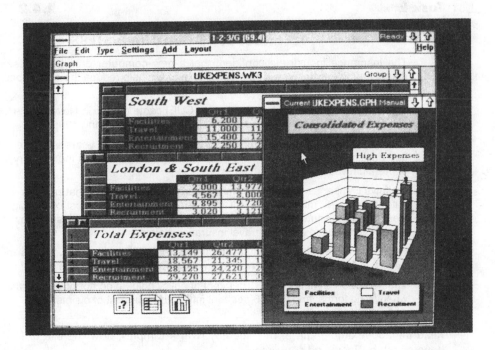

The spreadsheet package shown here (Lotus 1-2-3) can perform complex calculations quickly and display numerical information effectively in charts and graphs.

Use of Business Systems

9. The use of business software packages can readily be seen every day. If, for example you visit a travel agency to book a holiday, the details such as the place, dates, hotel and costs are entered directly into a computer. Most building societies now enter data directly into a computer and bank statements, gas, electricity and telephone bills are also prepared by computers. Companies usually keep a register of their shareholders on computer so that it can be kept up-to-date as shares are bought and sold. Whilst multiple retailers like Sainsbury's use optical character reader (OCR) scanners at check-outs which read bar-codes on products. These are linked to computers which not only produce customer till receipts but also act as a stock control and re-ordering system. Customers can then use a Delta or Switch card to pay for purchases and through EFTPOS (Electronic Transfer of Funds at the Point of Sale) computer technology, their account is debited immediately and the store's account credited. Thus what we have there is a very fast and efficient business communication tool performing many tasks which were previously carried out manually.

Office Technology

10. Over a half of workers in the UK are employed in offices where one of the most significant developments in information technology has been **word processing** which is now used by many firms instead of typewriters. A word processor consists of an electronic keyboard with a built-in computer memory linked to a visual display unit (VDU). It can be used to insert, delete or move text and will automatically design page layouts, including margins, and carry out a spell check. Thus material can be quickly and easily corrected or altered on the screen before it is printed. When completed, the information can be filed (stored) away on magnetic tape or on a floppy or hard disk until it is needed again.

11. Word processors have many uses and can produce a vast range of material including letters, graphs, charts and diagrams. They are particularly useful for repetitive typewriting tasks such as standard letters which only require the name and address, date and time, or other simple information to be changed. Other uses might include the preparation of invoices, accounts, memos and reports.

Task 2   **2.4.2 (C3.4, T3.4)**

TECHNOLOGY TO TRAP FRAUDSTERS

The insurance industry is confident that a new computer data base designed to detect fraudulent claims will be a success, and will help reduce the cost of policy premiums.

The Claims and Underwriting Exchange (CUE) came on-line in November 94, and is due to be reviewed by the Association of British Insurers during 1995.

The system contains pooled information backdated for three years on home contents and building insurance policy holders, and covers 70 per cent of the industry in terms of premium value.

It allows companies to check for false information at the time that policies are taken out, and later for multiple claims. It is already being used by most of the big companies, and in the future, the plan is to expand it to cover motor insurance. There is already a database covering travel insurance claims.

Research shows that fraudulent insurance claims cost the industry as much as £600m in 1994, and add on average an extra 4p in the pound to the cost of a policy.

The AIB also estimates that 31 per cent of policy holders do not give accurate details when filling forms, and that 36 per cent inflate the true cost of claims.

Read the above article and from it identify, with examples, how the use of IT databases can benefit both business and consumers.

12. So far we have mentioned just a few uses of computers in business which, in most cases, you have probably already seen yourself. However, there are literally thousands of different applications which affect just about every type and size of organisation, including charities, educational establishments, government departments, hospitals, industrial and commercial companies, libraries, legal, military and sporting bodies and so on – the list is endless.

13. The following are examples of areas in which computers are used. They give an indication of both the incredible diversity of uses, and also the increasing impact of computers, not just on data capture and information processing, but on all business functions.

❐ Advertising and design	❐ Simulation models
❐ Market research	❐ Research and development
❐ Computer graphics	❐ Product design
❐ Television selling	❐ Packaging design
❐ Packing	❐ Customer records

- ❏ Computer controlled warehousing
- ❏ Stock control
- ❏ Distribution and route scheduling
- ❏ Production planning and control
- ❏ Automatic production lines
- ❏ Quality control
- ❏ Operational research techniques
- ❏ Scientific calculations
- ❏ Invoicing
- ❏ Customer ordering
- ❏ Automatic addressing
- ❏ Mailing lists
- ❏ Investment appraisal
- ❏ Automatic doors and lifts
- ❏ Fire and burglar alarms
- ❏ Security devices

Different Information Technology Applications

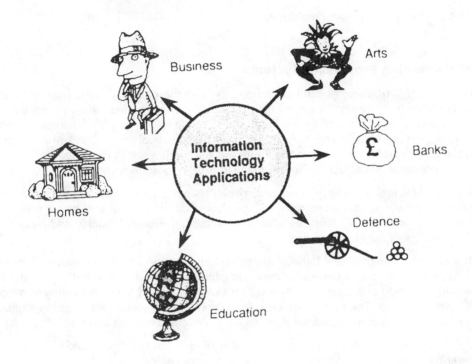

Multi-Media

14. Most computing applications are **single purpose** in that they use one medium to communicate with the user, namely text and graphics on the screen. Whether the application is as a word-processor, spreadsheet, database or training package it uses only one sense (sight). **Multi-media (purpose)** computing is simply the use of more than one medium. Data, graphics, video, photographs, speech, music and text can now be stored, manipulated and displayed on a p.c. and combined to form a very effective 'multi-media' communication tool.

15. Using broadband links it is possible for global networks (see Internet), interactive T.V. and video-conferencing all to be brought to virtually any p.c. anywhere in the world. For example, multi-media enables computer based

    - ❏ inter-active training
    - ❏ production of impressive promotion and marketing material (DTP)
    - ❏ electronic catalogues and associated software
    - ❏ e-mail systems with telephone access capabilities
    - ❏ desktop conferencing where business meetings can take place via p.c.s
    - ❏ engineering prototypes and technical manuals

Task 3   **2.4.2 (T3.4)**

1. Individually or in groups list at least 10 examples of the application of computers in the place where you work or study.

2. List at least 3 examples of the application of computers in the following types of organisation or activity and comment on how they might improve information processing.

    a) Banking   b) Central Government

    c) Local Government   d) Hospitals

    e) Libraries   f) Publishers

    g) Military bodies   h) Traffic control

    i) Engineering   j) Retailing

3. Identify examples of multi-media use.

Analysing Information Processing Systems

16. Developments in micro-electronic technology over the past fifty years have resulted in modern computers which are small in size (some portable), relatively cheap to purchase, extremely powerful, and capable of performing a wide range of routine and complex business functions. This has lead organisations to increasingly move away from manual information processing systems and replace them with computers. In the future this may well result in the 'paperless' office, but at present a combination of both methods is likely to exist in most organisations.

17. What matters is that a management information system is set up which can meet the organisation's needs by providing up-to-date data, ideally about both its internal and external environment. This will help to improve efficiency by enabling managers to respond quickly and make more informed decisions about current situations.

18. The cost of a computerised information processing system can vary considerably from a few hundred to many thousands of pounds, depending on the size of the organisation and the sophistication required. A local newsagent or a school, for example, would have very different needs to those of ICI, Shell or Asda. The costs involved include not only the initial investment in capital equipment, but also the costs of maintenance, running the system, and training and retraining staff.

19. Before choosing a system, therefore, a number of essential questions need to be asked, in order to determine whether or not it is fit for the purpose required, including:

     ❑ What is the job that needs to be done (amount and type of work, speed required etc)?

     ❑ What, precisely, does the system provide?

     ❑ What capacity does it have for information retention?

     ❑ Are the differences between the job and the system, small enough to make it worthwhile pursuing?

     ❑ If adopted, what changes, if any, are required in the way the business is run?

     ❑ How much will it cost to develop, install and use? Is it user friendly?

     ❑ Can confidential data be restricted and kept secure? Passwords are now commonly used with most systems.

     ❑ Will it be reliable? Who else is using it? What is the supplier's reputation like for training and after-sales service?

20. Only by analysing and evaluating systems in this way is it possible to determine whether or not the investment is likely to represent value for money, in terms of being be cost-effective, improving efficiency and helping the organisation to achieve its objectives.

Task 4   **2.4.3 (C3.4)**

M-WAY TOLLS

If technical problems can be overcome, sometime in 1995 nearly 2 000 volunteers are to be asked to 'test-drive' Britain's first motorway toll system in a trial before their planned introduction in 1998 which may have to be delayed.

During the experiment the drivers will use 'ghost' tolls and have small electronic charge units mounted on their windscreens. They will also have a phonecard-style electronic 'tag', or a device which will send a monthly statement.

Both will be activated by radio signals from overhead gantries, which will also be equipped with cameras to film 'dodgers' without tags.

The drivers will be selected through the DVLA records on the basis of how close they live to a motorway.

Britain's motorway network has about 2 400 entry and exit roads, each of which will require a toll point, expected to cost at least £150 000 to install.

To toll all Britain's motorways could be worth up to £500 million to contractors. There is also a maintenance contract and production of the in-car equipment which is likely to cost motorists as much as £50 each.

The tolls, which could cost up to £300 a year for the 12 million drivers who regularly use motorways, are likely to raise £700m annually to help pay for new roads. The basic charge of 1.5p-a-mile will increase at peak hours, just like phone charges, so that commuters using short parts of the motorway will pay dearly.

The Minister of Transport is expecting a rush of tenders from electronics firms throughout Europe for this major business opportunity.

A spokesman for the British Road Federation warned that the cost of installing the tolls could mean less money being spent on roads, and tolls will not be a panacea. They will not reduce congestion or pot-holes, provide badly needed by-passes or repair the 350 miles of motorway now urgently requiring attention. It might also push some motorists from tolled roads onto other highways which are free.

1. Discuss the criteria which could be used to evaluate the proposed investment in motorway tolls.

2. What, if any, alternatives are available?

3. Do you think that the 'test-drive' is a good idea? Justify your answer.

4. Outline the problems involved in installing the system.

5. What do you think is likely to be the reaction of drivers to the system?

Data Protection Act 1984

21. Nowadays, most large organisations keep detailed computer records which include, for example, customers' names and addresses, staff records which may contain information on previous employment and any disciplinary or other action. To control the possible misuse of this type of information and in order to prevent it causing harm to individuals, the **Data Protection Act** was introduced in 1984.

22. The main provisions of the Act are that:

❏ All organisations and individuals who hold personal records on computers must register with the Data Protection Registrar (the government's watchdog). Failure to do so can result in fines of up to £2,000.

❏ They must tell the registrar
   – what type of information they hold
   – what use is made of it

- to whom the information may be disclosed
- how it was collected.

❒ The Registrar has a duty to see that the data conforms to certain principles, namely:

- it must have been obtained openly and fairly
- it shall be held only for lawful purposes
- its uses and possible disclosure must be declared to the Registrar.
- it must be relevant to the purpose for which it is held
- it must be accurate and up-to-date
- it must be destroyed when it is no longer needed
- individuals are entitled to know what information is held about them and to challenge inaccuracies.
- it must be treated as confidential and protected against access by unauthorised persons.

❒ Organisations that do not comply may be liable to compensate individuals who may suffer as a consequence.

❒ There are, however, exceptions to the right to receive compensation, including:

- data that has been supplied by individuals themselves.
- data that has been acquired with 'reasonable care'
- data held for payroll or pension purposes.
- data held for statistical purposes, from which it is impossible to identify individuals.

Effects of the Data Protection Act

23. The Data Protection Act affects businesses and individuals in a number of both positive and negative ways. On the one hand it encourages businesses to hold accurate information which may then be sold to other organisations thus providing a potential source of income. On the other hand, meeting the needs of the Act is expensive. For example, the costs of employing a data protection officer to monitor and control the data input system and the time taken to oversee any additions, deletions and use of the information.

24. Although individuals have a right to request to see the personal details which an organisation holds on them and have any inaccuracies amended unless they do this they are likely to remain. Also most people 'suffer' at some time from receiving unsolicited communications (see direct mail Element 3.3 from organisations which have purchased information about them.

25. Under the terms of the Act, data for sale must have been gathered with the permission of the customers on that list. This permission is usually granted when buyers fail to tick the box that asks them to opt our of having further information sent to them. The European Union is currently seeking to have this changed so that customers will need to tick the box to opt-in.

Task 5	2.4.4 (C3.4)

COMPUTER LISTS 'MAY BREAK LAW'

Thousands of computer users could be breaking the law without knowing it, a court was told. Because there seems to be a conception that if you use computers in a small way or the data you hold is not particularly sensitive, there is no need to register – but this is not the case. The warning came after a hotel boss was fined £100 for keeping details of names, addresses and bill details on a computer without being registered under the Data Protection Act

continued...

Task 5 continued

COLLEGE FINED OVER PHONE CALLS LIST

A lecturer was so annoyed when he saw his name on a notice board he took action which resulted in the college being prosecuted. A summons was issued by the Data Protection registrar following a complaint to which the college pleaded guilty. The court was told that the college monitored phone calls from offices as a cost cutting exercise. A list was then pinned up on a staff notice board but the list of calls from room 8221 was attributed to one person. It was inaccurate because other people were based in the office and made calls. The college was fined £100 with £100 costs. The case being that it is an offence to publish material bearing personal details except in certain circumstances. The system has now been changed.

Thes articles refer to the Data Protection Act.

1. Why do businesses keep data on computer?

2. Outline its main provisions

3. Why is such legislation needed?

Impact of Information Technology on Businesses

26. The ability offered by information technology (IT) to gather, record, organise and act upon information quickly is vital in organisations. To gain maximum benefit however, IT needs to be properly managed and controlled. It should be seen as a dynamic and crucial resource supporting the organisation and helping it to achieve its objectives in the market place.

27. A properly managed IT system requires a clear organisation strategy with a number of key features.

   ❑ **That all managers can gain access** to information as and when required. This means that users and providers of technological expertise need to be linked by placing information systems staff alongside other key business functions like finance, production, personnel and marketing.

   ❑ **Information systems should be flexible** and able to adapt to the individual needs of the organisation in order to facilitate and control what goes on. They should also be fully tried and tested before being introduced to ensure that they work effectively.

   ❑ **Management styles must be receptive** to the opportunities offered by IT including the creation of a shared information culture and a willingness to use the specialist skills available.

   ❑ **All employees should have a broad overview of the business**, and made to feel part of it. This helps everyone to both better understand the business and also the use of IT in it.

   ❑ **Information systems personnel need to act as change agents** assisting management and meeting the needs of end users.

   ❑ **An IT action plan should be developed** with clear objectives, e.g., to improve customer response time by 50% or maximise the return achieved on overnight cash balances. Such objectives should be clearly linked to the organisation's overall mission and business strategy.

28. An action plan or policy should also consider strategies or systems which address potential problems including

   ❑ **security** – to prevent unauthorised access to data which might prove harmful to the organisation

   ❑ **any changes** to organisational procedures which may be needed when implementing it

   ❑ **accuracy of data** input and how quickly this takes place. Delays or inaccuracies may affect decision-taking which may be difficult or based on incomplete data

   ❑ **Maintenance and replacement** so that the system is always kept up and running and new technology (hardware and software) is introduced as it becomes available. Financial planning is needed to cover the costs involved.

   ❑ **Training needs** not just for managers, but for all staff whose IT skills need to be developed and kept up to date.

Organisational Benefits from IT

29. If IT is properly managed in an organisation, it is likely to result in a number of important benefits, including:

   ❑ Increased efficiency and effectiveness.

   ❑ More stimulating and satisfying work for employees who can be freed from routine, less interesting tasks and develop new skills.

   ❑ Increased autonomy, responsibility and feedback for individuals. Greater innovation. Better customer service.

   ❑ Increased flexibility and the ability to respond to change and market requirements.

   ❑ The highlighting of poor areas of work or employee performance.

   ❑ Improved communication and relationships.

   ❑ Access for people with disabilities.

   ❑ Better information and control over workflow and operations. Peaks, troughs, congestion and delays, for example, can be quickly identified.

The Effects of IT on Individuals

30. Together the above benefits should lead to reduced staff absenteeism and labour turnover, increased productivity and a competitive advantage for the business. It should be remembered, however, that new technology can also have its problems. For example,

   ❑ it can cause stress if information cannot be easily accessed or is 'lost' instead of stored.

   ❑ Learning to cope with change and developing the skills to use new equipment can also prove stressful for some people who may feel threatened as existing skills become redundant.

   ❑ In addition, VDUs are potentially harmful to health, hence the European regulations introduced in 1993 to reduce the effects on individuals of prolonged use.

Task 6	**2.4.5 (T3.4)**

In large firms today, virtually every junior and middle manager has a personal computer on their desk. This is often networked locally with the machines of colleagues, frequently with a modem installed to enable public electronic mail service and databases to be accessed. This helps to facilitate immediate and better control of business operations. It is important however, to ensure that back-ups are made to prevent a possible disaster should any of the files get corrupted. If managers want information about stock, sales, production or budgets, it is now usually available to them on screen within seconds. If they require up-to-date information about share prices or exchange rates, this can be readily obtained through the Prestel database. The time saved from using such electronic technology can make managers more effective, freeing them to concentrate on planning and decision-making.

Read the above article and from it:

1. Explain the meaning of the following terms 'networked', 'modem' 'Prestel database', 'public electronic mail', 'electronic technology'.

2. Identify the benefits to a manager of using computer technology.

3. From the article and your own knowledge and experience, can you suggest any possible disadvantages of using new technology.

4. If possible, use a wordprocessing program to type and print your own answer. Include a brief summary of the main advantages of using a wordprocessor instead of a typewriter.

Future Developments

31. As information technology becomes even more sophisticated, businesses will continue to make use of new and improved methods of communication. A few examples of how this might affect all of us in the future include:

    ❑ All staff will find themselves working increasingly with **computer based new technology**.

    ❑ More people will **work from home**, or from remote sites, contacting their offices and other businesses through view-data and other links.

    ❑ **Videophone**. This is a facility being developed which links a small TV screen to a telephone to enable two people to see each other as they talk.

    ❑ **Shopping from home** using Prestel could become quite common. It will soon be possible to talk to computers instead of operating them by keying in information.

    ❑ The use of **electronic mail** systems like Prestel, Datel and Fax could develop so that they are used not just by businesses but by all of us. This might eventually result in newspapers and postal services being replaced by viewdata systems.

    ❑ **The Internet** – A vast and ever growing global web of computer networks. The 'Net' provides an enormous amount of business, educational and other information which can be accessed via a computer. As it develops further it will become a **'superhighway'** capable of transferring very large amounts of information including video, still images, audio and text – at high speeds between users. It is likely to change the way businesses buy and sell products to each other and to other customers.

    ❑ **Virtual reality (VR)** is a very recent and developing form of technology which enables computers to create a synthetic world that looks as real as the world we live in. VR is a very sophisticated computer simulation which will soon radically change the way people learn e.g. learning history as if you were actually there at the time. Although still in its infancy VR is predicted to be a major growth area in the future. Its use in business will include design simulation.

Non-standard Systems

32. Currently, one of the biggest problems of IT is the incompatibility of different manufacturers' products. The growth, however, of IT generally and the development of large international markets like the European Union has lead to pressure on manufacturers to develop products to homogeneous standards so that systems and applications work more freely across trading and operational barriers. In 1992, the DTI introduced a 3 year **Open Systems Technology Transfer Programme** to help progress what is certain to be one of the most significant developments in recent years and likely to have considerable impact on all business in the future.

33. The greater IT compatibility from the development of 'Open Systems' will result in a number of important benefits for organisations including:

    ❑ the freedom to choose suppliers and products which best suit the needs of the business.

    ❑ better value for money from buying the most appropriate products at more competitive prices in the first place.

    ❑ the reduction of development and operational costs.

    ❑ easier handling and exchange of information both within and between organisations thus improving the overall efficiency of business operations.

195

Task 7   **2.2.3, 2.4.5 (C3.4)**

THE INTERNET

Modern organisations revolve around effective communication to find, win and develop business.

The **Internet** is a vast global computer network spanning more than 150 countries. It is literally a network of networks which already has over 30 million users and is growing rapidly. Developed initially for academic and research organisations it is made up of users. So no one actually owns it, each of whom keeps their own contribution up to date which can be scanned or typed in. The development of the World Wide Web (WWW) allows users easy access to a library of information including newspapers, magazines, software, announcements and company and product data.

E-mail is the most important application at present but the ability to provide information to customers, prospects and business partners offers important business opportunities. For example, the NET offers the scope to send a company's product catalogue, which can be updated daily or as required, to all customers who can browse and go on-line to get further information, check stock levels and place orders. Credit card numbers can be checked and dodgy ones broadcast to all traders.

The NET is only part of what will become the **'superhighway'**, the only part that currently exists. Although it gives users the ability to communicate with anyone, anywhere, the infrastructure is slow-speed, unlike that of the proposed superhighway.

The Superhighway will be capable of transferring very large amounts of information including video, still images, audio and text – at high speeds between users.

This will

❏ allow business organisations to create 'virtual corporations' and workforces, i.e. communicating from home to any destination, anywhere in the world, offices will not be needed.

❏ provide a medium for marketing products and services

❏ boost the use of electronic trading (EDI) and business to business communication.

❏ give consumers access to services such as video on demand, home banking and home shopping, plus a host of public and community information. You can already buy almost anything over the NET – from flowers and kitchens to holidays and insurance.

❏ it will bring the world to people's armchairs

❏ multi-media kiosks will become available in banks, libraries and other public buildings.

Companies are scrambling to establish consumer-to-business services, re-inventing ways to create products, attract customers, accept payments and provide support in this new medium. Electronic catalogues, on-line advertisements, information services and virtual shopping malls are the new storefronts; network navigators are the new Yellow Pages.

All over the world including the UK computerised shopping malls are springing up where you can browse round a number of shops on screen, look at products and hear a description of them. Computer shopping is obviously convenient, and, without the overheads involved in a shop or even in printing a catalogue, products should be cheaper.

VISA estimate 200 million dollars' worth of transactions – from a total of 600 billion dollars – took place over the Internet in 1994 and they expect that to reach 30 billion in 1995.

continued...

Task 7 continued

Some businesses however have been worried about the NET because of the risk of unauthorised access to a firm's software and computer database and also the confidentiality of E-mail messages. These problems are, however, being addressed and already it is possible to use a secure file server called a **'fire wall'** which protects confidentiality and restricts access to authorised users only.

There is little doubt that business will be one of the biggest users of the NET. A few years ago very few had a fax number, today they are seen to be essential. In a few years everyone will have an e-mail number as well.

1. Briefly explain what is meant by the Internet.

2. Explain how it differs from the proposed Superhighway.

3. Why is the W.W.W. important?

4. Discuss some of the potential benefits for businesses of these developments in communication.

5. Are there any benefits for consumers?

6. What factors about the Net are causing concern for businesses?

7. What other key factor, not mentioned in the article, do you think could have an effect on organisations joining the Net?

8. Briefly discuss, with reasons, what you feel is the likely future for and impact of such developments?

Summary

34. a) Information processing (IP) is an essential aid to decision-making which can be performed manually and electronically.

   b) Increasingly firms are now using computers for IP.

   c) The main purposes are receiving, sorting, analysing, storing, retrieving, communicating and distributing data.

   d) The advantages of electronic IP include: speed, accuracy, reliability, flexibility, and improved quality.

   e) Important business software includes databases, spreadsheets, desk top publishing, accounting and personnel packages.

   f) Word processing is one major application of computer technology in offices.

   g) There are literally thousands of uses of computers which can be applied to all types and sizes of organisation. The range of applications is increasing with the use of multi-media.

   h) Computerised IP systems are expensive to install and maintain, and therefore they need to be analysed and evaluated to compare needs with potential value for money.

   i) The Data Protection Act 1984 aims to protect individuals against the misuse of computerised information, and provides for compensation where someone suffers as a result of such misuse.

   j) To gain maximum benefit from information technology (IT) it must be properly managed as an integral part of the business' functions.

   k) IT can help to reduce absenteeism and labour turnover, and increase a company's productivity and competitive advantage.

   l) IT can, however, produce problems of stress and other potential health hazards.

Review Questions (*Answers can be found in the paragraphs indicated*)

1. Explain the difference between information processing (IP) and information technology (IT). (1–2)

2. In what ways have IP functions been changed by the use of computers? (4–7)

3. What are the advantages of using IT in business? (5)

4. Explain the main uses of word processing and at least three other business software programs. (10–13)

5. Distinguish between single-purpose and multi-purpose computer applications. (14–15)

6. How would you evaluate an information processing system? (16–20)

7. Outline the main features of the Data Protection Act and how it affects businesses and individuals. (21–23)

8. Describe the potential impact of IT on a business and its employees and the benefits which open systems could bring. (26–33)

9. What benefits can a business gain from the effective management of its IT systems? (29)

10. Identify some of the likely future developments which will impact on information processing. (31)

Assignment – Information Processing Research Project   Element 2.4

Consider, if possible by practical research, how each of the following types of organisation have been affected by developments in communication technology: – Banks – Supermarkets – Police – Schools/Colleges.

Present your findings in a word processed report.

1. Identify the main internal and external methods of communication in each.

2. Identify the main applications of information processing (include number processing, text and graphics) in each.

3. Suggest what you think were the main purposes behind each application.

4. Discuss the changes brought about and the positive and negative effects of each application for:

   i) the organisation as a whole

   ii) its employees

   iii) its suppliers and

   iv) its customers/clients.

5. Identify the effects of the Data Protection Act on the use and security of computer processed information in any two of the organisations.

6. Compare and contrast the different uses of IT in any two of the above types of organisation. Include a summary of the main advantages and disadvantages found.

---

9 Marketing in Organisations

The next 4 chapters are about the marketing activities of organisations. This chapter outlines some key marketing functions and principles which are considered in detail in Elements 3.2, 3.3 and 3.3.

- ❑ Marketing Defined
- ❑ Consumer, Industrial and Services Marketing
- ❑ Marketing Objectives
- ❑ Marketing Mix
- ❑ Marketing Research
- ❑ Branding
- ❑ Own Brands
- ❑ Packaging
- ❑ Marketing Principles

- ❑ Marketing Functions
- ❑ Customers
- ❑ Cost of Customer Services
- ❑ Customer Focus
- ❑ Growth of Organisations
- ❑ Market Growth
- ❑ Product Development
- ❑ Methods of Product Development
- ❑ Survival of the Small Firm

Marketing Defined

1. The term **marketing** is used to describe a whole group of business activities which are concerned with obtaining and keeping customers. The aim of good marketing is that organisations should identify, by **marketing research**, the products which consumers want and then produce and sell them at a profit. In marketing, product is a broad term used to mean goods or services supplied by business organisations.

2. The Chartered Institute of Marketing defines marketing as 'the management process which identifies, anticipates and supplies customer requirements efficiently and profitably'.

3. ❑ A marketing oriented business therefore puts the customer first. Instead of saying 'we only make two colours and sizes of paint (or paper, or pipes or whatever) – take it or leave it', they now ask customers what colours they require and in what sizes and then produce them.

   ❑ Everything the organisation does focuses on ensuring that the needs of customers are always met or exceeded. Whilst everyone in the organisation seeks to provide good customer service.

   ❑ Operating this way – trying to discover and meet customer needs – does not remove the risks of business but it greatly reduces them, thus improving a firm's chances of selling more and making a profit.

Different Types of Marketing

There are three broad categories into which marketing can be divided – consumer, industrial and services.

4. **Consumer Marketing**

   Where products are sold directly to the general public mainly through the retail trade, e.g. shops. This includes:

   ❑ **Consumer Goods** such as food and cosmetics, i.e., items which are bought frequently and are relatively cheap.

   ❑ **Consumer Durables** such as cars, furniture and washing machines which are expected to last several years and are relatively expensive to buy.

5. **Industrial Marketing**

   Industrial products are those sold to companies and manufacturers who use them to produce other goods and services. They can be consumer or durable and range in price from a few pence to thousands or even millions of pounds. Examples include nuts and bolts, raw materials, machinery, equipment and office supplies.

6. **Marketing in Service Industries**

   Services such as banking, insurance, plant hire, office cleaning, maintenance and repair, travel and transport can include either consumer or industrial marketing. Banks, for example, advertise their services to both the general public and businesses whilst garages repair cars owned by both individuals and companies.

7. **Types of Marketing**

Consumer Goods

Tea

Shirt

Computer

Car

Industrial Marketing

Packaging

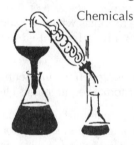
Chemicals

Timber

Marketing in Service Industries

Insurance

Restaurants

P O L I C Y

Shipping

Task 1	**3.1.1 (C3.2)**

Give at least 5 other examples for each of consumer, industrial and service products. Identify those which are sold to both business organisations and the general public.

Marketing Objectives

8. In Chapter one we considered the overall objectives of business organisations and how these are achieved through the planning and co-ordination of its functional activities. Each functional area

has its own set of objectives which for marketing are usually based on sales. Specific targets are usually set so that performance can be measured. Targets also serve to motivate individuals in the organisation.

9. The marketing objectives in any particular year or trading period would typically include some or all of the following:

    ❐ **Sales revenue** e.g. to achieve a turnover of £50,000

    ❐ **Unit sales** e.g. to sell 8,000 units

    ❐ **Profit** e.g. to earn an overall level of 10%

    ❐ **Market share** i.e. to increase business by attracting sales from competitors.

    ❐ **Rate of growth** of all or any of the above, e.g. to increase market share by 5%.

    ❐ **Market Penetration** i.e to find new markets or new parts of existing markets.

    ❐ **Quality assurance** i.e. to ensure that customers always receive goods and/or services that give them satisfaction. This may require quality systems or procedures which involve the setting of standards to reassure customers, e.g. 24 hour delivery, money-back guarantees.

10

Examples of Market Share

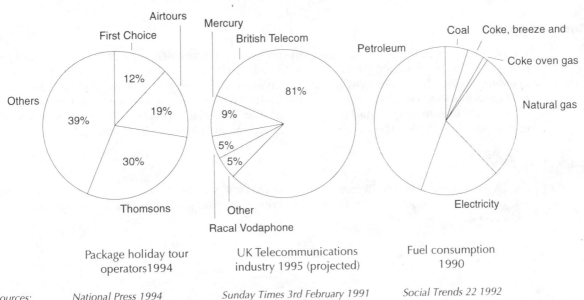

Package holiday tour operators 1994	UK Telecommunications industry 1995 (projected)	Fuel consumption 1990

Sources: *National Press 1994*   *Sunday Times 3rd February 1991*   *Social Trends 22 1992*

Product and Corporate Image

11. Some marketing objectives are more difficult to quantify but nonetheless important in helping an organisation to achieve its overall objectives. This would be the case, for example, if a firm wanted to develop its **corporate image**, that is, the way in which it is seen as a whole rather than by the individual products or services which it sells. Consider, for example, the low-cost image of Kwik-Save compared with the more up-market image of Sainsburys. Important in this is the **corporate identity** which is usually established through the use of logos which appear on letter headings, in advertising, on promotional materials, on vehicles and staff uniforms. The image projected can have an important influence on an organisation's sales.

Some organisations, such as BP and ICI, often use corporate advertising and/or extensive public relations activities which promote the company rather than its products. Whilst sponsorship and other activities are often used to change or reinforce the way in which consumers perceive a product, e.g. sport and health. Clearly any form of image development can also have the spin-off of producing extra sales.

> ### Task 2   3.1.1 (C3.2)
>
> A small manufacturer of cosmetics is seeking to increase its turnover and profit.
>
> 1. Consider the following marketing objectives and advise the company as to which you feel it would be best to pursue.
>
>   To improve customer service
>
>   To launch a new product
>
>   To Improve distribution
>
>   To identify new markets
>
> 2. Explain how each of these objectives can best be measured

Marketing Management

12. The organisation of marketing activities will vary from firm to firm. Large organisations usually have a specialist department with functional managers possibly covering market research, product development, advertising, sales and distribution. On the other hand, in smaller concerns, marketing may be just one of the many responsibilities of the owner, a partner, or director.

Market Appraisal

13. A business needs to know who is buying its products and also when, why and how they are being purchased. Just as importantly it needs to know who isn't buying them and why. This is the role of **marketing research**. If objectives are to be achieved data must be collected and analysed and a marketing mix devised which appeals to the various market segments that is, group of consumers which it decides to target. **Marketing segmentation** is explained more fully in Element 3.3. The **marketing mix** is outlined below and discussed in detail in Elements 3.2, 3,3 and 3.4.

Marketing Mix

14. The main activities involved in marketing a product or service are known as the 4 P's of the marketing mix, that is, product, price, promotion and place, any or all of which may be altered in order to increase sales.

15.

Marketing Mix

Product

16. Using the findings from market research firms can develop products to satisfy consumer needs, introduce new products or improve existing ones. This involves considering the design, quality and

technical specifications of products such as materials and features, the **product mix** (range) offered and how they are packaged. Product development is discussed in Element 3.2.

Price

17. Deciding how much to charge for goods or services is also very important and will be linked to the overall marketing objectives. A price must be set which:

   ❏ is competitive and attractive to customers so that they will buy the products, and

   ❏ covers the cost of production and maximises sales and profit for the firm.

   The price may also be affected by discounts, credit facilities, special promotions and pricing psychology, for example £1.99 sounds a lot cheaper than £2.03. Different pricing strategies are discussed in Elements 1.2 and 6.4.

Promotion

18. This includes sales promotion, advertising, public relations and personal selling which together are often referred to as 'marketing communications'. The aim of promotion is:

   ❏ to tell potential customers about the benefits of a company's goods or services.

   ❏ remind existing customers that the products are still on the market, and

   ❏ encourage both groups to buy or use them.

   Marketing communications are discussed in Element 3.3.

Place

19. This is about how products are made available to the consumer and involves:

   ❏ choosing the channels of distribution through which goods or services are sold. A manufacturer, for example, may use wholesalers or retailers or he may decide to sell his goods direct to consumers.

   ❏ ensure that they are available when required. If, for example, a product is out of stock, then sales may be lost to competitors.

   The different methods of selling products to consumers are discussed in Element 3.4.

Task 3　　　　　　　　　　　　　　　　　　　　　　3.1.1 (C3.2)

The following is an example of how the 4 P's of the marketing mix can be illustrated in the marketing of video recorders.

What facilities and services does the consumer require? (the product), for example remote control, 7 day timer, 12 month's guarantee.

How much is the consumer prepared to pay and what profit does the manufacturer require? (the price), for example £399.

How and when should the manufacturer inform potential customers about his product? (the promotion), for example television and newspaper advertising.

Where and how should the recorders be offered for sale? (the place), for example shops, mail order.

Produce your own example for any product or service with which you are familiar.

---

20. If a firm is to be successful in providing what consumers want at a profit then it is important that its market research and the 4 P's are carefully planned and co-ordinated to achieve this. The particular mix used at any time will vary depending upon the type of goods or services and the circumstances. Fashion clothing, for example, is always changing and therefore will require considerable product

development and promotion. On the other hand, manufacturers of some goods such as basic food-stuffs like tea and sugar will be more concerned with price and place, i.e. making the goods available to consumers at the right price. Whilst an increase in competition might mean that a firm must alter its prices or increase its promotion if it is to avoid a fall in sales.

21. The balance between an organisation's long, medium and short-term objectives will also affect the relative emphasis on the marketing mix. Lower prices, for example, may be used to increase market share but will also reduce profit levels and could cause competitors to retaliate. Thus this may only be suitable in the very short-term. In the longer-term it may be more profitable to develop new products or enter new markets e.g. selling overseas.

Task 4   3.1.1 (C3.2)

1. Select 3 supermarket companies and

2. any other 3 companies well known to you.

For each company, state, with reasons, where you feel the emphasis on the marketing mix is placed.

Marketing Research

22. This is the collection, analysis and interpretation of information about important areas in the marketing process to enable decisions to be made. It includes research about consumers, sales, advertising and promotion, competition, distribution and the analysis of key market factors such as market share, trends and developments.

23. This information is vital to enable organisations to develop products which are readily accepted because they meet consumer needs. Marketing research is discussed in detail in Element 3.2.

Branding

24. Nowadays many goods are mass-produced, standard in nature with few, if any, real differences between competing rivals. Therefore, most products are given **brand names** or trade marks to differentiate between them. These names are usually registered so that they cannot be used by anyone else. Branding is used in consumer, industrial and service markets.

25. Branding enables manufacturers to advertise the **characteristics** and **qualities** of their products and build **brand loyalty**. Thus, for example, when consumers go into a shop, they do not just buy butter or coffee but look for Anchor, Lurpak, Nescafé, Maxwell House or some other favourite brand. This also affects **price elasticity** because consumer loyalty makes brands less susceptible to falling sales following a price increase. (See Element 1.1.)

26. **Consumer Brands**

    Based on grocery outlets. Source: Neilsen

The Top Six Brands 1992 *(millions)**		Top Six Fizzy Drinks 1992 *(millions)**	
1 Coco-Cola	Over £400	1 Coco-Cola	Over £400
2 Persil	£235–£240	2 Pepsi Cola	£130–£135
3 Ariel	£230–£235	3 Lucozade	£85–£90
4 Andrex toilet tissue	£185–£190	4 Tango	£65–£70
5 Nescafé	£185–£190	5 Schweppes mixers	£50–55
6 Pampers	£170–£175	6 Lilt	£35–£40

Top Six sweets 1992	*(millions)**	Top Six snacks 1992	*(millions)**
1 Kit Kat	Over £150	1 Walkers Crisps	Over £170
2 Mars Bar	£85–90	2 Golden Wonder	£60–£65
3 Cadbury's Dairy Milk	£60–£65	3 Hula Hoops	£55–£60
4 Roses	£55–£60	4 Quavers	£30–£35
5 Twix	£55–£60	5 Skips	£25–£30
6 Snickers	£55–£60	6 KP Peanuts	£20–£25

*Figures give the researchers' range of sales revenue

27. Branding can also be used to project a product 'image'. 'Limmits', for example, suggests control as in a calorie controlled diet, whilst 'Gas Miser' conveys an image of economical heating.

> **Task 5**   **3.1.1 (C3.2)**
>
> 1)   What image is created by the following brand names?
>
>   a)   **Colour match** toilet rolls
>
>   b)   **Kwik-fit** car exhausts
>
>   c)   **Bonus Print** photographic developers
>
>   d)   **Tender Care** baby lotion
>
>   e)   **Pronto-print** printers
>
> 2)   Identify 5 other products or services whose name promotes an 'image' and state what that image is.

28. Some firms sell their products under a **'family'** brand name such as Kelloggs, Heinz, McVities, Fisons and Amstrad, thus increasing the cost-effectiveness of advertising and promotion. This is known as **brand stretching.** This can also produce the **'halo effect'** as successful promotion of one brand often encourages the purchase of others in the 'family' range. Whilst on the other hand disappointment with one product may discourage the purchase of others.

29. **Multiple branding** sometimes called **product segmentation** is another technique which is widely used by, among others, pet food suppliers Spillers (e.g. Bonus, Choice, Champ, Kenomeat) and Pedigree (e.g. Chum, Bounce, Chappie, Pal) and soap powder giants Unilever (e.g. Persil, Surf, Ra-

205

dion, Comfort) and Proctor & Gamble (e.g. Daz, Tide, Bold, Ariel). This involves selling broadly similar products under a **variety of brand names** in order to achieve sales in a number of **market segments.** It also **creates competition** within an organisation between the various brand managers.

Task 6	**3.1.1 (C3.2)**

1. Make a list of as many different brands as possible of tea, television sets, paint and cars.

2. From your list, identify any examples of multiple-branding and/or brand stretching.

Own Brands

30. Many retailers also sell goods which are specially made for them under their own brand name, which in many cases are a cheaper version of the well known brand. Examples include St Michael (Marks & Spencer), Boots, Tesco and Winfield (Woolworths).

31. Own brands are becoming **increasingly important** in attracting business because they are cheaper than famous brands (due to lower advertising and promotional costs); create store identity (through packaging) and customer loyalty (if you like ASDA's yoghurts you can only buy them from ASDA).

Task 7	**3.1.1 (C3.4)**

1) Referring back to Task 6, how many examples of 'own brands' can you identify for tea, television sets, paint and cars?

2) Why do you think that manufacturers of branded goods are prepared to produce similar products which retailers then sell at a lower price? the following news extract provides part of the answer.

BEATING THE RECESSION

The home market for Scotch Whisky represents only about 15% of total sales and exports were up by 6% in the first half of the year.

Invergordon Distillers Group exports went up even faster, by 14%.

It even increased home sales by 6%.

The secret is in supplies to supermarkets of own brand whiskies.

A 12% rise in sales to Tesco and Safeway is highly visible.

Packaging

32. An important part of branding is the use of packaging. Originally introduced to protect goods, packaging is now used to develop a **brands image** by making it distinct and easily recognisable. It is often an integral part of a product designed to add to its appeal through the use of colour, shape, size and logos all of which can have a significant effect on sales.

33. **Product differentiation** through packaging has become a vital aspect of consumer marketing since the development of self-service stores and impulse purchasing and is particularly important for successful advertising and sales promotion. In fact, with many products, the cost of packaging often represents a very high proportion of the total price as , for example, with boxes of chocolates and Easter eggs.

Marketing Principles

34. From what we have said so far it should be clear that a marketing oriented business puts the customer first. That is, it defines its objectives and policies in terms of customer needs rather than its own existing resources and skills. This involves certain key principles which are summarised below.

Analysing Market Needs and Opportunities

35. That is, using marketing research about products, markets and consumer motivation and buying habits to identify what consumers want. This is discussed fully in Element 3.2.

Satisfying Customer Expectations

36. By developing products, based on research data, which meet consumer needs in terms of features, price, performance or whatever the consumer regards as providing value and satisfaction.

37. The product must also be available when needed, in the required quantity and packaged to prevent damage or deterioration. An individual, for example, may simply want a single item at a fair price, whereas a wholesaler or retailer might expect large quantities, regular deliveries, a reasonable profit margin and possibly promotional or after-sales support.

38. Where appropriate an instruction manual and/or after-sales service and guarantees may also be important in the sales process.

39. In industrial markets maintenance and training may also be particularly important (e.g. computers, office equipment and machinery). All consumers will also expect problems or complaints to be dealt with quickly and efficiently.

Generating Income or Profit

40. The activities of the marketing mix must be used to maximise sales which are essential for business success. This is more likely to happen if products satisfy consumer needs and expectations.

41. It also requires

    ❐ the right price for the right market, that is perceived by the consumer as offering value for money

    ❐ good marketing communications to get information and the sales message across to consumers, and

    ❐ effective distribution channels which may involve either selling direct to consumers and/or using indirect methods via wholesalers, agents, retailers or whatever is most appropriate to maximise sales and profits.

Task 8   **3.1.1, 3.1.2 (C3.4)**

CARS AT A LOSS

Car sales grew in 1994 but the manufacturers paid a high price for success.

They spent record sums on discounts and free offers and sold thousands of cars at up to £3,000 below showroom prices just to 'move metal'. Many dealers also registered new models to boost figures artificially.

While the total of 1,910,933 new cars registered was 7.45 per cent up on 1993, motor chiefs admitted they needed to sell two million. By falling almost 100,000 short of that target the industry lost over £1 billion – even before discounts and incentives were taken into account.

And in real terms, sales were as low as 1.6 million say insiders, who claim up to 300,000 cars were registered by dealers so that they could be sold off as 'demonstrator models' at second-hand prices. High motoring taxation was partly blamed for slow sales figures, putting off private drivers from buying new.

Ford was the only major manufacturer to improve its market share, up 0.4 per cent to 21.9 per cent. It also had the three best-selling cars.

---

1. How do the problems in the motor trade illustrate the difficulty of generating profits in an industry?

2. What do you think is likely to happen if the current situation is repeated?

Manage the Effects of Change and Competition

42. In Element 4.2 we discuss the impact of change on organisations. We live in a world of constant change which takes place both inside and outside organisations.

43. **External change,** generally speaking, is outside the control of the organisation. For example, the government may raise taxes which can affect prices and the purchasing power of consumers; a political crisis in an overseas country could affect imports of raw materials or the export of finished goods; or competitors could introduce new products. If external change occurs, however, organisations must manage the situation and respond accordingly if business is not to be lost.

44. **Internal change,** on the other hand, is controllable because it affects the organisation's own resources and capabilities. For example, the need for change in order to increase productivity, improve quality, improve customer service, introduce new products or alter management structures.

45. Change can cause stress and place great demands on the staff who need to respond to it. Nonetheless, managing change is an important part of successful marketing and very necessary if the organisation is to remain competitive.

Co-ordinating Activities to Achieve Marketing Aims

46. That is, ensuring that all parts of the organisation are geared up to meet the objectives. For example, marketing communications can only be effective if the products are available when required. If production and/or distribution fail and there is no stock at the point-of-sale (e.g. warehouse, shop) then both existing and potential customers will be unable to make purchases. The sales opportunity will therefore be lost and both groups may decide to purchase another brand and remain with it in the future.

47. Likewise, promotional activities must be brought together and co-ordinated in a carefully organised plan to ensure that they produce maximum impact and benefit for the organisation.

Task 9	**3.1.1, 3.1.2 (C3.4)**

QE2 CRUISE FIASCO

Hundreds of passengers were left high and dry after their 1994 Christmas cruise on the QE2 was cancelled just hours after the Duke of York rededicated the luxury liner after its £30 million refit at a German shipyard.

The celebrations turned sour when it was revealed plumbing work being carried out in about 100 cabins by British sub-contractors had not been completed on time.

There was 'utter chaos' as nearly 800 anxious holidaymakers crammed into a departure lounge at Southampton docks to see if they would be allowed on board. Fights broke out and some holidaymakers burst into tears as Cunard officials told 300 of the 1,300 passengers that their £4,000-a-head dream trip was off.

The ship eventually sailed over 6 hours late. Passengers who did not sail were offered a full refund before Christmas, a free transatlantic cruise in 1995 and £250 spending money. They were also offered overnight hotel accommodation.

One American, visiting her family in New York for Christmas said 'It is disgusting. But the worst thing is that there are no Cunard officials to talk to.'

1. What was the QE2 cruise fiasco?

2. What did the company do about it?

3. How does this situation illustrate the problems of co-ordinating activities to achieve marketing aims?

Utilising Technological Developments

48. This could take place at any stage of the marketing process in order to improve products or services as the following examples illustrate.

49. Banks, retailers, building societies, travel, hotel and insurance companies all make extensive use of computer technology. Banks in particular are becoming increasingly automated. Credit cards, ETF-POS, EDI and 24-hour service all rely on it.

50. Manufacturing organisations producing vehicles, capital equipment, paper or whatever, are increasingly using robots and computers for product design and development, plus an array of new materials such as plastics and fibre optics.

51. All organisations are being affected by improved telecommunications including mobile telephones, fax machines, satellite links and increasingly the Internet. Computers are also changing the way information is collected and used in organisations.

Task 10	3.1.1, 3.1.2, 3.1.4 (C3.4)

SCAN FOR SUCCESS

In the past large retailers have spent heavily on IT mainly in the areas of stock management, the office and electronic point-of-sale equipment. In more recent times they have introduced bar-code scanners. This instrument has reduced ordering costs, lead to better stock level planning and increased the speed at which customers pay for goods. In the future IT is likely to be used increasingly to gain a competitive edge, develop customer loyalty and reduce queuing times at check-outs.

Safeway in Solihull, for example, is currently carrying out a trial using volunteer customers who can scan their own goods as they shop. They then simply present the receipt for payment at an express till. the scanner used can also provide information on the route shoppers take around the store, the order in which they select goods, and their most common purchases. Ultimately this could lead to a basic order being ready for collection when they turn up each week, which they only need to top up as required.

This approach could eventually be linked to loyalty schemes such as those introduced by Tesco, Asda and Safeway which use smart cards to record details of the amount of purchases. In return for regular shopping customers receive vouchers giving a cash discount on future purchases.

1. How are some supermarkets using technology to gain a competitive edge?

2. How is or could technology eventually be linked to customer loyalty?

3. What does the article reveal about the use of technology in marketing?

Enhance Customers Perceptions of the Organisation and/or Product

52. This can be achieved through successful advertising, promotion and public relations and by offering quality products supported by a high level of customer service. Marketing communications is discussed in Element 3.3 and customer service in Element 3.4.

Task 11

3.1.1, 3.1.2, 3.1.4 (C3.4)

HOOVER'S FREE FLIGHT FIASCO

Hoover has failed to halt a mass legal action over its free flights promotion, which has already cost at least £48 million. Thousands of customers want damages for disappointment and loss of enjoyment in addition to the value of the plane tickets they say they were unable to take up.

Hoover's promotion offered two tickets to Europe or the U.S. to customers buying appliances worth more than £100. While 220,000 have flown, there has been a flood of complaints from others that they have not received tickets or the flights they wanted. The offer expired at the end of April 1994.

Hoover has been bitterly criticised, but trading standards officers have already ruled out criminal action following a six-month inquiry into the promotion.

More than 3,000 customers joined together in a bid to force Hoover to deal with outstanding applications. Many bought shares in the American parent company Maytag in a bid to strengthen their position. The scheme has been described as one of the biggest marketing blunders of recent times.

1. In what sense was Hoover's promotion successful?

2. Why did it go wrong?

3. What has the promotion done to consumers' perceptions of the organisation?

Maximising Benefit to the Organisation

53. If the above principles are successfully implemented then they should result in improved sales, market share, reputation and profitability for the organisation. This involves careful planning to achieve objectives, managing existing successful markets, changing the marketing mix where necessary, developing new markets and possibly withdrawing from declining ones.

Marketing Functions

54. Having identified the key marketing principles it is important to recognise the functions which underpin them. These are summarised below.

55. **Managing change.** Marketing as a management function involves collecting and interpreting information about an organisation's markets, products and environment, including competitor activity. Any change must then be managed to ensure that an organisation and its products have a competitive edge.

56. **Co-ordinating marketing planning and control.** Objectives must be based on anticipated demand and the other organisational functions planned accordingly. For example, there is little point in developing new products if the organisation does not have the production capacity or skills to make them or the additional sales staff that would be needed to sell them. These problems need to be anticipated and planned for in advance. Production, finance and personnel need to be involved to establish what needs to be done and how it can be achieved.

57. **Implement the marketing mix** to ensure that product, price, promotion and place are all carefully considered. Innovation and product development are important to remain ahead of the competition.

58. **Branding** which is essential for marketing communications. Products and/or organisations must be differentiated and given an image which appeals to their targeted market segments. Promotional expenditure can then focus on and develop the strengths of the brand.

59. **Ensuring survival** of the business by generating sales, income and profit. Once an organisation has established which products it is best able to make then the marketing activities must be aimed at optimising sales at least cost in order to maximise profits. A successful organisation is likely to prosper and grow whilst others may struggle to survive and possibly go out of business.

Task 12   **3.1.2, 3.1.4 (C3.4)**

RUMBELOWS GET IT ALL WRONG

In February 1995 the closure of Rumbelows, the electrical goods chain was announced by parent company Thorn EMI. Rumbelows, with a market share of just 3 per cent , simply could not compete with Kingfisher's Comet, the Dixons Curry's group and the newly privatised electricity company stores in a market where profit margins are very thin due to oversupply.

Alan Sugar had pulled his Amstrad computers out of the high street in 1994 because of the cut-throat pricing needed to sell them.

In 1992 Rumbelows had over 500 outlets, in 1995 because of continuing loses this had already been reduced to just 285. One of the problems was that although the stores were usually prime high street locations they proved inconvenient and rarely had sufficient space to stock a full range of products. Hence rents, rates and delivery costs were high and despite competitive prices they could not attract sufficient customers to make a profit. Meanwhile other electrical chains were moving to convenient out-of-town shopping centres, where costs are lower, more space is available and customers can park and collect their own goods. Curry's, for example, moved over 300 stores whilst Rumbelows stayed put. Rumbelows had made no profit since 1988 and was heading for losses of £12million for the third consecutive year. By June 1995 all the 2,900 staff had been made redundant.

1. In what sense did Rumbelows get it all wrong?

2. What lessons can be learned in terms of how organisations implement their marketing mix?

Customers

60. Customers can be anyone who buys, uses or recommends an organisation's products. Whether an organisation is a manufacturer of baked beans, a charity such as Oxfam, provides a service such as a bank or garage, in the public or private sector they all have customers. Without customers there is no need for the organisation.

Task 13   **3.1.3 (C3.4)**

Consider the following list of customers and link them with a possible public or private sector organisation/business

patient	parent	pupil
passenger	guest	delegate
shopper	retailer	viewer
reader	supporter	member
applicant	tourist	motorist

Development of a Consumer Focus

61. In the nineteenth century and early part of the twentieth century, businesses were perceived as producing things, groceries and other products were sold as commodities with virtually no branding. Retailers had limited product ranges, sold from behind counters and purchasing took place at the point-of-sale. Demand exceeded supply and therefore manufacturers had little difficulty in selling their goods.

62. The many technical developments which took place, particularly in the first part of this century, however, lead to a rapid growth in mass production. Organisations were **production-oriented** concentrating on maximising production rather than producing what customers wanted.

63. In the 1920s and 1930s as output increased so did competition and consumer choice. Manufacturers responded by becoming **sales-oriented,** that is they increased their sales effort to sell the goods produced.

64. In the USA, however, production continued to exceed sales in many markets in the 1930s and 1940s and manufacturers recognised the need to do something about it. They decided that the best way to compete was to become **consumer-oriented**, that is find out what consumers wanted and produce it. Consumer satisfaction became fundamental to sales, profits and survival.

65. This marketing concept has developed in Britain from the 1950s onwards. Initially predominantly by fast Moving Consumer Goods (FMCG) manufacturers selling items like soap powders, toiletries, confectionery, tea, coffee and soft drinks. Nowadays it has spread to the service sector, public sector and charity organisations. Now marketing is usually seen as a key management function in all organisations with the focus very much on providing a high level of customer service.

66. Nowadays the majority of firms are

   ❐ **marketing oriented** i.e. through research they identify consumer needs and seek to develop products to meet them which are better than those of their competitors.

   Others are still

   ❐ **production-oriented** i.e. they aim to be successful by producing goods of the optimum quality at the lowest cost. They constantly pursue improved efficiency in production and distribution through the use of new materials and technology.

   Some are still

   ❐ **sales-oriented** believing that success comes from effective selling and promotion.

   Whilst others are

   ❐ **finance-oriented** believing that success comes from using assets and resources to optimise the return on capital employed.

Task 14
3.1.3 (C3.4)

Based on paragraph 66 what evidence is there to suggest how the organisation in which you work or study is oriented?

Cost of Customer Services

67. All customers require a variety of services. At the most basic level it includes a quality product at a fair price and readily available or promptly delivered. In many organisations and for many products it may go beyond this to include, for example, after-sales-service, guarantees, extended warranties, customer information desks, and consumer attitude research.

68. Too little customer service may alienate customers and provide opportunities for competitors. On the other hand, too much customer service is wasteful of an organisation's resources.

69. The costs associated with providing the customer service must therefore be weighed against the impact on the organisation in terms of profitability, productivity and accountability.

Customer Service versus Profitability

70. Most organisations must make a profit in order to survive. Even non-profit making organisations like charities or providers of public sector services need to at least cover costs and make a surplus. Basically no organisation can afford to supply goods and services unless it makes a profit.

71. To make a profit an organisation needs consumers. Customer services are designed to attract consumers. Since a failure to provide services could lead to a loss of business to competitors, the cost can be justified. Good customer service can improve sales and lead to repeat business, which in turn will enhance the organisation's reputation, gain new customers and keep existing customers loyal.

72. An organisation should, however, aim to ensure that the short-term costs of providing and/or improving customer services are more than offset by long-term financial gains from increased sales and profits.

Customer Service versus Productivity

73. Organisations will seek to improve productivity or efficiency in all areas of activity. Customer service is usually a cost in the marketing budget and therefore needs to be analysed to see how it can be reduced or controlled without jeopardising present or future sales volume and profit targets. This requires specific measurable standards of performance to be established against which progress can be measured.

74. For example, 95 per cent of all orders delivered within 24 hours; all correspondence answered within 72 hours; all maintenance requests dealt with within 48 hours; all telephone calls answered within 6 rings. These standards can be applied to all functions in the organisation.

75. Alternatively, or possibly as well as performance standards, an organisation may decide to try to determine the responsiveness of sales and profits to different levels of investment in customer service. This can be a more difficult measure of productivity to calculate because sales and profits can be affected by many factors other than customer service.

Customer Service versus Accountability

76. Rapid social change since the end of the Second World War has dramatically changed people's attitudes to and expectations of organisations. There is now much more concern about the impact of business activities on the community as a whole and the responsibilities which organisations should have towards both consumers and employees.

77. For example, concern about damage to the environment, pollution, energy conservation, recycling and the conservation of land must be considered by organisations if their reputation is not to suffer.

78. The growth of what is called 'consumerism' has come about largely because in the past consumers have been exploited or at least believe they have. This has lead to the growth of **pressure groups** such as the Consumers Association and its 'Which' magazines, **consumer programmes** on TV and radio such as 'That's Life', 'Watchdog' and 'Face to Face' and **legislation** such as the Sale of Goods, Trade Descriptions, and Monopolies and Mergers Acts.

79. Consequently, organisations are now more accountable than ever for their business activities. The cost of customer service therefore can be seen as an investment in recognition of this fact as they strive to satisfy consumer needs and expectations.

Task 15   **3.1.3, 3.1.4 (C3.4)**

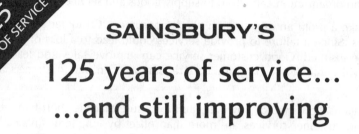

SAINSBURY'S
125 years of service...
...and still improving

We opened our first shop 125 years ago. Right from the beginning, our aim has always been to offer the very best value for money in food retailing. We believe that the customer comes first - and that goes for service as well as what we sell.

Our view is that you, the customer, deserve the best we can provide.

Our wish for you: a shorter queue

Everyone is allowed a birthday wish, and ours is to give you better service than ever. We've put our heads together over the past year. And we've asked **you**, the customer, what you would most like to see.

Top of the list was shorter queues at the checkout. So that's our priority from now on. Whenever there is more than one person waiting to be served, we'll do our best to open more tills.

At busy times it won't always be easy. But by training more of our existing staff to operate checkouts, and recruiting new staff as well, we believe you'll notice a big difference.

Service with a difference

We hope you'll notice a difference, too, in all sorts of other ways. Smoother running trolleys. Bags that are easier to open. Staff who serve you better because they have put themselves in **your** shoes, and learnt what your needs are.

Every customer is special to us, and we believe that each one of you needs - and deserves - the personal touch.

Give us your views

We need **you** to tell **us** what **we** can do to make shopping at Sainsbury's even better. Speak to one of our managers here. Or write to Terry Wells, Director of Customer Service, at Head Office. Or call our Freephone hotline on **0800 636262**.

Thank you for shopping at Sainsbury's

J Sainsbury plc Stamford House Stamford Street London SE1 9LL

SAINSBURY'S Where good food costs less

The above is a copy of a leaflet issued by Sainsbury's in 1995.

1. What does it reveal about the company's attitude to customers?

2. Why do you think the company operates in this way and what benefits is it likely to bring?

3. What costs do you feel are associated with it?

Customer Focus

80. In the 1990s many organisations have realised that it is no longer enough to have a small number of specialist staff providing customer service. Customer focus is one of the key business strategies now being adopted.

81. Customer focus is in effect an organisational ethos based on providing customer satisfaction. It involves everyone in an organisation being made aware of customers needs and the importance of meeting them with good customer service.

82. Whether it be seeking information, wanting to make a purchase, obtain a refund, make a complaint, requiring disabled access or whatever, customer needs must be dealt with quickly and efficiently.

83. It is also important to remember that customers are not just external to organisations. All staff will require customer service at the same time. For example, stationery, protective clothing or information.

84. Therefore, customer focus is about always putting people first and treating everyone as being important. Clearly, this means that customer service is no longer the role of a few specialist staff but everyone in an organisation. For example, it also includes how goods are delivered, accounts prepared, repairs or maintenance carried out.

Growth of Organisations

85. In Element 1.2 we considered different market conditions including those leading to monopoly, imperfect competition and oligopoly. Whilst in Element 2.1 we discussed the methods of growth and reasons why organisations wish to grow in size. From a marketing point of view growth can be achieved by developing markets or products.

Market Growth

86. This can take place in many different ways, for example

   ❐ **increasing sales volume and market share**, although these do not necessarily increase profitability which will be dependant upon the cost of achieving it, e.g. lower prices, substantial promotion.
   ❐ **expansion of geographical markets** and therefore sales, e.g. selling on a national rather than regional basis, exports etc
   ❐ **acquisition or merger**, thereby eliminating competition.
   ❐ **joint ventures** where two or more organisations agree to work together for their mutual benefit.

Product Development

87. New product development is vital for all organisations because it is a way of maintaining present and future success. Organisations need to innovate and change both in response to markets and to keep ahead in markets. This has become even more important with the increase in competition resulting from the growth of free trade opening up global markets, plus developments in telecommunications and computer technologies and increasingly sophisticated consumers demanding higher standards.

88. Product development is closely linked to market development because it provides the opportunity to

   ❐ stimulate sales enabling existing markets to be developed
   ❐ enter new markets or market segments
   ❐ counter competition more effectively
   ❐ gain greater dominance in the market by increasing market share and therefore profitability
   ❐ develop into new product markets to spread the risks of changing trends
   ❐ maintain a market position as an innovator which is particularly important with rapidly changing techniques such as electronics and telecommunications
   ❐ utilise spare capacity, for example in production, sales, distribution or where seasonal or cyclical peaks and troughs occur, e.g. Walls ice cream and sausages.

Methods of Product Development

89. This is discussed more fully in Element 3.2, but essentially product development can take place via innovation, modification or technical breakthrough.

90. In many organisations it is an on-going process which can result in

   ❐ **product improvements** which may range from improved quality, purchasing new technical or design features, or new ingredients, to the creation of new market segments such as razors for women and cosmetics for men

   ❐ **product additions** such as an extension of an existing product range, for example new flavours of soup, dog food or toothpaste

   ❐ **major innovations** resulting in completely new products with the potential to develop entirely new markets. For example, television, video recorders, satellite communication

91. It should be clear therefore, that long-term growth is highly necessary if an organisation is to survive in a competitive economy. If competitors grow too big then they may be able to eliminate organisations which remain static. Properly planned and controlled growth therefore, is the key to achieving stability and growth in sales and profits.

Task 16	**3.1.5 (C3.4)**

FIZZ GOES OUT OF COKE

In November 1994 Coca-Cola's share of the British market dropped below 50% for the first time. Since then sales of both Coke and Pepsi have continued to decline under pressure from a series of new competitive brands.

At the same time, supermarkets' own-label brands such as Sainsbury's Classic Cola and Safeway's Select, and Virgin Cola have taken close to 30% of the market.

Despite swingeing price cuts and a £4 million advertising campaign in the six weeks up to Christmas 1994, Coke has failed to stop Virgin making inroads into the market in once dominated, and has therefore launched a further £2.5 million campaign to win back its market share.

Richard Branson believes that his Virgin Cola, which was launched worldwide in 1995 , can overtake Coke. But a spokesman for Coke said 'Our total UK sales were 21% up last quarter. Business is extremely strong and growing.

'There's plenty of room for growth in the UK soft-drinks market.

'We welcome competition, because it gives consumers greater choice.'

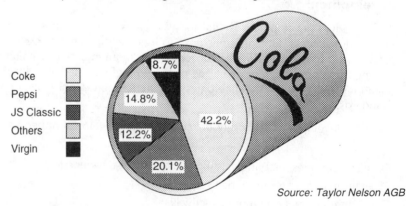

Source: Taylor Nelson AGB

1. What has happened to Coca-Cola's market share and why?

2. What has the organisation done to try to combat the new competition?

3. What does the article tell you about the effect of competition and product development in a market?

Survival of the Small Firm

92. Despite the advantages enjoyed by large firms, small firms still predominate in most forms of businesses. Small firms are especially important in certain industries such as agriculture, building, retailing and personal and professional services. It is also important to note that even within the same industry firms often vary considerably in size.

93. **Size of Manufacturing Units in the UK 1991**

Employees	Number of businesses	% of total businesses	Number of employees (000's)	% of total employed
1–19	121,077	77.4	532	11.2
20–99	25,886	16.5	1103	23.3
100–999	9,078	5.8	2298	48.5
Over 1,000	408	0.3	806	17.0

NB Figures based on Annual Abstract of Statistics 1992 edition.

The above diagram shows two important features:

❑ Small firms are typical of UK manufacturing. Nearly 94% employ less than one hundred people.

❑ Those small units employ over a third of the total labour force and therefore make a major contribution to the economy.

94. **Why Small Firms Survive**

Below are some of the reasons why small firms are able to survive.

❑ **Professional and specialist services or products**, for example accountants, solicitors, racing cars where demand is local or limited.

❑ **Sub-contracting** or making components for large firms. Many small firms produce goods for other large firms.

❑ **Personal services,** for example hairdressing, plumbing, window cleaning can be more easily supplied by small firms.

❑ **Limited markets**, for example 'corner shops' provide a local service.

❑ **Banding together,** for example Spar and Mace group together to gain the benefits of economies of scale such as bulk buying.

❑ **'Being one's own boss'.** Some entrepreneurs may accept smaller profits in order to enjoy the satisfaction of working for themselves.

❑ **Government assistance** or advice is offered to prospective and established small businesses on a wide range of problems.

Summary

95. a) Marketing is concerned with the way in which a business operates and includes all aspects of selling goods and services from initial market research to distribution to the final consumer.

b) Successful firms produce products which satisfy consumer needs.

c) The three main types are Consumer Marketing, Industrial Marketing and Marketing in Service Industries.

d) An organisation's marketing objectives may include specific targets for growth in sales, profit and market share.

e) The main activities in the marketing mix are product, price promotion and place.

f) Market research is necessary to discover information about all aspects of the marketing process.

g) Branding is used by manufacturers and retailers to differentiate products and promote customer loyalty.

h) Packaging is important not just to protect products but also to develop brand identity.

i) The principles of marketing include analysing market needs, satisfying consumer expectations, managing the effects of change and competition, co-ordinating activities, utilising technological developments, enhancing consumer perceptions of the organisation and its products and generating income and profit to maximise the benefits to the organisation.

j) The functions of marketing include managing change, co-ordinating planning and control, implementing the market mix, branding and ensuring survival of the organisation.

k) A production-oriented business concentrates on using resources to maximise the production of quality goods.

l) A sales-oriented organisation emphasises the use of effective promotion and selling techniques.

m) A finance-oriented business believes that success comes from efficient utilisation of assets and resources.

n) A market-oriented organisation identifies consumer needs and provides products to meet them.

o) Marketing has developed rapidly since the 1950s, particularly in FMCG companies.

p) The costs of providing customer service must be considered against the impact on an organisation's profitability, productivity and accountability.

q) Many organisations are now developing a customer focus ethos involving all staff in customer service.

r) The growth of organisations can come about by developing markets or products.

s) New product development is vital in a competitive economy and can provide numerous marketing opportunities.

t) Despite the benefits from economies of scale small firms continue to survive.

Review questions *(Answers can be found in the paragraph indicated)*

1. What is marketing? (1–3)

2. Explain, using examples, the 3 different types of marketing. (4–7)

3. Give examples of some typical marketing objectives. (8–9)

4. Distinguish between product and corporate image. (11)

5. Outline the 4 elements of the marketing mix. (14, 16–19)

6. What is marketing research and why do firms use it? (22–23)

7. Why are brand names used in marketing? (24–31)

8. Explain the difference between 'family brands' and 'multiple brands'. (28–29)

9. Why is packaging an important part of branding? (32–32)

10. Outline the principles of marketing which an organisation needs to implement. (34–35)

11. What are the main marketing functions needed to implement these principles? (54–59)

12. Distinguish between production, sales, finance and marketing-oriented organisations. (60–66)

13. What is customer service and in what sense is it a cost? (67–69)

14. Consider the costs of customer service in terms of an organisation's profitability, productivity and accountability. (70–79)

15. Explain what you understand by customer focus in an organisation. (80–84)

16. Why do organisations need to develop markets and products? (85–88)

17. Outline, with examples, three methods of product development. (89–90)

18. Give four reasons why small firms are able to survive. (94)

Assignment – Marketing in organisations   Element 3.1

You are asked to

1. **record a discussion** about marketing principles and marketing functions with supporting notes.

   Your discussion and notes should explain the ways in which business organisations manage to balance the interests of customers with the interests of their own organisation.

2. **prepare a report** which analyses the marketing activities of two business organisations, one profit making and the other not-for profit. Your report should explain how each organisation

   a) has achieved growth using both product development and market development

   b) uses marketing research to assess market needs and how this information is used by marketing personnel

   c) uses marketing and selling activities to generate maximum income and, where appropriate, maximum profit.

You may find it helpful to read the other chapters in this Unit and of Element 1.2 (markets) and 6.4 (pricing) before completing this assignment.

---

10 Marketing Research and Product Development

This chapter is about the collection and analysis of market information and its use in product development. It includes:

- Marketing Research
- Marketing Decisions
- Desk Research
- Field Research
- Sampling
- Research Methods
- Questionnaire Design
- Research Agencies

- Evaluating Marketing Research
- Analysis of Data
- Statistical Terms
- Normal Distribution
- Presentation of Data
- Product Development
- Product Withdrawal
- Product Design

Marketing Research

1. Businesses today have ready access to vast amounts of statistical data from both inside and outside the organisation. Much of this data is available on computers and therefore with the use of databases and spreadsheets can be very quickly and easily manipulated, to identify, study and solve many problems and to assist with decision-taking.

2. Internal information, for example, about sales, price, costs, exports, stock levels, can be analysed in such a way that they enable conclusions to be drawn and better informed decisions taken about such issues as capital investment, production and marketing. This process is assisted by external information from, for example, the local and national press, government publications and trade associations.

3. A firm which finds out about the people who buy, or may buy, its products is far more likely to be successful in selling them. This information can be used to improve the way in which goods and services are marketed. Market research is used to find this out and to provide information about past, current and future trends. It is now seen as an essential part of business planning by most successful companies.

4. **Marketing Research** involves collecting, recording and analysing information about products or markets in order to improve decision-taking. This includes for example:

   - **Consumer preferences**. The more a firm can find out about the people who use, buy or may buy their products, the easier it becomes both to produce what they want and then to persuade them to buy.

   - **Consumer behaviour and buying patterns**. This could include information about consumers age, sex, occupation, habits, likes and dislikes, where they live, which newspapers they read or when they watch television, which can all be used to improve the way in which goods and services are marketed.

   - **Market trends**. It is possible to discover whether the market is increasing or decreasing by studying changes in overall sales, market share, sales of new, existing or possible substitute products and the profitability of businesses in the market.

   - **Competitor activities**. In particular advertising, promotion, or product development which can all have an effect on sales and market share.

5. Marketing Research information then is used to find the answers to a number of questions. For example:

   a) Who might buy a product? – anyone, teenagers, parents.

   b) Who actually buys it? – most children's toys are bought by adults.

   c) Who uses it? – a lot of men's clothing is actually purchased by women.

   d) How often do they buy it? – weekly, monthly.

   e) Why do they buy it? – like smell, colour, sound, quality or shape.

   f) How did they find out about it? – TV, newspapers, friends.

   g) Where did they buy it from? – supermarket, mail order catalogue.

   h) Who are the main competitors? – locally, regionally, nationally.

   i) How do competitors products compare? – image, price, quality, packaging, promotion.

Task 1   **3.2.1 (C3.4)**

1. Choosing any two products which you or someone in your household has recently purchased, answer the questions listed in paragraph 5.

2. Are there any questions which you cannot answer or answers which you consider to be surprising?

3. Comment on your findings and in particular how they help you to understand why marketing research is important and necessary in business.

Marketing Decisions

6. Based on this type of information, it is possible for firms to **forecast** (estimate) the likely sales of their products or services. They can then make the important marketing decisions which are necessary to achieve these sales including:

   ❒ What type of product to **produce** (including features and packaging) and how much

   ❒ What **price** to charge, although clearly this must also be related to cost

   ❒ What sales and **promotional** methods to use, including the best place to advertise

   ❒ Which method of distribution to use, including the best **places** to reach most consumers

   ❒ The **timing** of decisions which will maximise sales from the marketing mix.

7. It is important to realise that research can help organisations to identify the optimum marketing mix of product, price, promotion and place. The price of own brand products such as Asda or Safeway tea or coffee, for example, is more important than that of a leading brand such as PG, Typhoo or Tetley, where promotion and marketing communications (see Chapter 11 Element 3.3.) to support the brand image are more important. This is because own brands are usually promoted as a cheaper alternative to leading brands. Many consumers are still prepared to pay a slightly higher price for a brand which is heavily promoted on factors such as extra quality and value which to some extent are seen as being reflected in the price. Consider, for example, you perceptions of a jumper selling at £8.99 compared with one at £19.99.

8. The process of market research involves six basis steps which are discussed in this chapter.

   ❒ **Defining** the problem to be researched i.e. what you want to find out
   ❒ **Determining** the most suitable research technique – within the budget available
   ❒ **Selecting** the sample for the study
   ❒ **Collecting** the data
   ❒ **Analysing** the data
   ❒ **Presenting** the results

Market Research Methods

Market research information can be obtained in two ways – using desk research or field research.

9. **Desk research** or secondary data involves studying existing information which can be found either:

   ❏ **internally** – within an organisation, i.e. a firm's own records, for example sales, stock or accounting records, customer complaints and feedback from sales representatives' reports, or

   ❏ **externally** – outside an organisation, i.e. published by someone else, for example by banks, newspapers, trade associations, governments, professional bodies and Chambers of Commerce.

Database Research

10. The knowledge which a business has about its existing and potential customers provides a valuable database for market research. Developments in information technology have made this area more useful for marketing purposes because it can help organisations to target customers, particularly by post and telephone, and by identifying opportunities for the sales force.

11. A database could, for example, contain:

   ❏ names and addresses of customers, with additional information such as size and type of business for companies, and demographic (age, size, race etc) and lifestyle characteristics (occupation, income, housing etc) for individuals.

   ❏ distinguish customers on the basis of what, when, why, how much and where they purchase, thus providing a customer profile. The analysis of postcodes is particularly useful in this respect.

   ❏ retailers, in particular supermarkets, are making increasing use of scanning techniques at the point of sale which record data on computers from bar-codes. This provides both rapid and valuable sales analysis and stock control information.

External Data Sources

12. Some examples of the many UK Government publications which a firm could study include:

   Annual Abstract of Statistics

   Population Trends

   Regional Trends

   Monthly Digest of Statistics

   Social Trends

   General Household Survey

13. Libraries also contain many other reference books from which marketing data can be obtained. Examples include Technical Journals, Dictionaries, Kompass Directories, The Stock Exchange Year Books and Extel's company records and 'Who owns Whom'!

14. Whilst sources of International Data include:

   International Yearbook of Labour Statistics

   International Travel Statistics, U.N. Demographic Year Book, U.N. National Statistical Year Book and various European Community Publications.

15. External data can be useful both

   ❏ to enhance an organisations own knowledge about its markets and also

   ❏ to identify potential opportunities and threats.

> **Task 2**   **3.2.1, 3.2.2 (C3.4)**
>
> Look in the reference section of a library and
>
> 1. Write brief notes on the content of each of the publications referred to in paragraphs 12 and 13.
>
> 2. Try to identify at least 5 potential sources of secondary data for a firm which is considering producing a new leisure product aimed at the 16–25 age group and state how each source will assist the firm in its decision-taking.

External Research

16. **Field Research** or primary data involves the collection of **new information** which could be about a firm's market, products, advertising, promotion, pricing, distribution or competition.

17. Most market research uses **quantitative** techniques to discover **how many** consumers are in a particular market, and how much they buy e.g. the total number of car owners and/or **qualitative techniques** to discover consumer attitudes and **why** they behave in certain ways, e.g. why they buy one make or model or car in preference to another.

Sampling

18. Except in some small industrial markets, it is not usually possible to ask all consumers (called the **population** or total market) what they think about a particular product or service. The time factor and cost involved would be too great. Therefore, market research surveys usually select a 'representative' cross section, or **sample** of people and question them.

19. Statistical theory can be used to calculate the minimum size of sample necessary to give the required degree of accuracy. Although generally the larger the sample, the greater the accuracy, this also increases the cost and therefore a balance between the two must be struck.

20. For practical purposes it is the selection of the sample which is more important than the size. The sample must be fully representative of the population being studied. If, for example a firm is carrying out market research to discover information about consumers of its products or services, it is important that the sample is balanced in terms of age, sex, type of occupation, social class and so on.

21. A carefully chosen sample should be **statistically reliable**, that is it should produce very similar results to those that would be achieved by asking everyone in the population. It has to be recognised, however, that a certain amount of bias may exist, that is any research may be distorted by a number of factors, for example samples which are poorly selected or too small, or questionnaires with complex interview questions or to which the responses might be misinterpreted. If bias takes place then the **validity** (accuracy and reliability) of the information collected will be reduced.

> **Task 3**   **3.2.1, 3.2.2 (C3.2)**
>
> 1. What would be the 'population' and what factors would you need to consider if you wanted to find out what influences the choice of brand or model for car owners in the UK?
>
> 2. How could you obtain this information?

Probability Samples

22. The two main types of sample are known as probability and non-probability samples. The main type of probability sample is called random sampling which can be simple, systematic or stratified.

23. **Simple Random Sampling** means that every member of the population has an equal chance of being selected. Names and addresses for example, may be chosen at random from the electoral register and

then visited for the interview. A slight variation to this is **systematic random sampling** which involves selecting every nth item or person, for example every 10th name in a telephone directory.

24. **Stratified random sampling** divides the population into groups (called strata) by, for example, age, sex, occupation or social class to provide a more representative cross-section of the whole. Each selected sub-group is then randomly sampled.

25. A major problem with random sampling is that only those selected are interviewed which often involves 'calling back' to complete them.

26.

Non-Probability Samples

27. These are samples where there is no way of estimating the probability of any particular item being included. This has the advantage of being cheaper and more convenient than probability samples.

28. **Quota Sampling** involves the interviewer in selecting a given number of the population who fulfil certain criteria such as age and sex. These are often used for street interviews when, for example, the quota may be to interview 25 males and 25 females in each of the following age groups: 15-24, 25-40, and 41-50.

29. **Purposive Sampling** involves deliberately biasing a sample depending on the market being investigated. Thus, for example, a manufacturer launching a new drug would want to discover doctors' likely reactions to it whilst a textbook publisher would seek teachers' opinions of a proposed book.

30. **Cluster Sampling** is often used to reduce the costs of interviewing such as travelling and involves selecting a random group which is concentrated in a particular area or region rather than individual respondents. Thus, for example, just a few streets or a particular town could be chosen.

31. **Convenience Sampling** involves gathering information from whoever is available when the survey takes place, regardless of their age, sex, background or other criteria, e.g. stopping passers-by to seek their views on bank charges. Whilst cheaper, this is clearly likely to be less reliable than other methods.

32. To help overcome this **judgement sampling** may be used whereby the interviewer selects respondents who are judged to be representative of the population in a particular market.

> ### Task 4   3.2.1 (C3.4)
>
> A national manufacturer of washing machines is planning to develop a new model to compliment its current range. It believes from an analysis of the sales of its existing products that the likely market is females in the 30-45 age group. To confirm this view it plans to obtain further information by carrying out a market research survey.
>
> 1. Suggest, with reasons, the type of sample which should be used to give the most accurate forecast of the potential market for the new product.
>
> 2. Indicate how changes in the age distribution of the population might influence its future strategies.

Research Methods

33. Methods of field research include the use of questionnaires, consumer panels, discussion groups, opinion polls, test marketing, retail audits, observation and motivational research. **Surveys** using questionnaires are by far the most commonly used method.

34. **Questionnaires** consist of a number of questions which are used to ask the opinions of existing or potential consumers. You or your parents for example, may have been stopped in the street and interviewed about a particular product or asked which television programmes you watch.

    Sometimes these surveys are also carried out on the telephone or by post and occasionally take place in a more informal environment such as in a person's home.

    Companies may also buy into an **omnibus survey** requiring specific questions to be asked in a survey which groups several (often unrelated) topics together.

35. **Example** – a simple questionnaire used in a restaurant to check customer satisfaction.

Please complete the reply section below and post it in the box provided.

(Please Tick)

1. How were you greeted on entering the restaurant?
2. How was the service?
3. How was the food?
4. Overall, how do you feel about your visit?
5. Will you visit again?

Name: _____
Address: _____ Post Code: _____

No. in party: _____
Day: ☐ Evening: ☐ (Please Tick)
Date: _____
Any other comments: _____

NAME OF OUTLET VISITED

Reproduced by kind permission of Burtonwood Brewery Plc

36. **Personal** interviewing, face-to-face, is time consuming and expensive, especially when random sampling is used. Interviewers may also introduce bias by misinterpreting questions and/or prompting respondents to answer in a particular way. They can, however, provide greater detail and accuracy plus high response rates. Body language can also be observed and noted if appropriate.

37. **Telephone** interviews are cost effective when a limited amount of information is required quickly. A growing use is for day-after recall of T.V. advertisements. They are also useful for obtaining a

response from busy business organisations. The sample, however, has an in-built bias if limited to telephone subscribers and may produce refusals if the call catches people unaware or at an inconvenient time.

38. **Postal questionnaires** provide a low-cost method of reaching vast numbers of potential customers across the country, including relatively inaccessible rural areas as well as towns and cities. But, although usually sent with a reply paid envelope, response rates are often as low as 5%. Also, respondents may take a long time to reply and not answer questions fully or accurately.

Questionnaire Design

39. Questionnaires will only be successful in providing the required information if they are well designed and relevant with unambiguous, easy-to-understand answers. A poor questionnaire is likely to produce bias, a poor response rate and consequently less reliable data.

40. Questions used can be dichotomous (closed), multiple-choice or open-ended.
    - ❑ **Dichotomous** questions require a simple yes or no response, e.g. 'Do you have a microwave?'
    - ❑ **Multiple-choice** questions offer the respondent a number of alternative answers, e.g. 'How often do you buy breakfast cereals?'

At least once a week	☐
Once a fortnight	☐
Once a month	☐
Never	☐

41. A mixture of the strengths of people's attitudes and opinions can also be obtained by offering a range of alternatives, e.g. 'prescriptions should be free for everyone'

Strongly disagree	☐
Disagree	☐
Agree	☐
Strongly Agree	☐
No particular view	☐

42. Dichotomous and multi-choice questions focus directly and are quicker and easier to answer and analyse.

43. **Open-ended** questions on the other hand, leave the respondent free to comment as they wish. Answers therefore may contain more information but prove to be lengthy and difficult to analyse.

44. Sometimes **prompt cards** and **skips** are used to assist respondents. These help to speed the response to questions and also make it easier to record and analyse answers particularly when numbered to facilitate data processing.

45. **A prompt card**

Which of the following dog foods do you regularly purchase? (Tick the relevant Boxes).		
Pedigree Chum	☐	01
Bounce	☐	02
Chappie	☐	03
Pal	☐	04
Chunky	☐	05
Shops own brand	☐	06
Other	☐	07

The above could be used for a postal survey. For a personal interview the respondent would merely be shown the list of names.

46. **A skip**

```
┌─────────────────────────────────────────────────────────┐
│                                                         │
│     Question 1                                          │
│              Do you own a dog?          yes   ☐         │
│                                                         │
│                                         no    ☐         │
│                                                         │
│          If your answer is no please go straight to Question 5. │
│                                                         │
└─────────────────────────────────────────────────────────┘
```

Task 5   **3.2.1 (C3.3)**

From re-reading paragraphs 25–38 and your own knowledge and experience identify the possible advantages and disadvantages of using questionnaires. Consider the differences between personal interviews, telephone and postal surveys in terms of:

- ☐ time
- ☐ cost
- ☐ speed
- ☐ accuracy
- ☐ ease of use
- ☐ accessibility of sample
- ☐ interview bias
- ☐ potential response rate.

Present your answer in the form of a simple chart or diagram.

47. **Consumer panels** are another method of field research. They involve the selection of groups of consumers who are **either questioned** about their reactions to new or existing products; **asked to record details** of their spending over a period of time **or to participate in user tests** where they try a particular product and say what they think about it.

48. The success of consumer panels, however, depends very much upon the personality, enthusiasm and reliability of the people involved. Since they can be quite time-consuming it is likely that they will not appeal to certain groups of the population and therefore may not be truly representative of the whole population.

49. **Focus groups** are sometimes used whereby a number of existing or potential consumers are brought together and asked to give their opinions of a particular products or service. Someone from the research organisation involved usually chairs the group in order to structure the discussion.

50. **Opinion polls** are used for a quick check on people's views or awareness of particular issues. They normally involve just a few (sometimes only 3 or 4) questions. A business may use these to, for example, quickly gauge the impact of a particular advertising campaign or product improvement.

51. **Test marketing** is sometimes used by manufacturers to gauge consumer reaction to a new product or promotion in a particular town or area before deciding whether or not to market it nation-wide. Manufacturers of mass produced goods such as tea, coffee, and cereals often base tests on ITV regions, e.g. Borders, Yorkshire or Ulster.

52. Although this is a relatively expensive form of research, it is more thorough and reliable than simply asking people what they might buy. However, the 'sample' area may not be truly representative of the total population and the results of a successful test launch may not necessarily be repeated nationally. Test marketing also means that competitors get to know about the product, advertisement or promotional idea and therefore may decide to develop something similar.

Task 6　　　　　　　　　　　　　　　　　　　　**3.2.1 (C3.4)**

Test marketing may also be carried out in other ways as the following news extract illustrates.

TROLLEY FOLLY

It was supposed to be the answer to a shopper's prayer, but the five-wheeled trolley invented by Sainsburys to cut accidents in the aisles is now consigned to the scrapheap.

An extra wheel fixed to one side of a traditional trolley to increase stability and aid steering drove customers round the bend when it went on trial at the firm's store in Somerford, near Christchurch, Dorset.

The store turned into an obstacle course, and a book for shoppers' comments was soon filled with angry complaints.

Sainsburys which has 317 stores, bowed to public pressure and halted the trial only six days after it had begun.

One disgruntled shopper said 'It's hard to believe anything could be worse than the trolleys we're used to, but this one was almost impossible to manoeuvre. I found that whenever I moved, it wouldn't. Going round corners was a nightmare, and I'm sure I hit other shoppers with it. When I first went into the store, I thought I'd got a duff trolley until someone said they were all like that.'

A spokesman for Sainsburys said: 'We would never introduce equipment which would prove unpopular with the majority of our customers. We frequently carry out trials of different types of equipment as part of our policy to offer the best new technology and service to customers.

---

1. In your own words, briefly outline the reasons for the research taking place and what benefits the firm gained from the trial.

2. Comment on the method used and its suitability for the purpose.

53. **Retail Audits** involve the use of sample surveys of retailers to analyse sales in order to gauge market size and shares, check price levels and assess the proportion of outlets stocking various brands. They are usually carried out by specialist research organisations who then sell the information to firms in the industry.

54. **Observation** involves monitoring consumer behaviour, particularly in supermarkets to study how people actually shop. This information is then used in the design of store layouts and use of shelf space, both of which can have a major impact on sales. Firms considering opening a new store may also use this technique to determine whether or not a particular location is likely to be busy.

55. **Motivational Research** involves the use of psychological techniques, including in-depth interviews and word association tests, to determine why particular products are purchased, or not. Often consumers themselves do not really know why they buy particular products.

Electronic Monitoring

56. Developments in information technology have already influenced the design of questionnaires so that nowadays answers are coded for rapid analysis. In future the anticipated growth of inter-active view data systems such as cable television and voice recognition computers is likely to lead to further electronic monitoring which could dramatically change the methods and speed with which much market research is carried out.

57. Personal interviewing, for example, could be supplemented and possibly eventually replaced, whilst consumer panels could use computers with direct links to a control point instead of completing conventional diaries. Information could therefore be instantly available. Thus, for example, a firm could ask people to answer questions on a particular advertising campaign whilst it is actually taking place.

Choice of Research Methods

58. We have seen that there are many market research techniques available, each of which has its own particular advantages and disadvantages. The method chosen to discover the information required by an organisation will clearly depend upon a number of different factors including: ·

- ❐ **Budget available**
- ❐ **Accuracy required** } Often the more accurate the method the higher the cost
- ❐ **How quickly the information is needed**
- ❐ **Complexity of the method** – simple methods may be less reliable but quicker, cheaper and easier to implement
- ❐ **Accessibility of the sample population** which could affect the time taken to arrange and complete the research and also its validity

---

Task 7   3.2.1, 3.2.2 (C3.2)

A local cash and carry wholesaler plans to carry out research to discover the following.

1. The size of its catchment area.

2. Which type of retailers use the warehouse and why.

3. Which other wholesalers/suppliers they use and why.

4. Whether its opening hours are convenient.

5. The main products which retailers buy and why.

6. Whether the layout of the warehouse influences the way purchases are made.

Suggest with reasons appropriate methods which it could use for each piece of information.

Market Research Agencies

59. We have seen that a firm can carry out its own market research, particularly where secondary data is required. When primary data is required, however, it is usual to engage the expertise of a specialist market research agency. In addition to carrying out ad hoc research for clients some of the larger agencies also undertake continuous research in particular market sectors. The findings are usually produced as reports which are circulated to subscribers at regular intervals and provide important information on, for example market size, growth, market shares, advertising, competition and trends.

60. Some well known examples of commercial research organisations include:

A.C. Neilson – which specialises in retail audits.

Gallup – famous for its political opinion polls and the weekly 'pop' charts.

Audits of Great Britain (AGB) – which uses consumer diaries to provide information on household expenditure.

Audit Bureau of Circulation (ABC) – which provides information on newspapers and other media circulation.

Joint Industrial Committee On Television Audience Research (JICTAR) – which produces weekly television viewing figures.

Mintel – which produces a monthly journal containing reports on various consumer markets such as banks and insurance.

Euromonitor – which produces Key Note Reports on a range of businesses, which include market sizes, growth trends, competitor analysis, market forecasts, current issues and a SWOT analysis.

Evaluating Market Research

61. The value of market research information will usually be measured in terms of the increased sales or profits which result from the application of the results. Ultimately, it is only worthwhile if this value exceeds the cost of the research. Thus, for example, take a company with current sales of 100,000 units at a profit of £5 per unit. The advertising manager believes from research costing £5,000 that a switch from poster to radio advertising will increase sales by 2–5% for the same level of expenditure. If we assume a 2% increase this equals £10,000 (£2,000 x 5) minus the cost leaving an extra profit of £5,000.

Analysis of Data

62. Different methods of marketing research lead to different forms of data collection. Open-ended questions, for example, cannot be analysed in the same way as closed or multiple-choice questions but they often provide more detailed information. In paragraph 50 we saw that the method chosen is usually a compromise between a number of factors. Clearly ease of analysis must also be considered especially since it can also affect the cost.

63. Developments in information technology and the increasing use of sophisticated data processing software packages has transformed the collection, analysis and storage of data in recent years.

64. As mentioned in paragraph 48, primary data obtained from market research surveys is now processed from questionnaires designed with numerically coded questions to enable the collation and analysis of answers to be carried out quickly and efficiently. The use of postcodes enables information to be identified by specific areas. Data can also be presented in a variety of interesting and more meaningful ways especially with desktop publishing packages.

Statistical Terms

65. The collection, recording and analysis of numerical data whether primary or secondary is called statistics. Thus, for example, we speak of economic statistics, population statistics and business statistics.

66. In order to understand the analysis and presentation of statistics it is important to be aware of some of the basic terms which are used. These include averages, trends, sampling, probability and frequency distributions.

Averages

67. An average is a value which is typical and representative of a set of data. Although it should be noted that an average is not necessarily identical with any of the numbers which it represents. For example, the average number of individuals per household in an area may be 3.5 but clearly in reality it is a whole number such as 1, 2, 3, 4 or 5.

68. There are several different types of averages which can be calculated from any set of data, the most frequently used measures being the arithmetic mean, median and mode.

69. **Arithmetic Mean**. This is the total of all individual values divided by the number of them. It is the most frequently used average, often abbreviated simply to mean, and useful because it takes into account all values and therefore can be used for further analysis.

70. Its main problem is that it can be distorted by extremes and therefore comparisons can be misleading. Consider, for example, the following two sets of numbers:

   ❐ 16, 20, 14, 24, 21

   ❐ 69, -47, 99, -2, -24

   Both have a mean of 19 but are clearly very different in their nature.

71. **Median.** This is found by taking the middle value of data arranged in order of magnitude (if there is an odd number of items in the set), or by the mean of the 2 middle numbers if there is an even number of items. It is a useful figure in that it helps to avoid the distortion by extremes. Consider, for example, the effect of an exam mark of 10 when all the others are between 45–65.

72. **Mode.** This is the value which occurs most frequently in a set of data. It is useful in that it can be used to represent data grouped in the form of a qualitative frequency distribution. Thus, for example, manufacturers interested in clothes sizes or shoe sizes could identify the numbers required for each size.

73. However, although the mode represents a typical value and is not affected by extremes, it does not use all of the values and therefore is not capable of further processing.

74. **Example – Mean, Median, Mode**

    In the following set of numbers:

    10, 14, 12, 13, 18, 14, 15, 10, 13, 10

    the mode is 10 because it is the value which occurs most frequently.

    If this data is rearranged in size order it would be

    10, 10, 10, 12, 13, 14, 14 , 15, 18

    hence the median is 13 because it is the middle value.

    Whilst the mean is calculated from the sum of the values, that is,

    $$10 + 14 + 12 + 13 + 18 + 14 + 15 + 10 + 13 + 10 = \frac{129}{10} = 12.9$$

Task 8   **3.2.2 (N3.3)**

6 employees had weekly incomes of £250, £150, £350, £400, £150 and £200 what would be the mean, median and mode incomes?

Trends

75. These refer to the **general direction** in which a measured variable is moving. Data may show a 'rising' or 'falling' trend depending on whether there is an increase or decrease over time. For example, current trends show a continuing decline in employment in manufacturing industries. Trends, for example sales, costs and inflation, are particularly important for business forecasting which is discussed in Chapter 19 Element 6.1.

Sampling

76. Demographic and economic statistics are concerned with establishing total values such as the size of the working population or level of unemployment. But much statistical theory used for market research is concerned with summarising and analysing information about individuals for example why they buy particular products. Sampling techniques are discussed in paragraphs 22–32.

Probability

77. Probability is one of the most important statistical concepts. It refers to the **likelihood of a particular uncertain event or outcome occurring.** For example, we speak of the probability of rain tomorrow, the probability of something breaking down or the probability of a business being successful. Likewise we tend to say that it is highly improbable that we shall win our fortune on the football pools.

78. Probability is usually measured on a scale from 0.0, such an event will never occur, to 1.0 such an event is certain to occur, for example death.

79. Probabilities are usually structured on the basis of the relative frequency with which an event has occurred in the past. Thus all events have a probability between 0 and 1, although we do not know precisely what it is because we cannot be certain about the outcome of any course of action which we choose.

80. However, by means of statistical analysis, it is often possible to assess the likely probability of an event occurring. This is important for business because it is this which enables possible outcomes from events or decisions to be structured on a 'calculated risk' basis rather than pure guesswork.

81. There are two probability theories:

   ❏ **Subjective theory** which essentially is based simply on what someone believes will happen.

   ❏ **Frequency theory** which is applied to events which happen 'regularly' or that can be repeated over and over again under the same conditions. For example, insurance companies, calculate premiums based on the probability of events such as fire, theft or accidents taking place.

Task 9   3.2.1, 3.2.2 (N3.2)

With some events it is possible to calculate the exact probability of it occurring.

Calculate the probability of:

1.   A tossed coin landing as a 'head' or 'tail'.

2.   Two six-sided dice thrown simultaneously, landing with a total score of 3.

3.   Test your calculations by recording 50 occurrences of each.

4.   Comment on your findings.

---

82. To get a better idea of what a set of probabilities look like, statisticians often present the information in a graphic form known as a **frequency (probability) distribution**. A set of data is called a distribution and the frequency is the number of times which any variable occurs in a distribution.

Normal Distribution

83. The dispersion of the values in a sample of a 'population' normally distribute themselves around a mean value. The greater the amount of data the more likely this is. This frequency distribution when plotted on a chart forms a bell shaped curve called a normal distribution.

84.

Normal Distribution Curve

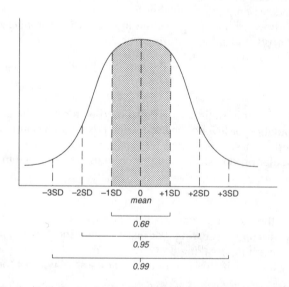

Mean = average of a set of data

Standard deviation (sd) measures dispersion of data around its mean value.

85. The normal distribution is very important because it is the pattern most frequently encountered in the real world. The areas under the curve represent probabilities which are available ready calculated in what is called a Z score table. Hence, it can be used to help make statistical inferences – either estimation or hypothesis testing – which can then be applied to the entire population.

86. **Estimation** involves calculating the unknown value of a population characteristic such as the average value of numerical data or a proportion having particular attributes. For example, the mean height of all adult females in Birmingham can be estimated by calculating the average height of a sample of adult females in Birmingham.

87. **Hypothesis testing** involves making a reasoned assumption, usually on the basis of observation and testing it. For example, the hypothesis that women are smaller than men or that salaries are determined by company size. These can be tested using the normal distribution curve, sample data or other statistical techniques before being accepted or rejected. A statistical hypothesis under test is referred to as the **null hypothesis.**

Skewness

88. When a distribution is not normal, that is the arithmetic mean does not fall in the middle, it is said to be skewed. This usually means that it is distorted by a few extreme values which is shown graphically as below.

89

Examples of Skewed Frequency Distributions

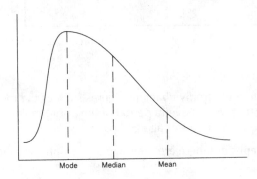 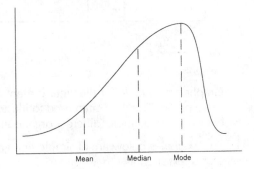

Positively skewed distribution   Negatively skewed distribution

Median = middle value of a set of data

Mode = value which occurs most frequently in a set of data

Presentation of Data

90. In order to make sense of data it is important that it is presented in such a way that it is easy to understand and makes the desired point(s) quickly and effectively.

91. The four main methods used to present statistical data are:

   ❏ Tables of figures
   ❏ Graphs
   ❏ Charts – Pie charts and Bar charts
   ❏ Diagrams such as Pictograms and Cartograms

92. **Tables of Figures**

   You will doubtless be familiar with information presented in tables like the one below. The problem with these is that the data may be difficult to interpret, absorb and retain. Hence, whilst statistical tables are useful, particularly when a lot of detailed information has to be presented, in general more visually interesting methods are to be preferred.

93.

Example of a Table of Figures
Participation in education (percentage of cohort)

Age Group	full-time		part-time	
	1988–89	**1992–93**	**1988–89**	**1992–93**
16	52%	71%	17%	8%
17	35%	55%	18%	11%
18	18%	34%	14%	12%
	1991–92			
21–24	6%			
25–34	4%			
35 & over	2%			

Source: Department of Education

94. **Graphs**

Graphs are suitable for the clear presentation of rapidly changing figures such as the movements in share prices. They are often used to illustrate changes over a period of time or to make comparisons between, for example, different organisations, countries or age groups.

95. The examples below are of simple **line graphs** but there are other types of graphs beyond the scope of this text such as:

❐ Lorenz curves
❐ Semi-Logarithmic and
❐ Layer Graphs

96. **Examples of Line Graphs**

Movement in the share price of ABC plc

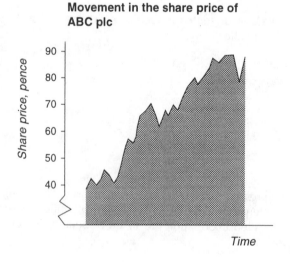

Labour market entrants from schools and colleges

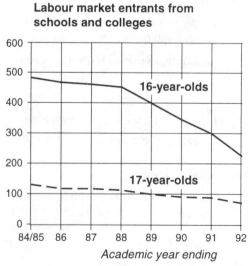

Source: Labour Market and Skills Trends 1993/4

Task 10

Study the share prices of any two companies over a time period of 1-4 weeks.

1. Plot the prices on a graph.

2. Comment on the trends and the reason(s) for any significant changes which have taken place

3. Identify and describe the trends in the 2 graphs in the example above.

97. **Charts**

The most common types of chart are pie charts, 'Z' charts and bar charts.

❑ **Pie Charts** are useful to illustrate in a circle divided into segments, how a total is made up, such as the breakdown of exports shown on the following page.

❑ **'Z' Charts**, so called because of their shape, are used to show 3 sets of data together. Current data, a cumulative total to show the position to date and the moving annual total which shows the trend. The latter is obtained by continually replacing a month from the previous year with the current month's data.

❑ **Bar Charts** are useful for summarising and comparing figures over a period of time or between items. Bar charts may also be presented in a number of different ways as the following examples illustrate. Here different formats are being used either simply to compare multiple data or to show the breakdown of a total into its component parts.

98. **Examples of Pie Charts and 'Z' Charts**

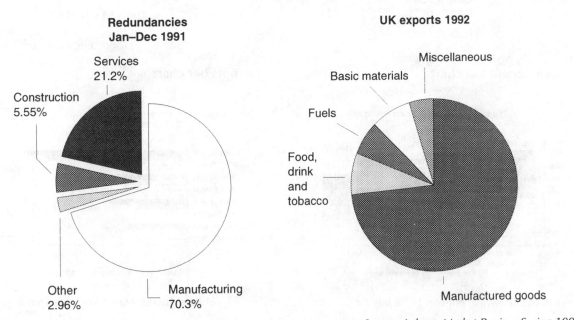

Source: Labour Market Review Spring 1992

235

'Z' chart for sales data

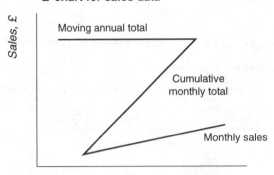

99.   **Examples of Bar Charts**

Multiple bar chart

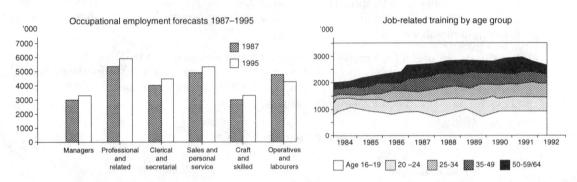

Component bar chart

Component bar chart

Multiple bar chart

Source: DFE Statistical Bulletin 14/92 July 1992

Source: Labour Market and Skill Trends 1993/4

The multiple bar chart shows the breakdown of a total figure into its component parts.

Task 11   **3.2.2 (N3.3)**

The age distribution of the population in 1991 was estimated as follows:

- ❏ 20% under 16 years of age
- ❏ 64% between 16 and 64 years
- ❏ 16% aged 65 years and over

In 1951 the figures were 23%, 67% and 10% respectively.

Show this information in the form of pie charts and comment on the figures.

Pictograms and Cartograms

100. **Pictograms** are similar to bar charts but use small signs or symbols to illustrate data. Ideally, these have some resemblance to the subject of the data and hence tend to be more visually appealing.

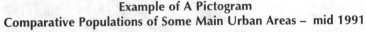

Example of A Pictogram
Comparative Populations of Some Main Urban Areas – mid 1991

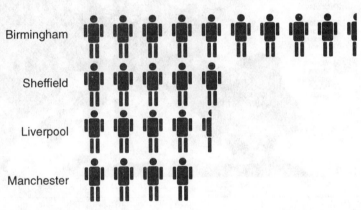

Based on preliminary figures from 1991 Census

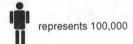 represents 100,000

101. **Cartograms** use maps to illustrate data. These are useful because they help us to put things in perspective. Many organisations, for example, use location maps to help clients to find them or to illustrate their spread of activities across the country or the world. The cartogram below is useful for illustrating the spread of some of Ford's multinational operations.

102.   **Example of a Cartogram**

**FORD OPERATIONS
IN EUROPE**

1 Belfast
2 Cork
3 Halewood
4 Treforest
5 Swansea
6 Bridgend
7 Langley
8 Leamington
9 Daventry
10 Southampton
11 Dagenham
   Warley
   Aveley
12 Enfield
13 Woolwich
   Croydon
14 Basildon
   Dunton
   Boreham
15 Oslo
16 Stockholm
17 Helsinki
18 Copenhagen
19 Amsterdam
20 Antwerp
21 Lommel
22 Brussels
23 Wuefrath
24 Cologne
25 Genk
26 Dueren
27 Charleville
28 Paris
29 Saarlouis
30 Zurich
31 Bordeaux
32 Madrid
33 Lisbon
34 Valencia
35 Vienna
36 Salzburg
37 Rome
38 Berlin

Ford is one of Europe's leading organisations, employing some 110,000 people in 15 separate national companies. Its products are sold through 2,520 main dealers and 1,460 sub-dealers across Europe. In addition there are 2,150 Ford customer service and repair centres.

Task 12   3.2.2 (C3.2)

1. Draw a simple sketch map to show the route to your School, College or place of work from an easily identified location such as a bus station, railway station or motorway junction.

2. Add any other helpful information and say why you have included it.

3. Comment on why such a map may be useful to visitors/clients both from inside and outside the area.

4. Finally, write a short memo to the head of your chosen organisation outlining the value of using pictograms and cartograms as methods of presentation.

103. We have considered just some of the many ways of presenting statistics. The method chosen will usually depend upon the data concerned and the preferences of the presenter.

104. The most important points to remember in presenting data are:

❏ The method chosen should be clear, concise and visually appealing.

❏ Complex or over-fancy illustrations can confuse and/or distract from the data presented.

❏ A clear title is essential and all components of the illustration should be labelled.

❏ If secondary data is used the source should be quoted.

❏ The units used should be indicated, for example, tonnes, thousands, £'s, hours.

Product Development

105. For a firm to remain successful **innovation** is essential. New products must be developed which cater for changing markets as consumers demand new and better quality products. As sales of one product decline it must be replaced by a new one if the firm is to survive and keep ahead of its competitors.

106. As shown in the following example, Proctor and Gamble Limited have regularly introduced **new** or **modified** fabric washing products, particularly during the 1980's and 1990's. Some other examples of recent successful new products include Body Shop, Red Rock Cider, Plax, Lucozade Sport, Mars Ice-Cream snacks, Radion Micro and Persil washing up liquid. Against this, however, it has to be recognised that an incredible 95% of new advertised grocery brands have failed in the past 10 years, whilst many of the top brands like Kodak, Del Monte and Campbells have been around since the 1920's.

Proctor & Gamble Limited Retail Fabric Washing Products

(with dates of national introduction)

Dreft	1937	Daz Ultra	1990
Tide	1950	Bold Ultra	1990
Daz	1953	Fairy Ultra	1990
Fairy Snow	1957	Ariel Ultra Liquid	1992
Ariel	1969	Ariel Color	1992
Bold	1972	Bold Ultra Liquid	1992
Daz Automatic	1979	Daz Ultra Liquid	1992
Ariel Automatic	1981	Daz Color	1992
Dreft Automatic	1984	Ariel Color Liquid	1993
Ariel Automatic Liquid	1986	Fairy Color Liquid	1993
Ariel Rapide	1988	Ariel Travel Wash	1994
Daz Automatic Liquid	1988	Dreft Ultra	1994
Fairy Automatic	1989	Ariel Future	1995
Fairy Automatic Liquid	1989	Ariel Future Color	1995
Bold Liquid	1989	Ariel Future Liquid	1995
Ariel Ultra	1989	Ariel Future Color Liquid	1995

Product Withdrawal

107. When sales of a particular product or service do decline, a firm will need to determine whether this is

   ❑ **temporary** due, for example, to circumstances such as economic recession, the weather or new competition. The sales of ice cream, for example, would suffer in a bad summer.

   ❑ **capable of being reversed** by changing the marketing mix, perhaps the price or methods of distribution.

   ❑ **due to obsolescence** brought about by new technology which makes the product out-of-date. Recent examples being the Sony Betamax VCR system which was replaced by VHS, records being replaced by CDs and standard locks currently being replaced by digital and swipe card systems.

   ❑ **permanent and irreversible** making it necessary to withdraw it from the market. Launderettes, for example, were very successful until quite recently. However, the increase in the number of people buying their own automatic washing machines is now forcing many launderettes to close down.

108. In the short-term if sales are expected to recover, a firm may allow **cross-subsidisation.** This means it will retain it in the product range using profits from other products to cover any losses. However, a product which is not selling well may become relatively expensive to produce due to reduced economies of scale from lower production runs. Therefore if volume continues to decline, the product may be withdrawn.

Task 13 3.2.3 (C3.4)

LYMESWOLD IS OFF

Lymeswold, which in 1982 became the first new British cheese for 200 years, was discontinued 10 years later because of falling sales in a very competitive market dominated by Brie and Camembert. The soft mould cheese was initially so popular that Dairy Crest built a new creamery at Aston, Cheshire, to cope with demand. But the new factory and equipment changed the nature of the product which has a short life and must be sold at its best. Consequently sales slipped and a relaunch failed to win back customers. The plant closed with a loss of 38 staff.

1. Why do you think that well-known products like Lymeswold Cheese and the Sinclair C5 electric vehicle have turned out to be unsuccessful?

2. Can you think of any other products or services which have been withdrawn from sale in recent years?

Try to identify at least 3 and consider what you feel are the likely reasons for their failure.

Product Design Strategy

109 An important stage in the creation of new products or the development of existing ones is that of design. The purpose of a **design strategy** in a business is to regularly review the features of all products in the range to ensure that they both meet customers requirements and are also cost effective to produce. This is particularly important in markets where **technology** is changing rapidly as, for example, with computers.

110. The main design factors which need to be considered can be summarised as performance, appearance, economy, and legal and environmental requirements.

111. **Performance**. To be successful, a product needs to be functionally efficient so that it does what it claims to do and what customers expect of it. Depending on the product, it may also need to be reliable, safe and easy and economical to operate and maintain.

112. **Appearance**. For many consumer products, for example, cars, houses and clothing, this is a very important factor. Essentially, unless a product looks appealing, even through the functional aspects may be good, it is unlikely to be successful. On the other hand, an attractive product is unlikely to be successful unless it functions well.

113. **Economy in production, distribution and storage.** If a business is to be competitive, then it must be able to manufacture its products at a reasonable cost. This may be affected by such factors as the raw materials, components and type of packaging used. For example, a manufacturer of soft drinks can use a variety of packaging techniques including glass bottles, plastic bottles, wax cartons and aluminium cans. Each of these is functionally sound but very different in terms of customer appeal, transport and storage. This is illustrated by considering the fact that glass is the heaviest and most fragile, although often favoured by customers because the product is visible inside. Wax cartons, on the other hand, are lighter, compact and easy to store and transport but generally less attractive to the eye.

114. **Legal requirements**. Nowadays, as discussed in Elements 1.3 and 4.1 there is a wealth of Health and Safety and Consumer Protection Legislation which has to be taken into account when designing products. Examples include seat belts in cars, safety foam in furniture and accurate descriptions about holiday accommodation.

115. **Environmental factors**. Apart from the recent introduction of environmental legislation, there is also a growing public concern about the effect of many products and manufacturing processes on the environment. This has to be taken into account in design if an organisation is to avoid losing out to its competitors. Well known examples include the switch to unleaded petrol, ozone friendly aerosol sprays, smokeless fuels and recycled products.

Task 14 **3.2.3 (C3.4)**

1. Consider the design features which you would regard as important to you when 'purchasing' each of the following.

   a) A consumer durable such as: A Television Set, Washing Machine or Table.

   b) A consumable such as: A convenience food or a fresh product

   c) A service such as an insurance policy, bank account or form of transport.

2. Using a recent example from your own experience, discuss and comment on how what you 'purchased' differed from the design features identified.

3. From your answers, what are the implications, if any, for each business concerned?

Summary

121. a) Marketing research is used to provide information to firms about consumers which can be obtained through desk or field research.

b) Desk research involves the analysis of existing data.

c) Field research is based on a 'sample' of consumers and uses questionnaires, consumer panels, focus groups, opinion polls, test marketing, retail audits, observation and motivational research.

d) To be effective questionnaires, which can be used in person, by post or by telephone, must be carefully designed.

e) Probability sampling uses simple, systematic or stratified random sampling.

f) Non-probability techniques include quota, purposive, cluster, convenience and judgement sampling.

g) The research method chosen will depend upon the budget available, accuracy required, and time, complexity and sample involved.

h) Important statistical concepts include averages, trends, samples, probability and frequency distributions.

i) The normal distribution curve is bell-shaped and shows the dispersion of data around the mean (average).

j) When a distribution is not normal, it is said to be negatively or positively skewed.

k) Statistical data can be presented as tables of figures, graphs, charts or diagrams.

l) The method chosen will depend on the data concerned and preferences of the presenter but should be clear, concise and visually appealing.

m) To remain successful firms must continue to innovate by introducing new or modified products.

n) A product design strategy is important to review products and take account of current technology and consumer needs.

Review questions *(Answers can be found in the paragraph indicated)*

1. What is market research and why do firms use it? (1–7)

2. Outline the process involved in carrying out market research. (8)

3. Explain the difference between desk research and field research. (9, 16)

4. Why is sampling used in market research and in what ways can it become biased? (18–21)

5. Briefly, explain 3 types of probability sampling. (22–26)

6. Describe 3 different types of non-probability sampling techniques. (27–32)

7. Briefly, describe 4 different methods of field research. (33–55)

8. Distinguish between dichotomous, multiple-choice and open-ended questions. (40–43)

9. Briefly discuss 5 factors which a company would need to consider before undertaking market research. (58)

10. Give 4 examples of commercial market research organisations. (59–60)

11. How can market research be evaluated? (61)

12. Briefly explain the statistical meaning of the terms averages, trends, samples and probability. (65–82)

13. What are the characteristics of a normal distribution curve and why is it important? (83–87)

14. What do you understand by a skewed distribution? (88–89)

15. Identify 4 different methods of presenting statistical data and give one key feature of each. (90–102)

16. What are the important points to remember when presenting data? (103–104)

17. Outline the importance of product development and its potential impact on product withdrawal. (105–108)

18. Why does a firm need a product strategy and what factors will influence it? (109–115)

Assignment – Researching the Product   Element 3.2

Based on market research from at least one qualitative and one quantitative method you are asked to prepare a presentation for the development of 2 products. These could be existing products or ideas of your own. Your proposals, which should be justified by reference to your research, should include

❏ change to the type of product

❏ features of the product

❏ packaging of the product

❏ sales outlets (place)

❏ product promotion

❏ selling price

❏ the timing of marketing communications and sales

Your presentation should be supported by notes and numerical information which explain why your chosen research methods are suitable for collecting information relating to the two products.

Whilst primary research is not essential it is certainly a most useful and informative method of research. The following guidance is included to help you should you decide to use this as one of your methods, in which case it may be more practical to work in a group.

Tasks

1. **Decide on the products to be investigated**

   These could be fast moving consumer goods, consumer durables, services or industrial products.

2. **Design a questionnaire**

   a) Information required. It is necessary to decide what questions you want to ask, and then to write them carefully in a clear and logical way. (It is recommended that your questionnaire is fairly brief, consisting of not more than 10–15 questions). The following example may help.

Crisp Survey   *Circle the answer

1.   When did you last buy a packet of crisps?

* Today   * Yesterday   * Within the last week

* Within the last month   * Over a month ago

2.   Which brand of crisps did you buy?

3.   Why did you buy that particular brand?

4.   Which flavour did you buy?

5.   How did you rate the taste of the crisps?

* Very good   * Good   * Fair   * Not very good   * Poor

6.   Would you buy the same brand again?   *Yes/No

7.   Would you buy the same flavour again?   *Yes/No

8.   What is your favourite flavour of crisps?

b)   *Question content.* It is possible to use different styles of questions. The example il-lustrates questions which require a simple *yes* or *no* response, those which give a choice of answers and those which leave the answer open-ended.

3.   **Select a Sample**

a)   When your questionnaire is ready, the next task is to select the type and number of people that you wish to interview. For example, if you are attending a college with 1,000 students, then you might decide to ask the opinions of 1 in every 20 students, i.e. 50 altogether. You could break this sample down further into various categories by interviewing 25 male and 25 female students and by dividing these into different age groups. Remember, if your sample is to be representative of all of the students you will need to select the people you interview very carefully.

b)   You will need to reproduce sufficient copies (and spares) of your questionnaire to cover the total number required.

4.   **Carry out the interviewing**

Once the sample has been selected you can begin the interviews. If it is a group assign-ment, each person should interview a small number of people, perhaps ten.

5.   **Analyse the results**

It will be necessary to count the answers to each question. When completed, the results can be presented in the form of tables, charts and diagrams. These are often much easier to understand than a long written description.

6.   **Present a report**

Each group member should now present their own report of the survey, word processed if possible.

This should contain full details of each person's contribution to the assignment in addi-tion to a summary of the work of the other group members. It should also give details of the problems involved in carrying out the research.

A suitable structure might be as follows:

a)   Title and purpose of report

b)   Introduction

c)   Body of report, i.e. presentation and analysis of data collected.

d)   Summary of findings including the value of the information discovered.

e)   Your conclusions and/or recommendations based on the findings.

The presentation of your research findings could be made to fellow students, assessors or a representative(s) from a business organisation.

11 Marketing Communications

This chapter looks at an important element of the marketing mix, namely promotion or communications. It includes

- ❐ Advertising
- ❐ Advertising media
- ❐ Sponsorship
- ❐ Advertising Agencies
- ❐ Advertising benefits
- ❐ Ethics of Advertising
- ❐ Public Relations
- ❐ Sales Promotion
- ❐ Trade Promotions
- ❐ Consumer Promotions
- ❐ Industrial Promotions
- ❐ Market Segmentation

- ❐ Consumer Characteristics
- ❐ Product Life Cycle
- ❐ Product Strategy
- ❐ Promotional Activities and Product Performance
- ❐ Direct Marketing Methods
- ❐ Direct Mail
- ❐ Telemarketing
- ❐ Selling off-page
- ❐ Selling off-screen
- ❐ Constraints on Promotional Activities
- ❐ Voluntary Control
- ❐ Legal Control

Promotion

1. A third element of the marketing mix is promotion or the **'communications mix'** which is an essential part of modern business activities. It comprises advertising, public relations (PR), sales promotion and direct marketing. Promotion focuses on the distinctive feature(s) of a product called the **unique selling point** (USP). The basic aim of the promotion then is to communicate information to customers and potential users about the products or services on offer and eventually to persuade them to buy.

Advertising

2. Over £7,700 million was spent on advertising in 1993 and it is an essential part of the promotional activities of any business if firms are not to lose out to their competitors. The largest advertising expenditure is on food, retail and mail order services, financial services, cars, drink, household goods and leisure equipment. It is through advertising that sales promotions are communicated to existing and potential customers.

    Advertising is also used by other organisations such as charities wishing to raise funds and the government to put across messages to the public, e.g. 'don't drink and drive!'.

3. **Consumer Advertising**

    Advertising is used by firms to **inform** potential customers about goods and services which they sell. This may include details of new lines, special offers or features, support seasonal, national or local events or coincide with a manufacturers promotion.

    However, the main object of advertising is to increase sales by **persuading** people to buy a certain brand of goods or buy at a particular shop.

    Advertising is also frequently used to raise **awareness** by keeping the name of a product or store before the public in order to maintain sales.

4. **Two Parts to Consumer Advertising**

   ❏ Advertising by **stores** who want to persuade as many customers as possible into their shops to make purchases, for example, MFI, Dixons, and ASDA.

   ❏ A massive volume of advertising is carried out by **manufacturers** to encourage consumers to buy their products. For example Kelloggs, Wrangler, Phillips, and Nike.

   Some firms such as BP and ICI also use **corporate advertising** where the image of the organisation rather than its products are promoted, although clearly this can have the spin-off of extra sales.

> ### Task 1   3.3.1 (C3.4)
>
> Make a list of advertisements shown on television and the number of times each is shown in one evening (or within a particular period of time).
>
> Consider and compare:
>
> 1. the time at which each is shown.
>
> 2. the age or type of person at which each is aimed i.e. target group.
>
> 3. Whether they are of national, or purely local interest.
>
> 4. What 'gimmick', if any, is used to catch people's attention.
>
> 5. Whether it is a retailer or manufacturer advertising.
>
> 6. Any examples of corporate advertising.
>
> 7. Any other interesting features.
>
> 8. Draw conclusions from your findings.

Advertising Media

5. The term media is given to the various methods which firms can use to advertise their goods and services. If a firm wants its advertising to be seen throughout the country, then it may well use the **mass media** such as television and newspapers which can very quickly reach millions of people everywhere.

6. Media have both **quantitative** characteristics, basically the **cost** and **coverage** (number of people likely to see or hear it), and **qualitative** characteristics. The latter includes

   ❏ the **usage** of the media; for example a daily newspaper is often quickly thrown away whilst a weekly newspaper or magazine may be kept for several days or weeks. Also

   ❏ the **creative scope**, that is, the opportunities for audio or visual effects from TV and cinema companies with newspapers and magazines

   ❏ the **vehicle effect** or how an audience perceives the media, for example *The Times* as representing quality and social class compared with the 'working class' *Sun*.

   ❏ the **user-friendliness** or how easy or difficult the media is to buy, schedule, control and evaluate. A TV advertisement for example, can often only be booked or cancelled many months in advance, whilst newspaper advertisements can be placed within a few days.

7. **Main Advertising Media**

   Some key features of various media can be summarised as follows:

   ❏ **Newspapers and magazines**. Printed media which represents a cheap way of reaching millions of people. Can be local, regional, national, daily or weekly and targeted to cater for particular groups or special interests, e.g. Financial Times, Woman's Own, Gardeners Weekly. Trade magazines, for example, the Grocer, National Newsagent, Nursing Times and Computer News may be used by manufacturers to inform potential customers about new products or special promotions.

- ❑ **Television**. More expensive but offers colour, sound and movement to catch attention. Can demonstrate product features and benefits. A very powerful local and national media, difficult to target accurately, but reaches vast audiences, which vary with the time of day and with different channels.

- ❑ **Cinema**. Some 75% of total audiences are in the 16–34 age group. Accurate targeting possible. With 'captive' audience in relaxed atmosphere. But advertisement may only be seen once.

- ❑ **Commercial Radio**. Popular with local business as a relatively cheap form of advertising. Portable but audio only. 'Spots' can be repeated.

- ❑ **Outdoor Advertising**. Includes large hoardings along main roads, posters on buses and shop windows and neon signs which are lit up at night. Cheap but sites vary in size, visibility and impact.

- ❑ **Leaflets**. Simple leaflets called **'flyers'** giving details of promotional offers or events are often placed on cars, handed out in the street, left on display in shops, libraries and other venues or used for exhibitions or direct mail. Relatively cheap and may be used for general distribution or specific targeting.

Task 2   **3.3.1 (C3.4)**

Collect three advertisements from three different publications aimed at a particular target group.

1. Say where they were published.

2. Identify the target group at which they were aimed.

3. State whether or not you think they are likely to be effective, giving reasons for your views.

4. Compare and contrast your findings with those from Task 1.

---

8. **Sponsorship**

This is a relatively recent but increasingly popular form of advertising and public relations. Many organisations now support a range of activities such as T.V. programmes, sports events, the Arts and charity fundraising by contributing towards the costs involved.

9. In return they can

- ❑ **gain favourable publicity** for the goods or service e.g. Carling and Littlewoods in football, Powergen ITV weather

- ❑ **promote an associated product image** e.g. Vernons Pools and 'Wish You Were Here'

- ❑ **obtain publicity not normally available/allowed** e.g. cigarette manufacturers use sponsorship to gain extensive T.V. coverage despite the ban on advertising.

10. Currently over 2000 British companies are involved in sports sponsorship spending over £230 million annually, particularly on football, cricket, rugby, motor racing, horse racing, darts and snooker. Sponsorship also includes grants to individuals who promote a company's products such as tennis or athletics stars as well as to teams who wear kit bearing a company's name.

11. The potential for mass media publicity associated with the arts, a sport, T.V. programme or other event, before, during and after it takes place is immense. The sponsors name may be repeatedly mentioned or shown over a long-time period making it a very cost-effective form of promotion, with the opportunity to target particular consumer groups such as sports fans.

12. Other Methods of Advertising

These include the advertising on beer mats, sandwich boards, bags and wrapping paper, the back of bus tickets, names on key rings, pens and calendars, and the use of the Yellow Pages telephone directory.

Task 3 **3.3.1, 3.3.2 (C3.4)**

A company which has recently moved into your area has indicated that it is seeking to provide sponsorship to a limited number of worthwhile local community organisations and/or sponsor specific local events.

1. List at least three reasons why you feel the company might wish to offer this sponsorship.

2. Identify a 'worthwhile' organisation and/or event which you feel should receive sponsorship.

3. Draft a letter to the company giving reasons as to why it should support your organisation/event. Include in your letter the benefits which you feel the company would gain from such sponsorship.

4. Try to identify at least 2 examples of local sponsorship such as those in the articles below.

SPONSORS HELP THE YOUNG

A major company has stepped in with a new sponsorship deal to help soccer players at Littos Albion football club. In October DLO at Littos will be main sponsors for a tournament of five-a-side football which should attract 250 youngsters in the eight to under-14 range. The firm is also providing shirts for the Littos youth squad. Club Chairman Jess Jones said: "One of our team trainers works at DLO and the club has several connections with the company."

SPONSORS REACTION

British Steel has ended its £10,000 a year soccer sponsorship of First Division Middlesbrough because German steel is being used to build the club's new stadium. The new ground is only five miles from British Steel's plant at Lackenby, and many of its workers support the club. But only 200 tons of local steel is being used compared with 1,800 tons from abroad, mainly Germany.

The company said: "We cannot support Middlesbrough football club if they don't support us." The club said it had no say in where the steel came from. Builders Taylor Woodrow said it was the cheapest offered.

---

5. Comment on how these and your own examples illustrate reasons why organisations may want to be involved in sponsorship and situations when it might be withdrawn.

Choosing Advertising Media

13. No organisation is likely to use all of the above methods of advertising. Where they advertise will depend on the cost involved, the type of goods or services being promoted, the size of the organisation, the market aimed at, the results expected and the budget available. The aim is to find the most effective combination of media to achieve its objectives at the lowest cost and with the most persuasive message possible.

14. Since advertising is expensive, to be effective it must be done where the maximum number of potential customers can see it, and be done well to attract the greatest number of buyers. When choosing a media, advertisers will always take into account the type of people they wish to reach, for example will they be male, female, young, old, rich or poor? It is the type of people who are likely to buy the product which determines how an advertisement is designed and where it is to be placed.

Cost of Advertising

15. This will depend on the media used and the size, or length of the advertisement. As a general rule, the bigger or longer the advertisement, the more it will cost. But the cost also depends upon the number of people who are likely to see it. For example, a television advertisement is most expensive at peak viewing times because the potential audience is greater; a full page in a national newspaper costs considerably more than a full page in a local newspaper because the larger circulation means that more people will read it.

16. **Some Typical Examples of Advertising Costs**

Regional Television	£12,000 for 10 seconds (peak viewing)
Local Radio	£250 for 30 seconds
National Daily Newspaper	(10cm x 2 columns) £2,500 per day
Local Evening Newspaper	(10cm x 2 columns) £200 per evening
Local 'Free' Newspaper	(10cm x 2 columns) £100 per issue
Oracle	£1,000 per page per week
Stands at Major Exhibition	£1,000 per day
Panel on side of Bus	£70 per space per month

    NB Rates vary depending on size/time/position/frequency of advertisement

17. Up-to-date information on the unit costs and size of audiences or circulation of all the main media (press TV, cinema, radio and outdoor) is published monthly in the **British Rate and Data (BRAD)**.

    Whilst the **Annual Willings Press Guide** provides comprehensive information on some 26,000 publications worldwide, plus an up-to-date database service.

18.

Expenditure On Advertising

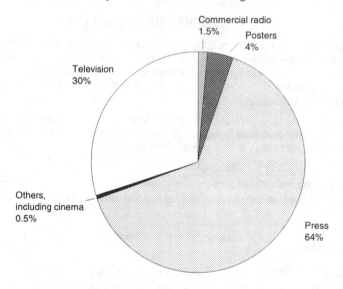

Task 4   **3.3.1 (C3.2)**

Which method(s) of advertising and promotion would you consider to be the most suitable and effective for each of the following. Be specific and give reasons for your answer.

1. A small local newspaper

2. A multiple shoe retailer

3. A large mail order company

4. A bank

5. A teenage magazine

6. To attract foreign tourists to your area

7. To introduce a new toothpaste

8. To sell a second-hand bicycle

9. To promote a school charity concert

10. To sell Rolls-Royce cars

Advertising Agencies

19. Firms can either arrange their own advertising or instead may use an advertising agency, for example Saachi and Saachi, J.Walter Thompson. These are specialist firms who employ experts to find the most effective way of advertising. An agency will plan and carry out an advertising campaign for clients for which they usually charge a fee. This involves the firm in **below-the-line** expenditure.

20. Alternatively, they may operate on an **above-the-line** basis, where their main income comes from commission received in the form of a discount from the media concerned. The firm may only have to pay for artwork or other specialist services.

21. Press, radio, TV, cinema and outdoor advertising media all offer agency discounts. In practice, a campaign will often involve both above and below-the-line expenditure.

22. Agencies carry out five main functions:

    ❑ **Market Research** is used to discover information on which to base the advertising. The success of a campaign can also be monitored through research.

    ❑ **Media Planning** – which involves selecting the most suitable media and booking it. For example, the time on television or space in the press.

    ❑ **Creating the Advertisement** – i.e. designing the advertisement and writing what is called the copy often with 'catchy' slogans. For example, 'The answer's yes at TSB', 'Mr Kipling makes exceedingly good cakes.'

    ❑ **Producing the advertisement** – for example making a film for television or drawing an illustration for the press.

    ❑ **Account Management** – agencies will look after a firms advertising budget and advise them on future campaigns.

Benefits of advertising

23. ❑ Consumers receive **information** about new and exciting products, enabling them to make comparisons.

    ❑ If firms sell more then mass production is possible. Producing larger quantities is cheaper and therefore leads to **lower prices.**

❏ Advertising promotes **competition** between firms and this results in lower prices and better quality products.

❏ Advertising **pays for ITV and Commercial Radio,** and keeps down the cost of **newspapers and magazines.**

❏ It can help to reduce sales fluctuations thus **aiding production planning.**

Ethics of Advertising

24. It is often argued that advertising is both **immoral** and **wasteful of resources** because:

❏ Initially it can lead to **higher prices,** for example if a product costs 10p to make and 2p to advertise, then this will mean a higher selling price.

❏ People may be persuaded to **buy goods which they cannot afford** and do not really want.

❏ Some products may be **harmful,** for example medicines, alcohol and tobacco. The advertising of cigarettes on television was banned in 1965 because it was felt that they were harmful to health.

❏ Advertising **can make people dissatisfied** by appealing to their ambitions, desires and emotions. For example, 'keeping up with Jones's, success with the opposite sex, or in a job; it encourages greed, or an easier life with more leisure.

❏ Advertising may lead us to believe that we can only achieve these by buying a particular product.

❏ It can be used to maintain **monopoly power** and prevent entry of rival products.

❏ It is used by 'charities' and in under-developed countries where **resources could be put to better use.**

Public Relations

25. In order to create goodwill, an organisation will often deliberately try to ensure that the public is kept informed about its trading and other activities. This is called **public relations** (PR) which can be defined as **the planned and sustained action to establish and maintain mutual understanding between an organisation and its public.**

26. The 'public' is very wide ranging and depending on the organisation could include not just existing and potential customers, but also suppliers, distributors, shareholders, trade unions, financiers such as banks, local and central government departments, pressure groups, employees and the general public.

27. PR should be used as an integral part of the 'Communications mix' and targeted at a wide range of media, most typically this will be newspapers, magazines, TV and radio. It is a highly specialist function, usually handled by a PR consultant or senior marketing personnel, which involves issuing regular 'press' releases, adapted for the chosen media, about the organisation's activities, products and employees. For example, the opening of a new shop or factory or a change of management. This has the added advantage that it is 'published' free of charge.

28. An organisation may use PR for a number of reasons, some examples of which are outlined below:

❏ To develop a **corporate image** and reputation by making sure that the public has a favourable impression of the organisation and knows about its strengths and achievements.

❏ To offset **bad publicity** in a positive and constructive way.

❏ To show that the organisation is a **leader** or innovator in its area of business e.g. reporting the latest advances in research or new product development which may be important in attracting employees and customers.

❏ To **develop community relations** by informing its customers and the public that the organisation is **socially responsible** and concerned about their interests e.g. support for charity events, environmental issues.

❏ To inform the public about **proposed actions** and policies, and possibly influence pressure groups, particularly where this may affect the social or physical environment. e.g. if plans to build a new factory are likely to produce major objections.

❏ To foster **good relations** with all levels of staff in an organisation. Good PR can enhance an employees sense of pride and commitment to an organisation and hence their level of performance.

❏ To **lobby** and improve relations with **opinion leaders** such as journalists, broadcasters, politicians, teachers, religious leaders, and other 'pressure groups' whose influence can affect the public's attitude towards a company and its products.

Task 5   **3.3.2 (C3.4)**

SHARE STATEMENT

The board of construction group M J Gleeson says it considers a fall in the company's share price is nothing more than a 'market adjustment' since it has out performed the sector for 12 months.

KEEP IN TOUCH PLEASE!

Tourists should have a contact point when they go abroad in case of urgent messages, and should register with the British consulate if away more than a few months, the Red Cross advises.

COUNDON SHOP TOP

Master butcher Geoffrey Saunders, manager of Dewhurst, Coundon, Coventry, and his staff are celebrating success in a national Best Kept Shop competition. Geoffrey and his team are Coventry district winners in the Dewhurst Group's Best Kept Shop competition, open to 1,400 shops throughout England, Scotland and Wales.

1. From the above examples of PR, identify the target 'public(s)'.

2. Collect 5 other examples of PR from a selection of local and national newspapers.

3. From these, identify what you feel is the main purpose of each 'story' and which members of the 'public' it is aimed at and/or most likely to influence.

---

29. A possible problem with PR is that, although the organisation submits the 'story' it has no control over the final content of the communication as this is determined by the editor of the media concerned. Nonetheless, this form of PR is very cheap and important in promoting a business and its products or services.

30. A further important aspect of PR is customer relations which in large organisations is often the responsibility of a separate department. Customer dissatisfaction must be dealt with promptly both to protect an organisation's reputation and to prevent the loss of future business.

31. PR can also be developed in other ways including the production of house magazines, loan videos about the organisation and its products and factory visits. The advantage of these methods is that although there is a cost involved, the organisation can actually control the PR content and invite direct feedback from the 'users'.

Task 6   **3.3.2 (C3.2)**

1. Which of the following would represent PR for a local company?

    a)   Sponsorship of a hospital Summer Fete.

    b)   An advertisement in the national press.

    c)   Use of direct mail to launch a new product.

    d)   Factory visits for organised groups

    e)   A promotional video for use in schools

2. For the organisation in which you work or study, suggest with reasons, the three most appropriate methods of PR.

3. Prepare a press release about an activity or event which is due to take place (or has recently taken place) where you work or study.

Promotional Budgets

32. There are a number of different ways of determining the amount to be spent on the various forms of promotion including advertising and PR.

    The following methods are amongst those commonly used.

    ❐ A percentage of last year's sales volume.
    ❐ A percentage of next year's planned turnover.
    ❐ With regard to the level of expenditure by competitors.
    ❐ The allocation of an arbitrary sum.
    ❐ Considering the objectives to be achieved and the cost of doing this.

    It is this latter method which would seem to be most logical and sensible although it may be more complex to work out.

Sales Promotion

33. Sales promotion involves many carefully planned events and activities which take place throughout the year to attract customers. With consumer goods and services promotional activities basically fall into three groups covering trade promotions, consumer promotions and window and point-of-sale displays.

Trade Promotions

34. These are aimed at distributors (retailers and wholesalers) to persuade them to stock a firm's products. Examples include:

    ❐ **competitions** offering prizes such as televisions and holidays
    ❐ **special discounts** usually for buying large quantities
    ❐ **bonuses** such as free extra packets per case
    ❐ **cash incentives** like money back in return for proofs of purchase
    ❐ **sales force incentives** may also be offered to encourage the achievement of sales targets.

Consumer Promotions

35. These are used to create interest and tempt potential customers to make a purchase. Examples include:

    ❐ **free gifts** like underfelt or fitting with carpets, small toys in cereal packets, keyrings
    ❐ **special price offers** such as 'sales' and the regular monthly promotions run by supermarkets

- ❑ **loss-leaders** where certain items like bread or sugar are sold at below cost to attract customers
- ❑ **free samples** either given out in-store or distributed door-to-door
- ❑ **competitions** offering holidays, cars and other prizes
- ❑ **loyalty incentives** such as the bonus cards issued by Tesco and Do-It-All, which offer regular customers discount vouchers, based on how much they spend, for use against future purchases.
- ❑ **personality promotions** where famous people like actors and footballers are used to open or visit stores.
- ❑ **coupons** offering money off.
- ❑ **premium offers** where goods like soft toys are offered at special prices in return for proofs of purchase.
- ❑ **credit cards** are often issued by large retailers like Debenhams and Dixons in an attempt to increase sales.
- ❑ **credit facilities** offered at low-cost or interest free can be as important as price with some products such as cars and electrical appliances.

36.

Tesco Loyalty Card

Do-It-All Loyalty Card

37. **Point-of-sale and Window Displays**

Displays or demonstrations are used to attract potential customers at the **point-of-sale**, that is, where they make their purchases. These are usually supported by related point-of-sale materials such as posters, banners, placards and showcards and often linked to some other promotional offer like a special price for maximum impact.

38. **Window displays** are very important in helping to attract customers' attention and encouraging them into a store. Often referred to as 'the silent salesman' they should be carefully planned and organised for effective promotion of the items on display.

Task 7	**3.3.3 (C3.2)**

1. Visit 3 local supermarkets and in each try to identify at least 4 examples of consumer and/or trade promotions.

2. Try to identify the USP for each product.

3. Identify any common features of the layout of each store and any major differences.

4. Comment on the different types of point-of-sale and window displays.

Industrial Promotions

39. Modified versions of some consumer promotions may also be suitable for industrial goods and services depending on the type of product.

Examples include:
- ❑ **Free gifts** displaying the company logo e.g. diaries, calendars and pens

❏ **seminars and demonstrations** to illustrate the features and benefits of products

❏ **catalogues,** technical and other promotional leaflets

❏ **trade shows and exhibitions** like the Business to Business Exhibition and Automotive Trade Show

❏ **free training** which is popular with computer sales

❏ **credit terms** using special low interest finance may be a big incentive with expensive items

❏ **sales force incentives** are frequently used, for example, payment by commission, bonuses or prizes.

Task 8   3.3.3 (C3.2)

Which types of sales promotion would you recommend in each of the following situations?

1. An educational publisher promoting a new textbook.

2. A company launching a new ice-cream product.

3. A manufacturer of industrial safety equipment.

4. The launch of a new automatic washing machine.

Market Segmentation

40. In order to market successfully, a firm needs to know what the total potential market is for its particular products or services and then try to identify the various **segments** or parts within it.

41. The total UK market for footwear for example, includes men's, ladies and children of all ages. A footwear manufacturer can therefore decide to carry out the activities necessary to supply the whole market or instead to target particular segments of it such as ladies or children only. The market can, however, be further sub-divided for example, children's' shoes include boys and girls and different ages such as the under 5's and 5-15. There are also many different types and qualities of footwear ranging from slippers to trainers to work shoes and specialist shoes such as those worn by dancers or footballers.

42. Thus, unless a market is either very small or dominated by one brand, it is unlikely that a particular product will be bought by everyone. Therefore, a manufacturer will usually select one or more specific market segments and devise a marketing mix which will appeal to those segments. Having identified a **target audience(s)**, tailor made marketing communications can be designed specially to appeal to that audience and influence its decision making.

Task 9   3.3.3 (C3.2)

1. How many market segments can you identify for each of the following products?

    a) Potatoes   d) Oil

    b) Computers   e) Paint

    c) Central Heating

2. Can you identify the market segments in the place where you are studying for your GNVQ?

Consumer Characteristics

43. Through research, markets can be analysed and classified according to the key factors which influence buyers' behaviour. The following classifications, all of which are of significance for marketing, are considered below:

- ❏ demographic
- ❏ geographical location
- ❏ geo-demographic
- ❏ benefits sought
- ❏ ethnic and religious influences
- ❏ behavioural factors
- ❏ life-style
- ❏ national characteristics, and
- ❏ socio-economic groups.

44. **Demographic** classification is important in providing basic information about buyers and consumers. For example, many products such as make up, nappies, 'pop' music and retirement homes are clearly aimed at **specific gender and/or age groups**, whilst others like newspapers and cars are targeted at different **socio-economic groups** (usually based on income and occupation). The **number of households** is important in determining the potential market for products such as the number who own fridges or washing machines, whilst the **size of households** can affect the demand for types of housing and family used items such as carpets and furniture.

45. **Geographical** classification considers the actual physical location of consumers for example, urban, rural, local or national. Particular regions of the country often have distinct tastes and purchasing patterns which can have important implications for advertising, promotion and product development.

46. **Geo-demographic** is the classification of small areas according to the characteristics of their inhabitants such as age, race and social class. It links purchasing power and how people live with where they live. Well known systems include MOSAIC, CDMS and ACORN (A CLASSIFICATION OF NEIGHBOURHOODS). The latter uses a full demographic database covering each of the 125,000 CENSUS ENUMERATION DISTRICTS, including post codes. This is linked to product usage data based on national surveys to provide detailed market segmentation data. Such data is now widely used for direct mail promotions and by firms like Tesco, Woolworths and Boots to study catchment area trends in relation to new site selection and store development.

47.

Acorn groups in Great Britain

Group		%
A	Modern family housing with manual workers	9.6
B	Modern family housing, higher income	7.4
C	Older housing of intermediate status	10.4
D	Very poor quality, older, terraced housing	9.2
E	Rural areas	5.8
F	Urban local authority housing	20.6
G	Housing with most overcrowding	2.9
H	Low income areas with immigrants	4.2
I	Student and high status non-family areas	4.3
J	Traditional high status suburbia	19.1
K	Areas of elderly people, often coastal resorts	6.4
Unclassified		0.2

48. The Post Office's Consumer Location System (CLS) combines several systems including ACORN and AGB Home Audit to analyse people's purchasing, reading and viewing habits and relate them to neighbourhoods to produce detailed 'consumer profiles'. It also identifies the most cost-effective ways of reaching specific target markets.

49. **Benefits sought** by consumers is another method of classification which is important for marketing products. Dried milk powder, for example, was originally developed as a standby for housewives who ran out of milk. It is now also sold as being of benefit to slimmers, weight watchers or consumers needing a fat-free diet and for single people and the elderly as being more convenient and less wasteful than fresh milk. This classification can provide a useful guide for product innovation and development.

50. **Ethnic and religious** classifications identify the characteristics of groups which represent distinct markets or parts of markets for certain goods and services. Many ethnic groups, for example, prefer brighter colours which could be important for packaging, whilst Jews, Asians and West Indians all have their own diet, retail outlets, entertainment facilities, communication media (eg own language newspapers) and culture.

51. **Behavioural** classifications cover product usage, for example the frequency of purchase, brand loyalty, and the differences between regular users and occasional users.

52. **Life-style** classifications attempt to determine the personality traits of consumers covering likes, dislikes, attitudes, opinions and interests. From this, for example, it may be found that a particular product only appeals to people who are introverts or extroverts. Acronyms are often used to describe lifestyles, for example DINKS (Double Income No Kids) and WOOPIES (Well-Off Older Persons), both groups with considerable discretionary income to spend.

53. **National classifications**. Although a product or service may be successful in the UK, it may require modification if it is to be sold in other countries. Thus firms who target this market segment must research it thoroughly in order to identify any factors which may influence its market-strategy. This could include for example, social, political and cultural differences; legislation, particularly that affecting consumer protection, health and safety and advertising; religious influences and the level of technological development. Firms planning to enter the Single European Market will need to be aware of some of these factors.

| **Task 10** | **3.3.3, 3.3.4 (C3.4)** |

SIMPLY CORNFLAKES

Kelloggs Cornflakes were launched over 70 years ago with an excellent and really innovative product with wide appeal. Over the years, heavy advertising expenditure, plus product and packaging updating have made and kept the brand successful.

Since the 1970's, however, there have been dramatic changes in the breakfast cereal market. This is illustrated, for example, by the fact that in 1979 there were 84 brands with a turnover of over £1m, whilst today there are more than 150. Thus many new and successful products have emerged to segment the cereal market. Faced with this development, Kelloggs has consistently spent more on advertising cornflakes than any other product (over £7.5 million in 1988-9 out of a total expenditure of almost £50m). It has also launched new 'added-value' products like Raisin-Splitz, Toppas, Smacks and Pop Tarts to appeal to new consumer groups wanting something different. Through market research, the success of cornflakes has also been re-assessed and the product relaunched in the 1990's as having something 'simple' in a market full of complex products. Thus today, cornflakes is re-emerging as a reliable old friend, targeted at the same customer with slogans like 'Have you forgotten how good they taste', and clearly re-establishing its own market niche.

The following questions are based on the above article:

1. Why have Kelloggs Cornflakes been so successful for over 70 years?

2. How has the product been affected by market segmentation?

3. What action has the company taken to re-establish the brand?

4. What do you understand by a 'Market Niche'?

5. What evidence, if any, is there to suggest that it could continue to be successful in the future?

54. **Socio-economic** classifications are shown in the table below. The basis being that consumer spending is related to social class, which is determined largely by the head of the household's income and occupation. Although still widely used, particularly by advertising media, classifications such as geodemographic, which take account of other factors are now considered to be more accurate.

55.

Classification of Consumers By Socio-Economic Groups

Social grade	Social status	Occupation of head of household	Approx % of total pop
A	Upper middle class	Higher managerial, administrative or professional	3
B	Middle class	Middle managerial, administrative or professional	12
C^1	Lower middle class	Supervisory, clerical or junior managerial	23
C^2	Skilled working class	Skilled manual workers	32
D	Working class	Semi and unskilled manual workers	20
E	Those at subsistence level	State pensioners, casual or lowest grade workers	10

Task 11   3.3.1, 3.3.3, 3.3.4 (C3.4)

1. Using the information in the table showing socio-economic groups, plus the information below on magazine readership, select the most appropriate publication in which to advertise the products a-e. Give reasons for your choice of publication.

    a) Lager

    b) A new DIY product

    c) Luxury holidays

    d) A foodmixer

    e) Male cosmetics

2. What additional information would you have found useful in completing this task?

56.

Readership of the most popular magazines: by sex and age, 1971 and 1990

	% adults reading each mag in 1990			% of each age group reading each mag in 1990				Readership (m)		Readers per copy
	Male	*Female*	*All adult*	*15-24*	*25-44*	*45-64*	*65 +*	*1971*	*1990*	*1990*
General magazines										
Radio Times	18	19	19	20	20	18	17	9.5	8.5	2.9
TV Times	18	19	19	21	19	18	15	9.9	8.4	3.0
Readers Digest	14	13	13	8	13	17	14	9.2	6.1	3.9
What Car?	7	1	4	6	5	3	1		1.8	12.2
National Geographic	5	3	4	4	4	4	2	1.1	1.7	
Exchange and Mart	5	2	3	5	4	3	1		1.5	8.2
Women's magazines										
Woman's Own	3	16	10	10	11	9	8	7.2	4.3	4.2
Bella	3	15	10	12	11	8	6		4.3	
Woman's Weekly	2	11	7	4	5	9	10	4.7	3.1	2.6
Woman	2	11	7	6	8	6	5	8.0	3.0	3.2
Best	2	11	6	9	8	5	3		2.9	3.1
Prima	2	10	6	7	8	5	2		2.6	3.0

Source: Social Trends 22, Reproduced by kind permission of the Controller of HMSO. 1992

Product Life Cycle

57. Just as we are born, grow up, mature and eventually become old and die, so the sales of many products have a similar life cycle. This involves six important stages which are illustrated below:

   ❏ **Development** – with the help of market research new products are designed. This is the most risky and expensive stage where the costs of research and technical development are incurred but no sales revenue is being earned.

   ❏ **Introduction** – once it has been developed, the product is advertised and brought to the market for sale.

   ❏ **Growth** – if the product is successful sales and the profit contribution will increase rapidly.

   ❏ **Maturity** – once established in a market the sales of a product do not grow so rapidly. A main reason for this is likely to be increased competition as other firms introduce similar products.

   ❏ **Saturation** – in time sales stop increasing, leading to

   ❏ **Decline** – eventually competition and other new products are likely to result in falling sales and profits. If this continues, the product may be withdrawn from the market.

58. **Stages in the Product Life Cycle**

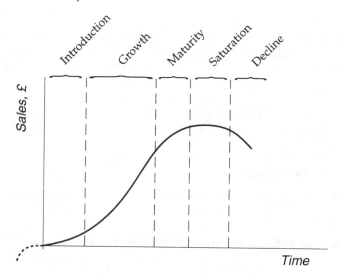

59. Changing consumer tastes and expectations, developments in new technology and the introduction of new and improved products can all affect the length of a life cycle which clearly will not be the same for all products.

Task 12
3.3.4 (N3.3, C3.3)

1. Draw a diagram to show the product life cycle over a 5 year period for a seasonal product the sales of which are growing.

2. Compare the life cycle of any three 'new' products with which you are familiar, perhaps a compact disc, car or soft drink. Discuss, giving reasons, the time which each is likely to take to complete the various stages of its product life cycle.

---

60.   **Cash Flow and the Product Life Cycle**

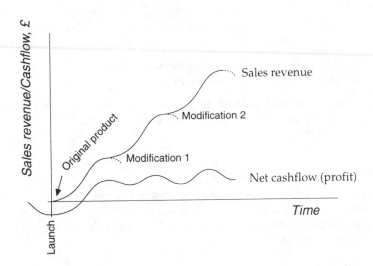

61. As the above diagram shows in the early stages of a product's life, the net cash flow is initially negative. This is due partly to the costs of developing and promoting the product but also because the full benefits from economies of scale are not gained at lower levels of production. The dotted line indicates the effects on sales revenue if the product life cycle is not extended.

62. **Extending the Product Life Cycle**

An organisation with a range of products is likely to have them at different stages of the life cycle. It needs to recognise this because of the implications for the rest of the marketing mix. Also, because it is possible to extend the life of an established product beyond the maturity stage by means of an **extension strategy**. This needs to be based on carefully planned marketing and production decisions and could involve strategies for any or all of the following.

❏ **More frequent use** of the product e.g. sales of Mars confectionery products in the Summer were increased by 'Cool Em' in the fridge advertising; frozen turkeys are now sold throughout the year and not just at Christmas.

❏ **Finding new uses or markets** for the product e.g. Johnsons baby powder promoted to adults; electric shavers for ladies; exporting Scotch Whisky; shampoo for different hair types.

❏ **Modifying the product** to retain its consumer appeal. This may involve changing its physical appearance, image or ingredients and relaunching it in new packaging on a regular basis, often with heavy promotional expenditure. For example, new styling or accessories such as central locking or electronic windows on cars, introducing new shoes and clothes as existing ones go out of fashion.

❏ **Technical developments** for example, new packaging techniques can also bring about new market opportunities like the use of plastic bottles and wax cartons for milk, fruit juices and wine; ring-pull cans for beers and soft drinks.

Likewise, the growth in the home freezer market and consequently frozen food means that many products such as meats can now be sold both fresh and frozen, whilst ice cream can be sold in larger quantities.

❏ **Wider product range**. It may also be possible for a firm to introduce associated products or variations to its present range. Examples include diet (Pepsi), slimline (Schweppes Tonic Water) and low-fat (Ambrosia 'light' Creamed Rice) versions of main brands; new flavours (Shreddies – Coco and Frosted); new sizes (Kleenex tissues pocket pack) and simplicity to create wider appeal (Shredded Wheat 'Byte Size').

> ### Task 13   3.3.4 (C3.4)
>
> Ask yourself why products like Coca-Cola, Persil, Whiskas, Dairy Milk, Weetabix and Heinz baked beans have been so successful as market leaders for so many years, whilst others fail.
>
> 1.   Identify at least two competitors for each of the products mentioned. Study and compare the different marketing methods used.
>
> 2.   Choose any 3 of the above or 3 examples of your own and briefly outline why you feel they have been so successful in extending the product life cycle.

Product Strategy

63. An organisation will usually achieve its marketing objectives through the range of products which it offers to its chosen market segments. The product strategy which it adopts will essentially depend not just on the position of these products in their life cycle, but also the market forces which affect them including the type of consumer.

64.   **Products and Market Forces**

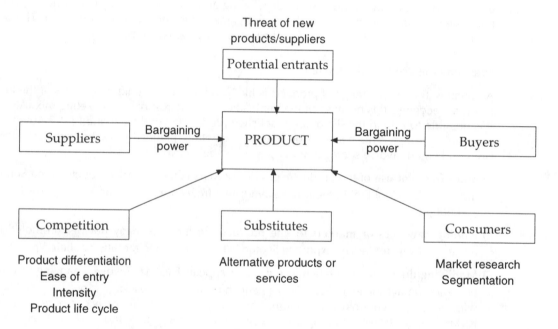

65. As shown in the diagram which is based on the model developed by Porter, there are a number of market forces which need to be considered in determining a product strategy. These include existing competition, potential for new entrants, availability of substitutes, power of suppliers, power of buyers and consumer analysis

66. **Existing Competition**. This may depend, for example, on the amount of product differentiation and therefore segmentation in a market. Thus, products like Coca-Cola and Heinz Baked Beans have created their own market segments. Other factors include the product maturity and ease of entry into the market which is considered below.

67. **Potential for New Entrants**. This is likely to depend on the existence of barriers, for example, high initial investment costs as with oil exploration or chemicals; government barriers like import tariffs; access to distribution channels such as wholesalers and large retailers, and again product differentiation. All of these factors make it difficult for new firms to enter an industry. Some markets, however, may be relatively inexpensive and easy to enter. For example, building trades, catering, nurseries, printing and retailing.

68. **Availability of Substitute Products.** This depends on whether or not there are other products which can perform the same function. Examples include butter and margarine; artificial sweeteners and sugar; savings accounts offered by banks and building societies.

69. **Power of Suppliers. An** organisation is dependent upon other businesses for the supply of goods and services which it uses. The power of these suppliers will usually depend on the actual number of firms involved. Some industries like British Telecom and Mercury for the supply of telephone services are dominated by a small number of very large and powerful firms. In this situation, lack of competition could cause potential problems. For example, if material costs are increased it could force a business to either raise prices or accept a lower profit and thus possibly reduced investment whilst labour problems or a delay in delivery could affect production. It could also lead to the possible threat of the business being taken over the supplier. In the 1960's and 1970's large companies such as General Motors and British Leyland chose this vertical integration as a way of controlling supplies and obtaining a larger share of the added value. In more competitive industries, the power of suppliers is of less concern to organisations.

70. **Power of Buyers.** Some sectors like the retail trades are dominated by a small number of very powerful buyers like Sainsburys, Tesco and Marks and Spencer. They may choose to takeover a supplier or if dissatisfied, stop buying from them with possible disastrous consequences for the firm. They can also negotiate large discounts which can squeeze a firm's profit margins.

71. **Consumer Analysis.** This requires the use of market research to ensure that the companies existing products and new product developments are meeting the changing need of final consumers. It can also involve identifying customer segmentation so that products can be more effectively marketed. Thus, different strategies may be needed to sell the same product to different consumer groups.

Task 14   **3.3.4 (C3.2)**

Choose any **two** products with which you are familiar and identify the market forces which affect them.

---

72. **Competitive strategies**

In most markets there will be a number of products jockeying for position. According to Porter there are 3 competitive strategies which a firm can use to achieve success in an industry.

☐ To produce **low-cost** products or services with wide appeal as with Ford or Vauxhall cars.

☐ To produce high-cost but **differentiated** products or services such as Mercedes cars.

☐ To **focus** products on a particular market niche, which is too small to attract bigger companies, as with Rolls Royce cars.

73.

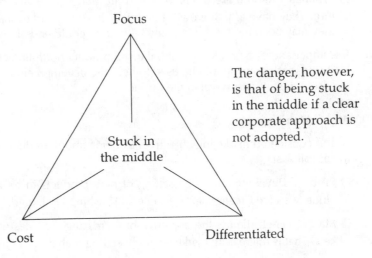

74. Market Analysis

Two major techniques used to analyse the product and market options available to organisations are the Boston Matrix developed by the Boston Consulting Group and the Ansoff Matrix, developed by Igor Ansoff.

75. Boston Matrix

This is a way of representing a firms product range in terms of market share and market growth. It uses a simple log scale according to a product's ability to generate income.

76.

Boston Matrix

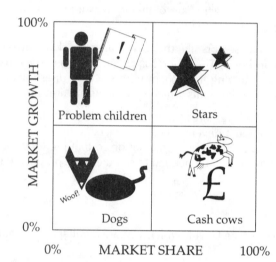

77. The matrix uses four categories of product:

- ❑ **Stars** are very profitable products with high market share and a high growth rate. They are usually at the early stages of the product life cycle.

- ❑ **Cash Cows** are established products which require little advertising. They have a high market share but low growth. These products generate a lot of cash and are usually 'milked' to help finance other products.

- ❑ **Dogs** have low market share and a low growth rate. They have little potential for development and should therefore be withdrawn from sale.

- ❑ **Problem Children** are products which are under achieving and therefore have an uncertain future. They have a high growth rate but only small market share. Therefore with a cash injection they may become stars but equally without it, could end up as dogs.

78. It is important for a firm to have a balanced product portfolio across the Boston Matrix. Cash generated from cash cows should be used to help the development of problem children and thereby help to ensure the future survival of the business.

79. Ansoff Matrix

Ansoff considered marketing objectives as being about products and markets and explained his matrix as follows:

- ❑ **Product Development** is the selling of new products in existing markets. Recent examples include Mars Ice Cream Snacks and Persil Washing-Up Liquid.

- ❑ **Market Penetration** is the objective of increasing the sales of existing products in existing markets. That is, increasing market share or setting higher sales targets.

❏ **Market Extension** involves increasing the sales of existing products but in new markets. Thus identifying a new age group or geographical area to which products can be sold.

❏ **Diversification** involves selling new unrelated products in new markets. An example is Pedigree Petfoods which is a subsidiary of Mars.

80.

Ansoff Matrix

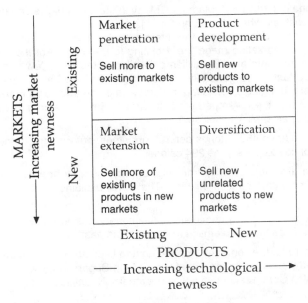

81. Thus, by examining the product life cycle, the external forces affecting a market and by using techniques like Boston, Ansoff and the SWOT analysis discussed in Element 3.1, an organisation can consider the many product options available to it. In respect of any particular product, this could include for example, decisions on whether to consolidate, expand, change its quality, features or performance, change the product mix or alter the branding. The product strategy will then provide a focus for the future direction of the organisation.

Task 15   **3.3.4 (C3.4)**

A LIGHTER MARS

The Mars bar was launched in this country in 1932 by American-born Forrest Mars. Using £25,000 borrowed from his chocolate magnate father, he set up a one-room factory in Slough, Berkshire. In his first year he sold two million bars at two old pence – less than 1p – each.

His family now controls 41 factories and has the world's fifth largest private fortune, estimated at £8 billion.

The business is now run by Forrest Jnr, John and Jacqueline Mars Vogel. Yet they still clock in and earn punctuality bonuses like every other Mars worker.

For 60 years Mars has helped us to 'work, rest and play' and is currently Britain's favourite chocolate bar, with annual sales of £55 million. But fierce competition in the 1990's has caused its market share to slip from 16 to 12.5 per cent which is why it is being given what its makers term 'image refreshment' involving a complete change of recipe and a multi- million pound relaunch. Out goes the traditional combination of 'glucose, milk and thick, thick chocolate'; replaced by a lighter, chewier and less malty-tasting confection. Out too goes the old advertising slogan in favour of 'Now

continued…

Task 15 continued

there's more to a Mars'. Fronting the £5 million campaign, which is focused particularly on the teenage market, will be TV and radio presenter Danny Baker. A company spokesman explained that 'Major consumers of chocolate confectionery are teenagers and young adults, and we want to keep the product in the forefront of their minds'.

If anyone can pull it off, Mars can. Many in the industry predicted that the firm would come unstuck when it renamed its Marathon bar Snickers two years ago. In fact, sales increased. Even so, the latest move is 'incredibly risky', according to Alan Mitchell of Marketing magazine. Pointing to the change of the recipe of Coca-Cola, which turned into a multi- million dollar flop in the US a few years ago, he warned: People's tastes are generally conservative. The new bar is very different in texture and taste, bringing a real danger that lovers of the traditional Mars will turn against it. The fact that the revamped product carries 15 more calories than the old one could also hurt sales, Mr Mitchell said.

Both bars have 452 calories per 100 grammes, but the replacement is bigger for the same price - 24p – so has 294 calories.

'People are turning away from big, sugary, gungey bars which are perceived as being unhealthy', said Mr Mitchell. 'That partly explains the Mars bar's drop in market share.

'Any company selling chocolate confectionery has to be wary of the health lobby, and Mars has had problems in this area in the past'.

In June 1992, the company won the right to keep its 'work, rest and play' slogan after the food watchdog Action on Information on Sugars complained to the Independent Television Commission that it was not medically justifiable.

The following are based on the case study.

1. Where would you place Mars bars on the Boston and Ansoff Matrixes?

2. What is 'new' about the new Mars bar?

3. What risks are associated with the relaunch of Mars bars?

4. Identify the examples of both the successful and unsuccessful relaunching of other well-known brands.

5. How and why will the new product be promoted?

Promotional Activities and Product Performance

82. To be successful, promotion must be cost effective, that is, it must bring in greater revenue than it costs. The promotional message, media, frequency and duration plus the other elements of the marketing mix must be carefully chosen and organised to produce the maximum impact and desired increase in sales at least cost.

83. The effectiveness of a promotional campaign on product performance should be measured against the objectives it was trying to achieve and therefore the full impact may not be easy to calculate. Typically, this is evaluated in terms of increased sales revenue as follows:

$$\frac{\text{Proportionate change in sales volume}}{\text{Proportionate change in promotional expenditure}}$$

84. For example, if from market research a firm discovers that 25% of the market is aware of a product and 10% have tried it, an advertising campaign might be launched with the objective of increasing these figures by 50% and 20% within 6 months. The success of such a campaign could only be measured by using market research techniques.

85. Other objectives, however, such as increasing consumer loyalty, product awareness, brand loyalty, repeat sales, pack recognition, brand image, or raising a firm's public profile may also be important but much more difficult to measure against objective criteria. Therefore, market research techniques such as questionnaires, consumer panels and psychological testing may be used for evaluation (see Element 3.2).

86. These can be used to seek answers to questions such as:

Did the activities

❏ attract attention?

❏ effectively provide information?

❏ influence consumer perceptions of the product?

❏ put the sales message or product image across?

87. Other methods used include 'keyed' (coded) advertisements in the press so that the response from particular newspapers or magazines can be identified, whilst with direct mail, the percentage response rate can be used as a measure. It must be remembered however, that increased sales may not necessarily come about immediately but could be spread over several months after the end of a campaign.

Task 16   **3.3.1, 3.3.3, 3.3.4 (C3.4)**

THINGS YOU DIDN'T KNOW ABOUT. . .

BISTO

Bisto was created by Cerebos in 1910, to simplify gravy making.

The initial appeal lay in its time saving: Bisto Browns, Seasons and Thickens In One – hence the anagram.

It wasn't until 1919 that an inspired piece of marketing transformed the product's future. Cartoonist Will Owen created the Bisto Kids and the "Ah! Bisto" slogan.

Such was the popularity of the "Bisto Kids" that cinema audiences in the 30s were treated to a 20-minute animated film entitled The New Adventures of the Bisto Kids, which was screened as suppport to the main feature.

Bisto became invaluable during the Second World War, when women used it to paint their legs, as an alternative to "American Tan" nylons.

The Bisto kids have undergone some changes since their early days. They were even known to sport flared trousers during the 70s.

Bisto's parent company Cerebos was sold to Ranks Hovis McDougall, in 1971.

Bisto gravy granules were launched in 1979.

Bisto's share of the £150m meat extract market, currently stands at 39% (Source: AGB Superpanel).

RHM's marketing budget in support of the Bisto brand, is set to top £7.5m for this year.

Independent research conducted on behalf of RHM, shows that 37% of homemade shepherd pies are made using Bisto as a "pour in" ingredient.

Bisto Fuller Flavour Gravy Granules was launched last year, following extensive research.

RHM is currently involved in a massive sampling exercise through door to door distributor, The Leaflet Company. Mini packs of Fuller Flavour Gravy granules are being delivered to one million UK households, each with a "10p-off coupon".

1075 tonnes of Bisto were sold during the four weeks leading up to Easter, last year – that's the same weight as 215 African male elephants.

Spontaneous awareness for the Bisto brands stands at 93%.

Bisto Original Gravy Powder and Traditional Gravy Granules are currently carrying on-pack promotions for celebrity cookery books endorsed by the NSPCC charity.

Reproduced by kind permission of Marketing Magazine

continued…

Task 16 continued

1. From the above information about Bisto identify the examples of:

   a) market research.

   b) the original and alternative uses of the product.

   c) product development.

   d) market share.

   e) brand identification.

   f) promotional activities.

   g) consumer awareness.

   h) the promotional budget.

   i) it's unique selling proposition.

2. Comment on the marketing strategies used to extend the product life cycle and keep Bisto a successful brand.

3. How might the information in the article be of use to a competitor?

Direct Marketing Methods

88. A rapidly growing form of promotional activity in both consumer and industrial markets involves the use of direct marketing methods. That is the use of direct media to reach a target market. It includes direct mail, telemarketing, selling off-screen and selling off-page.

89. Direct Mail can be sent either by door-to-door distribution (mail drops) or more commonly through the post (mail shots). Mail shots are often referred to as 'junk mail' but despite this they are often successful and cost-effective because they can be used to target particular market segments. Firms use market research and computer databases to obtain and record information about existing and potential consumers. Then, by carefully analysing this data, they can more accurately target mail shots thus increasing the potential response rate.

Task 17   **3.3.5 (C3.4)**

Read the following news item and complete the tasks which follow:

THE BUYERS WHO CAN'T RESIST JUNK

Junk mail may be seen as a nuisance by many people – but it sells.

More than a quarter of adults who receive it go on to buy goods and services offered, a report by market analysts Key Note reveals. Over half of the items that land on the country's doormats are received unsolicited. Direct mail accounts for almost 20 per cent, free newspapers another 18 per cent and leaflets and coupons a further 16 per cent.

Junk mail is ditched unopened by 44 per cent of adults and eight per cent have asked to be taken off a mailing list. But the study shows that 26 per cent use it for purchases.

1. Define 'junk mail'.

2. Identify the examples given of junk mail.

3. How much junk mail is never read?

4. What evidence is there of the success of junk mail?

5. How might this information be of value to business organisations?

90. The term **'junk mail'** came about from poor or non-existent selection in the use of data. But many firms have now recognised that by using the 'right' database which extends from just a list of names and addresses to include age, marital status, income, social background, interests and/or other potentially relevant factors such as records of past purchases or enquiries can lead to efficient customer orientated marketing which is targeted, personalised and therefore maximises sales opportunities and above all is cost effective.

91. Businesses can gather this information from their own customer database, advertising response cards, exhibition enquiries or specialist directories. The Direct Marketing Association publishes a directory which lists organisations who sell database information.

92. The dramatic growth of direct mail in recent years therefore is largely due to the increasing development and availability of sophisticated electronic databases. These make it so useful that it is now seen as a major promotional tool.

93. The features of direct mail can therefore be summarised as:

❏ advertising and selling combined
❏ precise targeting of customers using selective databases
❏ timed and controlled to meet agreed objectives
❏ powerful personalised communication to promote sales
❏ results are measurable and therefore effectiveness can be evaluated.

94.   **Example of a Direct Mail letter**

Dear Miss Brown,

YOU HAVE WON A CASH PRIZE!

It's very good news! Lucky Number **143267565** was entered for you in the **FREE £1,000,000.00 Money Match Prize Draw**. And now we are very pleased to be able to name **you** as **a CASH PRIZE Winner**.

Within the next few days, you will receive Official Notification of the TAX-FREE Prize you have definitely won.

It can be the **£100,000.00** First Prize, **DOUBLED** to **£200,000.00** when you return your Prize Claim on receipt - or the **£50,000.00** Second Prize, the **£10,000.00** Third Prize, or one of **FIVE £1,000.00** Fourth Prizes, **TEN** Fifth Prizes each of **£500.00** or a **SURPRISE CASH Prize**.

Keep a lookout for our Official Notification envelope - it's marked "Personal - Official Winner's Notification". **To claim your Money Prize - simply fill in and return the Prize Claim in the envelope**.

It costs nothing to claim the prize your Lucky Number **143267565** has **WON**, Miss Brown.

If **you** don't claim your Prize - what could be **your very** lucky number **indeed**, will go to someone else. Be sure to claim the CASH PRIZE **you have certainly won**. Simply look out for the Notification envelope, **then fill it in and post your Prize Claim by return**.

Yours sincerely,

Loretta Green   Loretta Green
                         Competition Director

P.S. **Claim the Prize you've won - post your Prize claim as soon as you receive it**!

Task 18   **3.3.5 (C3.2)**

Collect 3 examples of direct mail and comment on

❏ the target market for each

❏ the impact they have on you and

❏ how you feel they could be improved.

---

95. **Telemarketing**

This involves inviting consumers to buy goods or services by responding directly to T.V. advertisements or approaches to them by telephone. One T.V. shopping channel already exists and others are likely to follow as this method of marketing develops. Consumers can place an order by telephone or post. Telephone calls are usually unsolicited and often aimed at obtaining an appointment for a sales representative to call. Double glazing companies for example, frequently use this method. Premium Bonds are also sold this way.

96. **Selling off-page**

This involves the use of press advertising to promote sales. Frequently this takes place at weekends, increasingly in the growing number of newspaper and magazine supplements.

97. **An example of direct marketing**

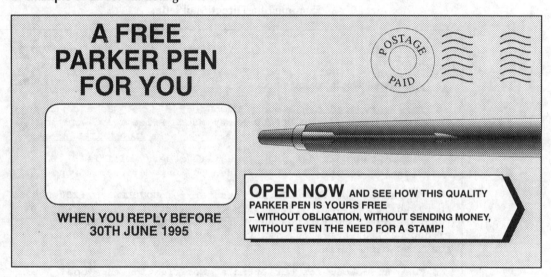

All communication is by post or telephone. The consumer has an incentive to respond and can make contact 24 hours a day, 7 days a week.

98. **Selling off-screen**

This involves the use of computer links and is likely to be the growth industry of the future. With the development of networks like the Internet and Superhighway (see Element 2.4) it will soon be possible to sell almost anything directly by computer. Initially this will be largely between businesses but eventually it will also extend to domestic consumers.

99. In June 1995 Britain's three biggest cable T.V. companies TeleWest, Nynex CableComms, and Bell Cablemedia announced the launch of an interactive multi-media trail in 2,000 homes. The aim is to determine demand for services such as home shopping, home banking, video-on-demand and educational programmes. Viewers will be able to order products or ask for information with a flick of their remote control.

The trial will run for up to two years after which the cable companies will decide whether to expand the service across all their franchise areas. BT has launched similar trials in 2.500 Colchester and Ipswich homes. It could decide to launch a nationwide service by as early as spring 1996.

Task 19 **3.3.5, 3.4.1 (C3.4)**

Discuss with reasons whether or not you feel each of the following is an example of good direct marketing.

☐ A gardening catalogue sent to the Occupier: 41 Nelson Court, a high rise flat in London.

☐ A letter received by Jane Bird from her local bank which contains a personalised loan offer.

☐ An advertisement for a new CD, available only by post, which 17 year old Gurbir Singh hears on his favourite local radio station.

☐ A telephone call to Mary Thomson offering to quote for the cost of new windows. She lives in a 1950's property which has recently been double-glazed.

100. **Constraints on Promotional Activities**

Manufacturers and retailers cannot say anything they like in advertisements or other promotional activities, otherwise this might lead to all sorts of misleading claims to entice customers. Therefore advertising is carefully controlled to protect consumers. This control takes two forms, voluntary control consisting of a list of rules drawn up by the industry itself and which advertisers have agreed to follow, and legal control enforced by laws passed by the government. Consumer Protection legislation is discussed more fully in Element 3.1. See also paragraphs 103–109.

101. **The Advertising Standards Authority. (ASA)**

This is a body which is financed by the industry itself to act as a 'watchdog' to ensure good practice in newspaper, magazine and billboard advertising. It issues 'The British Code of Advertising Practice' (CAP), which is a list of guidelines aimed at ensuring that all advertising is 'legal, decent, honest and truthful'; monitors advertisements and investigates complaints. It also has the power to ban advertisements or have campaigns withdrawn where organisations breach the Code.

102. **The British Code of Sales Promotion Practice** is similar to the ASA but essentially covers promotion other than advertising. This includes, for example, personality promotions, coupons, reduced prices, free offers, charity promotions and competitions.

Task 20 **3.3.7 (N3.3, C3.4)**

ASA GETS TOUGH

In the first major shake-up since 1988, the Advertising Standards Authority has updated its Code of Practice to stop firms targeting teenagers with slimming products, who then often diet unnecessarily.

Advertisers also face a crackdown on the use of 'sexual stereotypes', particularly female ones, to sell products. This follows concern about ads such as one for the Calvin Klein men's perfume Obsession, featuring Kate Moss, and an outcry over a poster for the T.V. premiere of the film Indecent Proposal. The new rules introduced on February 1 1995 state that 'particular care should be taken to avoid causing offence on the grounds of race, religion, sex, sexual orientation or disability.'

The rules have also been extended to include all electronic media, including computer games, for the first time. Celebrities can no longer advertise or endorse medicines. And firms are banned from advertising alcoholic drinks where more than 25% of the audience is under 18. Nor can they make speed the main message for car promotions – or portray fast driving in a way that might encourage motorists to break the law. Concerns about the advertising of sweets to children are also covered for the first time. Campaigns must not encourage youngsters to eat or drink near bedtime, or to replace main meals with sweets or crisps and other snacks.

continued…

Task 20 continued

SURE WIN ADS LOSE OUT

Adverts claiming to offer a way to win the lottery have come under fire. The Advertising Standards Authority upheld a complaint against Chartsearch Ltd of London, offering a 'mathematically proven system'. The watchdogs ordered changes in the advert and said people were as likely to hit the jackpot using a pin and a blindfold as complicated betting systems.

COMPLAINTS EXPOSED

Nearly five times as many complaints about 'indecent' advertising were upheld in 1994 compared to 1993. Of 1,700 cases 697 were upheld by the Advertising Standards Authority against 144 out of 1,297 in the previous year. But a spokesman said 'There is no evidence that advertisers are more indecent in their approach. The number of adverts complained about was similar – it is just the number of people writing to complain that has risen'.

1. Summarise the main changes introduced to the ASA's Code of Advertising Practice and explain why it was felt they were needed.

2. Calculate

    a)   the increase in the total number of complaints about advertising from 1993 to 1994.

    b)   the percentage change in the total number of complaints.

    c)   the increase in the number of complaints about 'indecent' advertising from 1993 to 1994.

    d)   the percentage change in the number of complaints about 'indecent' advertising.

    e)   Comment on your calculations and say whether or not you agree with the view expressed in the article 'Complaints Exposed.'

3. The media often reports situations where the ASA has asked advertisers to withdraw or modify advertisements. Try to find two relatively recent examples and comment on the action taken and why.

Legal Control

103. **The Broadcasting Act (1990)**. This was introduced to provide for the regulation of both independent television (ITV) and radio. It set up an **ITV Commission** which controls the issue of licences and generally regulates ITV including local cable and satellite services. The Commission has a Code of Practice which includes advertising standards and methods. It also has the power to investigate complaints and ban advertisements which do not comply with the Code. A **Radio Authority** was also set up to issue licences and oversee all independent radio services again including advertising.

104. **The Trade Descriptions Acts (1968 and 1972)**. These aim to ensure that traders tell the truth about goods and services. The descriptions used in advertisements must be accurate and truthful. If the law is broken, offenders may be fined or imprisoned. Altogether about 60 laws have been passed which affect advertising in some way.

105. **The Consumer Credit Act (1974)**. This states that advertisements for goods sold on credit must include the cash price, the credit price and the true rate of interest.

106. **The Sale of Goods (Amendment) Act 1994** states that goods advertised must meet the description applied to them e.g. shoes advertised as made of leather, or trousers of cotton must be just that.

107. **The Consumer Protection Act (1987)** makes it an offence to give false or misleading price indications e.g. advertising that goods were previously sold at a higher price when they were not or omitting to show VAT to give the impression that goods are cheaper than they actually are.

108. Other examples of legislation include the

    ❏ **Food and Drinks Acts (1955–1995)** which aim to ensure that food labelling on products is clear and truthful and the

    ❏ **Medicines Acts (1941 & 1968)** which cover claims which manufacturers of medical products can make, particularly where doctors or nurses are used to endorse products in advertisements.

109. **Trading Standards Departments** have been established by local Councils to investigate consumer complaints about faulty goods or services and enforce the consumer protection laws when necessary

---

Task 21   **3.3.7**

DIY STORE FINED

Texas Homecare was fined £2,400 with £1,000 costs by St Albans magistrates after being found guilty of eight charges of overcharging under the Trade Descriptions Act. The case was brought by Hertfordshire Trading Standards Department.

MFI FINED OVER PRICES 'CON'

The furniture giant MFI has been ordered to pay nearly £27,000 in fines and costs for misleading customers during sales promotions. The company was convicted of breaching consumer protection laws following an inquiry by trading standards officers. Swansea magistrates heard the firm made false claims of huge discounts at a store at Llansamlet and issued misleading sales literature and newspaper adverts.

TIMESHARE THIEVES

A Timeshare shark who wrecked the holiday dreams of seven customers has been jailed for a year after admitting seven charges of theft. He was also banned from being a company director for five years.

He gave himself up after being exposed on BBC's 'Crimewatch'. His clients paid him almost £25,000 for timeshare apartments in Gran Canaria – but they never got them, Gloucester Crown Court was told.

1. Why do consumers need protection from unfair trading practices?

2. What legal protection is currently available?

3. How do the above news reports illustrate the enforcement of the law?

Summary

110. a) Promotion involves all the activities used by businesses to maintain and increase sales and comprises sales promotion, advertising, PR and personal selling.

    b) Advertising is used to inform potential customers about goods and services and to persuade them to buy.

    c) Advertising media includes press, television, cinema, commercial radio, outdoor advertising and leaflets or 'flyers'.

    d) Other methods may include names on carrier bags, key rings, pens, 'Yellow Pages' and sponsorship whereby organisations support events in return for publicity.

    e) Because advertising is a very specialised business, firms frequently use an advertising agency to carry out campaigns for them.

    f) PR is used by organisations to keep their 'public' informed and to create goodwill and a favourable selling climate.

    g) Sales promotion covers trade promotions, consumer promotions and window and in-store displays to assist purchase at the point of sale.

h)   Some methods of sales promotion include reduced price offers, competitions, free gifts, trade fairs and exhibitions, coupons and low-cost credit facilities.

i)   Market segmentation identifies consumer characteristics according to demographic, geographical location, geodemographic, benefits sought, ethnic, religious, behavioural, life-style, national and socio-economic classifications.

j)   Most products have a life cycle of sales covering their development, introduction, growth, maturity, saturation and decline.

k)   With careful planning and development, this life cycle can be extended.

l)   A product strategy can be developed following analysis of the range and market forces which affect it.

m)   The Boston and Ansoff Matrixes can be used to help analyse the various options available.

n)   The effectiveness of promotional activities should be evaluated against the objectives set and their impact on product performance.

o)   Direct marketing methods are a rapidly growing form of promotional activity. They include direct mail, telemarketing, selling off-screen and selling off-page.

p)   There is both voluntary and legal control of what can be said or shown in advertisements, and other promotional activities.

Review questions *(Answers can be found in the paragraphs indicated)*

1)   What do you understand by the 'communications mix'? (1)

2)   What are the main purposes of advertising? (2–3)

3)   Name 10 different advertising media including two examples of mass media. (5–12)

4)   In what sense is sponsorship different from most other forms of advertising? (8–11)

5)   Outline the main factors which a business should consider when choosing advertising media. (13–17)

6)   Is advertising harmful or does it benefit consumers? (23–24)

7)   Explain, with examples, what you understand by public relations. (25–31)

8)   Outline the various methods of determining promotional budgets. (32)

9)   Distinguish between trade promotions, consumer promotions, point-of-sale and window displays. (35–38)

10)   Explain what is meant by market segmentation. (40–42)

11)   Describe 6 ways in which markets can be classified. (43–55)

12)   Briefly describe the stages of the product life cycle. (57–58)

13)   Outline the relationship between cash flow and the product life cycle (60–61)

14)   What can a firm do to extend the life cycle of a product? (62)

15)   What factors will influence a firm's product strategy? (63–72)

16)   Briefly describe the Boston and Ansoff Matrixes (74–79)

17)   Why is it necessary to evaluate the impact of promotional activities and how can this be done? (82–87)

18)   Explain what you understand by direct mail marketing. (88–94)

19)   Briefly outline 3 other methods of direct marketing (95–99)

20)   With examples, explain the two main ways in which consumers are protected from false or misleading promotional activities. (100–109)

Assignment – Comparing Marketing Communications   *Element 3.3*

1. You are asked to prepare a report, comparing the advertising, publicity, public relations and sales promotion methods of two business organisations. One of these should be involved in direct marketing, for example, Direct Line Insurance, Betterware household goods, Virgin Personal Equity Plans, First Direct Banking, Portland Holidays or Daewoo Cars.

2. The report should for each organisation

   a) explain why it uses particular types of marketing communications to promote its products and image.

   b) evaluate how marketing communications help it to reach its target audience.

   c) evaluate the effect of marketing communications in terms of product sales, consumer and brand loyalty and length of the product life cycle.

   d) identify any marketing communications which may contravene the Advertising Standards Authority's Code of Practice and explain why these may need controlling.

3. In addition, for the direct marketing organisation your report should identify and explain the reasons for the recent growth in this method of marketing communication, including changing customer needs and developments in technology.

4. Your report should be word-processed, if possible, and illustrated as appropriate with some examples of marketing communications used by each organisation.

12 Sales and Customer Service

This chapter considers the different methods which organisations can use to sell to customers and the role of customer service in helping to achieve customer satisfaction. It includes:

- ❏ Direct sales methods
- ❏ Indirect sales methods
- ❏ Chain of distribution
- ❏ Consumer choice
- ❏ Distribution management
- ❏ Comparing sales methods
- ❏ Personnel selling
- ❏ Sales campaign methods
- ❏ Responsibilities of sales persons

- ❏ Customer service
- ❏ Customer views
- ❏ Types of customer
- ❏ Customers with special needs
- ❏ Customer service by business sector
- ❏ Satisfied and dissatisfied customers
- ❏ Monitoring customer satisfaction
- ❏ Importance of customer service
- ❏ Improving customer services

Sales Methods

1. In Element 3.3 we considered the importance of marketing communications in informing customers about an organisation's goods and services and persuading them to buy. The sales method used is also an important part of this process. An organisation may choose to sell direct to consumers or indirect using a range of different distribution channels.

Direct Sales Methods

2. Some of the main methods used by organisations to sell direct to consumers include TV, radio, factory and farm outlets, telesales, door-to-door, pyramid and mail order using catalogues, newspapers and magazines. Other methods include automatic vending machines, party selling, trade fairs and exhibitions.

3. **Television.** In recent years there has been an increase in the number of organisations who advertise products on TV and invite consumers to purchase direct from them by telephone, usually via Access or Visa, or by post. The growth of cable television and interactive multi-media developments mean that this method of selling is likely to increase further. It is particularly popular for products such as insurance, CDs, holidays (currently via teletext), pop concerts and home banking.

4. Whilst British Sky Broadcasting provides a range of satellite channels such as sport, films and news, plus a specialist home shopping channel which advertisers can use to target consumer groups. The choice of satellite channels is expanding steadily and includes Eurosport (sport), CNN, (news), MTV (pop videos) and TV Asia (for Asian viewers.)

5. **Radio.** This is also a popular media for direct sales again inviting customers to respond to advertisements by ordering goods via post or telephone. The number of commercial radio stations has grown rapidly in recent years making it easier for organisations to target consumers .

6. **Factory and farm outlets**. Some organisations invite consumers to visit their premises to purchase direct. That is, they have a factory shop or other sales outlet. Examples which you might have come across include textile mills, pottery and kitchen unit manufacturers.

7. Many firms also have shops where fresh produce can be purchased or sometimes just one product is offered for sale such as eggs or flowers. Another variation on this is the opportunity to buy direct by picking-your-own strawberries, peas or other produce.

Task 1 3.4.1 (C3.4)

1. Have you ever bought anything direct from a TV or radio advertiser or factory/farm outlet?

2. If yes, describe what it was and why you chose it and the reasons for purchasing this way. If no, find a friend or relative who has, and describe the product(s) and reasons for purchasing this way.

3. Were any difficulties experienced with the purchase and if so what?

4. Comment on whether or not you (they) would purchase goods this way again.

8. **Telesales.** This is a relatively cheap method of contacting consumers. Some manufacturers use it to save the time and cost of sending sales representatives, particularly where regular repeat business is involved or for customers who may purchase infrequently or only place small orders. Frozen foods and other grocery products are frequently sold to retailers in this way.

9. To maximise efficiency and sales potential highly trained staff are used who can quickly establish stock levels to assess customer needs and give information on prices, discounts, special offers and delivery.

10. Telesales are also used by the media to sell advertising space, particularly to support special editorial features and also by organisations such as double glazing companies to obtain appointments for sales staff.

11. **Door-to-door** selling takes place when a sales person calls at someone's house and invites them to buy goods. Examples include the Encyclopaedia Britannica, double glazing companies, Betterware household items, Avon cosmetics and charity organisations offering toiletries and stationery. Although a salesperson sometimes calls at the request of the householder they usually call without a prior invitation. This **cold canvassing** generally has a poor ratio of sales to calls.

Task 2 3.4.1 (C3.4)

KLEENEZE SHINES ON DOORSTEP

More agents than ever are signing up to sell mops and brushes on the doorsteps, says Kleeneze chairman Robin Klein.

He now has 8,500 people selling his wares and claims 300 a week are joining. New agents have their own credit limits and report direct instead of through more senior agents.

More than a third of the sales force quit after the network was tightened up last summer.

The Innovations mail order division rescued the group with operating profits up 22%. Group pre-tax profits fell from £849,000 to £680,000.

1. Outline Kleeneze's direct selling network and how it is being restructured.

2. What do you think were the reasons for the change and what impact has it had?

12. **Pyramid selling**. This is a method of selling goods by using a hierarchy of organisers, distributers and sales staff each of whom buys into the organisation at a particular level.

13. For example, the central organisation may recruit a small number of regional organisers, each of whom contracts to buy a franchise to sell certain goods as well as a minimum quantity of the goods themselves. Each organiser then recruits a number of sub-distributors who buy a small share and so on. This continues down to the sales person at the bottom of the pyramid who actually sells the goods door-to-door or to friends.

14. Most people in a pyramid make money from the right to sell the product rather than actually selling it. In the 1960's and 1970's many people lost a lot of money due to pyramid selling and therefore

protection was introduced by the Fair Trading Act 1973. This makes it an offence to take or ask for payment for recruiting others into a pyramid scheme. Also anyone joining a scheme must receive a written contract setting out their rights.

Task 3   **3.4.1 (C3.3)**

Draw a simple diagram to illustrate how pyramid selling is organised.

---

15. **Mail order organisations**. We have already mentioned TV and radio as a means of selling products by post which may be one of several sales methods used by an organisation. Some businesses, however, specialise in direct selling by mail-order.

16. Organisations which sell by mail-order may range from

   ❏ **single-product businesses** who advertise in newspapers or specialist magazines. Newspapers themselves often offer holiday or household items at special prices to their readers.

   ❏ **department or chain stores** which have a section to supply goods by post e.g. Harrods, Lilly Whites, Mothercare, Next.

   ❏ **manufacturers and wholesalers** who advertise in the weekend colour supplements of national 'quality' newspapers to reach the more affluent consumers. They also send catalogues and leaflets by direct mail to consumers. Typical products offered include books, CDs, glass, cutlery, pottery, watches, commemorative medals/coins and electrical items. Companies who specialise in this type of business include Scotcade, Kaleidoscope (a subsidiary of W.H. Smith) and the Bradford Exchange.

   ❏ **catalogues**: about 18 million people regularly buy a whole range of goods and services through mail order catalogues like Littlewoods, Great Universal Stores, Freemans and Kays. These organisations offer products direct to the public via an illustrated colour catalogue often containing over 20,000 items ranging from socks to car insurance. Orders are either placed direct by post or telephone or through agents who receive commission on the value of sales.

Task 4   **3.4.1 (C3.4)**

1. Name 2 costs, besides advertising, which would be heavy in a mail order business, which are not normally incurred by a shop retailer.

2. Look at a mail order catalogue and answer the following questions.

   a) What happens if the goods are found to be unsuitable when delivered?

   b) How are the housewives who run the agencies paid?

   c) Are they full-time employees of the firm they represent?

   d) Do you have to pay for the goods in cash or can they be bought on credit?

   e) How are the goods delivered?

3. Why do you think that mail order is one of the fastest growing sections of the retail trade?

Other Methods of Direct Selling

17. **Automated vending machines**

The sale of goods through automated slot machines is another growing form of direct selling. They are common sights nowadays in schools, clubs, motorway service stations, outside shops and launderettes. They have the advantage of being open 24 hours a day and sell a wide range of goods, including drinks, chocolates, milk and cigarettes.

18. **Party selling**

Party selling involves housewives who are asked to hold coffee parties to which friends, neighbours and relatives are invited. In return they receive commission on sales, or free gifts, from the firm. Well known examples of party selling firms include Tupperware (polythene goods), Sarah Coventry (jewellery), Pippa Dee (women's clothing) and Dee Minor (children's clothing).

19. **Trade fairs and exhibitions**

Trade fairs and exhibitions are huge market places for the display and sale of goods which take place throughout the world and are very important, particularly for manufacturers. They usually take place in special halls or centres like Olympia in London or the National Exhibition Centre near Birmingham. Examples include annual events like the Daily Mail Ideal Home Exhibition, the Motor Show, International Boat Show and the Royal Agricultural Show.

20. GMEX Exhibition Centre in Manchester

Indirect Sales Methods

21. Where organisations do not sell direct to consumers they must use other methods to distribute and sell their products. Distribution is the physical process of getting goods from manufacturers to consumers. It involves the storage, transport and handling of goods which together can represent a significant element of a firm's costs which can often be reduced by using indirect sales methods.

22. **Distribution objectives**

The objectives of distribution are to get the right quantity, in the right place, at the right time and in the right condition. By right means what is right for the consumer. A supermarket customer, for example, looking for a half-pound pack of a particular brand of butter will expect to find it. If it is out-of-stock then they are likely to purchase another brand. Thus, if distribution fails, all the other elements of the marketing mix will have been in vain. Therefore a supplier will seek to develop a distribution network which best meets these objectives.

Task 5

DISCOVER THE DAEWOO DIFFERENCE

direct

We do not use a traditional dealer network. We sell our cars directly to you through our wholly owned distribution network. Cutting out the middleman means we can offer highly specified cars at extremely competitive prices.

Our staff are not on commission and we have fixed prices, so you're not pressured and don't need to haggle to get a good deal. And forget hidden extras – delivery, number plates and 12-months' road tax are all included in the price.

With every car we sell, you get a 3 year/60,000 mile warranty:

3 year/60,000 mile free servicing inclusive of all labour and parts: 3 year Daewoo Total AA Cover and a 6 year anti-corrosion warranty. We'll also give you this guarantee: for 30 days or 1,000 miles after buying a

hassle free

Daewoo you can return the car and we'll change it or give you a full refund. How's that for a comprehensive package?

Daewoo provides the most courteous car service you can imagine. The mechanic assigned to your car will call you to discuss the work required beforehand. You can arrange to deliver your Daewoo at a convenient time, or we can

peace of mind

collect it. And on those occasions when you need to keep mobile we can arrange a free courtesy car while yours is being serviced. Now that's what Daewoo call a courteous service.

But what we have to offer you doesn't end there. We know you'll enjoy discovering the complete Daewoo experience.

courtesy

A different kind of car company?

That'll be the Daewoo.

1. What is the Daewoo difference?

2. What benefits does it bring to consumers?

3. Compare this with the service offered by a local car dealer.

4. Daewoo spent a lot of money on market research before launching their car in the UK. Try to find out more about both the research and the the sales methods subsequently adopted by the company. A visit to a local branch of Halfords may help you.

23. Chain of distribution

In industrial markets there is often a direct link between the manufacturer and customer but in consumer markets , although direct methods are now widely used, distribution more commonly involves the use of wholesalers and retailers as shown in the following diagram. Methods of selling goods abroad are discussed in paragraph 35.

The Chain of Distribution

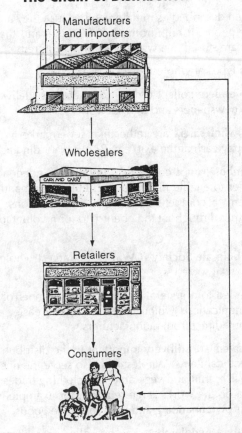

Economy in the distribution of goods is clearly illustrated by the following two diagrams:

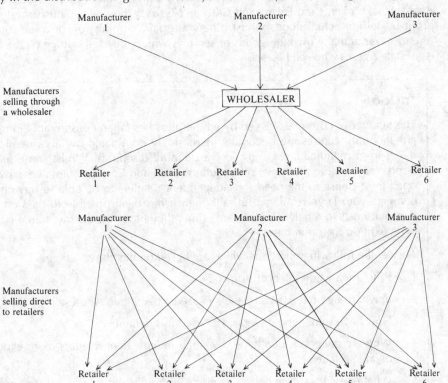

In the above example it can be seen that many extra deliveries are necessary if a manufacturer sells direct to retailers rather than through a wholesaler.

Wholesalers

24. Wholesalers are often described as **middlemen** because they are the middle link in the chain of distribution. They buy goods in bulk from manufacturers and then sell them in smaller quantities to retailers. The goods are stored in a warehouse until required.

25. There are four main types of wholesalers:

    ❑ **Traditional wholesalers** collect orders from retailers, deliver the goods and allow trade credit, e.g. W H Smith (newspapers and magazines)

    ❑ **Cash and carry wholesalers** are rather like supermarket warehouses where retailers go to buy their goods and pay cash at the exit, e.g. Booker, Nurdin and Peacock.

    ❑ **Voluntary or symbol groups** consist of a number of independent retailers who join together with a local wholesaler to enable him to buy in bulk from manufacturers. This leads to lower prices and it helps them to compete with bigger organisations. Sometimes a number of voluntary groups join together throughout the country to form voluntary chains, for example, Spar, VG and Nisa.

    ❑ **Co-operative Wholesale Society (CWS)** is the largest wholesaler in the UK and supplies goods for co-operative retail societies.

26. Several factors have led to a general decline in the number of wholesalers in particular improved transport and communications which make restocking easier and the development of large retail organisations who buy direct from manufacturers.

27. Despite this, wholesalers are still very important in the distribution of certain products, for example, newspapers and electrical items. Wholesalers also serve the needs of independent retailers, particularly in the grocery, fish, fruit and vegetable and clothing trades. When the wholesaler is eliminated someone else has to do the work. Large retailers, for example, who buy direct from manufacturers have to provide their own financing and storage for the goods.

28. It should be noted that 'middlemen' may be called merchants, agents, brokers, factors or wholesalers depending on which type of trade they work in. Examples include Corn Merchant, Insurance Agent, Stockbroker, Coal Factor and Cash and Carry Wholesaler. Thus some 'middlemen' make a profit by selling actual goods whilst others are paid commission or a fee for the work they do. Agents never actually own the goods or services which they sell but are paid for negotiating a sale, e.g. Estate Agents who sell houses.

Task 6   3.4.1 (C3.4)

The number of customers served by wholesalers has fallen considerably in recent years. Modern shopping centres are becoming increasingly dominated by large retailers who now buy direct from manufacturers and receive quantity discounts. Whilst some manufacturers, like Boots, sell direct to their own retail outlets. Cash and Carry Wholesalers have therefore developed in response to the need for independent retailers to be able to buy cheaper in order to compete with large retailers. But, although it has been possible to pass on the savings from transport costs to retailers, at the same time, they have lost the traditional facilities of delivery and credit on their purchases.

Answer the following questions which are based on the above article:

1. Who are a wholesalers customers?

2. In what sense have large retailers caused a decline in wholesaling?

3. How have some wholesalers adapted to this decline?

4. Why are the goods purchased by small independent retailers more expensive than those of large retailers?

5. What main advantage does a retailer gain from using a cash and carry wholesaler?

6. What services does a retailer give up in order to gain this advantage?

Retailers

29. The retail trade is referred to as the last link in the chain of distribution because it brings goods and services to the final consumer.

30. There are many different types of **retailers** each of which provides particular services for consumers.

   ☐ **Independent traders** offer personal counter service but their prices are often higher than other shops.

   ☐ **Self-service stores** are often independent but frequently join group wholesalers, like Spar, to enable them to compete with larger shops.

   ☐ **Supermarkets** offer cut prices and a wider choice of goods, e.g. ASDA, Tesco.

   ☐ **Superstores and hypermarkets** are very large supermarkets usually located away from town centres, which sell a vast range of merchandise, e.g. Carrefour.

   ☐ **Department stores** are found in the centre of large towns and cities and offer a large range of goods and have facilities such as toilets and restaurants, e.g. Debenhams, Harrods.

   ☐ **Multiple retailers** (those with more than 10 branches) specialise in selling a wide variety of one particular type of merchandise, e.g. Burtons, Dixons.

   ☐ **Variety chain stores** are multiples which sell a variety of goods, e.g. Woolworth, British Home Stores.

   ☐ **Discount stores** concentrate on selling durable household goods at cut prices, e.g. Comet, Argos.

   ☐ **Co-operative stores** are best known for the dividend which they give to customers.

Task 7   3.4.1 (C3.2)

1. Suggest with reasons, the most appropriate distribution channel(s) for each of the following products:

   a) the sale of Asda's own brand tomato sauce

   b) the sale of paperback books

   c) the sale of industrial machinery

   d) the export of whisky to Europe

   e) the import of bananas from Jamaica

2. Outline the possible channels of distribution for each of the following services:

   a) package holidays abroad

   b) car insurance

   c) plumbing

   d) theatre tickets

   e) bank loan

Consumer Choice

31. The particular distribution channel chosen by consumers will depend upon a number of factors including:

   ☐ Geographical location, e.g. close to, home, near a bus station, easy car parking

   ☐ Preferred method of payment, e.g. acceptance of cheques, credit cards or provision of credit facilities

   ☐ Personal preference, e.g. to shop in markets, supermarkets, corner shop or by mail order

❑ Brand and/or store loyalty i.e. how much effort consumers will go to to buy specific brands or from certain stores

❑ Frequency of use, i.e. whether the product or service is a regular purchase such as tea and bread or occasional like a TV or Video.

Distribution Management

32. Distribution is expensive and a firm must take decisions in respect of a number of important issues in order to achieve its overall objective of getting goods or services to final consumers.

33. These decisions include:

❑ **Distribution chain**, for example, whether to sell direct or via wholesalers and retailers. If wholesalers are used it must consider how to ensure that its products are 'pushed'. Thus advertising and sales promotion may be needed so that customer demand 'pulls' the products and forces retailers to stock them. This is particularly important with the launch of a new product.

❑ **Method of transport** such as whether to move goods by road, rail, sea or air. In addition, whether to have its own fleet of 'vehicles' or contract out. Efficient journey planning to reduce costs is also important.

❑ **Market Penetration**, for example, whether a firm's objective is to have the product stocked by all retail outlets or just selected ones such as chemists or supermarkets.

❑ **Location of warehouses** near to major transport routes may be important. Alternatively a firm may choose to have production facilities in several locations to reduce warehousing and transport costs.

❑ **Communication methods** like telephone or fax may be important for ordering and restocking products.

❑ **Type of packaging** used which may depend on the method of transport chosen.

❑ **Promotional policy**. Distribution can also be used as an important part of a firm's promotion. Thus, for example, fast cheap or free same day delivery, linked to telephone or fax ordering could give a firm an important competitive edge.

Task 8   3.4.1 (C3.2)

A car accessory company has recently developed a new technically advanced car polish. It has decided to sell this by mail order and through a selected number of specialist retail outlets.

1) Outline the main distribution factors which the management must consider.

2) Discuss the possible implications for the other elements of the marketing mix.

Comparing Sales Methods

34. Distribution management then is about comparing different sales methods to determine what is best for the product. It is also important, however, to evaluate the effectiveness of the method chosen. If it is not proving successful then another method may need to be considered. In 1994, for example, Amstrad decided to stop selling its computers through high street retailers like Dixons and changed to selling them direct. Cutting out retailers not only enabled Amstrad to control the quality of sales advice but also to cut prices whilst increasing profit margins.

Methods of Selling Goods Abroad

35. An organisation can sell goods abroad in a number of different ways including:

❑ **Direct sales from UK** – this would involve running an export sales department and probably mean sending representatives abroad to meet foreign buyers.

❏ **Foreign distributors** sometimes goods can be sold in bulk to foreign buyers who will sell and distribute them in that country.

❏ **Overseas agents** – these may be appointed abroad to represent the firm and sell goods on its behalf. They are usually paid a commission on sales for the work which they do.

❏ **Export houses** – these are specialist organisations which can assist a firm in three main ways:
They act as merchants buying a company's products and selling them overseas on their own account.
They act as agents responsible for handling all or part of a firm's overseas sales. For example, promotion, transport, distribution.
They act as agents for foreign buyers making contact with UK firms who can supply the goods required.

❏ **Overseas Subsidiaries** – instead of exporting, a firm may choose to set up its own factory in a foreign country. A multi-national company is one which owns and controls business operations outside the country in which it is based. They are in effect holding companies with shares in many individual overseas subsidiaries each of which is subject to the company law of the country in which it is located. Examples include: Ford, General Motors, IBM and the world's largest EXXON (Esso).

❏ **Licensing Agreement** – alternatively a firm may decide to allow a foreign producer to manufacture its goods under licence. In return the licencing firm receives a special royalty payment. Coca-Cola is sold world-wide on this basis.

Personal Selling

36. Personal selling offers a two-way means of communication. By meeting customers 'face-to-face', sales staff can present the benefits of and, if appropriate, demonstrate an organisation's products or services. They can also deal with any queries and overcome objections which is particularly important with complex or expensive products. The most difficult task is to 'close-the-sale' having obtained an order.

37. Personal selling is widely used in **consumer markets** for both goods and services as the following examples show:

Van deliveries e.g. milk, coal.
Double glazing, encyclopædias. } These are often sold direct
Financial services e.g. Insurance, Pensions } to consumers' homes

Retail outlets, e.g. clothing, footwear, cars
Exhibitions e.g. Ideal Home, Motor Show.

38. It is also used by manufacturers whose sales representatives call on wholesalers and retailers. Nowadays, the power of mass advertising has reduced the need for selling in consumer markets and turned many company representatives into 'order-takers'. Consequently, some firms now telephone customers for orders to reduce selling costs. (See telesales, paragraph 8.)

39. Personal selling is particularly suited to **industrial markets** where products such as machinery, aircraft, chemicals and plastics and services like cleaning and maintenance are very specialised and may require modification or individual design to suit specific needs. Negotiations on technical specifications, finance, delivery and installation may be of paramount importance and require considerable selling skills.

Sales Targets

40. Personal selling is a relatively expensive form of promotion and therefore an organisation must ensure that it is carried out in a cost-effective way. Therefore in order to achieve this, sales staff are usually set specific targets to achieve, such as a particular level of sales revenue (e.g. £2000); number of unit sales per week or month (e.g. 100) or a target ratio of orders to calls (e.g. 1:5) depending on the product or service. They are then often rewarded with commission, bonuses or prizes if these targets are met or exceeded.

Task 9   **3.4.1, 3.4.3 (C3.2)**

Explain from your knowledge of advertising and personal selling why you agree or disagree with the statement 'Mass advertising often reduces the need for actual selling and consequently many company representatives have essentially become just 'order-takers'.

Sales Campaign Methods

41. The preparation of a sales campaign requires careful planning and the co-ordination of key resources if it is to be successful and cost effective. A campaign is usually directed at the sales force, distributors, wholesalers, agents and/or retailers as appropriate and likely to be supported by a variety of different types of marketing communication as part of an integrated promotional plan. Advertising, sales promotion and PR, for example, could be used to create awareness and develop interest.

42. Examples of sales campaign methods include

☐ **Sales letters** which may be sent to existing or potential customers giving details of new products, of special offers and/or indicating that a member of the sales force will be contacting them. Retailers, for example, often write to customers who have credit accounts or loyalty cards. Manufacturers and wholesalers also use mailing lists of customers to create leads or encourage sales (see Direct Mail Element 3.3).

☐ **Sales memo**. Whilst letters may be sent to customers, memos could be sent to members of the sales force, for example to provide information about a campaign and/or possibly to motivate them by giving details of incentives for achieving targets.

☐ **Sales conferences** may be regional, national or even international and held either at the organisation's premises or in a hotel where the sales force is brought together. These are often major events held for a specific purpose such as the launch of a new product or organised annually to outline the organisation's objectives and targets and the promotional strategy to achieve them.

☐ **Sales meetings**. Whilst conferences are likely to involve the whole sales force or a large part of it and are held infrequently, sales meetings are more likely to take place locally and on a regular basis. The frequency will clearly depend on the organisation and its products. In fast moving consumer goods markets, for example, where new promotional offers are introduced every few weeks then weekly or fortnightly meetings may be needed.

Task 10   **3.4.2 (C3.2)**

Choose any product which you personally purchase on a regular basis. Assume you are the brand manager for the product and are planning a special campaign to increase market share by attracting new customers.

1. Prepare a sales letter to be sent to potential customers giving details of a special offer which you have devised.

2. Send a memo to the sales force giving details of the campaign and an incentive for them.

3. Comment on whether or not you feel a sales conference and/or meeting would assist your campaign.

Your product could be one bought by direct or indirect sales methods.

Responsibilities of Sales Persons

43. Sales staff are vital in any organisation whether it be a retailer, wholesaler, manufacturer, supplier of services, or whatever. It is they who have contact with the customer providing the vital link needed to sell the products. Consequently sales staff have a number of responsibilities including presenting

an appropriate image, customer care, product knowledge, point of sale service, sales administration and effective communication which ideally should form part of a training programme.

44. **Presenting the appropriate image**

The first impression of an organisation is often based on the way an individual looks, talks and/or answers the telephone in response to an enquiry. A clean, smart appearance is therefore essential for anyone who meets customers. Many organisations such as banks, building societies, supermarkets and other retail chains now provide uniforms. Where these are not supplied they often set standards in terms of appearance and dress which reflect the organisation's image, e.g. a smart suit for men.

45. **Customer care.** Customers are the most important people in any business, because without them there would be no business. Looking after them is therefore vital. Customer care involves putting customers first, seeking to meet their needs and expectations and providing a level of service which meets specific standards of quality. Making customers feel as if they and their business matter and treating them accordingly is therefore an important responsibility for any sales person.

46. **Product Knowledge**

In order to be able to help and advise customers efficiently and effectively it is essential that sales staff know as much as possible about the products they are selling. Apart from specific training, this knowledge can be gained from many sources, for example

❑ manufacturers leaflets, labels or packaging

❑ point-of-sale promotional materials

❑ trade magazines

❑ information gained from other staff and by

❑ trying the product personally.

Sales persons who show an interest in what they sell and can bring out the key selling points are more likely to clinch a sale.

Task 11   **3.4.3 (C3.4)**

Assume that you work for an organisation which sells the following goods and services:

1. Cars
2. Car hire
3. Car insurance
4. Car accessories (tyres and exhausts)
5. Car polish

1. Identify at least three specific sources of product knowledge about each product.

2. List at least five selling features of each.

Sales Administration

47. In addition to product knowledge sales staff also need to be aware of how **sales administration systems** operate in order to be able to complete a sale. In Element 2.2 we outlined some of the systems needed in order to facilitate the selling of an organisation's products. Efficient sales administration is important both to enable customers to make purchases and also to ensure that the organisation receives payment.

48. Depending on the organisation and its products this could include

❑ the processing of documents such as orders and invoices

❑ arranging credit clearance

❑ monitoring credit control

❑ managing customer accounts

❑ organising delivery schedules

❑ security of stock and money and

❑ using databases and mail shots to prospect for future business.

49. Sales staff need to be aware of such systems so that they can offer an efficient **point-of-sale service,** for example knowing

❑ how to wrap goods

❑ whether credit cards are accepted and if so the procedure involved

❑ what to do if a customer pays by cheque

❑ information about guarantees, delivery and after-sale service.

50. Correctly handled sales administration will give customers a positive image of the organisation thereby increasing the chances of securing current and future business which is good for income generation and profit. On the other hand, customers on the receiving end of poor administration or inefficient sales staff will be left with a negative impression and are more likely to be dissatisfied.

Task 12   **3.4.3, 3.4.5 (C3.4)**

SERVICE WITH A SNARL

A survey to rate standards of service in 2,500 businesses nationwide suggests that smiling sales staff with an eagerness to help are vanishing from the High Street. Many big name stores were criticised for making customers feel less than welcome. With rude, unfriendly and unhelpful service, with limited eye contact and few smiles from staff.

Supermarkets, the report says, were 'seriously short of smiles' with shoppers facing long check-out queues and rarely given help packing large loads. In many stores the main problem was getting staff to acknowledge customers' presence in the store. A third of the staff were either chatting or too busy with other duties. And they were familiar only with their own territory, unsure of the overall store's layout.

'Staff were bored and did not seem pleased when I did make a purchase,' one researcher says in the report.

Even the big fast food chains who pride themselves on friendly and efficient service, were below average on friendliness, politeness and helpfulness. In 15% of cases, researchers were served food they had not requested.

Better service was on offer, however, at gas and electricity showrooms, banks, post offices, estate agents and railway stations. Electricity staff come out tops in the study, rated as friendly, willing to explain and inspiring confidence.

A spokesman for research group Grass Roots said that service in some areas was certainly better than ten years ago. He added, however, 'There is no room for complacency when a quarter of all customer contact staff cannot raise a smile.

'Good service comes only from well-managed, well-trained and well-motivated staff and there is still clearly a big job to be done by management.'

Most of the companies involved said that the findings did not reflect their own feedback which suggested that customers were happy.

1. What does the article reveal about customers needs and how they were handled by sales staff?

2. What can be done about it?

3. Why do you think that the companies criticised, who were named in the research, disagreed with the findings?

51. It is also necessary for sales staff to know the organisation's policy on what to do if a customer returns goods or makes a complaint. In this respect some awareness and understanding of current legislation is important when dealing with customers, for example, the **Sale of Goods (Amendment) Act 1994** and **Trade Descriptions Acts 1968 and 1972** (see Element 1.3).

"Yes madam I know I said it was unbreakable but . . ."

Communicating Effectively

52. Much of what we have said about a sales person's responsibilities depends upon their ability to communicate effectively. In particular being able to identify customers' needs and get across information about the product being sold to meet those needs plus the services offered by the organisation. Poor communication can cause misunderstandings and consequently lost sales.

53. For example, if staff are rude or give the impression that they do not care or cannot be bothered customers may well 'pick up' this message and choose to go elsewhere.

54. Sales personnel, therefore, need to be good, clear speakers, able to communicate with all types of customers. Technical jargon should be avoided. Body language is also important, as is telephone manner, both of which can easily convey the wrong impression to a customer (see Element 2.3). Equally a customer's body language can also reveal a lot about what they are thinking.

Task 13   **2.3.1, 2.3.2, 3.4.3 (C3.4)**

1. Consider the following types of body language and comment on what they would tell you about a customer.

2. Comment on what you feel a sales person should do in each situation.

   a) A person who repeatedly keeps looking at their watch.

   b) Someone who taps their fingers on a counter.

   c) A blank expression on someone's face.

   d) A couple, each of whom is looking at different brands of a similar product.

3. Can you identify two situations where you have been a customer and demonstrated very definite body language. Briefly describe the situation and how the sales person reacted.

Customer Service

55. Customer service concentrates on acknowledging and appreciating how vital customers are to an organisation. This understanding is then reflected in the way that the business operates and how customers are handled and treated by individual members of staff. An important part of providing customer service is having an awareness of different customer needs and ensuring that these are then met. Effective internal and external communication is also essential in this process.

Customer Needs

56. Customers have a variety of different needs which an organisation must be able to meet if it is to successfully sell its goods or services and keep them satisfied.

57. These may include the need

   ❏ for **clear and accurate information** e.g. about the range of products stocked, prices, features, delivery or availability in order to determine if it meets their needs, or possibly an answer to a query on their account.

   ❏ to **purchase products quickly and easily** which they have decided meet their needs.

   ❏ to know how to **obtain a refund** or exchange goods where these are faulty with the minimum of fuss.

   ❏ to know **how to complain** about products bought or the service they have received where they are unsatisfactory.

   ❏ to receive **after-sales service** e.g. installation, repairs and/or training for goods like TVs, fitted bedrooms, carpets or industrial machinery.

Types of Customers

58. All customers are individuals each with their own particular needs which an organisation must try to meet. They can be different, for example, in terms of

   ❏ **age** – e.g. young, old.

   ❏ **sex** – male, female.

   ❏ **health** – e.g. poor, physically fit or having special needs or disabilities.

   ❏ **personality and temperament** – e.g. patient, impatient, confident, shy, calm, emotional.

   ❏ **aptitude** e.g. numeracy, literacy, communication, language.

   ❏ **socio-economic grouping**, i.e. income and occupation and therefore the way in which they spend their money (see Element 3.2)

   ❏ **nationality** – overseas customers may speak little or no English whilst cultural differences may make it more difficult to comprehend their needs.

59. Therefore it is important not just to recognise that these differences exist but also to consider what can be done to make it easier for particular customer needs to be met. Staff need to be trained to provide appropriate attention to a wide range of different types of customers whilst often special facilities can also be introduced which will help to maximise the business potential.

Task 14	**3.4.5 (C3.2)**

1. Identify from your own experience examples of each of the customer needs in Paragraph 57.

2. Comment on how you felt about the way in which the organisations concerned dealt with your needs.

Customers with Special Needs

60. Some customers may have needs which require special attention if their business is not to be lost. This could included for example customers who are physically or mentally handicapped, blind or partially sighted or have hearing difficulties. An organisation can take positive steps to help such customers by providing, for example, disabled access, lifts, automatic doors, special toilets, car parking, and hand rails on stairs.

Task 15	**3.4.5 (C3.4)**

1. Study six local retail outlets and compare the provision for disabled customers. Present your findings in the form of a graph and comment on any major differences and their potential impact on each business.

2. Now carry out a similar study by considering for other local public access buildings such as a cinema, theatre, museum, town hall, library or leisure centre. Include the place where you work or study as one of the buildings considered.

Customer Service by Business Sector

61. Most organisations today recognise the importance of their customers and try to be sensitive to their needs and expectations. Successful companies, like Marks and Spencer and Sainsbury's, put the customer first and clearly demonstrate this by placing great emphasis on good customer service and care.

62. Today's consumers have increasingly high expectations and customer service is about exceeding these expectations, not just meeting them. It involves

   ❐ providing an appropriate range of products and/or services,

   ❐ dealing promptly with problems and complaints,

   ❐ having good and clear communication systems,

   ❐ treating people with integrity and courtesy,

   ❐ building effective relationships with customers and

   ❐ setting standards for the handling of customers (customer care.)

63. Customer service then means more than just a smile or saying 'have a nice day' it is about an on-going commitment to provide continuous improvement. It is about being 1% better at 100 things not 100% betterat one thing.

   To achieve this means that the customer service culture must apply not just to an organisation's **external customers** but also to its **internal customers** (staff). Thus customer service is the responsibility of all staff at every level from the most junior to the most senior.

64. The type of customer service which an organisation provides will clearly vary according to the goods or services which it supplies. It can also vary according to its main objectives.

65. As discussed in Chapter 1 organisations in the private sector seek to make a profit in order to survive and develop and provide a return on their investment to its business owners. Therefore, it is essential to be successful that they both identify and meet customer needs. Failure to do this could result in a loss of customers and business to competitors. Increasingly, therefore, private sector organisations are putting an emphasis on customer service, including monitoring customer satisfaction and seeking ways to improve it. The importance of this marketing approach to business is discussed more fully in Elements 3.1 and 3.2.

66. Organisations in the public sector operate for the benefit of the nation and therefore, generally speaking, they do not have the same profit motive or threat of competition.

   However, to ensure that they give attention to customer service the government has introduced the **ombudsman scheme** to investigate and monitor complaints across a range of public and private sector business and the **Citizen's Charter** to establish measurable standards for public sector organisations. Your college will have a **student charter**.

67. These have changed the attitudes of public service organisations resulting in them being much more responsive to consumer needs and expectations. They are now required to provide customer service in the same way as private sector organisations.

Task 16   **3.4.5 (C3.4)**

Evaluating Customer Care

1. Identify at least two organisations in both the public and private sectors which you feel offer really good customer care.

2. What do they offer which determines this?

3. What standards do you look for or expect from such an organisation?

4. Who benefits from these standards and how?

5. How do you rate your college/employer in terms of customer service and why?

6. Identify five key areas for improvement.

Satisfied and Dissatisfied Customers

68. A satisfied customer is one who is pleased with their purchase and the service received. They are usually easy to deal with and will usually come back to make future purchases.

69. Unfortunately, however, there are a number of reasons why some customers may be dissatisfied and in this situation they must be handled carefully to prevent losing both their current and future business.

   Some dissatisfied customers will complain so that at least the organisation knows about the problem and can take action to deal with it. Others, however, may simply remain dissatisfied and not only never return but also tell their friends, relations, business colleagues or whoever which may cause a loss of further business.

70. Some of the main reasons for customer dissatisfaction include:

   ❏ **faulty goods** e.g. damaged, marked, broken;

   ❏ **poor service** e.g. lack of information, poorly trained staff;

   ❏ **limited services** e.g. credit cards not accepted, no delivery or after-sales service;

   ❏ **poor complaints procedures** e.g. difficult to get problems rectified, feel guilty for complaining or have to 'fight' for their rights.

71. Even where an organisation does have a clear, helpful complaints procedure such as Marks and Spencer all customers are different and some are unpleasant to deal with even at the best of times. When complaining they may become very angry or aggressive. It is important therefore that the sales person does not react by arguing (even if they think the complaint is unreasonable) but instead remains calm and polite in order to defuse the situation.

Task 17　　　　　　　　　　　　　　　　　　　　　**3.4.5 (C3.4)**

1. Investigate and compare how complaints are handled in at least three different types of organisation, e.g. a small local shop, a multiple store such as Burtons or Dixons, a variety chain such as British Home Stores, a service organisation perhaps a bank or dry cleaners, a privatised utility like gas or electricity or a public sector organisation like the local council. You could also include the college where you are studying and/or your place of work or work experience.

   Present your findings in the form of a table with appropriate comments on any major differences in approach.

2. Outline what you feel would be the 'best' procedure for handling a complaint from an irate customer returning a faulty alarm clock.

3. Now explain how you would deal with a customer returning a woollen jumper which has shrunk in the wash. This is the customer's rather than the shop's fault because the washing instructions have not been followed correctly.

   NB: 2 and 3 could also be carried out as role plays.

Monitoring Customer Satisfaction

72. As mentioned in paragraph 68 whilst many dissatisfied customers do complain many others do not and thus it might seem reasonable to assume that in effect they are satisfied. This may not be the case, however, and therefore it is important that an organisation monitors satisfaction by finding out what customers think about its products and service.

ASDA TALKBACK

We'd like your ideas on how to improve this store. Please complete the section below with any comments or suggestions you may have.

....

....

....

....

....

....

Do you use ASDA for your main grocery shopping?　Yes ☐　No ☐

BLOCK CAPITALS PLEASE

Title |＿＿＿| Initials |＿＿| Surname |＿＿＿＿＿＿＿＿＿＿＿|

Address |＿＿＿＿＿＿＿＿＿＿＿＿＿＿＿＿＿|

|＿＿＿＿＿＿＿＿＿＿＿＿＿＿＿＿＿|

|＿＿＿＿＿＿＿＿＿＿＿＿＿＿＿＿＿|

Postcode |＿＿＿＿＿＿|　Tel |＿＿＿＿|　|＿＿＿＿＿＿| (Home)

Post your comments in the box in the store foyer or post it free (no stamp required). ASDA Talkback never release information to other companies, but we may wish to mail you with information on further developments at your local ASDA. Please tick the box if you do NOT wish to receive this information. ☐

Thank you for helping us.

09192

73. This can be done in a number of ways including:

☐ **analysing sales performance** e.g. amount of repeat business, trends, increasing, decreasing;

☐ **customer feedback** e.g. analysing complaints and refunds to identify common problems; having suggestion boxes or inviting open comments or using anonymous shoppers to pose as customers;

☐ **market research** e.g. customer satisfaction surveys using questionnaires to investigate attitudes and opinions, consumer panels, focus groups, opinion polls, test marketing (se Element 3.2.).

Task 18   **3.4.5, 3.4.6, (C3.4)**

1.   In your place of work and/or study identify and describe the main methods used to obtain and monitor customer feedback.

2.   Comment on whether or not you feel that they are effective in meeting the needs of customers and the organisation and how they might be improved.

Importance of Customer Service

74. We saw earlier that successful companies put the customer first and therefore try very hard to ensure that their needs are met. This often involves extensive training in order to make staff aware of customer needs, to give them product knowledge and to develop the personal skills needed to deal with a variety of problems and situations.

75. By operating in this way an organisation is more likely to benefit from

☐ **satisfied customers** whose needs are met

☐ **repeat business** because satisfied customers are more likely to return to buy again

☐ **additional business** because satisfied customers are likely to recommend friends and relatives

☐ **customer loyalty** because good service makes them feel that they are dealing with a reputable organisation which cares about them and their needs. They are also less likely to have cause to complain.

☐ **improved staff morale** because satisfied customers are likely to be happier and easier to deal with than those who are dissatisfied and have reason to complain. Staff are also more likely to enjoy working for a business which promotes a customer care image which may increase job satisfaction.

76. These benefits together are likely to enhance an organisation's reputation and result in increased turnover, market share and profit potential. On the other hand a failure to meet customer needs can result in business being lost to competitors.

Task 19 3.4.3 (C3.4)

CUSTOMER CARE THE VITAL SPARK

To be successful in the next decade businesses will need as a minimum to develop a total customer-care culture coupled with continuous improvement programmes.

Customer care includes both internal customer relationships and after sales service throughout the useful life of the product.

To support this strategy, companies will have to be more innovative in the products or services offered. This will demand greater investment in creative R and D, to develop appropriate process technology, as flexible as possible to allow faster and easier response to future market needs. Management of such a complex situation will require excellent information technology systems.

This cannot work however, unless they invest in a motivated, effective, skilled, trained and flexible workforce. To achieve this requires total commitment to communication, involvement, encouragement, teamwork, training and a significant change in management attitudes and styles.

Employees also need to understand and be committed to the process of continuous improvement and customer care. They must not be suspicious or fear its effects.

Sound human relations policies are therefore needed covering management style and attitude as well as recruitment, training, development, succession planning, appraisal and communication.

Discuss the key message in the above article and why organisations need to respond to it.

Improving Customer Services

77. The information gathered from the monitoring of customer satisfaction can be used to help to develop and improve customer services or introduce new ones.

   It enables an organisation to provide what customers want and see as important and to raise standards beyond their expectations. This could, for example, involve the introduction of a customer care programme supported by appropriate staff training at all levels in the organisation.

78. In endeavouring to improve customer services it is important to remember that

   ❑ customers must perceive that they are getting good service e.g. Chairmen Richard Branson (Virgin) and Tom Farmer (Kwik-Fit) will deal directly with customer complaints themselves which is excellent public relations.

   ❑ Customers are not interested in an organisation's problems e.g. British Rail blaming snow or leaves on the line for poor service.

79. The **essential components of a customer care programme** include

   ❑ development of customer care policies, and training programmes

   ❑ internal customer care audits/reviews

   ❑ identification and implementation of ways to improve customer care

   ❑ conducting and analysing customer surveys to provide management information and identify issues/problems

   ❑ reviewing complaints procedures and effectiveness

   ❑ introducing friendly systems and procedures

   ❑ implementing a 'customer care culture' e.g. 'guide dogs only' rather than 'no dogs allowed'.

   ❑ setting measurable objectives and targets and monitoring progress e.g. response time to enquiries, reduction in number of complaints.

> **Task 20**   **3.4.3, 3.4.4 (C3.4)**
>
> 1. For the place where you work or study devise a customer care programme. Include in it specific examples of how you would monitor customer satisfaction, any improvements which you would introduce and measurable targets which could be used.
>
> 2. Comment on how this would improve the overall level of customer service currently provided by the organisation.

Summary

80. a) An organisation can sell either directly or indirectly to its consumers.

     b) Direct methods include TV, radio, factory outlets, telesales, door-to-door, pyramid and mail order.

     c) Indirect selling may involve the use of wholesalers, retailers or agents.

     d) There are many different types of retailers each providing particular services for consumers.

     e) Goods may be exported directly or through foreign distributors, overseas agents, export houses, overseas subsidiaries or licensing agreements.

     f) Personal selling is widely used in both consumer and industrial markets and sales staff usually have to achieve targets.

     g) Sales campaigns may be directed at the sales force, distributors, wholesalers, agents or retailers.

     h) Methods employed can include sales letters, memos, conferences and meetings.

     m) Sales persons are responsible for presenting the appropriate image, customer care, product knowledge, sales administration, point-of-sale service and effective communication.

     n) Customer service is about acknowledging and appreciating how vital customers are to an organisation.

     o) Customers may have a variety of needs including information, products, refunds, complaints and after-sales service.

     p) Staff need to be trained to provide appropriate attention to a wide range of customers including those with special needs.

     q) Organisations in the private sector must be responsible to customer needs if they are to survive. Whilst the Citizens' Charter sets standards for public sector organisations.

     r) Organisations can monitor customer satisfaction by analysing sales performance, customer feedback or carrying out market research.

     s) A customer care programme can help to improve customer service, enhance an organisation's reputation and increase sales and market share.

Review questions *(Answers can be found in the paragraphs indicated)*

1. List and briefly describe six different methods of direct selling. (2–20)

2. Outline the chain of distribution. (23–30)

3. Why are wholesalers generally less important today than they used to be? (26)

4. Identify the key features of four different types of retail outlet. (30)

5. Identify at least five factors which need to be considered in distribution management. (32–33)

6. List and briefly describe the main methods of selling goods abroad. (35)

7. Why is personal selling used in some markets and not others? (36–39)

8. Distinguish between the uses of sales letters, memos, meetings and conferences. (42)

9. Discuss the key responsibilities of sales persons. (43–54)

10. What do you understand by customer service? (55)

11. Briefly explain the main needs of customers. (56–57)

12. In what sense are all customers different and why might some have special needs? (58–60)

13. Why might there be differences as well as similarities between customer service provided by private and public sector organisations? (61–67)

14. What are the main reasons for customers being dissatisfied? (68–70)

15. Why should organisations monitor customer satisfaction and how could this be done? (72–73)

16. Why is good customer service important and how could it be improved? (74–79)

Assignment – Sales methods and customer service   Element 3.4

You are asked to prepare a report which

1. Compares the sales methods of business organisations. Your comparison should include the suitability of different sales methods to meet the needs of the organisation and its customers.

2. Describe the methods used by one organisation for one sales campaign.

3. Explain the responsibilities of a sales person when providing customer service. Specifically this should include their responsibilities in conforming with the Sales of Goods and Trades Descriptions Acts.

4. Explain the importance of sales administration work including how it contributes

   a) To a positive or negative customer impression and

   b) to the business's need to generate income or make a profit.

5. Conclude with a summary which

   a) evaluates the customer service provided in the same or different organisations in terms of meeting the needs of customers and the organisation.

   b) contains proposals for improvements to customer service so that it better meets their needs.

Your report should ideally be based on information obtained from existing business organisations although it could be based on the operation of a simulated business such as Young Enterprise, a Practice Firm or case study material.

You will find it useful to consider an unsuccessful organisation, (e.g. Ratners, Rumbelows) and compare the performance of its sales operation to that of a successful one to draw out what makes good customer service and effective sales work.

13 Human Resourcing

This Chapter is about the rights and responsibilities of employers and employees, the role of trade unions and staff associations and employers methods for gaining employee co-operation. It includes:

- ❏ People and Business
- ❏ Employer/Employee Expectations
- ❏ Employment Rights
- ❏ Employment Legislation
- ❏ Contracts of Employment
- ❏ Health and Safety at Work
- ❏ Equal Opportunities
- ❏ Pregnant Worker's Directive
- ❏ Rights of Redundant Employees
- ❏ Termination of Employment
- ❏ Dismissal Procedures
- ❏ Unfair Dismissal
- ❏ TURER
- ❏ Employer/Employee Responsibilities

- ❏ Industrial Relations
- ❏ Trade Unions
- ❏ Collective Bargaining
- ❏ Employers Associations
- ❏ Industrial Action
- ❏ Joint Consultation
- ❏ Staff Organisations
- ❏ Multi-skilling
- ❏ Teamwork
- ❏ Quality Circles
- ❏ Share Ownership
- ❏ Job Security
- ❏ ACAS

People and Business

1. People are an essential and very valuable resource in any organisation. But they are also expensive to employ and in some 'people intensive' organisations like schools and hospitals, can represent over 70% of the total operational costs. People are also individuals and everybody is different in terms of personality and needs. Since a large part of each day is spent at work, it should be both interesting and enjoyable if employees are to be motivated to always give of their best. A business's success can very often depend upon the quality of the staff it employs. Their efficiency, loyalty, attitude and enthusiasm can make the difference between the success or failure of the organisation.

Employer and Employee Expectations

2. The relationship between employers and their employees therefore is very important. Whether or not this is a harmonious one depends to a large extent upon the various rights and responsibilities of both parties and how these are implemented.

3. It would not be unreasonable for most **employees**, for example, to expect
   - ❏ a fair wage for the work they do
   - ❏ to be treated fairly by managers and others in the organisation
   - ❏ to work reasonable hours in a clean and safe environment
   - ❏ to receive some paid holidays and
   - ❏ to receive appropriate training for the job.

4. Likewise in return, an **employer** could reasonably expect employees to
   - ❏ be punctual, sociable and co-operative
   - ❏ obey all reasonable instructions
   - ❏ treat facilities and equipment with care and respect
   - ❏ be loyal and trustworthy and perform a fair amount of work each day.

Task 1   **4.1.1 (C3.1)**

1. With a colleague discuss what you feel are some other reasonable rights and expectations which both employees and employers might have of each other. If possible relate your views to your experience in a job or from work experience.

2. Comment on why you think such rights and expectations are important.

Employment Rights

5. Many of the expectations identified in paragraphs 3 and 4 are actual rights and responsibilities covered by legislation which affects both employers and employees.

   Summarised below these are the right to:

   ❏ A contract i.e. a written statement of Terms and Conditions of Employment.
   ❏ An itemised pay slip.
   ❏ Notice of Termination of Employment.
   ❏ The guaranteed payment of wages.
   ❏ A safe working environment.
   ❏ Be treated fairly and without discrimination.
   ❏ Not to be unfairly dismissed.
   ❏ Time off for public duties e.g. a local councillor, justice of the peace or school governor.
   ❏ Reasonable time off for trade union duties.
   ❏ Statutory Sick Pay.
   ❏ Compensation if made redundant.
   ❏ Maternity benefit and the right to return to work for female employees, regardless of hours worked or length of service.

6. Some statutory rights such as health and safety and contracts apply to anyone at work whilst others such as unfair dismissal and redundancy pay only apply to employees who have been continuously employed for at least two years.

   The legislation in which these rights are contained is considered below:

Employment Legislation

7. When an employer makes an offer of a job and the employee accepts it in return for a consideration (payment of wages/salary), then a legal agreement called a contract exists. As with all contracts this gives both parties a legal obligation to comply with the terms laid down.

8. The **Trade Union Reform and Employment Rights Act 1993** (TURER) states that an employee must be given a written statement of the main terms and conditions of their employment within two months of starting a new job. Any changes to the statement must be notified in writing within one month. TURER also contains other rights which are discussed in paragraph 47.

9. The **Contract of Employment Acts 1972-82** state that a contract should include details of the following:

   ❏ Employer's and employee's name
   ❏ Job Title
   ❏ Date the job started
   ❏ Rate of pay e.g. £15,000 pa, £5 per hour
   ❏ Frequency of payment, for example weekly, monthly
   ❏ Hours of work e.g. 8–4 Mon–Fri
   ❏ Holidays e.g. 25 days per annum plus Bank Holidays

- ❏ Place of work
- ❏ Sickness benefits i.e. entitlement to time off with pay
- ❏ Grievance procedure i.e. dealing with problems at work
- ❏ Trade Union Collective Agreements where the employer is bound by these
- ❏ Disciplinary rules
- ❏ Period of notice required to leave the employment
- ❏ Pension rights.

10. Sometimes not all this information is given directly to employees but instead is kept in a 'conditions of service' booklet to which they must be able to refer at any time.

11. **An example of a standard contract of employment**

Perkins Newman Ltd
5 Hampson Square, Buttermere

Contract of Employment
Particulars of Terms and Conditions of Employment pursuant to the
Employment Protection (Consolidation) Act 1978

Employee's name . . . .

1. **Continuous Employment**
   Your continuous service dates from . . . .

2. **Job Title**
   You are employed as . . . . Based at . . . .

3. **Salary**
   Your salary is . . . . per annum, paid monthly in arrears by credit transfer.
   Any changes or amendments to this will be confirmed in writing within one month of them occurring.

4. **Hours of Work**
   Your normal hours of work are . . . . hours a week, normally worked over a five day period (Mondays to Fridays inclusive).
   Occasional Saturday working may be required for which time off in lieu will be given.

5. **Leave**
   You are entitled to . . . . days paid holiday per annum in addition to statutory holidays.
   The leave is to be taken at a time convenient to the employer.

6. **Sickness**
   Notification of absence should be made on the first day of sickness, in writing or by telephone.
   If you are absent for a period in excess of five working days, a doctor's certificate must be submitted to the Personnel Office.
   Payment for periods of absence due to authorised sickness will be made in accordance with the current Statutory Sick Pay Scheme.

7. **Notice**
   After 1 month's service you are required to give the Company 4 weeks notice to terminate your employment.
   You are entitled to receive the same period of notice from the Company.

8. **Grievance Procedures**
   If you wish to raise any grievance relating to your employment, you should do so in accordance with the Grievance Procedure shown in the Employee Information Binder which can be obtained from the Personnel Office.

9. **Disciplinary Rules**
   The Company rules form part of your conditions of employment. These are shown in the Employee Information Binder and it is your responsibility to familiarise yourself with these and observe them at all times.
   If you are dissatisfied with any disciplinary decision taken against you, you should raise this in accordance with the Appeals Procedure shown in the Employee Information Binder.

10. **Pension Scheme**
    Details of the contributory Company Pension Scheme, for which you are eligible, may be obtained from the Personnel Office.

Signed by the employee . . . . Date . . . .

Signed on Behalf of the Company . . . . Date . . . .
Personnel Manager

Task 2   **4.1.1 (C3.2, C3.4)**

Choosing any job in the organisation where you work or study or any other well known to you compare the contract of employment with the example above. Comment on any differences in the layout and content including significant additions, for example, a confidentiality or exclusivity clause.

---

12. Other legislation which has been introduced to protect employees and improve their conditions of employment includes the **Health and Safety at Work Act 1974, Equal Pay Acts 1970 and 1983**, **Sex Discrimination Act 1975** and **Race Relations Act 1976**. The European Commission has also introduced a number of directives which affect employees at work.

    The government has also announced proposals for legislation to eliminate discrimination against disabled people.

13. **Health and Safety at Work Act 1974**. The purpose of this Act is to protect employees or members of the public from health and safety hazards at work. The Act makes everyone concerned with work activities responsible for health and safety, including:

    ❏ Employers, the self-employed, employees
    ❏ Manufacturers, designers, suppliers and importers of articles and substances for use at work
    ❏ Those in control of premises, for example Headteacher in a school.

14. The Act requires employers to:

    ❏ Maintain safe plant equipment and systems of work
    ❏ Provide safety training and
    ❏ Produce a Safety Policy Statement of which all employees must be made aware.

    Employees are responsible for taking reasonable care at all times and for co-operating with the employer on safety matters.

15. The **Health and Safety Commission** was set up to enforce the Act. It employs Health and Safety Inspectors who visit firms. They may make recommendations to help firms or, where hazards are found, issue improvement orders (requiring an unsafe system to be altered within a specified period of time, usually 21 days), or prohibition orders (stopping the use of unsafe practices immediately). Anyone who breaks the law may be prosecuted and could be fined up to £20,000 or face a 6 month prison sentence. In Northern Ireland the Health and Safety Agency performs a similar function.

16. The European Commission has set up a new pan-European Agency for Health and Safety located in Bilbao, Spain 'to provide the community with technical, scientific and economic information on health and safety'.

17. **Enforcement of Health and Safety Legislation**

ACTION AGAINST BLAZE FIRM

A Castleford chemical company is to be prosecuted by the Health & Safety Executive in connection with a fire earlier this year which killed 5 workers.

SAFETY CHARGE

The Royal Ordnance Company in Waltham Abbey, Essex is to be prosecuted for failing to ensure employees' safety after an explosion at the plant in January when toxic fumes were released over a wide area.

Health and Safety Law

What you should know

Your health, safety and welfare at work are protected by law. Your employer has a duty to protect you and to keep you informed about health and safety. You have a responsibility to look after yourself and others.
If there is a problem, discuss it with your employer or your safety representative, if there is one.

Opposite is a brief guide to health and safety law. It does not describe the law in detail, but it does list the key points.

HSE
Health & Safety Executive

© Crown copyright 1989   Printed by HMSO, Edinburgh Press   ISBN 0 11 701424 9   Dd 290487 160004 8/89 (288627)   Price £3.30 (excl. tax)

Your employer has a duty under the law to ensure, so far as is reasonably practicable, your health, safety and welfare at work.

In general, your employer's duties include:

- making your workplace safe and without risks to health;
- keeping dust, fume and noise under control;
- ensuring plant and machinery are safe and that safe systems of work are set and followed;
- ensuring articles and substances are moved, stored and used safely;
- providing adequate welfare facilities;
- giving you the information, instruction, training and supervision necessary for your health and safety.

Your employer must also:

- draw up a health and safety policy statement if there are 5 or more employees, including the health and safety organisation and arrangements in force, and bring it to your attention;
- provide free, any protective clothing or equipment specifically required by health and safety law;
- report certain injuries, diseases and dangerous occurrences to the enforcing authority;
- provide adequate first-aid facilities;
- consult a safety representative, if one is appointed by a recognised trade union, about matters affecting your health and safety;
- set up a safety committee if asked in writing by 2 or more safety representatives.

Employers also have duties to take precautions against fire, provide adequate means of escape and means for fighting fire.

In many workplaces employers may have other specific duties:

- to take adequate precautions against explosions of flammable dust or gas and when welding and soldering containers which have held an explosive or flammable substance;
- to maintain a workroom temperature of at least 16°C after the first hour of work where employees do most of their work sitting down;
- to keep the workplace clean;
- to provide, maintain and keep clean washing and toilet facilities and accommodation for clothing and to supply drinking water;
- to see that workrooms are not overcrowded and that they are well ventilated and lit;
- to ensure that floors, steps, stairs, ladders, passages and gangways are well constructed and maintained, and not obstructed;
- to take special precautions before allowing employees to enter and work in a confined space;
- to ensure that employees do not have to lift, carry or move any load so heavy that it is likely to injure them;
- to guard securely all dangerous parts of machines;
- to see that employees, especially young people, are properly trained or under adequate supervision before using dangerous machines;

- to ensure that lifting equipment (hoists, lifts, chains, ropes, cranes and lifting tackle) and steam boilers, steam receivers and air receivers are well constructed, well maintained and examined at specified intervals;
- to give employees suitable eye protection or protective equipment for certain jobs;
- to take proper precautions to prevent employees being exposed to substances which may damage their health;
- to take precautions against danger from electrical equipment and radiation.

As an employee, you have legal duties too. They include:

- taking reasonable care for your own health and safety and that of others who may be affected by what you do or do not do;
- cooperation with your employer on health and safety;
- not interfering with or misusing anything provided for your health, safety and welfare.

If you think there is a health and safety problem in your workplace you should first discuss it with your employer, supervisor or manager. You may also wish to discuss it with your safety representative, if there is one.

If the problem remains or you need more help, health and safety inspectors can give advice on how to comply with the law. They also have powers to enforce it. The Health and Safety Executive's (HSE's) Employment Medical Advisory Service can give advice on health at work and first-aid. Contact them at the addresses below.

Name and address of enforcing authority (eg the HSE or your Local Authority's Environmental Health Department)

Address of HSE's Employment Medical Advisory Service

You can get advice on general fire precautions etc, from the Fire Brigade or your fire officer.

The main Act of Parliament is the Health and Safety at Work etc Act 1974, but for particular purposes the Factories Act 1961, the Mines and Quarries Act 1954, the Offices, Shops and Railway Premises Act 1963, the Nuclear Installations Act 1965, the Agriculture (Safety, Health and Welfare Provisions) Act 1956, the Fire Precautions Act 1971 and other Acts and Regulations made under any of these may be equally relevant.

Useful HSE publications:

A Guide to the Health and Safety at Work etc Act 1974 (HS(R)6);
A guide to the Offices, Shops and Railway Premises Act 1963 (HS(R)4);
A guide to agricultural legislation (HS(R)2);
The Factories Act 1961 - A short guide;
The Essentials of Health and Safety at Work - A booklet for small firms;
Safety Representatives and Safety Committees.
Your employer may have copies which you can inspect. They are also available from HMSO and Government bookshops and booksellers.

Task 3

4.1.1 (C3.2)

Study the Health and Safety Executive notice and then describe what you think is your own responsibility for the health and safety of both yourself and the people with whom you attend school/college or work.

Workplace (Health, Safety and Welfare) Regulations 1992

18. Sweeping changes to Health & Safety legislation were introduced in January 1993 when 6 new EU Directives came into force affecting virtually all employers, employees and the self-employed.

    The regulations which are discussed below cover:

    ❒ Health and Safety management.
    ❒ Work equipment safety.
    ❒ Manual handling of loads.
    ❒ Workplace conditions.
    ❒ Personal protective equipment.
    ❒ Display screen equipment.

Health and safety management

19. Designed to encourage a more systematic and better organised approach to dealing with health and safety, the Regulations require

    ❒ a recorded assessment of the risks to employees.

    ❒ arrangements to manage health and safety covering planning, organisation, control, monitoring and review.

    ❒ the provision of health surveillance where necessary.

    ❒ specialist staff to ensure compliance with the law and to deal with problems.

    ❒ the setting up of emergency procedures.

    ❒ the provision of easily understood information to staff.

Work equipment safety

20. These Regulations govern the use of equipment at work which can be anything from a simple hand tool like a hammer, to complex plant such as an oil refinery.

    They aim to ensure that:

    ❒ equipment is suitable and safe to use.
    ❒ maintained in good working order and
    ❒ staff are properly trained to use it.

Manual handling of loads

21. These Regulations apply to any manual handling operations which may cause injury at work including lifting, pushing, pulling, carrying or moving loads by hand or other bodily force.

22. They require the following 4 key steps:

    ❒ avoidance of hazardous operations where practicable.
    ❒ adequate assessment of hazardous operations. that cannot be avoided.
    ❒ measures taken to reduce the risk of injury to the lowest level possible.
    ❒ information about loads for employees with additional training if necessary.

Workplace conditions

23. These Regulations replace previous legislation including parts of the Offices, Shops and Railway Premises Act 1963 and the Factories Act 1961.

24. They apply to all workplaces and define specific standards in 4 broad areas covering the

    ❑ working environment, e.g. ventilation, temperature, lighting and room dimensions.

    ❑ safety, e.g. floors, ability to open and clean windows, doors, falling objects and passage of pedestrians and vehicles.

    ❑ housekeeping, e.g. maintenance of equipment, cleanliness and removal of waste.

    ❑ facilities, e.g. toilets, washing, eating, changing, clothing storage and rest areas.

Personal protective equipment (PPE)

25. These Regulations set out the principles for selecting, providing, maintaining and using PPE. They cover all clothing and equipment designed to be worn or held to protect against a hazard. PPE should be a last resort where risks cannot be controlled by other means.

26. The Regulations require that:

    ❑ risks are assessed to ensure PPE is suitable.

    ❑ PPE must always be used, maintained in working order and stored correctly.

    ❑ employees must be provided with information, instructions and training about PPE.

Display screen equipment

27. These Regulations only apply to employees who regularly use display screen equipment as a significant part of their normal work, e.g. typists who use a word processor.

28. The main provisions are:

    ❑ all workstations must be assessed for risk.

    ❑ risks identified must be reduced.

    ❑ workstations must comply with minimum standards.

    ❑ work must be planned so that there are breaks or changes of activity.

    ❑ users have the right to free eye-tests and special glasses if needed.

    ❑ users must receive information and training about the risks.

Task 4   4.1.1 (C3.4)

The 1993 Health & Safety legislation will clearly have a major impact on organisations.

1. Re-read the section and identify the key measures which organisations must implement.

2. What potential costs could an organisation face?

3. Comment on why you feel such legislation is needed.

Equal Opportunities

29. **Equal Pay Acts 1970 and 1983** (and corresponding legislation in Northern Ireland). Under these Acts, women are entitled to receive equal pay with men when doing the same or broadly similar work.

30. **Sex Discrimination Acts 1975 and 1986.** These Acts make it unlawful to discriminate between men and women in employment, education and training, and the provision of housing, goods, facilities and services, and in advertising. Northern Ireland has similar legislation.

31. The **Equal Opportunities Commission** was set up in 1975 (1976 in Northern Ireland). It advises people of their legal rights and may give financial help when a case goes to a Court or Tribunal.

32. **Race Relations Act 1976.** This Act makes in unlawful to discriminate against someone on the grounds of colour, race or ethnic or national origin in employment, education and training, and the provision of housing, goods, facilities and services and in advertising. The **Commission for Racial Equality** was set up to investigate and eliminate discrimination and to promote racial harmony. It also provides advice and may assist individuals who have complaints.

*"An employer must not discriminate
when selecting employees."*

Reproduced by kind permission of the Commission for Racial Equality.

| **Task 5** | **4.1.1, 4.1.2 (C3.4)** |

From the following 5 situations, identify those which may represent some form of discrimination (i.e. adversely affect one particular group of people) at work and explain why in each case.

1. An Asian owned company making ladies clothing has an entirely Asian workforce. Notice of vacancies in the company is spread by 'word of mouth' i.e. existing employees tell people they know such as family and friends.

2. A male Afro-Caribbean trainee working on a Youth Training programme has opted to learn motor vehicle skills. He is told that whilst working in the workshop he will have to have his hair, which is a long Rastafarian style, tied back or enclosed in a hat. He claims this is racial discrimination.

3. A large organisation runs a crèche for the benefit of its female employees. A male employee is told that he cannot put his child in the crèche.

4. A canteen in an organisation has stringent Health & Safety rules and does not allow anyone with a beard to work in the kitchens.

5. A company employs both full-time and part-time staff. The part-time staff, mostly females, are employed on 10 hours a week contracts, but they are told that they must be available, if the company needs them, for up to 30 hours a week.

Pregnant Workers Directive

33. The Management of Health and Safety at Work (Amendment) Regulations 1994, introduced in January 1995 enforced important European Union Legislation affecting female employees.

34. The regulations apply to 3 groups:

    ❏ those who are pregnant

    ❏ those who have recently given birth (up to 6 months)

    ❏ those who are breast-feeding.

    They require that a Risk Assessment is carried out to take account of risks to new and expectant mothers within their work activity.

35. If any risks are revealed, employers should first refer to any legislation covering it (e.g. COSHH) and then follow the hierarchy of measures outlined below to remove the risk.

    1) Temporarily adjust the employee's working conditions and/or hours or if that is not reasonable

    2) Offer the employee alternative work or if that is not possible

    3) Suspend her from work (with paid leave) for as long as is necessary to protect her health and safety and that of her unborn child.

36. Employees must inform their employer in writing that they are pregnant and if requested must supply a doctor's certificate confirming it.

Returning to work

37. An employee entitled to maternity leave shall not work nor be permitted to work, for at least 2 weeks after the birth of her child. 'Childbirth' means the birth of a child whether living or dead after 24 weeks of pregnancy.

Task 6   4.1.1, 4.1.2 (C3.4)

1. What is the new legislation which has been introduced affecting female workers?

2. Which groups of female workers does it affect?

3. What action must an employer take?

4. Draw a simple flow chart to illustrate what an employer must do.

5. With examples comment on how the new legislation may impact on employers.

Termination of Employment

38. A contract of employment will terminate naturally when someone dies or retires from a job. Whilst some contracts are only made for a fixed period (e.g. 12 months) and therefore automatically end at the agreed time. A contract of employment may also be legally terminated by giving a period of notice, which usually depends on seniority and length of service, as will happen when someone leaves for another job. Minimum periods of notice are laid down by law but can be varied by mutual agreement.

39. There will, however, be occasions when employers seek to summarily (i.e. without notice) terminate an employee's contract and dismiss them. Since the **Industrial Relations Act 1971**, employees have had statutory protection against arbitrary (unfair) dismissal by an employer. These provisions are included in the **Employment Protection (Consolidation) Act 1978** as amended by the **Employment Act 1980**.

40. Under this legislation there are 5 reasons for dismissal that are considered 'fair':

    ❏ **Gross Misconduct** – i.e. dishonesty, negligence or wilful disobedience which represent a breach of contract.

    ❏ **Redundancy** – i.e. where workers are surplus to requirements, possibly due to reorganisation or a decline in business. (See also Chapter 14 Element 4.2.)

❑ **Incompetence** – i.e. unsatisfactory work demonstrating an incapacity to do the job. To be fair, the employer must be able to show that suitable written warnings have been given.

❑ **Continued employment would break the law** e.g. a chauffeur who has lost his driving licence could not continue working.

❑ **Some other substantial reason** e.g. refusal to accept a change in duties, particularly if this makes a worker surplus to requirements.

41. **Rights of Redundant Employees**

Where an employee is being made redundant they are entitled to certain rights (see also Chapter 14 Element 4.2.)

❑ the right to redundancy pay

❑ the right to be given notice

❑ where alternative work is offered, the right to a trial period (normally 4 weeks) without jeopardising their right to a redundancy payment. This enables the employee to see if the job is suitable and employers to assess their capability.

❑ the right to paid time off work to look for another job or to arrange training. A maximum of 2 days per week would not be considered unreasonable.

Task 7	**4.1.1, 4.1.2 (C3.4)**

MARCONI JOBS CUT

Marconi Radar Systems has announced 540 redundancies because of a fall in orders. The Gateshead factory will close with loss of 450 jobs and another 90 will go at Chelmsford.

REDUNDANCY CARE

Employers are showing a more caring approach to redundant workers, according to a survey carried out for the Institute of Directors. It reveals that companies are realising that, with redundancy playing a prominent part of corporate life, severance pay is no longer enough, and employees need practical help. There are clear signs that many companies and organisations now have a formal policy for counselling and training to help employees find new jobs.

PILKINGTON JOB LOSSES

Recession-hit glass giant Pilkington shed 3,000 UK jobs last year – part of a world-wide cut of 12,400 in its workforce. Accounted for by redundancies and business sell-offs in a drive to reduce costs in the operating companies and at the centre. Market conditions in the flat and safety glass industry during what has become the longest recession since the Second World War have been the worst anyone can remember. The major users of the group's products – the building and automotive industries – have been particularly hard hit. No improvement in trading conditions is yet apparent.

From the above newspaper articles:

1. Identify the reasons for the redundancies.

2. What can firms do to help employees to cope with redundancy?

3. Discuss what action a firm could take which might possibly help to avoid making employees redundant.

Dismissal Procedures

42. The ACAS Code of Practice on dismissal states

    ❏ that all firms should have a clear dismissal procedure (such as that shown on the following page) including the opportunity to appeal and

    ❏ all employees should be made aware of it.

43.

Dismissal procedure

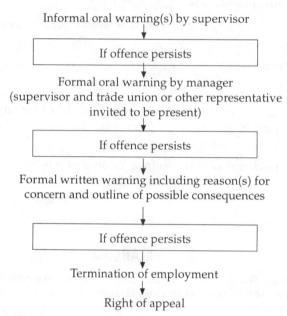

Informal oral warning(s) by supervisor

↓

If offence persists

↓

Formal oral warning by manager
(supervisor and trade union or other representative
invited to be present)

↓

If offence persists

↓

Formal written warning including reason(s) for
concern and outline of possible consequences

↓

If offence persists

↓

Termination of employment

↓

Right of appeal

Unfair Dismissal

44. If someone feels that they have been unfairly dismissed or unfairly made redundant, they can appeal to an Industrial Tribunal and, if successful, get their job back or receive compensation. **Industrial Tribunals** are independent judicial bodies set up to deal with complaints from employees on infringements of their rights under a number of Acts, including Contracts of Employment, Equal Pay, Unfair Dismissal, Sex Discrimination and Redundancy Payments.

Civil Legal Action

45. As an alternative to appealing to an industrial Tribunal an individual may decide to seek compensation for unfair dismissal by taking the employer to court. This may be expensive because it will involve using a solicitor to prepare the case and possibly a barrister to present it in court. It is usual, however, for costs to be awarded in successful cases.

46. To save time, and to reduce costs and possible bad publicity employers may sometimes try to prevent a case reaching the courts. Instead, they may offer an 'out of court' settlement, or alternatively, suggest arbitration whereby an independent person or body will determine an outcome which both parties agree to accept.

Task 8   **4.1.3 (C3.4)**

TOP SQUASH COACH WINS SEX BATTLE

An industrial tribunal has ordered the Squash Rackets Association to pay coach Katherine Moore £5,000 compensation for sex discrimination, including £1,500 for injury to feelings.

Miss Moore began coaching with the Women's Squash Rackets Association in 1980. But when the administration of men's and women's squash was amalgamated some years later she was excluded from a regional coaching post, the tribunal decided.

They also said that she may have been victimised because she encouraged members of the association to fight for pay equality.

RACE CLAIM IS SETTLED

A race discrimination claim by a Nigerian woman against the Legal Aid Board, was settled on undisclosed terms at a Manchester Industrial tribunal.

Mrs Christianah Obasaju, Wadhurst Walk, Brunswick, an administration assistant, complained after she failed to win a promotion.

SACKED STAFF VICTORY

Eight workers who lost their jobs with the Bollin Cafe in Prestbury, Macclesfield, were awarded a total of over £11,000 by a Manchester industrial tribunal after claiming redundancy money and holiday pay.

Reports of Industrial Tribunal cases like these regularly appear in both national and local newspapers. Try to find examples to illustrate complaints under at least 3 different Acts of Parliament and discuss what impact (if any) you feel the case could have on the organisation concerned.

Trade Union Reform and Employment Rights Act 1993 (TURER)

47. This was introduced with 2 main objectives:

   ❑ to strengthen the rights of individuals at work and the democratic rights of trade union members and

   ❑ to increase the competitiveness of the economy and remove obstacles to the creation of new jobs. It made significant changes to several areas of employment law and introduced new rights for employees.

48. **The main features of the Act are summarised below:**

Health and Safety Protection – anyone victimised or dismissed because of a health and safety issue is entitled to claim compensation.

Unfair dismissal – if an employee has made a claim against an employer under current legislation and is subsequently dismissed or made redundant it will automatically be considered as unfair.

Compensation for failure to re-employ – if an employer ignores a Tribunal order to re-employ someone unfairly dismissed additional compensation can be awarded.

Transfer of undertakings – this incorporates EU Acquired Rights Directives which protect the existing rights and conditions of employment for staff who transfer from one employer to another e.g. following a merger or takeover.

Redundancy consultation – in an effort to gain their agreement employers must inform and consult trade unions in relation to any proposed redundancies.

Maternity rights – all pregnant employees are entitled to 14 weeks maternity leave and protection against dismissal because of it.

Industrial action – unions must hold a postal ballot before taking industrial action, inform the employer in writing that it is taking place and the result, and give 7 days notice of any impending action.

'Citizen's Right' – any individual deprived of goods or services by unlawful industrial action has the right to bring proceedings to stop it happening. Help is available from the Commissioner for Protection Against Unlawful Industrial Action.

Employment particulars – all employees working more than 8 hours per week must receive a written statement of their main conditions of employment, including pay, hours and holidays within 2 months of starting a job.

Itemised pay statements – these should be given to anyone working over 8 hours per week. In firms employing less than 20 there is a 5 year qualifying period.

Tribunal matters – an agreement in a dispute between an employer and employee can be enforceable where the employee has received appropriate independent legal advice. Tribunals have been made more informal to speed up cases.

ACAS – is now able to charge for some services (see Chapter 12).

Union members' rights – individuals have the right to join a union of their choice. An employer cannot automatically deduct trade union subscriptions (under 'check-off' arrangements) without an employee's written consent within the last 3 years.

Internal trade union affairs – unions must provide members with an annual written statement about its financial affairs. The annual return to the Certification Officer must contain details of pay and benefits given to union leaders.

Task 9   **4.1.1, 4.1.2, 4.1.3, 4.1.4 (C3.4)**

TURER is a major piece of legislation which affects us all. From paragraph 48, identify those features of the Act which relate to:

1. individual employment rights

2. trade unions and industrial action

3. general employment matters.

49. Two other important measures in the Act were:

❐ the **abolition of Wages Councils** which set statutory minimum hourly rates of pay. The government considered these to be outdated by the move away from traditional, industry-wide collective bargaining where pay was fixed without any regard to the skills and performance of employees and the need to contain costs in order to create jobs.

❐ **changes in the management of the Careers Service** which is being opened up to local education authorities, TEC's and other private organisations to enable it to offer a more flexible, responsive service for local communities. Quality standards and performance indicators are to be set for guidance in consultation with employers.

Employer and Employee Responsibilities

50. So far in this chapter we have concentrated on the legislation which applies to both employers and employees at work. It is important therefore to briefly consider how it affects the responsibilities of each party.

Employer Responsibilities

51. These can be summarised as

   - ☐ **clarifying business objectives** so that employees know what the organisation is trying to achieve and more importantly what is expected of them, in terms of their contribution to ensure that it is successful.

   - ☐ **Making training and professional development available** to ensure that all staff have the skills needed to be able to do their job effectively.

   - ☐ **Negotiating pay and conditions** either directly with employees themselves or their representatives which usually means a Trade Union or Staff Association (see paragraphs 54 and 75.)

   - ☐ **Having a clear disciplinary procedure** so that employees know what will happen if they fail to comply with their terms of contract. The procedure recommended by ACAS was shown in paragraph 43.

   - ☐ **Having a simple grievance procedure** so that employees can complain if they have a problem with a manager, colleague or some other aspect of their work.

   - ☐ **Complying with legislation** to promote equal opportunities and thus prevent discrimination in terms of sex, race, pay and in the future disability.

   - ☐ **Implementing health and safety regulations** to ensure that employees work in conditions which at least comply with certain minimum standards, thus reducing the risks of accidents or hazardous situations occurring.

Employee Responsibilities

52. These can be summarised as:

   - ☐ **to comply with their contract of employment** which sets out the main terms and conditions of their employment.

   - ☐ **to comply with health and safety regulations** and procedures at work. By law employees must take care of themselves and others in the workplace, use safety devices where provided (e.g. protective clothing, guards on machines, eye goggles) and co-operate with their employer in observing safety requirements including training where necessary.

   - ☐ **not to use discriminatory behaviour** in the workplace, e.g. racial abuse, sexist comments, which not only cause offence but may be against the law.

   - ☐ **to work towards organisational objectives** by doing what is required of them at work to the best of their ability to ensure that tasks are completed on time, targets met, thus increasing the chances of objectives being achieved.

   - ☐ **to meet customer needs** whether internal or external to the organisation. For example, internal customers could include staff requiring stationery stock, protective clothing, petty cash, salary information or attention to a maintenance problem. Whilst external customers could include a patient visiting a hospital, a shopper waiting to buy a newspaper, a student visiting a college or a telephone call requesting information about products or services. The important point is that customers are the lifeblood of an organisation and should always be dealt with efficiently and treated with courtesy and respect.

Task 10   **4.1.1, 4.1.2 (C3.4)**

In the organisation where you work or study

1. Identify an example(s) of how the employer undertakes the responsibilities summarised in paragraph 51.

2. Now try to identify, if possible, examples of how employees fulfil their responsibilities as summarised in paragraph 52.

3. Finally comment on how, if at all, you feel that the responsibilities of employers and employees have an impact on you as an individual.

Industrial Relations

53. The term **'Industrial Relations'** covers every aspect of the relationship between a firm's management and its workers. People are crucial to the successful running of any business and therefore it is important that workers are happy in their job. Industrial Relations then is about preventing conflict (disagreements) at work. It is largely concerned with employees conditions of service, working environment and pay.

Trade Unions

54. A trade union is a **group of workers who have joined together** to bargain with their employers about pay and conditions of work. If one man in a firm tries to negotiate his own wages, he will have little power, and if he goes on strike it will have little effect on the firm. However, if 1,000 workers join together in a union then they are in a much stronger bargaining position.

55. Unions have an important role to play in negotiating pay and conditions, giving advice and information, defending employees' rights, including legal representation where necessary, and resolving conflict. Employees, however, do not have to belong to a union unless they want to. Some organisations, however, have a **closed shop** whereby the union(s) and employer come to an agreement that all employees should be union members to work there. However under the **1990 Employment Act** this cannot be enforced and anyone refused a job for not joining a 'closed shop' can complain to an Industrial Tribunal.

56. The early trade unions developed in the 18th and 19th Century and there are about 300 in Britain today, with a total membership of nearly 10 million people. In 1979 trade union membership reached a peak of 13.2 million. 80% of the current membership is in the largest 23 unions.

57. In recent years, the number of trade unions has been declining mainly because a lot of smaller unions have joined with others to form larger unions. The number of union members has also fallen because of the increase in unemployment and move away from manufacturing and public service industries where traditionally membership was usually high.

58.

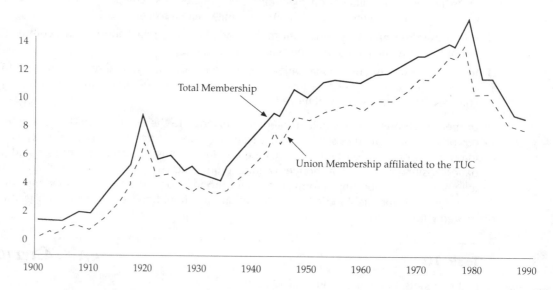

Trade Union Membership 1900-1990

59. **Types of Trade Unions**

The four main types of trade unions are craft, industrial, general and white collar.

❏ **Craft Unions**

These are the oldest type of union and tend to be quite small. They represent workers in particular skilled crafts or trades, for example, Society of Shuttlemakers, National Graphical Association

(NGA) and Associated Society of Locomotive Engineers and Firemen (ASLEF). As traditional skills have been replaced by new technology the number of craft unions has declined.

❑ **Industrial Unions**

These unions represent any workers in a particular industry, for example National Union of Mineworkers (NUM) and National Union of Seamen. Because they frequently represent all workers in an industry, these unions can often be very powerful.

❑ **General Unions**

These are the largest type of union and represent groups of unskilled workers in many different jobs and industries, for example TGWU (Transport and General Workers Union) which has over 1 million members and GMB (General Municipal, Boilermakers and Allied Union) with 860,000 members. In 1993 public sector unions NUPE (National Union of Public Employees), NALGO (National And Local Government Officers' Association) and COHSE (Confederation of Health Service Employees) merged to form UNISON, with nearly $1\frac{1}{2}$ million members.

❑ **White Collar Workers**

This is the most recent and rapidly growing type of union. They represent professional and clerical workers in a wide range of commercial and service industries, for example, National Union of Teachers (NUT) and National Union of Journalists (NUJ).

60. **The Growth of Trade Unions**

MERGER AGREED

Public sector unions NUPE, NALGO and COHSE have joined forces to create an organisation with nearly $1\frac{1}{2}$ million members.

Called Unison, it links workers in local government, health care, further and higher education, gas, electricity, water, transport and the voluntary sector. Each group still has its own identity.

The TGWU is also talking, tentatively, about merging with the GMB, a move which would also encompass $1\frac{1}{2}$ million members.

---

61. **Aims of Trade Unions**

The following is a list of some of the **main aims** which unions seek to achieve for their members:

❑ Better pay and working conditions

❑ Shorter working hours

❑ Longer holidays

❑ Improved Health and Safety at work

❑ Better Education and Training

❑ Job security

❑ Worker involvement in decision making

❑ Equal pay and equal opportunities

Task 11	**4.1.4 (C3.1)**

Discuss what you feel are the main advantages and any possible disadvantages of joining a trade union. Ask friends and colleagues whether in a union or not, to ascertain their views.

Collective Bargaining

62. To achieve their aims, trade unions negotiate with employers by a process known as collective bargaining. Each side seeks to get the best deal and reach a collective agreement which they both find acceptable.

63. **Example**

- ❏ The trade union demands a wage increase of £20 per week for all members.
- ❏ The employers offer £10 per week
- ❏ Further bargaining takes place between the two sides.
- ❏ Both the trade union and the employers agree to an increase of £15 per week.

64. Sometimes a settlement may also include a productivity agreement or points about changes in conditions or hours of work. A **productivity agreement** is a wage increase in return for workers producing more. This enables workers to get higher wages without increasing the costs to the employer.

Employers' Associations

65. Just as workers may be members of trade unions so employers can belong to an employers association. These are formed by firms in the same industry and represent them in negotiations with trade unions.

They also provide other services for members, for example statistical information, and advice or help with recruitment, training, health, safety and industrial relations problems.

66. **Examples**

- ❏ Engineering Employers Federation
- ❏ British Decorators Association
- ❏ Road Haulage Association
- ❏ Building Employers Confederation
- ❏ National Farmers Union

Task 12   4.1.4 (C3.4)

At the top of the trade union movement is the Trades Union Congress (TUC) to which most unions belong. It represents trade unions generally and speaks for the common interests of all its members. The employers equivalent of the TUC is the Confederation of British Industry (CBI) whose members include both companies and employers associations. Both the TUC and CBI are powerful pressure groups representing millions of people. Find out all you can about the role and functions of each of these organisations.

Industrial Action

67. If trade unions and employers cannot reach an agreement, either side can take industrial action to put pressure on the other. The main types of industrial action are outlined below.

- ❏ **Work-to-Rule**. This involves following every single rule and regulation in such a way as to slow down work and add to the employers costs, for example, a bus driver may cause problems by refusing to drive a bus with a faulty petrol gauge.
- ❏ **Go Slow**. This occurs when workers deliberately work slowly.
- ❏ **Overtime Ban**. Workers may also refuse to work more than their normal hours which may delay an urgent order.
- ❏ **Sabotage**. Sometimes workers will deliberately damage machinery and equipment thus delaying work.
- ❏ **Sit-Ins**. This happens when workers refuse to leave their place of work in protest at some action by their employer. Sit-ins are often used to delay or stop a firm selling or closing down a factory.

❏ **Boycott**. This occurs when union members refuse to handle certain goods or materials or refuse to work with other employees.

68. **Strikes**

If everything else fails then as a 'last resort' workers may decide to strike, i.e. withdraw their labour and refuse to work.

❏ An **official** strike is called by a union which sometimes also provides strike pay for workers. However, some strikes are **unofficial** because they take place without the backing of the union. Unions can be liable for damages if an industrial dispute is deemed unlawful.

❏ A **'lightning' or 'wild cat'** strike is a sudden walk-out as an expression of workers anger.

❏ Union members who refuse to join a strike are known as **'scabs'**.

69. Workers on strike usually **picket** their firm which means that they stand outside the gates trying to persuade people, not in the union, from going to work. By law only 6 persons may picket at any one entrance to a work place.

70. **Lock-Out**. This is the employers version of a strike. A firm may literally lock the gates to prevent its employees from getting to work.

71. **UK Working Days Lost Through Industrial Disputes 1980–1993**

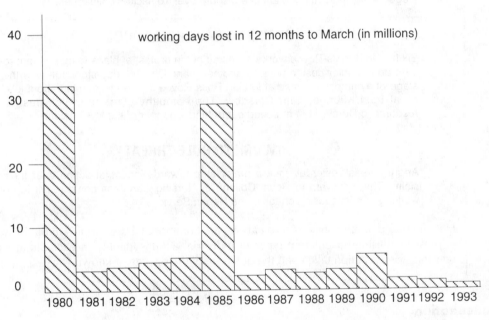

Source: Employment Gazette, Department of Employment

72. **Reasons for Disputes**

Some of the main reasons why workers take industrial action are summarised below:

❏ **Pay and working conditions**

❏ **Demarcation** – these are disputes between unions over which workers should do which jobs. For example, if a plumber fills a hole in a wall, the union may be annoyed because it is a plasterer's job. The problem is often caused because there are different rates of pay for different jobs and unions want to protect the jobs and wage rates of their members.

❏ **Victimisation** – when a worker feels that they are being 'got at' by the firm.

❏ **Threat of redundancy** – where employees may lose their jobs because there is no work for them.

❏ **New technology** and how it is introduced, for example computers, robots – particularly where this may result in the loss of jobs.

Task 13   **4.1.3, 4.1.4 (C3.4)**

200 IN 'SLEEP-IN'

More than 200 workers at the Temperatures factory at Sandown, Isle of Wight, staged a 'sleep-in' at the plant in a dispute over 10 sacked colleagues.

STRIKE TO SAVE ROLLS JOBS

Six hundred Rolls-Royce workers walked out in protest at plans to make them redundant and transfer design work to another plant. The $1\frac{1}{2}$ day stoppage was the first stage of a campaign aimed at forcing Rolls-Royce to change its mind about job losses at East Kilbride, near Glasgow. The company plans to switch design and research to Derby. Staff marched out behind a banner of the MSF union.

WORK TO RULE THREAT

Angry nurses yesterday took a major step towards industrial action over their pay claim. The move at the Royal College of Nursing Congress could result in nurses working to rule, causing chaos in the Health Service.

Headlines and articles such as those above are common. Find examples in the local or national press to illustrate 5 different types of industrial action. Identify in each situation the main reason(s) for the action taken and the outcome of the dispute, if known.

Joint Consultation

73. To help avoid labour problems or concerns leading to a dispute many organisations have regular meetings with unions. This enables any grievances to be aired and provides an opportunity for issues surrounding wages and salaries or working conditions to be discussed. It also enables employment issues such as potential redundancies or growth to be discussed. Overall, such meetings can lead to a spirit of co-operation and understanding between unions and employers, thus producing a positive approach to industrial relations.

74. In addition to union meetings, many organisations also have laid down **grievance procedures** which individual employees can use if they have a problem. This enables them to discuss it with management in order to reach a solution.

Staff Organisations

75   In some organisations trade union membership is relatively high, and often the power of the unions can be an important factor in industrial issues. Whether or not this is the case, however, it is important that staff are consulted about management proposals which may affect them, e.g. introduction of new technology, reorganisation, relocation or redundancy. This consultation should take place at the earliest opportunity both to involve staff and to dispel fears caused by rumours. Equally, if employee participation and initiative are encouraged, management can benefit from their views and ideas. This can also help to boost morale in an organisation and ease the process of change.

76.   Sometimes this participation is encouraged through **consultation committees** that may be formally established or convened on an ad hoc basis to discuss a particular proposal. In some organisations a **staff association** may exist. This may be formed essentially to organise social activities for staff, or be recognised by employees for formal consultation purposes. In the latter case it may fulfil some union functions, and therefore agreed procedures will be laid down about the frequency of meetings, matters covered and other issues such as whether or not an officer of the association can be present at a disciplinary interview. Staff associations can often act as pressure groups on management, regardless of their official status.

> ### Task 14   4.1.3, 4.1.4, 4.1.5 (C3.2)
>
> In the place where you work or study find out:
>
> 1.   what trade union(s), if any, represent the employees;
>
> 2.   if there is a staff association and, if so, what its main functions are;
>
> 3.   what the arrangements are for joint consultation in the organisation;
>
> 4.   if there have been any industrial disputes in the past two years and, if so, the reasons for them, any action taken and the outcome.

Multi-skilling

77.   In paragraph 72 we identified one of the main reasons for industrial action as being demarcation disputes, that is, disputes over 'who does what'. Prior to the 1990s many unions, in order to protect jobs, insisted that only their members could perform particular tasks, so such disputes were very common. This union policy was wasteful and lead to overmanning and inefficiency.

78.   To overcome this problem, multi-skilling has now become a common feature negotiated into many recent union agreements. Multi-skilling involves training employees to do a range of different tasks in the workplace instead of just one narrow task.

This system of job enlargement helps to motivate staff who get more variety at work, and often get paid more because they are more highly skilled. It also provides greater flexibility which increases the efficiency, productivity and competitiveness of the organisation.

79.   A well known recent example of multi-skilling is the Japanese car manufacturer Nissan's plant at Sunderland where all employees are trained to perform a variety of tasks. Whereas British car plants have traditionally had anything up to 500 different job classifications involving many unions, Nissan has three classifications and just one union to negotiate with.

Teamwork

80.   Employees' co-operation, job satisfaction, motivation and output can often be increased in organisations if tasks are carried out not by individuals, but by people working together in groups or teams. A team is essentially a group of people selected by management to work together win order to achieve a common objective. The Volvo car company in Sweden is an example of an organisation which has moved from an assembly line method of production to group working. (See Chapter 14 Element 4.2.)

Quality Circles

81. Sometimes called quality control circles, these originated in the USA but are also widely used in Japan, where they have been extensively applied in relation to just-in-time production methods. Quality circles consist of groups of shopfloor workers who meet regularly to discuss production problems, for example rising costs or wastage, identifying their causes and looking for solutions.

82. This form of participation, with management support, has been found not only to raise quality awareness, but also to improve employee co-operation and motivation. This results from a greater recognition, responsibility and involvement in decisions about the business, which in some organisations has been extended to include other important issues such as health, safety and environmental issues.

Share Ownership

83. In recent years there has been a growing trend towards companies involving staff in share ownership schemes. Often shares are given as a year end bonus based on the company's profits. They serve to motivate staff and encourage them to work harder. They also help to reduce conflict in organisations and improve the competitive edge because employees stand to benefit directly from harmonious working relationships and better company performance.

Job Security

84. The high levels of unemployment and redundancies experienced in the 1980's and 1990's has lead to many workers feeling less secure in their jobs. Both public and private sector employees have suffered. Therefore to improve job security it is important that workers and employers co-operate together for their mutual benefit.

Advisory, Conciliation and Arbitration Service (ACAS)

85. Where unions and employers cannot agree in a dispute they may request the help of ACAS. This is an independent body set up by the government with a general duty to help promote and improve industrial relations. ACAS is run by a council consisting of a chairman and nine members – three nominated by the TUC, three by the CBI and three independent members. ACAS in Northern Ireland is known as the Labour Relations Agency.

86. ACAS provides four main services:

    ❐ It gives **free advice** to unions and employers on any industrial relations issues.

    ❐ It offers a **conciliation** service. This involves trying to persuade the two sides in a dispute to start talking to each other again.

    ❐ If both sides agree ACAS can offer **arbitration**. An independent third party listens to all the arguments and then makes a decision which both sides agree to accept.

    ❐ If both sides do not want a binding agreement ACAS can arrange **mediation**. This involves getting the two sides together with a third party who puts forward proposals for a solution. It is then up to the two sides to decide whether to accept or ignore it.

87. Since April 1994 ACAS has been allowed to charge clients for certain services, including the cost of holding conferences, seminars, self-help clinics for small businesses and for some of its advisory publications.

Task 15   **4.1.3, 4.1.4, 4.1.5 (C3.3, N3.3)**

ACAS STATISTICS

	1990	1991
Requests for collective conciliation received	1,260	1,386
Conciliation successful or progress achieved	964	1,056
Completed conciliation cases by cause of dispute:		
Pay and terms and conditions	570	496
Recognition	159	174
Changes in working practices	67	46
Other trade union matters	50	91
Redundancy	109	233
Dismissal and discipline	147	144
Others	38	42
Total	1,140	1,226
Individual conciliation – cases received:		
Unfair dismissal	37,564	39,234
All discrimination cases	3,516	6,214
Wages Act	8,114	11,763
Other employment protection provisions	2,877	3,394
All jurisdictions	52,071	60,605

1. Comment on the trends in the above figures.

2. What do they reveal about the role of ACAS?

3. Try to obtain the most recent figures and comment on whether or not the use of ACAS has changed. Copies of the ACAS Annual Report are available free by calling into any ACAS office.

Legislation Affecting Employers and Unions

88. The **Trade Union and Labour Relations (Consolidation) Act 1992** brings together much existing employment legislation, including major measures concerning:

    ❏ the legal status of trade unions;

    ❏ the rights of trade union members (including rights to vote in the election of union leaders);

    ❏ organising, or taking part in, industrial action or picketing; including 7 days notice of proposed industrial action;

    ❏ protection for employees and workers against closed shop practices;

    ❏ collective bargaining;

    ❏ procedures for handling redundancies; and

    ❏ the constitution and powers of the ACAS, and other statutory industrial relations institutions.

89. The **Trade Union Reform and Employment Rights Act 1993** which revised existing legislation and introduced some new rights for employees is discussed in paragraph 47.

Task 16   **4.1.4 (C3.4)**

Modern governments have tended to get more involved in the whole structure of industrial relations. No government wants industrial disputes which slow down production, thus damaging the economy. Equally, workers do not want to lose wages, whilst employers do not want to lose profits. as consumers, we do not want to suffer the inconvenience of a bus or electricity strike or of not being able to buy goods because of industrial action. Therefore, peaceful industrial relations are of benefit to everyone.

1. Identify the possible consequences of industrial action for employers, employees and consumers.

2. Consider what effects you think it might have on other firms and on the economy as a whole

---

Summary

90. a) People represent an important resource and cost to a business.

   b) Both employers and employees have rights and responsibilities towards each other at work, many of which are statutory.

   c) Employees statutory rights at work include the right to a contract outlining the main terms and conditions of their employment.

   d) A number of Acts provide protection for employees covering Health and Safety; Equal Pay; Sex Discrimination; Race Relations; Unfair Dismissal and Redundancy.

   e) Six new Health and Safety Regulations introduced in 1993 all require the assessment of risks, introduction of controls and monitoring procedures.

   f) The Management of Health and Safety At Work (Amendment) Regulation 1994 introduced the Pregnant Workers Directive.

   g) The fair termination of an employee's contract may be due to misconduct, redundancy, incompetence, where continued employment would break the law or some other substantial reason.

   h) TURER introduced major changes to the rights of individuals and trade union members at work.

   i) A trade union is a group of workers who have joined together to protect and improve their pay and other working conditions.

   j The four main types of union are craft, industrial, general and white collar.

   k) Negotiations between unions and employers are known as collective bargaining.

   l) Employers may also join together by becoming members of an employers association.

   m) Industrial action by workers may include a work-to-rule, go-slow, overtime ban, sabotage, sit-in, boycott or strikes, whilst employers may lock-out their workers in a dispute.

   n) The main reasons for disputes include pay, working conditions and demarcation issues.

   o) Staff organisations may be used to improve consultation and participation in decision making.

   p) Multi-skilling and teamwork are important features of modern business.

   q) Share ownership, quality circles and job security and other ways of improving employee co-operation.

   r) ACAS is an independent body which can offer help when unions and employers cannot agree in a dispute.

Review questions *(Answers can be found in the paragraphs indicated)*

1. Give some examples of what both employers and employees could reasonably expect of each other at work. (2–4)

2. What are the statutory rights of employees? (5–6)

3. What is a contract of employment and what does it include? (7–11)

4. Outline the main Health & Safety legislation affecting employees at work. (13–28)

5. Give brief details of three other laws which protect employees at work (29–32)

6. In what ways are pregnant workers protected from risks at work? (33–37)

7. What rights do redundant employees have? (41)

8. In what circumstances can a contract of employment be terminated? (38–40)

9. Describe the ACAS Code of Practice on dismissal of employees. (43)

10. If someone feels that they have been unfairly dismissed, what action can they take? (44–46)

11. Explain why TURER was introduced and identify some of its key features. (47–49)

12. Summarise some of the main responsibilities of employers and employees at work. (50–52)

13. Explain what a trade union is. List the 4 main types of union and give an example of each. (59)

14. List the main aims of trade unions. (61)

15. Who takes part in collective bargaining? (62–64)

16. What is the employers equivalent of a trade union? (65–66)

17. List 6 different types of industrial action and list 4 main reasons for industrial disputes. (67–72)

18. How can organisations benefit from consultation with employees? (73–76)

19. How can teamwork, multi-skilling, share ownership, job security and quality circles affect industrial relations in an organisation? (72–82)

20. Briefly describe the functions of ACAS. (85–87)

Assignment – Investigating Human Resourcing   *Element 4.1*

Choosing one or more organisations well known to you prepare a report which:

1. analyses the terms and conditions outlined in employees' contracts of employment

2. analyses 2 working environments to check whether they comply with or contravene

    a) Health and Safety Regulations

    b) Equal Opportunities legislation in terms of race, sex or pay

3. describes the procedures which are available to employers and employees to uphold their rights a) if health and safety regulations are breached and/or b) discrimination takes place

4. explains, with examples, the role which trade unions and staff associations can play in negotiating pay and conditions and providing advice, information and legal representation for aggrieved parties

5. explains how, in one organisation, employer responsibilities are met for 2 of the following

    ❏ negotiating pay and conditions

    ❏ handling disciplinary procedures

    ❏ handling grievance procedures.

6. Explain how employees are encouraged to work towards organisational objectives and meet the quality standards through share ownership, quality circles or job security.

To help you with the assignment you could make use of any pamphlets, leaflets or posters designed to give advice to employers and employees.

14 Job Roles and Change

This chapter is about job roles and responsibilities in organisations and the impact of change on working conditions. It includes:

- Job roles
- Directors
- Managing Directors
- Executive/Non Executive Directors
- Company Secretary
- Managers
- Production Operatives and Support Staff
- Assistants
- Teams
- Teambuilding
- Team Roles
- Authority, Responsibility and Delegation
- Authority and Leadership
- Types of Authority
- Job Activities and Responsibilities
- Reasons for Change

- Internal Influences
- External Influences
- Changes in Working Conditions
- Contracts
- Hours of Work
- Flexi-time
- Shift work
- Holidays with Pay
- Sick Pay
- Redundancy
- Evaluating Change
- Barriers to Change
- Conflict
- Resistance to Change
- Implementing Change
- Predicting Change

Job Roles

1. There are literally many thousands of different types of jobs ranging from work in factories, offices and shops to a whole spectrum of other occupations such as those in farming, transport, involving labouring, repair and maintenance and so on. Each job involves a range of different duties, skills and responsibilities which vary depending on the level in the organisation concerned.

2. The main job roles in most organisations, however, can be broadly summarised as those of directors, managers, supervisors, operatives, assistants and team members.

Directors

3. The highest level of management in a company is the **Board of Directors** whilst other organisations such as schools, colleges and hospitals usually have a Board of Governors. These bodies are responsible for formulating policy and by law are required to safeguard the organisation's assets and protect it against inefficiency and fraud.

4. **Directors' duties and responsibilities** include:

- safeguarding shareholders' capital and ensuring a reasonable return on their investment
- setting objectives and targets and formulating policies to achieve them
- ensuring that policy conforms to the company's Memorandum and Articles of Association
- organising the company and its resources
- monitoring and controlling the company's activities

321

❏ continuously reviewing policies and amending as necessary

❏ determining the distribution of company profits.

Managing director

5. The managing director or chief executive of an organisation has specific duties and responsibilities to fulfil involving:

❏ providing leadership and taking urgent decisions

❏ appointing senior staff

❏ implementing policy to achieve agreed objectives

❏ promoting and maintaining staff morale and the goodwill of the organisation

❏ personal involvement with key customers, suppliers, and with trade unions for negotiation on major issues

❏ overall supervision, control and co-ordination of the company's day-to-day operations

❏ chairing certain meetings, including those of the Board of Directors unless there is a separate chairperson.

Executive and non-executive directors

6. Company directors may be either **executive** i.e. full-time, with functional responsibilities, actively involved in the day-to-day management of the company. They determine the organisation's long-term plans and objectives, set targets for achievement and implement the board's policy decisions. This involves communicating and delegating duties to managers, monitoring and reviewing tasks and reporting back to the board on progress, *or*

47. **Non-executive** i.e. acting in a part-time capacity, attending board meetings, but taking no part in the daily running of the company. Although they may not have practical knowledge and understanding of the company they can bring a broader, independent view to decision-taking and introduce new ideas and links to other organisations.

Task 1	**2.3.1 (C3.4)**

From a selection of at least six company reports (usually available in a library), compare and comment on the numbers, functions and roles of the directors.

Company secretary

8. The company secretary is not a director but is an executive officer who acts as secretary to the Board. They are often responsible for the general administration of a company but their main duties are to fulfil legal requirements such as:

❏ the administration of directors and shareholders meetings including arranging the dates and time, preparing the agenda, recording minutes and ensuring that any action points are followed up

❏ ensuring that the company meets its legal requirements including complying with the Memorandum and Articles of Association, making periodic returns (e.g. Annual Accounts), keeping statutory books (e.g. Register of Members) and special returns (e.g. reporting changes in company directors).

Task 2   **2.3.1 (C3.4)**

NO ONE WANTS TO BE A BOSS!

Many junior executives are no longer reaching for the top because the incentives are not big enough, according to a recent survey.

It reveals that most companies have trouble filling senior posts, especially from inside their organisations.

This management malaise is not just in Britain but throughout Europe, according to the survey of 500 chief executives of top companies in ten European countries.

Their answers indicate that because of the demands of business life and the lack of incentives, tomorrow's executives may not be able to meet the demands of industry.

The quality of managers is improving but their jobs are getting harder and the incentive to reach the top is less than it was ten years ago.

A grim report on the survey, says: 'There is little sign of the situation improving and in the years ahead industry may well suffer from a shortage of really effective leaders.'

Chief executives in all ten countries believe the pressures on management have drastically increased in the past decade. And there is widespread belief that the status of managers in the eyes of the community has declined.

Most top men say school-leavers are not as good as they used to be and that schools are not preparing pupils for careers in industry.

The answer, most executives believe, lies in closer liaison with educational authorities.

Read the above article and answer the following questions which are based on it.

1. Why are people no longer interested in becoming managers?

2. What consequences could this have for industry in the future?

3. If you were the Chief Executive of an organisation, what action would you consider taking to prevent your own firm suffering?

Managers

9. In Element 2.1 we identified different levels of management in organisations. At the top is the chief executive and board of directors. Below the Board we get **senior** and **middle** managers with foremen or supervisors at the **first** or junior level of management.

10. The efficiency and effectiveness of each functional area in an organisation will often depend very much upon the leadership qualities of the specialist managers involved. Work needs to be planned, organised and co-ordinated. Tasks must be delegated to suitable individuals and/or teams also must then be motivated, encouraged, supported, complimented or, if necessary, reprimanded to ensure that objectives are achieved.

11. It is managers then who ensure that staff work efficiently by taking operational decisions, setting targets, solving day-to-day problems, monitoring progress and keeping them informed of developments. Thus the role of managers is crucial to the success of organisations.

Task 3   2.3.1 (C3.2)

1. List the names of three directors, governors or managers in your place of work or study.

2. Identify some of the key tasks which they carry out. Job descriptions or if possible interviews may help you.

3. Comment on their role compared with the following 'managers':

    a) a shop manager

    b) a pub landlord/lady

    c) a lecturer/teacher

    d) a sports team captain

Production operatives and support staff

12. First-line managers are responsible for supervising the activities of a number of either production operatives or business support-staff.

13. **Production operatives** or 'shop-floor' workers are those whose job role involves the **direct operation** of machinery and equipment to produce goods or services, for example cars, plastics or furniture assembly. Although this usually means that they work in factories it can also include job roles in service industries such as fast food production.

14. **Support staff** are those whose job roles **support the internal working** of an organisation, for example, receptionists, clerks, and other office staff, security guards, cleaners, till operators or shelf-fillers in a supermarket and caretakers in a school or college. It also includes staff whose job roles support the organisation's **external operations,** for example, van drivers, service engineers and customer service staff.

15. Without this basic work the production of goods or services which is the essence of business would not exist. The most important asset in any organisation is its people, the majority of whom will be employed at the operator level performing essential tasks which enable the business to function effectively.

Assistants

16. The role of an assistant may exist at all levels in an organisation. Managers, for example, often have assistants or **deputies** who work with them. They carry out tasks for the managers which may include attending meetings or other activities on their behalf. Other examples where the term is often used include **sales staff** in shops; a director or manager might have a **personal assistant** who performs clerical and administrative duties; whilst van drivers, bricklayers, and plumbers often have assistants to help them with their work, frequently referred to as **'mates'**.

Task 4   4.2.1 (C3.2)

In the place where you work, study or know from work experience identify two examples of production operatives, support staff and assistants.

17.

Hierarchical or Tall Structure showing job roles

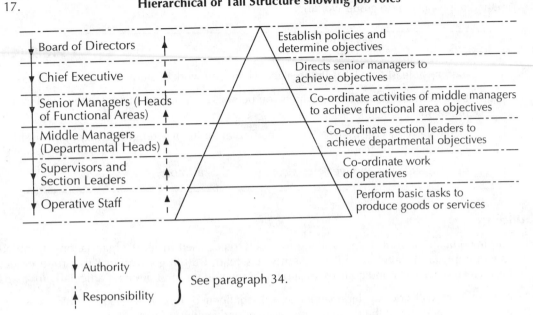

Board of Directors	Establish policies and determine objectives
Chief Executive	Directs senior managers to achieve objectives
Senior Managers (Heads of Functional Areas)	Co-ordinate activities of middle managers to achieve functional area objectives
Middle Managers (Departmental Heads)	Co-ordinate section leaders to achieve departmental objectives
Supervisors and Section Leaders	Co-ordinate work of operatives
Operative Staff	Perform basic tasks to produce goods or services

↓ Authority

↑ Responsibility
} See paragraph 34.

Teams

18. In practice, most people do not work as individuals in an organisation but as part of a team. Recognition of the importance of primary groups has lead to most organisations including teams as part of the formal organisational structure. A team is essentially a group working together to achieve a common objective. Team members with the various skills needed to complete tasks are usually brought together by management. By considering the social needs of workers, job satisfaction can be improved which helps to create a happier and more efficient workforce thereby increasing motivation and output.

19. When recruiting new staff, therefore, organisations need to take account of how individuals will fit into existing teams and indeed this ability may be an essential part of a job description.

Benefits of Team Membership

20. Some of the benefits of team working include:

❑ **commitment** – the sense of purpose and belonging to a group. A 'team spirit' and close personal relationship often develop with colleagues not wanting to let each other down.

❑ **co-operation** – in a good team members will enjoy working together to get things done, often helping each other if necessary.

❑ **responsibility** – teams are more able to solve problems and take decisions in order complete tasks than a person working alone. Less supervision is usually needed.

❑ **support** – members can provide each other with advice and encouragement when required, sharing the skills and experience which each possesses.

21. All these can help an organisation to achieve it objectives and targets. On the other hand, if a team does not work efficiently together, relationships between individuals often become difficult. This can result in advice and support being ignored, a general lack of co-operation and even conflict. Consequently, output and performance can be affected with problems such as work being completed badly or not on time.

22. For almost any organisation to operate successfully, teamwork is essential. A football team or cricket team, for example, can only be successful if everyone works for the good of the team. In businesses there are many teams ranging from the senior management team to clerical support teams, and teams in functional areas such as marketing, production, finance and personnel. The Volvo car

company in Sweden is an example of an organisation which has moved from an assembly line method of production to group working.

Task 5   **2.3.2 (C3.2)**

1.   Identify at least ten teams in the place where you work or study.

2.   Now consider two teams to which you belong. For each, identify and comment as appropriate on:

     a)   what you consider to be the particular skills or strengths which each individual brings to the team;

     b)   the strengths and weaknesses of the team as a whole.

Team building

23. The importance of good team working is widely recognised in most organisations. Consequently staff training and development frequently has team building as one of its prime objectives. Residential outward bound courses are a popular method for this training, particularly for managers.

24. A good team will develop independence, self-confidence, trust and tackle problems as a group, whilst taking account of the strengths, weaknesses and feelings of each of its members.

Forming teams

25. An important part of team building begins with the selection of individual staff who have the skills, experience and personality to fit together. Each member will have a particular contribution to make but it is the performance of the team as a whole which produces the desired results.

26. Although most teams are usually selected entirely by management, sometimes existing team members are allowed to be involved. This is useful in ensuring that new members are more readily accepted into the team.

27. The effectiveness of a team often depends upon the manager's leadership skills. A good leader should be able to secure the interest, loyalty and involvement of all members of the team, providing any necessary guidance and support to ensure that delegated tasks can be completed.

28. Another important factor is what is called the **group dynamics**. In other words, how individuals in a group interact with and influence both other members and the group as a whole which will depend on factors such as the group size, how long it has been established, the task involved, physical environment, motivation and leadership. A good leader needs to be aware of the group dynamics and where possible use it to increase the efficiency and effectiveness of the group.

Team roles

29. Good teamwork is essential if an organisation is to achieve its objectives. Although teams will vary in size, each member will have a specific role to perform. This will clearly vary from team to team and will depend on the objectives and tasks that have to be completed.

30. Some of the roles which might exist in an effective team include:

     ❑ **leader** or someone to co-ordinate the team's activities and monitor progress

     ❑ **innovator** or ideas person who helps with creativity and problem-solving

     ❑ **doers** or workers who implement decisions and ensure that tasks get completed

     ❑ **analyst** or someone who is able critically to assess progress, and identify potential problems.

     ❑ **supporter** or someone who can help to develop the team's harmony and remain calm in a crisis.

31. Clearly teams vary in size and therefore in large teams roles may be performed by more than one person. On the other hand, in small teams individuals may perform two or more roles.

32. Size may also affect the efficiency and effectiveness of teams. Small teams may lack certain knowledge, skills or experience, whereas large teams may not interact as well together, increasing the potential for disagreement or even conflict. The 'right size' team therefore is that which provides the necessary balance needed to get things done and achieve its objectives.

> ### Task 6   2.3.1, 2.3.2, 2.3.4, 2.3.5 (C3.2)
>
> In Task 5 you identified two teams to which you belong and considered the strengths and weaknesses of each.
>
> 1. Taking the same teams analyse the roles and tasks of each team member.
>
> 2. Identify and describe the role(s) which you perform and your personal contribution to the overall function of the team.

Authority, responsibility and delegation

33. The managing director or chief executive of an organisation needs to tell his managers what is expected of them in order to enable specific tasks to be achieved. The managers in turn will also pass instructions 'down the line' to their subordinates. This is known as **delegation** and is essential because it is impossible for one manager to maintain direct control over all staff, especially in a large organisation.

34. To enable instructions to be carried out, managers must also be given **authority** over their subordinates. That is, they must have the power to make decisions such as telling staff what to do and then expecting them to do it. However, a manager is still ultimately **responsible** for the actions of his subordinates. So although he may delegate the task, he is still accountable to the organisation for ensuring that it is properly completed.

Effective delegation

35. A number of conditions are necessary for successful delegation including the following:

- ❑ Tasks must be clearly communicated so that subordinates understand the type and limits of authority.

- ❑ Delegated work should be understood and checked or authority might be undermined.

- ❑ Managers must be prepared to let subordinates make mistakes (within reason and carefully controlled).

- ❑ They must also be willing to trust subordinates. A manager is judged by the work of his team and must delegate to obtain results.

- ❑ Managers must also be approachable, willing to listen to subordinates and discuss their ideas with them.

> ### Task 7   2.3.1, 2.3.2, 2.3.3 (C3.4)
>
> A firm is reviewing its management structure. The Board of Directors is concerned that some managers are doing too much routine work themselves rather than creating time for planning, co-ordination and more effective control. Some are reluctant to delegate tasks partly because they think that they can do jobs better themselves. Others do not plan properly, fear the ability of their subordinates or have insufficient staff.
>
> 1. Identify in the above some of the main advantages and disadvantages of delegation.
>
> 2. Can you add any others not mentioned?

Authority and leadership

36. It is important to understand the difference between authority and leadership. **Authority** is connected with acceptance by subordinates and therefore closely related to leadership. It is concerned with the issuing of orders.

    Whilst **leadership** is the art of organising the work to be done, and motivating people to achieve objectives. The better the leadership, the greater is personal authority.

37. **Leadership skills** include:

    ❏ organisational ability

    ❏ delegation

    ❏ energy and enthusiasm

    ❏ man-management

    ❏ tact

    ❏ self-discipline

    ❏ communication

    ❏ decision-taking

    ❏ motivation

    ❏ integrity

38. Whilst some of these skills will be inherent in a person's personality and character, others will need to be developed through training and experience.

Types of leaders

39. Studies of leaders' behaviour have identified 5 main styles of leadership – autocratic, democratic, bureaucratic, paternalistic and laissez-faire.

    ❏ **Autocratic** leaders are authoritative and expect unquestioning obedience to orders with no opportunity for employees to be involved in the decision-making process. The group is dependent upon the leader and usually unable to operate independently. This can cause frustration because it stifles people's initiative and relies upon the qualities of the leader to work successfully.

    ❏ **Democratic** leaders believe in consulting employees and allowing them to share in decision-making. This participation helps to increase workers' job satisfaction, morale and commitment to the organisation's objectives. It relies, however, on good communications, is usually time-consuming and can lead to the undermining of management control.

    ❏ **Bureaucratic** or constitutional leaders manage by acting in accordance with the 'rule book'. Thus there is little opportunity for workers' initiative and flexibility but what is expected of them is always clear and consistent.

    ❏ **Paternalistic** leaders are common in Japan. They manage by showing concern for workers' welfare in return for loyalty and hard work.

    ❏ **Laissez-faire** leaders set clear objectives for subordinates and then allow them, within very broad parameters, the freedom and responsibility to achieve the objectives. This style of leadership motivates enthusiastic workers but its success is dependent upon the competence and integrity of employees.

Task 8   **2.3.1, 2.3.2, 2.3.3 (C3.2)**

Can you give examples from your own experience of each of the 5 types of leader identified above. State your reasons in each for:

1)   why you think they operate in this way.

2)   If you think they are successful and

3)   whether or not it is the most appropriate form of leadership.

Types of authority

40.   Authority can come about in several different ways:

❐   **Legal** authority – from the internal rules and regulations laid down by the organisation. For example, a manager has authority over others because of their position in an organisation.

❐   **Personal** authority – which is connected with the personality of a superior who in the eyes of subordinates is seen as having authority, even though this is not necessarily acknowledged by management.

❐   Authority **by reputation** – usually based on knowledge. For example, people who become authorities on particular subjects such as economics, law or North Sea oil.

❐   **Economic** authority – a right conferred by economic circumstances. For example a shopper deciding whether or not to buy a particular product.

Task 9   **2.3.1, 2.3.2, 2.3.3 (C3.2)**

Discuss the importance of leadership and authority in a school, college or any other organisation with which you are familiar. Identify why you think they are necessary and how they could be made more effective.

Job Activities and Responsibilities

41.   Whatever their level whether a senior manager, operative or assistant, the actual work which people do and responsibilities which they have will depend upon the size, type and function of the organisation concerned. The smaller the organisation the more complex jobs are likely to be as individuals are asked to perform a wide variety of different tasks. Whilst in a large organisation specialist staff may be employed at different levels to perform specific tasks. As individuals' job roles extend as they progress upwards in an organisation they will move increasingly from handling daily routine tasks to making more strategic decisions.

42.   This can be illustrated, for example, by comparing the way in which particular activities are likely to be performed in a 'corner shop' run by a husband and wife who share most tasks between them compared with the head office of a large retailer with branches throughout the country.

43.

System	Corner Shop	Supermarket Head Office
Mail	Owner opens 3-4 letters daily, posts 3-4 per week	Mail room, three members of staff handling up to 1,000 incoming and 500 outgoing letters per day
Filing	Single Filing cabinet; Invoices and other documents kept in box until weekend	Central filing department with three staff
Accounts	Largely cash business. Keeps own records of receipts and payments, uses a local Accountant to prepare annual accounts	Fully computerised accounts department with ten members of staff. Prepares budgets and accounts invoicing, credit control etc.
Ordering	Some telephoned daily, others given to sales representatives when calling, also visits cash and carry wholesaler	Central purchase department, four members of staff each responsible for different product ranges. Most deliveries to central warehouse others direct to shops.
Stock control	Visually checks stock daily or weekly	Warehouse manager with team of six members of staff. Computerised Records
Personnel	Interviews and employs own staff	Personnel management, six members of staff deal with all aspects including recruitment and selection
Written communications	Internal not usually required, talks to staff. External handwritten on headed paper	Central typing pool using word processors, twelve members of staff.
Customer complaints	Dealt with personally by owner	Customer services department with three members of staff deals with most complaints

44. Whatever the size or type of organisation, however, employees main responsibilities are likely to include some or all the the following:

❑ **identifying business objectives** a task which is usually carried out by senior managers or directors

❑ **working with others** which applies to all staff at all levels in an organisation and is essential if it is to operate successfully. Who people work with, however, will depend upon their position and job role in the organisation

❑ **meeting targets** which again can apply to all staff at all levels

❑ **monitoring performance** which is usually the responsibility of a supervisor or manager and is needed to ensure that targets are being achieved

❑ **implementing change** which is an important part of the role of managers but which can impact on staff throughout an organisation (see paragraph 88)

❑ **to provide training** which is needed to ensure that the organisation can operate effectively and has the skills required to be able to meet its objectives. This is often the responsibility of a training or personnel manager to determine and arrange

❑ **to give advice** which is likely to be the responsibility of a whole range of staff across an organisation depending upon their job role. For example, a manager or supervisor may give advice on the best way to carry out a task, a health and safety officer on issues relating to an employee's working environment, an office junior may be advised by more experienced colleagues

❑ **disciplining staff**, perhaps for poor work, being late or failing to carry out instructions may be the responsibility of a supervisor, manager or director as appropriate depending on who in the organisation is being disciplined

❑ **handling grievances** again could be the responsibility of a supervisor, manager or director depending on the organisations grievance procedure and the nature of the problem (see Element 4.1).

Task 10
4.2.1, 4.2.2 (C3.4)

Referring back to tasks 3 and 4 identify who is responsible for each of the responsibilities listed in paragraph 44.

Reasons for Change

45. We live in a dynamic, exciting world where change is always taking place and affects both individuals and organisations. As individuals, we regularly experience change in our everyday lives as just a few examples help to illustrate. In recent years, our lives have been changed by the impact of the European Community and technological developments such as computers, satellite communications and lasers, whilst in the future, Sunday trading and the Channel Tunnel are likely to have dramatic effects on us.

46. Our concern, however, is with the impact of change on employment in business organisations. In order to survive and prosper in a competitive and rapidly changing environment, organisations also need to change. This may be brought about by many influencing factors which may be internal or external to the organisation.

47. **Internal influences** may include:

   ❏ **new products or services** which require changes in order to introduce them.

   ❏ **management** changes, due perhaps to a merger, take-over or the appointment of new staff. This may affect the management style and culture of the organisation.

   ❏ **quality assurance** systems which are becoming increasingly important in organisations in order to meet changing customer expectations. Therefore a business must organise itself to ensure that its products are always of the required quality. This puts new demands on workers to achieve the required standards.

   ❏ **productivity and profitability** improvements which often require changes in systems or procedures in order to control or reduce costs and/or increase output.

   ❏ **customer service** is now more crucial than ever for organisations in competitive markets because they can only survive and prosper if they satisfy consumers. The impact of change on our lifestyles means that consumers now have higher expectations of the level of service and satisfaction from what they buy.

48. **External influences** may include:

   ❏ **political** factors including legislation or other government measures. Organisations are forced to change in order to meet, for example, health and safety, environmental or consumer protection requirements.

   ❏ **economic** factors such as changes in levels of unemployment and interest rates which can have a major impact on demand.

   ❏ **social** factors including changes in lifestyles and environmental issues which organisations must respond to if they are not to lose out to competitors.

   ❏ **technological** progress such as word processing in the office or robots in the factory can change working materials, methods and practices and create the need for **new skills**.

   ❏ **trade unions** which can influence wage rates, working conditions and other aspects of industrial relations.

   ❏ **competition** and changes in consumer tastes and demand all impact on business organisations, making change necessary in order to respond. Therefore they must regularly review their working arrangements to identify ways of improving their competitive advantage.

   ❏ **media** reports which can influence consumers' and employees' perceptions of an organisation and its goods or services.

Task 11   4.2.3, 4.2.4(C3.2)

1. In the organisation in which you work or study or one well known to you, identify any internal and external changes which have taken place during the past 12 months.

2. Discuss the reasons for the changes and the effect on working conditions generally.

3. Comment on how, if at all, they have affected you.

Employment and Change

49. To meet these challenges of change in a flexible and responsive way requires organisations to redefine their objectives, develop and invest in new products and services and introduce new systems and techniques of production and marketing. Change can therefore be expensive, particularly where it involves the cost of buying and installing new technology and training staff to use it.

50. Change will inevitably have a major impact on an organisation's workforce which can cause problems for management. Whilst change is necessary for progress and can often bring new life and vitality into an organisation, it is often feared, frequently resisted and therefore also represents a potential source of conflict (see Element 4.1).

Task 12   4.2.3, 4.2.4 (C3.4)

FORD LOOK EAST

In response to the global success of companies such as Hitachi, Nissan and Sanyo, UK companies are beginning to show an increasing interest in Japanese management practices.

American owned Ford is actually introducing Japanese-style working in a drive for efficiency.

Employees will in future work in assembly line groups, eat in classless cafeterias and be encouraged to join in daily keep-fit workouts.

It is hoped that this will increase output, reduce costs, including those for supervision, and also help to overcome problems of boredom and job dissatisfaction. The move comes as part of a major cost-cutting reorganisation at the company's 14 British plants, which employ 38,000 people.

To keep the production lines moving, the multi-skilled work groups have already taken over repairs from maintenance staff at Dagenham, Essex, and Halewood, Merseyside. Rising unemployment and Conservative government legislation have weakened the trade union movement, making the fear of long strikes a thing of the past. Stockpiles of large parts have therefore been run down and suppliers are being signed up on ten-year rather than one-year contracts.

With the closure of executive and management dining rooms, even Ford UK chairman Ian McAllister now must queue in a self-service cafeteria with the rest of the staff.

Rover have already followed the lead of Sunderland-based Nissan by adopting Japanese- style work practices.

The following questions are based on the above information.

1. Why have Ford introduced Japanese working practices?

2. What changes will it bring for their employees?

3. What potential benefits will it produce?

4. Identify the type of production method which Ford has introduced.

5. Comment on the environmental conditions which helped to bring about the need for and implementation of the new working methods.

Changes in working conditions

51. Having considered some of the main reasons for change in organisations it is important to consider how these have impacted on working conditions. In particular here we shall consider fixed short-term term contracts, long term contracts, shift working, flexi-time, holiday pay, sick pay and redundancy terms.

Contracts

52. In Chapter 13 Element 4.1. we discussed the Contract of Employment which legally employees are entitled to receive from their employer outlining the main terms and conditions of their employment. In Chapter 17 Element 5.2. we considered the different types of employment which people are likely to have including full and part-time.

53. It is important to note here that whereas in the past it was quite usual for an employee to spend most of their working life with one or just a few employers this has now changed. Increasingly people are likely to have to regularly change jobs, learn new skills and even experience periods of unemployment during their working life. Many jobs have changed from permanent full-time to fixed short-term contracts perhaps for just a few months or for 1 to 2 years. Even longer contracts are now often fixed for say 3 or 5 years although sometimes they are what are known as rolling contracts. That is, there is an option to renew them again at the end of the fixed period.

Hours of work

54. Most workers in the UK now work full-time for five days a week, although the actual hours and days of work depend upon the type of job, for example, most shop workers are expected to work on Saturdays, with a day off during the week. Teachers, on the other hand, work Mondays to Fridays.

55. The basic working week is in the range of 37.5 to 40 hours for manual workers and 35 to 38 for non-manual workers. The actual hours worked, however, average nearer 41 for men and 37 for women due largely to overtime, most of which is worked in manual occupations.

EU Directive on hours

56. Britain, like Ireland and Denmark generally has few restrictions on working hours for adults and leaves it to employers and staff to decide the matter themselves, that is except for a few jobs such as driving of goods and public service vehicles where hours are limited for safety reasons.

    But this will change under a European Directive agreed in 1993 which introduces:

    ❑ a maximum working week across the Union, including overtime, of 48 hours, averaged out over a period of three months.

    ❑ except in certain industries, including transport and the merchant marine.

    ❑ an entitlement for all workers of a minimum of four weeks paid holiday each year.

    ❑ a minimum daily rest period of 11 hours and a weekly break of 35 hours.

    ❑ restrictions on night workers doing overtime where it could present a health and safety risk.

57. The Government has opposed proposals, but it could be 1996 before the result of the appeal against the working week restriction is known. It believes that

    ❑ the extra staff needed to cover the 'lost' hours would impose crippling costs on employers.

    ❑ it cannot be justified on grounds of health and safety.

    ❑ it will introduce unnecessary restrictions and bureaucratic rules.

    ❑ whilst some 2.5 million workers who regularly work overtime, which takes them above the new limit, could face a pay cut. This group includes many construction and postal workers, security guards, hotel and catering staff, agricultural workers and maintenance staff.

Task 13   **5.1.2 (C3.2)**

1. Identify in the place where you work or study the basic hours of work and holiday entitlement for different types of employees.

2. Find out how much overtime takes place and if so in what particular jobs.

3. Is flexitime and/or a shift system used at all?

4. How, if at all, do you think the new EU Directive is likely to impact on the organisation?

Flexitime

58. In recent years, many firms have started to introduce a system which allows flexible hours of work. Employees, particularly those in office jobs, are allowed to vary the time at which they start and finish work. Usually everyone must work a 'core time' perhaps from 10.00am – 4.00pm each day with an hour for lunch. They can then choose the rest of their hours to suit themselves.

59. The great advantage of flexitime to firms is that it **reduces absenteeism and leads to happier, better motivated workers.** Employees benefit because it enables them to avoid rush hour travel and fit in appointments, for example dentists, doctors or hairdressers. Married women with children find flexitime particularly useful. However, it also means that firms must keep strict records and could have some problems, for example, it may prove difficult to arrange staff meetings at a convenient time and staying open longer hours may incur extra costs such as heating and lighting.

Shiftwork

60. To enable a firm to operate its machinery for longer periods, often 24 hours a day, it will use different groups of workers in rotation. This is known as shift work. For example workers operating a three shift system might work 2.00pm-10.00pm 10.00pm-6.00am or 6.00am-2.00pm. In return for this they are usually paid an extra shift allowance.

Task 14   **5.1.2 (C3.2)**

JOB FLEXIBILITY RULES

In a speech at Exeter University in January 1995, Howard Davies, Director-General of the Confederation of British Industry said that British workers must face up to the new flexible labour market where 'womb to tomb' employment, a lifetime spent with one employer, is becoming the exception rather than the rule.

Employees could no longer rely on jobs for life and had to adopt more flexible working practices and conditions. Increased skill levels and less reliance on state provision of benefits were also vital if the UK was to compete successfully against the rest of the world, he said.

Rising part-time, temporary and self-employment meant that full-time permanent employees now made up less than two-thirds of the workforce. Increased labour market flexibility meant greater worker mobility was needed and, to facilitate this, the UK had to climb from its position near the bottom of the European skills league.

'The UK has been improving its skills levels, and is continuing to do so, but then every other country is striving to do just the same.'

Although job flexibility means more people will experience periods of unemployment and need benefits to support themselves he said they should not rely solely on the state.

continued...

Task 14 continued

> 'More and more individuals will be expected to make provisions for their own lives, including allowing for periods of unemployment, and especially retirement. This will be intended to provide a system which does not outstrip the nation's ability to pay, or the working population's willingness to pay. That way, it will be possible to safeguard the interests of the worst off.'

1. Explain what is meant by 'womb to tomb' employment and what is happening to it.

2. Why are increased skill levels and less reliance on state benefits important in the UK?

3. Comment on the impact which increased labour market flexibility is likely to have on individuals and the nation as a whole.

Holidays with pay

61. There are no general statutory entitlements to holidays in the UK which are an important fringe benefit frequently determined by collective agreements, between trade unions and employers. Recent decades have seen a considerable increase in holiday entitlements. Manual workers holidays, for example, have increased on average from 2 weeks in 1961 to over 4 weeks in 1994 plus additional days for bank holidays. Non-manual workers tend to have slightly longer holidays than manual workers.

62. Holidays also frequently increase with the length of service in an organisation e.g. one day for every month worked in the first 2 years and one extra day for each year thereafter up to a maximum of 30 days.

Sick pay

63. Nowadays when employees are off sick many organisations will still pay some or all of their wages. The amount paid and period of time involved, however, is likely to vary with the length of service and seniority in the organisation.

64. After 5 days sickness (the first 4 do not count) the majority of full-time employees are eligible for statutory sick pay (SSP). This in effect is a state benefit which an employer pays to the employee and then claims most of the money back from the government. SSP is payable for a maximum of 28 weeks.

Task 15   **4.2.3 (C3.4)**

1. Identify and compare the holidays and sick pay arrangements for any two local organisations.

2 Comment on your findings.

Redundancy

65. Under the Employment Protection (Consolidation) Act 1978 redundancy is defined as occurring when employees are dismissed from their job because

   ❑ an employer ceases to trade or closes a place of business (e.g. a branch of a firm) where an employee worked.

   ❑ the business no longer needs people with particular skills or fewer of them.

   ❑ employees are no longer needed due to other reasons e.g. a reorganisation resulting in fewer workers being needed . (This provision was introduced under TURER 1993 see Element 4.1.)

66. Dismissal for redundancy is usually considered to be fair as long as

   ❏ **it is genuine** i.e. an employee is being dismissed for one of the reasons above and not because they are not good at their job.

   ❏ **it has been carried out in accordance with the organisation's procedures** i.e. people made redundant are chosen on the basis of agreed criteria which is known to employees. e.g. last in first out or other factors agreed with trade unions such as age, length of service, aptitude, domestic circumstances, transferability of skills, standard of performance.

   ❏ **trade unions** (where recognised by the organisation for negotiating purposes) **have been consulted**. Under European legislation where there are no recognised unions then employers must still give prior warning to and consult with employees about a fair basis for selection and seek to redeploy where possible.

   ❏ **there is no suitable alternative work available**. An employer is expected to consider this before making anyone redundant.

   ❏ **selection does not contravene the Sex Discrimination or Race Relations Acts**, for example, employees must not be chose for redundancy simply because they are women or black.

Notification of Redundancy

67 Under the **Trade Union and Labour Relations (Consolidation) Act 1992** trade unions must be given written notice of any intended redundancies. Where an employer intends to make more than 10 people redundant within a short space of time then the Employment Department must also be informed. Failure to do so could result in a fine of £5000.

Redundancy Terms

68. Once the decision to make people redundant is made then the employer needs to consider the terms on which redundancy will be made.

Statutory Rights

69. All employees (full or part-time) over the age of 18 who have worked for 2 years or more with their current employer are entitled to receive statutory redundancy payments calculated as follows:

   ❏ Service under the age of 18 does not count

   ❏ For each year of service between 18 and 22 an employee receives half a week's pay

   ❏ For each year of service between 22 and 41 the employee receives one week's pay

   For each year of service between 41 and 64 the employee receives $1\frac{1}{2}$ week's pay

   ❏ Part years of service do not count

   ❏ In the last year of service before retirement age the redundancy entitlement is reduced by one-twelfth for each month worked.

70. For the purpose of calculating statutory redundancy weekly pay is limited to £205, maximum service to 20 years and the amount of pay to 30 weeks. This means that the current limit is £6150.

Example

71. Mary Smith joined ABC Company on 31st August 1986 at the age of 17 (date of birth 31.5.69). She is made redundant on 28th June 1995 after being employed for 8 years 10 months. She earns £195 per week. Her statutory redundancy entitlement therefore is 6 weeks at £195 i.e. £1170 which is calculated as follows:

   ❏ half a week's pay for each year between 18 and 22 i.e. $4 \times \frac{1}{2} = 2$

   ❏ one week's pay for each year over age 22 i.e. 4

   ❏ The calculation is based on her actual weekly pay because she earns less than the statutory maximum of £205.

> ## Task 16 $\qquad$ 4.2.3 (N3.3)
>
> Fred Jenkins (D.o.B. 12th November 1928) is made redundant after working for Fraser Brothers since he left school in 1942. His current earnings are £278 per week. Calculate his statutory redundancy pay entitlement. Explain how you arrived at the figure.

Contractual rights to a redundancy payment

72. Many employers offer more generous terms for redundancy than the statutory minimum. Called **enhancement** this usually takes one of 2 forms:

   ❑ Calculations based on a weekly figure higher than £205.

   ❑ a figure calculated on all years worked which may also include those under the age of 18 and any part-year service.

Evaluating change

73. Although change may be regarded by many people as a good thing to others it can be seen as unnecessary and threatening. Therefore, in order to evaluate the effect of changes to working conditions it is helpful to consider the costs and benefits to both businesses and individuals. This is probably best seen by examining the barriers to change and why they exist, the reasons for potential conflict and resistance to change and then considering a strategy for implementing change successfully.

Barriers to Change

74. Most individuals and groups are basically fairly traditional and conservative in their outlook and therefore do not generally welcome change. There are various reasons for this which can broadly be defined as behavioural, psychological and social and economic.

75. **Behavioural factors** relate to people's reactions to physical routines, for example:

   ❑ **individuals become set in their ways** and used to established patterns and conventions.

   ❑ **training may have to be undertaken** to adjust to new situations. Staff may have new tasks or jobs which they have to learn.

76. **Psychological factors** are those which affect the way people feel about their jobs, for example:

   ❑ **even minor change can be seen as threatening** and produce stress and frustration. This is because its effects are generally unknown, uncertain and unpredictable. Therefore, people often fear that change will mean more work, less jobs or reduced job security.

   ❑ **innovation often takes place so rapidly** that individuals feel unable to cope and adjust to new events. Older workers in particular may be psychologically incapable of accepting radical change.

   ❑ **status, authority and power are often overturned.** Reorganisations, for example may result in managers being redeployed in less senior posts, leading to loss of self-esteem.

77. **Social and economic** factors include the relationships with other workers and fear of unemployment, for example:

   ❑ **social structures and relationships may be disrupted** if redundancies, reorganisations or relocations take place.

   ❑ **the consequences may be quite devastating** both for individuals and the local community, particularly if change leads to job losses.

Task 17   **4.2.4 (C3.2)**

Referring back to Task 11, discuss the likely behavioural, psychological, social and economic effects of the changes which you identified.

Conflict

78. Conflict is possible in all walks of like whether it be disagreements between friends, parents, relatives or workmates, a complaint about a faulty product or service or at the extreme, war between nations. The potential for conflict in organisations comes about because they consist of various 'stakeholders' – namely owners, managers, employees and society – each of which has a number of different objectives which are not always compatible with each other.

79. **Owners** including shareholders in a business are interested in protecting and increasing the value of their investment, and the return in the form of profits.

80. **Managers** have a responsibility to run the business efficiently and to ensure its survival, growth and profitability. This may lead to conflict with shareholders who may want higher dividends rather than retained profits and employees who want higher wages.

81. **Employees** are interested in job security, better wages, holidays and working conditions and improved promotion prospects which may lead to conflict with management trying to control costs and increase efficiency.

82. **Consumers and society** where the interests may be in consumer satisfaction from lower prices and/or better quality products. Whilst higher standards of living require increased productivity and economic growth. But other factors are also important such as a better environment, less pollution, safer products and equal opportunities.

83. Other sources of conflict may result from:

    ❐ Proposed change

    ❐ Breakdowns in communication

    ❐ Poor organisation or

    ❐ Bad management

84. Whilst some conflict in an organisation may be a good thing because it can lead to the generation of new ideas, serious or prolonged conflict is likely to be damaging and lead to inefficiency. Therefore conflict must be managed in order to achieve consensus, that is ,a broad agreement which minimises the problem and enables the organisation to function effectively.

Task 18   **4.2.4 (C3.2)**

In the organisation in which you work or study:

1. Identify the 'stakeholders'.

2. Discuss any potential sources of conflict between them.

Resistance to Change

85. The fear of change can bring about considerable resistance in organisations, even though employees may actually recognise the need for change. This resistance can result in conflict which can be shown in a number of different ways, in particular industrial action and low morale.

86. **Industrial action** may include working-to-rule, strikes, go-slows or essentially refusing to accept new working practices. Even if it does not lead to industrial action, discontented employees are

likely to be more disagreeable and may clash with management or even each other, making control and smooth operation difficult.

87. **Low morale** can lead to increased labour turnover, low productivity and a general feeling of dissatisfaction amongst staff. Consequently, customers may suffer due to shortages, inefficiency and poor service or reduced quality, all of which could ultimately lead to lost business.

Task 19	**4.2.4 (C3.4)**

PLASTIC PAY STOP

Leading retailers may stop accepting debit and credit cards as banks threaten to charge more for processing transactions.

They have warned that they may insist on shoppers paying with cash or cheques unless the banks back down.

Tesco said yesterday it was 'very close' to refusing to accept cards, Sainsbury's said it was 'considering what steps to take' and W H Smith said action was being considered. The Office of Fair Trading confirmed that it was investigating complaints from retailers about the increases in card fees. The British Retail Consortium says stores will either have to stop accepting plastic, absorb the extra costs or pass them on to customers at a time when they are struggling to attract more shoppers.

Stores say they have invested millions of pounds in the new technology needed to accept cards because the banks assured them plastic payments would be no dearer to process than cheques. But planned increases could make the handling charges twice as expensive. The banks say they have been operating the service at a loss and need to put up their charges simply to cover costs.

They point out stores have also benefited from the new technology, which means guaranteed payments, reduced paperwork and is popular with shoppers.

TEACHERS BOYCOTT

Teachers fed up with too much testing and not enough teaching could wreck the government's new testing arrangements.

The 180,000-strong National Union of Teachers will shortly announce the results of voting on a boycott of this summer's English tests for 14 year olds.

Whilst leaders of the 127,000-member NASUWT will decide soon whether to ballot members on a boycott of national curriculum tests.

NAS-UWT general secretary Nigel de Gruchy said pupils faced tests at 7, 11, 14 and 16, plus the GCSE which was 'far too many' and overloaded teachers with work. The Government's determined to press ahead with nationwide testing of pupils despite criticism of a lack of preparation time and insufficient classroom trials.

The two articles illustrate some of the problems associated with change. In each situation:

1. Identify the nature of the change(s) and the main reason(s) for it being resisted.

2. Explain how the resistance is being demonstrated.

3. Comment on whether you feel that the proposed change(s) is a 'good thing' and whether or not it should be implemented.

Implementing Change

88. The fear of change can be exacerbated by:

    ❑ poor communication which leads to ill-informed rumour and gossip and

    ❑ authoritarian management with formal hierarchical chains of command which people often find intimidating. Therefore in order to successfully implement change, managers need to be aware of the reasons for any likely opposition and develop a strategy to overcome them.

89. The strategy should include:

    ❑ **considering the likely effects** of change and planning for it well in advance

    ❑ **adapting a flexible, democratic management style** even though this may be within a formal organisation structure, in order to create a climate where change is easier to achieve

    ❑ **identifying clear goals and targets** so that everyone knows what is to be achieved and the timescale involved

    ❑ **establishing genuine consultation and participation** in advance of impending change and agreeing a programme for introduction. Trade unions should be involved where appropriate and **negotiation** of change in return for incentives such as more pay, holidays or conditions may sometimes be necessary

    ❑ **selling the benefits** of change, for example, better working conditions, a more profitable and therefore financially sound and secure business and the opportunity to use new technologically advanced equipment

    ❑ **practical support** for staff including, for example, training or re-training, and new work or counselling for those being made redundant or asked to take early retirement

    ❑ **monitoring and reviewing progress** to regularly assess progress towards the goals and identify and overcome any difficulties.

90. Even following the above strategy, change may still take time to implement fully but nonetheless should be achievable with minimum disruption and still retaining staff morale. The alternative strategy of simply 'pushing' change on people often with threats and coercion is likely to prove to be self-defeating and could have disastrous consequences for the organisation.

91. The availability of new technology, for example, or withdrawal of a competitor from the market might represent opportunities. On the other hand, the introduction of new technology or new products by competitors may represent threats.

Predicting Change

92. It is important if organisations are to take full advantage of the opportunities offered by change that managers are able to anticipate when it is likely to take place and plan to meet it. Trends need to be identified and analysed and acted upon.

93. Management must be alert to the unexpected so that it can take advantage of the opportunities which change offers and minimise any potential threats. Once the trends are identified, decisions must be made and plans adjusted accordingly in order to respond effectively. This is likely to impact on all business functions. Personnel, for example, will need to develop a revised manpower plan, whilst finance and production will need to consider future investment needs.

94. If firms do not change in order to respond to market needs, then they are likely to go out of business. Consequently, there are large numbers of both individual bankruptcies and company liquidations every year.

Task 20 4.2.4 (C3.4)

BUSINESS FAILURES ROCKET

Business failures in England and Wales in 1992 reached their highest level since the recession started more than 3 years ago. Over 63,000 businesses collapsed, a rate of over 100 a day and an increase of 44% on 1991. Larger companies were also badly hit – over 24,000 failing – an average 67 a day, a 12% increase. DTI figures show that there were nearly 40,000 bankruptcies of firms run by one person or a partnership in 1992. But although 6,028 businesses collapsed in the 3 months to the end of December, this was substantially less than the record number of 6,699 in the previous quarter. Falling markets and bad debts, however, means that 1 in 38 companies was still going to the wall and only 1 in 5 was working to full capacity

MANAGEMENT BUYOUT

BP Chemicals has sold its Croydon-based foams business to its management in a £20 million deal backed by 3i, the investment capital group, Prudential Venture Managers and Barclays Bank. The new company, Zoetfoams, employs some 158 people

MORE BUY-OUTS

The first quarter of 1992 saw the second highest start to a year in the UK management buy-out market, according to accountants KPMG Peat Marwick. There were 12 large MBOs totalling £570m Only the record year of 1989 was higher in terms of total funds raised for MBOs over £10m.

BUTE BUYOUT

A Management buyout of the UK's largest dedicated flexible printed circuit manufacturer will secure 80 jobs on the isle of Bute and may create another 30 over the next three years. Graseby Flexible Technology, based in Rothesay, is returning to local ownership in a £1.4m project assisted by the Highlands and Islands Enterprise network.

From the above articles:

1. Discuss the extent of the problem of business failure and the reasons for it.

2. Why are management buy-outs on the increase?

3. Currently around 400,000 new businesses are starting up each year, 1 in 3 run by women. From the articles, discuss their prospects for survival and how they might be affected by future change.

Summary

95. a) The main job roles in an organisation usually include directors, managers, production operatives, support staff, assistants and team members.

   b) The highest level of management in a company is the Board of Directors, which may include executive and non-executive directors.

   c) The Board is responsible for formulating policy to achieve objectives and safeguarding the company's assets.

   d) Below the Board there are usually different levels of management responsible for planning and controlling the work of production operatives and support staff.

   e) Most people do not work as individuals but as members of a team.

   f) Good teamwork depends very much upon the personality and roles of the individual members.

g) To achieve objectives, managers need to delegate work along with appropriate authority.

h) Authority can be legal, personal, by reputation or economic, whilst leaders can be autocratic, democratic, paternalistic or bureaucratic.

i) The actual work which people do and responsibilities they have will depend upon the size, type and function of the organisation concerned.

j) This could involve identifying business objectives, working with others, meeting targets, monitoring performance, implementing change, training, giving advice, discipline and handling grievances.

k) Change is always taking place and affects both individuals and organisations.

l) Organisational change may be internal brought about by factors such as new products or management, or external resulting from environmental forces.

m) Changes in working conditions include fixed short-term and long-term contracts, shift working, flexitime, holiday pay, sick pay and redundancy.

n) Change in an organisation can be evaluated by considering the costs and benefits involved.

o) Proposed change can often by resisted leading to barriers and conflict.

p) To successfully implement change, therefore, managers need to develop appropriate strategies.

Review questions

1. Outline the main duties and responsibilities of directors in an organisation (3–5)

2. Distinguish between the role of executive and non-executive directors in a company (6–7)

3. By law, companies must appoint a company secretary. What role do they perform? (8)

4. Why are managers needed in an organisation? (9–12)

5. Explain with examples why production operatives and support staff are important in organisations. (13–16)

6. Describe the important factors in developing a good team and enabling it to work effectively (18–19)

7. What are the benefits and potential drawbacks of team working? (20–22)

8. Briefly explain the importance of group dynamics, team size and team roles. (24–32)

9. Briefly explain the terms 'authority', 'responsibility', 'delegation' and 'leadership'. (33–42)

10. What differences, if any, exist between the activities in a large and small business organisation? (43–46)

11. Why do organisations need to change (47–48)

12. Distinguish between the internal and external influences for change (49–50)

13. In what ways can change affect working conditions? (51–72)

14. In what way is redundancy different from the other changes identified? (65–67)

15. Explain what is meant by redundancy terms (68–72)

16. Briefly describe the main barriers to change (74–77)

17. Why does potential conflict exist in an organisation? (78–84)

18. How do employees demonstrate resistance to change? (85–87)

19. Outline a possible strategy for implementing change. (88–91)

20. Why do managers need to be able to predict potential change? (92–94)

Assignment – Job Roles and Change   Element 4.2

Choosing one or more business organisations which you know well and/or can readily visit you are asked to

1. Prepare a report which identifies 5 individuals with job roles at different levels in an organisation ranging from director to operative or assistant.

2. Your report should describe the responsibility of each person in respect of

    ❑ identifying and meeting targets

    ❑ working with others

    ❑ training

    ❑ discipline and

    ❑ implementing change in working conditions.

3. Explain why working conditions are subject to change.

4. Explain in depth one reason for changes to working conditions.

5. Finally prepare a plan to implement change to working conditions. Identify in it those job roles which have a responsibility for implementing the change.

You will find it helpful in completing this assignment to personally interview job holders, if possible, as well as studying job descriptions, organisation charts and some of the systems and procedures in the organisation(s) concerned.

---

15 Recruitment Procedures

This chapter looks at the recruitment of staff in organisations and covers:

❑ Recruitment

❑ Selection

❑ Job Advertising

❑ Application Forms

❑ Letters of Application

❑ Curriculum Vitae

❑ References

❑ Shortlisting

❑ Purposes of Interviewing

❑ Employer Interview Preparation

❑ Candidates Interview Preparation

❑ Interview Process

❑ Interview Bias

❑ Headhunting

❑ Legal Obligations in Recruitment

❑ Ethical Obligations in Recruitment

1. If an organisation is to operate successfully and achieve its objectives the importance of recruiting the 'right' staff must not be underestimated. Recruitment is also both time consuming and expensive, involving the personnel department and other staff, the costs of advertising, administration and candidates expenses such as travel and accommodation. It is even more expensive however, if unsuitable staff are appointed and therefore, ideally, a business should establish systems and procedures for recruitment and selection which help to minimise the potential for mistakes.

Recruitment

2. Before recruiting staff an employer must first of all decide:

❑ What skills and personal qualities are needed

❑ How to attract suitable applicants.

❑ Whether the post can be filled internally by existing staff or whether it requires new staff external to the organisation.

❑ Whether full or part-time staff are required.

❑ Whether the post is permanent or temporary.

Task 1   **4.3.1 (C3.4)**

External recruitment allows organisations to select staff with the qualities and skills required which may not exist within it, and to avoid jealousy often caused by internal appointments, particularly promotion. It also introduces 'fresh blood' with different experience and new ideas. On the other hand, it costs less to make internal appointments, the staff are already known and they know the organisation and how it operates. It also helps to motivate staff, particularly where opportunities for promotion exist.

1. Summarise the advantages of both internal and external recruitment.

2. Suggest some possible disadvantages of both the internal and external recruitment of staff to fill vacant posts.

---

3. **Job Description**

Once these decisions have been taken, an employer usually prepares a simple description of the job skills concerned. This will give the title of the job, an outline of the main purpose followed by a more detailed list of the main duties and responsibilities which it involves. It may also identify the section or site where the job is located and its position within the organisational structure.

4.   **Examples of job descriptions**

TITLE	TRAINEE SALES ASSISTANT
PURPOSE	To perform a range of general duties as specified by the store manager
DUTIES will include	Dealing with customers Selling Taking money Checking stock Filling shelves Moving stock

TITLE	JUNIOR OFFICE CLERK
PURPOSE	To undertake general clerical duties. Responsible to the office manager.
DUTIES will include	Completing relevant paperwork Filing Answering the telephone Some word processing General reception duties

TITLE	CLERICAL ASSISTANT Monday–Friday, 9am–5pm £7,000 pa
DUTIES	To work in the general office and to help out on reception when required. To undertake filing, photocopying, invoicing and filling in order forms, mail handling, answering the telephone and any other administrative tasks when asked to do so by the Office Manager.
Responsible to	Office Manager

5.   **Person specification**

From the job description an employer can draw up a person specification. This is a checklist of the personal qualities, experience and skills which are needed in order for someone to be able to do the job.

6.   **Examples of person specifications**

JOB TITLE	TRAINEE SALES ASSISTANT
QUALITIES/ SKILLS	Good appearance Ability to get on with people Good general education Honest Numerate Physically strong Age 16–17

JOB TITLE	JUNIOR OFFICE CLERK
QUALITIES/ SKILLS	RSA 1 Typewriting/Word Processing 3 GCSEs grade C, including English Good appearance Good telephone manner Reliable Age 16–18

345

Job Title	Clerical Assistant
Appearance	Needs to be smart, as will sometimes have to meet customers.
Qualifications	Level II Business qualification and GCSE Maths and English.
Experience	None necessary as training will be given.
Personality	Must have a polite and friendly manner. Must be outgoing.
Special Aptitudes	Must be able to work well in a team and be able to communicate well with others. Neat and tidy hand writing and ability to word process are also required.
Interests	Will show an enthusiasm for team games and sports.
Circumstances	Must live locally.

Task 2   **4.3.2 (C3.2)**

If you are working either full or part-time, consider your own job. If not, consider a job that a member of your family or a friend has or any job with which you are reasonably familiar, for example, teacher, caretaker, bus conductor or cleaner.

Prepare a job description and person specification, including as much detail as possible.

7. A person specification normally cover a range of factors including:

❑ **physical** demands of the job in terms of health, strength, eyesight and physique

❑ **intellectual** requirements in respect of the level of academic ability needed

❑ **aptitude**, that is any special skills or abilities which the job demands e.g. numeracy, communication, word processing, foreign languages

❑ **education and qualifications** – often a minimum of attainment is set, e.g. four GCSEs Grade C and above, Advanced GNVQ, degree or equivalent

❑ **experience** which may be broad or specific to the job e.g. at least two years' relevant experience

❑ **disposition** which covers the personality, characteristics, social conditions and other significant factors e.g. ability to work on own initiative, as a member of a team, or willing to work away from home

❑ **pay, working conditions and prospects** which must be commensurate with the grade, level of skills, qualifications and responsibilities of the post if suitable applicants are to be attracted. They may also vary according to the current availability of labour and the 'going rate' for the job.

8. Thus by preparing a job description to outline the purpose and duties of a job – and a person specification – to identify the skills and qualities needed to perform it – an organisation is better able to:

❑ prepare a suitable job advertisement
❑ match potential applicants with job vacancies
❑ brief interviewers involved in selection
❑ match business objectives to jobs and
❑ train and develop job holders in the required skills, updating them where necessary.

Selection

9. The employers next task is to attract and select suitable applicants for the job. Where the vacancy is at supervisory or middle-manager level, existing staff may well be promoted.

10. Places where job vacancies may be advertised include:

- ❏ Local Careers Offices
- ❏ Newspapers
- ❏ Trade Magazines
- ❏ Job Centres
- ❏ Private Employment Agencies
- ❏ Local Schools and Colleges
- ❏ Local Radio or Television
- ❏ Vacancy Boards or Windows
- ❏ Notices 'at the Factory Gate'
- ❏ In-house Magazines
- ❏ Internal Bulletin/Memo
- ❏ Noticeboards.

Job Advertising

11. Many firms use advertisements in the national or local newspapers to fill job vacancies. The advertisement gives details about the job itself and usually includes some key characteristics which the successful applicant is likely to possess.

12. A job advertisement should include:

- ❏ title of the post, e.g. Sales Manager, joiner, chef.
- ❏ target group – qualifications, experience, age
- ❏ outline of the main duties
- ❏ benefits, e.g. salary, pension, car, canteen
- ❏ reply arrangements – how, to whom, a closing date

13. Examples of Job Advertisements

SCHOOL LEAVER WANTED
for
General Office in City Centre

Duties include
Filing, Word Processing, Photocopying
and Reception Work

Training given. Good pay and prospects.

Apply in writing only, to:
Personnel Manager
Mr. N. Selby
Crompton & Co
57 High Street
Leicester

Warehouse Manager/ Manageress

**If you are looking for a challenge
If you thrive under pressure
Then this could be the job for you**

We need a highly motivated experienced warehouse manager/ess to take charge of our warehouse and distribution centres for all our retail outlets. Dealing in 1000's of lines of footwear, clothing and accessories. Product knowledge is not essential but an advantage, although organising, team building and motivation of approx 40 staff is essential. Age 30-50 years, current driving licence non-smoker (due to new company policy) 5 day week

In return we offer an attractive employment package including an excellent salary, profit share, private health care and free parking. We are an equal opportunities employer.

Initial enquiries and application together with a copy of your current CV to:

Vivien Royle

Skelton House
Exchange Quay, Salford, Manchester M5 3EQ

Wanted:
GIRL/MAN FRIDAY
FOR BUSY OFFICE

Location: $\frac{3}{4}$-mile from town centre.
Non-smoking office.
Salary: £8,750 p.a.

As a result of continued growth and expansion we are establishing a new manufacturing facility for our Fabricated Products Division.

We are therefore looking for an office all-rounder with VDU skills and a good telephone manner, as customer contact will be frequent. An understanding of basic credit control would also prove a distinct advantage, although training will be given. The successful applicant will play an important role within a small but busy Sales Office.

If you think you have the ability to cope in an often hectic environment, then please apply in writing to:

MRS. PAMELA DIXON
OXY Containers Limited
Old Road
ROCHDALE OL6 1ER

OFFICE JUNIOR

We require a Clerical Assistant to work in our busy Sales Office. The successful applicant must have experience of using a word processor and possess the ability to work without supervision.

Must be prepared to cover the duties of an Office Junior upon commencement with a view to progressing in a rapidly expanding Company offering good career prospects.

All applications in own handwriting together with an up to date CV to:

Mr. J. Smith
Gordons Computers
Chester Road
RHYL
CLWYD

Closing date for applications Friday, January 21, 199

Due to anticipated response, we regret that successful applicants only will be notified.

CAREER OPPORTUNITIES

FOR YOUNG PEOPLE WITH GNVQ, A LEVEL OR BTEC QUALIFICATIONS

TUX Home Shopping is a recognised UK market leader in the dynamic, competitive world of Home Shopping – a highly complex and sophisticated operation, relying heavily on a diverse range of management skills and disciplines.

We now have career opportunities for six young people aged 18 – 20, with the ambition and drive to ultimately join our Stock Control or Merchandise Administration/Support teams. Candidates must have GCSE Maths, be educated to advanced GNVQ or equivalent in a business related subject. We will give you the opportunity to undertake further part-time study.

The successful candidates will spend approximately 6 months training in key areas of our business, eventually specialising in Stock Control.

Starting salaries are circa £8,800 and we offer excellent working conditions, a 35 hour week, and other generous benefits including substantial staff discounts.

Please reply with full personal and educational details, no later than Friday, 21st January 199- to:

Mr. M. Carey
Personnel Officer
TUX Home Shopping Ltd
Milton House
Peebles Street
Chorley LA7 2UP

This is a re-advertisement.
Previous applicants need not re-apply.

TUX
HOME
SHOPPING
GROUP

Task 3   **4.3.1 (C3.2)**

Comment on how each of the advertisements in paragraph 7 meet the requirements of a good recruitment advertisement as explained in paragraph 6.

14. Potential applicants who enquire about the post are often sent additional information including the job description and application form, where used, and some details about the organisation itself.

15 Usually people are asked to reply in writing either by letter, by requesting an application form or by sending in a curriculum vitae (CV) which is a summary of their education and career to date. Sometimes they may be required to telephone or call in person for an interview.

16. The actual method(s) of recruitment and selection used in any organisation will usually depend on its own needs and experiences, the type of job concerned and the personnel systems and procedures which it adopts. It will also depend on the costs involved, particularly those for advertising.

17. For example, a small business which recruits staff only occasionally is likely to advertise locally, not have a standard form and therefore request replies by letter, CV or personal call. A larger company, on the other hand, may advertise locally and nationally for a wide range of posts. It will save time with a form which quickly identifies key selection criteria and may, where appropriate, request applicants to supply additional information in a supporting letter.

Task 4   **4.3.1 (C3.2)**

Consider the different methods of applying for a job referred to in paragraphs 9 and 11.

1.   Identify the main method(s) used in the organisation where you study or work.

2.   Consider, with reasons, which method is likely to be the easier and which the most difficult

     a)   for an employer to deal with and

     b)   for applicants to use.

3.   Discuss, with reasons, which method(s) you would personally prefer when applying for a job.

18.   **Application form**

Name (print in capitals)	**HENLEY ENGINEERING LTD APPLICATION FORM**
In full with post code	Surname: HUSSAIN Christian name(s): SAJID
	Home address: 19 EDGWICK CLOSE, BINLEY WOOD
	COVENTRY CV6 4ED
	Telephone no: (0203) 616477
	Nationality BRITISH Date and place of birth: 12/8/74
	BIRMINGHAM
	Name and address of parent or guardian:
Primary and secondary	MR K HUSSEIN, 19 EDGWICK CLOSE, BINLEY WOOD, COVENTRY CV6 4ED
	Schools attended and dates: COUNDON COMPREHENSIVE SCHOOL
	COVENTRY 1986—1991
	BINLEY PRIMARY SCHOOL
If not yet taken say so	1979—1985
	Exams taken and passes: GCSE MATHEMATICS, ENGLISH LANGUAGE,
	BUSINESS STUDIES, HISTORY, BIOLOGY,
	SPANISH, ART & DESIGN
	Other ESB SENIOR GRADE ONE
Give full details, including dates	Previous employment (including part-time and holiday jobs:
	SATURDAY JOB ON FATHER'S MARKET STALL SELLING CARPETS —
	SINCE 1989. YOUTH TRAINING — HARGREAVES ENGINEERING 1992—1993
Cross out yes or no	Are you willing to travel if necessary? YES/NO
	Have you a current driving licence? YES/NO
	Reason for applying: ALWAYS WANTED TO WORK IN AN OFFICE
	Name and address of two referees:
	MR J SMITH (HEADMASTER) MR T JONES (YOUTH LEADER)
	COUNDON COMPREHENSIVE 30 WESTVIEW
	COVENTREY CV6 3LJ FITTON HILL, COVENTRY
Are you fit to do the job?	Details of serious illnesses: CHICKEN POX 1980
	Any special skills ———
Spare-time activities	Interests SPORT: CRICKET, RUGBY. YOUTH CLUB. CYCLING
	Signature Sajid Hussain Date: 24 MAY 1995

There are many different types of application form, some requesting four or more pages of information. Each organisation which uses them will design one to suit its own recruitment and selection procedures.

19.

Letter of application

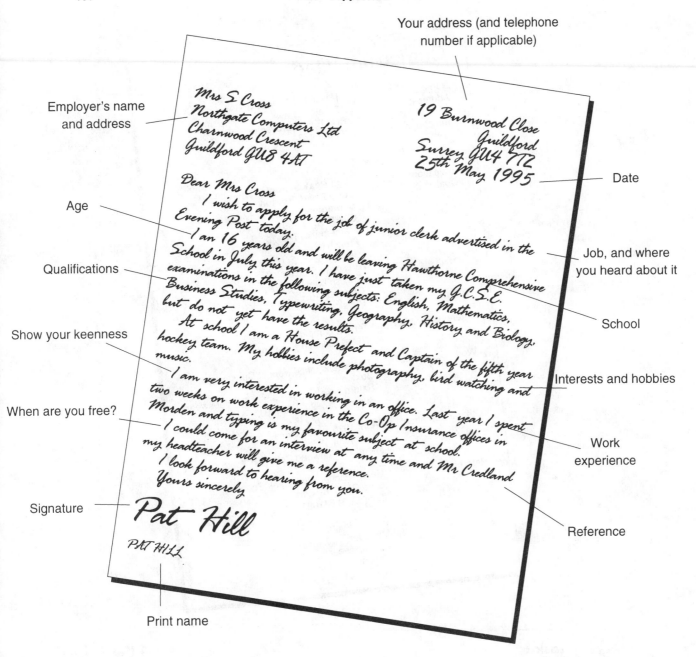

Your address (and telephone number if applicable)

Employer's name and address

Date

Age

Job, and where you heard about it

Qualifications

School

Show your keenness

Interests and hobbies

When are you free?

Work experience

Signature

Reference

Print name

Mrs S Cross
Northgate Computers Ltd
Charnwood Crescent
Guildford GU8 4AT

19 Burnwood Close
Guildford
Surrey GU4 7TZ
25th May 1995

Dear Mrs Cross
I wish to apply for the job of junior clerk advertised in the Evening Post today.
I am 16 years old and will be leaving Hawthorne Comprehensive School in July this year. I have just taken my G.C.S.E. examinations in the following subjects: English, Mathematics, Business Studies, Typewriting, Geography, History and Biology, but do not yet have the results.
At school I am a House Prefect and Captain of the fifth year hockey team. My hobbies include photography, bird watching and music.
I am very interested in working in an office. Last year I spent two weeks on work experience in the Co-Op Insurance offices in Morden and typing is my favourite subject at school.
I could come for an interview at any time and Mr Credland my headteacher will give me a reference.
I look forward to hearing from you.
Yours sincerely

Pat Hill

PAT HILL

It is important that letters or applications have a clear structure to them and are neatly presented.

Task 5

4.3.3 (C3.2)

1. Write a letter of application for one of the posts in paragraph 13.

2. Ask a colleague to comment on your letter and say in particular what they feel are its strengths and weaknesses and whether it is clear and well presented.

3. Reverse roles and prepare a written evaluation of a colleague's application letter.

20. **Curriculum vitae**

Curriculum Vitae

Name:	MALCOLM O'CONNER
Address:	15 Eaton Grove
	BUXTON, Derbyshire
Telephone:	(0298) 47321

Date of birth

14 August 1975

Education:
Qualifications:

High Peak School
Long Road, Buxton
September 1986 – July 1991
GCSE June 1991
Mathematics (A)
French (B)
Biology (B)
Business Studies (C)
English Language (A)
Chemistry (E)
Physics (D)

Interests/hobbies:

Tennis, camping
stamp collecting, reading

Work experience:

Two weeks office work at Dunstons, Buxton
Saturday sales assistant at BJ Menswear, Buxton. Jan '90 – July '91.

Other information:

April 1990: Team captain for tennis
November 1986–91
Member Eastwood Common Youth Club

Referees:

Head Teacher, High Peak School
Long Road, Buxton
Tel: (0298) 611021

Mr B Salmon
Manager
BJ Menswear
Manchester Rd, Buxton
Tel: (0298) 46274

Task 6   4.3.4 (C3.2, T3.1)

1. Prepare your own curriculum vitae if possible using a word processor. Include in it as much information about yourself as possible. If required it could be more detailed than the example shown above, including comments if appropriate.

2. Ask two colleagues to comment on its clarity, quality of presentation and the amount of information which it gives about you. Make a note of their views.

3. Repeat the exercise by preparing a CV, for someone who has worked for a number of years, perhaps a relative or family friend.

21. **References**

❑ Most employers will require anyone applying for a job to give the names of two people who know them well to act as referees. For example, teacher, youth leader, vicar or former employer.

The firm will then send details of the post and ask them for a confidential opinion on the character, attendance, punctuality and suitability of the applicant for the job.

❐ Some employers also accept **testimonials**. These are not confidential, and are usually headed 'To whom it may concern'. Copies can be given to any employer when applying for a job.

❐ References tend to be more useful because they are confidential. However, their value depends on how honest the referee is prepared to be. Many people do not like to identify weaknesses when writing references and therefore often they do not disclose potentially relevant information.

22.

Examples of 2 Different Types of Reference
A form for completion

Applicant's name: *John Bond*   TGY/YYO/LP/1720784

1/   Are the employment details shown overleaf correct?   YES ✔ / NO ☐

If no, what are the correct details? _____

Dates employed: From *Nov 199–* To *Present*   Job Title: *Sales Supervisor*

2/   Has he/she left your service?   YES ☐ / NO ✔

If so, please state reason for leaving. _____

3/   If he/she is remaining in your employment, is there any objection to he/she being employed on a part-time basis as a company representative of the society?

Would need permission of directors

4/   To the best of your knowledge:

a)   Is the applicant of good character?   YES ✔ / NO ☐

b)   Have you ever known him/her to be guilty of an act of dishonesty?

_____   YES ☐ / NO ✔

5/   Do you know of any reason why he/she should not become a representative of the company?

_____   YES ☐ / NO ✔

6/   Any additional information which may reflect on the applicant's suitability for this position.

Following reorganisation in Sept 199– now responsiblee for

North East region

_____

Authorised signatory *Joe Smith*   Date *20th Aug 199–*

For and on behalf of *BLUE PRINT SERVICES LTD*   (Employer Name)

A Reference Letter

CONFIDENTIAL

Mr. O. Berry
Principal
Caiteshall College
Willenhall
Derbys
DE1 1JP

Denton College
Daventry Road
Dell Green
Denton
DV5 6FQ
0704 - 31422

Our Ref: MB/JVB
14 July 199

Dear Mr. Berry

Mr. John Bond

I have known Mr. Bond since September 1990, when he was appointed to the position of Lecturer in Business Studies. He left the college in December 1993.

Mr. Bond was an extremely loyal, hard working and most reliable member of staff who carried out his duties promptly and efficiently. He always showed considerable initiative, examples of which include the introduction of the Young Enterprise Scheme and a residential weekend for GNVQ students. He was also involved in preparing a programme of visits for a variety of full-time students. Other significant developments in which he was involved included devising a business studies Audio-visual package for schools and he was very active in both industrial and school liaison.

Mr. Bond relates well to both staff and students and sets extremely high standards.

Apart from his academic developments, he was also closely involved with student activities, particularly climbing, and formed a very successful Outdoor Pursuits Club.

I am pleased to support his application, for which I feel he is very well suited. I am certain that he would make a tremendous contribution, be committed, and involve himself in many activities. Should you need any further information, I would be pleased to supply it.

Yours sincerely

Mary Brown

Mary Brown
Head Of Business Studies
Denton College

23.

Example of a Testimonial

```
Johns Clothing Store
71 High Street
Purbeck
Surrey
SU2 PE1

Ref: KM/JR/20/2/9
20th February 199

To whom it may concern
Re: John Tudor

This is to confirm that the above named
individual was employed by this company as a
sales assistant from May 1990 until July 1994.
During this time John was a very willing and
hardworking employee who relates well to
customers. He was always punctual and his
attendance record was excellent.

I would be pleased to supply further information
on request.
```

Ken Murphy

```
Mr. K. Murphy
Manager
```

Task 7   **4.3.1 (C3.2, C3.4)**

1. Write a short reference on one of your colleagues. Identify in it what you feel are the key points about their performance at school/college/work, their personality and other factors such as attendance and punctuality. Mention any particular successes or responsibilities and any weaknesses which you feel they have.

2. Show the reference to them and comment on their reaction. In particular whether or not they feel that it is fair and accurate.

3. Repeat the exercise with a colleague writing a reference for you.

4. Based on what you have learned from this task give your opinion on the extent to which you feel references are useful in the selection of employees.

Shortlisting

24   Whichever application method is used the employer wants to find out as much as possible about the people who are applying for the job. This information is then matched against the personnel specification to select a shortlist of suitable candidates for interview. Applicants who do not meet the criteria on grounds of qualifications, experience or other reasons such as poor presentation, will be rejected at this stage.

Depending on the size and type of organisation concerned shortlisting may be carried out by an individual, the personnel section or a representative group of the final interview panel.

25.   Most applications are quickly rejected with only the 10 or 12 best candidates being considered in real depth. These are then usually reduced down to a final shortlist of perhaps 4–6 people who are invited for interview.

Purposes of Interviewing

26. Interviewing is the last and most critical part of the selection process and should always be seen as a two-way exchange of information and ideas to allow the candidates and the organisation to find out about each other.

27. An interview should therefore

    ❏ enable employees to determine the suitability of a candidate for the job, and assess how they would relate to other staff and fit into the organisation.

    ❏ enable candidates to find out all the relevant information about the job and organisation to ensure that they really want it, e.g. opportunities to ask questions, meet potential colleagues, see the actual work environment.

    ❏ be seen as fair so that candidates feel that they had an equal chance and leave with a favourable impression of the organisation.

Task 8   4.3.1 (C3.2)

In the place where you work or study or have undertaken work experience find out

1. What information is supplied to people who respond to job advertisements.

2. If any additional information is sent to candidates who are shortlisted for interview.

3. Identify what, if anything, it tells you about the organisation which you did not already know.

4. Comment on how the total amount of information supplied would assist candidates. Is there any other information about the organisation which you feel would be helpful to candidates?

Employer Interview Preparation

28. Once the shortlisting process has taken place a number of important tasks must be carried out prior to the interview itself. These include:

    ❏ **Selecting the date, time and place**.

    ❏ **Determining the panel** members and ensuring that they are available. A 30–40 minute interview with a small group is commonly used.

    ❏ **Inviting the shortlisted candidates** usually by letter and ask them to confirm that they can attend. Brief details of the interview arrangements may also be included.

    ❏ **Take up references** (see paragraphs 21–23).

    ❏ **Complete the internal arrangements** for the day(s) as appropriate including informing reception, booking refreshments, lunch and organising site tours.

    ❏ **Prepare interview questions**, being careful to avoid any potential discrimination. Questions should be clear, concise and relevant to the job concerned. As part of their equal opportunities policy many organisations have these typed up to ensure that all candidates are asked the same questions. In order to give candidates the opportunity to discuss their abilities and achievements open-ended questions should be asked wherever possible.

    ❏ **Brief everyone involved** in the interviews with copies of the applications and details of the questions and interview arrangements. Decide who is asking which questions and chairing the interview.

    ❏ **Ensure privacy** on the day by using a location where the interview will not be interrupted by telephones or other distractions.

    ❏ **Arrange the seating** in the room prior to the interview start-time so that it is obvious who sits where.

29. Good preparation saves time during the interview, helps the candidates to feel more at ease, makes it less stressful for interviewers, gives a good impression of the organisation and most importantly increases the chances of selecting the best candidate for the post.

The Interview Procedure

30. The interview can now proceed, usually in a format similar to that outlined below.

    ☐ **Introduction** – the chair person opens the interview by welcoming the candidate, inviting them to sit down and introducing the members of the panel.

    ☐ **Questions** – members of the panel will ask questions in turn.

    ☐ **Follow-on questions** may be asked where the candidates answers are unclear or too concise to reveal the information being sought.

    ☐ **Body language** (see Element 2.3) used by the interviewers may give important signs to the candidates of how their responses to questions are being received.

    ☐ **Candidate questions** are usually invited at the end of the interview (see paragraph 34)

    ☐ **Closing the interview** is carried out by the chair who may ask the interviewee if they are still a firm candidate, thanks them for attending and informs them of when they are likely to receive a decision.

    ☐ **Feedback** on how they performed may be offered to unsuccessful candidates and this can be very useful in helping to prepare for future interviews.

Candidates preparation for interview

31. The interview is important for the employer, who wants to find the best person for the job. It is also an opportunity for the candidate to find out more about the job and whether it is what they want. Therefore, it is very important to prepare for it, just as an employer does. You may be nervous on the day, but good preparation will show that you are interested, increase your confidence and thus your chances of getting the job.

357

32. **Before you go**

- ❏ Find out as much as possible about the firm.
- ❏ Be prepared to answer questions.
- ❏ Make sure you know the time and place of the interview.
- ❏ Work out what you need to ask the employer.

33. **The Big Day**

- ❏ Dress sensibly – look neat and tidy.
- ❏ Be punctual.
- ❏ Take your interview letter with you.
- ❏ Remember and *use* the interviewer's name.
- ❏ Be pleasant and polite. Shake hands, wait to be asked to sit down, say thank you, smile.
- ❏ Don't smoke, unless invited to.
- ❏ Listen carefully.
- ❏ Speak clearly and answer questions fully – *not* just 'yes' and 'no'.
- ❏ Show that you are interested in the job – be enthusiastic and confident but not too assertive.
- ❏ Have some questions to ask – take a list with you if you wish.
- ❏ Don't forget the importance of body language (see Element 2.3).
- ❏ Try not to over-sell yourself by talking too much.

34. **Some questions you could ask**

If an employer has not already told you, the following are examples of possible questions:

- ❏ What training will I be given?
- ❏ Will I be paid weekly or monthly?
- ❏ What are the prospects for promotion?
- ❏ Who will I be working with?
- ❏ When will I be expected to start?
- ❏ When will I know the outcome?

35. **What questions might you be asked?**

- ❏ Why do you want to work here?
- ❏ How did you hear about the job?
- ❏ What are your interests and hobbies?
- ❏ What were your favourite/best subjects at school?
- ❏ What appeals to you about this job.
- ❏ What kind of books or newspapers do you read?

Reproduced by kind permission of the Further Education Unit, from the publication Recording Achievement

Task 9   **4.3.6 (C3.2)**

For one of the job advertisements in paragraph 13 prepare what you would consider to be a suitable answer to each of the following questions.

1. What particular personal qualities do you feel you can bring to this post?

2. In what ways has your GNVQ course prepared you for this post?

3. Have you had any work experience which you feel is relevant to this post? If so in what ways.

4. How do you feel that a knowledge of information technology would help you in this post?

5. As you know we are an Investor in People company. If appointed what particular skills do you feel you would need training in during your first year?

The Interview Process

36. Interviews are carried out in many ways depending on the size of the organisation. In smaller businesses it may be the owner or a departmental manager who interviews, whilst in larger concerns it will be the job of the personnel officer, usually with the help of a panel of senior executives who have appropriate 'technical expertise'

37. Many employers also ask candidates to take an aptitude test so that they can assess whether or not someone is suitable for the type of work, for example, police cadets, nurses, apprentice engineers.

38. Sometimes the selection process, particularly for very senior posts, may take place over several days, often involving aptitude and personality tests, practical exercises or presentations followed by an interview with directors or other senior executives. Some interviews, particularly for overseas posts will also involve the candidate's spouse. Some organisations may have an initial screening interview and invite the most promising candidates back for a second interview.

39. During the interview itself, or immediately afterwards, panel members will usually make notes on the candidates answers. This serves both as a reminder when selecting at the end, whilst also providing

a record for future reference. This is useful should any candidate request 'feedback' or claim that they have been treated unfairly.

40. Once all the interviews are completed the panel will have a discussion to select the best candidate who is then offered the post, usually by telephone and/or letter. This is usually made subject to a satisfactory reference unless one has already been taken up. It may also be conditional on passing a medical examination.

41. Sometimes no candidate matches the organisations specification. In this situation appointments are not made and the post is re-advertised.

Task 10   **4.3.5, 4.3.6 (C3.1)**

1. As a group, carry out a mock interview using one of the jobs in paragraph 13 and the questions from Task 8, paragraphs 27 and 28 and some of your own if you wish. You will need to select an interviewee, form a small interview panel, decide who will act as chairperson, what roles each person will play (e.g. personnel manager, appropriate line manager) and then allocate the questions for each to ask.

2. Afterwards discuss the interview and make a note of the key lessons which you learned. You may wish to repeat the exercise by reversing roles before drawing your conclusions, or interview several candidates and give reasons for selecting the best.

Recruitment Agencies

42. Sometimes for very senior positions, specialist private recruitment agencies are used to advise organisations on the appointment process. They can be used to advertise and/or select the most suitable applicant for the post.

43. Alternatively they may be asked to use their knowledge and informal contacts in the area of specialism covered to actually approach (**'headhunt'**) one or more potential individuals and invite them to take up a post. Headhunters receive a commission for their work which is sometimes referred to as 'poaching'.

Temp Agencies

44. Sometimes an organisation may employ temporary staff itself through its usual recruitment and selection procedures. Alternatively it may use a 'temp' agency such as Alfred Marks, Brook Street or Hays. Temp agencies tend to specialise in particular types of work such as accounting, computing or secretarial work and have a 'pool' of suitably qualified staff who can be called upon at short notice.

45. The employer usually pays a fee to the Agency but saves the cost of advertising and selecting staff. The Agency will also agree the hourly rate with the employer although the employee will receive slightly less to cover the costs of administration.

Task 11   **4.3.1 (C3.2)**

1. Using a copy of your local Yellow Pages and/or Thomson Directory find the names of at least two agencies which could help if your organisation required temporary staff for the following jobs: construction worker, HGV driver, a laboratory technician, VDU operator, secretary, computer specialist, accountant, sales marketing person, warehouse staff, receptionist.

2. In the press find examples of at least 4 different jobs where a recruitment agency is being used in the selection process.

3. Discuss the problems associated with attracting and recruiting suitable people to particular jobs.

4. Comment on why you think that some organisations choose to recruit from or with the help of agencies whilst others prefer to recruit directly themselves and the advantages/disadvantages of each method.

Legal Obligations in Recruitment

47. Care must be taken when recruiting staff to ensure that the processes used do not infringe the current employment legislation in respect of equal opportunities and contracts.

48. Equal opportunity laws make it illegal for employers to discriminate on the grounds of sex or race when recruiting staff (see Element 4.1). Thus, for example, questions on an application form or at an interview about a person's marital status, domestic circumstances, ethnic views or physical appearance are all potential forms of discrimination and should therefore be avoided.

49. It is, however, legal to advertise for a particular sex or race where such requirements are a 'genuine occupation qualification' for the job concerned.

50. These include:

     ☐ **Authenticity**, e.g. where a coloured actor is required for a part in a play.

     ☐ **Privacy or decency**, e.g. a female attendant for a ladies toilet or swimming pool changing room.

     ☐ **Provision of care**, e.g. female housemistress in a residential girls school.

     ☐ **Overseas culture**, e.g. advertising for a man because some countries, particularly in the Middle East, have attitudes to women which would prevent them from performing work effectively.

     ☐ **Ethnic groupings**, e.g. where someone from the same race is needed in order to be able to understand and relate effectively to the needs of the people involved, such as an Asian to work in an Asian community project.

51. Other legislation aimed at promoting equal opportunities includes the

     ☐ **Disabled Persons Acts 1944 & 1958** which requires employers with 20 or more full-time staff to employ a proportion (currently 3%) of registered disabled persons.

     ☐ **Companies (Directors' Report) Employment of Disabled Persons Regulations 1980** which requires every directors' report to contain a statement describing the company's policy for disabled persons in respect of recruitment, training and career development.

     ☐ **Rehabilitation of Offenders Acts 1974, 1975 & 1986** which make it illegal to discriminate against an ex-offender after a period of time has elapsed and the sentence is deemed to be 'spent'. They must be treated as if the offence was not committed, except where the sentence exceeds 30 months. Any sentence over 6 months carries the maximum rehabilitation period of 10 years with reduced periods for shorter sentences.

     ☐ **New Legislation** is being introduced in 1995 aimed at preventing employers from treating disabled persons less favourably than others, unless there are justifiable reasons. A consultant document 'Disability on the Agenda' was issued in July 1994.

52. Many medium to large organisations have well-developed equal opportunity policies which include specific procedures which must be followed when recruiting staff.

Task 12   4.3.7 (C3.4)

Consider each of the following interview questions and, with reasons, say whether or not you think they would infringe current equal opportunity legislation.

1. Can you tell the panel Mr Jones why you were in prison from 1981-1982?

2. Generally speaking, Mrs Smith, the company does not employ people over the age of 55. Can you tell us why you think we should consider employing you at the age of 57?

3. What arrangements do you make for your children when they are ill and have to miss school Mrs Jenkins?

4. I notice that you are registered as disabled Mr Patel. If appointed how do you think that your disability will affect you in the job?

5. If appointed Mr Johnson, you would be working in a small team. At present, 3 of the 4 members come from different ethnic backgrounds to yourself. How do you feel about this?

---

53. Under the contract of employment legislation (see Element 4.1) new staff are entitled to a written statement of the main terms and conditions of their employment within 2 months of starting a job. When offering a job a legal contract is formed and therefore most organisations send a letter which confirms the essential details such as the salary, start date, holidays and hours. These are then included along with additional information in the contract when it is issued.

Ethical Obligations in Recruitment

54. When an organisation prepares a job description and person specification and advertises a post, it is essential that the information given is both accurate and honest. For example, if the holiday entitlement is 4 weeks plus bank holidays, but the information supplied to applicants omits to mention that this is only after 2 years employment and starts at 2 weeks this is clearly misleading and unfair to applicants.

55. Likewise both the application for a job and the interview process itself are based on the honesty and integrity of the candidate. Application forms usually require a signature confirming that the information supplied is correct. Withholding or giving false information, for example about qualifications or previous experience, therefore means that any contract of employment would not be legally binding and thus could lead to instant dismissal.

56. A candidate's answers to interview questions must also be honest. Equally, when a candidate asks a question about the organisation or job itself he or she is also entitled to expect the employer to reply honestly. They should also be able to expect details of their applications, including the interview itself, to be treated in a confidential way.

Interview Bias

57. Despite following rigorous selection procedures it is still the case that mistakes are made and the 'wrong' or unsuitable candidates do get appointed.

58. This may be due to any of a variety of reasons. Some candidates, for example, usually due to nerves or stress do not perform very well in interviews whilst others excel. Also, a good candidate may simply have an 'off-day' and therefore not come across very well to the panel.

59. All of us, interviewers included, can also be influenced by a number of subjective factors which can affect the way we judge people. These factors include appearance, clothes, hair, shoes, hands, manner, e.g. body language, accent, voice quality, social background, e.g. attending the same school or university, supporting the same political party or living in a particular area.

60. Thus, for example, it is quite frequently assumed that someone who is smartly dressed with a refined accent is harder working, more reliable and intelligent than someone with, say, a strong regional accent and more flamboyant dress.

61. Studies have shown that most interviewers form an impression within the first few minutes of an interview and then spend the rest of the time trying to find evidence in the candidate's answers to support it. This natural tendency for subjective bias is one reason why many organisations use other more objective selection techniques to judge a person's suitability for a post.

62. The interview, however, is still probably the best method to judge whether or not a person has the inter-personal skills which will enable him or her to fit into an organisation. It also provides an opportunity for both the organisation and candidate to clarify information and hopefully helps each to make the right decision.

63. Interestingly, many universities and colleges no longer interview students but offer places on the basis of the application form, reference and subject to achieving the required examination results.

Task 13   **4.3.5, 4.3.6 (C3.1, C3.4)**

1. Consider your most likely immediate reaction to the following candidates as they arrive for an interview. What type of judgement would you make about their personality traits?

    a) John has a pony tail and ear ring in one ear.

    b) Jane wears heavy make-up and has bleached spikey hair.

    c) Tony has red hair.

    d) Peter has neat short hair and is wearing a very smart double-breasted suit.

    e) Mary has a very limp handshake. She is wearing a light-weight raincoat and stiletto heeled shoes.

2. Discuss your reactions with those of one or more of your colleagues and comment on any differences or similarities in your reactions.

3. Do you have any friends or classmates who would fit the above descriptions? If yes, do you think that this has influenced your thinking in any way?

4. Do you think your views would be any different if the candidates were applying for a job in computing as opposed to a job as a sales manager? Explain your answer.

5. Comment briefly on whether or not this simple exercise helps you to understand the concept of subjective bias, including how it might result in discrimination at interviews.

Summary

64. a) Recruiting the right staff is a vital but expensive and time-consuming process.

    b) A job description gives details of the main duties involved in a job, whilst a person specification outlines the skills and experience needed to do the work.

    c) Information about job vacancies can be found in many places, including newspapers, careers offices, job centres, and private employment agencies.

    d) Applications for jobs may be made using a letter, an application form or a curriculum vitae.

    e) To find out more about applicants for jobs, employers usually ask for references.

    f) Short-listed candidates are usually invited to an interview.

    g) It is important that both employers and candidates prepare for interviews both beforehand and on the 'big day'.

    h) Interviews enable employers to assess the suitability of candidates, who in turn can find out about the organisation.

i) Sometimes, for very senior posts, a recruitment agency may be used to 'headhunt' potential candidates. Temporary staff may also be recruited via an agency.

j) Care must be taken when recruiting staff to ensure that the processes used do not infringe legislation, particularly in respect of equal opportunities.

k) The recruitment process relies heavily on the honesty and integrity of both employers and candidates.

l) Mistakes can still be made in recruitment, sometimes because of subjective bias which is a human factor which can effect an interviewers judgement.

Review Questions *(Answers can be found in the paragraphs indicated)*

1. What key factors should an organisation consider before recruiting staff? (2)

2. Explain the difference between a job description and a person specification. (3–7)

3. List at least eight ways in which a job could be advertised. (10)

4. Why do recruitment and selection methods vary with the type and size of organisations? (16–17)

5. List six pieces of information which should be included in a letter of application for a job. (19)

6. Why are referees used in the selection process? (21–22)

7. What is the purpose of shortlisting? (24–25)

8. Outline the main reasons why interviews are the most commonly used method to select staff. (26–27)

9. In what ways does an organisation need to prepare before interviewing potential staff? (28)

10. What benefits does interview preparation bring to an organisation? (29)

11. How and why should a candidate prepare for an interview? (31–35)

12. How are candidates usually selected at interview? (36–40)

13. Explain what you understand by headhunting and why it is sometimes used in recruitment. (42–43)

14. Briefly outline an employer's legal obligations when recruiting staff. (47–53)

15. Explain your understanding of the term 'the ethics of recruitment'. (54–56)

16. Briefly discuss why many organisations choose to use objective tests as part of their selection process. (57–63)

Assignment – Getting a Job   **Element 4.3**

1. From a newspaper advertisement, select any job for which you would like to apply.

2. Prepare a possible job description and person specification for the job.

3. Prepare a letter of application which could be sent with the CV that you prepared for Task 6.

4. Outline the arrangements which the employer will need to make after the closing date in order to prepare for the interview.

5. Assuming that you have an interview, describe how you would prepare for it.

6. Carry out a mock interview with one or more of your colleagues, who will need to prepare some questions for this. Appraise your performance and comment on whether or not you found it useful in preparing for the job.

7. Ask your colleague(s) to appraise your performance in the interview, stating whether or not you would have got the job and why.

8. Now, repeat 6 and 7 by reversing roles with your colleagues.

---

16 Production in Business

This Chapter is about the function of production in a business and the way in which it can be organised, controlled and improved in order to add value. It includes:

- ❏ Production and Operations Management
- ❏ Added Value
- ❏ Costs of Production
- ❏ Production and Marketing
- ❏ Production Planning and Control
- ❏ Product Design Strategy
- ❏ Value Analysis
- ❏ Stock Control
- ❏ Economic Order Quantity
- ❏ Organisation of Production
- ❏ Job Production
- ❏ Flow Production
- ❏ Batch Production
- ❏ Just-in-Time Production

- ❏ Human Resource Management
- ❏ Labour Turnover
- ❏ Productivity
- ❏ Quality of Service
- ❏ Quality Assurance
- ❏ Reasons for Adding Value
- ❏ Production and Change
- ❏ Technological Developments
- ❏ Other Aspects of Change
- ❏ Innovation
- ❏ Research and Development
- ❏ Training and Development
- ❏ Ways to Improve Performance

Production and Operations Management

1. The **production function** in a business involves the planning and co-ordination of work to ensure that goods (or services) of the right quality are produced on time, in the required quantities and at minimum cost. In recent years, the growth of service industries and increasing use of new technology to replace labour in the manufacturing sector has lead to the term **operations management** often being preferred to that of **production management.**

Added Value

2. Production is a broad term used to cover all the processes of adding value in the provision of goods and services, whether in the public or private sector. Added value is the difference between an organisation's sales revenue and the cost of its bought-in components, materials and services. (It excludes therefore the cost of labour, land and capital.)

3. An organisation will seek to increase its added value and this can be achieved in a number of different ways including better marketing, improved planning and control, value analysis, improved purchasing and stock control (see Element 6.2), the organisation of production (e.g. just-in-time), improved productivity, quality control and the more effective use of human resources. The importance of the buying function is discussed in Element 6.2.

Costs of Production

7. The costs of production in a business involve those of:

   - ❏ **initial production** which uses materials, equipment and labour.

   - ❏ **waste** from scrap and faulty products.

☐ **maintenance** of equipment which should be preventative by means of regular servicing rather than reactive to breakdowns. This helps to ensure that machines are normally only out of operation as part of the overall production plan.

☐ **inspection** which is necessary for quality control.

☐ **prevention** costs which may include, for example, staff training, extra maintenance or investment in new equipment.

5. Additional costs may include those related to the:

☐ **investigation and servicing** of complaints.

☐ **loss of sales** and **customer goodwill.**

☐ **replacement or repair** of faulty goods.

☐ **rework** where this is undertaken

Task 1   **5.1.1 (C3.2)**

1. Identify and compare the main costs of production in any two local organisations. You could include the one chosen in the assignment at the end of Chapter 1.

2. Comment on your findings.

Production and Marketing

6. Depending on the type of organisation involved, production can be initiated from one of 3 key sources:

☐ to meet demand anticipated in response to the marketing effort.

☐ to replenish low stock levels.

☐ to complete an individual customer's order.

7. Like many business functions, marketing and production are closely linked. A business must decide on the type and quality of product it wishes to make and sell and then invest in the resources needed, including equipment of the appropriate capacity and labour with the necessary skills, to produce it. If either of these are a problem then they will restrict the marketing effort.

8. There would, for example, be no point in promoting demand for a product which a business cannot supply. Whilst new products or changes to existing ones must be developed in response not just to identified market needs but also in relation to the production capacity and capability of the organisation.

Task 2   **5.1.1 (C3.4)**

NO SUNSHINE FOR BREWING GROUP

Poor summer weather deterred drinkers from visiting riverside and garden pubs of London brewer Young.

The bleak economic climate also hit beer sales in the City, leading to a fall in half-year profits from £3.1m to £2.5m. Chairman John Young tells shareholders: 'These results take into account the very difficult economic times in which we live.'

continued...

Task 2 continued

FAIR-PLAY CHARTER AT XEROX

Photocopying giant Rank Xerox is hoping to set new standards in the industry with the introduction of its own version of the Citizen's Charter – the Rank Xerox Commitment.

The move is in response to the recent consumer initiative, the Campaign for Clear Copier Contracts.

It is an attempt to woo the customer back. Over the past year total UK market sales have fallen by a quarter. Rank has a third of the UK market.

PROFIT WARNING

Chocolate and confectionery group Thorntons warned today that annual profits will marginally under-perform current market estimates. It blames lower sales on the election and the hot weather.

Comment on how the above articles illustrate the importance of the need for the production and marketing functions of a business to work together.

Production Planning and Control

9. If an organisation operates in a stable market where sales do not fluctuate widely then production can operate at a fairly steady level. Manufacturers of **fast moving consumer goods**, for example, such as tea, sugar or soap powder are likely to experience a relatively regular demand. Some markets, however, are less stable and therefore close liaison with the marketing function is necessary so that production levels can be adjusted in response to changes in demand. **Seasonal items**, for example, such as ice cream and refrigerators where sales rise rapidly in warm weather and fashion items such as clothing and compact discs are subject to potentially quite erratic fluctuations in demand.

10. Therefore, for effective operations management, production must be planned, co-ordinated and controlled. Progress must be monitored to check that production schedules are being met and corrective action taken when necessary. This is essential to ensure that sufficient raw materials, equipment and labour are available when required so that production can run smoothly and costs are kept to a minimum. To achieve this involves establishing and implementing appropriate policies and systems for key factors such as:-

   ❏ Product design
   ❏ Purchasing (see Element 6.2)
   ❏ Stock Control
   ❏ Organisation of production
   ❏ Quality control
   ❏ Supervision and motivation of employees

Product Design Strategy

11. In Element 3.2 on Marketing, we considered the importance in business of market research and the need for a product strategy. An important stage in the creation of new products or the development of existing ones is that of design. The purpose of a **design strategy** in a business is to regularly review the features of all products in the range to ensure that they both meet customers requirements and are also cost effective to produce. This is particularly important in markets where technology is changing rapidly as, for example, with computers.

12. The main design factors which need to be considered can be summarised as performance, appearance, economy, and legal and environmental requirements.

13. **Performance**. To be successful, a product needs to be functionally efficient so that it does what it claims to do and what customers expect of it. Depending on the product, it may also need to be reliable, safe and easy and economical to operate and maintain.

14. **Appearance**. For many consumer products, for example, cars, houses and clothing, this is a very important factor. Essentially, unless a product looks appealing, even through the functional aspects may be good, it is unlikely to be successful. On the other hand, an attractive product is unlikely to be successful unless it functions well.

15. **Economy in production, distribution and storage.** If a business is to be competitive, then it must be able to manufacture its products at a reasonable cost. This may be affected by such factors as the raw materials, components and type of packaging used. For example, a manufacturer of soft drinks can use a variety of packaging techniques including glass bottles, plastic bottles, wax cartons and aluminium cans. Each of these is functionally sound but very different in terms of customer appeal, transport and storage. This is illustrated by considering the fact that glass is the heaviest and most fragile, although often favoured by customers because the product is visible inside. Wax cartons, on the other hand, are lighter, compact and easy to store and transport but generally less attractive to the eye.

16. **Legal requirements**. Nowadays, as discussed in Elements 1.3, 3.4 and 4.1 there is a wealth of Health and Safety and Consumer Protection Legislation which has to be taken into account when designing products. Examples include seat belts in cars, safety foam in furniture and accurate descriptions about holiday accommodation.

17. **Environmental factors**. Apart from the recent introduction of environmental legislation, there is also a growing public concern about the effect of many products and manufacturing processes on the environment. This has to be taken into account in design if an organisation is to avoid losing out to its competitors. Well known examples include the switch to unleaded petrol, ozone friendly aerosol sprays, smokeless fuels and recycled products (see Element 1.2).

Task 3   **5.1.1 (C3.4)**

1. Consider the design features which you would regard as important to you when 'purchasing' each of the following.
   a) A consumer durable such as: A Television Set, Washing Machine or Table.
   b) A consumable such as: A convenience food or a fresh product
   c) A service such as an insurance policy, bank account or form of transport.

2. Using a recent example from your own experience, discuss and comment on how what you 'purchased' differed from the design features identified.

3. From your answers, what are the implications, if any, for each business concerned?

Value Analysis

18. A technique widely used to aid decision-making in product design is that of value analysis. It is used to help businesses to improve efficiency and reduce production costs by evaluating whether all the materials or components in a product have a value commensurate with its cost. If, for example, complex expensive components are used it may be possible to replace them with simpler lower cost items without impairing the product's safety, quality or performance. Value analysis is particularly useful for mass produced items where a small saving on each part can result in a substantial reduction in overall costs.

Stock Control

19. Most organisations need to carry stocks whether it be raw materials, components, finished goods or stationery. If too much stock is held this takes up storage space and ties up cash, whilst a shortage of stock can cause delays in production and possible loss of sales.

20. Very often stocks constitute a high proportion of working capital and therefore must be controlled to ensure that they do not exceed an optimum level. Proper stock control should ensure that stock is

always available when needed. The amount of stock required will clearly depend upon the type of product and the **rate of stockturn**. Fruit and flowers, for example, which are perishable but sell quickly will be kept in different quantities to durable items such as toys or jewellery.

21. Therefore stock records need to be kept which record the movement of stock into and out of an organisation. It is also necessary to set maximum stock levels and a re-order level at which an order will be placed with a supplier. These levels will depend upon how frequently the item is used or sold, and how quickly stock can be replaced.

22.
Stock Record Card

Midland Auto Spares Ltd

Stock Card

Item:	Wheel trims (speciality)			
Ref no:	4721		**Max stock:**	50
Location:	Row 4A		**Min stock:**	20
			Re-order level:	30

Date 19___		Receipts		Issues		Balance
	Qty	Supplier		Qty	Customer	
1 Sept						
2 Sept						
3 Sept						
10 Sept	30	Car Distributors Ltd		10	A1 Garages	40

23.
Stock Control Graph

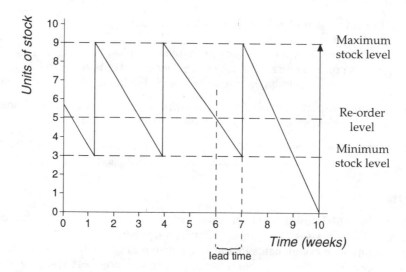

24. A simple stock control graph like that shown above can be used to illustrate when ordering should take place and how much should be ordered.

- ☐ Each vertical line represents a new delivery of stock.
- ☐ The slanting lines represent the using up of stock.
- ☐ A new order is placed when stock falls to the re-order level.
- ☐ The delay between placing an order and the stock being delivered is called the **lead time**.
- ☐ The minimum level is the buffer or amount of stock kept in reserve.

Task 4   **5.1.1 (N3.3, C3.4)**

The following questions 1-4 are based on the stock control graph in 23 above.

1. What are the minimum and maximum stock levels?

2. At what level of stock are new orders placed?

3. What is the stock level at week 5?

4. How long is the lead time?

5. Read the following article and use it to illustrate the potential impact on a company if stock levels are too high.

UNSOLD BRICKS PILE UP

Stockpiles of bricks continue to block the road to recovery for building materials and forest products group Ibstock Johnsen. Falling prices have knocked first-half profits by more than half to £3.1m and the interim dividend from 2.25p to just 0.5p. Ibstock has a brick stockpile of six months in the US. It needs to clear these stocks before it benefits from a housing recovery, if and when it comes. Stocks in the UK are still running at over four months. 'We don't expect any recovery in demand during 1993'. says managing director Ian Maclellan. He added that prices had fallen a further two points in the second half, and admitted: 'We have done our fair share of price-cutting.' Brick plants are being closed – Ibstock shut two last year and Tarmac four. But Mr Maclellan believes the industry needs to take a further 500m bricks out of production or 'two companies the size of Ibstock to reduce the general over-capacity.' He said Ibstock had reduced production and stock levels were 10m lower than last year's at 87m bricks or 17 weeks' sales.

---

25. **Pareto Rule**

The Pareto Rule or Law is important in a number of areas of business activity including stock control. It states that many business situations have an 80/20 characteristic. That is, 80% of the value of items in stock is represented by 20% of the items. Thus stock control should concentrate on the important 20% high value items with less concern about the remaining 80%. Another example is that often 80% of sales turnover comes from only 20% of the product range. This again has implications for stock control.

Economic Order Quantity

26. In order to minimise total costs, supplies are often purchased on the basis of the optimum or **economic order quantity** (EOQ). That is, the **cost of storage** such as warehousing – security – insurance – deterioration – obsolescence – pilferage and interest on capital tied up **balanced against the costs of ordering** including – administration – transport – handling – inspection and accounting. Generally, the larger the order is, the lower will be the unit costs due to quantity discounts but the higher are the costs of storage and vice versa.

27. It is possible, using a simple mathematical formula, to calculate the quantity which minimises total costs.

$$EOQ = \sqrt{\frac{2CD}{H}}$$

Where   C = Cost of placing an order (Order costs)
              D = Annual rate of demand (Quantity)
              H = Cost of holding one unit of stock for a year. (Average unit stock value)

28. **Example**

The annual demand for an item is 10,000 units. The cost of holding one unit in stock for a year is 15p and an order costs £30 to deliver.

$$EOQ = \sqrt{\frac{2(30)(10,000)}{0.15}} = 2,000 \text{ units}$$

Many businesses now use computerised record systems which automatically control stock and can be used to calculate EOQ

Task 5   **5.1.1 (N3.2)**

From the following information, calculate the EOQ. A supermarket sells 60,000 packets of sugar annually. Delivery costs are £25 per order and the cost of holding a unit in stock is 12% of the total cost.

29. **Costs of Stockholding**

The EOQ can also be shown graphically as follows:

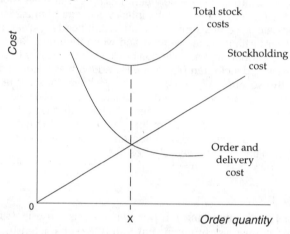

This illustrates how order and delivery costs fall as larger and less frequent deliveries are made. But this increases the average length stock is held and therefore the costs involved. The EOQ shown as OX occurs at the minimum point on the total cost curve.

30. Whilst the EOQ is a useful method it ignores the lead time needed for stock replacement and therefore 'buffer stocks' may need to be kept which will represent a further cost. Without this, there is a risk of a 'stock-out' situation which could lead to lost production or sales.

Organisation of Production

31. The scheduling of production involves organising the activities in a manufacturing plant or service industry to ensure that the product or service is completed at the expected time. In order to achieve this, production can be organised in 3 basic ways – using job, batch or flow production. In practice, however, more than one method may be used.

32. The method chosen will depend upon a number of factors such as

❏ **the type of product**, for example whether it is durable or perishable.

❏ **the size of the business,** thus for example many small firms may never have sufficient demand or the capital investment required to operate on a large scale.

❏ **the size and location of the market** and therefore the volume of production required.

❏ **the frequency of demand,** that is whether the product is a regular purchase such as toothpaste or infrequent such as central heating equipment.

Job Production

33. This method is used when a single product or small 'one-off' orders are made from start to finish to a customers own individual requirements. Generally, there is no repetition of products or tasks and each order must be planned and controlled separately.

34. Because products are non-standard this is invariably the most expensive form of production, often very labour intensive and requiring considerable flexibility and technical skills. Examples could include exclusive luxury goods like jewellery, houses, ships, racing cars, and closer to home, birthday cakes at a local bakers.

Flow Production

35. This method uses a series of repetitive processes and is common where mass produced standardised products pass along a conveyor belt or assembly line. Flow production makes maximum use of the division of labour and is particularly cost effective for large scale production. The longer the production run, the lower will be the unit cost due to the wider spread of fixed costs. Nowadays, assembly lines are usually highly automated as businesses make increasing use of robots and other forms of computerised technology.

36. Careful organisation and planning is needed to ensure continuous flow from one process to the next and to avoid 'bottlenecks'. That is, problems and delays which can be caused when machines have differing production capacities. Examples of goods produced by this method include cars, television sets, chocolates and many tinned and packeted goods.

Batch Production

37. This method falls between job and flow production. Some repetition is involved so that complete batches or units of production can be made at any one time according to demand. All items in a batch will move simultaneously from one process to another.

38. Careful planning and monitoring of production is required to reduce the costs of changeover, including any necessary re-tooling and to prevent staff and machines lying idle for long periods. Units costs are slightly higher than with continuous flow because production runs are shorter. Examples include wallpaper firms which produce batches of different designs, paint manufacturers make colour batches, housing estates are also built by this method whilst bakery firms produce fresh batches of bread daily.

39.
Example – Flow and Batch Production

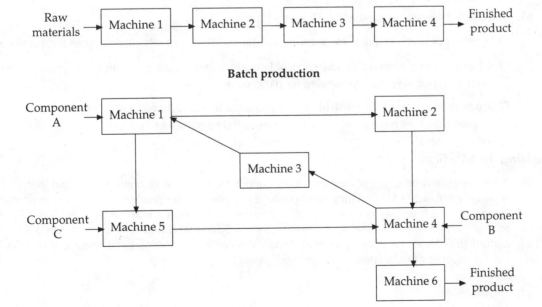

Flow production

Batch production

Task 6   **5.1.1 (N3.2)**

From the items in your own home and place of study or work, try to identify at least 5 examples of goods or services which have been produced using:

1. job production

2. flow production

3. batch production

4. Now select one item from each list and discuss the factors which the supplier would take into account to determine the choice of production method.

Just-In-Time Production

40. A recent development in production methods is that of **just in-time** (JIT) which originated in Japan. It has proved to be so successful in increasing productivity that it is now being adopted by many UK businesses. Although it is often referred to as **supply chain management**, based on working with suppliers to achieve quality and efficiency. The idea behind JIT is to reduce production costs by always keeping stocks of components, materials and work-in-progress to an absolute minimum.

41. JIT means that:

     ❒ finished goods are produced just-in-time for them to be sold.

     ❒ the components or raw materials needed to produce finished goods arrive just when required for use.

42. To work effectively JIT, sometimes called stockless production, requires 3 conditions to be met:

     ❒ All sources of uncertainty must be removed from the manufacturing system in order to remove the need to keep buffer stocks. This means, for example, that unreliable suppliers or equipment cannot be tolerated.

     ❒ The time needed to set up machines must be drastically reduced so that products can be produced in smaller batches which also has the effect of reducing lead times. This might be achieved by simplifying the production process.

     ❒ Bottlenecks must be eliminated to prevent production holdups.

Benefits of Just-In-Time

43. The major benefits of introducing JIT are that:

     ❒ **lower stock levels require less working capital** and therefore release resources for use elsewhere.

     ❒ **it forces an organisation to address problems.** Bottlenecks, for example, or problems with equipment and suppliers must be tackled for JIT to work.

     ❒ **production is easier to control.** Since products are sold immediately rather than stored, any problems such as quality, will quickly come to light and can be rectified.

Organising Just-In-Time

44. JIT is dependent upon a smooth flow of production and success through people and therefore work is usually organised by grouping workers in teams around the product they make. In practice this means that each worker is **multi-skilled** and trained to perform a number of operations. The Japanese car company, Nissan, set up its new factory in Sunderland on this basis with just 3 job classifications in order to overcome potential demarcation problems. Many large retailers now relay on JIT for the supplies of many products, e.g. Netto, Benetton.

Task 7   **5.1.1 (C3.2)**

Mary Carter is production manager at Holcombe Products Ltd, a manufacturer of pet foods. She is planning a new automated production line which requires 3 different types of machine. The capacity of each machine is as follows:

Machine X processes 40 units per minute

Machine Y processes 60 units per minute

Machine Z processes 80 units per minute

1.   Which machine will limit the production capacity of the line.

2.   Discuss the potential bottlenecks, and/or under-utilisation which could arise, which need to be considered in the planning process.

3.   Suggest the proportion of each type of machine which could be installed to achieve an efficient production run.

Human Resource Management

45. Value-added can be influenced by the effectiveness of an organisation's human resource management policy. For example the efficient use of employees helps to reduce costs whilst appropriate working conditions can increase productivity. A problem in any of the following areas therefore could indicate a personnel problem which must be addressed:

   ❑ the rate of labour turnover
   ❑ the level of absenteeism
   ❑ the level of productivity
   ❑ the quality of work or service
   ❑ the level of wastage
   ❑ the safety record

Labour Turnover

46. Labour turnover is the term used to describe the movement of people into and out of an organisation. This can be an important indication of job satisfaction, which we considered at the beginning of this Chapter.

Reasons for Labour Turnover

47. Some of the most common reasons why employees leave an organisation include:

   ❑ **Voluntary** or avoidable reasons such as better pay, better prospects or job dissatisfaction. This can be a key indicator of discontent in an organisation.

   ❑ **Involuntary** or unavoidable reasons such as retirement, ill-health or death. Many women leave employment because of pregnancy or a change in their partner's career.

   ❑ **Management action**, for example, redundancy or dismissal due to poor performance or bad discipline

Task 8   **5.1.1 (C3.2)**

Choose any organisation well known to you and try to discover information about its labour turnover. Consider the number of people it employs, make comparisons with previous years and if possible identify the main reasons for any changes.

Measuring Labour Turnover

48. One method of measuring the rate of labour turnover over a period of time is the wastage or separation rate which can be expressed as:

$$\frac{\text{number of employees leaving during a period}}{\text{*average number employed during the period}} \times 100$$

49. NB * The average number can be calculated by taking the average of the number employed at the beginning and end of the period. The figure can be calculated to include or exclude the unavoidable turnover.

50. **Example**

$$\frac{700}{3,500} \times 100 = 20\% \text{ labour turnover}$$

A 20% per annum figure means that a firm would have to plan to replace its workforce over a 5 year period. It may also be a cause of concern as to why so many people are leaving

51. Another statistic which can be used is the stability index:

$$\frac{\text{number with 12 months' service}}{\text{Total number of employees 12 months ago}} \times 100$$

This indicates the extent to which a firm is losing or retaining its experienced staff.

52. Whilst statistics should be treated with caution, a high labour turnover may indicate trends which identify problems in the organisation overall or in particular departments or areas of work. It may also be an indicator of poor staff morale.

Importance of Labour Turnover

53. A certain amount of turnover is healthy for an organisation because it can create promotion opportunities and may help to **reduce an ageing workforce.** Whilst new staff can inject **new life**, **new ideas** and may respond better to **change**.

54. On the other hand, if the turnover is very high, it can cause instability, of lead to a **loss of experienced and skilled staff**, and impose **increased costs** on an organisation. This is because the recruitment, selection and training of staff is expensive and time-consuming and when staff leave it can result in reduced efficiency, lost production and higher costs of temporary overtime until new appointments are made. Therefore personnel managers need to devise policies which aim to keep turnover to an acceptable level.

Task 9	**5.1.1 (N3.2)**

Calculate the labour turnover and stability index from the following information and comment on the figures

Number of employees beginning Jan 1994:	5,000
Number of employees end Dec 1994	4,600
Number of employees leaving during the year:	
Voluntary:	500
Involuntary:	100
Redundant:	120
Number of employees with more than 12 months service:	3,900

Personnel Policies to Control Labour Turnover

55. Suitable policies to recruit and retain good staff by increasing morale and job satisfaction could include:

   ❑ Improving recruitment and selection processes

   ❑ Improving working conditions

   ❑ Introducing or improving training programmes

   ❑ Job enrichment, enlargement and rotation

   ❑ Introducing career structures to provide promotion prospects

   ❑ Reviewing pay structures or methods e.g. introducing bonuses.

   ❑ Promoting a corporate feeling e.g. worker participation

   ❑ Strategies for improving industrial relations and raising morale e.g. better communication.

   ❑ 'Exit' interviews to discover why people are leaving and thus identify particular problems.

Absenteeism

56. The number of working days lost each year can have a major effect on the efficiency and profitability of an organisation. Although some absenteeism, such as training and development activities, is authorised most is not, and therefore needs to be monitored and controlled as much as possible.

57. The main reasons for absenteeism in most organisations are:

   ❑ **sickness** e.g. colds, flu, back injuries

   ❑ **stress** which is a problem generally on the increase

   ❑ **family problems** e.g. sick children, bereavement

   ❑ **job dissatisfaction** and low morale which can result in people taking time off because they are bored or unhappy

   ❑ **industrial accidents** which can be reduced by stringent health and safety practices.

Task 10   5.1.1 (C3.4)

1. Try to discover the level of, and reasons for, absenteeism in your place of study or work. Comment on any particular problem areas. In a school or college this could be an investigation into staff and/or student absences.

2. Try to identify the impact on your organisation of staff (and/or students in school or college) being absent from work and in particular how, if at all, it affects you personally.

3. Suggest ways in which absenteeism could be reduced, particularly in the problem areas identified in 1.

Productivity

58. An important measure of the efficiency of production is referred to as productivity. It shows the relationship between the output of a system and the factor inputs – in terms of materials, labour and capital – used to produce it, taken either individually or together.

$$\text{Productivity} = \frac{\text{Outputs}}{\text{inputs}}$$

59. The most commonly used factor for productivity calculations is labour, that is, output per employee. Essentially, this is because in most cases it is easy to quantify by simply counting the number of

workers engaged in a particular process. Another reason is that in the past, labour has tended to be the major factor input. Thus, for example, the weekly, monthly or annual productivity of a car assembly plant could be measured as:

$$\text{Productivity} = \frac{\text{Number of cars produced}}{\text{Average number employed}}$$

An increase in productivity occurs when the output per employee is raised. This is usually achieved by making better use of, or increasing the amount of capital.

60. It has been found that labour is a good measure of productivity showing in particular the benefits of technological improvements as they have increasingly been used to displace workers in the production process. It has to be remembered, however, that an increase in the productivity of labour may be due to other factors such as better organisation of production or increased efforts or skills, as well as the introduction of new techniques. Also, the relative importance of labour is declining with the growth of new technology.

61. Improvements in productivity, which are important not just for individual organisations but for raising a country's standard of living and promoting its economic growth, can come about in 2 main ways:

❒ **Increasing output as costs remain constant**. That is, boosting output without using additional resources.

❒ **Reducing costs whilst maintaining output**. Possibly by using less and/or cheaper labour or materials.

Task 11	**5.1.1 (N3.2)**

1. Compare the output per shift of the following 3 coal mines and identify the most efficient pit on the basis of the information given.

   A   which employs 70 workers produces 250 tons per shift

   B   which employs 48 workers produces 200 tons per shift

   C   which employs 50 workers produces 210 tons per shift

2. The figures relate to the coal face workers only. Comment on whether or not you feel all employees, including management and administrative support staff, should be included in the productivity calculations.

Quality of work or service

62. Quality is something which everyone recognises and is familiar with but a concept which is not always easy to define. Essentially it is about the way in which products or services are perceived by customers relative to the alternatives available. Some organisations, for example, like Sainsbury's and Marks and Spencer are immediately associated with quality because they have clearly identifiable standards which demonstrate a degree of excellence.

63. In a manufacturing situation, a widely used definition of quality is that of 'fitness for purpose' whilst in a service environment the 'best possible standard' is often used. But, however, it is defined quality is about the attributes of a product or service which are needed in order to satisfy a customer.

64. A quality approach to business helps to reduce costs of production because it results in fewer returns, less waste, re-work and delays. It also saves time and trouble dealing with production problems and/or customer dissatisfaction. It is therefore essential that a quality control system exists to ensure that goods and services consistently meet the required standards (see Element 2.2).

65. Since a business's success often depends on the quality of staff that it employs, their efficiency, loyalty, attitude and enthusiasm can make the difference between a firm making a profit or a loss. Whether they are employed as managers, clerks, receptionists, sales staff, factory workers or cleaners, poor work or service from staff can lead to lost business.

66. The need for quality is now widely recognised as being essential if firms want to survive and prosper. Hence the importance not only of good selection and recruitment procedures, but also of a commitment to training and development. Many organisations have now become 'Investors in People'. This is a TEC sponsored initiative to encourage the development of all employees in an organisation in order to help it to achieve its objectives (see Element 5.3).

Quality Assurance

67. Quality assurance is a term used to describe an approach to production and the checks and audits which are carried out to ensure that quality control procedures are followed.

68. This approach involves working with suppliers to ensure that materials and components meet the required standards of, for example, safety, reliability and performance. Some companies, for example, Marks and Spencer and Ford actually set their own very rigid standards for the quality of their products and then carefully select manufacturers who can meet them. They also insist that suppliers are organised in such a way as to ensure quality output and carry out regular checks to verify that standards are being maintained. They will also reject complete batches if just one item is found to be below standard.

Task 12	**5.1.1 (C3.2)**

1. Identify at least 6 organisations which you feel offer quality products and/or services.

2. Explain what they offer which determines this.

3. What standards do you personally look for or expect from such an organisation?

4. Who benefits from these standards and how?

5. Can you identify any areas for improvement in the products or services of the organisations concerned?

Wastage

69. High levels of wastage may indicate a number of potential personnel problems in an organisation, for example:

- ❒ **careless work** possibly due to poor supervision or because workers are simply not motivated
- ❒ **inadequate training** so that staff are unable or do not know how to perform tasks correctly
- ❒ **job dissatisfaction** possibly caused by boredom, poor pay, ineffective management or environmental conditions

Safety

70. In paragraph 57 we mentioned that industrial accidents, and therefore absenteeism, can be reduced by stringent health and safety regulations. If a firm has a poor safety record it could indicate a problem in terms of policy and/or enforcement of safety standards in the workplace. Consequently this particular aspect of human resource management would need investigating and appropriate action taken.

Reasons for Adding Value

71. A business needs to aim to add value in production in order to enable it to

- ❒ **survive and grow** which are basic objectives of any business organisation
- ❒ **meet customer requirements** which is essential if it is to be successful in the market place
- ❒ **meet competition** which could come from home based or overseas organisations. Competitive factors could include quality, price, design and availability.
- ❒ **improve profit levels** which is more likely to happen if the business is operating more effectively and succeeding in meeting customer requirements and beating competition.

Task 13   **5.1.1, 5.1.2 (C3.4)**

> Employers are losing in the region of £4 billion to £9 billion a year through workplace accidents and work-related ill health, says a new authoritative HSE report.
>
> This sum equates to between £170 and £360 per annum for every employee or between 5-10 per cent of all UK industrial companies' gross profits in 1990.
>
> It covers the costs incurred from lost output, damage to materials or finished goods, having to recruit and train replacement staff, and paying sick pay or compensation awards to affected staff.
>
> Based on findings from a special health and safety supplement to the ED's 1990 Labour Force Survey, plus a series of in-depth company case studies of accident losses, the report provides the most comprehensive estimates of the costs of accidents at work ever undertaken in the UK or, as far as is known, abroad.
>
> The overall cost of work accidents and ill health to the nation is estimated at between £11 billion and £16 billion a year.
>
> HSE hopes the report will draw employers' attention to the true costs of work accidents and ill health, and indicate the gains available from better health and safety management and training.

From the above article and your own knowledge and experience of health and safety explain the benefits to an employer to better health and safety management and training and why this is the most cost effective way of reducing accidents.

Production and Change

72. In Element 4.2 we considered the concept of change, the internal and external factors which can bring about the need for change in an organisation and how it can be managed. Managers need to be alert to and take advantage of the opportunities which can come about from change and also to minimise any potential threats. The availability of new technology, for example, or withdrawal of a competitor from the market might represent opportunities. On the other hand, the introduction of new technology or new products by competitors may represent threats.

Technological Developments

73. We live in an age of computerised technology the rapid growth of which has made many products obsolete whilst at the same time creating opportunities for **new products and services**. For example, the growth of **telecommunications** products like the telephone, facsimile machines and satellite broadcasting and financial services like cash machines and EFTPOS. If you compare a modern hi-fi system with a 1950's record player, you will see dramatic changes whilst products like colour televisions, the Sony Walkman, battery watches, video recorders, compact discs and microwave ovens, were still being developed. The micro-chip has completely transformed the computer industry and lead to a rapid growth in **information technology** (see Element 2.4) which is beginning to alter not only products but work patterns.

74. The same is also true of industrial markets where people and heavy, bulky machinery have been replaced by **robots** and much smaller computer controlled **production systems**, enabling firms to develop new, better or cheaper products.

75. The major changes can be summarised as:

❐ **Communication** is much quicker and more accurate using television, satellite links, word processing, facsimile and electronic mail.

❐ **Information processing.** The use of microcomputers to store, retrieve, transmit and process data on discs or tapes.

❐ **Management information systems** (MIS) are available which can be used to provide essential information needed by managers to enable them to make decisions, e.g. weekly or monthly sales figures, production costs, output achieved, sales of different products.

- **Computer aided design** (CAD) is used to design new products.
- **Computer aided manufacture (CAM).** Much equipment is now automatically controlled by computers. Robots have been introduced making work faster and more accurate.
- **New materials** are now used, which are often lighter or stronger than those they replaced, such as carbon fibre composites in the Aerospace industry, new plastics in cars, high-fibre, cholesterol free protein in foods, and synthetic fibres in clothing.

76. The resulting effects of technological progress include:

- More goods can be produced and of a higher quality.
- Reduced production costs possibly leading to lower prices for consumers.
- Stock records, payrolls, accounts and other data can be prepared and processed on computers.
- Men have been replaced by machines leading to increased unemployment in many industries.
- New range of services, for example banking from home, cash-points and a general growth of tertiary industries.
- New technology makes jobs cleaner, easier and safer for workers.
- Increased leisure time because more work   Technological change is also important because it raises consumer expectations as they expect and demand more sophisticated and innovative products not just with electronic equipment but with all products.

77. Technological change is also important because it raises **consumer expectations** as they expect and demand more sophisticated and innovative products not just with electronic equipment but with all products.

Task 14   **5.1.3, 5.1.4 (C3.4)**

NEW PRINTING TECHNOLOGY

Computer technology is now widely used in the production of national and provincial newspapers.

Journalists, for example, can type and edit articles directly into computer terminals where colour pictures or graphics can also be added. Where production plants are some distance from editorial offices, pages are transmitted by facsimile. Other technological developments include full-colour printing and the use of plastic-plate processes. London Docklands has become an important location for printing plants. The Financial Times moved there in 1988 with about 200 production workers compared with 650 at its former City of London facility. News International which publishes 3 daily and 2 Sunday newspapers has over 500 computer terminals, one of the largest systems in the world.

1.   From the above information, discuss the impact of new technology on the printing industry.

2.   Find the names of the newspapers published by News International.

3.   Comment, if possible from a site visit, on how newspapers in your locality are now produced and how their format has changed in recent years. Also, describe how new technology has altered the type of work which is now performed.

4.   Identify the two largest employers in your area. Are they capital or labour intensive?

5.   Find out the total numbers employed in each organisation and whether, with reasons, these have increased or decreased over the past five years.

78. **The rate of technological change** means that it may be the most difficult environmental factor to identify, often developing very quickly and in a short space of time completely changing the character of an industry, as for example with cars. Nonetheless, an organisation must not only be aware of this but also consider the extent to which it can develop and apply new technological advancement and keep ahead of its competitors.

Task 15   **5.1.3, 5.1.4 (C3.4)**

BLOCKED CHUNNEL

The Channel Tunnel launch date has had to be delayed again and it will now not open before Autumn 1994 - over 12 months later than originally planned.

The Anglo-French Trans-Manche Link (TML) consortium of 10 builders blamed problems over safety work on the shuttle trains which will run between Folkestone and Calais for the setback. This means operator Eurotunnel will have to ask banks and shareholders for more cash, adding to the £8.9 billion already being spent in a protracted row over construction costs. A final settlement increases the original contract price for the fixed equipment in the tunnel from £620 m to £1.14 bn (at 1985 prices). This will be raised mainly from a rights issue of over £500m part of which will be taken by TML instead of cash.

At £64.50 one-way for a car and its occupants, the loss of the summer's peak business will cost £70 million a month. And while independent analysts have raised estimates for the company's first year losses from £444m to £500m and predict the venture will not break even until 1999, Eurotunnel says it expects to be making £971 million by 2003. Although construction of the tunnel itself is virtually complete, a full service involving passenger and freight traffic between London, Paris and Brussels will not now be running until 1995.

1.   Why was the Tunnel launch date delayed?

2.   What effect did this have on the Eurotunnel consortium?

3.   What effect could the delay have had on other business organisations both in the UK and Europe?

4.   When fully operational what impact is it likely to have on individuals, business and the economy as a whole?

Other Aspects of Change

79. Technological change has partly been responsible for bringing about other aspects of change which have had an impact on production in business. For example, in Element 5.2 we will consider the impact on **work patterns** such as the growth of working from home, increase in female employment, need for employees to work more flexibly, multi-skilling, the need for regular re-training to update skills and the increase in the contracting-out of work as organisations, particularly in the public sector, seek greater efficiency.

80. In Element 4.1 we considered the main **legislation** which affects employers and employees covering such areas as health and safety, discrimination, equal pay, redundancy and unfair dismissal, whilst in Element 1.3 we identified some of the environmental legislation which affects organisations. In addition to the **Environmental Protection Acts 1990 and 1995** which controls, air, water and noise pollution there is also other significant legislation such as the **Pollution of Rivers Act 1951,** which prohibits the discharge of refuse and pollutants into rivers, the **Chemical (Hazard Information and Packaging) Regulations 1993 (CHIP)** which classifies over 1400 common hazardous substances and controls how they should be labelled and supplied, and the **Clean Air Act 1956** which prohibits the emission of dark smoke from chimneys.

81. In addition, local councils can also influence production through, for example
     ❏ **bye-laws** which might put restrictions on trade
     ❏ **planning permission** which can control or restrict development in an area
     ❏ **parking or other restrictions** which can influence access and location.

82. In paragraphs 62–68 and also Element 2.2 we considered the importance of quality and the introduction of standards such as BS 5750 (ISO 9000) which many large firms now insist that their suppliers have and the environmental standard BS 7750, which could reduce costs and increase efficiency by, for example, leading to organisations finding new and better ways of getting rid of waste.

Innovation

83. The practical refinement and development of an original invention into a usable technique or product, is called innovation. It can be a lengthy and expensive process but is nonetheless an important means of improving an organisation's market performance, for example, by reducing costs or improving quality. Innovation is also a key contributor to a nation's economic growth. Consider, for example, the success of Japan through innovation in its electrical and photographic consumer products such as videos, camcorders, computers and cameras.

Task 16	**5.1.5 (C3.4)**

Consider the following products in terms of your own knowledge and experience of innovation. Take each in turn and discuss the extent to which they have changed over the past 10-20 years.

1. Breakfast cereals
2. Cars
3. Building materials
4. Packaging materials for food and drink
5. Computers.

Research and Development (R&D)

84. An important factor in bringing about innovation and change is that of research and development (R&D). The extent to which organisations develop and introduce new and improved products, production processes and distribution techniques, often depends upon the level of investment in pure and applied scientific research.

85. **Pure research** is often undertaken by Universities and government agencies (e.g. Medical Research Council, Economic & Social Research Council) to add to the general level of scientific knowledge and understanding. The important point is that it often has no practical application and therefore no financial return is expected from the investment. Despite this, business organisations often contribute to University research and also undertake some pure research themselves in their own laboratories.

86. **Applied research** on the other hand is concerned with developments which should have some commercial value. Therefore, it is used to meet particular needs and/or to share problems. As such it should at the very least pay for itself over a period of time. If successful, a major breakthrough can very quickly change the whole nature of a business. Radical innovations may result in lower manufacturing and distribution costs and thus either increase profits and/or reduce the price to the consumer. Whilst new or improved products may lead to an increase in market share.

87.

Savings from Innovation

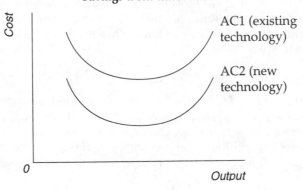

Task 17   **5.1.4, 5.1.5 (C3.4)**

NO MORE SPECS

Wearing glasses or contact lenses could become obsolete for anyone under 45 within ten years, say doctors.

Research into eye surgery in Britain is advancing so fast that it will soon be possible to use lasers to treat millions suffering from vision defects.

Surgeons are achieving a 95 per cent success rate with laser surgery to correct short-sightedness (myopia) and are confident they will be able to cure long-sightedness (hyperopia).

Surgery normally costs around £1,000 an eye and is available at some private clinics. Clinical trials on more advanced techniques to treat astigmatism are described as 'extremely promising'.

Around 25 million Britons currently wear glasses. About three million have contact lenses. An estimated 12 million people suffer from myopia and nine million from astigmatism.

SECRET TAG THAT COULD COST SHOPLIFTERS £1BN

A revolutionary anti-theft tag could save retailers £1 billion a year, it is claimed. The slim magnetic strips – described as a 'quantum leap' in security technology – can be inserted into packaging or hidden behind bar codes on any goods, including basic food items. They are automatically deactivated as goods are paid for at the checkout. The tags, developed by the Centre for the Exploitation of Science and Technology, cannot be detected by shoplifters.

A spokesman for the Co-operative Wholesale Society, which plans to use them in a pilot scheme in Slough said: 'Our security people estimate these could deter 75 per cent of shoplifting offences.'

Read the articles and from them:

1. Identify the benefits from investing in research.

2. Explain who will gain most from the research and why.

---

88. Large organisations are often better able to afford to invest in R&D because their monopoly profits provide the necessary resources. Often they will have a specialist R&D department run by a senior manager. Although the amount of investment will depend upon an organisation's objectives and strategy, it should be related to profit forecasts resulting from the commercial potential if successful. Pharmaceutical companies, for example, often spend millions of pounds to develop new drugs.

89. In Britain, the highest level of R&D spending in relation to their gross output takes place in the high-technology manufacturing industries of aerospace, chemicals, instrument engineering and electrical and electronic engineering. The latter includes office machinery, telecommunications and data processing equipment.

90. **Development**

Successful research will lead to the need for development into a practical application. In the case of new or improved products, organisations will clearly want to launch them as quickly as possible in order to give them a competitive edge. The time scale involved will depend upon the type of product, the costs involved and the amount of testing necessary for health and safety purposes. New drugs, for example, often have to be tested over several years to ensure that they do not have any harmful side effects.

33. **Problems of R&D**

The following factors are important for organisations which invest in R&D.

☐ **provision of finance** which will depend upon the type of product(s), the size of the organisation and its financial strength and the rate of technological change in the industry concerned.

❏ **budgetary control** to try to ensure that resources are not wasted. But unfortunately there is no direct correlation between expenditure and results because the time required and eventual outcomes are usually unpredictable.

❏ **personal involvement** and interest of researchers which is often so intense that it makes control and direction to a commercial end difficult.

❏ **prioritising** may be difficult where a number of projects are being undertaken at the same time and the resources for some must be stopped or reduced.

❏ **management decisions** about the potential of any particular project, whether to continue it and for how long, or alternatively to stop it, even though considerable resources may have already been invested.

Training and Development

92. In order to ensure that an organisation has the necessary skills to achieve its objectives, it is important not only that it recruits the 'right' staff, but also that it has a policy for regularly training those staff. **Training is the process of developing the knowledge and skills of employees to enable them to perform their jobs more efficiently**.

93. Most training takes place **'on-the-job'**, i.e. people learn at work either from other people or by themselves, often from experience. This is relatively cheap and the easiest method of training to arrange because it takes place in the organisation itself. Most employees learn at least part of their job in this way. The growth of work-experience as an integral part of courses for students in schools and colleges illustrates the value and importance of this method of training.

94. One of its major drawbacks, however, is that the quality depends very much on the skills and experience of the instructor concerned, and his or her ability to teach (although, of course, the instructor can also be trained), and bad habits or methods can be learned just as easily as good ones.

95. Training can also take place **'off-the-job'** either inside (in house) or outside a firm, for example, a course may be held in a firm's own training school, at a local college (day release or evening class), in a specialist training centre or in a hotel (particularly if the course is residential). The important thing is that employees learn their skills away from the job.

96. Although off-the-job training costs more it does have the advantages that training is carried out by specialist qualified trainers, it enables the trainees to mix with people from the same or other organisations, and may be less pressured or stressful, enabling learning to take place at the individual's own pace.

97. **Types of Training**

There are five main types of training which firms may carry out.

❏ **Induction** – that is, all new staff should be introduced to the firm generally and told about the business, for example the goods which it makes and sells, the general organisation and what their particular job involves.

❏ **Basic skills** – whilst all new staff should receive induction training, junior staff in particular should also undertake an organised training programme. This should be designed to teach them basic skills required in their job and thus to develop them into more efficient and effective employees.

❏ **Re-training** – regular refresher or updating courses should take place for all staff. For example when new technology, Health and Safety measures or new products are introduced.

❏ **Management trainees** – many larger companies run special management trainee courses, for example ICI and Marks and Spencer. Often people with a University degree or GCE 'A' levels are recruited to undertake an intensive training programme. Staff who join the firm from school at 16 can usually join the scheme after a few years basic training.

In any organisation staff with potential should be developed to take on additional responsibilities so that they are prepared when promotion opportunities arise.

❒ **Management** – regular training for executives in the latest management techniques should form an essential part of any firm's overall training plan to ensure that its business operates efficiently.

Task 18   **5.1.5 (C3.2)**

Depending on where you work or study you will have experienced different types of training. For anyone new to an organisation, initially induction training is the most important.

1.   From your own experience and knowledge, draw up an induction programme for someone new to your organisation. List all the important factors which you feel it should cover and briefly explain why.

2.   Discuss the importance of training and in particular how induction or other training you have experienced could be improved

---

98. **Training Needs**

As organisations change and develop, different skills are required. Training, therefore, should always be linked to the manpower plan, and seen as an on-going process which takes place throughout an individual's career.

99. Situations where training and re-training may be needed include:

❒ **technological change** which creates the need for new skills and/or updating existing skills.

❒ **Introduction of new equipment** and/or processes

❒ where **reorganisation** occurs and people take on new or different roles

❒ development of particular individuals in **preparation for promotion** into more senior posts

❒ where **competitive pressures** create the need to make more efficient use of manpower in order to cut costs

❒ where **skill shortages** exist, not just locally, but nationally e.g. marketing and sales, IT and computing, textiles and electronic engineering

❒ to further **develop individuals** employed for their particular skills

❒ to **change attitudes** and inculcate the culture of the organisation in all staff

Possible Benefits From Training

100. **For the employee:**

❒ Feel valued by the organisation.

❒ Opportunity to develop skills and knowledge.

❒ May improve promotion prospects.

❒ May improve job satisfaction because they are more competent to do their job.

❒ Makes them better able to cope with change by increasing understanding of, reasons for, and providing the knowledge and skills to adjust.

❒ Increases general proficiency and confidence.

101. **For the employer:**

❒ Improves quality and motivation of staff.

❒ Brings in new ideas and skills that could improve efficiency, productivity and profitability.

❒ Better health and safety helping to reduce accidents and raise standards.

- More effective use of staff, more quickly and at less cost.

- Helps to develop individual, team and corporate competence and improve performance in terms of output, quality and speed of operation.

- Helps to develop a positive culture in the organisation, e.g. employees oriented towards quality and improved performance.

- Provides higher levels of service to customers.

- May increase commitment to the organisation if employees are better able to identify with its mission and objectives.

Training costs

102. The costs of training employees may include not just the direct cost of the programme itself, but also the cost of replacing staff while they are away, or the effects of work being delayed or not being completed at all.

103. A hospital, for example, could clearly put patients at risk if it does not replace nurses who are being trained; the training of doctors or surgeons could increase the waiting time for treatment. Similarly, a business which, for example, takes sales representatives 'off the road' for training may risk losing orders.

104. Most organisations usually set a training budget which is used to develop the skills required to achieve its objectives. Generally speaking the potential benefits from training should outweigh the costs incurred. Despite this, however, in times of recession many organisations still regard training as one of the first areas in which to cut costs in order to make savings.

Evaluation of training

105. Training, therefore, like many other investment in a business, needs to be evaluated to ensure that it is worthwhile and cost-effective. Any training programme should have specific objectives against which evaluation can take place.

106. Some examples of **training objectives** are:

- To reduce the risk of accidents by making all staff aware of the organisation's health and safety policy.

- To ensure that all managers understand the processes involved in strategic planning.

- To enable VDU operators to use the current software package.

- To develop the leadership and supervisory skills of first-line managers.

107. It is not, however, always easy to measure the improvements in performance, if there are any, that come about from training. This is partly because they may not be immediate or direct, as for example when the objective is to change attitudes, improve motivation or increase job satisfaction. The benefits of training should therefore form part of any employee appraisal system. Overall, the cost-effectiveness of training has to be evaluated in terms of the financial gains and success of the organisation.

Task 19   5.1.5 (C3.4)

1. Consider, with reasons, what training is likely to be necessary in a small engineering company which is planning to introduce new technology in its factory and offices. It is well established and currently employs 50 people (40 in the factory), many of whom have been with the firm for 5 years or more.

2. Discuss how the training could be evaluated.

Ways to Improve Production

108. Change has become a fact of life in organisations today. It has always existed but it is the pace at which change now takes place which makes it so important. Also, as we have seen in this chapter change impacts not just on the process of production, but on human resource management, and customer and supplier relationships creating a need for on-going research, development and training in order to keep ahead of competitors.

109. In summary, the main ways to improve production and add value are by

- ❑ raising productivity
- ❑ a commitment to total quality
- ❑ investing in research and development
- ❑ investing in training
- ❑ investing in physical resources
- ❑ reducing pollution and waste
- ❑ improving working conditions

Summary

110. a) Operations management is concerned with the planning and co-ordination of production in conjunction with the other business functions.

  b) Production processes add value to goods or services. Added value is the difference between an organisations sales revenue and the cost of its bought in components, material and services.

  c) Marketing and production are closely linked and can be used together to increase added value.

  d) Production planning involves the co-ordination of product design, purchasing, stock control, the organisation of production, quality control and the supervision and motivation of employees.

  e) Value analysis is used to improve efficiency and reduce production costs.

  f) Proper stock control is vital to avoid supply shortages or the tying up of large amounts of capital.

  g) Total costs of stockholding can be reduced by calculating the economic order quality.

  h) Production can be organised using job, batch, flow or just-in-time methods.

  i) Value added can be influenced by the effectiveness of an organisation's human resource management policy. This could be reflected in the rate of labour turnover and levels of absenteeism, productivity, quality, wastage and the safety record.

  j) Added value is important for organisations to survive, grow, meet customer requirements, meet competition and improve profit level.

  k) Technological developments, particularly the use of computers can quickly change an industry and consumer expectations.

  l) The need for change can also be brought about by new legislation and quality standards which in turn can impact on work patterns.

  m) Research and development is important for bringing about innovation.

  n.) Training needs.may be brought about by many factors involving technological change, new equipment, reorganisation, skill shortages and competitive pressures.

  o) Value can be added to production by raising productivity, total quality, research and development, training, investing in physical resources, reducing pollution and waste and improving working conditions.

Review questions *(Answers can be found in the paragraphs indicated)*

1. Explain what is meant by added value and how it can be increased. (2–3)

2. What are the costs of production in a business? (4–5)

3. In what sense are marketing and production interdependent in a business? (6–8)

4. Outline the key factors to be considered in production planning and control (9–10)

5. What factors need to be taken into account when developing a product design strategy? (11–17)

6. How can a business control its stock levels? (19–24)

7. Explain, with the use of an example, the concept of an economic order quantity (26–30)

8. Distinguish between job, batch and flow methods of production. (31–39)

9. Explain the main benefits and features of just-in-time production. (40–44)

10. How can an organisation's human resource management policies have an effect on added value in production? (45–70)

11. Why is productivity important to organisations? (58–61)

12. Identify the main reasons why business organisations need to add value. (71)

13. In what ways does technological change affect organisations? (73–78)

14. What other aspects of change can impact on production? (79–82)

15. Why is research and development important for innovation and what problems does it bring? (83–91)

16. What is training and why is it needed? (92–99)

17. How can the costs of training be justified? (100–104)

18. Summarise the main ways in which value can be added to production. (108–109)

Assignment – Analysing Production in Business **Element 5.1**

You are asked to prepare a report which

1) describes ways in which businesses can add value

2) explains why they add value through production

3) identifies and gives examples of changes in production

4) analyses the effects of changes in production on any business organisation of your choosing including the reasons for the change(s) taking place and its effect on the business, its employees, customers and suppliers.

5) describes at least 3 examples of ways in which businesses may improve production.

17 Employment Trends

This chapter considers the types of employment in the UK, the changing nature of employment in recent years and likely future trends. It covers:

- ❏ Labour Market
- ❏ Sources of Information
- ❏ Working Population
- ❏ Occupational Distribution
- ☑ Types of Employment
- ❏ Full-time
- ☑ Part-time
- ☑ Job Share
- ☑ Permanent/Temporary Work
- ❏ Contracting-out
- ☑ Temp Agencies
- ❏ Self-employment
- ☑ Sub-contracting

- ❏ Methods of Payment
- ❏ Fringe Benefits
- ☑ Employment Features and Trends
- ❏ New Contractual Arrangements
- ❏ Future Employment Trends
- ❏ Skill Shortages
- ❏ Training to Develop Skills
- ❏ Wage Differentials
- ❏ Employment and the European Union
- ❏ Economic, Social and Political Effects of Unemployment
- ❏ The Government and Unemployment

Labour Market

1. Labour is defined as the total of human effort used in the production of goods or provision of services. It includes both the number of hours worked and the physical and mental skills used. The total supply of labour depends initially upon the size of the population, which in turn depends on factors such as birth rates, death rates and migration. It also depends upon peoples' geographical mobility, motivation, interests and abilities, the cost of training, the time needed to develop skills and wage rates offered.

2. A firm or industry which uses a proportionately large amount of labour and relatively small amount of capital is said to be **labour intensive**, that is, it has high labour costs. Publishing, for example, is labour intensive, whereas printing is **capital intensive** because it uses more capital than labour. Rapid developments in new technology are increasingly enabling many organisations to replace labour and become more capital intensive.

3. The labour market consists, on the supply side of individual workers or trade unions negotiating for them on a collective basis, and on the demand side of firms that require labour as a factor input in the production process. The demand for labour, therefore, is indirect in that it is derived from the demand for production.

Sources of information

4. Throughout this text we have identified a variety of sources of data which organisations can use to find out about the markets and environment in which they operate. Information about employment trends and workforce performance is available from government publications produced by the Central Statistical Office and Employment Department. Collectively such information is usually referred to as LMI i.e. Labour Market Intelligence.

5. **Examples include:**
   - ❐ Monthly Digest of Statistics
   - ❐ Annual Abstract of Statistics
   - ❐ Employment Gazette
   - ❐ Labour Market and Skills Trends ⎫ published monthly
   - ❐ Employment News ⎭

6. **Other sources include:**
   - ❐ Local TEC's and Job Centres
   - ❐ Local Authority Economic Development Units
   - ❐ CBI Quarterly Industrial Trends Survey
   - ❐ Newspapers, journals and magazines such as the Economist
   - ❐ Health and Safety Executive
   - ❐ Equal Opportunities Commission
   - ❐ UK and EU National and Regional Computer Based Data (e.g. SECOS)

7. The International Yearbook of Labour Statistics, produced by the International Labour Office provides information on employment, unemployment, hours of work, wages, consumer prices, occupational injuries and labour costs for 180 countries, some covering a 10 year period.

Labour Force Survey (LFS)

8. The LFS is conducted quarterly by the Office of Population Censuses and Surveys on behalf of the Employment Department. It covers a sample of 60,000 households in Britain and asks questions about employment, self-employment, hours of work, unemployment, education and training, qualifications and other information including age and ethnic origin. Monthly features about the data are published in the Employment Gazette.

Use of data

9. If an organisation is to both attract suitably skilled labour whilst still controlling costs to remain competitive then LMI can be useful for this purpose. It enables it to compare its own policies with other organisations and national trends on a range of issues.

10. **Examples could include:**
    - ❐ hours of work and wage rates in the industry
    - ❐ fringe benefits such as holidays and working conditions
    - ❐ training budgets and number of days training per employee
    - ❐ equal opportunities such as the proportion of male and female workers or the ethnic mix of the workforce
    - ❐ health and safety including the number of accidents and absence from work caused by such problems.

Task 1	**5.2 (C3.4)**

1. Visit a local library and identify 10 potential sources of employment data.

2. Briefly describe each source and the type of data which it provides.

3. How might the information be of interest to a company considering building a new factory in your area?

Working population

11. Not everyone works, however, and therefore it is the number of people who work or are available for work that provides the supply of labour. The **working population** therefore consists of everyone with a job, those registered as unemployed and the self-employed.

12. In the UK the total working population has gradually increased since the war and is now approximately 28 million, of which over 15 million are men. The main reason for this is the increase in the number of women who now work. The working population, as a proportion of the total population, has increased from 45% in 1976 to over 50% in 1993. However, approximately 3 million people are unemployed.

13. The size of the working population depends upon the

   ❒ size of the total population

   ❒ number of people in the 16–65 age group

   ❒ number of married women who return to work

   ❒ number of people over 16 still in full-time education

   ❒ number of people of retirement age still at work.

14. Changes in the composition of the working population are important because it also affects the demand for goods and services. For example, working women have more money to spend on clothes and leisure activities, but have less time for shopping and therefore buy more ready prepare 'convenience' foods rather than fresh food.

15.

Manpower in Britain 1980–90

Thousands (as at June), seasonally adjusted

	1980	1985	1986	1987	1988	1989	1990
Employees in employment [a]	22.965	21,414	21,379	21,586	22,266	22,670	22,864
Self-employed	2,103	2,614	2,633	2,869	2,988	3,253	3,298
Unemployed [b]	1,274	3,019	3,121	2,839	2,299	1,791	1,618
Armed forces	323	326	322	319	316	308	303
Work-related govt training programmes [c]	–	176	226	311	343	462	424
Workforce [d]	26,759	27,743	27,877	28,077	28,347	28,486	28,509

Sources: Dept of Employment and Northern Ireland Dept of Economic Development
a Part-time workers are counted as full units
b Figures are adjusted for discontinuities and exclude school-leavers
c Not seasonally adjusted
d Comprises employees in employment, the self-employed, the armed forces, particpiants in work related government training programmes and the unemployed (including school leavers)

16. The key points which can be identified from this table include:

   ❒ In 1990 the total workforce had increased to 28.5 million.

   ❒ A substantial increase in self-employment to nearly 3.3 million.

   ❒ Wide fluctuations in unemployment during the period.

Task 2	**5.2.1 (N3.1, N3.3)**

1. Using some of the many sources of government statistics available in libraries update the manpower information table with data since 1990.

2. Comment on any changes and trends since 1990 and try to give reasons as to why they have taken place.

Occupational distribution

17. The number of people employed in different jobs is referred to as the **occupational distribution**. Occupations can be classified under three main headings:

   Primary – agriculture, forestry, fishing, mining and quarrying

   Secondary – manufacturing and construction

   Tertiary (Services) – transport, distribution, financial services, catering and hotels, and national and local government.

18.

Changes in the Occupational Distribution of the Working Population in Britain between 1980 and 1991 from *Britain '93 – An Official Handbook*

Industry or service (1980 Standard Industrial Classification)	Thousands (as at June)				Per cent (1991)
	1980	1983	1987	1991	
Primary sector	**1,099**	**998**	**820**	**703**	**3.2**
Agriculture, forestry and fishing	373	350	321	272	1.3
Energy and water supply	727	648	499	431	2.0
Manufacturing[b]	**6,937**	**5,525**	**5,167**	**4,720**	**21.7**
Construction	**1,243**	**1,044**	**1,013**	**939**	**4.3**
Services	**13,712**	**13,501**	**14,889**	**15,381**	**70.7**
Wholesale distribution and repairs	1,173	1,150	1,240	1,217	5.6
Retail distribution	2,177	2,005	2,123	2,143	9.9
Hotels and catering	972	963	1,113	1,230	5.7
Transport	1,049	912	902	913	4.2
Postal services and communications	437	433	448	415	1.9
Banking, finance and insurance	1,695	1,875	2,337	2,658	12.2
Public administration	1,980	1,918	2,046	1,923	8.8
Education	1,642	1,592	1,708	1,741	8.0
Health	1,258	1,294	1,315	1,467	6.7
Other services	1,327	1,359	1,657	1,674	7.7
Total	**22,991**	**21,067**	**21,889**	**21,743**	**100.0**

Sources: Department of Employment and Northern Ireland Department of Economic Development.

[a] Figures are not seasonally adjusted.

[b] In June 1991 employment in the main sectors of manufacturing industry included 691,000 in office machinery, electrical engineering and instruments; 678,000 in mechanical engineering; 544,000 in food, drink and tobacco; 439,000 in textiles, leather, footwear and clothing; 474,000 in paper products, printing and publishing; 497,000 in timber, wooden furniture, rubber and plastics; 303,000 in chemicals and man-made fibres; and 220,000 in motor vehicles and parts.

Note: Differences between totals and the sums of their component parts are due to rounding.

19. The above table shows the main changes in the distribution of the working population between 1980 and 1991. These can be summarised as follows:

   ❏ A fall in the numbers employed in primary industries
   ❏ A fall in employment in the secondary industries
   ❏ An increase in employment in the tertiary sector.

20. In fact these changes have been taking place throughout the twentieth century. The main reasons for these are:

   ❏ The increased use of new technology and mechanisation which has improved productivity and replaced labour. For example, fertilisers and tractors have helped to increase output in agriculture, computers and robots in manufacturing industries.

   ❏ The general growth of the service sector in the UK, particularly insurance, banking and financial services although 1993 and 1994 have seen many redundancies in these areas due to increasing automation.

Types of Employment

21. Your grandfather probably worked full-time, walked or cycled to work and had only one or two jobs in his whole working life. Your grandmother possibly never worked at all. However, it is now increasingly likely that the average person will change their occupation at least 3-5 times during their working life, i.e. they will be **occupationally mobile** and also experience some periods of unemployment. Work is also increasingly likely to involve more **geographical mobility of labour**. That is, people may have to move to a different area in order to find jobs.

22. This is because as society changes so the demand for goods and services changes with it. Further developments in new computerised technology will also continue to change both what we buy and how it is made. Therefore, as some industries decline new ones, demanding different skills, will develop to take their place.

23. The type of employment is also likely to vary with people no longer automatically being employed in full-time permanent jobs. Instead part-time and temporary work is increasingly likely, as also is the growth in self-employment. This paragraph mentions a number of different types of employment which are explained below. The breakdown between full and part-time employment is show in the following diagram.

24.

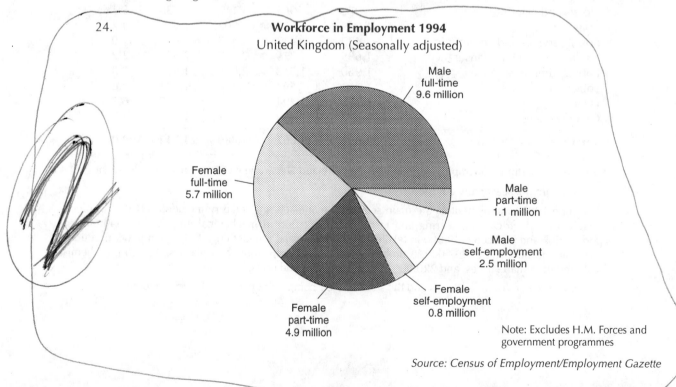

Workforce in Employment 1994
United Kingdom (Seasonally adjusted)

Male full-time 9.6 million
Female full-time 5.7 million
Male part-time 1.1 million
Male self-employment 2.5 million
Female self-employment 0.8 million
Female part-time 4.9 million

Note: Excludes H.M. Forces and government programmes

Source: Census of Employment/Employment Gazette

25. **Employers**

    Most people work for someone else. Whether it be the government, a large multi-national company or small local shop they are classed as employed and have a contract of employment with that organisation.

Full-Time

26. Most workers in the UK still work full-time for five days a week, although the actual hours and days of work depend upon the type of job, for example, most shop workers are expected to work on Saturdays, with a day off during the week. Teachers, on the other hand, work Mondays to Fridays.

27. The basic working week is in the range of 37.5 to 40 hours for manual workers and 35 to 38 for non-manual workers. The actual hours worked, however, average nearer 41 for men and 37 for women due largely to overtime, most of which is worked in manual occupations.

Part-time

28. Where people work for less than 16 hours per week they are usually classed as being part-time. Although the official Department of Employment figure includes anyone working less than 30 hours.

    The number of part-time jobs have increased by over 35% in the past 10 years, and now at almost 7 million represent over a quarter of the total UK workforce. Many part-time jobs are being taken by females, particularly mothers returning to work and the number of such jobs is expected to continue to rise.

29. Many of these jobs are, however, replacing ones which previously were full-time. A well-known example is the Burton Group which announced in late 1992 that it was replacing 1000 full-time posts with 3000 part-time ones. The Gateway Supermarket chain has pursued a similar policy in recent years.

30. The **benefits to employers** of employing part-time staff include

    ❏ increased flexibility of the work-force because staff can be employed at busy times e.g. lunchtimes, evenings, weekends rather than during the 'normal' 9-5 day.

    ❏ reduced wage costs because less overtime is needed, often expensive because it is paid at time and a half or double-time.

    ❏ reduced national insurance costs because these are related to wages/salaries

    ❏ part-time staff can be asked to work extra hours to help overcome short-term staffing problems and

    ❏ they can be used to meet skill shortages. Many further education colleges use part-time staff with particular specialist skills for just a few hours a week.

31. Many **employees** also **prefer part-time work** because

    ❏ It can fit around their domestic circumstances e.g. working mums hours can often be organised around children at school.

    ❏ It provides an income whilst leaving time for leisure and other activities.

    ❏ It is preferable to being unemployed.

    ❏ Hourly rates are often the same as for full-time workers.

    ❏ It provides extra income for people who cannot or do not want to work full-time, e.g. students, pensioners.

Job Share

32. Some organisations allow 2 (or occasionally more) people to share a full-time job. That is, each works part-time, receiving half the total salary for the job for working half the required hours. There may be some overlap in the hours to improve communication and ensure a smooth transition from one person to the other.

Task 3   5.2.2, 5.2.3 (C3.4)

Source: *Institute for Employment Research 1994 from Labour Market and Skill Trends 1995/6.*

1. Identify and comment on possible reasons for the key trends in the above data including the predictions for the year 2001.

2. Compare, examine and comment on the trends in the organisation where you work or study or any other organisation which you know well.

Permanent and Temporary Work

33. Most jobs are **permanent** in that whether people work full or part-time they are continuously employed for an indefinite period of time. This gives them a certain amount of job security with a guaranteed regular income and the possibility of a long-term career.

34. Some jobs, however, are **temporary** in that they are only available for a limited period of time to meet a specific need. Whether full or part-time at the end of the contract period temporary employees are automatically laid off.

35. Examples of temporary employment include

   ❏ **fixed-term contracts** which may be for a few weeks, months or several years, e.g. an employee may be taken on to cover a maternity leave or to fulfil a special order.

   ❏ **Casual work** where people are taken on as and when required usually for fairly short periods. The building trade is a good example, particularly when labourers are needed.

   ❏ **Seasonal work** for example jobs in tourism, fruit picking or special times such as Christmas when work is only available for specific periods.

   ❏ **Temporary workers** may sometimes be taken on for an unspecified period to meet a specific need e.g. to cover absenteeism through sickness or holidays.

Contracting-out

36. Nowadays it is becoming increasingly common for contracting-out (or out-sourcing) to take place. That is, instead of employing their own staff one organisation contracts with another to supply the labour to do jobs such as cleaning, catering and computer maintenance. This trend is particularly prevalent in the public sector where the government has encouraged it. The BBC, for example, now has many programmes made by private companies, whilst the Civil Service, Local Authorities, Universities and Colleges must invite private firms to bid for contracts such as cleaning and waste disposal in the search for efficiency savings.

Task 4   **5.2.1, 5.2.2, 5.2.3 (C3.4)**

OUTSOURCING BECOMING MORE POPULAR

According to a recent survey nearly half of British companies are likely to contract out the services of part of their organisation in the next five years.

As more and more businesses look for ways to improve efficiency, outsourcing of organisational functions is gaining popularity, with 43 per cent saying they would probably call in the services of external providers for one or more of their departments in the near future.

Only 33 per cent of the companies interviewed said they would not be outsourcing any function in the next five years.

Top of the list for outsourcing was information technology, followed by legal departments, human resources and staffing arrangements including security. Marketing and accounting services are also seen as potential outsourcing functions.

1. Explain, with examples, what is meant by outsourcing. Include local examples if possible.

2. Why is it becoming more popular?

3. Comment on why you think the trend is likely to continue to grow and the likely impact on jobs.

Temp Agencies

37 Sometimes an organisation may employ temporary staff itself through its usual recruitment and selection procedures. Alternatively it may use a 'temp' agency such as Alfred Marks, Brook Street or Hays.

38. Temp agencies tend to specialise in particular types of work such as accounting, computing or secretarial work and have a 'pool' of suitably qualified staff who can be called upon at short notice. The employer usually pays a fee to the Agency but saves the cost of advertising and selecting staff. The Agency will also agree the hourly rate with the employer although the employee will receive slightly less to cover the costs of administration.

Task 5   **5.2.1. 5.2.2 (C3.4)**

1. Using a copy of your local Yellow Pages and/or Thomson Directory find the names of at least two agencies which could help if your organisation required temporary staff for the following jobs:

    Construction worker, HGV driver, a laboratory technician, VDU operator, secretary, computer specialist, accountant, sales/marketing person, warehouse staff, receptionist.

2. In the local press find examples of at least 4 different temporary jobs.

3. Comment on why you think that some organisations choose to recruit from agencies whilst others prefer to recruit directly themselves and the advantages/disadvantages of each method.

Self-employment

39. This is discussed in more detail in Unit 8 but it is important to note here that an increasing number of people, particularly those who cannot find a job or are made redundant, are deciding to become self-employed. That is, choosing to work for themselves rather than an employer.

40. Many small businesses, however, fail and therefore if considering this option it is important to carry out research to evaluate the idea, its market potential and from this develop a business plan. A typical business plan outlines the objectives of the business, sales and marketing ideas, production plans and the resources needed including finance and financial data needed to support it.

Sub-Contracting

41. In some industries, for example building and construction, it is common to find sub-contracting. That is, self-employed individuals and/or companies working for someone else. A general building company, for example, might win a contract to build a new leisure centre. In order to be able to complete the job, however, it needs to sub-contract some of the work to decorators and electricians because it does not employ such workers itself. This specialisation and sub-contracting helps to increase efficiency and reduce costs.

Task 6   5.2.1. 5.2.2 5.2.3 (C3.4)

Not everybody who is self-employed works full-time.

Can you think of any jobs and situations where people may be self-employed on a part-time basis.

Try to identify examples from the organisation where you work or study and others from the local area.

Methods of Payment

42. Regardless of how they are employed, there are a number of different ways in which workers may be paid:

   ❏ **Hourly or time rates.** Often wages are paid on the basis of so much per hour, for example £4.00 This method is often used to pay factory workers.

   ❏ **Flat rate.** This is a fixed amount per week or month, for example £850 per month. Most office workers are paid in this way.

   ❏ **Overtime.** If an employee works more than the usual hours, they may be paid overtime, which for example, may be paid at time-and-a-half or double-time (perhaps for working Sunday).

   Example

	Wages
Basic £4.00 per hour for 38 hours	£162.00
3 hours at time-and-a-half (£6.00 per hour)	18.00
3 hours at double-time (£8.00 per hour)	24.00
	£204.00

   ❏ **Piece-Work rates.** This is another common method of payment in factories. The work is broken down into 'pieces' and a worker is paid for each 'piece' produced. The more they produce, the more they are paid. For example a sewing machine operator may be paid 25p for each sleeve sewn on a coat. If she sews 500 sleeves in a week, she would earn £125.00.

   ❏ **Commission.** People who work in selling are often paid only for what they sell. This is usually a percentage of the value of the total sales, for example, a person might be paid commission at 10%. If they sell £1500 worth of goods in a week, they would receive £150.

   ❏ **Fees.** Professional people like dentists, solicitors and accountants charge a fee for their services, for example, £55 per hour or per visit.

   ❏ **Bonus.** Often employees are paid an additional amount for completing a particular job on time, for example, motorway workers. Other forms of bonus include extra payment to workers at Christmas or holiday times as a reward for hard work or loyalty (for staying with a firm).

   ❏ **Profit Sharing.** Sometimes at the end of the financial year, a firm will give employees a share of its profits. This may be given in cash or in the form of a number of the company's shares.

Task 7   **5.2.2 (C3.2)**

Consider which method of payment you feel is most appropriate and state why in each of the following situations:

1. A door-to-door salesman

2. The Chief Executive of a large public limited company.

3. A shop assistant required to work alternate weekends.

4. A long distance lorry driver.

5. A shop floor operative working on a three-shift system.

Fringe Benefits

43. In addition to money, many organisations offer other incentives to their workers. These are called **'fringe benefits'** or **'perks of the job',** some examples of which include:

   ❏ Company cars – sales staff, senior managers and directors often have the use of a car.
   ❏ Luncheon Vouchers (LVs) – which can be used to help pay for meals in cafes and restaurants which accept them.
   ❏ Canteens – large firms often provide subsidised low-priced meals for employees.
   ❏ Transport – many firms provide free coaches or cheap transport for their employees.
   ❏ Pension Schemes
   ❏ Help with house purchase, for example low interest loans.
   ❏ Medical facilities, for example nurse on premises.
   ❏ Life Assurance.
   ❏ Sports facilities
   ❏ Good Holidays
   ❏ Discounts on firm's products or services.

44. Fringe benefits can often be of more value to an employee than an increase in pay. This is because most are usually tax free. They may also be used to indicate a person's status in an organisation. A director, for example, would have a higher value car than a Sales Representative, although this perk is now taxable.

Task 8   **5.2.2 (C3.2)**

1. Identify the main methods of payment and any fringe benefits offered by the two organisations studied in the assignment at the end of Chapter 1.

2. Comment on the differences between them.

Employment Features and Trends

45. In the past two decades, jobs have changed substantially and this trend is expected to continue as increasing competition, particularly from Europe, and technological advance bring about more sophisticated products and methods of production leading to the need for new skills. The impact of these changes on the working population includes de-skilling, unemployment, new jobs/skills, wider educational opportunities, new working patterns and new contractual arrangements.

46. **De-skilling**

This has come about because many traditional crafts, for example, printing, tailoring and joinery, have declined or been eliminated as machines have taken over from people. Nowadays, most clothing, publications and furniture no longer rely on the skills of highly trained workers. Whilst robots and computer-aided machines are being used on manufacturing production lines to perform many lower level skills.

47. **Unemployment**

This is a key problem not just in the UK but throughout Europe. New technology increases productivity and leads to the need for less workers. Machines are replacing people and redundancy is becoming more common and socially acceptable. The growth in unemployment has lead to the development of a range of government education and training programmes aimed at helping unemployed people to get back to work.

48. **New jobs/skills**

The rapid development and application of electronic and micro-electronic technologies has created the need for highly skilled specialists, scientists and technicians to develop and maintain computer hardware and software. At the same time, the leisure and tourism industries have also developed as hours of work have been reduced and paid holidays increased. Manual workers' holidays, for example, have increased on average from 2 weeks in 1961 to 4 weeks in 1990.

49. **Wider Education and Training Opportunities**

The Government has introduced measures to make further and higher education more accessible and responsive to the needs of the UK economy. Thus more people will have the opportunity to participate in education and training and therefore to improve their qualifications and skill levels.

50. The number of young people entering higher education, for example, rose from 1 in 8 in 1980 to 1 in 5 in 1990 and is expected to reach 1 in 3 by the year 2000. Whilst National Vocational Qualifications (NVQs) and General National Vocational Qualifications (GNVQs) are designed to make qualifications more relevant to the needs of employment by basing them on standards of competence set by industry.

51. **Work patterns**

Perhaps the most significant developments taking place are in the patterns of work.

New technology has lead to completely new methods of work and in the 1990's the development of **working from home**.

❏ People now need to be more **flexible** and ready and willing to adapt to changes. The concept of the traditional **working week** is becoming more difficult to define. It is estimated that three quarters of the UK workforce now operate flexibly.

An increase in the number of **temporary and part-time jobs**, often replacing full-time permanent positions, in order to cut costs as well as create flexibility. Some organisations also allow **job sharing** whereby two people perform a full-time job between them.

The growth of **self-employment** which has been strongly encouraged by the Government to help regenerate the economy out of recession. Many examples can be found in the catering, construction, retail and transport industries.

❏ In the past, it was common for people to have only one or perhaps two jobs in their working life. Increasingly, now and in the future, **people have many different jobs** often requiring re-training or an updating of skills and probably with some periods of unemployment in-between jobs.

❏ The **early retirement** of people from work in their 50's is another factor likely to continue as people prefer leisure to work.

❏ **More women are joining the workforce.** Modern domestic appliances have changed the role of women in the home, whilst the changing nature of work away from heavy manual tasks, the introduction of equal opportunities legislation, the desire to achieve higher standards of living, the increase in single-parent families and changing social attitudes towards women working have added further impetus.

Task 9   **5.2.1, 5.2.2, 5.2.3, 5.2.4 (C3.4)**

STAY AT HOME COMMUTERS

Commuters could soon be a thing of the past. Up to 4 million office workers, roughly 1 in 6 of the working population are expected to plug into their computer terminals by 1995. Companies leading the way in introducing teleworking for staff include telecommunications giant BT, computer firms IBM and ICL, photocopier manufacturer Rank Xerox, chemical company ICI and Prudential Insurance.

BT has announced that junior managers, potentially 8,000 people, will have the right to apply to work from home, and reckons that as many as 1,000 will opt for the deal by the end of 1993. The company calculates that productivity per worker could rise by an average of 45 per cent. Although teleworkers find that household bills for heating, electricity and phones tend to rise, they are still well in pocket because they don't have to pay travel costs. On average, they could be almost £15 a week better off working at home for four days a week and the environmental benefits to the nation would be worth £10.3 billion a year. Some staff miss the companionship of fellow workers so BT has started providing videophones for discussing problems and removing the feeling of isolation. IBM says one in ten of its staff work from home using computer terminals, alongside their work in the office. It is considering introducing telecommuting on a more widespread basis, as it is time-efficient and gives staff more flexibility.

Rank Xerox found the cost of keeping workers in an office, commuting costs and other expenses came to two-and-a-half times their salaries. Sixty were re-employed as freelances and now work from a terminal at home.

National Westminster is very keen on the concept and has several thousand staff members working mainly or wholly from home. It is happy to consider introducing teleworking 'where it fits in and works'.

For staff who cannot work at home, the CBI suggest high technology 'neighbourhood offices' where staff from different firms share resources like telephones, fax machines and video conferencing. The idea being that 'they could drive in with their neighbour each morning and use shared facilities, enjoy meeting people while working for their own respective company. The CBI is also convinced that ending the wear and tear on workers' nerves caused by commuting will give companies better employees in the long run.

BT which is a world leader in piloting 'Teleworking' believes that it can be applied to many jobs, especially where work is highly structured and easily monitored, including those in mail order, ticket agencies, credit checking.

With the help of the above article and by carrying out research in your own area, answer the following. If possible, present your findings in the form of a word processed report. Use examples throughout to illustrate the points which you make.

1.   Explain in full the meaning of teleworking.

2.   Identify its potential benefits and drawbacks.

3.   Teleworking potentially represents the most dramatic change in working practices ever. Consider the likely impact on both individuals and businesses in your locality and on the economy as a whole, assuming it develops as anticipated.

New contractual arrangements

52. As jobs have changed so have the nature of contracts of employment. As discussed in Element 4.1 a contract exists when an employer makes an offer of a job which an employee accepts on consideration of payment. Either party can end the contract by giving the appropriate notice which can vary from one week to several months.

53. The vast majority of jobs are still full-time but the recent rapid growth of temporary and part-time posts now means that employees often do not acquire any employment rights such as protection against unfair dismissal. This is because such rights are usually acquired on the basis of continued employment of at least 2 years. Thus, for example, temporary workers are usually appointed to a fixed term contract offering them employment for a specific period of time such as 6 or 12 months. Traditionally this type of contract has been used for seasonal work like tourism but it is now becoming a normal feature of current employment patterns.

54. Where new employees are appointed to an organisation then clearly they accept the contract offered as it stands. Sometimes, however, organisations seek to alter the contracts of existing employees to meet changing needs.

55. Examples might include:
    - ❏ increasing or decreasing the hours of work
    - ❏ reducing the rate of pay
    - ❏ altering holiday entitlements
    - ❏ moving a job location possibly to another part of the country
    - ❏ introducing new work patterns e.g. shifts or Sunday working
    - ❏ requiring additional or different duties and responsibilities
    - ❏ introducing new technology which changes the nature of a job.

56. Clearly where change is to take place it should be negotiated with employees and/or their trade union representatives in order to avoid breach of contract by employers and potential conflict, stress and dissatisfaction which can affect employees motivation and morale

57. If employees refuse to accept new contracts then they may find themselves being made redundant. If, however, a contract is changed unreasonably or unfairly then they may seek compensation from the courts or an Industrial Tribunal. Alternatively they may themselves choose to walk out and claim 'constructive dismissal' or continue working under protest whilst trying to seek redress.

58. To help ease some of these problems many organisations now include a clause in contracts to the effect that employees must be flexible and adapt to the changing needs of the organisation. If negotiation fails an employer may choose to give notice to employees of proposed changes so that in effect the existing contract ceases and the employee either accepts the new one or leaves. If the changes are 'reasonable' and correct notice is given this practice is likely to be considered as legal if taken to court.

| **Task 10** | **5.2.2, 5.2.3, 5.2.4 (C3.4)** |

BA STRIKE CALLED OFF

The threat to British Airways flights from Gatwick airport was lifted when staff called off a planned strike.

The 1,200 employees were angry that staff previously employed by Dan-Air were being asked to take a 25 per cent pay cut. A BA spokesman said those affected had been offered compensation to change their rates of pay, or could remain on their present terms and conditions if they chose.

'JOB DUMPING' DENIED

Confectionery giant Nestle Rowntree's has defended its move to cut up to 550 workers in Glasgow before switching production to Newcastle and then later to Dijon in France.

continued...

Task 10 continued

It denied that the decision has anything to do with a similar move by Hoover who cut 600 jobs - again in Dijon, France - and announced the creation of 400 new posts in Cambusland, near Glasgow.

Scottish workers voted to accept pay cuts and union curbs for some in the Hoover deal to ensure the new plan.

The Nestle announcement added to concerns about European 'dumping' with firms shutting down factories in one country and moving their work elsewhere to reduce labour costs.

COUNCIL JOB CUTS

Birmingham City Council is to save £40m by cutting 3000 jobs.

The authority which has a workforce of 54,000 - many part-timers - hopes the job losses can be achieved by encouraging staff over 50 to retire with a golden hand-shake.

But unless the offer is taken up by the end of January, compulsory redundancies will be inevitable, council leaders warned.

The Council blames the government for enforcing an £879 million spending ceiling.

UNION ANGER AT TRANSFER PLAN

The Co-operative Bank plans to transfer 133 of its staff to an outside company as part of a £21.5m "strategic partnership" plan.

But union leaders claim terms and conditions for workers will not be the same and there will be no trade union representation.

The banking union BIFU is taking legal advice on the move is unhappy about the consultation, claiming the plan has come like a bolt from the blue,

The articles and advertisements on the previous page illustrate some aspects of the contractual changes which many workers are now starting to face.

1. Identify the aspects involved and the potential impact on the employees concerned.

2. Consider the need for change from the employers point of view.

3. Collect similar articles and advertisements from your local news media and comment on any local trends particularly in respect of the major employers in the area.

Future Employment Trends

59. Notable trends include:

☑ the proportion of jobs in the **service sector** which now accounts for over 70% of jobs in the UK is continuing to rise, whilst those in manufacturing declines.

☑ it is likely that the **growth of private sector** output and employment will continue to increase at the expense of the public sector, particularly with the increase in privatisation.

☑ the number of **part-time jobs** which have increased by 35% in the past 10 years, and now at almost 7 million total over a quarter of the UK workforce, are likely to continue to rise. Many part-time jobs are being taken by mothers returning to work.

☑ the number of **self-employed** is also expected to keep rising. In 1993 it was 3 million compared with 1.2 million in 1979.

60.

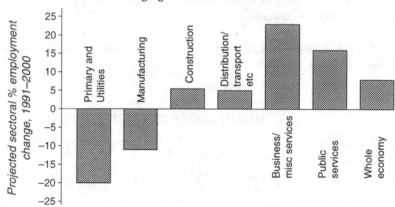

A Changing Industrial Structure

Source: IER

61.

An Ageing Workforce

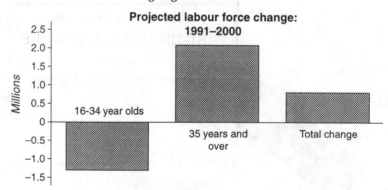

Source: Labour Market and Skills Trends 1993/4 Department of Employment

62. Projected changes by 2001 include:

❏ a **growing labour force** to 28.8 million, an increase of 700,000 compared with 1992.

❏ an **ageing workforce** with 1.8 million more people in the 35-54 age group but 1.2 million fewer aged 16-34.

❏ an **increasing number of women** in the workforce, up to 50% of the total by 2001. In 1991 the government launched Opportunity 2000, an initiative to promote equal career opportunities for women in employment.

❏ a **growth** in the number of **higher education** students by about 50% to 1.5 million.

Task 11   **5.2.1, 5.2.2, 5.2.3, 5.2.4 (C3.4)**

EMPLOYMENT BOOM FOR WOMEN

Eight out of ten of the new jobs created in Britain in the next 12 years will go to women, according to Department of Employment predictions. The number of people in work is forecast to grow by 1.4 million by the year 2006 - but only 300,000 of these will be men.

This will have important implications for employers including the increasing demand it will bring for workplace childcare, nursery places and flexible working arrangements. But it will also severely affect family life, with the upheaval caused by a complete reversal of the traditional male and female roles of provider and carer in many homes.

The Government forecasts continue a 20-year trend where the number of working women has increased by a third from 8.7 million to 11.7 million.

The proportion of working-age women with jobs is forecast to rise from the 1994 level of 71 per cent to 75.4 per cent by 2006.

Involvement is expected to grow fastest in the 25-44 age group - those most likely to raise families.

70.7 per cent of women aged 25 to 34 are currently in some form of employment, but that is expected to rise to 80.6 per cent. For those aged 35 to 44, the increase will be from 77 per cent to 85.2 per cent.

The workforce is forecast to rise from 27.1 million to around 28.5 million by 2006. The fact that the majority of the extra jobs will be for women will see the female proportion of the total workforce rise from 44 to 46 per cent.

Most of the jobs will be in the service industries such as catering, leisure and retail, as well as caring occupations and on a part-time basis. This has the advantage of fitting in with family responsibilities but the disadvantage of being low paid.

However, high levels of unemployment are likely to be maintained for more than a decade.

While the number of people in work will rise by about 1.5 million, the working age population will rise from 34.6 million to 36.2 million between now and 2006 - an increase of 1.6 million.

These figures could, however, be affected considerably by the positive effects of the Single European Market on manufacturing employment, the greater movement of workers between the European Union countries, together with the possible influx of migrants from Hong Kong and even Eastern Europe.

Another factor identified by the study is a general increase in the age of the working population, in line with the trend for the population as a whole.

This means that the 'ageism' which exists in many organisations will have to be overcome while demand for young workers could mean that they receive premium salaries whilst some jobs, such as check-out operators in supermarkets and office clerks may need to move away from traditional employment patterns.

Concern expressed about the need to protect the rights of increasing numbers of part-time workers has lead recently to new legislation being introduced.

Read the above article, which is based on media reports, and complete the following:

1. Outline the reasons for the headline 'employment boom for women'.

2. What are the implications of this for employers?

3. How could it affect family life?

4. Many of the new jobs created are likely to be part-time in service industries. With the use of examples explain these terms. Why was new legislation needed to protect part-time workers?

continued...

Task 11 continued

5. What are the governments predictions in respect of future unemployment?

6. The last paragraph refers to 'ageism', 'premium salaries', and 'traditional employment patterns'. Explain each of these terms and try to illustrate your answer with the use of local examples.

7. Now using two organisations which you know well investigate the differences in employment between them. Identify the main employment features and trends and why they have come about.

8. Finally consider how the issues raised in the article could affect each of the organisations over the next ten years.

Skill shortages

63. These exist when there are insufficient people available with the skills needed to perform jobs which need doing. The **'skills gap'** is measured by the difference between the total demand for a skill and the total supply.

64. There will always be some mismatch between the supply of and demand for skills because:

❐ demand changes with new technology, new products and new firms whilst

❐ supply alters as people join or rejoin the labour force. Because learning new skills requires training supply cannot usually respond immediately to changes in demand.

Task 12   **5.1.3 (C3.3, N3.3)**

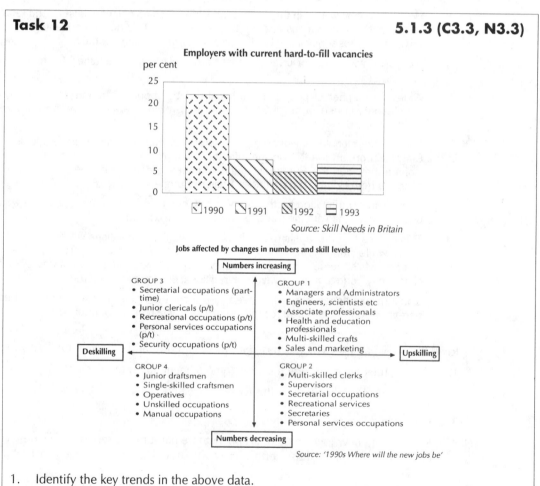

1. Identify the key trends in the above data.

2. Why is this information important and who needs to know about it?

65. Since 1990 the Department of Employment has carried out a major annual survey to identify skill needs based on hard-to-fill vacancies in some 4,000 organisations employing over 25 people. In 1990 the figure was over 22% but in 1993 this had fallen to nearer 6%. It is, however, likely to increase again as the economy recovers from recession.

66. The main areas of skills shortage for several years have been in:
   - ❏ hotel and catering
   - ❏ textiles
   - ❏ electrical and electronic engineering
   - ❏ health associate professionals
   - ❏ sales representatives and
   - ❏ information technology and computing.

Training to develop skills

67. The effect of increasing computerisation and other forms of automation means that the level of skills needed by employees is also increasing and therefore training and development is necessary. The survey suggests that approximately 80% of employers provide some form of training. On average this amounts to about 5 days off-the-job for the 40% of employees who receive training, making an average of about 2 days per employee overall. The amount of off-the-job training has tended to be reduced in the 1990's due to the effect of the recession.

Wage differentials

68. The wages which workers receive for different jobs will vary for a number of reasons. As a general rule, wage rates are determined by **supply and demand**. That is where there are a lot of workers who are able to do a particular job, wages are likely to remain low. Where there is a shortage of workers, wages are likely to be higher.

69. The following examples explain this in more detail and also include other reasons for what are called **wage differentials.**

   - ❏ Certain types of work require **highly specialised skills** for which people may need to study or train for many years. Therefore, once qualified they receive higher rates of pay, for example, doctors, solicitors and accountants.

   - ❏ **Unskilled workers** receive lower rates of pay because very little knowledge or training is needed to do the job, for example, cleaners and labourers.

   - ❏ Managers, supervisors and foremen are usually paid more than workers because they have a **responsible** job.

   - ❏ Regional differences such as **a high level of unemployment** in an area like Northern Ireland or the North East of England is likely to keep wages lower because there will be more workers available for each job.

   - ❏ Likewise, where **skill shortages** exist, as for example in catering, textiles, sales and technology, wages may be higher to attract labour.

   - ❏ From time to time the **Government** also controls wages, particularly in the public sector industries.

   - ❏ Whilst equal opportunities **legislation** means that women must now receive the same pay as men for similar work whereas in the past they would probably have been paid less.

   - ❏ The **power of the trade unions** in an industry can also affect the wages of workers, for example, car and print workers get higher wages because the unions are well organised, whilst in retailing and catering, unions are weak and therefore wages relatively low.

Task 13   5.1.4, 5.2.2, 5.3.3 (C3.2)

Consider the following list of occupations: chauffeur, gardener, finance director, dentist, road sweeper, coal miner, lorry driver, electrician, receptionist, computer programmer. State with reasons, in which you would expect to receive the highest and in which the lowest wages.

Employment and the European Union

70. It is increasingly recognised nowadays that good human resource management is about co-operation and working together in the mutual interests of organisations and employees. This has been emphasised in recent years by the impact of factors such as technological change, the weakening of trade union power and the recession of the early 1990's. Industrial relations issues are therefore now dealt with more by negotiation and consultation with the emphasis on avoiding conflict wherever possible.

71. Worker consultation and participation is being increasingly encouraged throughout Europe as illustrated by the Maastricht Treaty. Among the aims of its Social Chapter are to:

    ❑ raise and standardise working conditions

    ❑ introduce minimum wages, minimum holidays and maximum working hours

    ❑ increase rights for part-time workers and

    ❑ increase equal opportunities and worker consultation.

72. Although at the present time the UK government does not support all of these, nonetheless it is likely that eventually they will be introduced via EU directives (see Element 1.3).

Task 14   5.2.1, 5.2.4 (C3.4)

VICTORY FOR PART-TIMERS

A decision by the House of Lords in March '94 means that part-timers now qualify for compensation in the event of redundancy or unfair dismissal after two years service instead of five, giving them equality with full-time employees.

There are about 5.8 million work part-time - defined as between eight and 16 hours a week - and 4.7 million of these are women.

A test case was brought by the Equal Opportunities Commission on behalf of a part-time school cleaner, sacked just before she would have qualified for employment protection rights.

The judges decided that, because most part-timers are female, the five-year rule was in breach of European sex equality laws.

Employment lawyers were studying the implications but, because the Government accepted EU equality laws on to its statute book in 1978, it may have to accept liability from that date.

It could mean employers facing a bill for millions of back-dated claims.

Individuals would have to instigate industrial tribunals to establish they has been made redundant or unfairly dismissed. But unions believe thousands of cases could be in the pipeline.

It is the second recent case of EU regulations being used to overturn national law. The same device was used to win compensation for servicewomen sacked for becoming pregnant. Back-dated claims have flooded in and could cost taxpayers £100 million.

continued...

Task 14 continued

FEWER WOMEN MANAGERS

New statistics suggest that the number of women managers is falling in Britain.

The latest national management salary survey published by the Institute of Management and Remuneration Economics shows that the number of female managers and directors in the UK's largest organisations is on the decline.

They number 9.5 per cent - down from a high of 10.2 per cent. Only 2.8 per cent of directors and 9.8 per cent of managers are women.

Many companies do not use human resources as effectively as they could and many women are overlooked for promotion and engaged in jobs well below their full capacity.

BETTER DEAL FOR WORKING WOMEN

Almost a quarter of the nation's workforce is now covered by the Opportunity 2000 campaign, launched in 1991 by the Prime Minister, which has achieved "practical improvements" for women.

The number of employers joining the campaign has grown from 61 to 141 and includes Government departments, banks, supermarkets, British Rail, and BT.

Every organisation joining Opportunity 2000 reviews its policies towards its female employees, with the aim of improving their career opportunities.

WOMEN TO WORK LONGER

The retirement age for women is being raised from 60 to 65, bringing them into line with men.

All women now under 44 will be affected by the change, which will be phased in over ten years starting in 2010.

By 2020, Britain's pension age will be broadly in line with most European countries. In the United States it is being raised to 67.

The move reflects the Government's determination to encourage more people to make private or company pension arrangements rather than relying on the State.

Making women work five years longer to qualify for the state pension will ultimately save the Treasury at least £5 billion a year.

Increasing financial demands from an ageing population mean an ever-shrinking workforce might eventually be unable to support its pensioners. Spending on the state pension has rocketed from £21 billion in 1978 to £26 billion in 1993.

Women also generally live longer than men and spend more of their lives than they used to in paid employment.

Read the above articles and then consider what they reveal about the following:

1. attitudes towards equal opportunities

2. the potential impact of EU legislation on employers

3. the role of the Equal Opportunities Commission

4. the potential impact of future employment trends and work performance.

Economic Effects of Unemployment

73. These include the:

-   ❏ **Cost to the exchequer**. It is estimated that the payment of benefit, loss of tax revenue and provision of training schemes means that it costs the government between £8,000-£10,000 per annum for each unemployed person.

- ❑ **Waste of resources.** Unemployment means that the economy is operating below its full potential and a valuable resource is being 'lost', i.e. the skills, knowledge, production and income of the individuals concerned.

- ❑ **Inequalities of income distribution**. Despite receiving benefits, unemployed people are still worse off financially than those in employment.

- ❑ **Growth of the 'underground' or black economy**. That is, economic activity which takes place but is not declared for tax purposes. This is always going on but is more likely when people are unemployed because they often do 'jobs on the side' to supplement income

Social Effects of Unemployment

89. These include the:

- ❑ **Work ethic.** Unemployed people become demoralised and lose the will to work.

- ❑ **Loss of status. A** jobless person loses the status which a job gives.

- ❑ **Crime and vandalism**. The frustration, boredom and deprivation of unemployment often leads to mindless vandalism and increases in theft and other crimes.

- ❑ **Health**. Unemployed people experience falling living standards. This can lead to poor nutrition, depression and general ill health. Personal relationships can also suffer.

Political Effects of Unemployment

90. Unemployment is an important political issue which can have a major effect on how people vote in local and national elections. It also influences government policies. The government proposals on how unemployment can be tackled. 'Competitiveness and employment' is discussed in Element 5.3.

Task 15   5.2.4 (C3.4)

£12BN DOLE MISERY

The Government is likely to spend about £12 billion on unemployment in 1993 as the nation's dole queues continue to grow.

That would cover the cost of the Channel Tunnel – the biggest and most expensive project undertaken in Britain – almost one-and-a-half times. Unemployment reached 3 million in January 1993 when the number out of work for more than a year leapt to 1,030,000, the highest total for five years. A fifth of those are between 18 and 24.

The total, which rose by 75,000 in the three months to January, has more than doubled since October 1990. Long-term unemployment is climbing everywhere but London, the South and East Anglia are worst hit.

Analysts believe unemployment will continue rising throughout the year and could peak at around 3.3m in mid-1994.

The previous jobless record was 3,124,000 reached in July 1986.

The DSS rule of thumb on unemployment benefits is that every 100,000 people joining the dole queues adds about £350m to benefit payouts.

MPs and Trade Union leaders have called for an urgent package of measures to give people the hope that comes through quality training, help to get the long-term unemployed back to work, and investment in areas like construction that will generate jobs and growth.

1. Identify the key trends in unemployment.

2. Find out what actually happened to unemployment in 1994. Did it peak?

3. What is the cost of unemployment to the government and economy?

4. What action could be taken to alleviate the problem?

Effects of Unemployment on Organisations

76. These include:

- ❐ **Reduced demand** which can result in falling sales and profits.

- ❐ **Wage rates** are forced lower because there is a large pool of labour available. This may not be the case in skills shortage areas such a high technology.

- ❐ **Trade union power** is reduced because they have less members and the threat of further job losses. Thus, it is easier for organisations to introduce change without strong resistance.

The Government and Employment

77. The Government plays an important part in the labour market.

- ❐ It is a **large employer of labour.** The government pays the wages of workers in the public sector and in recent years it has issued 'guidelines' saying that their pay increases should not be in excess of a certain percentage, a range of 1–3%.

- ❐ **Wages Councils** were set up to decide minimum wages and working conditions in some areas of work where unions are weak, for example, catering, retailing, clothing and agriculture. These were abolished in the Trade Union Reform and Employment Rights Act 1993.

- ❐ It can introduce **prices and incomes policies** which attempt to limit price increases and prevent large pay increases. The present Conservative government has not used this policy. It has, however, in recent years limited public sector pay rises to no more than 1–3%.

- ❐ It may pass **new laws** which affect both workers and employers. For example the Employment Protection Act 1975 which set up ACAS, the Health & Safety at Work Act 1974, and the Trade Union Act 1984 which states that before taking industrial action, a union must first obtain the support of its members through a secret ballot (vote).

- ❐ Through its **regional policy** it offers financial incentives and other measures which can influence business location and attract inward investment, and therefore affect employment in particular industrial areas.

Task 16   **5.2.3, 5.2.4 (C3.4)**

THE DAY A TOWN ALMOST DIED

Over 15,000 jobs came under threat when the Dutch owned truck and van maker Leyland-DAF fell into receivership in February 1993. Administrators moved onto plant sites to try to save its UK operation after banks refused to approve a £100m three-year restructuring plan for the parent company. More than 5,500 Leyland-DAF jobs in Birmingham, Glasgow and Leyland, near Preston were at risk, plus 10,000 more in UK component suppliers. In Leyland, where 2,200 are employed, shopkeepers were steeling themselves for a shutdown.

Greengrocer Barbara Smith said: 'If the factory closes it will turn this into a ghost town. Many businesses will go to the wall.'

DIY shop boss Gordon Watson said: 'Men who are paid off won't have much to spend. I heard the maximum even a long-server will get is £4,000.

The Leyland plant, is the UK's most modern truck assembly line.

But from booming world sales of around 69,000 heavy trucks in 1989, the market has slumped to about 30,000 a year as recession-hit firms hang on to ageing fleets. Last year was the worst since the war, even though Leyland DAF captured a quarter of the UK market.

continued...

Task 16 continued

Although the Dutch company is the major shareholder of Leyland DAF, 30 per cent is in the hands of private investors and institutions. The BAe-owned Rover Cars group has 10.9 per cent.

If Leyland sinks it will hand over a massive sales opportunity to Germany's Mercedes-Benz. An industry expert said: 'There are signs that the UK business is picking up, so for Leyland to die now would be tragic.

An Amalgamated Engineering and Electrical Union spokesman said: 'A campaign of action will be launched which will probably include a march through Leyland and the lobbying of Parliament. We also aim to get local MPs involved.

With unemployment nudging 3 million, a fierce political row erupted in the Commons over whether the Government should intervene. Trade President Michael Heseltine said he was 'ready to work closely' with DAF to save some of the business, but rejected Labour calls for direct aid.

Whitehall feels a significant part of Leyland's UK business can survive and be sold – despite its Dutch parent company being close to collapse.

A key question will be whether the UK factories can be protected from the Continental creditors of the parent firm, which took over Leyland Vehicles in 1987 but has suffered losses of £301 million in the past three years.

Lancashire County Council leader Louise Ellman urged Mr Heseltine to work with the authority and its economic development agency, Lancashire Enterprises, in mounting a rescue package.

She said: 'This is a major manufacturing concern. If it is allowed to die it will devastate a major part of Lancashire.

After lengthy negotiation, the receivers revealed management buyout plans which involved the loss of some 1500 jobs at Leyland and 1000 at Birmingham. Twelve months later LDV (former Leyland Daf Vans) at Birmingham, bought for £40m, announced profits of £8.6m on a turnover of £80m, plus a 100 new jobs.

Whilst Leyland Trucks at Leyland where 45 temporary workers had been recruited, was still in profit and expecting a turnover of £150m. Production was up by 20%.

Recovery continued into 1995 as LDV's first quarter sales increased by over 30%. LDV expected to sell 15,000 vans in the year compared with 20,000 in the 1989 peak.

From the article and your own knowledge of Leyland-DAF or similar local situations, complete the following:

1. Identify the element of change which caused the collapse of Leyland DAF.

2. Describe the economic impact on the Community of Leyland as a result of the collapse and how it will affect the supply of and demand for labour.

3. Discuss the likely social and environmental impact.

4. Could the situation have been prevented?

5. Do pressure groups have a valid role to play in such situations?

6. Does any group stand to gain from the situation?

7. Prepare the case for and against 'letting Leyland die' and comment on which key factors and why, should determine the final decision in such situations.

8. Now carry out some practical research in your local area to identify a recent major change. Briefly describe the situation and how it came about.

9. Finally, analyse the problems associated with it and what action was or is being taken to alleviate them.

Summary

78. a) Labour is the total human effort used in the production of goods or provision of services.

 b) Information about employment trends is available from a wide variety of sources including the Labour Force Survey.

 c) The supply of labour depends upon the working population which consists of the number of people who work or are available for work.

 d) The occupational distribution of the working population has seen a reduction in employment in the primary and secondary sectors with a rapid growth in service industries.

 e) Most workers are still employed in full-time jobs but there is a major trend towards part-time and temporary work. Self-employment is also on the increase.

 f) The methods of paying workers include by hourly rates, flat rates, overtime, piece-work, commission, fees, bonus or profit-sharing.

 g) Many firms provide fringe benefits for workers, for example cheap canteen meals or free travel.

 h) Employment trends resulting from change include de-skilling, unemployment, education and training opportunities, new jobs and work patterns.

 i) The structure of industry has also changed, in particular the rapid growth of the service sector.

 j) Further predictions include a growing but ageing workforce, with an increasing number of part-time workers and women in employment.

 k) Skill shortages exist where there are insufficient people available to perform jobs which need doing.

 l) This may require the training and development of existing workers to keep their skills up to date.

 m) Workers usually receive higher wages in jobs requiring greater skills or carrying more responsibility.

 n) Unemployment has important economic, social and political effects.

Review Questions *(Answers can be found in the paragraphs indicated)*

1. What determines the supply of labour? (1–3)

2. Identify 10 sources of data on employment trends. (4–8)

3. What is size of the working population and what factors influence it? (11–13)

4. Describe the main changes in the last 20 years in the occupational distribution of the population. (17–20)

5. Distinguish between occupational and geographical mobility of labour. (21–22)

6. What are some of the main features of full-time employment? (25–27)

7. Why has the growth of part-time employment come about? (28–32)

8. With examples explain the difference between permanent and temporary work (33–35)

9. In what situations might an organisation decide to sub-contract work, contract-out or use a temp agency? (36–38,41)

10. Name 4 methods of paying wages to employees. (42)

11. Use examples to explain the meaning of fringe benefits. (43–44)

12. Briefly describe the effect on the working population of industrial change. (45–58)

13. What are the likely future trends in employment? (59–62)

14. Why do skill shortages exist in particular industries? (63–66)

15. Explain why a solicitor is likely to be paid more highly that a bus conductor. (68–69)

16. Why do workers in some industries like retailing and catering receive relatively low wages? (68–69)

17. In what ways does the EU impact on employment? (70–72)

18. Distinguish between the economic, social and political effects on unemployment. (73–75)

Assignment – Investigating employment   Element 5.2

You are asked to prepare a report using a variety of information sources which

1) identifies and explains different types of employment and

2) evaluates how at least 4 types of employment have changed in a business and the effects of these in terms of employee and business needs.

The report should illustrate both national and regional trends in

❑ employment in at least one manufacturing and one service industry

❑ full-time and part-time employment

❑ male and female employment

❑ differences in pay

and explain the implications for

❑ employed and unemployed people

❑ communities

❑ government revenue and expenditure.

18 Competitiveness of UK Industry

This chapter examines the competitiveness of UK industry and both business and government strategies to improve it. It includes:

❏ Business Environment	❏ Business Competition Strategies
❏ SWOT Analysis	❏ Governments Competitive Strategies
❏ Environmental Scanning	❏ Government Policy/Legislation
❏ PEST Analysis	❏ Current/Recent Initiatives
❏ Competitor Analysis	❏ Growth, Competitiveness and Employment
❏ Britain's Competitive Position	❏ Competitiveness: Helping Businesses to Win
❏ Productivity	❏ Competitiveness: Forging Ahead
❏ International Trade	❏ Single Regeneration Budget
❏ Imports and Exports	❏ Training and Enterprise Councils
❏ Balance of Payments	❏ Vocational Qualifications
❏ Barriers to Trade	❏ Investors in People
❏ Exchange Rates	❏ Training
❏ Movement Towards Free Trade	❏ Inward Investment
❏ Overseas Markets	❏ Evaluating Competitiveness

The Business Environment

1. In Chapter 1, we saw that an organisation operates within a range of both internal and external constraints which can affect its ability to meet objectives. But whilst internal factors can usually be controlled because they relate to the organisation itself, external factors cannot because they relate to its environment and competitors.

2. Two techniques commonly used to assist organisations to assess their environment and plan for the future are known as SWOT and PEST.

   ❏ **A SWOT analysis** is used to highlight an organisation's internal strengths and weaknesses, measured against its competitors, and any key external opportunities and threats.

   ❏ **A PEST analysis** is used to scan the political, economic, social and technological environment within which the organisation operates in order to identify changes and trends.

Swot Analysis

3. A SWOT analysis requires management to look closely and analytically at every aspect of its operations and then develop suitable strategies to achieve the desired objectives. It can be carried out either by line managers, although this may not always produce objective analysis, or by using external consultants.

4. **Strengths**

These are the advantageous aspects of the organisation on which its future success can be built. Examples might include:

❏ a well motivated, skilled workforce,
❏ well established products,

❏ a good reputation and

❏ modern production technology

5. **Weaknesses**

These are the factors which could hinder the future success and potential growth of an organisation. Therefore, it is important that they are investigated and remedial action taken. Examples might include:

❏ poor industrial relations which could disrupt production,

❏ outdated equipment or production techniques,

❏ poor quality control leading to high wastage or complaints about faulty products,

❏ poor management information systems,

❏ inadequate research and development and therefore limited product innovation.

6. If a strong financial position exists, then in the examples quoted it should be possible for management to implement remedies. If, however, finance itself is a weakness, then it would have to be a key priority for action.

7. **Opportunities**

Usually, but not always, strengths and weaknesses relate to the organisation itself whilst opportunities come about as a result of external factors which affect it. They may be identified from planned research or just purely by chance but either way it is important that organisations seek out, recognise and grasp appropriate opportunities when they arise.

8. Organisations which fail to do this may miss out and find that their competitors are leading the way, turning opportunities into potential threats. Examples may include:

❏ new market openings which could be met from existing resources,

❏ opportunities for new products or services as a result of new legislation or trends, or

❏ developments in technology which present opportunities for improved production techniques or administrative systems.

9. **Threats**

Most threats come from outside organisations and therefore outside the control of management. Examples might be:

❏ increasing competition,

❏ changing technology,

❏ economic factors like rises in interest rates and

❏ political factors such as the introduction of new legislation.

Nonetheless, it may be possible to overcome them. For example, controlling costs by finding alternative suppliers or substituting raw materials to reduce the effect of price increases.

10. But threats can also exist within an organisation. Examples might be:

❏ an ageing workforce which resists change,

❏ management complacency which can lead to an acceptance of what is happening now and therefore a failure to recognise potential opportunities and threats, or

❏ a lack of financial or other management information needed for decision-making and control in an organisation.

11. One of the main reasons why Japanese manufacturers are so successful in selling goods like audio-visual equipment, cars, motor cycles and photographic equipment in both the USA and Europe is that they have been much quicker than Western companies to take advantage of technological innovation.

Task 1   **5.3.1 (C3.2)**

Choose any organisation to which you belong, such as a school, college, business, church, social or sports club.

1. Briefly explain how you fit into the organisation, for example, student, employee, treasurer, team captain.

2. Carry out a SWOT analysis on the organisation identifying at least 3-5 key factors under each heading.

3. Comment on your findings including how you think the SWOT is likely to influence the future development of the organisation.

Environmental Scanning

12. As stated earlier, an organisation does not operate in isolation but is part of the environment with which it interacts. The environment consists of a range of factors or constraints which are external to the business but which have a direct or indirect influence on its decision taking and ability to achieve its objectives. The environment can represent either or both opportunities and threats depending on the industry and the way they are managed. Therefore it is important for strategic planning that managers are aware of these factors and are alert to the impact which they can have on the organisation so that plans can be amended or abandoned accordingly.

13. One way of doing this is by means of **environmental scanning** which is a term used to describe the activities involved in the gathering, analysis and communication of information which firms need in order to keep up-to-date with changes in the business environment.

14. Consideration of the business environment is important in strategic planning because it

    ❏ provides a base of objective data which enables more informed planning, forecasting and decision-taking.

    ❏ enables more effective resource allocation.

    ❏ makes an organisation aware of the changing needs and wishes of its customers.

    ❏ provides training and development for executives thereby increasing their skills in handling problems and change and facilitating new approaches.

    ❏ enables better understanding of government decisions and therefore effectiveness in dealing with them.

    ❏ enables an organisation to improve its image with the public by showing that it is sensitive to its environment and responsive to it.

15. In addition, environmental scanning would include continuous monitoring of all factors which have a direct impact on an organisation including consumers, distributors, suppliers, competitors – for customers and suppliers, trade unions, government regulations, and product and process developments.

16. Information about the business environment may come from a wide variety of sources. Within an organisation it is available from, for example, reports, memos, meetings, management information systems, sales and technical staff, and advisory committees. Whilst sources outside the organisation include stock market reports, trade and technical journals, press reports, market research, government publications, consumer studies, suppliers, banks and trade associations.

Task 2 **5.3.1 (C3.2)**

From which source is an organisation most likely to find the following information:

a) Sales trends

b) Data on market share

c) The organisation's objectives

d) Customer views on the product range

e) The current share price.

17. **Pest Analysis – A Framework for Environmental Scanning**

Political	Economic	Social	Technological
General level of stability	Unemployment	Lifestyles and leisure time	New products and services
Party system	Economic growth	Culture	Telecommunications
Government policies – monetary, fiscal, industrial	Inflation	Demography	Growth information technology
	Taxation	Fashion	
Economic planning – public versus private sector control	Interest rates	Education	New manufacturing processes
	Exchange rates	Pressure groups	New materials
Legislation		Environmental issues	Consumer expectations
European standards/directives			Rate of change

Competitor Analysis

18. A business is always under potential threat from its competitors and if it gets any element of the marketing mix wrong, it could lose business. For example, if for whatever reason customers become dissatisfied with the product or the price is increased, then they may decide to switch to a competitor's product which they could then prefer to buy in future. Likewise, if a competitor has a promotional offer or customers cannot buy the product in the usual place (eg the local supermarket is out of stock) then again they may decide to switch to another product or organisation.

19. Therefore, as well as considering the general environmental factors, which to a greater or lesser extent affect all businesses in all industrial and commercial sectors, strategic analysis also requires a close study of an organisation's competitors. It needs to consider the intensity of competition, what it is based upon, whether it is likely to increase or decrease and how it can be reduced. Also, increasingly for many organisations competition may come from overseas markets, particularly the EU.

20. Four key factors which should be examined are:

❏ **The entry of major competitors into the market**

This may represent a threat to an organisation's market share and therefore to profits. On the other hand, it may stimulate demand and lead to an overall growth in the market. If the new entrant has researched the market it could be entering into what is sees as a growth area or to seize an opportunity because current organisations are weak.

❏ **The exit of major competitors out of the market**

This may assist an organisation by helping it to achieve its market share and profit targets. On the other hand, it may indicate that the market is in decline and therefore could become unprofitable in the future.

❏ **Availability of substitutes**

If alternative products become available this can seriously affect a market and signal the need for action. For example, the sales of record turntables were seriously affected by the introduction of compact discs.

❐ **Strategic policy changes for major competitors**

Awareness of major changes in competitors' strategies is also important. For example, the introduction of new products or heavy promotional expenditure can both affect an organisation's market share. An awareness of how they might react to your strategies is also important.

Task 3   5.3.1 (C3.4, N3.3)
Where people go on holiday

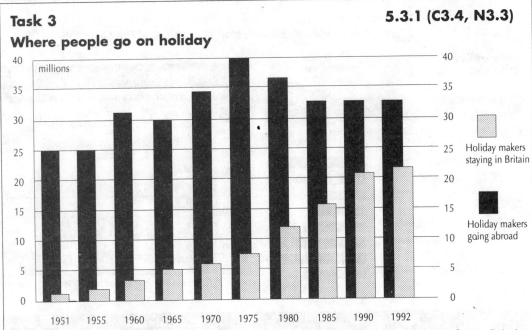

The graph above shows the number of people taking holidays of four or more nights in Britain and abroad over the last 40 years.

Overseas destinations 1992

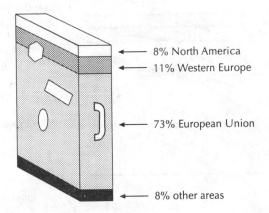

- 8% North America
- 11% Western Europe
- 73% European Union
- 8% other areas

There's a fair chance people going on holiday this year will plump for a trip to Spain, Greece or Florida. But that hasn't always been the case. Before the 60's, the cost of foreign travel meant most people holidayed in Britain.

1. From the above information, identify the main trends in the holiday market.

2. How is this information of value to holiday companies?

3. On the basis of this information plus other relevant data which a PEST and competitor analysis would reveal present a graphical and written report of likely future trends in the holiday business.

Britain's Competitive Position

21. Looking to the future it is likely that global competition will increase and therefore it is important that Britain improves its workforce performance if it is to compete effectively. The following data summarises Britain's competitive position in world markets. The key to achieving this lies in addressing many of the issues identified in this chapter and others such as the skill shortages discussed in Element 5.2.

22. The information below is reproduced with kind permission of *The Guardian*.

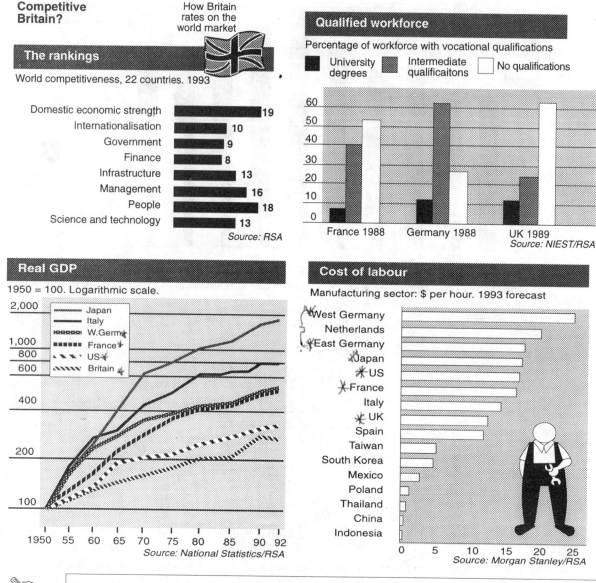

Competitive Britain?

How Britain rates on the world market

The rankings

World competitiveness, 22 countries. 1993

Domestic economic strength	19
Internationalisation	10
Government	9
Finance	8
Infrastructure	13
Management	16
People	18
Science and technology	13

Source: RSA

Qualified workforce

Percentage of workforce with vocational qualifications

■ University degrees   ▨ Intermediate qualificaitons   □ No qualifications

France 1988   Germany 1988   UK 1989

Source: NIEST/RSA

Real GDP

1950 = 100. Logarithmic scale.

Japan
Italy
W.Germ
France
US
Britain

1950 55 60 65 70 75 80 85 90 92

Source: National Statistics/RSA

Cost of labour

Manufacturing sector: $ per hour. 1993 forecast

West Germany
Netherlands
East Germany
Japan
US
France
Italy
UK
Spain
Taiwan
South Korea
Mexico
Poland
Thailand
China
Indonesia

0   5   10   15   20   25

Source: Morgan Stanley/RSA

Task 4

5.3.1 (C3.3, N3.3)

Identify the key trends from the above data and comment on the significance for workforce performance and the potential implications for the UK economy.

Productivity

23. In Element 5.1 we discussed the importance of productivity (output per factor input) as a measure of the efficient or effective use of resources in an organisation covering labour, quality, wastage and safety. An organisation will usually seek to continually improve productivity because it increases the use of resources, helping to reduce costs and increase output and thus improve profits.

24. For example, consider a bottle manufacturer currently producing 10,000 bottles per week with labour costs of £1,000 i.e. 10p. per bottle. The company introduces the latest computerised equipment which with the same workforce increases output to 20,000 bottles. The labour cost per bottle is now only 5p. If these are sold at the same price then the extra profit would be 20,000 × 5p. i.e. £1,000. Thus the company would have extra profit to either distribute to shareholders, increase wages, lower prices to attract more customers or to invest in further equipment.

25. This simple example illustrates the benefits of increased productivity. It is this which leads to economic growth and prosperity if repeated in organisations throughout the country and is the main reason for the growth of developed countries since the war.

26. Unfortunately, however, increased productivity can also produce problems for organisations. In our example, if the company cannot increase sales to match the new level of output then it will require less workers to produce an output of 10,000. Thus a loss of jobs could result. If workers are not laid off the relatively low productivity may make the firm uncompetitive which could lead to losses and possibly eventual closure.

27. In the 1980's manufacturing productivity in Britain grew at an average of 4.7% a year which was faster than in all other leading industrialised countries.

Productivity in the economy as a whole fell very slightly in 1990 but has been rising slowly since the start of 1991, reflecting the decline in employment relative to output.

Task 5   **5.3.2 (C3.4)**

TROLLEY CHIPS

A revolutionary checkout machine could transform supermarkets and bring an end to queuing within 5-10 years. It could also dramatically reduce the number of checkout staff.

A new electronic scanner has been developed by the British Technology Group in collaboration with a South African government agency.

Instead of the present time-consuming process which requires every item to be individually checked at the till, the new machine will be able to 'read' the entire contents of a trolley in one go and add up the prices within seconds.

Each food wrapper will have a tiny in-built radio chip which, when passed through a scanner, forms a circuit with a radio base which can instantly register what has been bought.

ROBOT BANKING COMES TO BRITAIN

The first of 10 nationwide employee-free banks was launched by the Co-op Bank in May 1994.

They are aimed at eliminating queuing and inconvenient opening hours which irritate many working people.

The Tardis-style Bank Point Kiosks will be fully automated and open 24 hours a day, with a 'phone link to the Co-op's round-the-clock home banking facility.

Link cash machine and withdrawal and deposit facilities will be available and entry will be gained by a cash card swipe mechanism.

The Bank is also closing another 30 of its 300 in-store Handibank counters as it moves remorselessly towards holes in the wall.

In 1979 it boasted 750 in-store, six-day-a-week Handibanks with full banking facilities. Many customers have therefore 'lost' this convenient banking facility.

It is still opening traditional-style branches and sees Bank Point Kiosks as complementing its existing 110 outlets.

continued...

Task 5 continued

JOBS CUT FEAR

Britain's finance industry has cut 100,000 jobs in the past four years, according to the Banking Insurance and Finance Union today.

It warned that thousands more jobs were at risk in 1994 and that the pace of closing High Street branches was accelerating.

With the industry back in healthy profit, BIFU appealed for the cuts to stop. It wants the banks and the other institutions to share their profits with staff and customers – by keeping open branches, improving service, cutting queues and giving job security.

It says staff want to provide an accessible and friendly service and customers don't necessarily want more technology and high-pressured selling.

Complaints about bank services had soared after a new regime of charges and the Bank Ombudsman had recently warned about high-pressured selling techniques. BIFU believed things would get worse as banks imposed targets and performance pay on staff.

The union was not ruling out possible industrial action to oppose further job cuts which it says will plunge workers morale even lower.

From the developments outlined in the articles identify:

1. the likely effects on productivity and competitiveness;

2. the potential impact on employees and consumers.

3. Finally, consider any other individuals, groups or organisations which might be affected by developments.

Improving productivity

28. In developed industrial economies where there is a shortage of skilled labour great importance is attached to the productivity of labour and as shown on the diagram Britain lags behind some of its key competitors.

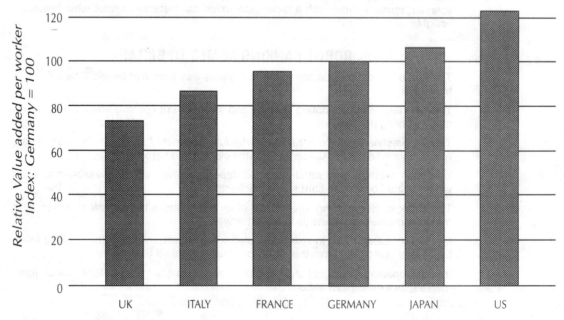

29. Productivity, however, may be affected by a number of other factors. Thus, for example, an increase in the productivity of labour may be due to:

- ❏ the introduction of new technology, particularly the use of advanced manufacturing systems including CAD/CAM and robots.
- ❏ better organisation which improves work flow
- ❏ encouraging workers to work harder
- ❏ reduced absenteism through improved health, safety and welfare
- ❏ economies of scale
- ❏ education and training and
- ❏ specialisation.

Task 6   5.3.2 (C3.2)

Fringe benefits are sometimes referred to as the 'carrots' used by employers to encourage staff to work harder. On the other hand, an employer may also use 'sticks' or punishment such as demotion, transfers, redundancy or withholding performance related pay. Consider a firm which you worked for or one well known to you. Make a list of the important 'carrots' and 'sticks'. Say briefly with reasons, which of each you think is most important in improving productivity.

International Trade

30. All the countries of the world are dependent upon each other to a certain extent. Very few can hope to produce everything they need because every country has a different climate, physical and geographical conditions (rivers, mountains, soil etc) and resources (raw materials, machinery, labour and capital). Therefore countries need to trade with each other which explains why many goods we buy today have been made in foreign countries. Britain is the world's fifth largest trading nation.

31. The **benefits from trade** include:

- ❏ **Higher standard of living.** International trade is very important to a country because it enables it to have a higher standard of living. Trade widens the choice of goods in the shops because countries can buy foods, raw materials and finished goods which they cannot produce themselves.

- ❏ **Economies of Scale.** Also, each country can concentrate on producing those goods which it can grow or make most easily and therefore this often means that they are cheaper due to economies of scale.

- ❏ **International co-operation.** Trade also helps to develop International understanding and closer political and economic ties. The European Union, for example, was a logical development from the trading links which already existed in Europe. The benefits and impact of EU membership are discussed in Element 1.3.

Imports and Exports

32. The goods and services bought from abroad are called **imports** and those sold abroad **exports.** As shown in the following diagram the UK's main imports are food, raw materials and manufactured goods. The main exports are manufactured goods including machinery, vehicles and chemicals.

33. **UK imports and exports 1992**

	Exports (fob) £m	Exports (fob) per cent	Imports (cif) £m	Imports (cif) per cent
Non-manufactures	**17,561**	**16.2**	**25,503**	**20.3**
Food, beverages and tobacco	8,713	8.0	13,426	10.7
Basic materials	1,965	1.8	5,092	4.0
Fuels	6,881	6.4	6,985	5.5
Manufactures	**88,672**	**81.9**	**98,729**	**78.4**
Semi-manufactures	30,484	28.1	32,339	25.7
of which: chemicals	14,996	13.8	11,615	9.2
textiles	2,456	2.3	3,944	3.1
iron and steel	3,007	2.8	2,524	2.0
non-ferrous metals	1,753	1.6	2,591	2.1
metal manufactures	2,211	2.0	2,571	2.0
other	6,061	5.6	9,095	7.2
Finished manufactures	58,188	53.7	66,389	52.7
of which: machinery	30,690	28.3	31,801	25.3
road vehicles	8,895	8.2	12,121	9.6
clothing and footwear	2,427	2.2	5,633	4.5
scientific instruments & photographic apparatus	4,455	4.1	4,255	3.4
other	11,721	10.8	12,579	10.0
Miscellaneous	**2,065**	**1.9**	**1,661**	**1.3**
TOTAL	**108,298**	**100.0**	**125,896**	**100.0**

SOURCE: Monthly Review of External Trade Statistics

Differences between totals and the sums of other components are due to rounding. See Monthly Digest of Statistics for most recent figures

Balance of Payments

34. A nation must keep an account of its financial dealings with the rest of the world. This is called the **Balance of Payments.** It is a record of all the money which flows into or out of a country and it is rather like a bank account. If the account does not balance then the government may need to borrow money, repay loans or use its gold and foreign currency reserves to solve the problem.

35. The Balance of Payments which is published monthly is made up from three accounts.

   ❒ The **Balance of Trade** or **visible balance.** This is the difference in the value of all the actual goods which are imported and exported.

   ❒ The **Balance on Current Account**. This includes the visible balance and also the invisible items of trade, that is services such as transport, banking, tourism and insurance which are not physically taken in and out of the country.

   ❒ The **Transactions in External Assets and Liabilities.** This lists all the lending to, borrowing from, and investment between countries, trade credit and any other capital flows.

36. A **balancing item** is also shown which includes any errors and omissions which occur in compiling the accounts. Adding together the totals on the Current Account and External Assets and Liabilities Account plus the balancing item, gives the **balance for official financing.**

37. **Britain's balance of payments 1988–1992**

	£m 1988	£m 1989	£m 1990	£m 1991	£m 1992
Current account	–21,480	–24,683	–18,809	–10,284	–13,406
Visible trade balance	4,863	2,171	541	2,632	4,786
Invisible transactions balance					
Current balance	–16,617	–22,512	–18,268	–7,652	–8,620
Financial account					
Transactions in assets and liabilities					
British external assets	–58,458	–90,089	–82,187	–18,925	–84,976
British external liabilities	68,812	109,503	93,148	25,652	93,295
Balancing item	6,265	3,097	7,308	924	301

Source: United Kingdom Balance of Payments 1993 Edition.

Differences between totals and the sums of their component parts are due to rounding. See Monthly Digest of Statistics for most recent figures.

38. The ideal situation for any country is to pay for its imports by the value of goods and services which it sells abroad. Traditionally, Britain has for many years had great difficulty in doing this and usually has a deficit on its Balance of Trade. However, this has always been reduced by a surplus on invisible trade but still, in recent times, leaving a deficit on the Current Account. This can be seen in the figures above.

Task 7   5.3.1 (N3.3, C3.4)

The following article is based on newspaper reports

TRADE BALANCE DIVES INTO RED

According to Department of Trade and Industry figures, in May Britain had its second worst Current Account deficit on record at £561 million. This was despite a £600 million net contribution from invisibles like banking, insurance and tourism. The visible trade gap doubled between April and May as the bill for imports leapt by £375 million to £7,450 million while export earnings fell £282 million to £6,290 million.

Demand for foreign goods rose by seven per cent across the board, with purchases of capital equipment and intermediate goods rising as fast as imports of consumer goods.

However, since the country is now growing faster than almost any other major economy in the world, it is hardly surprising that we are buying more from others than they are prepared to buy from us.

The set-back for exports reflects sluggish world demand but may also have something to do with the 5% rise in the price of sterling since the beginning of the year. Even so, exports are still running at levels 6.5% higher than a year ago.

The following are based on the information in the article.

1. How much was the deficit on the Current Account and how is it calculated?

2. What was the net contribution from invisible trade?

3. Calculate the size of the visible trade deficit in May.

4. Give 3 examples of invisible items.

5. Explain why 'invisibles' are vital to Britain's trade.

6. Explain fully and in your own words why Britain is importing more than she is exporting. Comment on the most recent figures available and any important trends.

Barriers to Trade

39. Despite the benefits which trade brings, a country may still decide to restrict it by imposing protective measures such as:

   ❒ **Tariffs** (or customs duties) which are put on imported goods in order to make them more expensive.

   ❒ **Quotas** which are physical restrictions on the amount of particular goods which can be imported into a country.

40. Tariffs and quotas are usually placed on imported goods which are already produced in the UK. This protects the home market and encourages us to 'Buy British'. They may also be placed on goods that we cannot produce ourselves but wish to restrict for one reason or another. (see paragraph 18).

41. Other methods of protection which a country might use include:

   ❒ **Embargoes** – this is the complete banning of trade between one country and another.

   ❒ **Subsidies** – a government may provide finance to enable home goods to be sold at a lower price and thus reduce the demand for imports.

   ❒ **Exchange controls** – a country may decide to restrict the supply of foreign currency thus reducing the volume of imports which can be purchased.

Reasons for Protection

42. There are five main reasons why a country may decide to impose barriers to trade:

   ❒ **To reduce unemployment** – imported goods might result in job losses in some industries.

   ❒ **To prevent dumping** – this takes place when surplus foreign goods are sold abroad at a lower price than in the home market. This creates unfair competition.

   ❒ **To provide for self sufficiency** – a country might wish to protect industries in case of war.

   ❒ **To protect 'Infant' industries** – young industries may need protection from foreign competition to enable them to develop and grow.

   ❒ **To correct Balance of Payment problems** – a country may want to reduce imports in order to correct a trade deficit.

Task 8   **5.3.1, 5.3.3 (C3.4)**

EXPORT TONIC

Sales of British medicines abroad have earned a record £1.2 billion – almost £14,000 for every worker in the drugs industry.

Figures from the Association of the British Pharmaceutical Industry reveal that output rose by 6.8 per cent – a marked contrast to a fall in UK manufacturing as a whole Nationally the industry employed over 87,000 people up by 23 per cent since 1970 One in five is a scientist or technician involved in research and development. A record £1.2 billion was invested in such work last year. An ABPI spokesman says: 'A lot of the success of the industry is in its international competitiveness. The foundations are laid in the amount of money companies are prepared to invest in research and development. That means we are able to compete with the Japanese the Americans and Europeans.'

---

continued...

Task 8 continued

CHINA CONTRACT

GEC Alsthom is close to winning a £290m contract to fit out the Shajiao C power station in southern China. A letter of intent with the project managers has already been signed, and detailed negotiations on the contract terms are in progress. If GEC is successful, it could mark the start of several weeks of big orders for UK companies.

AIRBUS ORDER

The four-nation Airbus consortium of which Britain is a member, has won a £300 million order for six ultra-long range A340-200 passenger jets. Up to 300 UK companies will gain some £60 million from the contract with Philippine Airlines, announced at the Farnborough Air Show.

JOBS WASTELAND

An MP claims that so many manufacturing jobs have been lost that Britain can no longer produce the goods its population needs. Lawrence Cunliffe says his Leigh constituency has seen thousands of jobs go in recent years in the mining, textile and engineering sectors. 'Even in the depth of the recession we are still running an enormous trade deficit because imported goods are taking the place of home-made products in our shops, at a terrible price for employment'. The collapsing pound may make these imports dearer, but the damage has already been done. Mills, heavy engineering factories and collieries cannot be reopened quickly – industrial vandalism takes decades to repair.' Over the last 13 years, 2.4m manufacturing jobs have been lost throughout the country, leaving just 4.6m he said. 'All over, local factories which used to be landmarks are lying derelict and skilled workers are thrown on the scrap heap at an early age.'

TOURIST ATTRACTIONS

A recent study shows that the Japanese see in us a combination of solemnity, propriety and long traditions, which they feel builds a character similar to their own. Their admiration has seen the number of big-spending UK visitors from Japan climb from 132,000 in 1978 to some 600,000 in 1992 – spending £300 million.

From the above news extracts:

1. Identify examples of visible and invisible exports.

2. What arguments are there to support the idea of free trade?

3. Are there any arguments in favour of protection?

4. Comment on any key factors which are or may be considered important for the development of trade.

Tackling Balance of Payments Problems

43. If a Balance of Payments deficit persists then, in addition to the measures of protection already mentioned the government can also consider:

   ❏ **Measures to stimulate exports**. The ongoing help for exporters is outlined in paragraph 70 but the government could also choose to introduce specific measures to assist exporters such as tax relief or encouraging banks to provide cheap loans.

   ❏ **Deflation of the economy**. A government may choose to increase interest rates, increase taxation, reduce public expenditure or introduce a credit squeeze in order to reduce demand in the economy and consequently the level of imports. This could work but may result in unemployment due to falling demand.

❑ **Devaluation of the pound.** Another measure is to allow the value of the pound to depreciate in value against other currencies thereby making exports cheaper and imports dearer. This can work but could also lead to domestic inflation.

Rate of Exchange

44. Since the Balance of Payments is a record of the **total currency flow** into or out of a country a further term which must be understood is the rate of exchange. This expresses the value of the pound in terms of other currencies used by the countries with which we trade. For example £1 = 197 (Spanish) pesetas or £1 = 1.48 (American) dollars. If you have had a holiday abroad you will have bought foreign currency yourself to spend whilst away. Similarly, businessmen must also buy foreign currency to pay for imports or investments, whilst at the same time, customers abroad buy pounds to pay for the goods and services which we export to them.

45. Thus we have both a demand for foreign currency and a supply of it. At the equilibrium exchange rate the two will balance out. The equilibrium is linked to the Balance of Payments because in a deficit situation, less domestic currency is required causing it to depreciate.

46.

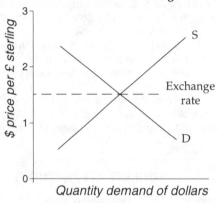

Quantity demand of dollars

47. In the above graph, for example, the demand curve (D) for £'s is downward-sloping, which means that if the £ falls in value, British goods and services will become cheaper for Americans to buy. This will produce an increase in demand for them and therefore also more £'s.

48. The supply curve (S) of £'s is upward-sloping, which means that as the dollar price of the £ rises, USA goods and services become cheaper in Britain, causing an increase in demand for them. Hence the supply of £'s offered also increases to pay for them. The equilibrium rate of exchange between the two currencies is determined by the interaction of demand and supply, in this case, £1=$1.50.

Fixed and Floating Exchange Rates

49. How the price will respond to this trading pressure will depend on whether the exchange rate is floating or fixed.

❑ Under a **floating exchange rate** the exchange rate is allowed to vary until supply and demand is in equilibrium. In a completely free market, this is called **'clean floating'.**

❑ Under a **fixed exchange rate,** the government will intervene in currency markets to keep the price fixed by buying or selling its foreign exchange reserves or by borrowing abroad.

❑ The ERM is a system of **semi-fixed exchange rates** within agreeds bands (see Element 1.3). Britain left the ERM in 1992 in order to be able to reduce interest rates and revitalise the economy.

50. In order to help promote trade after the Second World War under the **Bretton Woods** agreement, countries agreed to fix their exchange rates to the US dollar. The pound, for example, was fixed at £1 = $2.80. This system was supervised by the IMF but abandoned in 1973 since when most of the world's currencies have been floating. But this has led to a system called **'dirty floating'** whereby governments still intervene to try and stabilise the system by buying and selling currency.

Importance of the Rate of Exchange

51. Movements in exchange rates can have important effects on business profitability for a number of reasons:

   ❏ They can affect the costs of imported raw materials making it difficult to forecast costs of production.

   ❏ They can also influence the selling price of imported goods and services.

   ❏ Profit margins on exports can increase or decrease substantially if the value of currencies change between the contract and delivery date.

   ❏ If exports are priced in foreign currencies, sales could be lost if the relative values change.

   ❏ They can increase the risk of investing in overseas assets, such as foreign government bonds, shares in foreign companies or buildings and land, because future returns are subject to exchange rate fluctuations.

Task 9	5.3.1, 5.3.3 (N3.1, C3.2)

Munir Shortt Ltd, a Manchester based import/export company has asked you to advise it on contracts which it has negotiated with 2 of its main overseas customers.

The first contract signed in June was for the export of £20,000 worth of china tea sets to the USA. The buyer agreed to pay $30,000 at the time when the exchange rate was £1 = $1.50. The order was duly delivered and paid for in October as agreed. At this time the exchange rate was £1=$1.42

The second contract, signed in July, involved the import of 10,000 electronic games from Japan at a price of £10 each payable in yen. In July the exchange rate was £1=200yen. Delivery took place in November, and payment in December at which time the exchange rate was £1=190yen.

You have been asked to:

1. explain in each situation how the firm was affected, if at all, by the change in the exchange rates.

2. outline the potential advantages and disadvantages to the company of negotiating its contract in sterling or in a foreign currency.

3. Using information from the Financial Times or other quality   newspapers, plot the value of the dollar and yen against the pound over a 3-6 month period and comment on the relative values including reasons for any significant fluctuations and whether or not this information is useful to the company.

Movement Towards Free Trade

52. Despite these many barriers recognition of the economic importance of **Free Trade** has been clearly illustrated since the end of the second World War. Nations throughout the world have been involved in negotiations in an attempt to reduce trade barriers and make trade easier. The result of these negotiations is shown by the International Monetary Fund (IMF) 1944, the General Agreement on Tariffs and Trade (GATT) 1948 (replaced in 1994 by the World Trade Organisation), the formation of the European Free Trade Area (EFTA) in 1959, the European Economic Community in 1957 (now called the European Union, or EU – see Element 1.3), and the European Economic Area (EEA) in 1994.

53. **IMF.** Most of the countries of the Western World are members of this organisation. Each member pays a contribution to the Fund (25% in gold and 75% in its own currency). The main aim is to encourage trade by using the Fund to provide short-term loans to members with a Balance of Payments deficit. It also wants to see stable (fixed) exchange rates.

54. **GATT** was established with the aim of helping to increase world trade by reducing tariffs and other barriers. It now has some 117 members and since 1947 has completed 7 rounds of multi-national trade agreements. The 8th, the Uruguay Round, was launched in 1986, and concluded in 1993.

55. Initially GATT was very successful but since the recession of the early 1970's what is often referred to as the 'new protectionism' has emerged. That is, trade is not restricted by tariffs but by 'hidden' controls such as import licensing, domestic price subsidies and technical specifications all of which create unfair competition. The latest agreement will replace it with a tougher policing body known as the **World Trade Organisation**.

56. **EFTA** was formed to abolish tariffs on manufactured goods between its members who are Austria, Finland, Iceland, Norway, Sweden and Switzerland. Members are allowed to impose whatever restrictions they choose on non-member countries.

Task 10   5.3.2, 5.3.3 (C3.4)

EUROPEAN ECONOMIC AREA (EEA)

January 1st 1993 was not only the date for completion of the single market programme but also that originally proposed for the creation of the European Economic Area (EEA) which eventually came into effect on 1st January 1994.

The (EEA) is made up of all European Union states and the countries of EFTA (European Free Trade Association: Austria, Finland, Iceland, Norway, Sweden and Switzerland) together with Liechtenstein. Switzerland did not join the EEA following a referendum.

The agreement does not grant automatic EU membership to the countries, although Austria, Finland, Sweden and Switzerland have already applied. Norway is expected to follow. In effect, most EU legislation, including the four freedoms – movement of goods, services, capital and people ,now extends to all 18 countries making up the EEA.

The EEA is a market of some 380 million consumers and offers tremendous scope for specialisation, growth and prosperity.

EFTA is the EU's main trading partner, with EU states supplying over 60% of EFTA imports and taking more than 58% of its exports in 1990. Trade between the two groups of countries is concentrated on manufactured goods, which represent 85% of total EFTA imports. The aim of the EEA is to strengthen trade and economic relations between the European Union and EFTA countries.

The EEA opens up the affluent markets of the EFTA states to EU countries and widens the scope of the single European market by promoting trade between the two groups of countries. Britain currently exports goods and services worth about £8 billion to the members of the EFTA but it is estimated that as trade and tariff barriers come down in those countries, Britain's gross domestic product could be boosted by up to two per cent. British fishermen will also be allowed to catch more cod off northern Norway.

The EEA also creates the world's largest trading alliance – bigger than the US and Japan combined. It is estimated that the EU and EFTA together account for over a third of world trade. As part of the deal, the EFTA nations contribute more than £1 billion to a special fund to help develop the poorer regions of Spain, Portugal and Greece.

The two blocs have set up a joint ministerial council to provide consultation on new legislation, but without voting rights, and a joint court to settle disputes.

It also reduces the likelihood of the Union turning into an exclusive, bureaucratic, European fortress surrounded by tariffs and barriers erected against competition from the outside world. It also takes it nearer to Britain's goal of an outward-looking, confederal Europe of nations. This deal should also help hasten the inclusion in the free trade zone of the newly-liberated countries of the old Soviet bloc.

continued...

Task 7 continued

Answer the following questions which are based on the above article.

1. Why was the 1st January 1993 an important date?

2. Who are the members of the EEA?

3. Why was the EEA formed, and how does it operate?

4. What benefits arise from its formation?

5. How will Britain in particular benefit from its formation?

6. What future trade development could now take place?

Other Overseas Markets

57. Although EU, EFTA and the EEA represent Britain's major trading partners, there are several other important overseas markets, particularly in terms of their purchasing power and growth potential. Broadly, these can be grouped as Western Industrialised, Third World, New Industrialised, Eastern Bloc and Oil Exporters.

58. **Western Industrial Economies** are the advanced, wealthy nations of Western Europe, North America, Japan and Australia. These countries have sought to promote free trade agreements and trade is now well developed between them.

59. **Third World or Developing Countries** are those whose level of economic development is not yet sufficiently advanced to generate the savings necessary to finance industrialised investment programmes. About 70% of the world's population live in developing countries which include Africa (except the Republic of South Africa), Asia (except Japan) the Soviet Republics and Central and Latin America (except Argentina, the Caribbean and Pacific Islands).

60. The criteria usually used to distinguish developing countries include low levels per head of population of

    ❏ National income

    ❏ Net average per capita income

    ❏ Energy available and literacy

    ❏ They also tend to face problems of over-population, poverty, disease and a heavy dependency on one or a small number of products.

    ❏ They earn foreign currency mainly from primary production (usually agriculture) and have to rely to a large extent on international aid for capital investment and technical knowledge.

    ❏ Consequently, their effective demand for imports is limited.

61. **Oil Exporting Countries** such as the Gulf States of Iraq and Kuwait are extremely wealthy, although it is not usually evenly distributed amongst the population. Hence they tend to provide markets for luxury items and arms rather than general consumer goods.

62. **Newly industrialising countries** are developing countries which have moved away from reliance on primary production and established manufacturing capabilities as part of a long-term programme of industrialisation. Examples include Brazil, Mexico, Hong Kong and Taiwan. They represent a potential opportunity for exporters, although trade barriers often make it difficult. But they can also be a threat often regarded as offering unfair competition because they use low-cost labour to produce relatively inexpensive goods such as textiles, shoes and electrical goods which have lead to declining home industries and heavy unemployment.

63. **Eastern Bloc or Communist Economies** have experienced considerable change in recent years. Communism involves a centrally planned economy where strategic decisions concerning production, distribution and trade are taken by the government as opposed to the price system of a free

market economy. True communism still exists in a few countries like Bulgaria and Romania but many former communist states such as China, the former USSR, East Germany, Poland, Hungary and Czechoslovakia are now introducing market economies. These will present new and major opportunities for exporters throughout the 1990's.

Task 11   **5.3.1 (N3.3)**

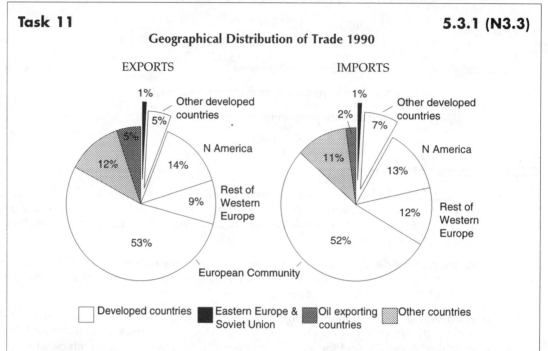

Geographical Distribution of Trade 1990

Consider the above pie charts and the following facts about the geographical distribution of Britain's trade.

- In 1970 trade with developed countries accounted for 73% of exports and a similar proportion of imports.

- In 1970 non-oil developing countries accounted for 17% of exports and 15% of imports.

- In 1972 around 1/3 of trade was with the 11 countries which now make up the European Community.

- In 1990 non-oil developing countries accounted for 13% of exports and 12% of imports.

1.   Identify from the above the key trends in Britain's distribution of trade.

2.   From your knowledge of, and research into overseas markets, comment, with reasons on trends since 1990, and likely future trends.

International Marketing

64.   The world population explosion, plus the movement towards free trade and demand for higher standards of living has lead to increased opportunities for exporters. We have already outlined the benefits arising from foreign trade which for individual companies could also include the following:

    ❐ An opportunity to increase or maintain sales when the domestic market is stagnant or shrinking.

    ❐ The chance to benefit from economies of scale achieved through higher levels of output/sales.

    ❐ Possibility of obtaining government advice and financial backing.

    ❐ Possibility of charging different prices in overseas markets.

65.   On the other hand, exporters face a number of problems which increase the risks involved in business. Some of these also exist in home trade but require special attention when sending goods overseas. The difficulty of obtaining market information and political or economic uncertainty abroad can increase these problems, examples of which include:

❏ Customer remoteness making good communications important.

❏ Different languages and cultures.

❏ Supplying a suitable product, for example with foreign measurements and safety standards.

❏ Import regulations will be different in every country with the possible burden of tariffs and quotas.

❏ Difficulties in obtaining payment and a longer delay in receiving it.

❏ Fluctuations in exchange rates.

❏ Increased costs of transport, insurance and documentation.

❏ Products/services need to be adapted to meet different tastes, customs and climates.

Task 12   5.3.2 (N3.1)

Consider any home produced product which you use regularly.

1. List at least 10 factors which are important in marketing the product concerned.

2. State with reasons which factors you feel are most important.

3. Try to list at least 10 factors which would need to be considered if the product was to be successfully marketed abroad.

4. State, with reasons, which factors you feel are most important.

5. Now compare and comment on any differences between your two lists.

Help for Exporters

66. In order to reduce the risks associated with exporting and in order to encourage trade, help is supplied by the Department of Trade and Industry, Consular Officials, Chambers of Commerce, the Confederation of British Industry and banks.

Department of Trade and Industry (DTI)

67. This government department runs the British Overseas Trade Board (BOTB) which aims to promote trade. It offers a wide range of advice and services for exporters. The Head Office is in London and it operates in England through seven regional offices. The Northern Ireland Department of Economic Development, Welsh Office Industry Department and Industry Department for Scotland all assist exporters in their respective areas.

68. **BOTB Services for Exporters** include:

❏ Assessment of overseas markets for potential exporters

❏ Help with market research

❏ Organisation of and/or support for overseas trade fairs and exhibitions

❏ Information on trade restrictions and regulations abroad

❏ Issue of export licences where required

Export Credits Guarantee Department (ECGD)

69. The ECGD is a separate department within the DTI which provides insurance cover for exporters. It will also guarantee loans and overdrafts taken out to finance exports. The main risks insured against are:

❏ That the buyer does not pay

❏ That a government may take action which prevents payment, for example exchange control

❏ That a government may cancel an export licence

❏ The possible effects of war

❏ Rises in costs and currency fluctuations

Consular Officials

70. These are UK diplomats appointed by the government who are based in Embassies in most countries throughout the world. They can give advice and assistance to exporters and also help with import documentation.

71. **Other sources of help include:**

   ❑ **Chambers of Commerce** which can often provide information about overseas markets and help with export procedures and documentation.

   ❑ **Confederation of British Industry (CBI)** which provides up-to-date information about export opportunities.

   ❑ **Banks** which provide information and advice, short and long-term loans and special facilities for dealing with payments from abroad including the discounting of Bills of Exchange.

Task 13	**5.3.2, 5.3.3 (C3.2)**

Carry out an investigation and then prepare a brief report on the assistance available locally for firms who wish to engage in overseas trade.

Business Competitive Strategies

72. Every organisation is different – in terms of its focus, size, structure – as is every market and the level of competition within it. All businesses, however, face competition to a greater or lesser degree and therefore must devise appropriate strategies to deal with it if they are to survive and prosper.

73. Examples of how an organisation could seek to compete include

   ❑ increasing the **scale of production** to reduce costs and benefit from other economies of scale in finance, marketing and management. It is nonetheless still possible for small firms to compete in niche markets and/or by utilising technological developments.

   ❑ **improved marketing,** for example making use of research and development to bring about innovation and change and ensure that customer needs are always being met (see Elements 3.2 and 3.4)

   ❑ the introduction of **new technology** which could, for example, range from Fax or E-mail to improve communications, EDI to improve purchasing and sales systems, CAD or CAM to robotics to automate production to new materials such as fibre optics.

   ❑ developing **human resources** by, for example, providing training in the skills needed to use new technology efficiently, promote customer care, improve quality and reduce waste. Changing structures and/or management styles could also be part of this development, for example giving increased delegation and responsibility to individuals actually doing the job, or flattening organisational structures to focus more on team working and customer needs.

   ❑ tightening **financial control**, for example endeavouring to reduce labour, production and marketing costs through budgetary control.

Task 14	**5.3.2 (C3.2)**

BRITISH STEEL LEADS THE WAY

British Steel, which in June announced soaring annual earnings to make it the world's most profitable steel producer, expects results in the 1995/6 financial year will be even better.

The chairman told shareholders at the company's AGM that 'British Steel is making real progress towards its goal of being a world class, internationally based steel company and, with further benefits from selling prices and our continuing drive on competitiveness leading to further progress.'

continued...

Task 14 continued   **5.3.2 (C3.2)**

> He added 'While in the USA and Europe there has been some recent easing in economic growth, market conditions remain good and our own performance continues to improve at a very satisfactory rate.'
>
> British Steel is a world leader in terms of profits, productivity and competitiveness and intends to remain so, although there is no room for complacency.
>
> Booming exports by Britain's manufacturers pushed up the demand for steel by nine per cent during the year to March 31, helped profits jump sevenfold to £ 578m. 'Efficiency savings last year alone exceeded £ 70m and there is more to come.'

1. What evidence is there of British Steel's competitiveness?

2. What is its goal and how does it intend to achieve it?

Governments Competitive Strategies

74. Throughout this text you will find reference to the influence of the government on organisations. The three main factors are **State ownership** which is discussed in detail in Element 2.1, and **Government policies and legislation**, all of which can impact on competitiveness.

75. In some countries, the level of **political stability** can also have a major impact on business. Italy, for example, frequently has changes of government whilst the economy of the former Yugoslavia was devastated by the outbreak of civil war in 1991. Third World and Middle-Eastern countries are also politically volatile.

76. The **political party** in power in a country both locally and nationally is also important because of the different policies which may be adopted. In the UK, for example, the labour party believes in a far greater level of government intervention in, and control of, the economy and business including nationalisation whilst the conservative party allows greater freedom and has carried out substantial privatisation and deregulation (see Element 1.3) to promote competition.

Task 15   **5.3.2 (C3.4)**

INTERNATIONAL ENVIRONMENT

> Cable and Wireless PLC is a major international telecommunications company which operates in highly complex and volatile markets affected by diplomacy, nationalism, politics, war, economics, high technology, intense competition and rapid innovation. Its research and development, production and pre- and after-sales service costs are enormous whilst its products are non-standard and usually tailor-made to meet the needs of large, powerful buyers. These in turn are heavily influenced by many unpredictable environmental factors such as diplomatic pressure, international funding, political loyalties and reciprocal trading which bear no direct relationship to the actual economic costs and functional benefits normally associated with the supply of telecommunications equipment.

1. Explain the meaning of PLC

2. Outline the distinguishing features of the market in which Cable and Wireless operates.

3. Why is environmental scanning important to the success of the Company.

4. Is a PEST analysis appropriate for the company?

5. What other types of information might assist the company in its strategic planning and where might it be obtained?

Government Policies and Legislation

These can be summarised as follows:

77. **Control of the Economy**

    This was discussed in detail in Element 1.3. Sufficient to note here that the Governments use of **fiscal** measures (ie taxation and public expenditure) and **monetary** measures (mainly interest rates and credit controls) can have an important impact on businesses because they affect the cost of borrowing and level of consumer expenditure (ie demand) and therefore profits. In recent years output, productivity and exports have improved whilst inflation has remained low.

78. **Company Legislation**

    Element 2.1 outlines the Government's control on both private and public limited companies through the Companies and Insolvency Acts.

79. **International Trade**

    This element examines the assistance given to exporters through the BOTB and ECGD. The Government also influences overseas trade through its foreign exchange and balance of payments policies, customs duties and export documentation.

80. **Employment and Training**

    Element 4.1 outlines some important legislation which affects the employment of people. The Government has introduced several laws, both to protect employees and also to improve their working conditions. Training is encouraged through Government funded schemes co-ordinated by TECs.

81. **Industrial Relations**

    In Element 4.1, the role of ACAS is discussed. This is a body which seeks to improve industrial relations and settle disputes quickly. The Government has also passed laws like the Trade Union Act 1984 which states that a trade union must hold a secret ballot before taking industrial action.

82. **Location of Industry/Industrial Policy**

    Element 1.3 discusses the assistance given to firms to influence the location of firms. In particular, the Government provides grants, tax relief and other benefits to encourage businesses to move into or expand in the Development Areas. Inward investment is discussed in Chapter 18, paragraph 120.

83. **Marketing and Consumer Protection**

    Element 1.3 includes an outline of the various laws which exist to protect consumers. The Office of Fair Trading is responsible for consumer affairs and consumer credit, whilst the Monopolies and Mergers Commission investigates proposed mergers which may not be in the public interest. Environmental protection legislation has also recently been introduced (see Element 1.2).

84. **European Standards/Directives**

    The impact of the UK's membership of the European Union was discussed in Element 1.3. Increasingly, all UK standards and legislation will be common throughout the Union and European directives are so wide ranging that they affect all businesses to a greater or lesser extent.

Task 16

VAT IN THE EUROPEAN UNION

	Standard rate	Basic foods	Public transport	Children's clothes	Domestic fuel	Newspapers & magazines	Books
UK	17.5%	0%	0%	0%	8%	0%	0%
Belgium	20.5%	6%	6%	20.5%	12–20.5%	6%	6%
Denmark	25%	25%	0%	25%	25%	0–25%	25%
France	18.6%	5.5%	18.6%	18.6%	18.6%	2.1%	2.1%
Germany	15%	7–15%	7–15%	15%	15%	7%	7%
Greece	18%	8%	8%	18%	18%	4%	4%
Ireland	21%	0%	0%	0%	12.5%	12.5–21%	0%
Italy	19%	4–9%	9%	19%	9%	4%	4%
Luxembourg	15%	3%	3%	3%	12%	3%	3%
Netherlands	17.5%	6%	6%	17.5%	17.5%	6%	6%
Portugal	16%	5%	5%	16%	5%	5%	5%
Spain	15%	6%	6%	15%	15%	3%	3%

In recent years there has been much talk about the likelihood of VAT being imposed on many items currently zero-rated particularly books, newspapers and even basic foods.

1. Discuss and compare VAT rates in the EU.

2. Comment on the potential impact on the economy and business competitiveness if the government changed any of the above VAT rates.

Current/Recent Government Initiatives

85. The government and European Union have tried to improve the labour market in recent years by introducing a number of measures aimed at helping to combat high levels of unemployment, develop the skills of the workforce for the future and thereby improve the UK's competitive position.

86. These measures include

- ❒ **strategy White Papers** outlining potential actions e.g. Growth, Competitiveness and Employment, 'Competitiveness Helping Business to Win' and 'Competitiveness Forging Ahead.'

- ❒ **improving the co-ordination** of economic development and regeneration by establishing integrated regional offices with a single budget and merging the departments of education and employment.

- ❒ **encouraging better training** to raise skill levels particularly by setting up TEC's and LEC's, the reform of Vocational Qualifications, introducing National Targets for Education and Training (NTET's), promoting Investors in people and giving National Training Awards.

- ❒ **Increasing the flexibility of labour** particularly by offering training opportunities to school leavers and the unemployed.

- ❒ **removing burdens on employers and workers** including barriers which hinder employment. The Trade Union Reform and Employment Rights Act (TURER) 1993 introduced important new rights for employees, trade union members and members of the public. (TURER is discussed in Element 4.1)

Growth, Competitiveness and Employment

87. This White Paper – Growth, Competitiveness and Employment – presented to the European Council Summit in December 1993 proposed a series of measures to stimulate economic growth and jobs in response to current low growth and high levels of unemployment (17 million). It recommended that

the European Commission set itself a target of creating 15 million new jobs by the end of the century and achieve an annual growth rate of 3 per cent until the year 2000.

97. The White Paper suggested possible ways of meeting these targets. In the spirit of subsidiary, however, it did not prescribe actions to be taken. Instead, it offered member states a choice of options to be selected according to prevailing national conditions.

89. The Council responded favourably to the White Paper and committed itself to an action plan based on its proposals. The plan includes measures to be taken at both national and EU level although the commitment to create 15 million new jobs by the year 2000 was removed at the UK's request. The Government's 'Competitiveness' White Papers represent the UK's response.

'Competitiveness' Helping Business to Win

90. A White Paper issued in May 1994 which set out what the UK needs to do to compete successfully in world markets as we approach the 21st century and highlights the need for open trade to encourage competition and create more jobs and included a range of important initiatives aimed at raising the skill levels of the workforce, including

❏ improving education and training

❏ increasing wage and labour market flexibility

❏ ensuring better use of public funds to combat unemployment

❏ providing training for young school leavers

❏ simplifying Single Market legislation affecting all businesses and cutting red tape

'Competitiveness' Forging Ahead

91. Issued in May 1995, this updated the first Competitiveness White paper, and announced new Government policies. It acknowledges that whilst principally improving competitiveness is a task for business itself it must be a priority and the government has a vital role to play.

92. The main proposals in the paper cover support for small businesses, technology and education and training, for example

❏ **revised national education and training targets** which now include the core skills of communication, numeracy and IT (see paragraph 104).

❏ **a review of the 16–19 qualifications framework**

❏ **improved careers advice** and guidance for adults

❏ encouraging individuals to take responsibility for **lifetime learning**

❏ **measures to encourage training** in small business

❏ an **improved benefits system** through the introduction of the Jobseekers' Allowance and **increased incentives to work**

❏ encouraging TEC's and LEC's to develop strategies for **improving management skills** in business e.g. through commitment to Investing in People (see paragraph 108).

❏ providing **funding for a network of Business Links**. These are one-stop shops offering help and advice to encourage business start-ups and development including exports, design, innovation and technology (see Element 8.3)

❏ **improving efficiency, effectiveness and competition in the public sector** where necessary by, for example, further privatisation, contracting-out, deregulation and national comparisons of local authorities' performance in key services.

❏ substantial expenditure to encourage **innovative and technology based developments** in industry and education.

❑ measures, including financial support and trade missions, to introduce at least **30,000 extra firms to exporting** by the year 2000

❑ measures to encourage the **provision of financial help to business**, particularly SME's and to encourage prompt payment by organisations

❑ **improving communications and the physical infrastructure** by, for example, privatising the railways, developing information superhighways, and initiating a national debate on transport priorities.

Single Regeneration Budget

93. In April 1994 the Government created 10 new **Integrated Regional Offices** bringing together the existing regional offices of the Departments of Transport, Trade and Industry, Employment (Training, Enterprise and Education Directorate) and Environment.

94. It also introduced a **Single Regeneration Budget (SRB)** to replace the budgets of the various departments. The aim is to encourage local initiatives and partnership to overcome disadvantage and promote regeneration in employment, education and skills, economic development, housing, environment, crime prevention and aid to ethnic minorities. Local authorities, TEC's and Business Leadership Teams will be key partners, together with voluntary groups, schools, police, health authorities, small firms and others.

95. The new offices will co-ordinate UK and EU funds and provide business with a key focal point for comprehensive and easy access to government services in the regions. Senior Regional Directors are accountable to the relevant Secretary of State for the programmes their offices carry out.

96. **Department for Education and Employment (DFEE).** In July 1995 the departments of education and employment were merged into one. The DFEE aim is to increase competition and the quality of life. The new department is seeking to increase education and skills throughout life, advance understanding and knowledge and promote a flexible and efficient labour market.

Training and Enterprise Councils (TEC's)

97. Introduced in March 1989 TEC's are funded by the Government to co-ordinate and develop training and enterprise in specific areas. They are private limited companies with up to 15 directors of whom at least two thirds are local business executives and the rest are from Local Authorities, Trade Unions, education and voluntary organisations.

98. 80 TEC's cover England and Wales e.g. Eltec (East Lancashire), Powys Tec, Avon Tec, Letec (London East) and Tyneside Tec, whilst in Scotland there are 22 local enterprise companies (LEC's).

99. TEC's are responsible for researching into local labour market needs and skill shortages and then organising a range of existing and new programmes to meet the needs identified. These programmes include Modern Apprenticeships, Training for Work, Business Growth Training, Small Firms Counselling and the Enterprise Allowance Scheme which TEC's manage and adapt locally within broad government guidelines.

100. The Government has asked TEC's to take the lead locally in maintaining the commitment of employers and education in working to achieve the NTET's. The possibility of merging TEC's with local Chambers of Commerce is also being considered.

Task 17	**5.3.3 (C3.2)**

1. Identify the name and address of your local TEC.

2. Write brief notes on any 5 programmes which it co-ordinates including details of the programmes themselves and how they are delivered.

3. From its Annual Report and any other publications outline how it plans to achieve its mission and the progress towards NTET's.

Reform of Vocational Qualifications

101. **National Vocational Qualifications** (NVQ's) were introduced in 1988 and more than 600 are now available. NVQ's are based on real work standards which have been set by industry indicating what an individual is actually competent to do in a job. There are initially 5 levels ranging from basic tasks at Level I to higher technician and management skills at Level IV and professional jobs at level V.

    General National Vocational Qualifications (GNVQ's) were introduced in 1993. They are designed to lead on to work and higher education by developing knowledge and skills in broad vocational areas such as business studies and engineering.

102. The new qualifications have been developed by industry lead bodies often **Industry Training Organisations** (ITO's). These are independent bodies covering sectors which employ about 85% of the workforce. They act as the focal point for training matters in their sector and have a role of ensuring that standards are established and maintained and skill needs met.

103. **Qualification Levels**

    Advanced Level

    Leading to Higher Education or advanced craft, technical, supervisory or administrative jobs.
    To reach Advanced level you must get:

    ❑ two GCE A levels (or one GCE A level and two AS qualifications, or four AS's); or

    ❑ one Advanced GNVQ (the vocational A level); or

    ❑ one NVQ at Level 3.

    Intermediate Level

    Leading to Advanced level or to basic craft or clerical jobs.
    To reach Intermediate level you must get:

    ❑ five GCSE's at grades A to C; or

    ❑ one Intermediate GNVQ; or

    ❑ one NVQ at Level 2.

    Foundation Level

    Leading to Intermediate level or very basic jobs.
    To reach Foundation level you must get:

    ❑ four GCSE's at grades D to G; or

    ❑ one Foundation GNVQ; or

    ❑ one NVQ at Level 1.

Task 18   5.3.3 (C3.2)

1. Identify the qualification level which you have personally reached.

2. State with reasons which level you are seeking to achieve.

National Targets for Education and Training (NTET's)

104. The importance of training and development has gained increasing prominence in the 1990's with the introduction of NTET's which were launched in 1991 by the CBI in its document 'World Class Targets'. NTET's quickly received the support of the Government, employer organisations, training and education bodies and trade unions.

105. NTET's came about from the recognised need for action to fill the skills gap brought about by the challenge of technological change and need for flexible working necessary to meet global competition and more sophisticated consumer demand. They set realistic, achievable targets for young people, adults and employers which identify where the country as a whole should be by the year 2000 if it is to have the necessary skills to compete in world markets with the like of Japan and Germany.

Task 19   **5.3.3(C3.3, N3.3)**

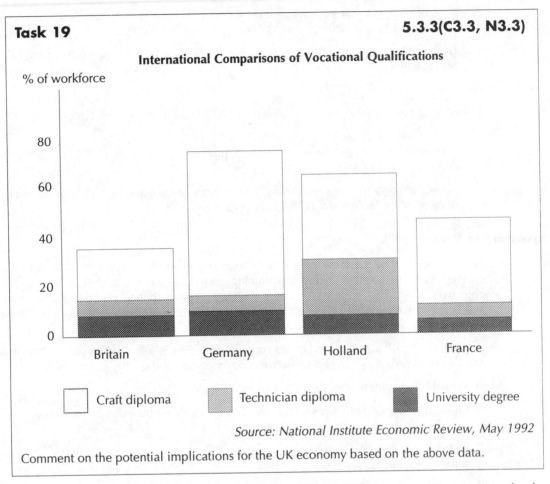

International Comparisons of Vocational Qualifications

Source: National Institute Economic Review, May 1992

Comment on the potential implications for the UK economy based on the above data.

106. A new National Advisory Council for Education and Training Targets (NACETT) was set up by the Government in 1993. It is an independent employer-led body and includes members from education and trade unions. It monitors and reports publicly on progress towards the targets which includes identifying barriers and ways to overcome them. It will also regularly review and update them. The targets shown below are the result of the first such update.

The Targets

107. **Aim**

To improve the UK's international competitiveness by raising standards and attainment levels in education and training to world class levels through ensuring that:

1. All employers invest in employee development to achieve business success.

2. All individuals have access to education and training opportunities, leading to recognised qualifications, which meet their needs and aspirations.

3. All education and training develops self-reliance, flexibility and breadth, in particular through fostering competence in core skills.

Targets for 2000

Foundation Learning

1. By age 19, 85% of young people to achieve five GCSEs at Grade C or above, an Intermediate GNVQ or an NVQ level 2.

2. 75% of young people to achieve level 2 competence in communication, numeracy and IT by age 19; and 35% to achieve level 3 competence in these core skills by age 21.

3. By age 21, 60% of young people to achieve two GCE A levels, an Advanced GNVQ or an NVQ level 3.

Lifetime Learning

1. 60% of the workforce to be qualified to NVQ level 3, Advanced GNVQ or two GCE A level standard.

2. 30% of the worforce to have a vocational, professional, management or academic qualification at NVQ level 4 or above.

3. 70% of all organisations employing 200 or more employees, and 35% of those employing 50 or more, to be recognised as Investors in People.

Investors In People (IIP)

108. IIP was launched by the Government in 1990 to encourage employers of all sizes to improve their business performance by linking the training and development of their employees to business objectives. It is a key initiative to deliver the targets run on behalf of the Department of Education and Employment by local TEC's and LEC's who help organisations to work towards the standard and award it.

109. To achieve the IIP standard employers training provision is accessed to ensure that it involves all employees, is linked to business objectives and meets specific quality standards.

110. The benefits to business from IIP include:

    ❐ changes to working practices which can lead to improved business performance
    ❐ better motivated employees
    ❐ better staff induction
    ❐ increased customer confidence
    ❐ external scrutiny of training to ensure that it is linked to business need
    ❐ increased profits from a higher quality, better trained workforce.

National Training Awards

111. These were first made in 1987 designed to promote good training practices and to recognise exceptionally effective training.

     The competition is open to employers, education and training providers and to individuals who have made exceptional progress in their own careers through training. Around 80 corporate awards and approximately 20 individual awards are presented annually to national winners, who are selected from 200 regional commendations.

INVESTORS IN PEOPLE

A survey of nearly 1,900 companies in the first national evaluation of IIP revealed increased planning, skills auditing and better staff induction as among the benefits.

Since its launch in 1990 over 12,000 organisations had made a formal commitment to work towards the Investors in People (IIP) standard whilst by April '95 over 1,200 had achieved it.

Three-quarters of those employers who had achieved the Standard believed that it had led to an improvement in business performance. The most frequent outcome was that training and development had become more specific and targeted and between a third and a half had introduced job appraisal systems and skills audits; companies involved with IIP commonly used formal methods to assess training needs, while non-participants tended to rely more on informal requests by line managers or the employee themselves. Those involved were also more likely to have formal, strategic planning processes such as mission statements, business plans, personnel/human resource development strategies, and a formal training budget. They were also more likely to place greater emphasis on medium to long-term strategy, rather than on levels of current business activity and profitability. Some employees said it was too early to assess the impact of IIP whilst others who had not really changed their current practices said it had no impact.

A new business-led body Investors in People UK was set up in January 1994 to promote and market the initiative with a view to meeting the Government's National Targets.

1. Briefly describe the potential impact on an organisation committed to IIP.

2. Why might it have little impact?

3. What evidence if any if there of the Government's commitment to IIP?

4. How does IIP fit into NTET's?

Training for young people

112. About 70% of 16 and 17 year olds who leave school to enter the labour market go into **Youth Training (YT)**. A weekly training allowance is paid whilst trainees in a job receive a full wage. YT is run by TEC's through a range of training providers who are responsible for arranging the trainees pay, work placement, training programme and for looking after their general welfare. All schemes provide the opportunity to obtain specific job skills and qualifications to a minimum of NVQ Level II.

113. A **Modern Apprenticeship Scheme** will replace YT from 1995-6. The intention is to have 150,000 young people on the scheme at any one time and for around 40,000 to achieve NVQ's at level 3. They are expected to cost £1,250m over three years (compared to £700m per year expenditure on YT). The apprenticeships will be piloted in 1994-5. One major difference from the old style apprenticeships is the abolition of 'time serving' to be replaced by the achievement of work based competence. The scheme will be funded through youth credits and the Youth Training programme phased out.

114. **Accelerated Modern Apprenticeships** are available for people aged 18/19 who have already completed a full-time course such as GNVQ or 'A' level. Because of this further education trainees should be able to reach a minimum of NVQ level 3 faster than those on the standard apprenticeship. It is estimated that if employers come forward, there will be about 37,000 accelerated Modern Apprentices in training at any one time with about 30,000 qualifying to NVQ level 3 each year.

115. **Youth Credits** give young people who have left full-time education to join the labour market an entitlement to train to approved standards. They carry a monetary face value and can be presented to an employer or training provider in exchange for training.

116. **Workfare schemes** for young unemployed are being piloted in 2 areas from April '94. 20,000 people aged 18--24 and unemployed for more than one year are likely to be involved. Workfare schemes oblige the jobless to work in return for benefit, and the Employment Department has indicated that those refusing to participate in proposed trials would have their benefit withheld.

    The scheme includes personal interviews and assessments plus help with job search. It also offers a £200 grant to buy clothing and equipment necessary for return to work after long absence.

117. Two other measures to help increase training opportunities were:

    ❑ making Further Education and sixth form colleges independent from local authorities and giving them financial incentives to increase recruitment

    ❑ providing for an increase in the numbers of young people taking up higher education opportunities.

Task 21   **5.3.3, 5.3.4 (C3.4)**

NEW APPRENTICESHIPS

Announced in 17th November 1993 Budget, The Modern Apprenticeships initiative aims to boost the numbers of young people with technician, craft and supervisory skills in the workforce, and so help close the skills gap between Britain and its main international competitors.

Three distinct but equal pathways are now available to young people:

- to continue with their general education
- to study for a broad vocational qualification (GNVQ)
- to undertake work-based training leading to an NVQ.

Fourteen industry sectors, through their Industry Training Organisations (ITO's) designed prototypes to start in September 1994, in advance of the introduction across all sectors in 1995.

The ITO's are designing the Apprenticeships in conjunction with TEC's who will arrange delivery under contract to the Employment Department (ED). 42 TEC's are providing 1,750 places. Each trainee will have a training plan, and a formal written agreement with the employer (or group of employers) underwritten by the TEC. This will set out each party's rights and obligations, and the commitment to see the training through.

The time needed to become qualified will be flexible dependent upon the young person's ability. Training will include core skills, supervisory skills, and/or entrepreneurial skills and offer both breadth and flexibility.

To ensure consistency and quality, all the prototypes will have to meet formal criteria set by the ED covering training content and outcomes, trainees' rights and expectations, and funding and administration.

The industry sectors developing the prototypes include business administration, chemicals, childcare, engineering, IT, retailing and travel.

---

1. Why are Modern Apprenticeships being introduced?

2. What are the main features of the scheme?

3. Why do you think that ITO's are piloting the scheme?

Training for unemployed adults

118. Through the TEC's and Employment Services the Government provides a range of training programmes and support for the unemployed. Examples include Training for Work, Job Match, Community Action, Work Trials, Job Centres, Job Clubs and the Restart Programme and the new Careers

Service. The schemes are usually run by approved training organisations such as further education colleges, private training providers and voluntary organisations.

119. These schemes are outlined below.

❑ **Training for Work** aims to help long-term unemployed people to find jobs and to improve their work-related skills Each participant receives an individually adapted package of training and/or structured work activities based on an assessment of their needs. The programme is expected to help up to 320,000 people. In April '94 the age limit was increased from 59 to 63.

❑ **Jobmatch** helps people unemployed for over two years to use part-time jobs as a way into full-time work. A £50 per week allowance is paid for six months.

❑ **Community Action** is a scheme to provide 40,000 long-term unemployed people with part-time voluntary work and effective help with jobsearch. Placements last for up to six months and priority is given to disabled and people aged under 25 who have never worked.

❑ **Work Trials** allow people unemployed for more than six months to try out a job for up to three weeks while claiming benefits and travel expenses. 60,000 places will be available by 1997–8.

❑ **Information and advice** about job hunting and training opportunities is provided for example by:

Job Centres – which exist in most towns to help people to find jobs. They also offer a comprehensive service to employers recruiting staff including advice, assessment and short-listing.

Job Clubs – which offer help with job search including access to telephones and newspapers.

Re-start Programme – which offers job search advice and training opportunities.

Careers Service – this has been revised under Turer to enable it to offer a more flexible service responding to local needs.

Task 22   **5.3.3, 5.3.4 (C3.4)**

CAREERS 'PATHFINDERS'

In April 1994 the first 13 'Pathfinder' organisations start their 3 year contracts to deliver the new look Careers Service. Most of the services are being run following successful bids by new companies or partnerships involving local education authorities, TEC's and local employers. The aim is to provide a more responsive service to help young people to make effective, realistic career choices.

New ways of achieving this include increasing work placements, integrating guidance, recruitment and referral services, reviewing schools career guidance, involving local employers at Board level and developing business and enterprise provision. During 1994/95 Careers Service expenditure will be £143m. In addition the employment department is making £34.5m available to provide careers guidance earlier, for 13-14 year olds in Year 9 and 10 in preparation for making informed decisions about career choices in Year 11.

---

1. What are the key features of the new careers service?

2. Why was there a need to reform it?

3. How, if at all, do you think the changes will affect you?

4. From your own knowledge and experience what do you feel will be the impact on the area in which you live?

5. Why do you think employers might want to be involved in the new careers service?

6. If you are in a pathfinder area, or there is one nearby, try to visit the offices and write a brief report on the changes which have taken place following TURER (see Element 4.1).

Inward Investment

120. Britain is recognised as an attractive location for inward direct investment where some 13,000 overseas companies currently operate. This reflects its membership of the EC and proximity to other European markets, its stable labour relations and comparatively low personal and corporate taxation. Overseas-owned firms are offered the same incentives as British-owned ones.

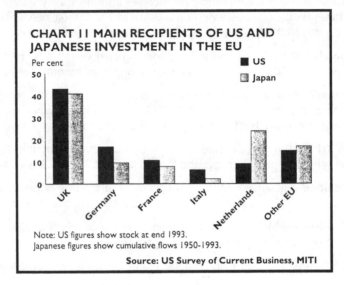

CHART 11 MAIN RECIPIENTS OF US AND JAPANESE INVESTMENT IN THE EU

Note: US figures show stock at end 1993.
Japanese figures show cumulative flows 1950-1993.

Source: US Survey of Current Business, MITI

121. Britain attracts about a third of all inward investment in the European Union including around $^2/_5$ of both Japanese and USA manufacturing investment. For example, Toyota has invested £840 million in two new plants in North Wales and Derbyshire. Ultimately creating 3,000 jobs, the new Carina E is now set to accelerate Britain's export drive and improve our balance of payments. In total in 1993/4 over 400 inward investment projects created or safeguarded some 96,000 jobs. It can also increase exports (or reduce imports) introduce new technology and products and bring new management styles and attitudes. Overseas firms now provide 17% of all manufacturing jobs in the UK.

Task 23   **5.3.3, 5.3.4 (C3.4)**

In July 1995 the Government agreed to pay an £ 80m subsidy to the American-owned company, Ford, to secure a £400m investment by Jaguar. The grant would create some 6000 jobs at Castle Bromwich in the West Midlands which is an area of high unemployment.

Without the subsidy the car would probably be produced in America. But pressure is being put on the EU Fair Competition Commissioner to veto it. The new car would rival medium-sized models from Mercedes and BMW, and much of the pressure that the subsidy would be 'anti-competitive' comes from Germany.

The EU has consistently turned a blind eye over massive subsidies to firms on the Continent. There is a belief in some quarters that the EU allows them because it fears civil unrest in countries such as Italy and Spain if they were banned and unemployment followed.

British Steel, which has not received any taxpayers' cash since it was privatised in 1985, has waged a war on subsidies to over-manned and inefficient producers in Italy, Germany and Spain.

In 1994 there was dismay when £ 400million aid to the ailing former East German manufacturer Ekostahl was allowed.

continued...

Task 23 continued

> Elsewhere, there is anger over big subsidies to loss-making state airlines, while British Airways has stood on its own financial feet since privatisation. The Spanish government has said it plans to inject £700 million into Iberia. In 1988, the French Government wiped out debts of £1.5 billion for Renault, which underwent major restructuring.
>
> Since then state investment has been channelled through banks and private companies via low-interest loans.
>
> The UK has become a magnet for inward investment because wage costs are highly competitive. Industry is enviably strike-free and the government's opt-out from the Social Chapter means that firms are not handicapped by Continental-style social burdens.

1. Why did the Government agree to pay a subsidy to Ford?

2. Who is objecting to the proposal and why? Is it justified?

3. In what sense could the objection be said to be unfair on the UK?

4. Why is the UK attractive for inward investment?

5. Finally comment on whether or not you feel subsidies should be allowed and the extent to which you feel they are likely to create unfair competition.

Evaluating Competitiveness

122. Whether an organisation is competing in the UK, EU or global markets it needs to evaluate its strategies and success in that market place. Equally, as a trading nation the government will compare the UK's performance against that of other nations.

123. An individual organisation is likely to compare itself, for example, in terms of

- ❏ **Market share**. As discussed in Element 3.1 increasing this may be one of its marketing objectives.

- ❏ **Sales.** These can be compared either in terms of total sales volume and/or total sale revenue.

- ❏ **Productivity.** As discussed in paragraph 23 this is an important measure of labour efficiency which also has an impact on production costs.

- ❏ Other measures of **efficiency** which could be compared include the return on capital employed, profit on turnover, and capital turnover. (See Element 7.4)

- ❏ **Product quality** is also important because it is likely to influence sales, particularly where it gives a competitive edge and/or encourages repeat business.

- ❏ **Service** which could range from efficient ordering and delivery procedures to after-sales. Many firms e.g. car manufacturers set up distribution networks in overseas countries to improve their level of service.

124. Many of these measures can also be used to compare the UK against other countries for example, the share of world trade, and production. The government also needs to compare factors and strategies which can affect trading conditions, competitiveness and economic growth such as inflation, interest rates, unemployment, investment and taxation. Competitiveness is vital for growth, which in turn impacts on the standard of living of us all.

Task 24

5.3.1, 5.3.4 (C3.4)

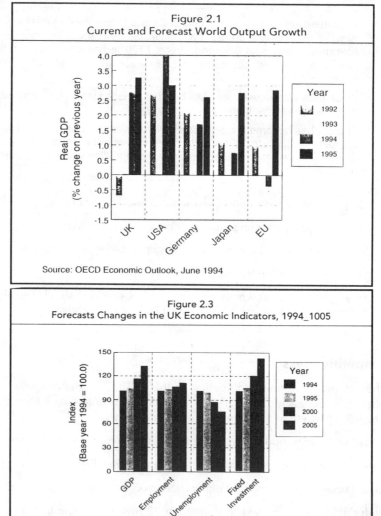

Figure 2.1
Current and Forecast World Output Growth

Real GDP
(% change on previous year)

Year
1992
1993
1994
1995

UK USA Germany Japan EU

Source: OECD Economic Outlook, June 1994

Figure 2.3
Forecasts Changes in the UK Economic Indicators, 1994_1005

Index
(Base year 1994 = 100.0)

Year
1994
1995
2000
2005

GDP Employment Unemployment Fixed Investment

Economic Indicator

Source: Cambridge Econometrics – Regional Economic Prospects, July 1994

Source: NW England Economic Assessment 1994/5

1. What do the above diagrams tell you about the UK Economy and its future development?

2. Why and how might such information be of interest and importance (a) to organisations and (b) the government?

Summary

125.a) A SWOT analysis highlights an organisation's strengths and weaknesses, measured against the competition and any key external opportunities and threats.

b) Environmental scanning provides important planning data.

c) A common method considers the political, economic, social and technological (PEST) factors which impinge on an organisation.

d) Britain needs to improve its workforce performance in order to be more competitive in world markets.

e) Productivity is important for economic growth and prosperity.

f) New technology, education and training and specialisation are factors which can increase labour productivity.

g) International or foreign trade is the buying and selling of goods and services between different countries throughout the world.

h) Specialisation and trade results in a higher standard of living, economies of scale and international co-operation.

i) The Balance of Payments Account consists of:

1. Visible exports – visible imports = Balance of Trade
2. Balance of Trade + invisible balance = current balance
3. Current Balance + external assets and liabilities + balancing item = Total Currency flow
4. Total Currency Flow = Balance for Official Financing

j) A country may restrict trade to prevent unemployment and dumping, remain self-sufficient, to protect 'infant' industries or to solve its Balance of Payments problems.

k) The rate of exchange which can be floating or fixed, expresses the value of the pound in terms of other currencies.

l) Free Trade is encouraged by the IMF, WTO, EFTA, EU and more recently the EEA.

m) Exporters face many additional trading problems including language and market differences, transport and packaging, documentation, insurance, import regulations, obtaining payment and fluctuations in exchange rates.

n) Exporters can obtain help from the BOTB, ECGD, Consul Officials, Chambers of Commerce, CBI and banks.

o) A business can improve its competitiveness by increasing the scale of production, improving marketing, introducing new technology, developing human resources and tightening financial control.

p) Government policies and legislation can affect competitiveness.

q) In the UK these includes State ownership, monetary and fiscal policy, company legislation, employment and training, industrial relations, location of industry, international trade, marketing, consumer protection and European directives.

r) The EU has proposed a series of measures to stimulate economic growth and jobs, which the government has responded to with recent White Papers and initiatives.

s) Some of its main measures include the Single Regeneration Budget, TEC's, NVQ's, GNVQ's, NTET's. IIP and National Training Awards.

t) TEC's provide a range of training for young people including new Modern Apprenticeships and Youth Credits.

u) Help for the unemployed includes Training for Work, Jobmatch, Community Action, Work Trials, Job Centres, Job Clubs, Restart and an improved Careers Service.

v) Inward investment is important for creating jobs in the UK.

w) Both individual organisations and the government need to evaluate their strategies for competitiveness.

Review questions *(Answers can be found in the paragraphs indicated)*

1. Use examples to explain how a SWOT analysis can benefit an organisation. (1–11)

2. What is environmental scanning and why is it important? (12–17)

3. What is competition analysis? (18–20)

4. With the use of an example explain why increasing productivity is important to business organisations and why it might create problems. (23–27)

5. What action might an organisation take to improve the productivity of labour? (28–29)

6. List three benefits from trade. (30–31)

7. Give 4 examples of goods which the UK imports and 4 which it exports. (32–33)

8. What is the Balance of Payments and how is it calculated and financed? (34–35)

9. Briefly explain 4 methods of protection and give 4 reasons why a country might use protection measures. (39–43)

10. Explain what determines the rate of exchange and the difference between fixed and floating exchange rates. (44–50)

11. Give brief details of 3 attempts to promote 'free trade' since 1945. (52–56)

12. Identify the UK's main overseas markets. (57–63)

13. What factors are likely to cause problems in International Trade? (64–65)

14. What sources of help are available to firms in the export trade? (66–71)

15. What strategies might a business adopt to be competitive? (72–73)

16. In what main ways can the government influence business competitiveness? (74–84)

17. Outline some current government initiatives to help promote competition. (85–92)

18. Explain the significance of the government integrated Regional Offices and Single Regeneration Budget. (93–95)

19. What is the role of TEC's? (97–100)

20. Discuss the relationship between NVQ's, GNVQ's and NTET's. (101–107)

21. In what ways do IIP and National Training Awards encourage more effective training? (108–111)

22. Outline the main government schemes available to assist young people in the Labour Market. (112–117)

23. What help is available to provide training and support for unemployed adults? (118–119)

24. Why is inward investment important to the UK? (120–121)

25. In what ways can competitive strategies be evaluated? (122–124)

Assignment – Competitiveness of UK Industry   Element 5.3

You are asked to produce a report which

1. includes a set of league tables, supported by a summary, comparing the performance of the UK economy with at least 3 of its major competitors. The tables should compare economic growth, investment, inflation, the exchange rate, share of world trade and productivity. The supporting summary should explain and justify your choice of performance indicators.

2. describes how one business faces foreign competition including the strategy it uses to improve its performance in a competitive world market evaluated in terms of its effects on both its employees and the business.

3. evaluates business strategies and government strategies to show how these may hinder or help businesses to compete.

To illustrate your understanding of the competing and sometimes conflicting strategies you may find it helpful to build up a file of newspaper and other media stories on the performance of UK industry. Information of this type is usually readily available on a monthly or quarterly basis when government statistics are published but also at a time of public debate such as the Budget or an election when you may find it easier to complete this assignment.

19 Added value and the money cycle

This chapter is about the link between the trading cycle of a business and its money cycle, plus the factors which need to be considered when selling or buying products.

It includes:

❒ Added Value and Trading
❒ Trading Cycle
❒ Distribution of Added Value
❒ Work-in-progress
❒ Money Cycle
❒ Trading/Money Cycle Link
❒ Purchasing or Procurement

❒ Purchasing Function
❒ Purchasing Trends
❒ Factors when Selling
❒ Buying Methods
❒ Factors when Buying
❒ Choosing a Supplier
❒ Vendor Appraisal

Added Value and Trading

1. In Element 5.1 we said that added value is the difference between the cost of materials, goods or services bought from others, and the value of goods or services supplied. We also discussed added value in production, why it is needed, and some of the different ways in which an organisation will seek to increase it.

2. Although in talking about production it is easy to think only of manufacturing, the term production process can be used to refer to any organisation whatever it supplies. Hence, whether an organisation is involved in manufacturing, the re-sale of goods, or provides services, the creation of added value is just as important because it represents a profit.

3. In Element 6.2 we considered in detail financial transactions and the supporting documents used by organisation in the process of trade. Here we consider the **trading cycle or production process** which organisations go through in order to achieve added value.

4.

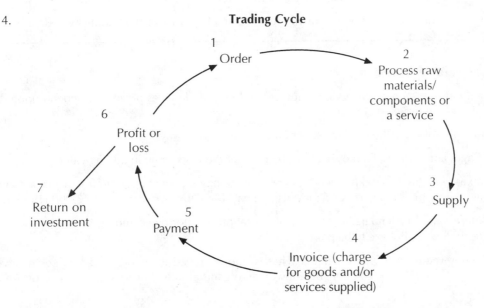

Trading Cycle

1 Order
2 Process raw materials/ components or a service
3 Supply
4 Invoice (charge for goods and/or services supplied)
5 Payment
6 Profit or loss
7 Return on investment

5. When an order is received an organisation will process the necessary materials or components in order to supply the customer.

6. The customer will then be charged accordingly and the organisation will expect to receive payment. It can then determine whether it has made a trading profit or loss. That is, whether the revenue received from supplying the goods or services is greater or less than the cost involved.

7. This is an on-going cycle in that profit from one order is likely to be used to help finance further orders. That is, an organisation has to invest in raw materials, work-in-progress and finished stock (see paragraph 11) which are constantly being 'turned over' as goods are sold. It will also need to invest in capital items such as the plant, machinery and equipment needed to produce goods. It will therefore need to consider not just the profit or loss it makes from supplying goods or services, but the return on the actual investment.

8. The **Return on Investment** or **Return on Capital Employed (ROCE)** is one of the most significant ratios used to measure the efficiency of a business. This is discussed in detail in Element 7.4 where the capital employed in a business is explained as its total assets minus its debtors. The ROCE is the ratio of net profit to capital employed.

Task 1   **6.1.1 (C 3.4)**

DIAL-A-TYRE AT KWIK-FIT

Kwik-Fit chairman Tom Farmer is looking at ways of building on his new operation, which sells motor insurance by telephone.

Initially launched in Scotland, Kwik-Fit Insurance went nationwide in spring 1995. Private motorists are offered a computerised choice of quotes from a panel of 16 insurers. With a credit card, cover can be clinched on the spot.

The insurance operation which is 77 per cent owned by the group is expected to add to profits in the year from March 1996.

Costs of the telephone marketing centre are covered by commission from the insurers. So logically the next step is to offer other goods by phone, starting with car tyres.

'It's impossible for us to carry the whole range, so there is a huge mail-order business for specialist tyres,' says Farmer. From September, customers will be able to order tyres and have them fitted at their nearest Kwik-Fit.

---

1. How does the above article illustrate the concept of added value?

2. In what ways is Kwik-Fit seeking to add value?

3. Comment on whether or not you feel this article illustrates the trading cycle in a business.

Distribution of Added Value

9. How the distribution of the added value created from trade takes place will depend upon the type and size of organisation concerned.

10. It could, for example, be used in one or all of the following ways:

   ❑ **Wages and salaries.** Employees must be paid for the work done in adding value.

   ❑ **Taxes.** Sole traders and partnerships are liable to pay income tax on profits, whilst a company is liable for corporation tax. VAT may also be payable if turnover exceeds £46,000 (1995/96).

   ❑ **Interest paid to lenders.** Where an organisation has borrowed money to finance its activities then interest will have to be paid on the loan.

   ❑ **Money required to pay off debts.** That is, money owed for goods and services received. Although a period of credit may be allowed an organisation will need to pay its debtors on a regular basis.

   ❑ **Dividends paid to shareholders.** Investors who purchase shares in a company will usually do so in the expectation of receiving a share of the profits, called the dividend.

❑ **Profits retained in the business.** In Element 7.1 we discuss sources of finance, one of which is to reinvest some of the profits back into the organisation.

Task 2   **6.1.2 (C 3.4)**

PROFITS CLIMB, BUT BPB CUTS DIVIDEND

As forecast, plasterboard maker BPB Industries today cut its dividend despite a profits recovery.

The profit recovery was due to cost-cutting, improved sales at higher prices and a good performance in building materials. Paper and packaging was the one blackspot.

Full-year profits climbed from £37.8m to £57.5m after sliding for three years. The final dividend is cut from 7.35p to 4.8p, reducing the total from 11.25p to 7.5p to conserve cash.

BPB is cautious about the future pointing out that recovery in the UK and US is being offset by recession in mainland Europe.

---

1. What has happened to added value at BPB?

2. How has this been achieved?

3. Why, therefore, is it cutting the dividend on shares?

4. Does this tell you anything about the way in which added value is distributed in an organisation?

Work-in-progress

11. This is the term used to describe any goods which are still in the process of being made. They are sometimes referred to as **semi-finished goods**.

12. Work-in-progress is often included in a balance sheet, along with stocks of raw materials and **finished goods**, that is those which are completed but not yet sold.

13. The important point is that although stocks are used to add value they also tie up capital in a business, the potential significance of which we will now consider in the money cycle.

Task 3   **6.1.2 (C 3.2)**

In the place where you work or study, can you identify any examples of finished goods or work-in-progress?

Money Cycle

14. In Element 7.2 we discuss the importance of **cash flow** and the need for a business to predict how much money it thinks it will receive and how much it thinks it will pay out over a specified period of time, usually a year.

15. This cash flow or money cycle will correspond to the trading cycle as the following diagram illustrates.

Money cycle

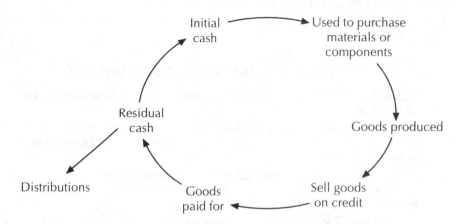

16. Initially cash is necessary to purchase the materials needed to produce goods. It is important to realise though that in business goods are usually bought and sold on credit, that is the goods are supplied but payment for them is not made until a later date. Consequently, to help cash flow most businesses will also seek to delay their own payment to suppliers. When goods are paid for the organisation will then have cash for distribution.

Task 4	**6.1.3 (C3.2)**

Can you think of a situation where you personally, or someone well known to you, have had a cash flow problem?

1. Explain briefly what caused the problem.

2. How was it handled?

3. Comment on how, if at all, it helped you to understand the concept of the money cycle.

Trading/Money Cycle Link

17. It is important to understand the close link between a business's trading cycle and its money cycle. That is, it is revenue from sales which produces cash. However, although a business may have high sales and is making a healthy profit, it still may not prosper and survive.

18. This is because regular payments must be made such as wages and salaries, repayment of loans, and other expenses such as rent, telephone or electricity bills which create a cash out-flow, and also because it is payment for those sales which bring a cash flow into the business.

19. If customers are slow to pay for products supplied then this may mean that the organisation has no residual cash, and begins to experience serious cash flow problems.

20. In the **short-term** it may be able to overcome this by borrowing, delaying payment for bills or running down stocks.

21. In the **long-run**, however, creditors may decide not to supply any further materials or goods without prompt payment or even advance payment which may have serious consequences for the organisation. For example, this may in turn cause problems with production or distribution leading to reduced sales and an even lower supply of cash. It is money therefore, which is the lifeblood in any business.

22. Hence in paragraph 32 we discuss the important factors to consider when selling products, particularly where these are supplied on credit. In paragraph 46 we consider the associated risk of bad debts.

Task 5

REXAM PROFITS SHOCK

The UK-based packaging and printing group Rexam, formerly known as Bowater, saw its shares drop 73p to 422p following a shock warning in August that its 1995 profit will be 'close' to 1994's £231m. Analysts had forecast £250m to £270m following a buoyant AGM in May.

The US market accounts for 33pc of group sales and 43pc of profits, but demand there has suddenly turned sharply down, and earlier stock-building of packaging materials, spurred by shortages and sharp rises in pulp polymer prices, has been transformed into destocking.

Raw materials prices are levelling off and shortages disappearing. Consequently companies are no longer buying ahead to get things more cheaply. However, growth is expected to resume in 1996 because underlying demand is still rising and current investment spending should bear fruit.

Rexam has passed on 95pc of the increases in raw materials costs. But the result had been lower volume growth, only half that expected and less than that enjoyed by competitors who had not passed on price increases to the same extent.

1. Why did Rexam issue a profits warning?

2. What impact did it have?

3. What is likely to happen in the future?

4. a) What impact is the situation likely to have on the company's trading and money cycles?

   b) How, if at all, does it help to illustrate the link between the two?

Purchase or Procurement

23. Every organisation purchases supplies whether it be

    ❑ for **manufacturing,** e.g. raw materials and components
    ❑ for its **own use,** e.g. stationery and furniture
    ❑ or for **re-sale,** e.g. finished goods purchased by wholesalers, retailers or mail-order companies.

24. Many organisations also purchase services such as cleaning, grounds maintenance, transport and security.

25. Various terms are used to describe the purchasing function and the people who carry it out. Retailers, for example, generally refer to buyers, in the public sector the term is usually **procurement** officer, whilst in industry there may be **purchasing** or **supplies** officers or buyers.

Purchasing Function

26. Whatever it is called, purchasing is an important function in any organisation, but particularly in a manufacturing business where the cost of raw materials and components often constitutes a large proportion of the total costs of production. In a service industry, purchasing will be more concerned with consumables including paper, stationery and office equipment such as computers and photocopiers. These form a relatively small proportion of total costs but are nonetheless important.

27. A successful buyer aims to get the right goods, at the right price, in the right place, in the right quantity, of the right quality, at the right time. If this is achieved then it should lead to increased sales and profits. Very large firms may employ a number of specialist buyers each dealing with the purchase of different goods or materials. A supermarket, for example, might have buyers for fashion goods, hardware and fresh foods.

28. The chief buyer, merchandise director, or purchasing or procurement manager is responsible for supervising the purchase of all supplies, materials and equipment for the organisation. This will include:

❏ **Finding the best sources of supply**, reliable suppliers, the 'right' quality, styles, sizes and prices.

❏ **Bulk-buying** i.e. buying in large quantities to save time and money.

❏ **Controlling the ordering process** to ensure that orders are efficiently progressed for delivery when needed.

❏ **Handling purchase requisitions** which are written requests from other departments or branches to the purchasing department specifying particular items which they require for example stationery, cleaning materials or merchandise.

❏ **Rationalising** the range of materials purchased in conjunction with the design and quality control managers.

❏ **Providing Reports** to the Management Accountant about price movements and, where appropriate, the availability of new materials for standard costing purposes.

❏ The purchasing department may also be responsible for maintaining a store or warehouse and an efficient system of **stock control.**

Purchasing Trends

29. In the past decade there have been a number of important trends in purchasing which have lead to closer links being developed between buyers and sellers.

30. These trends include that

❏ purchasing is now **more specialised** and professional with highly trained personnel involved

❏ it is **more centralised** in organisations to promote consistency, reduce queries and problems, and gain economies of scale

❏ It is becoming **increasingly computerised** and therefore based on sophisticated management information

❏ there are **new philosophies and methods** being used, e.g. just-in-time(based on very precise delivery arrangements, see Element 5.1), zero-defects (rewarding employees for producing quality goods with no faults) and materials management (based on ensuring a flow of raw materials or components to ensure efficient production)

❏ more and **improved analysis of suppliers performance**, e.g. increased emphasis on monitoring product quality and delivery schedules.

31. It is now widely recognised that effective purchasing can make a direct contribution to the efficiency and profitability of an organisation by controlling or reducing costs, ensuring reliable sources of supply and reducing the amount of capital tied up in stocks.

Task 6

6.1.2 (C 3.4)

Prepare a brief report on the purchasing function in the organisation where you work or study. If possible, include in it the type of supplies purchased, the sources of supply, the criteria used for selecting supplies, and the structure/systems used.

Comment on which, if any, of the current trends in purchasing are a feature of the system(s) in place.

Factors when Selling

32. Wherever an organisation is on the chain of distribution, whether it be an importer, manufacturer, agent, wholesaler or retailer, it must consider a number of important factors when it supplies goods or services. These include cash, credit, payment terms, credit control, credit worthiness and bad debts.

Cash

33. The term cash is widely used to mean immediate payment for products as opposed to credit, and therefore also includes payment by cheque and credit card (see Element 6.2). The majority of both small and large retailers do most of their business on the basis of cash sales, whereby money is paid into the till and goods are taken at the same time. Some retailers, however, are very dependant upon credit sales.

Credit

34. On the other hand, the majority of business transactions are undertaken on credit and relatively few with the use of cash. As mentioned in paragraph 16, raw materials, components, finished goods, equipment and ancillary items are supplied to customers, who are then allowed a period of time, usually up to 30 days, in which to pay for them.

35. In Element 7.1 we discuss the importance of trade credit as a source of additional short-term finance for businesses. Delaying payment like this also means that organisations have the chance to sell goods and pay for them out of the proceeds.

Task 7	**6.1.4 6.2.4 (C3.4)**

1. List at least 5 retailers whose business is based mainly on cash sales. Now list a further 5 who need to be able to offer credit facilities if they are to be successful.

2. In the place where you work or study, try to identify at least 5 examples of items which are frequently bought and paid for with cash rather than involving credit. See Element 6.2 if you need help.

Payment Terms

36. The terms of a business transaction refer to the various aspects which both parties need to agree upon. Payment terms mean how much time buyers are allowed to pay for their goods and are usually shown on quotations, tenders and/or price lists. Cash discount may be offered off the invoice price to encourage prompt payment.

37. Examples of payment terms include

5% 15th of month following delivery	5% can be deducted if payment is made on the 15th of the month following the month of delivery
$2\frac{1}{2}$% monthly	$2\frac{1}{2}$% can be deducted if payment is made buy the end of the month following delivery
$7\frac{1}{2}$ seven days	$7\frac{1}{2}$% can be deducted if payment is made within 7 days
Net Cash	no cash discount allowed
Net monthly account	no cash discount allowed and payment has to be made in full by the end of the month following the month of delivery.

38. Other payment terms could include

- ❑ **cash with order (CWO)** – payment when placing an order
- ❑ **cash on delivery (COD)** – payment when goods are delivered

Task 8   **6.1.4 (N 3.2)**

1. Goods are invoiced to a business customer for £1,000. The payment terms are 5% monthly. If the account is settled by cheque before the due date how much will be paid?

2. If instead the terms had been 3% monthly what would have been the **difference** in the amount due?

Credit Control

39. If an organisation allows credit then it must control its Trade Debtors in order to ensure that customers pay promptly and also to minimise the risk of bad debts.

40. Credit control involves:

   ❏ **assessing the creditworthiness** of new and, periodically, established customers

   ❏ **encouraging prompt payment** through reminder letters or cash discounts

   ❏ **efficient record-keeping and administration** to monitor the payment of accounts and ensuring prompt follow-up

   ❏ **pursuing slow payers** through reminder letters and telephone calls

   ❏ **seeking to recover bad debts** by chasing outstanding accounts if necessary by taking legal action.

41. The purpose of credit control is to improve an organisation's liquidity and profitability by minimising the amount of funds which an organisation has to tie up in debtors. It requires a clear policy on how much time customers are to be allowed to pay, and the action to be taken when they do not pay up on time.

42. Large organisations often employ credit controllers whose job is to regularly review customers accounts to ensure that payment is being made and credit limits are not exceeded.

43. In Element 7.1 we discuss the use of factoring whereby businesses can sell their debts to a factoring company which buys them for less that they are worth. Rather than waiting and taking the risk of a bad debt this brings some money into the business immediately which can than be used for further production.

Creditworthiness

44. An important part of any credit control system is not allowing credit until customers have been vetted to check that they are able to pay.

45. A person or organisation will often be given a **credit rating** which will help to determine how much they should be allowed. This will be based on information from bank and trade referees and/or from a specialist credit reference agency which, for a fee, will verify the creditworthiness of organisations or individuals. These agencies collect data from a range of sources including any court summonses which may have been issued.

Bad Debt

46. This is the term used for money owed to an organisation which is unlikely to be paid, perhaps because a customer has become insolvent and has insufficient assets to pay the debt.

47. No matter how good their credit control, unfortunately most businesses incur some such losses from time to time. It is possible to take out insurance against bad debts although this will involve paying the cost of the premium.

48. Bad debts are usually written off as a business expense (cost) in the profit and loss account. In addition a provision for bad debt may be created in the profit and loss account which is subtracted form the closing figure in the balance sheet.

Task 9   **6.1.4 (C 3.4)**

CREDIT COSTS

The heavy use of credit to buy Christmas gifts and January sale bargains often results in a difficult period in February for many individual consumers and small firms, particularly seasonal businesses such as shops and hotels. The Finance and Lending Association which represents most stores offering credit recorded a 65 per cent year-on-year increase for store card lending to £527m in November 1994 while spending on credit cards and deferred payment schemes is also substantially increased in December and January.

The advice is to ensure that the bank and other creditors are made aware of any difficulties and are supplied with all information on request. Professional lenders will in most cases work with an honest individual to avoid formal insolvency.

In the case of small businesses trade creditors often adopt a sympathetic attitude to cashflow problems as long as they are honestly dealt with.

1. What are the key points in the above article?

2. Why should they be of interest to businesses?

Buying Methods

49. An organisation will need to make decisions about how it wants to make purchases. Essentially, this will usually be done in one or a combination of 3 main ways.

- ❐ **Regular contracts** to ensure that supplies are available continuously when required and at a known price which is particularly important where flow production techniques are used.

- ❐ **Hand-to-mouth buying** whereby supplies are only purchased when needed which reduces storage costs and avoids tying up large amounts of capital. Unit costs, however, are likely to be higher because smaller quantities are being bought and at current prices (see Element 6.3).

- ❐ **Speculative buying.** Sometimes a business may decide to buy stock in excess of its normal requirements in order to take advantage of anticipated future price rises.

Factors when buying

50. Whatever an organisation is buying whether it be material or components for production, services or supplies for its own use, or goods for resale, it needs to consider a number of key factors in its selection of suppliers. These could include, for example, the specification, quality, price, delivery or after-sales service which will need to be taken together to determine the 'best' source of supply.

51. **Specification.** This is a detailed description of the product required which could include, for example, the quality, features and precise identification of goods/services as for example with own brands (see Element 3.1). It may also include precise delivery arrangements, particularly where Just-in-Time is used.

52. **Quantity.** Ensuring that products are readily available in the required quantities both at present and in the future.

53. **Price.** An important part of the price could include discounts which may be given for buying in quantity, cash payment and/or prompt payment. Stable prices may also be important to avoid rapid fluctuations which can influence costs.

54. **Delivery.** An organisation will need to know the date when goods are likely to arrive and whether or not any additional costs are involved.

55. **After-sales.** This can be particularly important when purchasing equipment which may require servicing, maintenance or advice as, for example, with photocopiers and computers.

Task 10   **6.1.5 (C 3.4)**

Consider anything which you have recently purchased.

1. Comment on whether or not any of the factors identified in paragraphs 51–55 influenced your purchase.

2. Were there any other factors which were important to you?

Choosing a Supplier

56. The process of identifying reliable suppliers is clearly of considerable importance to organisations. Therefore, once a need is identified and a specification drawn up, buyers can use numerous sources of information to help them.

57. For example, they could visit the trade shows, investigate trade journals or directories, 'surf' the internet, speak to sales staff, look at their existing records or advertise for tenders. The latter is very common in public sector procurement where the purchase of materials and supplies are often based on 3–5 year contracts.

58.   **Examples of advertisement for contracts and tenders**

SILKERBY CITY COUNCIL

CONTRACT FOR TECHNICAL SUPPLIES

Tenders are invited for the supply of the following materials for the period 1st August 1995 to 31st July 1996:

Dry Stone, Pre-cast Concrete and Cast Iron Bollards, Sand, Portland Cement, Ready Mixed Concrete

Tender documents returnable by 2pm Friday 25th August 1995 can be obtained from the Purchasing Co-ordinator, City Treasury (Audit), Civic Centre, Main Street, Silkerby S1 2SS

•Contracts & Tenders

GREATER FARNSFORTH POLICE AUTHORITY The Authority wishes to upgrade its tandem Cyclone mainframe computer and seeks tenders for the supply of suitable hardware. Invitation to tender documents can be requested form Mr P M Boulton, Computer Operations Manager, Greater Farnsforth Police, Computers and Communications Branch, PO Box 49, Main Post Office, High Road, Farnsforth F3 0AB. Deadline 2.00pm 29th September 1995.

---

59. The number of suppliers to choose from will vary from product to product, but the increasingly rapid developments in digital, cable and satellite communication, improvements in transport, particularly air and motorways, plus the promotion of free trade and trading unions such as the World Trade Organisation, European Union and European Economic Area mean that global markets are becoming increasingly accessible and important. These are creating new opportunities for buyers whilst creating new competition for supplying organisations.

60. Once the various proposals have been evaluated against the agreed criteria then a choice will be made as to the most suitable purchase. At this stage further negotiation may be needed to alter certain product specifications and/or other details such as price and delivery.

61. The 'buyer' may also decide to have a number of suppliers to protect the organisation from being too dependent on one supplier. There may also be an evaluation system agreed to ensure that everything is satisfactory before future orders are placed.

Task 11   6.1.5 (C 3.4)

100PC BRITISH

The Truckmaster range of replacement silencers and fittings for commercial vehicles will in future be 100 per cent British made, say UK distributors Timax Exhaust Systems based in Lancashire. Until now 15 per cent of the product was sourced from overseas suppliers.

CUSTOMER-SUPPLIER LINK FOR PROFIT

Cultivating links between customers and suppliers can lead to improved profits for both parties according to the CBI. Organisations are increasingly discovering the benefits of working together as a team. By co-operating more closely they are able to drive down total costs, enhance quality and improve services, while maintaining or increasing profitability.

1. What do the two articles tell you, if anything, about the importance of buying in an organisation.

2. Would they in any way help a buyer who is seeking new sources of supply?

Vendor Appraisal

8. The importance of good purchasing to a business has led to the development of **vendor appraisal** techniques which can be used to identify and assess potential suppliers. Key factors such as price, reliability, quality, and delivery times are used and weighted according to their importance to the firm. Each potential supplier is given scores for each factor which are then added together to give an overall rating.

9. The score may not be the only basis for selection of suppliers and a more detailed evaluation may be necessary, particularly if inputs are purchased from abroad and therefore foreign exchange and exchange rates are significant. It is, however, nonetheless useful in helping to narrow down the choice.

Task 12   6.1.5, 6.2.1 (C3.3, N3.3)

Choose any product or service which you use on a regular basis. Carry out a vendor appraisal by identifying at least 4 places (including your usual one) where you could purchase the item concerned and assessing them under a range of 5-10 factors such as opening hours, price, accessibility and availability.

Weight each factor according to its importance to you. Present your findings in a tabular form and comment accordingly.

Summary

64. a) Added value is important because it represents a profit on the production process.

     b) An organisation's trading cycle includes orders, processing, supply, invoicing and payment leading to a profit or a loss and return on investment.

     c) Added value can be used to pay wages and salaries, taxes, interest on loans, debts, dividends and a retained profit.

     d) The money cycle involves the flow of cash into and out of a business.

     e) It is closely linked to the trading cycle because trade generates the cash in-flow needed to meet the cash out-flow.

     f) Every organisation purchases supplies whether it be for manufacturing, its own use, or resale or services.

g) Materials or components can represent a major cost of production and therefore the purchasing function is very important.

h) When selling products an organisation needs to consider cash, credit, payment terms, credit control, credit worthiness and bad debts.

i) When buying products it needs to consider the specification, quantity, price, delivery and after-sales.

j) Vendor appraisal techniques can be used to select suppliers.

Review Questions *(Answers can be found in the paragraphs indicated)*

1. Outline what you understand by the trading cycle in business and how it creates added value. (1–7)

2. What is the difference between a trading profit and return on investment? (7–9)

3. In what ways is added value distributed? (9–10)

4. Explain the difference between finished and semi-finished goods. (11–13)

5. Briefly describe the money cycle in a business. (14–16)

6. Explain the link between the trading and money cycle in business. (17–18)

7. What problems can occur in a business if customers are slow payers, and how can they be overcome? (19–21)

8. Discuss the function of the chief buyer in an organisation. (26–28)

9. Briefly describe some current purchasing trends. (29–31)

10. Outline some key factors which an organisation should consider when selling its products. (33–44)

11. What factors would it need to consider when buying supplies? (50–55)

12. How might an organisation go about choosing a supplier? (56–63)

Assignment   Element 6.1

You are asked

1. to draw a diagram which illustrates the trading cycle of the goods or services provided by one business. your diagram should be supported by appropriate annual figures for the business which show

   ❐ the accumulated costs of goods and or services bought from other businesses

   ❐ the final value of the goods or services when sold to the customer and

   ❐ the resulting added value (profit).

   The figures should be supported by commentary which suggests how the profit could be distributed and explains why it might be either

   ❐ retained in the business

   ❐ used to pay off debts or

   ❐ paid to shareholders.

2. Produce a spreadsheet which shows how the money cycle for the same goods or services mirrors the trading cycle and starts and ends with cash.

3. Prepare notes to explain

   a) why the finance department in the same business would have to consider the credit worthiness and payment terms offered to customers, and

   b) Why the quantity ordered, price paid and delivery date are significant in terms of both the trading and money cycles.

You will find it helpful to refer to Elements 5.1 and 7.2 to assist you with this assignment.

20 Financial Transactions and Documents

This chapter is about financial record-keeping in a business and the use and analysis of trading accounts. It includes:

- ❐ Need for Accounts
- ❐ Business Documents
- ❐ Purchases Documents
- ❐ Sales Documents
- ❐ Export Documents
- ❐ Payments Documents
- ❐ Payments in the Future

- ❐ Wages and Salaries
- ❐ Payslip and Payroll
- ❐ Pay in Arrears
- ❐ Bank Charges
- ❐ The Bank Statement
- ❐ Importance of Correct Documentation
- ❐ Security

Need for Accounts

1. All organisations need to keep records of their financial transactions whether they are profit-making businesses or non-profit making charities and Local Authorities. These financial records are called accounts and there are a number of reasons why they must be kept.

    - ❐ To **confirm the details of transactions** between buyers and sellers.

    - ❐ To **record financial transactions** called book-keeping. It is important to record sales and purchases to keep track of money owed to and by the business and thus determine its assets and liabilities and whether it is trading at a profit or a loss. Computers are now widely used in business for this purpose.

    - ❐ To **provide management information** as a basis for decision-taking, monitoring performance and control and thus to assist in planning to meet business objectives.

    - ❐ To **provide information for owners and shareholders.** Company directors and managers are entrusted to act honestly and efficiently and are accountable to shareholders for results.

    - ❐ To **meet legal requirements** such as determining the liability for **tax** e.g. corporation tax, value added tax.

    - ❐ The Companies Act 1985 and European **legislation** make it a requirement **for companies** to disclose accounting and other information about the business.

    - ❐ **Business evaluation.** Customers, suppliers, employers, creditors, potential lenders and prospective investors are all parties likely to be interested in an organisation's accounts to enable them to assess the likely business risks and/or potential profitability.

Task 1	**6.2.1 (C3.2)**

1. Identify which of the above reasons for keeping accounts apply to the organisation in which you are working or studying.

2. State which, if any, do not apply and say why.

Business Documents

2. The buying and selling of goods is called a transaction. This often involves considerable paperwork. Therefore, special documents are frequently used for purchases, sales, payments and records in order to make the process as quick and efficient as possible. They provide a record of each transaction and make communication easier. Each of these documents has a particular purpose in passing information between buyers and sellers and, although they may vary from firm to firm, the basic principles are the same.

3. In a typical business transaction some or all of the following documents could be used:

   Purchase Documents – enquiries, quotations, estimates, orders, goods received note

   Sales Documents – acknowledgement of order, advice note, consignment note, invoice, proforma invoice, statement of account, credit note, debit note

   Payment Documents – cheques, standing orders, direct debits, bank giro, credit cards, petty cash vouchers.

   Receipt Documents – sales receipts, cheques, paying in slips and bank statements.

4. Since organisations are involved with both purchases and sales they will need documents and systems for handling both. For example, placing orders for supplies, receiving goods and invoices and making payments; receiving orders, delivering goods, sending invoices and collecting payment.

| **Task 2** | **6.2.1 (C3.2)** |

Choose any 5 goods or services which you have purchased in the last week. List what they were and briefly describe the process involved in making the purchase including any paperwork involved.

Purchase Documents

5. **Enquiry**

   When a business wishes to buy goods it will frequently send an enquiry to several firms asking them if they can supply the goods and requesting details of the price, quality and delivery dates. The enquiry may be by letter or on a specially printed form, verbally to a sales representative when he calls, over the telephone or at a trade exhibition.

6. Names and addresses of suppliers may be obtained from:

   ❏ Catalogues

   ❏ Price Lists

   ❏ Telephone Directory – Yellow Pages

   ❏ Trade Directories

   ❏ Trade Journals, for example 'The Grocer', 'The Hardware Trade Journal', 'Retail Confectioner', 'Shoe and Leather News'.

7.

Example of an enquiry

ENQUIRY

R Fisher & Company
'Pet Place'
Martin Street
SHEFFIELD   S30 5AP

Tel: 56353

Ref: RSW/AED

TO: The Albion Supply Co Ltd
Ashfield Avenue
West Street Corner
Middlesborough
MR16 3AL

Directors: R Fisher
M E White
L Taylor

Date: 21 July 199-

Dear Sirs

ENQUIRY NO 76139/S

We are interested in purchasing the following and would be pleased to receive your best prices and delivery:

100 Cases 'Happy Pet' Dog Food   400 gm size

25 Cases 'Contented' Cat Food   400 gm size

50 Cases 'Purr' Cat Food   400 gm size

Yours faithfully

R.S. Warren

R S Warren
Office Manager

---

8.   **Quotation or Tender**

The firms approached will usually reply by giving a quotation for the goods required and these are compared to see which is the most favourable.

9.   The quotation will give details of the price, any TRADE or CASH discount allowed, when delivery can be made, and any *terms* or special conditions under which the goods will be sold. (See paragraph 12.) General enquiries, not about a specific item, might be dealt with by sending a price list, some descriptive leaflets, or a general catalogue instead of a quotation.

10. **Example of a quotation**

QUOTATION

Directors

K Jones
K Moore
S Wickstead

Telephone 88226

THE ALBION SUPPLY CO LTD
Ashfield Avenue
West Street Corner
MIDDLESBOROUGH
Cleveland   MR16 3AL

Your Ref: RSW/AED
Our Ref: DC/BA

23 July 199-

Messrs R Fisher & Co
'Pet Place'
Martin Street
SHEFFIELD
S30 5AP

Dear Sirs

Quotation No 48973

Thank you for your enquiry no 76139/B dated 21 July for dog and cat food. We have pleasure in quoting as follows:

100 Cases 'Happy Pet' Dog Food   400 gm size – £5.45 per case delivered

25 Cases 'Contented' Cat Food   400 gm size – £5.75 per case delivered

50 Cases 'Purr' Cat Food   400 gm size – £6.00 per case delivered

Less 20% Trade Discount
Plus 17½% VAT

Delivery – by our own van 2 weeks after receipt of order

Terms – 5% Cash Discount of payment within 28 days

We trust our offer will be of interest to you and look forward to receiving your order.

Yours faithfully

D. Coyne

D Coyne
Sales Manager

---

11. A firm's buyer or purchasing officer must be familiar with certain terms and conditions used by a supplier which affect delivery and packing costs. These can include:

❐ Carriage Paid – the price includes the cost of delivery

❐ Carriage Forward/ex Works – the price quoted does not include the cost of delivery

❐ Returnable Empties – firms who supply goods in expensive packing or containers, for example wooden crates, often make a charge for them. This is refunded if the containers are returned in good condition.

12. Trade discount

This is a form of discount given by one firm to another for goods which are to be re-sold. For example, retailers usually receive trade discount from manufacturers and wholesalers. The amount of trade discount is deducted from the invoice for the goods and may vary with the quantity bought so that bigger discounts are often given for larger orders.

13. Cash discounts

To encourage prompt payment for goods bought, cash discount may be allowed provided that payment is made within a specified period of time, for example 28 days. Net Monthly Account on an invoice means that no cash discount is given.

14. Trade and cash discount example

ABC Co Ltd bought £1,000 worth of goods which were delivered on 1 August 19..

Terms are 20% trade discount and 5% within 30 days.

Total cost	= £1,000 less 20% trade discount
	= £1,000 less £200
	= £800
Cash discount	= 5% of £800
	= £40
Therefore amount paid	= £760

15. Estimates

An estimate differs from a quotation because it is used for items where no price list exists. It therefore deals with enquiries for special items that must be made instead of supplied from normal stock. It will be based on the cost of materials and labour, and the other expenses involved in making the item. Estimates are often used for building work where each job is different and therefore no standard price applies.

16. Order

From the suppliers catalogues, quotations or estimates received the best terms will be selected and an order placed for the goods. The best terms are dependent not only on price, but also factors such as trade discount, cash discount, quality and delivery time. Goods should be described in detail usually repeating the wording of the quotation or estimate to avoid any confusion. The quantity, price, discounts, sizes, place and date of delivery and all relevant information should be included.

17. Usually an order must be signed or counter-signed by someone with the authority to sanction the expenditure involved. Also they are often processed by the Accounts Department where copies are kept for checking against the subsequent invoice.

18.

Example of an order

```
                              ORDER

                        R Fisher & Company
                            'Pet Place'
                           Martin Street
                        SHEFFIELD   S30 5AP

    TO:  The Albion Supply Co Ltd              ORDER NO A245
         Ashfield Avenue
         West Street Corner
         Middlesborough
         MR16 3AL

    Please supply:                          Date: 24 July 199-

    Dear Sirs
```

QUANTITY	DESCRIPTION	SIZE	COST
100 cases	'Happy Pet' dog food	400 gm	£5.45 per case
25 cases	'Contented' cat food	400 gm	£5.75 per case
50 cases	'Purr' cat food	400 gm	£6.00 per case

```
    Delivery Instructions:

    Prompt delivery               SIGNED:  P. Wood
    Carriage paid                 for R. Fisher & Company
```

Task 3
6.2.2 (C3.2)

1. Imagine you are working in a sales office and a customer telephones to make an enquiry about some goods which he might order. He asks you to send him a quotation giving any trade discount and any terms.

    a) What information should be included in the quotation?

    b) Explain, using examples, what is meant by trade discount and terms.

2. Why might a retailer decide to buy from a manufacturer whose quotation is not the lowest figure he received? Give examples of the factors which he would consider besides the actual figure quoted.

Goods Received Note

19. This may be used to provide a record of goods received. A copy will be kept by the warehouse or goods inward department with copies sent to notify the department that ordered the goods, and to accounts for checking off against the invoice before payment is made.

20.   **Example of Goods Received Note**

R Fisher & Company				

Goods Received Note

Top Copy: Accounts
Blue Copy: Purchasing
Yellow Copy: Warehouse

Received by ___J. SMITH___   Signature ___J Smith___
Checked by ___R. BOWEN___   Signature ___R Bowen___
Carrier ___Supplies vehicle___   Date _____

Quantity	Description	Supplier	Order No.	Stock location

Comments:

	Accounts Use Only
Date Received	_____
Authorisation for Payment	_____
Amount of Payment	_____
Cheque No.	_____
Payment Sent	_____

Sales Documents

21. So far the documents mentions are those used by organisations for the purchase of goods and services. Once an order is received then the supplying organisation is likely to use some or all of the following documents.

22. **Acknowledgement of Order**

Many firms will acknowledge the order in writing to say that it has been received and is being attended to. Also, if the goods are not available immediately, then a date of delivery can be given.

23. **Advice Note**

If goods are likely to be in transit for a while then often an advice note is sent to tell a customer that the goods ordered are on their way. It gives details of the date of despatch, quantity and description of the goods, and how they have been sent, for example British Rail or Parcel Post.

24. **Delivery or Despatch Note**

When goods are delivered in the suppliers own vehicle the driver has a delivery note which gives details of the quantity and description of the goods and states the number of packages. The customer can check the items delivered against the note so that any errors or damage can be quickly spotted. This is particularly useful when orders are delivered in several parts. When checked the delivery note, which is in duplicate, is signed and one copy kept as proof of delivery.

25. **Consignment Note**

These are used when a firm does not deliver goods itself but sends them by road or rail transport. Details on it include:

❏ Weight and description of goods

❏ Delivery address

❏ Who pays for the carriage

❏ Whether the goods are sent at owner's risk.

When the goods are delivered they must be signed for to acknowledge receipt, with a note made of any damages or shortages.

26. **Invoice**

An invoice is sent by the supplier to his customer when goods have been bought and includes

❏ A description of the goods

❏ The quantity supplied

❏ The price charged

❏ The total cost

27. Trade Discount (if any) is deducted and VAT and carriage charges (if any) are added. Where goods are supplied on credit, special terms such as cash discount are usually shown on the invoice. Many invoices include the abbreviation E&OE (Errors and Omissions Excepted) on the bottom left hand corner. This indicates that if a mistake is made on the invoice, the firm is not bound by it and is able to correct it later. British firms registered for VAT must by law show their VAT number on all invoices.

28. **Pro-Forma Invoice**

A pro-forma invoice is similar to a quotation and is used as follows:

❏ For goods sent on approval or on a sale or return basis. Mail Order catalogue firms use this type of invoice to show how much must be paid if goods are kept.

❏ Where goods must be paid for before they are despatched or when they are sold cash on delivery.

29.   **Example of an invoice**

INVOICE

THE ALBION SUPPLY CO LTD
Ashfield Avenue
West Street Corner
MIDDLESBOROUGH
Cleveland MR16 3AL

Invoice No 6342

Date: 4 August 199-

To: R. Fisher & Company
'Pet Place'
Martin Street
SHEFFIELD
S30 5AP

VAT Registration No
112 5965 85

Quantity	Description	Price		VAT Amount	VAT Rate
100 cases	'Happy Pet' dog food	£5.45	£545.00		
25 cases	'Contented' cat food	£5.75	£143.75		
50 cases	'Purr' cat food	£6.00	£300.00		
			£988.75		
	Less Trade Discount 20%		£197.75		
			£791.00	£138.42	17.5%
	Plus VAT		£138.42		
	Total		£929.42		

Terms:	5% cash discount for payment by 14th of month following month of delivery	Your Order No A/245
Delivery:	Carriage paid	Date: 24 July 199-
E & OE		

Task 4   **6.2.2, 6.2.3 (N3.2)**

Copy and complete the invoice below using the following information:

Today ABC Co Ltd supplied K. Richards and Co Ltd, 54 Nottingham Road, Mansfield with 5 wooden stools (catalogue No 421) at £15 each less 25% trade discount, and 10 padded chairs (catalogue No Y714) at £35 each less 25% trade discount. The order number is X275. The terms are 5% 7 days, 2½ % 14 days and net thereafter.

		INVOICE	No. _____

To: .... Date ....
.... VAT Registration No 143271
.... Your Order No ....
....

Cat No	Quantity	Description	Unit Price	Total Price
		% VAT		
Terms:			£	

30. Statement of account

Several invoices may be received during the month from the same supplier and therefore each invoice is not paid as it arrives, but one cheque is made out to settle the account. This is done when the Monthly Statement comes. It shows the balance outstanding (amount owed) at the beginning of the month, adding any invoices or debit notes, and deducting any payments received, cash discount or credit notes. The balance at the end of the month is the amount owed and the statement is really a request for payment of the account.

31.   **Example of a statement**

STATEMENT

THE ALBION SUPPLY CO LTD
Ashfield Avenue
West Street Corner
MIDDLESBOROUGH
Cleveland MR16 3AL

Tel: 88226   Account No: 12345

To: R. Fisher & Company
     'Pet Place'
     Martin Street
     SHEFFIELD
     S30 5AP

Terms: 5% cash discount   Date: 31 August 199-
        if paid by 28 September

Date	Invoice Ref	VAT Rate	Debit	Credit	Balance
4 August	6342	17.5	929.42		929.42
					£929.42

N.B. Any other invoices during   The last amount
      the month would also be   in this column
      shown on the statement   is the amount due

32. **Credit note**

A credit note is sent by a supplier to a customer to make an allowance which is deducted from the original invoice. This might happen where:

❐ There is an overcharge on an invoice

❐ Goods are lost in transit

❐ Goods are returned as damaged, faulty, incorrect or short

❐ Empty packing cases or delivery pallets etc., which have been charged on the invoice, are returned.

Credit notes are usually printed in red to distinguish them from other documents.

33. **Debit note**

Debit notes are sent to customers to notify them of an increase in the amount owed, since it is easier to send a separate document rather than alter the invoices and accounts. For example, a debit note may be sent to correct a mistake on an invoice or to charge for packing cases or delivery pallets which have not been returned.

Task 5   **6.2.2, 6.2.3 (N3.2)**

1. Calculate the total cost of the following order. £1,000 worth of goods delivered on 4th August 19..

   Terms are 20% trade discount and 5% within 30 days.

2. The firm had a debit note for £50 and a credit note for £125. What would be the balance shown on the August statement?

3. If the firm settled in full by 5th September, what would be the amount paid?

34. VAT is a tax on sales and is added to the selling price of most goods and services at the standard rate of $17\frac{1}{2}\%$.

    As the name suggests, it is a tax on the value added to items at all stages of manufacturing and distribution. For example, when a manufacturer sells goods to a wholesaler, VAT is added to the invoice. When the wholesaler sells the goods to retailers, he also adds VAT to his invoice. Finally, the retailer includes VAT in the selling price so it is the final consumer who actually pays it.

35. **Example**

Manufacturer sells a stool for	£8.00
Plus VAT at 17.5%	£1.40
Total selling price	£9.40
Wholesaler sells stool for	£12.00
Plus VAT at 17.5%	£2.10
Total selling price	£14.10
Retailer sells stool for	£22.00
Plus VAT at 17.5%	£3.85
Final price to customer	£25.85

36. Therefore it can be seen that VAT has been passed on at each stage until the stool is bought by the final customer. The manufacturer, wholesaler and retailer can claim back the VAT paid from the Government. Therefore only the final consumer actually pay it.

Task 6   **6.2.2, 6.2.3 (C3.2)**

Match the documents in List A with the correct definition in List B. Use each letter once only. You do not have to use every definition.

List A Documents		List B Definitions	
1	Advice note	a	Used when goods are sent on approval
2	Statement of account	b	A request to a firm asking them to supply goods
3	Order	c	Summary of a customer's transactions with the selling firm
4	Debit Note	d	Used when goods are delivered in a firm's own vehicle
		e	Used when goods are damaged and/or returned
		f	Is sent to rectify an undercharge
		g	Informs the buyer that goods are being delivered

Export Documents

37. It should be noted that some or all of the following additional documents may be used by firms which are involved in overseas trade. Export documents are necessary for the movement of goods, for invoicing the customer, for receiving payment for the goods delivered, and to satisfy various government regulations, both in the United Kingdom and overseas.

   ❑ **The Bill of Lading.** This is used when goods are sent by sea. The shipping company provides a printed form which the cargo owner completes giving details of the:

   i) Name of the ship and port of loading

   ii) Description of the cargo and its destination

   iii) Charges payable

   At the destination, a copy of the Bill of Lading is presented by the importer to claim the goods at the dockside. It provides a 'document of title' (i.e. proof of ownership) which is important because the goods may have been sold whilst at sea.

   ❑ **The Air Consignment Note or Air Waybill**. This is used as a receipt for goods sent by air. However, it is not a 'document of title' like a Bill of Lading.

   ❑ **The Customs Declaration.** This is used for statistical purposes. It gives details of the type and value of the goods. This information is used in compiling the monthly trade figures.

   ❑ **The Shipping Note.** This document is sent to the Port Authorities when goods are delivered to the docks. It gives details of the goods, name of ship and destination port, and acts as a docks receipt.

   ❑ **The Certificate of Origin.** This provides evidence of where the goods were made. It is important because goods from some countries (for example outside the EC) will be subject to customs duties.

   ❑ **The Insurance Certificate**. This provides proof that goods have been insured against loss or damage during transit.

   ❑ **Consular Invoice**. Some countries require a copy of an export invoice which must be signed by the Consul in the importing country. This helps to speed up the customs procedures.

   ❑ **Import Licence**. Often this is required from the importing government before the goods are allowed into the country. It can be used to enforce quotas.

   ❑ **Export Licence.** This must be obtained before certain types of goods are allowed out of the country, for example, works of art or firearms.

38. Business documents are therefore a very important means of communication between an organisation and its customers. Developments in computer technology have made the issuing, monitoring and recording of such documents and transactions much quicker and easier for firms. Technology is also having an increasing impact on the methods of payment discussed below.

Payment Documents

39. The most common methods used by businesses and individuals to pay for goods and services are cheques and cash. Other methods include standing orders, direct debits, bank giro and credit cards. For many organisations the largest payments they make are the wages and salaries to employees.

40. **Cheques**

   A cheque is simply a written instruction to a bank by a person with a current account to transfer money from their account to someone else's. The name of the company or the person to whom the money is to be paid is called the **payee**. The **drawee** is the name of the bank, whilst the customer writing and signing the cheque is called the **drawer**. Each cheque has a serial number, sorting code and the customer's account number to help the bank in identification and sorting.

   There is also a counterfoil on which to record the date and amount of the cheque and to whom it is made payable.

41.   **Example of a cheque**

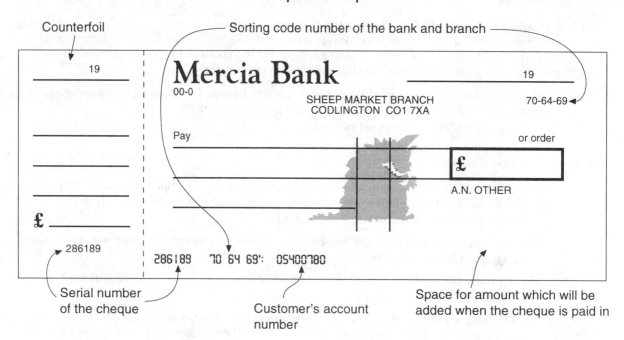

Counterfoil

Sorting code number of the bank and branch

Serial number of the cheque

Customer's account number

Space for amount which will be added when the cheque is paid in

42. An important feature of cheques is that they may be open or crossed. A crossed cheque is so called because it has two parallel lines across it. Crossing a cheque makes it much safer because it means that it must be paid into a bank account. Thus, if stolen it can be traced. For extra security, 'A/c payee only' is often added between the lines. This means that the cheque can only be paid into the payee's account. On the other hand, an open cheque can be cashed over the counter. It will be paid to whoever presents it at the bank on which it is drawn.

43. **Cheque cards**

These are issued by banks to reliable customers, and guarantee that their cheques will not 'bounce', provided that:

- ❑ they are not made out for more than the limit printed on the card – usually £50 or £100
- ❑ they are signed in the presence of the payee and the signature matches that on the card
- ❑ the card number is written on the back.

44. Therefore, it is not possible to 'stop payment' on any cheque given with a cheque card. Most businesses, including shops, garages, hotels and restaurants, will not accept cheques unless they are backed by a cheque card.

45.   **Example of a cheque card**

Front   **Reverse**

Task 7   **6.2.4 (C3.1, C3.2)**

Working in groups of two or three, visit a local shopping area and complete the following. You will need to make rough notes which can be copied up later.

1. List the commercial banks in the area.

2. Obtain leaflets from at least one of them on the services offered.

3. Make a list of five or six services which you and/or a business might use. Briefly explain each one.

4. Name the two most common types of bank account and explain the differences between them.

5. Find out what you would need to do to open a bank account.

46. **Standing orders**

A customer can request their bank to make regular payments on their behalf. These are known as standing orders which the bank will carry out until they are cancelled. They are used for paying rates, mortgages, insurance premiums, hire purchase instalments and other regular bills. If the amount to be paid by standing order changes, the customer must instruct the bank to pay the new amount.

47. **Direct debits**

These are similar to a standing order but, instead of instructing the bank to make regular payments on their behalf, the customer gives permission for a payee to withdraw money from their account. Direct debits are used when the amount is likely to vary – for example, trade union subscriptions which increase each year, or credit payments which might alter if the interest rate changes.

48. Standing orders and direct debits avoid the need to write cheques and mean that the account holder does not have to remember to make payments.

49. **Bank Giro or Credit Transfer**

The use of this service enables money to be transferred within the banking system. Payments can be transferred directly into the bank account of a payee at a branch of any bank anywhere in the UK.

A form is filled in for each payment, and the payer gives the bank a cheque or cash to cover the amount involved. Rent, gas, electricity and telephone bills are examples of payments which can be made by Bank Giro. People who do not have a bank account can also use the Giro service.

50. Bank Giro is most useful when several payments are made at the same time, because it is cheaper and easier than sending lots of cheques. By writing one cheque, a customer is able to have any number of payments transferred. For example, this is very often used when a company pays its employees wages directly into their bank accounts. It provides a very safe and simple method of payment with less chance of a mistake, since wage packets do not have to be made up.

51. The transfer of most payments by standing order, direct debit and bank giro take place electronically via the bankers automated clearing service (BACS). This enables payments to be transferred automatically from one bank account to another.

52.   **Bank Giro Credit being used to pay an electricity Budget Account**

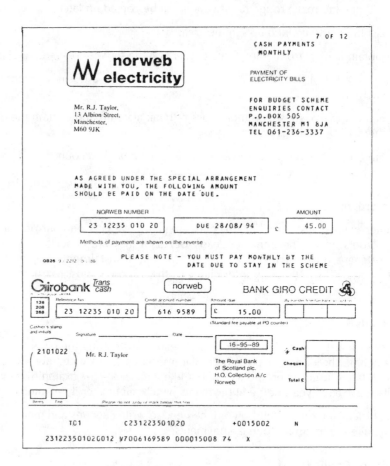

53. **Credit cards**

These are issued by most banks and some building societies e.g. ACCESS (Lloyds, Midland, NatWest, Royal Bank of Scotland) and VISA (Barclays, TSB, GiroBank, Leeds). Some are issued free of charge whilst others incur a small annual fee.

54. Credit cards enable the holder to buy goods or services at any shop, restaurant, garage etc which has joined the scheme. Each cardholder is given an overall personal limit, for example £750, which cannot be exceeded. Each organisation in the scheme is given a 'floor limit', for example £100, beyond which it cannot accept a credit card payment without first seeking authorisation from the credit card company. This is done either by telephoning the credit card company or by using a special machine with a direct computer link. The business receives payments from the credit card company. A small charge is made for this service (usually between 3% and 6%).

Payments in the future

55. In the future, banks will have less branches and make increasing use of post, telephones and automatic machines. Individuals and businesses will use cash and cheques to a lesser degree as more transactions are settled by credit cards and new methods of payment using computer technology, examples of which are DELTA, SWITCH, Electronic Data Interchange (EDI) and home banking.

More building societies will compete with banks by offering a wider range of financial services including current accounts with cheque books, personal loans and overdrafts.

56. DELTA (Barclays, Lloyds) and SWITCH (Midland, National Westminster, Yorkshire) like credit cards are systems of EFTPOS. Customers can use their Delta or Switch card to pay for purchases in shops and other organisations which are members of the scheme. This is much quicker and simpler than using cheques because the cardholder's current account is debited immediately. Retailers have to pay a fixed charge for transactions accepted on a Switch or Delta card but their account is instantly credited with the money.

57. EFTPOS operates using plastic cards which are 'swiped' through an electronic card reader linked to a computer network. This has the advantages of providing guaranteed payment to businesses in less time which reduces queues for customers. It also reduces security risks because there is less cash to handle.

58. As discussed in Chapter 7 (Element 2.3.) EDI will increasingly affect the methods used for purchasing and payment in business. As more and more businesses and financial organisations become involved whole transactions will become automated via computer networks making it a very quick, efficient and secure process.

59. **Home banking** involves the use of a special device which provides a link via a television set with the bank's computer. A customer can key into the computer to make transfers direct from their account to pay bills or to obtain up-to-date information. Business customers can also use this service which is now offered by several organisations, for example the Nottingham Building Society, the Royal Bank of Scotland and Giro Bank.

| **Task 8** | **6.2.2, 6.2.3, 6.2.4 (C3.2, N3.2)** |

On 7th March a manufacturer sold 200 cases of frozen food to a wholesaler at £12 per case less 15% discount, and an invoice was forwarded to the wholesaler together with the goods. A cash discount of 5% is allowed if payment is made within 7 days. The wholesaler paid the manufacturer on the 12th March by crossed cheque drawn on Midland Bank plc, Walsall.

1. What is trade discount and why is it given?

2. Why does the manufacturer offer cash discount to the wholesaler?

3. What was the total amount due to the manufacturer shown on the invoice?

4. How much did the wholesaler pay to settle the account on the 7th March?

5. What is a 'crossed cheque' and why are they used?

6. Suggest two other means of payment offered by a commercial bank and explain whether or not they are suitable for use in this situation?

Wages and Salaries

60. The money which people receive for work may be paid to them in cash, by cheque or directly into a bank or building society account by credit transfer. The term 'wages' is used when people are paid weekly, often in cash. A salary on the other hand is used to refer to a monthly payment, which is usually paid straight into an employee's bank account.

Payslip and Payroll

61. Details of how much an employee has earned and any deductions are given in the form of a *payslip* which everyone receives with their wages or salary. This is usually in the form of a slip of paper which tells an employee how their net pay has been calculated.

62. In addition an employer needs to keep a record of the wages and deductions for all employees. This is known as the *payroll*. Frequently nowadays computers are used which can calculate and print out the payroll and individual payslips.

Pay in Arrears

63. Many firms pay wages a week in arrears. This gives the wages department time to calculate the wages and make any necessary deductions, e.g. tax, national insurance, superannuation, trade union subscriptions.

64.
Example of a Wages Slip

Name	Date	Works Number	Tax Code	Basic Wage	Overtime	Tax	NI	Other Deductions	Net Wage
A VANN	28 Feb '95	43758	260L	200.60	25.40	53.90	14.20	4.70	153.20

65.
Example of a Salary Advice

Employee's Name	Pay Date (a)	Payroll Number (b)	NI Number (c)	Tax Code (d)	Basic Pay (e)	Overtime (f)	Total Gross Pay (g)
JONES S	28 FEB '95	04878341	YL979401B	260L	£770.94	£40.00	£810.94

NI (h)	Tax (i)	Superann (j)	Trade Union (k)	SAYE (l)	Other Deductions (m)	Total Deductions (n)	Month (r)
£31.22	£160.72	£48.66	£4.00	—	—	£244.60	Net Pay (s)

Taxable Pay to Date (o)		Tax to Date (p)		Superannuation to Date (q)			
£7597.31		£1581.37		£484.94			£566.34

A salary slip is similar to a wages slip but usually has more information on it as can be seen from above.

66. The letters used on S Jones' payslip are explained below:

a) *Payment* will be made on 28th February 1995

b) Firms usually give employees *individual reference numbers.*

c) Everyone, when they start work, is given a *National Insurance (NI) Number.*

d) A *Tax Code* is issued by the Inland Revenue and tells employers how much tax to deduct.

e) *Basic Pay* is the pay for a normal working week, say 40 hours.

f) Payments for working more than the normal working week are called *overtime.*

g) *Total Gross Pay* equals basic pay plus any overtime.

h) & i) are the *statutory deductions* from pay.

j), k), l) & m) are *voluntary deductions* from pay.

n) *Total deductions* includes the *total* of statutory and voluntary deductions.

o) *Taxable pay to date* shows how much S Jones has earned since April. His tax deductions are based on this figure.

p) *Tax to date* shows S Jones' tax since April 1994.

q) *Superannuation to date* shows the payments into the company's pension scheme since April 1994.

r) Month of *current tax year* beginning on 6th April.

s) *Net pay* is found by taking the total deductions of £244.60 from the total gross pay of £810.94, leaving £566.34.

Petty Cash

67. Most businesses pay for nearly everything by cheque. They also receive most payments in the form of cheques or cash which are then banked. These payments into and out of the bank are then recorded in the Cash Book for accounting purposes.

68. Every business, however, also needs to have some ready cash available to pay for small items of expenditure. Examples might be window cleaning, stamps, small stationary items, office tea, bus and taxi fares or entertaining customers. This money is called 'petty cash' the details of which are entered in a petty cash book. When expenditure takes place the details are recorded on a petty cash voucher to which receipts are attached.

69.

Example of Petty Cash Voucher

Petty cash voucher	Folio	*222*	
For what required	Date	*Jan 31st*	
	£	p
10 stamps (first class)	2	40
	2	40
Signature *J Jones*	Authorised by: *S Stanley*	

Task 9   6.2.4 (C3.3)

1. Make a list of five items which a business might purchase with petty cash.

2. Draw and complete a Petty Cash Voucher for two of the items you have listed in 1.

Receipt Documents

70. When a payment is made a receipt is usually needed as proof and for record-keeping purposes. The most usual receipt documents are simple sales receipts, cheques, paying in slips and bank statements.

Sales Receipts

71. If you buy goods or services from a retail outlet such as a supermarket, DIY store or insurance office you will usually be given a receipt for your payment. Likewise, when a business makes payments, particularly for cash, it will be given a receipt or *paid in full* may be written or stamped across the invoice.

Task 10   6.2.5 (C3.3)

Collect four examples of different sales receipts which you have been given.

Study these and the four shown on the following page.

Try to identify as many reasons as possible why receipts are given and why they are useful to both businesses and their customers.

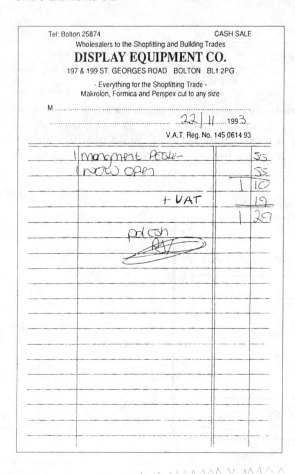

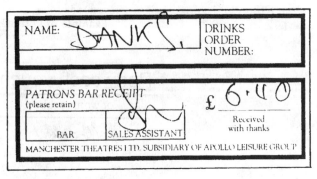

```
                    BOLTON 051
                  AT   C&A   WE
                  RECYCLE   HANGERS.

BOOTS THE CHEMIST LTD.,     21.02.94  0902 0902 051 9242
BOLTON
65 NEWPORT ST.     1105 1219 001     1968396  BRND SPORT    35.00
                                     1968703  BRND SPORT     9.99
NHS PRESCRIPTION 372        4.25
     TOTAL                  4.25     9242    2  **TOTAL**    44.99

     CASH                   5.00     4           VISA       44.99
     CHANGE                  .75
                   7/06/94  10:44
```

Cheque Receipt

72. Many organisations do not send a receipt when the payment is paid by cheque. The drawer will keep a record on the counter-foil and as cheques are usually crossed they must be paid into a bank account and therefore appear on a bank statement which in effect acts as a receipt. If requested a simple sales receipt would normally be given.

Paying In Slip

73. To pay into a bank account, a paying in slip is completed and this is handed, together with the cheques, notes and coins, to the cashier. When the items have been checked, the cashier will stamp and initial the paying in slip and the counterfoil (which acts as the customer's receipt).

74.

Paying-in slip

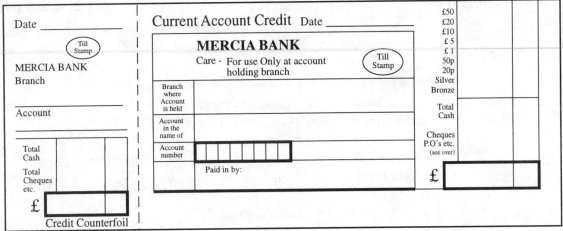

Bank Charges

75. Banks usually charge customers for the use of the current account. The charges will vary according to the number of cheques written, regular balance in the account and the other services which the bank provides. The charges are shown on a bank statement.

The Bank Statement

76. The bank keeps a record of every payment made into and every withdrawal out of a current account. At regular intervals, or on request, it sends a bank statement to customers which lists this information. The statement can be checked against the entries on cheque and paying-in slip counterfoils.

77.

Bank statement

BiS SPECIMEN ONLY Issued by Banking Information Service

IN ACCOUNT WITH

TITLE OF ACCOUNT   D K ARMSTRONG

BANK ...MOSS BANK LIMITED

BRANCH MANCHESTER

ACCOUNT NUMBER   22963714

STATEMENT NUMBER ☐ 4 ☐

DATE	PARTICULARS	PAYMENTS	RECEIPTS	BALANCE
	Balance Forward			
11 NOV	Balance forward			55.17
	226352	0.54		
	CD	25.00		
17 NOV	226351	6.86		22.77
	226354	8.93		
26 NOV	226350	21.50		7.66 DR
30 NOV	CITY OF MANCHESTER 321206 422631 BGC		216.97	209.31
	226356	30.00		
1 DEC	2 A/C SO	75.00		104.31
	STANDARD LIFE MC 101062 X21 DD	15.19		
2 DEC	66917325116 SO	65.13		23.99
	226357	41.50		
	226355	60.00		
10 DEC	BGC		33.72	43.79 DR
	226358	1.89		
	226359	5.99		
19 DEC	REMITTANCE		63.10	11.43 DR
	CHS	2.84		
	INTEREST	3.12		5.47

ABBREVIATIONS

BGC Bank Giro Credit	DIV Dividend	O/D or DR Overdrawn Balance	
DD Direct Debit	CHS Charges	SO Standing Order	
CD Cash Dispenser	ADV Separately Advised	TFR Inter-Account Transfer	

Task 11   **6.1.5, 6.2.4 (N3.2)**

1.   Enter the following 10 transactions on the Bank Statement below (or use a separate one if available). The balance b/f at 1 June was £115.50 and the account number is 07534217.

2.   Show the balance in the account at 30 June.

a)	6.6.199	Cheque no 117594 drawn	£4.50
b)	8.6.199	Cheque no 117597 drawn	£22.95
c)	10.6.199	Credit transfer received	£101.95
d)	11.6.199	Standing order paid	£12.00
e)	14.6.199	Cheque no 117596 drawn	£34.00
f)	14.6.199	Cash dispenser	£50.00
g)	18.6.199	Direct debit paid	£25.00
h)	19.6.199	Standing order paid	£20.00
i)	22.6.199	Cheque no 0907546 received	£13.90
j)	28.6.199	Bank charges	£3.70

MINSTER BANK   STATEMENT   R Jones Esq
14 High Street   OF   A/c No ....
ASHWORTH Notts   ACCOUNT   Date ....

DATE	DETAILS	DEBIT	CREDIT	BALANCE

Bank Reconciliation Statement

78.   To ensure that mistakes have not been made, when a Bank Statement is received it needs to be reconciled with the organisation's own record in the cash book.

79.   There may be differences between the two due to:

❒   clerical error – figures being wrongly entered or monies omitted

❒   cheques – not yet presented or cleared

❒   payments not yet entered in the cash book, e.g. bank charges, standing orders, direct debits or interest.

Importance of Correct Documentation

80. The use of business documents should enable an organisation to speed up its purchasing and sales procedures. Properly completed documents should enable it to operate more efficiently and effectively, thus providing a better service to its customers and suppliers.

81. Sometimes, however, they are not completed correctly. Errors and omissions can and do occur, e.g. prices, references or figures being wrongly entered or missed completely on orders, invoices or cheques. When this happens it can create confusion and consequently a range of problems for organisations. These may be minor, causing inconvenience but only needing time to correct or more serious resulting in false accounting or in extreme cases business failure.

82. Examples include:

    ❏ **incorrect purchases** – buying the wrong supplies which could be expensive in terms of time, lost production, re-ordering and waste.

    ❏ **incorrect sales** – late deliveries or supplying customers with the wrong items which may result in goods being returned and a loss of future business.

    ❏ **incorrect payment and receipts** – could lead to queries, money being 'lost', if customers are undercharged or payments delayed leading to poor cash flow, dissatisfied customers and suppliers.

    ❏ **incorrect accounts** – could result because the data used is unreliable, whilst errors in the accounts themselves can distort stock, purchases, sales and profit figures.

    ❏ **wrong information** about business performance will also result in making monitoring and control more difficult possibly leading to unexpected/unknown financial problems.

Security

83. Whatever methods are used to purchase and pay for goods and services, attention to security systems and procedures is essential to reduce the risk of theft and/or fraud.

84. Examples of measures which might be taken by a business include:

    ❏ **Authorisation of orders.** Usually orders can only be signed by specific people in an organisation. Sometimes they must be signed by more than one person and depending on the value of the order may require authorisation by a senior manager.

    ❏ **Checking procedures**. Deliveries, for example, are usually checked against the delivery note and likewise invoices checked against orders and goods received note to ensure that the business only pays for what it receives.

    ❏ **Authorised cheque signatories**. Only a small number of people in an organisation are usually allowed to sign cheques and the need for two signatories is quite common.

    ❏ **Crossed cheques** are now the norm. They must be paid into a bank account which helps to protect against fraud.

    ❏ **Physical devices** such as video cameras, screens and safes are used in many organisations to reduce the risk of theft, particularly of cash and goods.

    ❏ **Strict procedures** are usually laid down for the acceptance of cash, cheques and credit cards.

    ❏ **Segregation of duties**. For example to eliminate the opportunities for fraud, the responsibility for receiving goods and paying for goods is usually given to different people.

Task 12   **6.2.6, 6.2.7 (C3.4)**

SMEAR TEST BLUNDER

Almost 4,000 women are being recalled for cervical smear tests after a blunder by health chiefs. They will receive a letter advising them to see their doctor though experts said it was extremely unlikely that anyone's health had been put at serious risk. It has emerged that staff at a Family Health Services Authority in South-West London failed to key into computers a system for sending reminders about follow-up tests for women who had unsatisfactory or mildly abnormal smears. Those with more serious abnormalities did receive reminders.

GIRLS GUN TERROR

A girl cashier was held at gunpoint during a £45 raid at the Rushgreen Service Station at Lymm, Cheshire.

1. How do the above news items illustrate the importance of both the need for security in a business and also the problems which can be created from record-keeping errors?

2. Try to identify other examples from the media and/or your own experience and comment on the impact or potential consequences which each did or could have had on you and/or the organisation concerned.

Summary

85. a) All organisations whether profit-making or non-profit making need to keep a record of their financial transactions.

   b) In a typical business transaction any or all of the following special documents could be used to make it as quick and efficient as possible:

   i) Enquiry – a request for more information about goods

   ii) Quotation or tender – which will include details of any trade or cash discounts

   iii) Estimate – used where no price list exists

   iv) Order – a request for goods

   v) Goods received note – to provide a record of goods received

   vi) Acknowledgement of the order – to say that it has been received

   vii) Advice note – stating when the goods are likely to be delivered

   viii) Delivery or despatch note – used when goods are sent by the supplier's own vehicle

   ix) Consignment note – used when goods are sent by road or rail

   x) Invoice – which will take account of any debit or credit notes

   xi) Proforma invoice – similar to an invoice but not charged to a customers account

   xii) Statement of account – a request for payment

   xiii) Credit note – to make an allowance against an invoice

   xiv) Debit note – to correct an undercharge on an invoice

   c) VAT may well be added to an invoice, thus adding to the cost of the goods purchased. However, this is then added to the selling price so that in effect it is paid by the final consumer.

   d) Special documents must be used for exported goods.

   e) Goods and services may be paid for in many ways including cash, cheques, standing order, direct debit, bank giro, credit cards, EFTPOS. and EDI

f)   Receipts are usually given as proof of payment and may also be used for record-keeping purposes.

g)   Incorrectly completed documents can create confusion and problems for a business.

h)   Security systems and personnel are needed to reduce the risk of theft and/or fraud in a business.

Review Questions *(Answers can be found in the paragraphs indicated)*

1.   Why is it necessary for organisations to keep accounts? (1)

2.   Why are special documents used for business transactions? (2)

3.   Explain the difference between a quotation and an estimate. (8–10, 15)

4.   What is the significance of trade and cash discount in business? (12–14)

5.   Identify and explain some examples of sales documents which a business might use. (22–28)

6.   Explain the difference between an invoice and a proforma invoice. (26–28)

7.   Outline the content and purpose of a Statement of Account. (30–31)

8.   In what situations are credit notes used and what effect do they have on a customer's account? (32)

9.   Which documents would be made out to correct an undercharge on an invoice? (33)

10. Briefly explain how an organisation could be affected by VAT. (34–36)

11. Why are special export documents needed? (37)

12. List six documents which are used when goods are exported. (37)

13. Outline the main payment documents which are likely to be used in a business. (39–69)

14. In what ways are methods of payment likely to change in the future? (55–59)

15. Identify the receipt documents most commonly used in a business. (70–74)

16. Why is a Bank Reconciliation Statement needed? (78–79)

17. Why is the correct completion of documents so important for a business? (80–82)

18. How can a business reduce the risks involved in its buying and selling procedures? (83–84)

Assignment – Business Documentation   **Element 6.2**

1. Copy and complete the flow chart by filling in the words from the list below in the correct order.

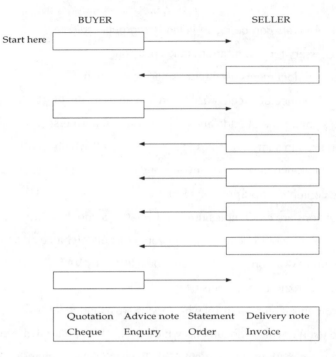

Quotation	Advice note	Statement	Delivery note
Cheque	Enquiry	Order	Invoice

2. Briefly explain the purpose of each document.

3. Suggest and briefly explain two other documents which could be used in a business transaction.

4–6 are based on a transaction between S. Bray and Quick Fit Ltd.

4. From the order on the following page, complete the invoice No. 123 dated 15 July 19--. VAT at $17\frac{1}{2}$ per cent is applicable to all the goods which are subject to 20% Trade Discount. A further 5% Cash Discount is offered if the invoice is paid within one month.

   Calculate the total cost of the goods ordered.

   For each calculation, show how you worked out your answer.

5. One of the central heating boilers was returned by S. Bray because it was faulty.

   a) What is the name of the document which Quick Fit Ltd would send to S. Bray?

   b) What will be the amount shown on the document?

6. On 31 July, Quick Fit Ltd sent a statement to S. Bray. Invoice No. 123 and the document in Task 4 were the only items shown on the statement.

   a) Calculate the balance owing on 31 July.

   b) S. Bray paid his account by cheque on 18 August 19--. How much did he pay?

ORDER

Quick Fit Ltd
12 Silver Road
CROYDON

To: S. Bray (Plumbers' Merchants)   No: 251
17 Farwood Road
GUILDFORD   10 July 19--

PLEASE SUPPLY THE FOLLOWING GOODS

Cat. No.	Quantity	Details	Unit Price
4/34	20 metres	Copper pipe 22 mm	£2.80
5/38	100 tins	Putty	0.90
30/46	4	Radiators 950 mm single	£45.80
3/94	2	Central Heating Boilers 40,000 BTU	£95.90

INVOICE

Quick Fit Ltd
12 Silver Road
CROYDON

To: Date

Your Order No.

VAT Registration No.
197476323

Cat. No.	Quantity	Description	Unit Price £	Total Price £
			% VAT	

Terms:

E and O E

21 Costing, Pricing and Break-even

This chapter considers the costs which a business faces and how these are used to determine pricing and break-even. It includes:

Element 6.3

❑ The cost of goods and services

❑ Direct and indirect costs

❑ Unit costs of production or service

❑ Standard costing

❑ Variance analysis

❑ Marginal cost

❑ Absorption costing

❑ Full costing

Element 6.4

❑ Pricing objectives

❑ Related pricing strategies

❑ Break-even analysis

❑ Selected operating point

❑ Margins of safety

❑ Stepped break-even chart

❑ Uses of break-even analysis

The Cost of Goods and Services

1. An organisation needs to determine how much it is going to charge for its goods and services. In order to do this it must calculate the costs involved in producing them and then determine the profit margin which it wishes to add. The rest of this chapter is about the costs associated with running a business, (usually classified as fixed or variable) and how these can be controlled to help maximise profits.

2. **Fixed costs** are those costs which do not vary in direct proportion to a firm's output. They have to be paid regardless of the level of output. Even if there is no output at all, a firm will still have fixed costs which it must meet. For example rent of premises, rates, heating, lighting, insurance, postage and telephone, cost of management, supervision, maintenance, administration and marketing. Fixed costs are also known as **indirect costs** or **overheads** because they are not directly involved in the production of goods or services.

3. <center>**Fixed costs and average fixed costs**</center>

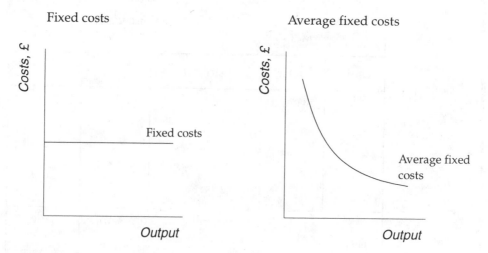

4. If we know the total fixed costs then we can calculate the average fixed cost (AFC) per unit of output. For example, if 10,000 units are to be produced and fixed costs are £20,000 then:

$$\text{AFC per unit} = \frac{£20,000}{10,000} = £2 \text{ per unit}$$

Clearly the higher the output, the lower will be the average fixed cost per unit as shown in the above diagram

> ## Task 1   6.3.1 (C3.2)
>
> The total output of goods or services which a firm is able to produce is known as its capacity. If a manufacturing firm with fixed costs of £20,000 has a capacity of 10,000 pa units but is currently only producing 8,000 units p.a.
>
> 1.   Name three fixed costs and three variable costs it is likely to have.
>
> 2.   Indicate the significance, if any, of it operating at less than full capacity.

5.   You could argue that some overheads, such as postage and packing, maintenance and depreciation, are not fixed but do vary with the level of production. **Depreciation** is discussed in Chapter 24 (Element 7.3.) but it is important to note here that a business must allow for the fact that assets, such as machinery, computers and vehicles wear out over time and need to be replaced. Therefore this cost of depreciation is usually spread over the useful life of the asset and charged annually in the accounts. For example, a machine costing £10,000 with a useful life of 5 years could be assumed to depreciate by £2000 per annum.

6.   **Direct costs** or the cost of production, on the other hand, vary directly with output. For example, if a firm produces more goods, it will need additional raw materials, labour, power and transport. Direct costs are also known as **variable or prime costs** because they can be clearly allocated to a particular product or service. Hence we have direct-labour and direct-material costs.

7.

Costs

Variable costs

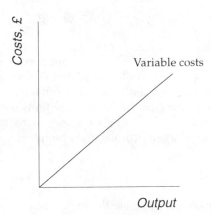

8.   **Semi-Variable costs**. It is better to consider some costs as containing both a fixed and a variable element. Thus, for example, an electricity bill will include a fixed standing charge irrespective of a firm's output, but the cost of electricity will vary with the number of units produced.

9.   **Example**

	Outputs	**Costs**
	(Units)	(£)
High Output	10,000	5,000
Low Output	5,000	3,000
Difference	5,000	2,000

Since each cost contains the same fixed cost if the figures are subtracted, we can calculate the variable costs needed to produce the extra units. That is, to produce an extra 5,000 units increases costs by £2,000 so the variable cost per unit is

$$\frac{£2,000}{5,000} = £0.40$$

The fixed costs for the high output can then be calculated as follows:

Variable costs = 10,000 units x 0.40p = £4,000

Fixed costs = Total costs – Variable Cost = (£5,000 – £4,00) = £1,000

10. **Stepped Fixed Costs**. These are costs which stay constant over a range of output and then suddenly increase at certain levels. Consider for example, a supervisor who can only effectively manage 10 workers. The employment of any additional staff therefore, would also require an extra supervisor, hence their salary would become a stepped fixed cost. This is shown graphically in paragraph 29.

11.

Stepped fixed costs

Stepped fixed costs

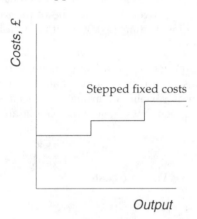

Output

12. **Unit Costs**. The total costs of production are made up by fixed costs plus variable costs. Therefore, by dividing this figure by total output the average unit cost of each item produced can be calculated. Thus, for example, a publisher would calculate the average unit cost of producing a book, a restaurant owner the cost of a meal and a wallpaper manufacturer the cost of each roll produced. These costs are particularly important because many firms use cost-plus pricing policies whereby they add a percentage profit margin to the unit cost to determine the selling price. The two basic methods of defining cost are marginal costing and absorption costing.

Task 2   **6.3.1, 6.3.2, 6.3.4 (N3.2)**

1. Using the same example, calculate the fixed costs and unit costs for the low level of output of 5,000 units.

2. Suggest two other semi-variable costs which an organisation could face.

Unit Costs of Production or Service

13. Costs can be measured in different ways depending on the product and organisation concerned. The unit cost of production in a manufacturing industry, for example, is usually calculated from the direct costs of labour, material and other expenses involved. Thus

$$\frac{\text{Total output}}{\text{Total costs}} = \text{unit cost of production}$$

14. In service industries it is not quite so straightforward and therefore costs are usually based on other units, for example

- ❑ cost per call unit e.g. telephones
- ❑ cost per labour hour e.g. hairdressers, car mechanics
- ❑ cost per passenger mile e.g. railways, airlines

Task 3   6.3.2 (N3.1, N3.2)

1. Calculate the unit cost of producing 1,000 widgets where the total cost is £380.

2. Assume that 200 are damaged and cannot be sold. What is the unit cost of the widgets sold?

3. If the total charge for a sales conference is £2,200, compare the rate per delegate if 30, 40 or 50 sales persons attend.

4. If the cost to the conference venue is £19.50 per head, what is the impact of 30, 40 or 50 delegates attending?

Standard Costing

15. Standard costing is the calculation of how much costs should be under defined working conditions and is best suited to repetitive manufacturing processes. Standard costs are usually based on the time (in standard hours or minutes) required to complete a certain volume of work. Thus, for example, standard costs would be established for labour, materials, production and sales. A proportion of indirect costs or overheads will then be added to these costs.

16. Costing is important because it provides an analysis of data which a business can then use for decision taking. For example, deciding whether to make products itself or to buy from someone else, or whether or not it can make sufficient profit to enable it to enter particular market segments.

Variance Analysis

17. The differences between the actual results achieved and the planned budget or standard cost are called variances. These are used to prepare **exception reports** for management which are used to quickly focus attention on potential problem areas in the business so that corrective action can be taken.

18. Variances can be:

- ❑ **negative (adverse)** which occurs when actual revenues fall short of the budget or standard, or when actual costs exceed budget or standard.

- ❑ **positive (favourable)** which occurs when actual revenues exceed budget or standard, or when actual costs are less than budget or standard.

19. The main variances cover Direct-Materials, Direct-Labour, Overheads and Sales-Revenue. Each of these is now considered in more detail including possible reasons for the variances.

Direct -Material Variances

20. ❑ **Material-price variances.** If the prices paid for materials are higher or lower than the standard, it could mean that the market price has changed or that the firms' buying policy needs attention.

21. ❑ **Material-usage variances.** If more materials have been used than the standard, this could reflect inefficiency, high wastage, theft or poor quality.

Direct Labour Variances

22 ❐ **Labour-rate variances.** The most usual problem in a business is that there has been an increase in the rates paid. This may be due to excessive overtime or because higher paid labour is being used. If the changed rates are to be the norm in the future, then the standard will need revising.

23. ❐ **Labour-efficiency variances**. This shows whether more or less time has been spent on production than the standard allows. This may necessitate remedial action to sort out problems which may be due to worker inefficiency, machine breakdowns, poor planning or material shortages.

Overhead Variances

24. ❐ **Overhead expenditure variances**. If expenditure is higher than the standard it could mean that the full-cost of overheads is not being **absorbed** (covered) in the price. Any inaccuracy must therefore be rectified and any permanent change in the overhead costs would require the standard to be changed. **Over-absorption** would take place if the actual overhead costs are less than the standard.

25. ❐ **Overhead volume variances.** If actual output is less than planned, this will produce a variance because the fixed overheads will not then be fully absorbed. On the other hand, over-absorption of overheads occurs when more is produced than planned.

Sales-Revenue Variances

26. ❐ **Sales price variances**. If the actual sales, based on the costs of production, are less than the standard cost, then this will be of concern to a business because it is likely to reduce profits. It may indicate that the cost of sales is higher than expected.

27. ❐ **Sales volume variances.** If the actual volume of sales are less than the standard or budgeted volume, then a firm will need to identify why and take action to correct it. Reasons might include increased competition, or problems with some element of the marketing mix.

Task 4   **6.3.2 (N3.2)**

A company has production and sales targets of 10,000 items for the current year. Its production levels are usually fairly even throughout the year but sales are subject to wide fluctuations with most taking place in the first half of the trading period.

After 6 months, its actual production is running at 6,000 units with sales of 4,500 units. The Board had recently decided to raise prices to cover the rising cost of raw materials.

1.   What variances, if any, should be brought to the attention of the Board?

2.   What are the implications for the Company and what action would you recommend?

---

28. **Marginal Cost.** The extra cost (addition to total cost) of increasing output by one more unit is called the marginal cost. Since, in the short run, fixed costs do not vary with output, marginal costs (MC) are entirely marginal variable costs. As shown in the following diagram MC initially falls reflecting increasing returns to the variable-factor input, but then rises as decreasing returns set in:

29.

Marginal cost

Marginal cost

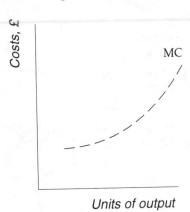

30. MC together with Marginal Revenue (MR), the addition to total revenue from the sale of one extra unit of output, determine the level of output at which a firm achieves its maximum profit. Since MR is, in effect the price, profit maximisation takes place at the level of output at which MC = MR.

Total Absorption Costing

31. Absorption costing involves ensuring that the total unit cost of a product includes (absorbs) all the costs of an organisation, both direct and indirect. It is relatively straightforward to calculate the direct costs of labour, materials and other expenses but much more complex to calculate the indirect costs such as administration and rent and rates.

Absorption Costing

32. In order to establish the true cost of a product then a share of the indirect costs must be allocated to each unit made. The basis of this allocation should ideally depend on the proportion of costs which any particular cost centre uses (i.e. absorbs).

33. Once the total overheads have been estimated there are many alternative methods for allocating them to cost centres. For example:

   ❑ **space used or units of output produced** could be used to allocate rent and rates;

   ❑ **value of assets or number of machine hours used** for depreciation or insurance

   ❑ **number of employees** in a cost centre for administration, health and safety and catering

   ❑ **direct material costs** for storage and material handling.

34. In practice more than one method may be used to suit the needs of the organisation and ultimately it is likely to be the cost accountant who makes the decision. What is important, however, is that if managers are to have effective responsibility for cost control, overheads must be apportioned on a basis which is easy to understand and seen as logical and fair to all concerned.

Full Costing

35. A simplified version of absorption costing, which is often used by small organisations, involves the allocation of overheads to cost centres on a more arbitrary basis. The underlying assumption made with full costing is that cost centres which have the highest variable cost also have the highest proportion of overheads allocated to them.

Example – Full Costing

36. XYZ Manufacturing Limited has four production departments. It has estimated costs for the next 12 months as follows:

Overheads

Rent and Rates	£45,000
Administration	£22,000
Depreciation	£16,000
Maintenance	£10,000
Heat, Light and power	£12,000
Indirect labour	£40,000
	£145,000

Department	1	2	3	4	Total
Direct Labour	12,500	10,000	15,000	7,500	45,000
Direct Materials	22,500	17,000	20,000	10,000	69,500
Overheads	?	?	?	?	145,000
					259,500

The total overheads are to be shared amongst the four departments using the **full-cost method**. The allocation is based on the proportion of direct material costs which each cost centre uses. Therefore the overheads for Department 1 would be allocated as follows:

$$\text{Apportioned overheads} = \frac{\text{Cost Centre basis}}{\text{Total basis}} \times \text{Total overheads}$$

$$= \frac{22,500}{69,500} \times 145,000 = £46,942$$

Task 5

6.3.2, 6.3.5 (N3.2)

1. Using the full-cost method complete the overhead allocation for XYZ Manufacturing Ltd on a direct material basis.

2. Now calculate the overhead allocation on a direct labour basis.

3. Comment on any significant differences between the two sets of figures and state, with reasons, which basis you feel would be the most appropriate to use.

4. The planned output for each department is:

   1 5000 units; **2** 7,500 units; **3** 8,000 units; **4** 2,700 units

   Calculate the unit cost for each using the figures in paragraph 41 and the allocation of overheads which you worked out for 1 above.

Example – Absorption Costing

37. XYZ decides instead to allocate overheads using the absorption rate method. The total floor space of 35,000 square metres is occupied as follows:

Department 1	6,000 sq m.
2	7,500 sq m.
3	15,000 sq m.
4	6,500 sq m.

Therefore the proportion of rent and rates allocated to each department would be calculated as follows:

$$\text{Overheads absorbed} = \frac{\text{Cost Centre basis}}{\text{Total basis}} \times \text{Overheads}$$

The cost centre basis in this situation is the chosen alternative method such as the value of assets, number of employees or, as in this case, the floor space used.

Therefore Rent and Rates absorbed by Department 1 = $\dfrac{6,000}{35,000} \times £45,000 = £7,714$

Task 6   6.3.5, 6.3.6 (N3.2)

1. From the above information calculate the allocation of rent and rates for Departments 2, 3 and 4.

2. Administration costs are allocated to departments on the basis of direct labour used. From the information in paragraph 36 calculate the amount of administration absorbed by each department.

Pricing Objectives

38. If an organisation is to maximise its sales and profit potential it must have sound pricing strategies which support its marketing and corporate objectives. Clearly pricing objectives will not be the same for all business but commonly they will include the following:

    ❒ **Profitability** a key objective clearly would be to set the price which achieves an overall level of profitability for the business. A target might be to increase this profit level.

    ❒ **Rate of return** – a firm may seek to obtain a specified return on its investment (capital employed) e.g. at least 10% or 20% pa.

    ❒ **Growth** – a price must be set which provides a steady profit over a period of years to enable the firm to survive and grow.

    ❒ **Competition** – the price charged should be competitive and attractive to customers. It can also be used to beat rivals in a price war or to discourage new firms from entering the market. In recent years many retail firms like Do-It-All and Currys have offered price promises like, 'never knowingly undersold'.

    ❒ **Market Share** – a price must be set which enables a firm to at least maintain its market share. Whilst lower prices may be used in an attempt to increase sales and market share by a quantifiable amount e.g. 10,000 or 10%.

    ❒ **Utilise capacity** – a price must be set which attracts business and avoids under-used capacity. Unit costs are lower when capacity is fully utilised because fixed costs are spread over a larger output.

Related Pricing Strategies

39. In Chapter 2 (Element 1.2.) we considered a number of different pricing strategies. It is, however, worth mentioning here the strategies which can be adopted to achieve each of the objectives identified in paragraph 38.

Profit and Rate of Return

40. All businesses, except perhaps in the short-term, need to make a profit in order to survive. Cost-plus pricing is often used to ensure that this happens. This involves determining prices by adding a profit mark-up (usually a percentage) to the unit cost of products. By using absorption costing all costs are included in the unit cost figure. The term 'mark-up' is usually used in the retail trade and **'cost-plus'** in manufacturing but both refer to the same method for determining prices.

Growth and Market Share

41. Typical strategies which are used to achieve these objectives include promotional or penetration pricing. These involve offering products for sale at lower than normal prices for a period of time in order to attract extra customers. This could be a few days, weeks or even months depending on the objective to be achieved.

Competition

42. In a competititive market price will be a very important factor and often it is determined largely by what other firms are charging for the same product. If products are priced very differently the consumer will tend to buy from the cheapest seller.

Under-used Capacity

43. To prevent this happening firms often sell some products whose price is based on marginal costs. Any unit sold at a price in excess of its marginal cost makes a contribution to fixed costs.

Unit Sales Price – Unit Marginal Cost = contribution

If an organisation produces and sells enough units to make a total contribution in excess of total fixed costs, it will make a profit.

44. Where a business is profitable at one level of production and sales in certain circumstances it can make additional profit by selling further production at any price above the marginal cost. An airline, for example, may be profitable if it flies with 70% of its seats sold at a standard fare. It can therefore make extra profit if it sells the remaining seats at a price which covers little more than the cost of the in-flight meal. The railways also operate a pricing structure which seeks to attract extra passengers at off-peak times when capacity would otherwise be very much under-utilised.

Task 7   **6.4.1 (C3.4)**

HOLIDAY PRICES SLASHED

Leading holiday companies such as Airtours and First Choice are continuing to slash summer prices. The package tour giants cancelled around 7% of holidays in July-September after heavy discounts in June failed to pull in customers. Over-capacity plus hot weather at home is causing a drain on profits. $1\frac{1}{2}$ million summer holidays remain unsold.

Many tour companies make 75% of annual profits in August alone. Further discounts on slow-selling destinations – Greece, Cyprus and Turkey – mean some will barely break even in the month. A number of smaller operators are expected to go out of business.

1. Why are the prices of summer holidays being reduced?

2. How does this article illustrate the importance of pricing objectives in a business?

Break-Even Analysis

45. This is an extension of marginal costing which is used to identify a businesses break-even point. That is, the point at which it makes neither a profit or loss because its total sales revenue equals its total costs. Linked with the concept of planning through budgetary control is the use of break-even charts. A break-even chart can be used to enable firms to analyse changes in sales volume, prices and costs as shown below.

A Output (no of units) produced) £	B Fixed Costs £	C Variable Costs £	D (B+C) Total Costs, £	E Sales Revenue £	F (E+D) Profit £	G (E+D) Loss £
0	2000	0	2000	0		2000
100	2000	500	2500	1000		1500
200	2000	1000	3000	2000		1000
300	2000	1500	3500	3000		500
400	2000	2000	4000	4000	NIL	NIL
500	2000	2500	4500	5000	500	
600	2000	3000	5000	6000	1000	
700	2000	3500	5500	7000	1500	
800	2000	4000	6000	8000	2000	

46. The above information shows a firm with variable costs of £5 per unit and a selling price of £10 per unit. In this situation the firm would need to sell 400 units before it reaches break-even point i.e. where total costs = total sales revenue. Beyond this point a profit can be made. However, if the firm sells less than 400 units it will be operating at a loss.

The break even point can be calculated using the following formula:

$$\text{Break-even} = \frac{\text{Total fixed costs (F)}}{\text{Contributions per unit (C)}}$$

Remember that C = selling price per unit (S) – Variable costs per unit (V)

Thus in the example above, we know that F = £2,000 S = £10 V = £5

$$\text{Therefore break-even} = \frac{2,000}{10-5} = \frac{2,000}{5} = 400 \text{ units}$$

Variable costs at break-even point = 400 × £5 = £2,000

47. This information can also be shown graphically on a break-even chart which illustrates a firm's profit or loss at different levels of output.

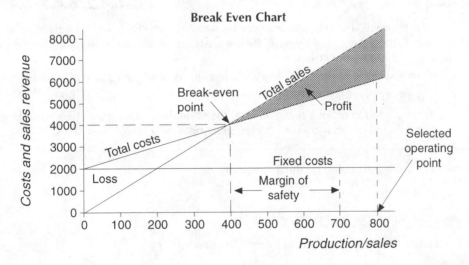

Break Even Chart

48. In the illustration the sales revenue of £6,000 would represent the sale of 600 items sold for £10 each. From the chart, we can also see that it would cost £5,000 to make this number of items. Thus the cost of producing each item would be £5,000 divided by 600 = £8.33. Thus the profit per item sold was £1.67 (£10-£8.33).

49. On the other hand, if sales were only £3,000 i.e. 300 items, we can see that the total cost would be £3,500. Thus to produce each item it would cost £11.67 (£3,500 divided by 300). At this level of sales, the firm would be making a loss of £1.67 per item.

50. As the firm sells more so the unit or average cost of producing each unit will fall. This is because the fixed costs do not change and therefore these costs are spread over a larger output.

$$\text{Unit cost} = \frac{2,000}{10-5} = \frac{\text{Total cost}}{\text{Output}}$$

Using the figures in the above example

a) At an output of 100 Unit Cost $= \dfrac{2,500}{100} = £25$ per unit

b) At an output of 500 Unit Cost $= \dfrac{4,500}{500} = £9$ per unit

Thus, although the variable cost per unit is still £5, the fixed cost per unit has fallen from £20 (£25–£5) to £4 per unit (£9–£5).

51. If the organisation has a specific target profit to aim at then the number of units which need to be produced and sold to achieve it can be calculated from the break-even analysis as follows

$$\text{Selected Operating Point} = \frac{\text{Fixed Costs + Target Profit}}{\text{Contribution per Unit}}$$

Thus, if in the above example we assume that a profit target of £2000 has been set then the

$$\text{Selected Operating Point} = \frac{2,000 + 2,000}{5} = 800 \text{ units}$$

52. The amount by which the selected operating point exceeds the break-even point is known as the **margin of safety.** Again in the example break-even is at 400 units, therefore the margin of safety is also 400 units (800 – 400). In other words it is the amount by which sales could fall from the planned level before the organisation ceases to make a profit.

Task 8	**6.4.2, 6.4.3, 6.4.4 (N3.3)**

Gary Carter owns a small garage where he services cars. Each week he usually has about 30 customers, the average bill being £100 per customer. Fixed costs are £400 per week, variable costs are about £60 per customer.

1. Give examples of possible fixed and variable costs which Gary will have in his business.
2. Construct a break-even chart. Identify and explain the break-even point.
3. If he wanted to make a profit of £900 per week how many customers would he need and what would be his margin of safety? Show both on a break-even chart.

53. Break-even analysis is based on the assumptions that

❒ all goods produced are sold

❒ costs and selling price remain constant

❒ fixed costs, technology and capacity remain constant.

54. In reality of course these variables can and do change. For example, fixed costs may rise as output and sales increase because new assets may be needed to provide the required capacity. In this situation the fixed cost line would show a series of steps indicating that the area of profit is reduced as capacity increases as shown on the following diagram.

55.

A Stepped Break-Even Chart

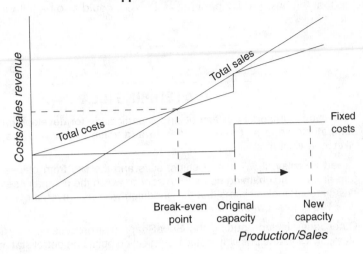

Uses of break-even analysis

56. Break-even analysis is useful to business organisations because it enables them to

☐ measure the profits and losses at different levels of production and sales

☐ analyse the relationship between fixed and variable costs

☐ predict the effect of changes in price on sales

☐ predict the effect on profitability of changes in costs and efficiency

☐ assess the effect of changes in capacity brought about by investment in new fixed assets (see diagram – stepped break-even)

☐ examine different production strategies, for example comparing capital intensive which produces high fixed costs and labour intensive which has lower fixed costs

☐ examine 'what if ' scenarios, for example, the impact on profit if sales fall by 10% (see diagram sales below production) or rent increases 20%, which will add to the fixed costs.

☐ when starting a business it can be used to help find the level of production and sales needed to cover costs or achieve a level of profit. It can therefore form part of the business plan.

57.

Costs and Sales Reviewing

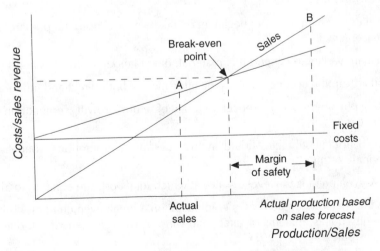

Because demand was less the anticipated the level of sales has fallen below the margin of safety which means that the business is operating at a loss. It could also be left with stocks of goods which it cannot sell.

Task 9   6.1.1, 6.4.5 (C3.4)

A FETCHING IDEA

Innovation is important in any business particularly for development and keeping a competitive edge as the latest idea to add value to the services of dry cleaners Sketchley illustrates.

Called Fetchley, it will collect shirts, suits and the like from offices, with a 48-hour turn-around and charging no extra. A service which the company believes is ideal for busy people. It also claims that the operation will break even if every van driver handles 100 orders a week.

Other ideas include putting the SupaSnaps film processing side into another 60 stores in 1995 and possibly installing collection points on petrol station forecourts.

Careerwear (Sketchley's uniform business) has recently designed new outfits for Lunn Poly, Alamo Car Rental and Alpha Flight Services. Sketchley's own staff go into new uniforms from September 1995.

---

1. What, if anything, does this article tell you about the use of break-even in business?

2. Who is added-value important to and in what ways is this illustrated in the article?

Summary

a) Costs in a business can be fixed, that is those which remain the same regardless of output, or variable – those which increase as output increases.

b) Dividing the total fixed and variable costs by total output gives the unit cost, whilst the marginal cost is the extra cost of producing one more unit.

c) Overhead costs can be allocated to unit costs using various methods including absorption costing and full costing.

d) Costs can be controlled by the use of standard costing and the monitoring of variances.

e) Standard costing is the calculation of how much costs should be under defined working conditions.

f) Differences between the actual results achieved and the planned budget or standards are called variances.

g) Variances, which can be negative or positive, are used to prepare exception reports for management.

h) The main variances cover direct material, direct labour, overheads and sales revenue.

i) Total absorption costing involves the allocation of both direct and indirect costs to unit costs.

j) Pricing objectives may be related to a rate of return, growth, competition, market share or utilisation of capacity.

k) Related pricing strategies could include cost-plus, promotional, penetration, market lead or marginal-costing.

l) Break-even point is the level of sales at which total costs are equal to total revenue.

m) This information can be shown graphically on a break-even chart and used to identify selected operating points, margins of safety and various 'what-if' scenarios at different levels of promotion and sales.

n) It can also form part of a business plan for a new business.

Review questions *(Answers can be found in the paragraph indicated)*

1. With the use of examples distinguish between direct and indirect costs in a business. (2–11)

2. Why are unit costs important and how do they differ from marginal costs? (12–30)

3. How do standard costs and variance analysis help businesses? (15–27)

4. What methods could an organisation use to allocate overheads to unit costs? (31–37)

5. Briefly explain key pricing objectives for a business organisation. (38)

6. Identify related pricing strategies to meet these objectives. (39–44)

7. At what point does a business break-even? (45–50)

8. Explain the significance of a selected operating point and margin of safety. (51–52)

9. On what assumptions is break-even analysis based and in what sense could they be unrealistic? (53–55)

10. Identify the uses of break-even and explain why it might help a new business. (56–57)

Assignment – Birchall's Target   *Element 6.4*

Birchall Enterprises Ltd is a manufacturer of high quality wooden doors which it supplies mainly to the building trade. Currently the company produces 4,500 doors per year which it sells for £100 each. Fixed costs are £165,000 per annum and variable costs £45 per door.

At a recent meeting of the board of directors, managing director John Clark said that the company must improve its present output and profits. Marketing director Bob Moss stated that he believed that the company could increase its current selling price by 10 per cent and still remain competitive. Production director Jill Bennett estimated that to double current production would increase the firm's variable costs by a third although fixed costs should remain the same. Finance director, Bill Dolby expressed concern about the likely financial implications and suggested delaying a decision.

The directors agreed that before reaching a final decision they would like to see some break-even details at the next meeting.

Complete the following tasks which are based on the above situation.

1. Explain the basic factors which are likely to influence Birchall's pricing strategy.

2. Is Birchall's a public or private limited company? How can you tell from the information provided?

3. a) What is a 'board of directors'?
   b) Briefly describe the main functions of the managing director in a company.
   c) Name two other directors who might be on the Board at Birchall's and outline their likely responsibilities.

4. a) With the use of examples, explain the terms fixed and variable costs.
   b) What are the company's current fixed costs?
   c) What are the company's current variable costs per door?

5. Suggest ways in which the company could reduce its fixed and variable costs.

6. Calculate the following for the current year:
   a) Total variable costs
   b) Total costs
   c) Total revenue
   d) The unit cost of producing: 500 doors; 4,000 doors

7. a) Draw a break-even chart and show on it Birchall's current break-even point.
   b) What is the break-even output?

8. a) Assuming that the company achieves its revised targets, calculate the new break-even point.
   b) How is the use of break-even analysis helpful in this situation?

9. a) What is the company's new sales target?
   b) Suggest reasons why the firm might not achieve its sales targets at the new selling price.
   c) What action could the firm take if sales do not meet their target?
   d) Advise the company whether, in your opinion, it should go ahead with the proposed new product and pricing structures.

10. Finally comment on why Birchall needed to make pricing decisions based on marketing, production and financial information.

22 Sources of Business Finance

In Elements 8.1 and 8.2 we discuss the importance of planning in business if objectives are to be achieved. This involves deciding which financial, human and physical sources are needed for a business and how they can best be obtained and organised. The next four chapters are about financial sources. This chapter considers the need for and sources of finance and covers:

- Need for Capital
- Assets
- Liabilities
- Provision of Finance
- Methods and Sources of Business Finance
- Loans and Overdrafts
- Security
- Cost of Borrowing
- Advantages and Disadvantages of Borrowing

- Company Finance
- Types of Securities
- Methods of Share Issue
- Shares and Dividends
- The Stock Exchange
- Share Prices
- Role of Merchant Banks
- Investment Appraisal
- Sensitivity and Risk Analysis

Need for Capital

1. **Capital** is vital to the running of a business. It includes everything that is used in a business from the money invested to set it up to the equipment purchased to help run it. A window cleaner for example needs to buy a ladder, bucket and wash leather. A retailer needs shop premises, fixtures and fittings, staff and a stock of goods to sell, whilst a manufacturer needs land, a factory, machinery and raw materials as well as money to pay expenses like wages, advertising, heat, light and transport before he can make and sell anything.

2. If a business is successful more capital may be needed for a variety of reasons. For example:

   - To restart the trading cycle and produce more goods/services
   - money may be 'tied up' in raw materials, work still in progress or stocks of finished goods or
   - owed by debtors who have not yet settled their account.
   - the business may be expanding and therefore need to buy new premises or equipment or
   - it may need to modernise its equipment and perhaps introduce computers or other forms of new technology in order to increase efficiency.

3. Within this short introduction we have identified three key types of capital (money invested in a business):

   - **Venture capital** which is needed to start a business venture or enterprise.
   - **Investment capital** which is used to finance the purchase of new equipment and other assets.
   - **Working capital** which is the finance used in the day-to-day running of a business and is calculated from the difference between current assets and current liabilities (see Element 7.4).

Assets

4. **Assets** are of two main types, fixed or current.

    ❑ **Current Assets** (or circulating capital) are those which are constantly changing from day-to-day for example stock of goods, debtors, cash and bank balances.

    ❑ **Fixed Assets** (or fixed capital) are those which remain the same over a period of time and are held for use in the business rather than for resale. Fixed assets can be **tangible**, for example: land, buildings, machinery, fixtures and fittings, furniture, equipment and vehicles; or **intangible**, for example: goodwill, copyrights, patents and trademarks.

Liabilities

5. **Liabilities** are also of two main types:

    ❑ **Fixed Liabilities** such as capital and long-term loans which remain the same over long periods.

    ❑ **Current Liabilities** such as creditors, bank overdrafts, and short-term loans which change from day-to-day

---

Task 1   **7.1.1, 7.1.2 (C3.2)**

Assume that you are thinking about 'starting up' in one of the following businesses. Taking each in turn, list three items of fixed capital and three items of circulating capital which you would need:

❑ mobile disco
❑ mail order
❑ florist shop
❑ painter and decorator
❑ travel agency

Provision of Finance

6. There are several factors which an organisation must consider whenever finance is required, in particular:

    ❑ why it is needed
    ❑ whether it is needed for a short (less than one year) or long (more than a year) period
    ❑ how much is required
    ❑ when it is required
    ❑ where it can be obtained from
    ❑ whether it is available within the organisation or must be borrowed
    ❑ what security, if any, is required
    ❑ what it will cost
    ❑ how it will be repaid
    ❑ the likely return on the investment.

Methods and Sources of Business Finance

7. If a business wishes to raise finance there are a number of sources from which this might come:

    ❑ **The public.** As we saw in Element 2.1 in a small firm, most of the capital required is provided by the businessman himself, possibly with the help of his family, friends or partner or by borrowing from a bank. Whilst in companies finance can be obtained by issuing debentures, shares or borrowing.

❏ **'Ploughed back' or retained profits**. An existing business might be able to make sufficient profits to enable it to provide its own additional finance.

❏ **Government Agencies**. Frequently it is possible for a business to obtain **grants or loans** from government agencies particularly in areas where unemployment is high. Examples of these grants or loans are DTI Regional Selective Assistance Grant, support from Training and Enterprise Councils or the Small Firms Loan Guarantee Scheme.

❏ **Business Mortgages**. Capital may also be obtained by borrowing from banks, insurance companies, building societies and other **financial institutions.** These offer business mortgages (e.g. for premises), short, medium and long-term loans and overdrafts usually at different rates of interest to those for personal borrowing. A mortgage is simply the name given to a long-term loan which is secured on property,

❏ **Factoring Companies**. When a firm sells goods it will invoice the customer and may have to wait several weeks or even months before it is paid. An alternative to this is to sell the invoices to a company which specialised in factoring for less than the full amount. This service has developed in recent years and is usually provided by banks or finance companies. A factor purchases the invoiced debts of a business, usually paying up to 80% of their value depending on the risk involved. The firm therefore gets its money immediately leaving the factor to collect the amount outstanding and deal with any possible bad debts. For example, a business has invoices outstanding for £1,000. It sells these to a factor and receives £800 for them.

❏ **Trade Credit**. Some traders build up credit with their suppliers in order to give them additional capital, particularly in the short-term. That is they buy goods and pay for them some weeks later by which time they may have already received the money for selling them.

❏ **Leasing or renting of equipment**. Leasing enables firms to acquire expensive up-to-date equipment without the large amounts of capital needed to buy it. Just as your family might rent a television set so a business can obtain goods in this way by paying an annual rental fee which includes maintenance. It is quite common for firms to lease major items like office equipment, machinery and company vehicles rather than buying them outright.

❏ **Hire Purchase**. It may be possible for a business to purchase some items like furniture, equipment and cars on credit rather than paying for them immediately. The firm will pay a deposit and pay the balance outstanding by monthly instalments over a period of 2–5 years thus spreading the cost. Specialist **finance companies** (often subsidiaries of banks) often provide the finance on hire purchase (HP) or credit sales. With HP the goods remain the property of the finance company until all payments have been made. With credit sales the goods belong to the purchaser immediately.

❏ **Venture Capital Companies**. For example 3i Group PLC. These meet the need for capital when funds are not readily available from traditional sources such as banks or the stock market. They provide finance in excess of £100,000 to small and medium companies in return for an equity stake in the business. Many of these companies are subsidiaries of other financial institutions including banks, insurance companies and pension funds.

❏ **Loans by Organisations**. A number of other organisations offer loans to businesses for example, Local Authorities seeking to attract industry into an area, and Finance for Industry (FFI), set up in 1973, which provides loans through its two subsidiaries, the Industrial and Commercial Finance Corporation (ICFC) and the Finance Corporation for Industry (FCI).

❏ **Membership fees**. Some organisations, particularly clubs, societies and professional bodies which often are non-profit making usually charge a fee or subscription to join or remain a member which provides an important source of finance. This fee may be in addition to any charges made for the use of facilities or resources. For example, golf, squash or health clubs, trade unions and employers and trade associations.

❏ **Charities**. It may be possible to receive a grant or other financial support from a charity organisation. For example, the Prince's Youth Business Trust helps young people (see Element 8.3), whilst the **National Lottery** is a potential major source of finance for many organisations, particularly in the areas of the arts, sports, heritage and charities themselves.

8. It is important to recognise that trade credit, leasing and hire purchase do not actually increase the amount of money coming into a business. Instead they enable a firm to have the use of additional capital without needing to lay out large amounts of cash. The difference between borrowed money and venture capital should also be understood. The former is usually **secured** on property or other assets and involves repayments of capital and interest, whilst the latter is **unsecured** and rewarded by dividends and capital gain from the sale of the equity if the company is successful and goes 'public'.

Task 2   7.1.2, 7.1.3, 7.1.4 (C3.2)

From the above sources of business finance, with examples:

1. Distinguish between the potential sources of venture, investment and working capital for any two of the business ideas in Task 1.

2. Identify those which are most suitable for

    a) Long-term borrowing (5–20+ years)

    b) Medium -term borrowing (1–5 years)

    c) Short-term borrowing (less than 1 year)

3. Distinguish between the internally generated and externally generated sources of finance.

Loans and Overdrafts

9. Two of the most popular methods of borrowing, particularly for new and small businesses, are loans and overdrafts, and therefore it is important to understand the difference between them.

10. A **loan** is a fixed sum of money lent for a stated period of time, for example £2,000 for three years. Each month part of the loan will be repaid plus an extra payment called interest. Loans are usually arranged to finance specific capital expenditure such as purchasing new equipment or premises.

11. An **overdraft** is where a bank allows customers to draw cheques which take more money out of their current account than they have in it. That is, they are allowed to overdraw or go into the 'red'. The bank will agree a limit on how much can be overdrawn, for example £800.

12. Overdrafts are usually cheaper than having a loan. This is because the size of an overdraft is likely to fluctuate as cheques and other items are paid in and out of the account. Therefore money is only borrowed when it is needed. Interest is charged daily but only on the balance outstanding. Overdrafts tend to be used for **short-term** or temporary borrowing where income, expenditure or both fluctuate a lot and therefore are intended for use as working capital.

13. The interest rate charged on an overdraft facility will depend on a number of factors including:

    ❑ an organisation's credit rating with the bank based on previous experience

    ❑ the security offered

    ❑ the current bank base rate.

    Thus, for example, if base rate is 8% the bank may charge anything between 3% and 10% above this depending on the perceived risk based on the credit standing and security.

Security

14. With bank loans and overdrafts some form of **security** or collateral may be needed to protect the bank and enable it to get its money back if things go wrong. This might be in the form of a mortgage on the premises or other business assets.

15. Alternatively, personal security may be used such as a life insurance policy, shares, a mortgage or an individual's own home or guarantees by a third party. It is possible to have an **unsecured loan** but usually this will involve a higher rate of interest and also the amount which can be borrowed and the time period involved are likely to be less.

Cost of borrowing

16. The interest charged on a loan is based on a percentage of the amount borrowed and may be calculated as simple or compound.

17. **Simple interest** is calculated on the original sum (called the principal) only using the following formula:

$$I = P \times \frac{R}{100} \times N$$

where I = simple interest
P = Principal
R = % rate of interest
N = Time period

18. **Example**

	£	
Loan	1,500	for 4 years
10% Interest	600	£150 pa × 4
Total Cost	2,100	

Repayments £43.75 per month (2100 ÷ 48)

19. **Compound interest** is calculated on the original principal plus all interest earned so far which is added to it. The formula used is

$$A = P\left(1 + \frac{R}{100}\right)^n$$

Where   A = compound sum
P = Principal
R = % rate of interest
n = time period

Thus, for example, a £100 loan earning 10% compound interest p.a. would accumulate to £110 at the end of a year and £121 at the end of 2 years and so on.

$$\text{i.e.} \quad 121 = 100\left(1 + \frac{10}{100}\right)^2$$

20. **Example**

Loan £1,500 borrowed at 10% compound interest for 4 yrs

	£
YEAR 1 PRINCIPAL	1500
end year 1 interest 10%	150
YEAR 2 PRINCIPAL	1650
end year 2 interest 10%	165
YEAR 3 PRINCIPAL	1815
end year 3 interest 10%	181.50
YEAR 4 PRINCIPAL	1996.50
end year 4 interest 10%	199.65
TOTAL PAID BACK	2196.15

Repayments £45.75 per month (2196.15 ÷ 48)

> ### Task 3　　　　　　　　　　　　　　　　　　　　　7.1.3 (N3.2)
>
> What is the total amount repaid and the monthly repayment on the following loans.
>
> 1.　A principal of £1,000 over 3 years with a simple interest of 9%.
>
> 2.　A principal of £750 over 4 years with a compound interest of 8%.

Advantages and Disadvantages of Borrowing

21. There are a number of factors which a business must consider when deciding whether or not to borrow money.

    ❏ It provides a **source of capital** to finance business development and growth.

    ❏ It requires a **regular outlay** in order to make the repayments.

    ❏ **Collateral** (security) may be required by lenders so that if the business becomes bankrupt, the loan is repaid from the sale of the asset. A mortgage, for example, is secured on premises.

    ❏ **Assets may be 'tied-up'** if they are used as security which may create difficulties if they need to be sold.

    ❏ A **higher rate of interest** is usually payable **on unsecured loans** because of the greater risk involved.

    ❏ **Further interest rate increases** add to the cost of borrowing. This could **cause problems** if it leaves the business with insufficient funds to pay off other debts.

    ❏ Investment decisions will depend on the **cost** of borrowing **relative** to the **anticipated rate of return** e.g. a 10% interest rate requires a profit of at least 10% to cover it.

Company Finance

22. When a limited company is formed, the Board of Directors must decide how much capital is needed to finance the trading operations. This capital is then divided up into smaller equal parts called shares. Each share therefore represents a small part of the business and these are then sold to raise the money required to trade. Shares normally carry some voting rights which enables their holders to have a say in how the company is run, but this varies according to the type of share.

Types of Securities

23. A security is simply a written or printed document acknowledging the investment of money. People who purchase securities are call **investors** and they can put their money into either stocks or shares. Generally speaking stocks are loans which carry a fixed rate of interest, whilst the return on shares varies. There are a number of different types of company securities, the most common being preference shares, ordinary shares and debentures.

Methods of Share Issue

24. As discussed in Element 2.1 a private limited company cannot issue shares to the general public. A public limited company, however, can issue shares in a number of ways.

    ❏ **Offer by prospectus.** This is a direct approach to the public which is usually handled by a specialist issuing house such as a merchant bank. The shares are sold at a fixed offer price.

    ❏ **Offer for sale.** Sometimes a company will sell its entire share issue to an issuing house which then sells them to the public at a slightly higher price to cover fees and expenses.

    ❏ **Offer by tender.** Rather than fixing the price in advance, companies sometimes issue shares to the public by inviting them to state a price at which they are prepared to buy them, subject usually to a set minimum. The issue price is then fixed according to demand and anyone offering less than this receives no shares.

    ❏ **Placing.** A large number of share issues are 'placed' by the issuing house with a selected group of its own clients, usually large financial institutions, rather than the general public.

- **Rights Issue.** Sometimes existing shareholders are offered the 'right' to buy additional shares in the company at a discount to the market price.
- **Bonus Issue.** Shares are sometimes issued free to existing shareholders in proportion to their holdings, e.g. 1 bonus for every 10 held. This makes shares more marketable by reducing their market price.
- **Scrip Issue.** Sometimes instead of paying a cash dividend, a company offers shareholders a choice of receiving it in the form of extra shares.

Task 4   **7.1.3, 7.1.4, 7.1.6 (C3.4)**

ALLIED RIGHTS OUT

The food and drinks group Allied-Lyons has ruled out a rights issue in order to cut borrowing of nearly £2bn, which represents about 66 per cent of share-holders' funds.

It will only tap investors for cash if it makes a major acquisition. Although a move is not imminent.

IT ASDA BE RIGHT

Asda, the fourth largest supermarket group, said 94 per cent of its £347m rights issue had been taken up by shareholders. The money raised will be used to cut debts to around £100m and to speed up the refitting of some stores for £2m each and relocation of some other poor performers at £12-£20m a time. Two years ago, Asda faced debts of nearly £1 billion. It is already investing £130m a year but still losing market share to new openings by Sainsbury, Tesco and Safeway.

BURTON RIGHT ON

Burton Group, which includes Top Shop, Debenhams and Dorothy Perkins, has had a 90 per cent take-up for its £163m rights issue.

Burton, which recently said that 20,000 full-time jobs were to go and 3,000 part-time staff hired instead, will use some of the cash to cut borrowings to around £160m.

BIG RIGHTS AHEAD

Recent successful rights issues include Asda the supermarket chain (£347m), High Street fashion group Burton (£163m) Trafalgar House (£204m) and Commercial Union (£438m). Kingfisher is also asking for £313m to buy French electrical retailer Darty.

The stock market rise has encouraged companies to raise new capital, support recession hit balance sheets and make acquisitions. But some are raising extra funds now because they are worried that the Government's heavy borrowing programme for the year will drain funds out of the market and lead to a cash shortage.

1. Explain what is meant by a rights issue.

2. Why do companies need to raise such funds?

3. What factors can determine the timing of such issues?

Shares and Dividends

25. Investors who purchase shares in a company stand to profit in two ways:
- Firstly, the shares in a successful company are likely to rise in price, thereby offering a **capital gain.**
- Secondly, they receive a share of the company's profits called a **dividend.**

26. The size of the dividend is dependent upon the amount of profit made and how much the directors decide to retain in the company before distributing the balance to shareholders. The Directors, however, will only declare a dividend if they judge that the Company has made sufficient profit to be able to do so.

Task 5	**7.1.3 (C3.4)**

MOWLEM PROFITS PLUNGE

John Mowlem today became the latest group to expose the dire state of the construction industry as it crashed £9.9m into the red, reversing a £7m profit. The interim dividend is slashed from 5.67p to 2p a share.

On the positive side, the company says borrowings have fallen and will continue dropping thanks to the £17.6m sale of its US scaffolding business. It is also closing its Canadian operation. The Board has focused its attention on reducing costs in all areas, the disposal of non-core assets and businesses, cash control within all companies and the maintenance of its strong and cash-positive contracting business.

Core businesses of contracting, housing and equipment hire in the UK all made operating profits, but less than in the previous two half-years. The group, which built and operates London City Airport, had a £2.5m loss on this business.

1. Identify Mowlem's core business.

2. What difficulties is the company experiencing and how are shareholders being affected?

3. How are the directors reacting to the current situation?

Preference Shares

27. These are so called because they receive a fixed dividend which is paid before all other classes of shareholders. The dividend is expressed as a fixed % on the nominal (original) value of the share, for example 8% £1 Preference Shares, means that the dividend is 8p per share p.a. Preference shareholders do not usually have any voting rights.

28. There are several types of preference shares which are as follows:

❏ **Cumulative Preference Shares**. If there is insufficient profit to pay the dividend in one year, then this will be made up in later years. For example, 1995 no profit, therefore no dividend on 8% £1 Preference Shares, then in 1996 if there is sufficient profit the dividend will be 16p per share.

❏ **Non-cumulative Preference Shares.** These are exactly the same as cumulative, but without the right to receive any arrears of dividend. Dividends are paid out of current year profits only, therefore no profit means no dividend.

❏ **Redeemable Preference Shares.** These shares are issued for a specified period and the company agrees to repay the capital at some future date, for example 10,000 £1 Preference Shares, Redeemable 1998 means that the company must repay this capital in 1998.

❏ **Participating Preference Shares.** In addition to the fixed dividend, these shares receive an additional dividend depending on the company's profits.

Ordinary Shares

29. These are by far the most common type of share. Once the preference shareholders have been paid, then the directors of the company decide how much of the profits to keep in reserve (i.e. money which is kept for future expansion or against a 'rainy day') and how much to pay as a dividend on the ordinary shares. Ordinary shareholders usually have voting rights and they also carry the greatest risk because profits and therefore the dividends may fluctuate considerably from year to year. These shares are often referred to as **'equities'** because they participate equally in the profits of the company.

Debentures

30. These are not shares in a company but long-term loans. They are issued in £100 units and secured against property or other assets. Debenture holders receive a fixed rate of interest, which must be paid whether the company makes a profit or not, and usually have a guaranteed repayment date.

The Stock Exchange

31. A company is not like a bank or building society and therefore it cannot give shareholders their money back when they ask for it because it has already been spent – on buildings, machinery, materials, wages, and all the other needs of the business. However, before buying securities investors naturally want to know that they can sell them again if they need their money back. This problem is overcome by having a Stock Market.

32. All the leading countries throughout the world except the Communist states have stock markets, for example Japan (Tokyo), USA (Wall Street, New York) and France (Paris). The UK's Stock Exchange is a highly organised financial market based in London, where over 7,000 different securities can be bought and sold, including shares in over 500 leading overseas companies.

Unlisted Securities Market (USM)

33. Often young companies going public will seek admission to the USM as a first step towards acceptance to the full Stock Exchange official list because it is cheaper and easier to do. This 'second tier' market was started in 1980 and shares are traded in exactly the same way as outlined above. The Stock Exchange considered that the USM no longer fulfilled its role of providing capital for smaller companies and therefore closed it at the end of 1995. In its place, the 'official list' now includes an Alternative Investment Market (AIM) to provide capital for smaller companies.

Share Prices

34. The price of stocks and shares varies from day to day according to the supply and demand, i.e. the number of people who want to sell shares and the number who want to buy. Thus if the demand for shares exceeds the supply, the price will rise. If the supply exceeds demand, the price will fall. So although you might buy a share for £1 it could go up in value if the company does well, to say £1.50. Prices may also be affected by some of the following factors.

Some Reasons Why Share Prices Fluctuate

35. ❑ **The recent company profit record**, rate of dividend paid and the growth prospects of the company's market(s).

    ❑ **Rumours and announcements** of proposed take-overs and mergers or trading difficulties.

    ❑ **Changes in Government policy**, for example restrictions on consumer spending will probably cause a fall in the share price of companies making consumer durable goods.

    ❑ **World political and economic events** will have some effect on the shares of companies which have a large export trade, for example a recession or boom in another country.

    ❑ **Changes in the rate of interest** on government securities will sometimes affect share prices. A rise in the market rate of interest might cause some 'switching' from shares to government securities.

    ❑ **Major events** such as a General Election, the Budget, or something affecting a particular company like the discovery of a new drug can all influence share prices.

    ❑ **Views of experts.** Articles by well-known financial writers can persuade people to buy or sell certain classes of shares.

    ❑ **Industrial disputes or settlements** which may affect production, sales and profits.

Task 6   **7.1.4 (C3.4)**

The trading results of public limited companies are often reported in the financial press, i.e. the Financial Times and business section of the Daily Telegraph, Guardian, Times and other newspapers. Look carefully at the following article which gives a report of the results of Eagle Industries and then answer the questions which apply to it.

EAGLES FIGHTING FINISH

A much improved second half performance from computer supplies group Eagle Industries caught City pessimists by surprise yesterday and sent the shares soaring 45p to 285p. The dividend cut and poor trading figures recently announced by UK competitor Hogan had led everyone to expect another set of poor results. But Eagle has managed to maintain its unbroken profits record by the narrowest of margins and delighted shareholders by increasing the dividend for the year ending December 1994. Profits are up from £16.8 million to £18.2 million against expectations of around £15 million. A final dividend of 6p brings the total payment for the 12 months to 9p. The group has pulled back losses in the rental division from £1.6 million to almost break-even despite continuing competition from the USA. Profits in the Microchip Division have improved slightly to £8.6m and would have been better but for the recent cancellation of a large export order. Expansion in Europe has helped the maintenance division to achieve another good performance whilst profits from commercial software have moved ahead due mainly to last year's takeover of the German company Fresco.

---

1. Why are shareholders of Eagle Industries delighted with the results?

2. How have the results influenced the company share price?

3. What do you understand by the 'City pessimists' and why were they caught by surprise?

4. How has the company managed to maintain its unbroken profits record?

5. What information, if any, is there in the article to suggest that the company could make even higher profits in 1995?

6. Assuming you are a potential investor give your views on the company as an investment possibility.

Economic Importance of the Stock Exchange

36. ❏ **It encourages people to invest** in securities because it provides a market where they can get their money back.

❏ **Companies can raise large amounts of money** for investment in new machinery and buildings. Firms cannot expand unless they can raise the necessary finance. Mass production could not take place, goods could not be produced as cheaply, leading to higher unemployment and a lower standard of living. Therefore ultimately our standard of living and way of life are affected by the Stock Exchange.

❏ **The Government can raise finance** for the nationalised industries and various essential projects by selling government bonds on the Stock Exchange. Without this finance there would be fewer and more costly state services and taxation would have to be increased to provide the funds. In recent years over 75% of new issues have been in gilt-edged securities.

❏ **Most people will gain from successful stock market investments** by the institutional investors, for example their pensions keep pace with the cost of living and life insurance benefits rise.

❏ **It provides a means of valuing companies** for takeovers and mergers because this is based on the share price.

The Role of Merchant Banks

37. Merchant banks provide services almost exclusively for businesses. These include:

    ☐ acting as **issuing houses** for new shares on the Stock Exchange and as **underwriters**. This means that before a share issue they agree a price at which they will buy any unsold shares. They also

    ☐ provide **loans** and offer

    ☐ **advice** on business problems.

Investment Appraisal

38. We have seen that capital investment is essential in any organisation providing the key to its future development and growth. There are a number of situations which we have identified when an organisation will need to make investment decisions but particularly when it is considering any of the following:

    ☐ **replacing existing tangible assets** such as plant, buildings and equipment which are old, and unreliable or technically outdated.

    ☐ **introducing new tangible assets** possibly in order to increase production, improve quality or reduce administrative or production costs due to financial constraints.

    ☐ **purchasing modern 'state-of-the-art' equipment** in order to operate more efficiently and keep up with or overtake competitors.

    ☐ **internal expansion** by acquiring new premises, launching a new product(s) or increasing research and development.

    ☐ **external expansion** involving another organisation such as a merger or joint venture.

39. In making investment decisions, it is important for managers to consider the various ways of achieving the desired objectives, to assess whether or not the benefits or return expected from the investment will outweigh the costs involved and then to choose between several uncertain alternatives. In order to do this, it is necessary to compare the immediate cash outlay with the income which the investment is expected to generate over a period of time.

40. There are a number of statistical techniques, not covered in this book, which can be used for this, the most common of which are payback, average rate of return and discounted cash flow (DCF). The latter can be calculated using either net present value (NPV) or internal rate of return (IRR).

Sensitivity and Risk Analysis

41. Investment appraisals are based on forecasts and assumptions about the future which clearly are uncertain. Therefore, in order to consider all the possibilities, businesses often use a **sensitivity analysis.**

42. This involves making a range of what/if assumptions – from the optimistic to the pessimistic – about possible alternative factors. In particular, the costs and time involved to assess how they would impact on the overall benefits from the proposed investment.

43. For particularly large or risky projects a **risk analysis** may be necessary. If, for example, heavy borrowing is involved then clearly assumptions about interest rates are crucial. Likewise, the purchase or sale of large assets may be affected by changes in market conditions. Thus, in these situations, a more detailed consideration of the risks is essential.

Summary

44. a) Capital is vital in any business for starting up, day-to-day operation and expansion or modernisation.

    b) Fixed assets remain the same over a period for use in a business, whilst current assets change from day to day.

c) A business can obtain capital by borrowing from the public, using retained profits, government grants and loans, borrowing from the financial institutions or venture capital companies, factoring, extended trade credit, leasing of equipment or by buying items on credit or hire purchase.

d) Bank loans and overdrafts are two of the most popular forms of borrowing and usually require some form of security.

e) The cost of borrowing is calculated by using either simple or compound interest rates.

f) Whilst borrowing provides a source of capital, it also involves a regular outlay, collateral, the 'tying-up' of assets and an increase in costs if interest rates rise.

g) A public limited company can raise capital by issuing shares on which it pays a dividend out of any profits.

h) Shares can be issued by prospectus, offer for sale, tender, placing, rights issue or bonus issue.

i) Capital investment is essential for the development and growth of organisations and is worth pursuing if the expected return exceeds the costs involved.

Review questions *(Answers can be found in the paragraphs indicated)*

1. Use examples to distinguish between venture, investment and working capital. (1–3)

2. What is capital gearing and why is it important in a company? (4–5)

3. List the main sources of capital available to a business.(7–12)

4. Outline the main features of an differences between a loan and an overdraft. (9–13)

5. With the use of examples, explain the difference between simple and compound interest. (16–20)

6. Outline some of the main advantages and disadvantages associated with borrowing. (21)

7. Identify ways in which a public limited company can issue shares. (24)

8. Why do investors put their money into shares? (25)

9. Distinguish between preference shares, ordinary shares and debentures. (27–30)

10. Why is capital investment essential for the growth and development of organisations? (38)

11. What key criteria is used to determine whether or not capital investment is worthwhile? (39)

12. Explain the difference between a sensitivity analysis and a risk analysis. (41–43)

Assignment 7.1 – Sources of Business Finance   Element 7.1

Using examples from the following types of business organisation:

sole trader, partnership, private limited company, public limited company, non-profit making (eg charity, trade union).

You are asked, with the aid of a chart or diagram, to

1. explain the difference between asset finance and working capital finance

2. explain the different methods of finance used by each type of organisation, including the

     ❑ usual sources

     ❑ characteristics

     ❑ appropriateness to different types of asset finance, and

     ❑ appropriateness to the type of organisation concerned.

---

23 Budgeting and Cash Flow

In Element 7.1 we considered the sources of finance available to a business both for the purchase of assets and also to provide day-to-day working capital. This chapter considers the importance of budgeting and cash flow.

It covers:

- Budgets
- Types of Budgets
- Current and Capital Budgets
- Cash Flow Budgets
- Master Budget
- Cash Flow

- Purposes of a Cash Flow Forecast
- Cash In-Flow
- Cash Out-Flow
- Cash Flow Timing
- Under Capitalisation
- Consequences of Poor Cash Flow

Budgets

1. A **budget** is a financial or quantitative statement relating to the use of resources to achieve specific objectives or targets over a given period of time. In other words it is a financial plan or forecast of income and expenditure.

2. As individuals, we all need to budget so that our income matches our expenditure. If we overspend this must be financed by using our savings, or borrowing possibly by having a bank loan or overdraft or maybe buying goods on credit and paying for them over a period of time. Alternatively, we may simply have to cut-back our expenditure and adjust our life-style accordingly, perhaps going out less or buying cheaper food and clothes.

3. To help reduce the commercial risks and in order to survive and prosper, a business must also undertake a similar exercise. This involves careful planning to produce budget forecasts for an agreed period, usually a financial year. The annual budget is then often broken down into shorter monthly or quarterly operating budgets for easier control. The use of computer-generated spreadsheets has greatly extended the scope for **budgetary control** (see paragraph 9).

| **Task 1** | **6.3.1, 7.2.1 (C3.4, N3.2)** |

1. Prepare two budgets, one to cover a month and another to cover 12 months, based on your own personal or family circumstances. List all the expected income and planned expenditure.

2. Distinguish between the fixed and variable costs in your budget.

3. Comment on any differences between the two totals in each budget.

4. Identify the main cost centres and any factors which could cause costs to exceed your planned budgets (see paragraph 11).

5. Outline your plans to deal with any surplus or deficiency.

Capital, Trading and Cash Flow Budgets

4. Budgets are usually split between planned expenditure on **capital** items such as premises, fixtures, fittings, machinery and vehicles and **revenue or trading** items such as raw materials, wages and other expenses including stationery, travel, telephone, light, heat rent and rates. The trading forecast will also include an estimate of sales against which production will be planned.

5. A further budget which is also prepared is that for **cash flow**. This is a forecast of the money which flows both into and out of a business. When it sells goods or services, it receives income but it also has a flow of money out in order to meet its fixed and variable costs such as payments to suppliers and workers. It is essential for success that there is a regular cash flow into a business. Therefore a system of control is important to ensure that a firm is able to pay its expenses and earn sufficient additional income to make a profit. (See paragraph 15.)

6. Whilst the revenue expenditure is likely to be based on the organisation's projected cash flow for the financial year, the capital budget also often involves additional funding in the form of loans, for example from banks or other external sources (see Chapter 22 Element 7.1).

Purposes of Budgets

7. Forecasts of income and expenditure are compiled by organisations for a number of reasons. These include:

    ❒ predictions about the future enable an organisation to **determine its objectives** and make plans to achieve them.

    ❒ forecasting creates opportunities to **appraise** alternative **courses of action**. Decisions need to be made on the best way to achieve objectives including the resources to be used and how they can best be co-ordinated.

    ❒ to **set targets** which will enable objectives to be achieved e.g. sales volume, for revenue and spending limits to control costs

    ❒ to **monitor performance** to ensure that targets are being achieved and to enable corrective action to be taken where this is not happening (see Budgetary Control.)

Types of Budget

8. Organisations may choose to use different types of budgets depending on their needs and circumstances.

    ❒ A **fixed budget** remains the same even if activity levels are different from those predicted.

    ❒ A **flexible budget** is one which is adjusted in response to changes in variable costs or levels of business activity.

    ❒ A **zero-based budget** is one which is calculated in relation to the needs of each activity rather than, as with many firms, on the basis of past spending with an adjustment for inflation. Before budgets are allocated, each activity is evaluated against its relevance to the business and perceived value-for-money.

Budgetary Control

9. As mentioned in paragraph 7, in order to monitor and control their activities, many firms set targets of achievement in line with their objectives and limits on spending for the various aspects of the business. The most common form of financial regulation is an accounting technique called budgetary control, which includes two broad stages – preparation and monitoring.

10. **Budget preparation**

    This involves:

    ❒ identifying the objectives from which targets are set, for example in terms of output, sales volume and profits. In a large business organisation these targets will be sub-divided so that there is an individual target to achieve for each factory, office, branch, geographical area or product.

    ❒ preparing initial budgets in line with these objectives. Thus, for example, budgets will be set for purchasing, production, distribution, personnel, administration and capital expenditure.

    ❒ reviewing and co-ordinating these budgets with adjustments for any anomalies, before

    ❒ final co-ordination and preparation. Thus, for example, if a firm has a production and sales target of 100,000 units it might allocate a budget for capital spending of £20,000.

Thus budgetary control involves the planning of expenditure on the basis of a business's expected income.

Cost Centres

11. The importance of controlling costs is often emphasised in an organisation by delegating budgets and giving managers and workers complete responsibility for the control of costs in their particular area of work. This helps to ensure that positive action is taken to keep waste and inefficiency to a minimum.

12. A **cost centre**, then, is any area of a business's activities to which costs can be ascribed. This may be to a department, a person, a geographical location or an item of equipment such as a photocopier. Once determined the next stage is to allocate all relevant costs. Variable costs such as a direct material and labour present no difficulty, but the apportionment of factory overheads and other indirect costs is more complex. Two commonly used methods are absorption costing and full costing. (See Chapter 21, Element 6.3.)

13. **Cost centre monitoring**

   Once a budget is allocated to a cost centre, actual performance must then be regularly checked by managers against targets to ensure that spending is within the limits set. Each department or section must be provided with information which it can use to assess progress against its budget. Any problems can then be identified and corrective action taken where necessary.

Master Budget

14. The individual budgets for trading, capital expenditure and cash flow are all incorporated into a master budget which includes a statement of the anticipated future profit and loss account and balance sheet.

Task 2   **7.2.3 (C3.4)**

From the following statement by a company executive, identify the potential advantages of using budgetary control in a business. Does this statement suggest any possible disadvantages?

> 'In line with the strategic plan and operational objectives, we ask each departmental manager to prepare a forecast of the likely expenditure needs for their area of responsibility. After adjustment, the agreed functional budgets are then co-ordinated into the master budget. Close monitoring provides regular information for managers which is so essential for the efficient control of activities and achievement of objectives because problems can be anticipated in advance. It also helps to ensure that resources are used in the most efficient and profitable way.'

Cash flow

15. ☐ **Cash flow** refers to the money which comes into and goes out of a business over a period.

   ☐ **Money** in a business can exist in many forms including notes, coins, and cheques and may be held within the organisation itself, as for example with petty cash, or in a bank account.

16. **A cash flow forecast** is a budget or estimate which identifies the anticipated income and expenditure and the time when it is likely to take place, usually, over a six or twelve-month period. This is then used for planning and control purposes.

   ☐ When cash shortfalls are predicted it will be necessary to negotiate bank loans or overdrafts. Equally, when cash surpluses are likely, arrangements can be made to utilise cash by investing it.

   ☐ A firm which suffers from cash deficiencies can quickly find itself unable to meet its current liabilities which could ultimately lead to liquidation. (See Elements 2.1 and 7.4.)

17. Cash flow forecasting is discussed in detail, including worked examples, in Element 8.2 as an essential part of business planning. You should therefore read the appropriate section in addition to the key points summarised here.

Task 3	**7.2.4, 7.2.5, 7.2.6 (C3.2)**

Consider your own personal cash flow during the past month.

1. List all the income which you received and expenditure which you made.

2. Comment on how you handled your finances during the month including your financial position both at the beginning and end of the period.

3. Explain whether or not prior knowledge about the importance of cash flow could have helped you.

Purposes of a Cash Flow Forecast

18. It is strongly recommended that a new business, of any size and regardless of whether or not it needs to borrow money, should prepare a simple cash flow for at least the first year's trading. Subsequently, once the business is established, it is good practice to produce these forecasts of income and expenditure on a regular basis – for example, monthly.

19. The main reasons for preparing a cash flow forecast include:

   ❏ **to support an application for finance** – since it will show the amount of money an organisation expects to have in (or owe to) the bank each month. This enables the level of overdraft needed or loan arrangement (if any) to be calculated and negotiated with the bank or other lender.

   An organisation's cash position can fluctuate rapidly and the fact that it has planned its cash flow and identified potential problems will **give a lender greater confidence** in its ability to repay as well as helping to determine the timing and amount of money required.

   ❏ **To highlight the importance of timing** – particularly if capital items are being purchased then the budget for these should be made available at a time when cash is available. Purchases made at the wrong time can put a drain on cashflow and may create the need for borrowing or other financial action to be taken (see paragraph 31).

   ❏ **financial monitoring and control** – monthly monitoring of actual income and expenditure against the forecast will give some measure of how a business is doing. This will assist **owners or managers** and give them greater **confidence** in running the business. Where cash flow problems do exist it allows remedial action to be taken. This might happen if, for example, a major customer goes bankrupt, sales or profit are below expectations or wage costs are higher than planned.

Cash In-Flow

20. Cash flows into a business from a number of sources including:

   ❏ **start-up capital** – as discussed in Element 7.1 a business needs cash to get started and initially much of this may come from the proprietor's own resources.

   ❏ **loans** can be used to supplement a proprietor's own capital. These may be obtained, for example, from a bank, venture capital company or government agency or, in the case of a company, by issuing debentures.

   ❏ **sales** are the lifeblood of a business and sales receipts will produce the major form of cash inflow. From time to time a business may also raise cash from the sale of assets such as premises or equipment.

   ❏ **interest receipts** may also produce cash for a business as, for example, when surplus funds are invested in a bank deposit account or other form of interest-bearing investment.

   ❏ **VAT** – where a business is VAT registered it will complete a quarterly return. If the balance which can be reclaimed exceeds the amount payable it will receive a cash in-flow.

Cash Out-Flow

21. The main cash flows out of a business are:

    ❐ **payments for assets** such as premises and machinery which are needed for production. The major out-flow may take place when a business starts up but further outflows will be needed, for example, when equipment is replaced or updated.

    ❐ **payments for raw material or stocks** which will take place on a regular basis and are essential for trading purposes.

    ❐ **wages and salaries** which are paid weekly or monthly to employees.

    ❐ **running costs** such as heat, light, water, rent, telephone, advertising and insurance all put demands on cash flow, as also do business rates (see Chapter 21 Element 6.3).

    ❐ **loan repayments** must be made on a regular basis, usually monthly, and will include a charge for **interest**. Where a business has an overdraft facility interest will be charged daily to its bank account when this is used.

    ❐ **VAT payments**. If a VAT registered business owes more each quarter than it can reclaim then the amount will be a cash outflow.

Example

22. John Dean has a business manufacturing packaging material for the food trade. At the 30th June he has £1,500 in his business bank account and debtors of £1,050 for sales that month. John also has outstanding bills, recently received, for electricity £85 and telephone £80 which he plans to pay in July. He also owes £550 for supplies received in June and £370 from May.

    He estimates that on average he will have purchases of £450 per month and will receive two months' credit. His rent of £750 per quarter due in October, is payable in advance. He also pays business rates of £40 per month by standing order and expects to pay his next electricity and telephone bills estimated at £95 and £85 in October. His annual insurance premium of £800 is paid in two equal instalments in August and February. John also pays transport costs of about £100 per month, miscellaneous expenses including maintenance of £35 per month and estimates wages and drawings at £500 per month. He is anticipating meeting a tax demand of £1,000 in September.

    His estimated turnover for the coming year is £1,050 in July £1,200 in August and September, £1,400 in October and November and £1,600 in December. He allows one month's credit and operates a strict credit control system. He also rents out a small workshop in part of his factory for which he charges £40 per month.

Six Month Cash Flow Forecast For John Dean
1st July – 31st December 199-

Cash-in	July	Aug	Sept	Oct	Nov	Dec	Total
Sales	1050	1200	1200	1400	1400	1600	7850
Rent	40	40	40	40	40	40	240
	1090	1240	1240	1440	1440	1640	8090
Cash-out							
Purchases	370	550	450	450	450	450	2720
Tax	–	–	1000	–	–	–	1000
Insurance	–	400	–	–	–	–	400
Electricity	85	–	–	95	–	–	180
Telephone	80	–	–	85	–	–	165
Transport	100	100	100	100	100	100	600
Rent	–	–	–	750	–	–	750
Miscellaneous	35	35	35	35	35	35	210
Wages & Drawings	500	500	500	500	500	500	3000
	1170	1585	2085	2015	1085	1085	9025
Balance b/f	1200	1120	775	(70)	(645)	(290)	1200
Monthly Surplus/(Deficit)	(80)	(345)	(845)	(575)	355	555	(935)
Balance c/f	1120	775	(70)	(645)	(290)	265	265

The opening balance for each month is taken from the previous month's balance. In the example the cash flow is forecast to fall considerably from £1,200 to £265 over the six months. The really difficult months are September, October and November when the cash flow is negative.

Therefore an overdraft or other form of finance will be needed to keep the business going with working capital. The reduction in cash flow could present further problems if, for example, there was an increase in maintenance costs because a machine needed expensive repairs or a major customer failed to pay.

Task 4   7.2.8, 7.2.9 (T3.3)

Hamilton Construction Limited, a small house building and restoration company, forecast the following cash flows over the next 12 months commencing in January. Turnover of £16,000 per month from January to March inclusive and wages of £3,000 per month; £28,000 per month from April to August inclusive and wages of £5,000 per month; and £14,000 per month from September to December and wages of £2,500 per month. All work is undertaken on strictly one month's credit.

The company had a cash balance of £17,000 at the beginning of January. Materials which are paid for on one month's credit are estimated at £5,000 per month from February to May, £10,000 per month from October to December. Current creditors total £25,000 for supplies bought in December, whilst debtors are £12,000.

A £20,000 investment in new equipment is anticipated in May. Corporation tax is estimated at £20,000 payable in July and VAT payments starting in March at £2,000 per quarter. Miscellaneous expenses are estimated at £2,500 per month.

1. From the above information, using a computer spreadsheet, prepare a 12-month cash flow forecast for the company.

2. Comment on any trends and action which the company may need to take to control its cash flow.

3. Use your spreadsheet to consider the potential impact on the figures if:
   a) the credit period allowed was increased from one to two months.
   b) wages and material increased by 10%.
   c) sales improved by 20%

4. Produce monthly and cumulative figures and discuss any reasons why this might be important.

5. Is there any other data which should be taken into account when preparing the cash flow forecast?

Timing and Cash Flow

23. In Element 7.4 we discussed the importance of the creditors ratio, debtors ratio, aged debtor and credit analysis and credit control. These can all have a major impact on an organisation's cash flow, as can the timing of cash flows discussed below in respect of purchases and sales, wages and salaries and VAT.

24. **Purchases and Sales**

When a business sells goods on credit it is usual to allow up to 30 days before payment is due. Likewise, when buying raw materials or stock it will expect to receive up to 30 days credit before having to pay. Thus there can be a significant cash flow time lag between actually completing work or selling a product and being paid for it. Therefore at times a business may need to delay payment for purchases for as long as possible in order to avoid or reduce cash flow problems.

25. **Wages and Salaries**

It is also usual for a business to pay employees wages and salaries in arrears and often not until the last day of each month. This helps to delay cash out-flow for as long as possible and often means that these payments can be made out of sales receipts for the month concerned.

26. **Other expenses**

There are many regular demands on a business which must be met. For example, gas, electricity, telephone and VAT are all payable quarterly. Loan repayments are usually monthly whilst some others such as rates can also be paid monthly. Although it may be possible to delay paying some of these there is the risk of being taken to court and/or having the service removed (e.g. telephone or electricity cut off) which could seriously damage any business. Therefore the cash flow forecast must take account of the timing of these payments which can usually be estimated fairly accurately.

VAT

27. Another potential cash out-flow is that of VAT which must be paid to the Customs and Excise department. A business collects VAT on behalf of the Government by adding it, where applicable, to the selling price of its goods or services. A business with a taxable turnover of less than £46,000 p.a. (1995/96) is not liable for VAT. Above this figure it must register, keep records and make quarterly VAT returns. Although the tax paid on supplies (INPUT TAX) can be claimed back it must collect the tax on sales (OUTPUT TAX). If output tax is greater then it must pay the difference owed. If input tax is greater it can claim back the difference.

Task 5	**7.2.5 (C3.4)**

Referring back to Task 4 explain with examples the significance of the timing of cash in-flows and out-flows.

Under Capitalisation

28. When a business is short of cash and, therefore working capital it becomes more difficult to build up stocks and take advantage of economies of scale such as bulk buying. Creditors are likely to press hard for their money, a situation which quickly becomes known to the potential suppliers. Creditors who have to wait for payment will soon stop supplying and the business goodwill soon suffers.

29. This **under-capitalisation** can come about if too much money is tied up in fixed assets or where apparent profits are taken out of the business before the cash has been received.

Under-capitalisation can be detected in the balance sheet by a large figure for creditors and small figures for stock and cash. A small amount of stock usually indicates that most of the creditors are old ones for stock bought some time ago.

30. Another common cause of under-capitalisation is due to **over-trading**. That is, a business trying to do more than is possible with its present facilities. It comes about when trade increases without any additional capital being available. Therefore in order to buy extra stock to meet demand usually involves increasing the level of creditors. Since there is no cash available to pay creditors until the stock is sold the business is under continual pressure to pay its way.

Consequences of Poor Cash Flow

31. Cash flow forecasting can clearly help a business to identify potential problems in advance, particularly deficit months, and take appropriate action. In fact, without such a document a business is in effect 'flying blind', itself often the cause of failure. If, however, the forecast is wrong or not properly monitored it can lead to difficulties including a **shortage of working capital** making it difficult to meet expenses.

32. Once this happens a business can very quickly find itself unable to meet its debts, suppliers will refuse to supply goods on credit and it may therefore risk **insolvency** and bankruptcy.

33. Although in the short-term a bank may allow an overdraft to pay off debts a business will also need to take other measures such as reducing costs and controlling the levels of stock, debtors and creditors.

Task 6   **7.2.10 (C3.4)**

Wholesale wine merchants, Sudlow's, have been experiencing excellent sales and the promise of profits well in excess of those forecast. The company approaches its bank for an overdraft to tide it through the current operating period.

The bank is concerned at the size of the overdraft requested because it feels that it may indicate a cash flow problem. However, after further discussion with the company, it agrees to lend half the amount requested and recommends the introduction of tighter credit and stock controls as a matter or urgency.

1. Why do you think that the bank was concerned in this situation?

2. How might the bank's recommendations be implemented and how will they assist with the cash flow problem?

3. What are the potential consequences if no action was taken?

Summary

34. a) A budget is a financial forecast of income and expenditure.

   b) Budgets can be prepared for revenue or trading expenditure, capital expenditure, and cash flow. Together these provide a summary of master budgets.

   c) These are used to help organisations to determine objectives, appraise alternative courses of action, set targets and monitor performance.

   d) Budgets can be fixed, flexible or zero-based.

   e) Budgetary control involves the careful preparation and monitoring of budgets which are usually allocated to cost centres.

   f) A cash flow forecast is an estimate or budget of the money which comes into and goes out of an organisation over a period.

   g) It is needed both to support an application for finance and also in order to assist with financial monitoring and control.

   h) The main cash in-flow come from start-up capital, loans, sales, interest receipts and VAT.

   i) The main out-flows are payments for assets, raw materials, stock, wages and salaries, running costs, loan repayments and VAT.

   j) An organisation's cash flow can be considerably affected by the timing of receipts and payments from sales and purchases, wages and salaries and VAT.

   k) Under-capitalisation may come about if an organisation has too much capital tied up in fixed assets or is over-trading.

   l) If action is not taken to correct poor cash flow it could result in insolvency and bankruptcy.

Review questions *(Answers can be found in the paragraph indicated)*

1. Briefly explain what you understand by a budget. (1–3)

2. Distinguish between capital, trading and cash flow budgets. (4–6)

3. Why are budgets needed in organisations? (7)

4. Distinguish between fixed, flexible and zero-based budgets. (8)

5. How does a system of budgetary control and cost centres help a firm to monitor its activities? (9–13)

6. What is a master budget? (14)

7. Distinguish between cash flow, money and a cash flow forecast. (15–17)

8. Outline the main purposes of a cash flow forecast. (18–19)

9. Briefly describe the main cash flows into and out of a business. (20–21)

10. Explain how an organisation can be affected by the timing of cash flows. (23–26)

11. What is under-capitalisation and why might it happen? (28–30)

12. Briefly explain the potential consequences of poor cash flow. (31–33)

Assignment – Budgeting and Cash Flow   Element 7.2

You will find it useful to also read Chapter 27 (Element 8.2.) before starting this assignment.

Geoff Dickens is planning next month to open a shoe shop close to the nearby town centre. He has read books on business studies and from them thinks that he really ought to prepare some 12 month budgets. However, because his understanding is limited and he knows that you are on a GNVQ course and are computer literate he seeks your help.

1. Explain to Geoff the difference between a capital, trading and cash flow forecast and why they are needed.

2. He estimates sales at £50,000 spread roughly equally, throughout the first year with purchases of £25,000. He needs your help in identifying the main cash in-flows and cash out-flows and roughly what these might be.

3. Explain to Geoff the significance of the timing of his cash flow and the consequences of a net cash out-flow over successive periods of the forecast.

4. Geoff knows that his quarterly rent is £900 payable in advance and that if his sales forecast is correct he will need to register for VAT. His sales and purchase estimates, however, have not taken account of VAT. Based on your own knowledge and experience and the information in this text estimate his other trading budget figures. Apart from an initial outlay of £15,000 on refurbishing and fitting out the shop, which he hopes to finance with a £10,000 bank loan, he does not envisage any further capital expenditure in the first year.

6. Using all the information gathered so far you are asked now, using a speadsheet, to prepare a capital budget, trading forecast and cash flow forecast for Geoff.

7. Finally, explain to Geoff how he could use the cash flow forecast to support his request for finance from the bank.

24 Financial Statements

This chapter considers the purposes of financial statements and their preparation in different types of organisation.

It covers:

❏ Purposes of Financial Statements	❏ Trial Balance
❏ Financial and Management Accounting	❏ Control Accounts
❏ Accounting Concepts	❏ Final Accounts
❏ Auditors	❏ Balance Sheet
❏ Double-Entry Bookkeeping	❏ Stock Valuation
❏ Journals	❏ Depreciation
❏ Ledger Accounts	

The Purpose of Financial Statements

1. In Elements 7.2 and 7.4 we consider the importance of forecasting, monitoring and controlling the financial performance of a business. This is necessary not just to assist **owners or managers with decision making**, but also in order to

    ❏ help **secure and maintain finance** from potential investors or lenders

    ❏ provide the **Inland Revenue** with financial data to assess liability for taxation

    ❏ fulfil **statutory obligations** e,.g. the Companies Acts which require accounts to be registered and/or published.

    ❏ **monitor performance** to ensure that the business is operating profitably.

2. The key financial statements used in most organisations include cash flow and budgets (see Element 7.2), the profit and loss account and the balance sheet. These are prepared from an organisation's accounting records which detail all its financial transactions and it is from these that it can determine whether or not it is operating profitably.

    As discussed in Element 6.2 to improve the efficiency and accuracy of these records special documents and are frequently used for purchases, sales, payments and receipts.

Financial and Management Accounting

3. Accountants are used to ensure that statutory records of business transactions are maintained and that accounting conventions, principles and practices are adhered to. It is necessary to distinguish between 2 different types of accounting – financial and management.

4. **Financial accountants** are essentially concerned with ensuring that a businesses accounts are a true and fair record of its financial transactions, as required by law.

5. They are responsible for:

    ❏ planning, monitoring and controlling all financial and accounting systems.

    ❏ the preparation of periodic and annual accounts, including the profit and loss accounts and balance sheet.

    ❏ safeguarding the assets of the business and

    ❏ maintaining an assets register.

Management accountants on the other hand are not covered by legislation but are concerned with the statistical analysis of accounts to ensure that managers are supplied with the information they need to assist them in making decisions in order to achieve objectives.

This could include:

- ❐ cash flow analysis,
- ❐ cost accounting,
- ❐ preparation of budgets and
- ❐ the evaluation of projects including the application of discounted cash flow.

} these are covered in Element 7.2

7. Management accountants also provide variance and control ratios relating to liquidity, utilisation of resources and overhead expenditure (which is discussed in Element 7.4).

Task 1   **4.21, 6.3.2 (C3.4)**

Look at a selection of advertisements for financial and management accountants in both the local and national press.

From these, identify which key skills are being sought by the organisations concerned and the responsibilities involved in each type of accounting.

Accounting Concepts

6. To ensure consistency in the way accounts are prepared, the Accounting Standards Committee (ASC) was set up in 1969 by the professional bodies involved. ASC was replaced in 1990 by an independent Accounting Standards Board. It issues **Statements of Standard Accounting Practice** on which the keeping of financial records is based, so that they represent a 'true and fair view'. The published accounts of a company must by law comply with these concepts which are summarised below.

7. **'Going-concern'**. A Balance Sheet is prepared on the basis that a business will continue to operate in the future i.e. as a going-concern.

8. **'Accruals' of Realisation**. The Profit and Loss Account must take account of any outstanding debts which have not yet been paid and payments received which do not appertain to the current financial year i.e. transactions must be recorded for the trading period to which they relate and not in the period where the money is paid or received.

9. **'Consistency'**. Methods used must be consistent to enable accounts to be compared both over a period of time and between other organisations.

10. **'Prudence'** or conservation. Accounts should reflect the least favourable position in a business. So, for example, projected income should not be over-estimated, whilst anticipated expenditure should take the likely maximum.

11. **Separate business entity**. A set of accounts should always be treated from the business' viewpoint and not the owners, regardless of the legal entity. In a limited company, the business is a separate legal entity but with sole traders and partnerships there is possible confusion between personal and business finances.

12. **Money-measurement**. All accounts are shown in money terms and include only aspects of the business which can be expressed in this way.

13. **Stability of cost.** Assets in the Balance Sheet are valued at their cost price.

14. **'Verification'**. All statements in the accounts should be based on verifiable evidence, i.e. can be proved to be true.

> ## Task 2 $\qquad$ 7.3.1 (C3.2)
>
> Mary Cox is a sole trader who owns a small 'corner shop' where she sells mainly groceries and fresh foods. At present she does her own book-keeping.
>
> Explain to Mary:
>
> 1. Why she should keep the business accounts separate from her own personal finances.
>
> 2. Why she should be aware of basic accounting concepts.
>
> 3. How an accountant could assist with her accounts.

Auditors

15. Whilst an organisation's own accountants prepare the financial statements, independent assessment is carried out by auditors of which there are 2 categories – internal and external.

16. **Internal Auditors** are company employees who are responsible for carrying out impartial monitoring of accounting and other systems and procedures thereby providing information and advice for management. They present audit reports with recommendations direct to appropriate senior management.

17. **External Auditors** are independent of the company and appointed to examine the accounts and business records at the end of the financial year to ensure that they represent a true and fair view of the profits, losses, assets and liabilities. External auditors' reports by law must be attached to a company's published accounts. Guidelines on standards are issued by the Auditing Practices Board.

> ## Task 3 $\qquad$ 4.2.1, 7.3.1 (C3.4)
>
> ### NHS FRAUDS GUIDELINES CRITICISED.
>
> Government guidelines for auditing the health service, issued following recent financial scandals, have been fiercely criticised for failing to provide adequate protection. The Institute of Internal Auditors, (IIA) the professional body for auditors in the NHS has demanded that the present system of internal audit be reformed after a damning parliamentary report on the loss of at least £43m by Wessex Regional Health Authority. This followed criticism of West Midlands Health Authority for wastage on a flawed computer scheme.
>
> Internal auditors are employed by a hospital trust or health authority to review systems of financial control. It is these accountants who are best placed to detect fraud or malpractice. But audits currently don't indicate whether expenses are illegitimate or wasteful.
>
> The NHS Management Executive draft guidelines on internal audit restrict the scope of the audit to purely financial matters. The IIA wants auditors to have a more comprehensive brief to cover the operational management of the health service where it says most mismanagement, waste and fraud occurs.
>
> Based on the article discuss the role of an internal auditor and why there is concern about NHS audits.

Double-Entry Book-Keeping

18. Book-keeping is essentially about recording the money paid out and money received in an organisation. Accounts are maintained using a system of double-entry book-keeping. The left-hand side of an account is known as the **debit** and the right-hand side as the **credit**. Although nowadays many organisations use computerised software or spreadsheets to prepare accounts the basic principles are still the same.

19. The double-entry system essentially means that all items (invoices, credit notes, etc.) are entered as both a debit on the left hand side (which represents an expense or asset) and a credit on the right hand side (which represents income or a liability) in the **books of prime entry**. So for example, if a business buys £2,000 of stock on credit, this will increase both the stock and creditors. If, on the other hand, the stock was purchased for cash, it would increase stock but reduce the cash balance.

20. The main books of prime entry which are used are the:

❑ **cash-book** in which receipts and payments of cash (which includes cheques and other forms of payment) are recorded, i.e. it includes cash and bank transactions.

❑ **Sales day book or sales journal** in which all sales on credit are recorded.

❑ **Purchase day book or purchases journal** in which all credit purchases of items used directly in trading are recorded.

❑ **Journal(s)** which are used for all other credit transactions, for example the purchase or sale of assets such as equipment or buildings or liability such as bank loans.

❑ **Ledger** – entries in all the other books of account are posted (transferred) to the Ledger, hence the system of double-entry.

Journals

21. Journals provide a quick and convenient way of recording mainly credit transactions which do not have their own book of original entry, e.g. assets bought or sold on credit, bad debts written off. They are usually balanced monthly and the amount transferred to the relevant account, such as sales or purchases, in the ledger.

Example

22. On 1st June a new £10,500 vehicle was purchased on credit from Radmoor Motors.

Journal

Date	Details	Folio	DR £	CR. £
1st June	Vehicle A\C Radmoor Motors Being purchase of new motor vehicle	URM RMV	10,500	10,500

23. The Purchases and Sales Day books are also journals used to record mainly credit transactions. They would appear as follows:

Sales (Journal) Day Book

Date	Customer	Folio	Invoice Number	Total excluding VAT	VAT	Total including VAT
1st Jan	Houghton Enterprises	X7	111	75.00	13.13	88.13
15 Jan	K. Clarke	P4	112	51.00	8.93	59.93
19 Jan	T. Packer	J102	113	130.00	22.75	152.75
25 Jan	E.Wise	L44	114	17.00	2.98	19.98
31 Jan	Totals			273.00	47.79	320.79

24. The above shows the layout for a typical Sales Journal. The columns are totalled at appropriate intervals and balance transferred to the ledger. A typical Purchase Journal would look the same but with suppliers instead of customers listed. The customer or supplier details will also be entered to individual accounts in the Ledger.

Ledger Accounts

25. Depending on the type and size of organisations and the number of transactions ledger accounts may be used for each customer, supplier, liability, asset or expense.

26. Typically ledger accounts are grouped into:

- **Purchase or creditors ledger** in which all puchases are recorded including details of individual supplier accounts, Purchases Returns Account and Sales Returns Account and Vat where applicable.

- **Sales or debtors ledger** in which all sales are recorded including individual customer accounts, sales returns and VAT where applicable.

- **Nominal or general ledger** in which all other income and expenditure is recorded under various headings such as wages, advertising, maintenance, heat and light.

- An **asset ledger** in which the purchase and sale of capital items such as premises and equipment are recorded; may also be used in a large organisation although it is often part of the nominal ledger.

27. At the end of each financial period, or more frequently if required, the ledger accounts and cash book can be balanced to produce a **trial balance.** A financial period may be monthly, quarterly, six-monthly or annually. Public Limited Companies, for example, publish accounts twice a year.

Example

28. The following transactions take place during the month of August in the business of S. Player.

1st August	Commenced in business with £1,000.
1st August	Purchased stock £200 cash.
2nd August	Bought fixture and fittings for £100 cash.
3rd August	Sales of £300 on credit to A. Booth.
8th August	Purchased £200 stock on credit from M. Quinn.
16th August	Cheque received for £100 from A.Booth in part payment.
21st August	Purchased £15 stationery and stamps for cash.
24th August	Sold £250 goods, received cheque.
27th August	Paid part-time assistant wages by cheque £30.
31st August	Paid window cleaner £5 cash.

These would be entered in the ledger and cash book as follows:

Ledger Accounts

Date		£	Date		£
		Capital			
31 Aug	Balance c/f	1,000	1 Aug	Cash	1,000
			1 Sept	Balance b/f	1,000
		Purchases			
1 Aug	Cash	200	31 Aug	Balance c/f	400
8 Aug	M. Quinn	200			
1 Sept	Balance b/f	400			
		Fixtures and Fittings			
2 Aug	Cash	100	31 Aug	Balance c/f	100
1 Sept	Balance b/f	100			
		A. Booth			
3 Aug	Sales	300	16 Aug	Cash	100
			31 Aug	Balance c/f	200
1 Sept	Balance b/f	200			
		M. Quinn			
31 Aug	Balance c/f	200	8 Aug	Purchases	200

Date		£	Date		£
		Stationery & Stamps			
21 Aug	Cash	15	31 Aug	Balance c/f	15
1 Sept	Balance b/f	15			
		Sales			
31 Aug	Balance c/f	550	3 Aug	A. Booth	300
			24 Aug	Cash	250
			1 Sept	Balance b/f	550
		Wages			
27 Aug	Cash	30	31 Aug	Balance c/f	30
1 Sept	Balance b/f	30			
		Window cleaner			
31 Aug	Cash	5	31 Aug	Balance c/f	5
1 Sept	Balance b/f	5			

Cash Book

DR | | | | | | | | | | CR

Date	Details	Folio	Cash	Bank	Date	Details	Folio	Cash	Bank
Aug 1	Capital		1,000		Aug 1	Purchases		200	
16	A. Booth			100	2	Fixtures & fittings		100	
24	Sales			250	21	Stationery/stamps		35	
					27	Wages			30
					31	Window cleaner		5	
					31	Balance c/f		680	320
			1,000	350				1,000	350
Sept 1	Balance b/f		680	320					

Trial Balance as at 31st August 199-

	DR	CR
Capital		1,000
Purchases	400	
Fixtures & Fittings	100	
A. Booth	200	
M. Quinn		200
Stationery & Stamps	15	
Sales		550
Wages	30	
Window cleaner	5	
Cash	680	
Bank	320	
	1,750	1,750

Task 4   7.3.1 (N3.2)

Using the example in paragraph 28 assume that a Sales (Journal) Day Book and Purchase (Journal) Day Book were completed. Prepare the appropriate entries. No VAT is payable.

Trial Balance

29. The trial balance is not part of the double entry book-keeping system. It is a summary of all the balances in the ledger accounts at the end of the financial period and can be set out either in **double column form** (each column totalling the same) as shown in the previous example or **single column form** (which should total zero). Although it provides a useful check it does not necessarily mean that the accounts are accurate and indeed it may not actually balance.

30. There are a number of possible reasons for this, for example:

❑ the wrong accounts could have been debited or credited

❑ entries could have been missed from the books

❑ two or more entries may cancel each other out

❑ wrong balances could have been brought forward from the previous financial period

❑ mistakes in addition may occur.

31. Once the accuracy of the accounting data has been confirmed in the trial balance a trading and profit and loss account and balance sheet can be prepared. Before this is done, however, some adjustment may be required for any prepayments or accruals.

32. ❑ **Prepayments** such as rent or insurance which may have been paid in advance relate to the next accounting period and therefore must be deducted from the expenses and carried forward.

❑ Likewise any **accruals** must be included. That is, expenses for the period which have not yet been paid or recorded in the accounts, for example an outstanding telephone or electricity bill.

Task 5   7.3.3 (N3.2)

1st Jan. A Trader starts a business with an £11,000 cheque.

1. He buys a second-hand van for £5,200 and pays by cheque.
2. He buys goods on credit from PRY Ltd., for £3,000.
3. He buys goods on credit from C. Dodd for £2,600.
4. He pays PRY Ltd. £3,000 – £500 cash plus a cheque.
5. He pays C. Dodd by cheque £2,548. Discount £52.
6. Sales for cash £10,000, cheque £3,000.
7. He pays wages to staff £1,600 cash.
8. He pays rent £800.
9. Closing stock 31st March, £420.
10. Depreciation of van 5% of cost.

You are required to make the above book-keeping entries in the books of account and draw up a trial balance for the trading period concerned.

Control Accounts

33. During a financial year a business may be involved in hundreds or even thousands of transactions each of which must be recorded with the obvious potential for error to occur. Therefore, often a separate system of control accounts is used to help identify and correct errors quickly. These

accounts may be outside the double-entry system or designed within it. Debtor and creditor control accounts are common where the majority of transactions involve credit sales and purchases.

Final Accounts

34. At the end of each financial period, any business needs to know whether or not it has made a profit. To provide this information, final accounts are prepared from the accounting records. From the trial balance we get the Trading and Profit and Loss Account which shows the gross and net profit (or loss) for the period concerned. An **accounting period** will vary depending on the type and size of the organisation concerned. It may be monthly, quarterly, half-yearly or annually as required.

- ☐ **Gross profit** is essentially the difference between sales and purchases, taking into account differences in stock values.

- ☐ **Net profit** is calculated by deducting from the gross profit overheads (expenses) such as rent, rates, advertising, insurance, depreciation and interest charges.

35. **Example**

Best Buy Stores

Trading and Profit and Loss Account for the year ending 31 December 19..

	£	£	£
Sales			17,400
Cost of sales:			
Opening Stock (1st Jan)		5,000	
Add Purchases		4,800	
		9,800	
Less Closing Stock (31 Dec)		4,600	5,200
GROSS PROFIT			12,200
Less Overheads:			
Administration			
Wages	3,800		
Lighting & heat	500		
Rates	810		
Rent	1,700		
Telephone	300		
Insurance	150		
Stationery	35	7,295	
Finance			
Interest on loan	100	100	
Selling			
Advertising	100		
Transport	200	300	5,695
NET PROFIT			4,505

533

Task 6 **7.3.2, 7.3.5 (N3.2)**

From the following information,

1. identify the accounting period used

2. prepare a trading and profit and loss account for the business of Trevor Jones.

Stock at 1st Jan £2,410	Purchases £18,000	Sales £29,550
Wages £8,420	Postage £120	Rent and Rates £1,160
Transport £490	Insurance £220	Stationery £80
Lighting and Heat £590	Stock at 30 June £2,500	

Balance Sheet – 'Statement of Affairs'

36. In addition to calculating the gross and net profit, a Balance Sheet must also be prepared which shows the financial position of the business at that particular time. A balance sheet consists of two lists – one of the **Assets** (things possessed or owned by a business) and the other the **Liabilities** (anything owed by a business). That is, it shows the **sources of funds** in a business and the **uses** to which those funds have been put.

37. **Example**

Balance Sheet of J Taylor's – Sole Trader as at 30 June 199..

Fixed Assets

Premises	14,800		
Fixtures & Fittings (8,000 less depreciation 800)	7,200		
Motor Vehicles (6000 less depreciation 1000)	5,000		
		27,000	
Current Assets			
Debtors	3,500		
Stock	7,000		
Cash	500		
	11,000		
Less Current Liabilities			
Bank Overdraft	2,000		
Creditors	2,000		
Unpaid expenses	1,000		
	5,000		
Working Capital		6,000	
Net Assets		33,000	
Financed By			
Capital		26,000	
ADD Net Profit	8,000		
LESS Drawings	3,000	5,000	
Long Term Liabilities			
Bank Loan		2,000	
		33,000	

38. It is important to note the following in respect of accounts.

   - ❏ A **Debtor** is someone who owes money to a business, for example for goods which they have bought.

   - ❏ A **Creditor** is someone to whom a business owes money, for example a supplier from whom raw materials have been bought.

   - ❏ **Drawings** represent money taken out of the business during the trading period.

   - ❏ On a balance sheet, the assets must always be equal to the liabilities.

   - ❏ The final accounts and balance sheet of a large company or other organisation are much more complex than the simple example of J Taylor but the basic information and presentation is essentially the same.

39. **Types of Assets**

   In Element 7.1 we identified the fixed assets of a business as being both tangible and intangible. Since assets are shown in the Balance Sheet it is important to understand the difference between them.

40. **Tangible Assets**

   These are assets which can be seen such as land, buildings, vehicles and equipment. Land and buildings may be freehold or leasehold. **Freehold** means that they belong totally to the business owner and **leasehold** that they are owned by someone else but used by the business for which rent is paid. Likewise other assets may be leased rather than purchased.

41. **Intangible Assets**

   These can be just as valuable, although they are not visible in the same way and include:

   - ❏ **Goodwill** – the difference between the value of a business's tangible assets and its market price and thus can only really be accurately valued when a business is sold. Essentially, it represents the value of the existing customer base in a business.

   - ❏ **Copyrights** – covered by the 1956 Copyright Act. They have the effect of granting to the owner automatic legal protection against their work being copied, for example: records, books, videos, computer software and advertisements.

   - ❏ **Patents** which give inventors of products or processes the right to have sole use for a specified number of years, if they register them with the Patents Office under the 1977 Patents Act.

   - ❏ **Trademarks** or brand names given to products to distinguish them from others. They are registered as copyright by firms to prevent them from being used by anyone else, which is important for marketing. (see Unit 3).

42. **Liquidity**

   Fixed Assets are usually shown on a Balance Sheet in order of liquidity with the least liquid first. That is, the asset which is most difficult to turn into cash without loss of value if the business went bankrupt or into liquidation. The most liquid asset, that is, cash itself, is shown last.

Task 7 7.3.4, 7.3.5 (N3.2)

1. From the following information, compile Trading and Profit and Loss Accounts and a Balance Sheet for the year ended 31 December 199.. for T Tucker.

Opening Stock £13,500	Purchases £40,000	Overheads £8,000
Premises £50,000	Vans £12,000	Debtors £3,200
Capital £75,000	Closing Stock £9,500	Cash-in-hand £300
Sales £60,000	Cash at Bank £13,000	Loans £1,000
Creditors £4,000		

2. Using the information from Task 5, prepare a Trading and Profit and Loss account for the three months ended 31st March, 199..

Take out a Balance Sheet as at 31st March, 199..

Stock Valuation

43. Where, at the end of a trading period, a firm has stocks of raw materials, components, work-in-progress or finished goods, then they must be valued for accounting purposes. Invariably this is done using one of the following methods – FIFO, LIFO, Replacement Price, Standard Price or Average Cost System (AVCO).

44. **First-In, First Out (FIFO)**

This method assumes that goods are withdrawn from stock in the order in which they are received. Thus the cost of goods sold is based on the cost of the oldest stock, whilst the closing stock value is based on the prices of the most recent purchases. FIFO is acceptable to the Inland Revenue for tax purposes because costs are related to those actually incurred and the closing stock value is close to the current market price.

45. **Last-In, First Out (LIFO)**

This method assumes that the most recently bought stock is used first. Therefore the cost of goods sold is based on the cost of the most recent purchases, whilst the closing stock is valued on the cost of the oldest goods available. LIFO is unacceptable for tax purposes because it understates the profitability of a business. However, this does not prevent a firm from choosing this method for its own internal use.

46. **Example**

FIFO		**LIFO**	
Sales (1,000 × £25)	25,000	Sales (1,000 × £25)	25,000
Cost of goods sold:		Cost of goods sold:	
500 × £15 = £7,500		1,000 × £17	17,000
500 × £17 = £8,500			
	16,000		
PROFIT	9,000	PROFIT	8,000
Closing Stock (200 × £17)	3,400	Closing Stock (200 × £15)	3,000

In the above example, under FIFO the cost of goods sold is based on those actually incurred, i.e. 500 at £15 and 500 at £17, whilst the closing stock of 200 is valued at its replacement cost of £17. On the other hand, using LIFO, the cost of goods sold is valued at its current cost of £17, whilst the closing stock of 200 is valued at £15 which is what it cost when purchased.

47. **Replacement Price Method**

This method is also unacceptable for tax purposes because it values all stock at the current cost of replacement rather than at actual cost.

48. **Average Cost System (AVCO)**

This is the simplest method of valuing stock acceptable for tax purposes. The total value of stock bought in a period is divided by the number of items purchased to give the value of each unit, thus smoothing out price fluctuations.

49. **Example**

Value of stock bought on

1st January	£5,000	(500 × £10)
1st March	£7,000	(500 × £14)
1st May	£7,200	(600 × £12)

Therefore the total cost of stock bought is £19,200 and the value of each unit

$$= \frac{19,200}{1,600}$$

therefore average cost per unit = £12.00

Thus, if the stock level at the end of the trading period is 400 its valuation = 400 x £12 = £4,800.

50. **Standard Price Method**

This method uses a pre-determined standard price to value stock. Thus, although it eliminates price fluctuations, it does not use actual costs.

Task 8   **6.3.1, 7.3.4, 7.3.5 (N3.2)**

1. Using the following information from a book retailer, calculate the value of the stock sold on 30 March using the methods of FIFO, LIFO and AVCO.

2. Comment on the effect which each method would have on a firm's gross profit.

Date	Details	Unit Cost	Total Stock	Valuation
1st March	Bought 50	£1.50	50	£75.00
10 March	Sold 10			
20 March	New delivery	£2.00		
(Price change)	Bought 20			
30 March	Sold 50			

Depreciation

51. The Balance Sheet shows the value of a business's assets at a particular point in time, i.e. how much each asset would be worth if it was sold for cash. Each year some fixed assets lose value due to wear and tear. For example, a two year old car will be worth less than a new one. Therefore in its accounts, a business will make an allowance (deducted as an expense in the Profit and Loss Accounts) for this called depreciation.

52. In T Taylor's Balance Sheet, the fixtures and fittings are estimated to depreciate (lose value) by £800 each year, whilst the motor vehicles depreciate by £1,000 each year. Eventually these will need to be replaced. The depreciation allowance saved each year can therefore be used to purchase new

items. The figure for depreciation is usually calculated by using either the straight line or reducing instalment methods.

53. **Calculation of Depreciation**

Using the '**Straight line**' or equal instalment method, the cost of the asset is divided by the length of time it is expected to be used before needing replacement.

Example

A machine costing £10,000 and expected to last 5 years would depreciate by £2,000 p.a.

Sometimes this formula is modified slightly by allowing for a resale or scrap value at the end of the period.

54. The **Reducing instalment** method is calculated by assuming that an asset depreciates by the same percentage each year.

Example

A machine costing £10,000 with a 20% annual rate of depreciation

Year 1	Cost	10,000	
Year 2	Worth	8,000	
Year 3	Worth	6,400	
Year 4	Worth	5,120	etc

The method chosen will depend on decisions which best suit the financial needs of the business.

Task 9   **7.3.4, 7.3.5 (N3.2)**

Which method of depreciation allowance would you recommend as being most appropriate for a new computer system costing £15,000?

Show possible comparative depreciation methods over a 5 year period and give reasons for the method chosen.

Summary

74. a) All organisations, whether profit making or non-profit making need to keep a record of their financial transactions.

   b) Financial statements are needed to secure and maintain finance for tax purposes and also to monitor performance.

   c) Financial accountants are used to ensure that a business's accounts are a true and fair record as required by law whilst management accountants are used to provide information to assist with decision making.

   d) To ensure consistency in accounts, the Accounting Standards Board issues Statements of Standard Accountancy Practice.

   e) Internal auditors may be employed to monitor accounts, whilst external auditors provide independent checks.

   f) Accounts are maintained using a system of double-entry book-keeping.

   g) This involves the use of books of prime entry including the cash book, sales day book, purchases day book, journal and ledger to which all other entries are posted.

   h) A trial balance provides a summary of all the ledger accounts.

i) A set of Final Accounts are prepared at the end of each accounting period, usually 6 or 12 months.

j) The Trading and Profit and Loss Account shows the gross and net profit (or loss) for the period concerned.

k) The Balance Sheet shows the assets and liabilities of a business at a particular time. That is, what it owns and what owes.

l) Stock can be valued using either FIFO, LIFO, Replacement Price, Standard Price or the Average Cost System.

m) The depreciation of assets can be calculated using the straight-line or reducing instalment methods.

Review questions *(Answers can be found in the paragraph indicated)*

1. Why is it necessary for organisations to keep a record of their financial transactions? (1)

2. Distinguish between the role of financial and management accountants. (3–5)

3. Briefly explain some of the main concepts used when preparing accounts. (6–14)

4. What are auditors and why are they necessary? (15–17)

5. Use a simple example to explain the double-entry system of accounting. (18–28)

6. Why is a trial balance used and in what circumstances might it not balance? (24, 29–33)

7. What is the difference between gross and net profit? (34–35)

8. Why is a Balance Sheet often described as a 'Statement of Affairs'? (43–50)

9. Briefly explain four different methods of valuing stock. (43–50)

10. Explain the difference between the straight-line and reducing instalment methods of depreciation. (51–54)

Assignment – Small Business Accounts   Element 7.3

1. P. Conner runs a mobile snackbar and has just completed his first year of trading. Answer the following questions based on his accounts.

Account for year ended 30. 9. 199 .

	£	£		£
Cost of Goods Sold:			Sales	30,000
Purchases	15,600			
	15,600			
Less Closing Stock	600	15,000		
Gross Profit		15,000		
		30,000		30,000

Answer the following questions in connection with the account above.

a) What is the name of the account and what is the trading period involved?

b) What percentage gross profit is the business making on its turnover?

c) If the business continues next year to sell the same types of goods in the same proportions, and sales increase to £40,000, what would you expect the gross profit to be?

d) If, when stock was taken on 30 Sept 199.., a batch of stock which had cost £300 was omitted, what effect would that have in the account given above?

continued...

Assignment continued

e) If the mistake is not put right, what effect will it have on next year's figures for the same account?

f) Why is the profit called 'gross' profit?

g) How would 'net' profit be calculated?

2. **P Conner Balance Sheet as at 30 Sept 199...**

	£	£		£
Capital	5,000		Mobile Van	8,600
Add Net Profit	6,000		Fixtures & Fittings	2,050
	11,000		Stocks	600
Less Drawings	6,500	4,500	Debtors	50
Loan (for 5 yrs)		6,000	Cash & Bank	500
Creditors		1,000		
Unpaid expenses		300		
		11,800		11,800

Answer the following questions in connection with the Balance Sheet above:

a) What is the total value of the fixed assets?

b) What is the total value of the current assets?

c) What percentage profit is P Conner making on his capital at the beginning of the year?

d) Why has P Conner's capital fallen in value by the end of the year?

e) Explain the difference between debtors and creditors.

f) What percentage profit has the business made on the total funds it is using?

g) Can the business pay its short-term debts in full? Give reasons for your answer.

3. Why are the above accounts needed?

4. What other useful information, if any, can be extracted from the Accounts?

5. P Conner has prepared the Accounts with the help of his father. Both attended college over 25 years ago. Show the Accounts in a more modern format.

6. The following details were extracted from the books of A Scratchwood, a local trader, for the year ended 31st December.

Capital £7,000, Motor vehicles £15,000, Fixtures and fittings £2,000, Creditors £8,500, Debtors £14,000, Drawings £70,500, Sales £590,000, Wages £50,520, Other expenses £12,950, Rent £16,160, Purchases £388,000, J. Williams (loan) £500, Bank deposit a/c £27,330, Bank current a/c £12,720,

Depreciation: Motor vehicle £3,000, Fixtures and fittings £180.

You are asked to prepare a Trial Balance, Trading and Profit and Loss Account and Balance Sheet from the above data.

7. Comment on how profit and loss statements and balance sheets can be used to secure and maintain finance from lenders.

25 Financial Monitoring

In Chapter 1 we referred to the importance of monitoring and controlling the performance of an organisation to ensure that it is achieving its objectives. In this Chapter, we are considering some of the methods used to do this. It includes:

- Users of Accounting Information
- Reasons for Monitoring Performance
- Comparisons and variance
- Monitoring and Measuring Performance
- Key Components of Accounting Information
- Interpretation of Final Accounts
- Types of Capital
- Ratio Analysis

- Profitability Ratios
- Performance Ratios
- Liquidity Ratios
- Overhead/Sales Ratios
- Shareholder Ratios
- Capital Gearing
- Other Performance Indicators

Users of Accounting Information

1. A measure of performance in an organisation is essentially a quantitative statement which is used to evaluate progress and to assist management in decision taking. Owners or managers must know what is going on if they are to be in a position to take action to ensure that objectives are achieved.

2. Such information may also be of interest to other people who wish to assess performance, such as

- **Shareholders and potential investors** to assess the likely return on their investment.

- **Banks or other providers of finance** to assess the potential risks of not being repaid.

- **Customers** who need to be confident of receiving supplies and after sales service if appropriate.

- **Suppliers, particularly creditors** who want to be sure that debts can be paid.

- **Government**, particularly for taxation purposes. The **tax authorities** need to be satisfied that the accounts supplied to them represent the true results of the business.

- **Competitors** who may wish to make comparisons.

- **Employees** whose jobs and wage increases may depend on it.

- **Financial advisors** and business analysts who need to be able to advise their clients.

Task 1	**7.4.1 (C3.4)**

1. Obtain copies of at least two company annual reports from a library or by writing to the companies themselves.

2. From them identify the information which you feel would be of interest to each of the groups mentioned in paragraph 2.

Reasons For Monitoring Performance

3. In addition to assisting decision making, an organisation also needs to monitor and control its performance for a number of other reasons including the need to:

❑ **Remain solvent** – i.e. to ensure that it is able to meet its debts when they become due. Forecasts of cash flows into and out of an organisation must be made and monitored so that problems can be anticipated and action taken if necessary in order to continue trading.

❑ **Achieve profitability** – i.e. it is not enough simply to meet its debts. At the end of the trading period it is important that an organisation also makes a profit in order to survive and prosper.

❑ **Establish tax liability** which must be paid on profits and minimise it by taking advantage of any allowances available.

❑ **Maintain finance** – regular repayments will have to be made to banks and other lenders if they are to continue to provide finance.

❑ **Provide comparison with targets** to check whether these are being achieved or exceeded. Progress can be assessed and corrective action taken if necessary.

❑ **Improve performance** – monitoring and control can provide opportunities to do this eg reducing costs, improving efficiency and output, reducing bad debts, increasing profitability.

Comparisons and Variance

4. In assessing its financial performance there are a number of comparisons which a business can make. In particular it needs to compare its results against

❑ the **forecasts made** at the beginning of the trading period. Levels of sales , costs and profits, for example, will have been predicted and targets set accordingly against which performance can be measured. (see Element 7.2).

❑ **previous year's performance** for the business. This can provide an indication as to whether or not the organisation is improving its sales, cost-effectiveness, profitability and return on investment.

❑ **internal comparisons** between divisions and product groups in an organisation may also be made to determine whether some are operating more profitably than others.

❑ the performance of **other businesses** in the same industry. This **inter-firm** comparison helps to identify variances (differences) between them.

By analysing and interpreting these variances it may be possible to find ways to improve business performance. This could include comparing factors such as turnover, market share, profitability, and return on investment. Much of this type of data is available by studying the published accounts of different companies.

Monitoring and Measuring Performance

5. There are a large number of different ways of monitoring and measuring performance. Some of those most commonly used include:

❑ **financial controls**, in particular keeping costs and budgets within agreed targets. Budgeting is an important part of an organisation's planning processes. (See Element 7.2.)

❑ **performance ratios** based on an analysis of the accounts, in particular the balance sheet, which are discussed in this chapter.

❑ **productivity measurement** which defines performance as a ratio of output to input (see Element 5.1.)

❑ **quality control** which can help to increase customer satisfaction and therefore sales and also reduce costs such as those of wastage and returns. (See Element 5.1.)

Task 2   **7.4.1, 7.4.2, 7.4.3 (C3.4)**

POUNDSTRETCHER CRISIS

Leeds based Brown and Jackson, which runs the Poundstretcher chain of discount stores warned that it would have to cease trading unless it raises sufficient working capital for the year.

The future of more than 220 Poundstretcher shops, employing over 4,000 people, was in jeopardy as a result of the financial crisis. The company's Directors had been unable to secure agreement with the group's banks to cover 1994's working capital, which was forecast to peak at £14 million in September.

Brown and Jackson said it strongly disagreed with the stance of its banks, who were also blocking a proposed £5.9m sale of stores. It was urgently reviewing options for the future of the business and talks were currently taking place with another company with a view to it taking a stake in the group.

Brown directors said that 'In the absence of adequate working capital facilities, the group would not be able to continue trading'.

'However, the group's bankers were presently completely secured; the group had facilities available to it and with the support of its bankers, could continue trading'.

But such public warnings may frighten suppliers. The shares tumbled from $6\frac{1}{2}$p to $2\frac{3}{4}$p.

Because of the cash crisis the company could not present its annual results on the normal basis of 'a going concern'. Instead it published unaudited management information showing a loss for 1993 of £12.7m on turnover of £170m. Unaudited results for the previous 12 months showed a loss of £6.6m.

Poundstretcher was forced to cut prices to clear slow-moving stock and costs increased as the management acted to improve the financial situation.

On current trading, it said like-for-like sales for the eight weeks to February 26th, were down one per cent on last year. 'The performance in 1993 shows that there is still a core of stores that require a significant increase in turnover in order to deliver an adequate return.'

After several months of negotiation a rescue package was agreed with South African stores group Pepkor, which injected £56m in return for a substantial shareholding. The news reassured the banks whilst the shares recovered again.

An extensive programme of updating, rationalisation and new store openings are underway. To enable the company to reduce borrowing further Pepkor agreed in June 1995 to inject up to £20m more giving it between 64% and 94% of the total equity. In its 1994 annual results Brown's losses were £7.2m before tax. Sales rose marginally to £151.8m.

---

1. What is working capital and why is it important in a business?

2. How does the 'Poundstretcher Crisis' illustrate the importance of monitoring performance in a business and what reasons are given?

3. What do the profit comparisons tell you about the business?

4. Which users of the information can be identified from the article and why are they interested in it?

5. Suggest with reasons other users who may also be interested in the information.

6. Why was the company unable to present its annual accounts in 1993 and what has it done instead?

7. Why was the further £20m needed and what impact will it have?

8. Why was the initial rescue package so important to the company?

9. Suggest ways in which the company's performance could be improved and the implication if it fails to do so.

Key Components of Accounting Information

6. An organisation should be able to extract the information which it needs for the purposes of monitoring and control from its accounting system (see Element 7.4). The key components are the forecasts which it makes in respect of its cash flow, budgets, profit and loss and balance sheet. These forecasts must be compared with the actual performance on an on-going basis and from year to year. From this an assessment of performance can be made.

Interpretation of Final Accounts

7. By examining the figures in the Trading Profit and Loss Account, and in particular the Balance Sheet, it is possible to discover the financial strengths and weaknesses of a business. They provide a summary of all the important financial facts and thus it is possible to see, for example, the amount and types of capital in the business, the net profit and how much is owed to the bank and other creditors.

Types of Capital

8. The assets in the Balance Sheet show how a business's capital has been spent for example to buy premises, stock or vehicles. It is also possible to calculate the capital owned, capital employed and working capital.

9. **Capital owned** is a measure of the value or net worth of a business.

CAPITAL OWNED = TOTAL ASSETS – CURRENT LIABILITIES

10. But this may not be all the capital in a business since money may be borrowed from a bank or goods bought on credit, in other words, someone else's capital may also be used. On the other hand, a business may also be owed money by its debtors. Therefore the actual **capital employed** that is used in a business may be slightly different from what is owned.

CAPITAL EMPLOYED = TOTAL ASSETS – DEBTORS

11. **Working capital** is the money which a business must have available to meet its day-to-day expenses such as staff wages, purchasing of stock and other overheads.

WORKING CAPITAL = CURRENT ASSETS – CURRENT LIABILITIES

12. Working capital is essential to ensure that a firm can operate efficiently and remain **solvent** i.e. in a position to pay its expenses. If a business is **insolvent** it means that the current assets are less than the current liabilities and thus it cannot pay its debts in full. For example, if current assets were £10,000 and current liabilities £12,000, then the firm would not have sufficient working capital to carry on the business.

13. In the short-term it may be possible to solve this problem by borrowing or extending credit, but if it continues for any length of time, the business may be forced to close down. In the case of an individual this is called **bankruptcy** or in the case of a company **liquidation.** (See Element 2.1.)

Task 3   **7.1.2, 7.4.4 (N3.2)**

1. From the following information, draw up the Balance Sheet as at 31 March 199.. for ABC Ltd. (See Element 7.3 if you need help.)

2. From it, identify the figures for capital owned, capital employed and working capital.

Creditors £15,200	Debtors £11,000	Stock £1,600
Land £14,000	Machinery £15,000	Depreciation £3,000
Bank £12,000	Cash £1,200	Capital £40,600
10-year loan £14,000	Premises £18,000	

Ratio Analysis

14. Simple statistics, however, are by themselves of limited value and therefore ratio analysis is used to assess the performance, profitability and solvency of a business. The use of ratios enables more meaningful comparisons to be made between companies of different sizes, the same company over a period of time and between several companies in an industry.

15. The key accounting ratios are:

   ❏ **Profitability and performance ratios,** including the return on capital employed, assessment of profitability and turnover of capital, which measure a business's level of activity and efficiency.

   ❏ **Liquidity (solvency) ratios** including the current ratio and acid test which indicates a business's ability to pay its debts.

   ❏ **Investment (or shareholder) ratios** which measure the returns on capital investment.

   ❏ **Capital gearing ratios** which measure how assets are financed.

Profitability Ratios

16. There are a number of ratios which can be used to assess the performance and efficiency of a business. Three which we shall consider here are the return on capital employed (or prime ratio), profit on turnover and turnover of capital.

17. **Return on Capital Employed**

   Investors in a business will obviously wish to see a return on their money which is assessed by determining the return on capital employed (ROCE) or **prime ratio**.

   $$\text{This is calculated as } \frac{\text{Net profit}}{\text{Capital employed}} \times 100$$

   Thus, for example, if we compare a company with capital of £30,000 and profits in Year 1 of £5,000 and in Year 2 £6,600

   $$\text{ROCE in year 1} = \frac{£5,000}{£30,000} \times 100 = 19\% \text{ approx}$$

   $$\text{ROCE in year 2} = \frac{£6,600}{£30,000} \times 100 = 22\%$$

   So, for every £100 invested in the business, in Year 1 £19 was earned in profit, and Year 2, £22.

18. These would probably be considered as satisfactory returns on capital, but if the return was less than about 10% then it would not be very good because it would be possible to invest money elsewhere, say in a building society and earn a similar rate of return but without the risks involved by investing in a business.

19. **Profit on Turnover (or Profit-Margin Ratio)**

   In order to compare a firm's profits with both previous years and those of other businesses, it is usual to calculate it in percentage terms. The profit margin is used to measure the return on turnover in a business and can be calculated on either gross or net profit.

20. **Example 1**

Turnover = £120,000
Gross Profit = £30,000
Net profit = £12,000

$$\text{\% profit} = \frac{\text{Gross profit} \times 100}{\text{Turnover}} = \frac{30,000}{120,000} \times 100 = 25\%$$

That is for every £100 of sales £25 has been earned as gross profit.

OR

$$\text{\% profit} = \frac{\text{Net profit} \times 100}{\text{Turnover}} = \frac{12,000}{120,000} \times 100 = 10\%$$

21. **Example 2**

	Year 1	Year 2
	£	£
Turnover	400,000	600,000
Gross Profit	100,000	120,000
Net Profit	50,000	66,000

If we compare the 2 years, at first glance, it would seem that most profit was made in year 2 but this does not take account of inflation or the quantity of goods sold and therefore we use a percentage comparison.

Gross Profit to Turnover

$$\text{Year 1} = \frac{100,000}{400,000} \times 100 = 25\%$$

$$\text{Year 2} = \frac{120,000}{600,000} \times 100 = 20\%$$

Thus the firm actually made less gross profit in Year 2.

Net Profit to Turnover

$$\text{Year 1} = \frac{50,000}{400,000} \times 100 = 12\frac{1}{2}\%$$

$$\text{Year 2} = \frac{66,000}{600,000} \times 100 = 11\%$$

From these calculations it can be seen that in year 1 for every £100 worth of goods sold, the cost was £75, the overheads £12.50 leaving £12.50 profit. Whilst in year 2 the cost was £80, the overheads £9 leaving £11 profit.

22. By calculating the percentage profit on turnover, a business can compare its trading results with previous years to see what progress is being made and to take action where needed. For example, they may indicate improved efficiency and better buying or inefficiency, higher overheads and overmanning (i.e. too many staff employed).

Performance Ratios

23. Other important measures of the efficiency of a business include capital (asset) turnover, the rate of turnover, creditors ratio and debtors ratio.

24. **Capital Turnover**

This is used to measure the extent to which an organisation has utilised its capital to achieve its sales. Any investment in capital should lead to an increase in sales which is calculated as turnover of capital rather than as a percentage. The higher the turnover of capital, the better the capital has been used.

$$\text{CAPITAL TURNOVER} = \frac{\text{SALES REVENUE}}{\text{CAPITAL EMPLOYED}}$$

Thus a company with capital of £250,000 and sales of £1 million would have a turnover of capital of 4.

Task 4   **7.4.5, 7.4.6 (N3.2)**

The return on capital, profit on turnover and capital turnover are all inter-related.

1. Calculate each ratio from the following information to show this relationship.

   ABC Company has capital employed of £400,000

   Sales of £800,000 and a net profit of £50,000

2. Comment on your findings

25. **Rate of Turnover**

Turnover is the value of sales over a period of time. The ratio of turnover or stockturn is a measure of how quickly those goods are sold (turned over). It can be measured in two different ways.

$$1. \quad \frac{\text{Value of total sales}}{\text{Average stock at selling price}} \qquad 2. \quad \frac{\text{Cost of goods sold}}{\text{Average stock at cost price}}$$

Thus if a business has annual sales of £24,000 and the average stock at selling price is valued at £2,000, then the rate of turnover, using method 1 is 12 times per year. In other words the stock is turned over about once a month.

26. There are several ways of calculating the average stock, but one of the most popular is as follows:

$$\frac{\text{Stock at the beginning of the year} + \text{stock at the end of the year}}{2}$$

Thus if we have £20,000 of stock at the beginning of the year and £16,000 at the end then our average stock is

$$\frac{20,000 + 16,000}{2} = £18,000$$

That is, at any particular time in the year the business would probably have about £18,000 worth of goods in stock. This is important because stock has to be financed and therefore ties up capital. On the other hand, too little stock might lead to lost sales.

27. The rate of turnover depends very much upon the type of business, since where fresh food is sold such as meat, fish and vegetables, stock must be turned over and replaced quickly. As a result, the business will have a high rate of stock turn, whereas a television, carpet or furniture trader might have goods in stock for several weeks or even months and therefore have a low rate of stockturn.

28. The rate of turnover in a business can usually be increased in two ways:

☐ By **cutting prices** so that customers will buy more or,

☐ By **increasing the amount of advertising** and sales promotion to attract more customers.

Task 5

7.4.5, 7.4.6 (C3.4)

Stock turnover is important to a business because of the costs of storage, finance and because high stock levels can cause liquidity problems if goods prove difficult to sell. Supermarket retailers like Tesco expect stock to turnover every 10-20 days, whilst manufacturing companies like British Steel would expect it to be nearer 90-100 days.

1. Identify the importance of stock turnover to a business.

2. Explain, with reasons, why you would expect Tesco and British Steel to have widely differing stock turnovers.

29. **Creditors Ratio (Average Payment Period)**

This indicates the average time taken by a business to pay its debts. It is important because it can indicate that a firm is having difficulty paying its debts which may eventually create problems with its suppliers. It is calculated as:

$$\text{Average payment period} = \frac{\text{Average trade creditors}}{\text{Total credit purchases}} \times 365$$

Up to 30 days is the normal period allowed by suppliers to pay for credit purchases.

30. **Debtors Ratio (Average Collection Period)**

This indicates the average time taken to collect payments for goods sold. It is important because it is a measure of a firm's credit control and can draw attention to potential bad debts. It is calculated as:

$$\text{Average collection period} = \frac{\text{Average trade debtors}}{\text{Total credit sales}} \times 365$$

31. **Aged Debtor and Creditor Analysis**

If a firm does not collect money owed to it efficiently, it may well experience cash flow difficulties and find itself unable to pay its own debts .If it allows 30 days credit it must try to ensure that payment is made during this period. For example, a firm with credit sales of £120,000 and average debtors of £25,000.

$$\text{Average collection period} = \frac{25,000}{120,000} \times 365 = 76 \text{ days}$$

32. Long delays in receiving payment can create cash flow problems with potentially serious consequences. Therefore, a system of credit control is essential using an **aged debtors list**. This will include names of outstanding debtors, the amounts owed, and the length of time it is overdue which is usually listed by 1, 2, 3 and 6 months.

33. Constant reminders, warnings and possibly legal action must be taken to chase outstanding accounts. Otherwise they may end up being written off as **bad debts** on the assumption that they will never be paid. The average collection period can also be used to improve the efficiency of a credit control department.

34. A business also needs to keep accurate records of its own debts and when they are due for payment. An **aged creditors list** can be used to control payments and make maximum use of the credit period allowed whilst avoiding the dangers of court action being taken.

Overheads/Sales Ratios

35. A large expense item such as the costs of administration or other overheads can be expressed as a percentage of sales.

    For example the ratio of administration costs could b 8% in one year but 12% in the following year. This would indicate a rise requiring investigation.

36. Likewise, if advertising and promotion costs increase from 5% to 10% it would indicate that the increase in advertising and promotion had failed to produce a proportionate increase in sales.

37. **Example**

    Sales £150,000, Administration £20,000, Marketing £8,000, Total overheads £60,000

$$\frac{\text{Administration}}{\text{Sales}} = \frac{20,000}{150,000} \times 100 = 13\%$$

$$\frac{\text{Marketing}}{\text{Sales}} = \frac{8,000}{150,000} = 5.3\%$$

$$\frac{\text{Total overheads}}{\text{Sales}} = \frac{60,000}{150,000} = 40\%$$

Liquidity (Solvency) Ratios

38. Sometimes working capital is a misleading measure of a firm's ability to meet its immediate debts and liquid capital is used instead. Liquidity refers to those assets which are available as cash or can be easily converted into cash, for example bank balances and debtors. The current and acid test are two **liquidity ratios** frequently used:

39. **Current (or Working Capital) Ratio = Current Assets:Current Liabilities**

    For example, a business with current assets of £15,000 and current liabilities of £10,000 would have a current ratio of 15,00:10,000 or 1.5:1. A ratio of 2:1 is generally considered as about ideal. A ratio of less than 1:1 would mean that a firm could not meet its immediate debts because current liabilities exceed current assets. Whilst a ratio of more than 2:1 means that too much capital is being tied up in stock or debtors are taking a long time to pay.

40. The current ratio calculation uses all current assets which includes stock but stock is not always easy to convert into cash, therefore the **Acid Test Ratio** or **Quick Ratio** is usually considered to be a better measure of liquidity.

    Acid Test Ratio = Current Assets less Stock : Current Liabilities

    This measures whether a business can meet its short-term liabilities without having to sell more or reduce its stock levels. Some assets are usually financed by borrowing which incurs interest charges. Consequently, if sales (and therefore revenue) fall, this may affect a firm's liquidity position.

41. For example, a company with current assets of £15,000, stock of £7,000 and current liabilities of £10,000 would have an acid test ratio of:

    $$15,000 - 7,000:10,000 = 4:5$$

    Thus it would have a problem if all creditors demanded to be paid at the same time. A ratio of 1 : 1 is ideal because a business can then meet its objectives without having to sell off stock, possibly at a discount, to obtain cash quickly.

Task 6   7.4.6 (C3.4)

From the following statement, identify some potential advantages and disadvantages of using ratio analysis to assess a company's investment potential.

'Ratio analysis is a technique which may be used to assist management decision-taking or to provide information about a company for shareholders, potential investors, banks, suppliers and customers. But whilst it enables a company's financial performance to be assessed and is useful to indicate trends over a period of time, it is not without its limitations. Since final accounts are prepared at a particular point in time ratios may not reflect the 'normal' situation in a business. Also, because companies can record information and value assets in different ways, comparisons may be imprecise.

Ratio analysis also ignores non-quantitative data about products and developments which may be equally important when assessing a company's growth potential.'

Shareholder Ratios

42. Most companies pay a dividend twice a year, an **interim** (for the first 6 months of their financial year) and a **final** (at the end). A dividend is declared as a percentage of the nominal (face) value of a share, for example, a 5% dividend would pay 5p on every £1 share in the company. Thus a shareholder with 1,000 shares would receive £50. However, because shares can increase or decrease in value, it is more meaningful to use various ratios in order to assess the return.

43. **Dividend Yield**

    The yield is the percentage return on the price paid for shares and is calculated as follows:

    $$\text{Yield} = \frac{\text{Nominal value of share}}{\text{Cost or market price of share}} \times \% \text{ dividend}$$

    Thus if the current market value is £1.50 then:

    $$\text{Yield} = \frac{100}{150} \times 5 = 3.3\%$$

    Generally, lower yields reflect a secure business with growth potential, whilst higher yields suggest riskier investments.

44. **Dividend Cover**

    This is a measure of the number of times a company's earnings cover the dividend payments on its shares. It is calculated as:

    $$\frac{\text{Net profit, after tax}}{\text{Declared dividend on ordinary shares}}$$

45. For example, a company makes a profit of £500,000 and has a tax liability of £200,000. The dividend on preference shares is £50,000 leaving earnings of £250,000 available for distribution. If a dividend amounting to a total of £50,000 is declared on its 100,000 ordinary shares, then it is said to be covered 5 times, i.e.

    $$\frac{250,000}{50,000}$$

46. Dividends can, however, exceed earnings, as for example when a company maintains its dividend despite sharply reduced profits. In this situation, the dividend is uncovered. Sometimes firms deliberately retain profits for future expansion, giving a higher cover. However, a high cover often implies a low yield especially with a quality share whose price may be at a premium to the market.

47. **Earnings per share (EPS)**

This expresses in money terms, the relationship between profits and the number of issued ordinary shares.

$$\text{EPS} = \frac{\text{Net profit after tax}}{\text{Number ordinary shares}}$$

In the previous example:

$$\text{EPS} = \frac{250,000}{100,000} = 2.5\text{p}$$

This figure is useful because it is the denominator of the price earnings ratio which is one of the most widely used investment statistics.

48. **Price/earnings ratio (P/E ratio)**

This is the share price divided by the earnings per share.

$$\text{P/E ratio} = \frac{\text{Market price per share}}{\text{Earnings per share}}$$

Thus a share with a market price of £1.50 and an EPS of 5p would have a P/E ratio of 30:

$$\frac{150}{5} = 30$$

49. Shares of companies with a good profits record tend to have a high P/E ratio and probably usually a low yield. On the other hand, companies with poor profits records will usually have a low P/E ratio.

50. Thus, a share selling at 75p with a P/E ratio of 10 would be less profitable than one selling at 75p with a P/E ratio of 5. Hence, when deciding whether or not to buy a particular share, the P/E ratio can be compared with that of similar companies to determine which is potentially the better buy.

Task 7   **7.4.6 (N3.1)**

Detailed information about share prices are shown daily in the Financial Times and quality newspapers like the Guardian, Independent and Daily Telegraph.

Using these sources:

1. Select 6 shares from each of any 2 sectors, eg Banks, Chemicals or Food Retailing and identify the current market prices, yield and P/E ratio for each share.

2. Comment on your findings and identify which of your chosen shares in each sector you feel represent the best value.

Capital Gearing

51. One of the indicators which may be used to evaluate the financial health and stability of an organisation is its loan gearing. This is simply a measure of the degree to which a business is financed by loans rather than equity capital. Often banks and other lenders will insist that a business applying for a loan puts up a proportion of what is needed as an indicator of its financial stability. In a company, capital gearing refers to the relationship between the amount of fixed interest borrowing (including preference shares and debentures) and equity investment (ordinary shares).

52. Two gearing ratios can be calculated from a company's balance sheet: Capital (CGR) or Income (IGR)

$$\text{CGR} = \frac{\text{Gross borrowing}}{\text{Equity investment}} \times 100$$

The IGR shows the relationship between interest charges and profit and is calculated as follows:

$$IGR = \frac{\text{Interest charges}}{\text{Profit before interest and tax}} \times 100$$

Task 8   **7.4.6 (N3.1, N3.2)**

Obtain copies of the annual reports of two public limited companies. From the accounting information given, calculate the CGR and IGR for 2 years and comment on any possible reasons for changes in the ratios.

53. An organisation with a high proportion of fixed interest securities is said to be **highly geared** because it is committed to making substantial interest payments. This may be beneficial to ordinary shareholders when the company is enjoying buoyant trading and high profits, but detrimental in poor trading. On the other hand, companies with **low gearing** may be unable to pay large dividends because profits are distributed to numerous shareholders and therefore the shares may prove unattractive to investors.

54. Hence there needs to be a balance between the two gears. Overall gearing will depend on a variety of factors such as the asset structure of the firm, the risk associated with the business, the growth rate of future sales and the effect of taxation on dividends.

55. The gearing adopted by an organisation will reflect its changing balance sheet structure as it develops. Expansion may be financed by issuing additional ordinary shares which reduces capital gearing rather than by borrowing which increases it.

Task 9	Capital Gearing		7.4.5, 7.4.6 (N3.2)
	Firm X	Firm Y	
Ordinary Shares	£ 9,000	5,000	
Fixed interest loans	1,000	5,000	
Total capital employed	10,000	10,000	
Year 1			
Trading profit	1,500	1,500	
Less loan interest (at 10%)	100	500	
Net Profit	1,400	1,000	
Return to shareholders	1,400	1,000	
	10,000	5,000	
Year 2			
Trading profit	700	700	
Less loan interest (at 10%)	100	500	
Net profit	600	200	
Return to shareholders:	600	200	
	10,000	5,000	

From the above information:

1. Identify how each of the companies are geared.

2. Calculate the returns on capital employed in each year.

3. State which company's gearing you feel is most beneficial to its shareholders.

Other Performance Indicators

56. Depending on the business, there are many other figures which may be used to measure performance. Even though some are less sophisticated than those discussed so far, nonetheless they can still be of assistance to managers, for example:

❑ Average overtime payments per employee can influence costs.

❑ Time taken to produce a quantity of products, eg number of cars per man/hour may prove a useful measure of efficiency.

❑ Customers per thousand population may indicate market penetration.

❑ Advertising costs per unit of sales may indicate value for money.

❑ Total output per employee may be useful in manufacturing industries.

❑ Turnover per square metre of floor or shelf space is commonly used in retailing outlets.

57. Some objectives, however, may be qualitative rather than quantitative and therefore performance may be more difficult to measure. Examples might include improving the corporate image, environment or welfare of the community.

Summary

58. a) The monitoring of performance is important to ensure that organisations meet their objectives.

b) Other people may also wish to assess performance, including shareholders, banks, customers, suppliers, the Government, competitors, employees and financial analysts.

c) Monitoring performance is needed to help ensure solvency and profitability, to meet tax requirements, maintain financial backing, make comparison with targets and to seek improvements.

d) This could include financial control, performance ratios, production, measurement and quality control.

e) Final accounts can be analysed to provide information on capital owned, capital employed and working capital in a business.

f) Ratio analysis can also be used to assess performance, profitability and solvency of a business.

g) Key performance indicators include the return on capital employed, profit on turnover and capital turnover.

h) Other performance ratios include rate of turnover, creditors ratio, debtors ratio and overhead/sales.

i) The current and acid test liquidity ratios are used to measure a firms' ability to meet its debts.

j) The success of a company can be evaluated from the dividend yield, dividend cover, earnings per share, and the price/earnings ratio.

k) Capital gearing provides a measure of the degree to which a business is financed by loans rather than equity capital.

l) Some indicators may be qualitative rather than quantitative and therefore performance may be more difficult to measure.

Review questions *(Answers can be found in the paragraphs indicated)*

1. Why and how can an organisation measure and monitor its performance? (1)

2. Who might be interested in an organisation's financial information? (1–2)

3. Why does an organisation need to monitor its performance and what comparisons could it make? (3–4)

4. What is the difference between capital owned, capital employed and working capital? (6–11)

5. Distinguish between the return on capital employed, profit on turnover and capital turnover. (16–22)

6. Why is the rate of turnover important in a business? (24–27)

7. What is the difference between the creditors ratio and debtors ratio? (29–30)

8. What do the current and acid test ratios reveal about a business? (38–41)

9. Briefly explain at least three shareholder ratios and why they are used. (42–50)

10. What is capital gearing and why is it important in a company? (51–55)

Assignment – Business comparison   Element 7.4

From the following 2 simplified sets of accounting information, using ratio analyses, compare, illustrate and explain the profitability, (gross and net), solvency and financial performance of the 2 businesses. Both companies operate in the same industry.

ABC LTD

Trading and Profit and Loss Account for the year ended 30th June 199-

Sales	450,000
Less cost of sales	340,000
	£110,000
Gross profit	
Less Expenses	34,000
Net profits before tax	76,000
Provision for taxation	30,000
Net profit after tax	46,000

Balance sheet as at 30th June 199-

Fixed assets		
Land and buildings	£164,000	
Less depreciation	40,000	124,000
Vehicles and equipment	36,000	
Less depreciation	12,000	24,000
		148,000
Current assets		
Stock	82,000	
Debtors	100,000	
Bank	10,000	
	192,000	
Less Current liabilities		
Creditors	48,000	144,000
Net assets employed		292,000
Financed by:		
Share capital (£1 shares)		175,000
Revenue reserves		57,000
8% debentures		60,000
		292,000

Note

- Opening stock was valued at £78,000
- Dividend per share is declared at 10%
- Current stock market price of share is £2.60

continued…

Assignment continued

XYZ LTD

Trading and Profit and Loss Account for the year ended 30th June 199-

Sales	95,000
Less cost of sales	60,000
Gross profit	35,000
Less expenses	17,500
Net profit before tax	17,500
Provision for taxation	7,500
Net profit after tax	10,000

Balance sheet as at 30th June 199-

Fixed assets		
Premises	25,000	
Less depreciation	2,500	22,500
Fixtures and fittings	5,000	
Less depreciation	1,000	4,000
Motor vehicles	12,000	
Less depreciation	4,000	8,000
		34,500
Current assets		
Stock	6,000	
Debtors	3,500	
Bank	5,900	
	15,400	
Less Current liabilities		
Creditors	3,800	11,600
		46,100
Financed by		
Share capital (25p share)		20,000
Revenue reserves		16,100
Bank loan		5,000
8% Debentures		5,000
		46,100

Note
- Opening stock was valued at £4,800
- Dividend per share is declared at 8%
- Current stock market price of shares is 75p.

26 Preparing a Business Plan

This chapter is about the need for planning in an organisation and the factors which need to be considered if the objectives of the plan are to be achieved. To help your understanding of the importance of business planning the rest of this chapter and Element 8.2 take you through the essential stages involved in setting up in business. They are specially written to enable you to apply the knowledge acquired throughout your business studies course and to demonstrate your understanding in a practical and meaningful way. Much of what is covered is revision and therefore may require you to refer back to earlier chapters for help. The tasks can be completed on an individual or group basis. This chapter covers:

- ❑ Corporate Strategic Planning
- ❑ Purpose of Corporate Planning
- ❑ Corporate Planning Framework
- ❑ Starting Your Own Business
- ❑ Why Bother?
- ❑ Purposes of a Business Plan
- ❑ Business Objectives
- ❑ Evaluating a Business Idea
- ❑ Legal Basics

- ❑ Legal Form
- ❑ Law of Contract
- ❑ Insurance
- ❑ Resources
- ❑ Importance of Timing
- ❑ Constraints of Business
- ❑ External Support
- ❑ Professional Advisers

1. We saw in Chapter 1 that a successful organisation requires a set of corporate objectives defining, for example, the market share, profit, or return on investment which it is seeking to achieve within its targeted market segments. The specific objectives of any particular organisation will depend upon such factors as its type, size and stage of development.

2. Thus, for example, when a new business is first set up its main objective may be to break-even simply in order to survive. As it becomes more established it will look to increase its profits and seek to identify new customers to enable it to increase its market share. A well-established business, on the other hand, may look for growth externally by taking over an existing business, or by expanding internally.

3. Other types of organisation, such as charities or theatres, may set objectives which, for example, seek to obtain government grants or subsidies or private sector sponsorship in order to supplement their income.

4. The important point is that all organisations need to set objectives to determine where they want to be in the future and to do this within a corporate planning framework to work out how to get there.

Corporate Strategic Planning

5. If an organisation is to achieve its set objectives, then clearly it must make plans and develop suitable strategies to do so. This requires a comprehensive and systematic corporate approach to planning. which takes into account the capability and resources of the organisation as a whole and the environment within which it has to operate.

6. By its very nature, corporate planning involves a long-term period of 3–5 years and often more, depending upon the type of organisation. A well formulated strategy can last several years, although the plan must be frequently reviewed and updated so that it can be modified as necessary.

Purpose of Corporate Planning

7.   Corporate planning is crucial to the success of an organisation and therefore is a key task of the Chief Executive and senior managers. It is used for a number of purposes which are essential to the organisation's survival and growth including:

☐ to identify all potential long-term objectives and decide which to pursue.

☐ to evaluate the organisation's internal resources including personnel, finance, marketing, production, purchasing and administration.

☐ to identify the organisation's internal strengths and weaknesses and possible external opportunities and threats which it faces. (See SWOT, Chapter 9).

☐ to scan the external environment within which the organisation operates in order to identify changes and trends. The ability to successfully achieve objectives will be affected by broad changes in the political, economic, social and technological environment which in turn can all have an influence on decision making. (See PEST analysis Chapter 9).

☐ to evaluate the present and likely future competitive situation and identify any threats. (See Competitor Analysis Chapter 9).

☐ to review the organisation's position in the market and identify any trends such as increasing or decreasing market share and whether or not the total market is increasing or decreasing.

☐ to manage and co-ordinate all activities and plans throughout the organisation.

☐ to establish a formal planning process with effective feedback and regular review and updating.

☐ to communicate with, involve and motivate all staff.

Task 1   8.1.1 (C3.2)

Choosing any organisation well known to you, such as a school, college or business, identify with examples 5 key reasons why it does or should plan.

Corporate Planning Framework

8.   There are certain common elements of corporate strategic planning which apply to any organisation. They are the mission statement, strategic plan, operating statement and monitoring and evaluation.

9.   **The Mission Statement** – determines the nature and direction of an organisation and says what it is about.

Based on a consideration of the environment in which the organisation operates, it should set out a clear view of the primary purpose of the organisation, its values and distinctive features and provide a rationale for its strategic plan. ICI, for example, is about chemicals and related products. MacDonalds is about hamburgers and fast food, Burtons about men's clothing and Prudential about insurance and financial services.

10. **Examples of Mission Statements**

Bolton College
'To promote, encourage and assist the enhancement of people and organisations through the provision of quality services in Education.'

ASDA
'ASDA's mission is to become the UK's leading value for money grocer with an exceptional range of fresh foods together with those clothing, home and leisure products that meet the everyday needs of our target customers.'

British Gas
'The aim of British Gas is to be a world class energy company and the leading international gas business.'

Task 2

8.1.1 (C3.2)

Consider the organisation in which you work or study.

1. Write down what you think its mission is.

2. Find out what the actual mission is as determined in its strategic plan.

3. Now compare the two and comment on any differences.

11. **The Strategic Plan** is based on the mission statement and develops clear intentions for the organisation in terms of its major objectives and targets and a timescale by which these are expected to be achieved, often 3-5 years. Once the strategy has been determined, an organisation can then make decisions about how it is going to be achieved. This includes decisions about its products and services, the markets and customers to be served, standards of quality and the resources needed.

12. **The Operating Statement** considers each aspect of the strategic plan and determines how it is to be implemented and achieved. It is a detailed action plan which relates the short-term strategy (usually annual) to the longer-term objectives.

13. **Monitoring and Evaluation** is required to allow the organisation to review the progress towards its objectives in a regular and systematic way. It also enables it to consider the continued relevance of its broader strategy and update it as appropriate.

14.

Strategic Planning Process

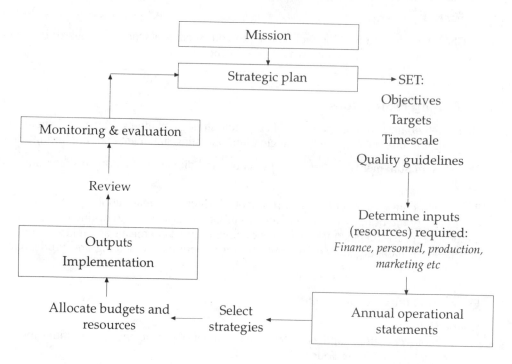

Task 3   **8.1.1 (C3.2)**

State with reasons, how each of the following situations could affect an organisation's strategic planning.

1. A threatened strike.

2. An increase in the number of customer complaints.

3. The introduction of a new product.

4. The appointment of a new board of directors.

5. Investment in production technology.

Starting Your Own Business

15. Around 500,000 new businesses are started every year in Britain. Of these two in five cease trading within the first three years whilst others grow and develop often to become household names like Body shop, Boots, Granada, Pilkington and Virgin.

16. Starting a business is always risky because so many factors cannot be controlled. For example, the state of the economy, level of demand, new legislation and competition. But the chances of success can be considerably improved by giving some thought beforehand to the problems which are likely to be faced. This will involve researching and evaluating the idea in order to collect data for use in producing a business plan.

Why bother?

17. More and more people are considering the option of self-employment. Setting up your own business is both exciting and challenging and if successful can be rewarding both financially and in terms of personal satisfaction. The idea of being one's own boss is appealing to many people, especially to those who may have suffered from redundancy and unemployment.

18. These, however, are not good motives unless they also have a sound business basis which can stand up to the harsh reality of the commercial market place.

19. Whether you are a writer, artist, builder, plumber, taxi driver, run a shop, office, factory, deliver services or whatever, going into business is not an easy matter. There is no such thing as a guarantee of success and it can mean long hours of hard work with few holidays. It also involves taking a financial risk because, no matter how well you have researched your idea, you could lose money.

Task 4   **8.1.1 (C3.2)**

1. List at least 4 reasons why people may want to start their own business.

2. What problems or drawbacks might there be?

20. Whatever the reasons for starting up, it is important for success to have clear business and personal objectives and to set goals which you want to achieve. A mission statement is also needed to indicate the clear direction of the business.

Task 5 8.1.1 (C3.2)

1. List 5 ideas which you believe would make a successful business venture. Include goods and services in your list.

2. Select one which you would like to run and write down the likely business and personal objectives associated with it. You will be asked to use your chosen business to complete the other tasks in this chapter and Element 8.2.

3. Write a mission statement for the business.

Purposes of a Business Plan

21. In paragraph 15 we said that two out of five new businesses fail within three years. Those that survive are the firms that have thought their concept through, have worked out all the eventualities and are 100 per cent committed to their new business. Drawing up a business plan is a crucial factor in all this. This simply sets out your expectations and forecasts on paper.

22. It is needed for a number of reasons:

   ❏ **to clarify your own thoughts** and objectives by writing them down.

   ❏ **to support an application for finance**. You cannot get a bank loan without a plan. Even if you do not need finance, a plan will help you to focus on the main issues that are likely to determine the success of your venture.

   ❏ **to monitor performance** and measure success by assessing progress against the plan.

   ❏ **to set targets** for sales and profit.

   ❏ **to identify the resources** which are needed and the costs involved.

23. A business plan therefore should:

   ❏ explain your idea and why you think there is a market for your product or service, its size and potential. Evidence of market research will help you here. One of the surest routes to business failure is to set up on the basis you think that there ought to be a demand when, in fact, no such demand exists.

   ❏ give details of any competition, its strengths and weaknesses and how you intend to counter it, for example by price or service.

   ❏ an outline of how you intend to market your product or service and the costs involved.

   ❏ include plans for premises and any capital equipment which is needed. A potential lender will want to see evidence that you know your way around the business. Include where you intend to obtain supplies, production plans (if appropriate) and reasons for your choices.

   ❏ give details of your own background and business experience and that of any others involved.

   ❏ state how much of your own money you are proposing to put in.

   ❏ state the amount of financial backing required and what return an investor could expect. They will want to know how you are going to repay the money borrowed and how soon before the business makes a profit.

   ❏ outline the security which you are able to offer.

   ❏ finally, you will need some fairly detailed financial forecasts, including a monthly cash flow and a profit and loss forecast for the first 12 months. The figures given for anticipated sales are absolutely critical because time and again people overestimate what these will be.

24. Preparing a business plan sounds a chore, but it is absolutely essential that you do it. Assumptions based on market research should underlie every figure. On the basis of this information, a bank manager or other financier will decide what form of help they are able to offer. And remember that preparing a plan is a continuing process. It should be regularly updated to keep lenders informed of your progress.

25. A typical business plan is presented in five key parts covering:

   ❐ objectives

   ❐ sales and marketing

   ❐ production

   ❐ resource requirements and

   ❐ financial support data.

Task 6   **8.1.1 (C3.4)**

'HIGHWAY' DISPLAY

Town centre traders are up in arms over a council blitz on shop front displays and advertising boards in Moor Street. One trader, greengrocer Jim Smith, was threatened with having stock from a display removed by the council if he did not move it himself. Said Mr. Smith, who owns Fruit World "I need these displays to advertise for trade. The display at the front gives me 30 per cent of what I sell. We can't survive without them."

The council say they are on the highway.

Mr. Smith said "But other shops have them in the town, and they haven't been told to move them."

A spokesman for the council's Development Services Department said: "It is a question of judgement about whether these displays constitute an obstruction. There are no hard and fast rules, we take each case on its merits."

He went on: "Sometimes these boards do add to the character of the street."

This is something of a special case because, although pedestrianised, it is still a highway.

He declined to comment on Mr. Smith's case, but did confirm they were still looking into it.

---

1. What impact is the above situation likely to have on the business plan for Fruit World?

2. What lesson does it give for business planning in general?

Business Objectives

26. We have mentioned the importance of objectives several times throughout this text. In producing your business plan you will need to identify:

   ❐ what you are trying to achieve

   ❐ how it can be done

   ❐ when it must be done by and

   ❐ how you will know when you have succeeded.

27. Typical objectives for your new business might therefore be:

   ❐ Initially, for the first 6–12 months **to survive** by selling enough goods or services to make sufficient profit to at least **break even**. This may be expressed, for example, as 'to achieve a turnover of £400 per week for the first three months of trading'.

   ❐ As the business develops and becomes more established you will set objectives which **increase market share and profits**. One objective may be to achieve a certain level of sales, eg 200 units per week or a specific turnover value such as £1,000 per week within six months of starting up.

   ❐ In the longer term you may have plans **to expand**, with objectives related to taking on new staff, entering new markets, and developing new products or services within a certain time period e.g. develop one new product a year.

❏ If successful, you may eventually have objectives relating to **further expansion**. For example, to develop from a sole proprietor to become a private or public limited company, to open new branches or locations, possibly to begin exporting or even to establish an overseas subsidiary.

Whatever the objectives, what is important is that they are realistic and have been carefully thought out in line with the business mission statement. Indicating the direction of the business in this way will give a clear purpose and focus, thus helping to identify priorities.

Task 7   8.1.2, 8.2.1 (C3.2)

For your chosen business idea in Task 5, list the main objectives which you would seek to achieve. Remember to include targets with measurable outcomes.

Evaluating a Business Idea

28. Once you have decided on your business idea and objectives, it is time to consider the likely market potential. Some simple **market research** will enable you to assess the viability of your idea. It is better to try and find out at this stage if it is likely to be successful rather than failing in the market place. Remember, if people don't want your idea, it is doomed to failure.

" WE SORT OF HAD OUR HEARTS SET ON SOMETHING ROUND. "

Reproduced with kind permission of Girobank Plc

29. In order to assess the likely consumer appeal

❏ discuss your idea with family, friends and potential customers,

❏ seek advice from your local Training and Enterprise Council, Enterprise Agency or Chamber of Commerce and

❏ study trade journals which are available from local libraries.

❏ try to assess the likely **demand** and identify key trends in the market for your product or service. Gardening products, DIY and health and vegetarian foods, for example are growth markets, whereas records and motor bikes are declining. Clearly it may be unwise to enter a declining market.

30. Other factors to consider are

    ❑ whether or not the market is big enough,

    ❑ can the potential customers pay a price that will enable you to make a profit and

    ❑ what quality standards are required.

31. It is also important to study the strengths and weaknesses of likely competitors from the point of view of image, price, design, quality, reliability, delivery dates and any other factor which might give them a competitive edge.

32. From research, identify the people who are likely to buy your product or service by age, sex, income, occupation and geographical location. Then consider whether what you are offering has a **Unique Selling Point (USP)** which differentiates it from competitors and which through advertising and promotion will persuade people to buy.

33. In markets where products are very similar, depending on what is being sold, examples of USP's might be better service, better prices, faster delivery, wider range, after-sales service, car parking, convenience of location or longer opening hours.

Task 8   **8.1.2 (C3.2)**

1. Taking the 5 business ideas listed in Task 5, list a possible USP for each.

2. For your chosen business, identify the potential competition.

---

34. You will also need to consider the likely **product life cycle** and your ideas for extending it or bringing in new products or services in order to secure your long-term future. Fashion items, for example, are often high profit but have a relatively short life cycle with limited opportunities for repeat sales. Looking ahead is therefore essential to determine where the business will be in 12 months time and what changes are likely to affect it.

35. Other important factors to consider include

    ❑ **any legal constraints**, particularly the increasing impact of European legislation, which might affect your business. Safety, labelling, descriptions, packaging and transport, for example, are all subject to legislation. The need for planning permission might also be important.

    ❑ **the state of the economy** both locally and nationally and how it affects your business. For example, are you setting up in an area of high unemployment and if so, how is this likely to affect sales.

Task 9   **8.1.2 (C3.2, C3.4)**

1. From your own knowledge and experience identify 5 growing and 5 declining markets.

2. Evaluate and compare the ideas identified in Task 5 in terms of likely consumer appeal, competition, life cycle, legal constraints and current economic conditions.

---

36. Once you have gathered and analysed the information you should be in a position to estimate the

    ❑ likely **number of customers**

    ❑ likelihood of **repeat business**

    ❑ likely **volume of sales** e.g. 100 units per week

    ❑ possible **value of turnover** e.g. if each unit sells at £5 then turnover will be £500 per week

    ❑ possible **profit** after deducting all expenses from the turnover.

Legal Basics

37. A wide range of legislation exists which is designed to protect consumers, employees, the general public and businesses themselves. It is therefore important that you have at least a basic understanding of the legislation and how it affects you and your business.

38. Examples, all covered elsewhere in this text, include:

Consumer Protection Act 1987

Trade Descriptions Acts 1968 and 1972

Data Protection Act 1984

Employment Protection (Consolidation) Act 1978

Employment Act 1980

Health & Safety at Work Act 1974

European Safety Directives 1992

Environmental Protection Act 1990

Monopolies and Mergers Act 1965

Restrictive Trade Practices Acts 1956 to 1968

Companies Acts 1948 to 1989

Insolvency Act 1986

Business Names Act 1985

Copyright Act 1956

Patents Act 1977

Trade Union Reform and Employment Rights Act 1993

Task 10

8.1.3 (C3.2, C3.4)

1. Briefly describe how each piece of legislation above might affect your proposed business.

2. Is there any other legislation which you feel could be important? State which and in what ways.

Legal Form

39. Your business can be structured in a number of ways. You may operate as a

☐ sole trader

☐ partnership

☐ limited company

☐ co-operative or

☐ franchise

40. Deciding which is best again requires good professional advice which can be obtained from accountants, solicitors, banks or other agencies. Before you start trading, you must decide on the legal form because it affects taxation and the accounting records which you are required to keep. Even if you are considering running your business from home, it may be advantageous to form a partnership or limited company.

> **Task11**
>
> **8.1.3 (C3.2)**
>
> 1. List the main features of operating as a sole trader, partnership, co-operative and limited company.
>
> 2. How does a franchise differ from the other legal forms of business?
>
> 3. State, with reasons, which form you would choose for your business idea.

Law of Contract

41. It is also very important to have a basic understanding of the law of contract. A contract is a legally binding agreement between two or more parties which if 'broken', gives the 'injured' party the right to claim some form of redress. A contract, which is usually written but may be oral, is valid as long as it has the essential features of offer and acceptance, consideration, intention, capacity and validity.

42. **Offer and Acceptance.** The offer is the terms under which a person is willing to sell or supply something. It will usually include the price, quantity, quality and also any delivery and payment terms. The offer must be accepted to form a contract.

43. **Consideration.** Both parties to a contract must show consideration which means that one must give a profit or benefit in exchange for a promise made by the other. In business, this usually means one party supplying goods or services in return for payment.

44. **Intention** to create a legally binding relationship. This is usually assumed to be the case in business agreements unless a contract states specifically that it is 'binding in honour only'. An example of this would be property bought 'subject to contract'.

45. **Capacity to contract.** For a contract to be binding, the parties to it must have legal capacity. For example, contracts signed by anyone who is under 18 (minors), mentally ill or drunk come into this category and are likely therefore to be declared void.

46. **Validity.** If a contract meets all of the above essential requirements, it is said to be valid and therefore legally enforceable. The only exceptions to this could be where a genuine mistake has been made, some material fact has been withheld (for example, not disclosing details of previous claims on an insurance proposal), deliberate misrepresentation has taken place (under, for example, a breach of the Trade Descriptions Act 1968) or where an unlawful act is intended, such as fraud.

> **Task 12**
>
> **8.1.3 (C3.4)**
>
> State, with reasons, whether or not each of the following situations represents a legal contract.
>
> 1. A bank manager agrees to invest money in your business.
>
> 2. She also agrees to introduce you to a local accountant.
>
> 3. A taxi driver agrees to take you to the nearby station.
>
> 4. The rail travel clerk agrees to sell you a ticket.
>
> 5. A friend agrees to collect you at the station.

Insurance

47. Insurance is essential from the start for almost all kinds of business, to give protection against some of the risks involved. Because premiums vary from company to company as does the promptness with which they pay up on claims, it is often worthwhile to use an **insurance broker** to advise you. They can check premiums and have knowledge of how efficiently claims are usually handled.

48. The main kinds of business insurance are

☐ **Premises, contents, stock and other assets** against fire, theft or damage. These should also be covered for 'consequential loss' caused by the interruption to business. If, for example, a bookshop's stock is destroyed in a fire, then it not only loses the value of the books, but also the loss of business until they can be replaced. This can be covered as can the cost of renting temporary premises if necessary.

☐ **Employer's liability** which is compulsory by law and must be displayed. This provides protection against claims for compensation from staff who have accidents at work.

☐ **Public liability** which is needed to compensate anyone else who may have an accident whilst visiting a firm's premises

☐ **Product liability** to protect against claims for compensation arising from injury or damage caused by the firm's products.

49. Other important types of business insurance include:

☐ **Fidelity Guarantee** to protect against the possible dishonesty of employees such as the stealing of goods and money.

☐ **Bad debt** and risks of losses due to customers not paying for goods bought on credit.

☐ **Motor vehicle**, for which third party insurance is compulsory by law to protect passengers or pedestrians injured in accidents.

☐ **Legal insurance** to protect against prosecution under Acts of Parliament, for example unfair dismissal and unfair trading.

☐ **Professional liability** insurance is needed in some professions such as surveyors and architects to protect against the consequences of mistakes.

50. Some business risks, however, cannot be insured against. For example, you cannot insure against making a trading loss or going out of business. This is because these may be caused by inefficiency, out-of-date stock, changes in fashion or even how hard someone works. These are factors which it is impossible for an insurance company to calculate and therefore are uninsurable risks.

51. Although insurance is expensive, it is a vital precaution because on the one hand you could pay out thousands of pounds in premiums without making a claim. On the other hand, a fire or legal action could wipe out your business overnight and the many years of hard work spent building it up.

Task 13

8.1.3 (C3.2)

1. Not all insurance companies provide insurance for businesses. Find the name and address of 5 companies which do offer such cover and the type of cover provided. You may need to contact a bank, insurance broker, the TEC, Chamber of Commerce or other local agency to obtain your information. Alternatively you could write to the British Insurance Brokers Association, 10 Bevis Marks, London, EC3.

2. Comment on your findings.

52.

Example of Employer Liability Insurance Certificate

Common Accident

CA Bonus

Head Office:
Common House
124 Jupiter Road
London EC1A 0XX

X01 99

X1 5030012/458

Certificate of Employers' Liability Insurance

(A COPY OF THIS CERTIFICATE MUST BE DISPLAYED AT EACH PLACE OF BUSINESS AT WHICH THE POLICYHOLDER EMPLOYS PERSONS COVERED BY THE POLICY)

POLICY No.   X1 00BZ4511 XXX

1. NAME OF POLICYHOLDER   THOMAS TANKENGINE

2. DATE OF COMMENCEMENT OF INSURANCE   15/04/19X1

3. DATE OF EXPIRY OF INSURANCE   14/04/19X2

WE HEREBY CERTIFY THAT THE POLICY TO WHICH THIS CERTIFICATE RELATES SATISFIES THE REQUIREMENTS OF THE RELEVANT LAW APPLICABLE IN GREAT BRITAIN, NORTHERN IRELAND, THE ISLE OF MAN, THE ISLAND OF JERSEY, THE ISLAND OF GUERNSEY AND ISLAND OF ALDERNEY, OR TO OFFSHORE INSTALLATIONS IN TERRITORIAL WATERS AROUND GREAT BRITAIN AND ITS CONTINENTAL SHELF

SIGNED ON BEHALF OF

CA Bonus plc
Authorised Insurer

MANAGER, CA BONUS plc

Resources

53. Having researched your idea you now need to consider the resources required for setting up and running the business. The essential resources can be summarised as:

  ❏ **physical resources** with which to operate, e.g. premises, equipment, raw material, stock and other consumable items such as stationery

  ❏ **human resources**, that is people to actually carry out the work

  ❏ **financial resources**, that is the money to pay for the physical and human resources

54. Another key factor is that of the **time** which anyone starting a business must commit in order to make it successful. It may take many months or years to get a business 'off-the ground'. Meanwhile, coping with all the planning, organising, and paperwork for monitoring and control is very time

consuming. This responsibility and involvement can easily take over your life, producing stress and family problems if time is not properly managed.

55. The actual mix of resources needed will depend upon the size and nature of the business as the following three examples illustrate:

   ❏ A window cleaner might work from home and therefore not need premises, but he would need ladders, a bucket, cloths, detergent and a car or van for transport. A relatively small amount of capital would be required to purchase these items and to possibly pay for someone to help him.

   ❏ A sandwich shop would need to rent or buy suitable premises and a range of specialist catering equipment. Because it is **labour intensive** it would also need to employ staff. Finance is therefore needed to pay for these and also to buy stock from suppliers.

   ❏ A wine bottling plant would be **capital intensive** requiring a large investment in premises and equipment which could be bought or rented, staff would be needed to operate it and, depending on the level of technology involved, some specialist skills may also be required. The costs of supplies and transport must also be considered.

56. Thus, for any business it is important to identify the resources needed and cost involved in order to develop an idea and bring it to the market. This involves estimating the physical, human and financial resources needed for the marketing mix, including design, production, sales and marketing.

Design

57. This refers to the features which goods or services must offer if they are to appeal to consumers. The greater the number of features, the higher the costs of design and production are likely to be. Many businesses today design or modify products with the aid of computers. In Element 3.2 we summarised the main design considerations as performance, appearance, economy and legal and environmental factors.

Production

58. Having decided on the type and quality of product it wishes to make or sell, a business must invest in the plant and equipment of appropriate capacity, and labour with the necessary skills to produce it at a competitive price.

Sales and Marketing

59. Having produced the goods it is necessary to ensure that they reach the final consumer by using the 'right' marketing mix. Depending on the product this is likely to involve the costs of advertising, promotion, distribution and customer services and may include after-sales service (see Unit 3).

Start-up Costs

60. The chart on the following page can be used it give a quick indication of the appropriate start-up costs of a business. This can be used in Element 8.2, Chapter 27 to help develop cashflow and profit and loss forecasts.

Importance of Timing

61. Timing is also of vital importance to business success. Often many months may pass between thinking about a new business and when it actually commences trading. No matter how keen you may be to start, do not be surprised if other people in the plan do not act as fast as you would like. Also, unexpected problems may arise which cause delays. Therefore, never underestimate the amount of time required before you begin trading and be prepared to be flexible in your planning.

62.

Business Start-up costs

Purchase of equipment and fixtures _____
Installation costs _____
Purchase or stock and raw materials _____
Installation of power supplies and raw materials _____
Property
– rent in advance _____
– rates _____
– planning fees _____
– fire and safety equipment _____
– insurance premiums (except transport) _____
Transport _____
– vehicle tax and insurance _____
– petrol, oil and servicing _____
Printing, stationery and postage _____
Advertising _____
Legal Fees _____
Bank Fees _____
Wages and National Insurance (including wages and yourself) _____
Any other expenses (e.g. licences, cleaning) _____
Total _____

Task 14   8.1.5, 8.1.6 (C3.2)

1. For the idea which you chose to pursue in Task 5, identify what essential resources you will need to start up in business.

   Use the list above to help you and add any others which you might think of, for example secretarial or other support services such as telex, fax, wordprocessing, reception and mail boxes.

2. An alternative to starting up yourself would be to buy an existing business. What factors would you need to consider in this situation?

Constraints on Business

63. The co-ordination of all these resources therefore must be carefully planned if a business is to be successful. It is also important to realise that this can take a lot longer than you expect. A new business may be slow to get off the ground and may not break-even for several weeks or even months. This is partly because no matter how well an entrepreneur may plan or how hard he may work, there are a number of constraints which may affect the business and prevent it from achieving its objectives. Therefore, developing a successful business may take considerable time, effort and perseverance.

64. Some of the potential constraints could include:

   ❏ **Production** which may be limited by a lack of skills or the level of technology. If either of these are a problem then they will restrict the marketing effort. There would, for example, be no point in promoting demand for a product which a business cannot supply. In the same way, new products or changes to existing ones must be developed in response not just to identified market needs, but also in relation to the production capacity and capability of the organisation.

   ❏ **Marketing** which may require considerable resources for advertising and promotion, particularly where competition is a major factor. If the marketing mix is wrong sales are likely to be affected.

   ❏ **Sales**, which are only one part of marketing, are the lifeblood of a business. If the price is wrong, customer base too small or number of outlets are too few then sales may fail to reach expectations.

❑ **Administration** which involves record-keeping and essential systems and procedures to enable the business to operate efficiently. If these fail, the business will suffer.

65. It may be possible to overcome some constraints in time, for example, if more capital can be raised, staff trained or new people employed, new sales outlets identified or the customer base increased.

66. Many constraints, however, cannot be controlled because they are external to the business. Examples would be the political (e.g. new legislation), economic (e.g. interest rates), social (e.g. environmental issues) and technical (e.g. developments in new technology) factors discussed in Chapter 9. Any of these could affect the success of a business and may require considerable resources to help offset them and enable the business to survive and prosper.

External Support for a Business Proposal

67. Having researched and evaluated a business idea and discussed its feasibility with others it is necessary to obtain external support for it before developing it into a full business plan. A good starting point is to discuss the idea fully with one or more professional advisors.

Professional Advisers

68. Whether starting from scratch with your idea, buying an existing business or entering into a franchise, professional advice may be essential in order to raise the necessary finance and to assist with the negotiation of the price. It is important to assess key areas of the business, consider all factors involved and seek as much advice as possible to ensure that the idea is a sound proposition. Once trading, professional advisers can save you time and money, freeing you to run your business.

69. Professional advisers you will probably need include:

❑ **An accountant** to help prepare the initial cash flow forms, a set of accounts and to complete tax returns including allowable expenses.

❑ **A bank manager** possibly for a loan but also to discuss your business idea. They have good local business knowledge and can direct you to specialist organisations for help and support. You will also need a separate bank account for your business.

❑ **A solicitor** to handle any legal issues such as the formation of your business, particularly if it is a company or partnership, but also if you buy or lease premises, have to sue a customer for non-payment or indeed if for any reason someone sues your business. Also for preparing employee and other contracts.

Task 15   8.1.4, 8.1.7 (C3.2, C3.4)

An accountant and solicitor will charge you a fee for their services. Operating a bank account also usually involves charges although advice is generally free. An insurance broker, however, does not charge you but instead receives commission from insurance companies on the policies sold.

Suggest how you might go about choosing each of these as your professional adviser and identify what you feel are the most important factors to consider.

---

70. Other sources of support and advice include:

❑ Training and Enterprise Councils

❑ Local Enterprise Agencies

❑ Local Authority Economic Development Units

❑ Local colleges including the one where you are currently studying

❑ Chamber of Commerce

❑ The Small Firms Service

❑ Other self-employed people and local business

Task 16   **8.1.3, 8.1.5, 8.1.6, 8.1.7 (C3.2, C3.4)**

You should now be in a position to draft out a proposal for your business idea. Include in it the legal, insurance and estimated resource implications and indications of possible support from external sources. Use a flow chart incorporating the above to illustrate your proposal and include on it any potential constraints.

Summary

71. a) An organisation needs to plan ahead and forecast its future markets, sales revenue, costs and resources required.

    b) It is important that this takes place within a strategic planning framework which determines the nature and direction of an organisation.

    c) This involves a mission statement, strategic plan, operating statement and monitoring and evaluation.

    d) Starting a business is risky and therefore requires careful planning to increase its chances of success.

    e) A business plan is needed to clarify ideas, set objectives and targets, identify resources, obtain finance and for monitoring and control.

    f) Realistic objectives give a clear purpose to a business and help to identify priorities.

    g) A business idea should be evaluated by carrying out some research into its market viability.

    h) A basic understanding of the legislation which affects a business is vital to avoid breaking the law.

    i) Insurance is needed to give protection against some trading risks, including employer's liability which is compulsory by law.

    j) Physical, human and financial resources, plus time are needed to set up and run a business.

    k) These resources need to be considered in relation to the marketing mix including design, production, sales and marketing.

    l) Constraints on a business and insufficient time for planning may prevent it from achieving its objectives.

    m) Once a business idea has been researched and evaluated support should be sought from professional advisors or other external agencies.

Review questions *(Answers can be found in the paragraphs indicated)*

1. Why is corporate planning necessary? (5–7)

2. Briefly describe the components of the corporate planning framework. (8–14)

3. Why could going into business be described as a risky and difficult matter? (15–19)

4. Why does a business need to plan? (21–24)

5. What are likely to be the initial objectives of a new business and how might they change as it develops? (26–27)

6. How can a business idea be evaluated and why is this necessary? (28–36)

7. Why is an understanding of current legislation important when starting or running a business? (37–38)

8. Outline the main kinds of insurance which a business is likely to need. (47–52)

9. Why is it not possible to insure against some business risks? (50)

10. Briefly describe the essential resources which are needed in a business. (53–55)

11. How do these relate to the marketing mix? (56–59)

12. Give examples of how internal constraints can affect a business. (63–65)

13. Why is it not possible to control some of the constraints which a business has? (66–67)

14. Why is external support needed for a business idea and where is it available from? (68–70)

Assignment – Getting Started   **Element 8.1**

Sharon Evans and Nina Patel are both 18. Since leaving school they have had a number of part-time jobs in the catering trade, but so far have not managed to find full-time employment. For the past six months they have been unemployed. After watching a television programme on healthy eating they have an idea for starting their own business.

Their idea is to produce a small range of quality vegetarian convenience foods, prepared using only fresh vegetables. This could be started from home with the minimum of capital investment. They envisage selling the products in returnable crock pots to the catering trade and in microwave containers for home consumption.

After carrying out some small-scale research they are convinced that there is a local market for the products. However, not knowing very much about business studies they ask you for some written advice about the problems which they may face and what they need to do to get started.

continued...

Assignment continued

1. Explain why they should prepare a business plan.

2. Propose what might be suitable objectives for the business in its first year of trading.

3. Suggest three sources of market research information which could be used to find out about the potential market.

4. a) Define what is meant by 'the catering trade'.

   b) Identify eight potential outlets in your area for Sharon's and Emma's products.

5. Describe what is meant by convenience foods and suggest four local competitors.

6. a) Describe the capital investment which will be needed to start the business.

   b) Suggest three sources of finance which could be used.

7. What other resources will they need to consider and why?

8. List and describe at least five major issues which the girls must resolve before starting up their business, including any legal or insurance implications.

9. List the likely overheads which must be covered.

10. Identify five agencies/organisations which help people to set up or run their own business and say how they might assist the girls with financial, legal, marketing and production matters.

11. Suggest a suitable brand name for the product range and describe four promotional methods which could be used to launch the business.

12. Identify the action which Sharon and Nina now need to take to complete their business plan.

27 Producing a Business Plan

Element 8.1, Chapter 26 covered the essential factors which need to be considered when evaluating a business idea and the collection of data for a business plan. This chapter takes you through the stages involved in actually producing and presenting a business plan. It covers:

- Marketing Plan
- Choosing a Trading Name
- Marketing Mix
- Selling Methods
- Sales Targets
- Marketing Budget
- Production Plan
- Organisation of Production
- Premises

- Resource Requirements
- Obtaining Finance
- Employing People
- Financial Data
- Budgeting and Cash Flow
- Profit and Loss Forecast
- Start-up Balance Sheet
- Taxation and National Insurance
- Monitoring and Reviewing Performance

1. In Element 8.1, Chapter 26 we considered the importance of setting realistic business objectives and what these might be for a new business. Initially this may be little more than being in a position to supply a product when required by the customer. But clearly the need to achieve a certain level of sales to gain a share of the market, break-even and then to make a profit are other objectives, but these may take a little longer to achieve.

2. In this chapter you will be asked to produce and present a business plan for one of the ideas which you developed in Element 8.1, Chapter 26. Therefore we will be looking in more detail at the marketing plan, production plan, resource requirements and financial data and forecasts needed.

Marketing Plan

3. All aspects of a business are concerned with marketing because everything which you do can have an important effect on sales and profits. Marketing is about the total approach to organising and running a business which places an overall focus on the needs of the customer. It includes not just the research needed to assess the demand for a product, discussed in Element 3.2, but a whole range of factors which create an impression of the business. These are essential in reassuring customers that they are dealing with a sound and professional organisation which provides value for money.

4. For example:
   - trading name
   - how the telephone or correspondence is answered
   - the design of business stationery and signs
   - having clean floors and windows in a shop or office
   - the personal appearance and body language of staff
   - the attitude to customers, staff and suppliers
   - how after sales service and/or complaints are dealt with
   - the packaging and presentation of products or services
   - selling techniques used
   - the unique selling point of the business eg better range of stock, friendlier staff, quality products
   - where, when and how advertising takes place
   - knowing about competitors products, prices and service to ensure that yours are at least as good, if not better.

5. In presenting the marketing plan it is important to cover the key elements of the **marketing mix** which are covered in detail in Unit 3: product, price, promotion and place. These need to be planned and considered against a marketing budget and the time schedule needed to achieve objectives.

Choosing a Trading Name

6. The name given to a business can affect the way in which it is perceived by its potential customers. Ideally the name should give customers some idea of the nature and scope of the business, for example, Bathroom World, Rigby's Chippy, Hedley Steelworks. On the other hand it may be just as important to have a name which suggests particular features of the business such as quality, service or value for money. Equally, you may prefer to use your own name.

Task 1   8.2.2 (C3.2)

1. Suggest, with reasons, a trading name for your business.

2. How, if at all, is your choice of name affected by the Business Names Act 1985?

3. Would you use the same trading (brand) name for the products or services which you sell? Give reasons for your answer.

Product

7. Appearance factors such as the size(s), shape(s), colour(s), label(s) and brand name of a product are all very important in attracting customers, as might be guarantees and after-sales service, depending on the product.

8.

Marketing a Product

— 'Handy' shape

SUPER COLA! — Brand name

— Attractive label

500ml — Convenient size

Price

9. Price, to a large extent, will be determined by 'what the market will bear' and the costs which you have to cover. If price is too low, profits may be low and the product could look cheap and inferior to its competitors. On the other hand, too high a price could mean that people will not want to buy. Therefore, it is important to establish a fair price which provides a reasonable profit and retains customer goodwill and future business.

10. **Calculating Prices**

    A simple five step approach to calculating prices is to

    1. Determine your annual salary, which should be at least sufficient to cover your personal and household expenses.

    2. Calculate your business costs for the same period.

3. Total your salary and business costs.

4. Divide the total by the estimated number of sales over the year. This gives the cost per item.

5. To the unit cost, add a margin of profit to give the price charged.

11. In many businesses, an **estimate or quotation** may be requested before a firm order is placed. Examples include builders, decorators, electrical repairs, carpets and office services. Calculating prices here involves ascertaining the costs of materials involved, estimating how long the job is likely to take to complete, relating this time to a proportion of your fixed costs, then adding your wages and a margin for profit.

12. Quotations should express clearly what work is to be carried out and include the terms of payment. They should also have a time limit (eg 30 days) so that the price can be adjusted if additional work is requested or to protect against increases in material or other costs due, for example, to inflation or higher wages.

Task 2   8.2.2 (N3.2)

1. Using the following information, calculate the price per item for a product. The desired profit is 50% on cost.

   Personal salary, £20,000, Wages £30,000, Materials £10,000

   Interest on Bank Loan £12,000, Stationery £400,

   Advertising £1,000, Rent and Rates £6,000. Heat & Light £1,600

   Insurance £2,000, Professional fees (Accountant and Solicitors) £2,000.

2. Consider some of the other factors which in practice may influence the price charged for a product or service and in particular the idea which you selected in Task 5, Chapter 24.

Promotion and Advertising

13. It is essential that people know about your business and what it offers. Promotional activities are used by businesses to maintain and increase sales. This may involve, for example, special offers, after-sales service, quality, price, gimmicks and other features which together offer customers a 'good deal'.

14. Advertising is then used to tell people and to persuade them to buy from you. You can arrange this yourself or through an advertising agency. What is important is choosing which media or mixture will attract most customers at least cost. Examples include newspapers, word-of-mouth, Yellow Pages, signage on vehicles, local radio and even television, depending on the success of the business. Whilst press releases are an important form of free advertising.

Task 3   8.2.2 (C3.2)

1. List and briefly describe at least 6 different methods of sales promotion and 6 different advertising media.

2. Decide on a 3 month promotional campaign for your business idea.

3. Choose appropriate media in which to advertise the campaign.

4. Prepare an advertisement for one of the chosen media.

5. State how you intend to measure and evaluate the success of the campaign.

Place

15. This is about distribution, that is, how products are made available to consumers. Distribution involves the physical process of getting goods from manufacturers to consumers. This includes the

storage, transport and handling of goods which together can represent a significant element of the firm's costs. The objectives of distribution are to get the right quantity, in the right place, at the right time and in the right condition. By right means what is right for the consumer.

Task 4   8.2.2 (C3.2)

Outline for your chosen business idea where any why you feel the emphasis on the marketing mix will need to be placed.

Selling Methods

16. There are many ways in which goods or services are sold and it is important to determine which is best for your business.

17. In making this decision several factors need to be considered including:

☐ the **type of market**, eg local government, industry or commerce or the general public

☐ the **cost** which will vary with the method chosen

☐ the **effort or time involved**, eg personal selling compared with newspaper advertising

☐ the **'normal' practice**, ie how customers would normally expect the goods or service to be sold

☐ **innovation**, ie whether or not a different approach might attract more customers.

Some Examples of Selling Methods

18. Products or Services used in the main by:

Industry or Commerce
Visiting customers yourself
Using a sales team or agents
Mail shots
In trade magazines or publications
At trade exhibitions
To wholesalers
Through Yellow Pages or specialist directories
By newspaper advertising
On bill boards or poster sites
To large companies for them to use your product as promotional aids
Local radio or TV

The Public
In your shop
To a shopkeeper – either direct or through his central buying organisation
Door to door
Party plan or home demonstrations
In a mail order catalogue
By leaflets or mail shot to householders
Shop window cards
Newspaper – especially 'small ads'
Exhibitions, craft and country fairs
Markets
Yellow Pages
Through agents or salesmen
TV, local radio, local cinemas

> ## Task 5
>
> ### 8.2.2 (C3.2, C3.4)
>
> Using the above list and any ideas of your own, determine with reasons the selling methods which you believe are best suited to your new business.

Sales Targets

19. It is important to set realistic sales targets which will enable the overall objectives in the business plan to be achieved. This involves considering all the information available, including the budget available for promotion and selling and then making decisions as to the likely level of sales which in a new business may take time to build up. Information from the trade press and other desk research or field research needs to be analysed in order to determine the market trends, growth potential plus the extent and type of competition.

20. Having done this it is possible to set targets which may be in terms of

   ❏ **turnover** e.g. £1000 per week or £50,000 per annum and/or

   ❏ **volume** e.g. 200 units per week or 10,000 units per annum.

21. Once targets are agreed they must be monitored to ensure that they are being achieved. Failure to meet targets could have serious consequences for income and therefore cash flow as well as affecting the potential profitability and future survival of the business.

Marketing Budget

22. Promotional budgets are discussed in Element 3.3, but it is necessary to note here the importance and difficulty of estimating the cost of marketing for a new business. Ideally you should consider the objectives to be achieved, the best ways to do this and then calculate the cost involved. In practice though, many small businesses simply set aside a small amount for advertising and publicity material based on what they feel they can afford.

23. From your marketing plan, however, you should be able to calculate the potential marketing costs for your business and budget for them just as you budget for other expenses. Never forget that the cost of an effective marketing campaign should be more than offset by the resultant increase in sales.

> ## Task 6
>
> ### 8.2.2 (C3.2)
>
> Prepare a marketing plan for your business idea. In it give details of your proposed 'marketing mix' and how you would plan this within an estimated budget during the first 12 months of trading.
>
> An outline of what to include is given below:
>
> ❏ a summary of the findings from your market research including information about competitors
>
> ❏ the target market identified and how this is supported by your research
>
> ❏ details of your product and its USP
>
> ❏ your sales and marketing targets
>
> ❏ your pricing policy and what this is based on
>
> ❏ an outline of your advertising and promotion plans, including how you are going to launch your business to gain maximum interest and publicity
>
> ❏ identify any promotional materials or equipment needed and where these can be obtained
>
> ❏ your proposed selling methods and ideas for distribution to the final consumer
>
> ❏ how any after-sales service will be handled
>
> ❏ an indication of the timescales involved including that needed for legal formation and 'start-up' planning.

Production Plan

24. The production plan is a statement of how a business intends to create the goods or services to satisfy demand. It will include the identification of suitable premises, the machinery, equipment and raw materials needed and the type and quantity of labour. Other factors not already considered include product design and development, production levels, quality assurance and the time-scale needed for production. In order to consider the requirement of a production plan it is important first to consider the production process.

Organisation of Production

25. The scheduling of production involves organising the activities in a manufacturing plant or service industry to ensure that the product or service is completed at the expected time. In order to achieve this, production can be organised in 3 basic ways – using job, batch or flow production. In practice, however, more than one method may be used. These are discussed in Element 5.1.

26. Having determined the method of production it is then possible to decide on the type of machinery, equipment, raw materials and labour needed to achieve the planned output. Initially, this may depend to a large extent upon what the business can afford.

27. Things to consider include:

   ❏ whether to buy new or second-hand equipment – the latter will be cheaper but may not be as good and may cost more to maintain

   ❏ level of computerised technology required – is this essential to be competitive, will it be cost-effective?

   ❏ what raw materials are needed and when? Quality required, possible substitutes

   ❏ are adequate supplies available at a price which is right for your business

   ❏ suppliers of raw materials – do they deliver, minimum order size, how often, how fast, prices, cash and carry or credit terms?

   ❏ level of stock required which is likely to depend on how quickly and easily supplies can be obtained

   ❏ additional labour required and when, eg full-time, part-time, casual, freelance

   ❏ level of skills, qualifications, experience or training needed

   ❏ cost of employing people compared with the contribution they will make

   ❏ whether or not to sub-contract some work out to other organisations rather than investing in additional sources yourself.

Task 7   8.2.3 (C3.2, C3.4)

Refer back to Task 14 in Element 8.1 and reconsider your list of essential resources in light of the issues raised in paragraph 27 above. Discuss, with reasons, any changes you would make or any additional information you would add.

Premises

28. Finding the right premises, in the right location and at the right price is seldom easy, but the choice of premises can be critical for business success, especially if it is dependant upon a lot of passing trade.

29. As a new small business it is likely that you will initially be renting rather than buying property. Depending on the type of business your choice of premises will be either a:

   ❏ shop;

   ❏ office;

❏ workshop/factory; or

❏ working from home.

30. Many small businesses are **run from home**. Examples, might include driving instructors, builders, insurance agents, mail order, office cleaners, sandwich suppliers, toy makers and childminders. However, whilst this is probably the cheapest, most convenient and quickest way to set up a business, it is nonetheless important that appropriate legal advice is taken in order to avoid potential pitfalls.

31. Examples might include

❏ the need for planning permission from the local authority;

❏ the conditions in your mortgage or property deeds which restrict or forbid business activities;

❏ any local by-laws in existence which might restrict your trade.

32. A **town centre site**, on the other hand, may be easier to find and more accessible for customers but will incur higher overheads, such as rent and rates and involve time travelling to work. Clearly,the choice of location will also depend upon the type of business concerned. A shop, for example, must be well located from the point of view of attracting the type of trade you are looking for and parking may be a major consideration. Whilst a factory may be better located near to a motorway for distribution and supplies.

33. When leasing property, it is important that

❏ a formal agreement is drawn up and checked by a solicitor,

❏ your proposed use for the premises is within the terms of the lease and allowed by the local authority,

❏ you know your rights as a lessee,

❏ you carefully consider the length of the lease in relation to the potential of your business.

34. In practice it may not be possible to find premises which meet your needs 100% and therefore you may need to compromise.

35. The actual search for premises may involve the following:

❏ contacting local estate and business agents

❏ following up advertisements in the press

❏ placing your own advertisement for property

❏ discussing your needs with the local council

❏ following up empty or for sale/to let properties

❏ asking around to find out by word of mouth of any existing properties which may become available.

36. There are a number of costs typically involved with property which you should be aware of including:

❏ **legal fees** – the costs of drawing up and checking a lease, including having to pay the landlord costs

❏ **survey fees** – a structural survey is often advisable, particularly with a full repairing lease, ie one where you are responsible for paying for any repairs to the property

❏ **advance rent** – three months in advance is often required

❏ **planning fees** – if planning permission or change of use is needed

❏ **business rates** – which are paid to the local council

- **installation costs** – such as water, electricity or security systems. Electricity boards often insist on a deposit from new businesses

- **insurance premiums** – which landlords often pass on to tenants

- **alterations** – the costs involved if you wish or need to alter the premises in any way, eg to meet health and safety, environmental health or fire regulations

- **'key money'** – this is a premium, eg £5,000, which sometimes has to be paid for the lease of sought-after properties, such as those located in the main shopping street or centre.

Task 8   8.2.3 (C3.2)

1. Briefly describe where you would choose to locate your business and why. Are there any restrictions which may affect your choice?

2. What potential costs would you face?

Product design

37. An important stage in the creation of new products or the development of existing ones is that of design. The main features which need to be considered, which were discussed in Element 3.2, are the performance, appearance, economy in production, distribution and storage, legal requirements and environmental factors.

Product development

38. It is also important to regularly review the features of all products to ensure that they both still meet customers requirements and are also cost effective to produce. This is particularly important in markets where technology is changing rapidly, as for example, with computers.

39. As discussed in Element 3.3, all products have a life cycle the length of which is affected by changing consumer tastes and expectations, developments in new technology and the introduction of new and improved products.

40. For a firm to remain successful therefore innovation is essential. New products must be developed which cater for changing markets as consumers demand new and better quality products. As sales of one product decline it must be replaced by a new one if the firm is to survive and keep ahead of its competitors.

Production Levels

41. Like many business functions, marketing and production are closely linked. A business must decide on the type and quality of product it wishes to make and sell and then invest in the resources needed, including equipment of the appropriate capacity and labour with the necessary skills, to produce it. If either of these are a problem then they will restrict the marketing effort.

42. There would, for example, be no point in promoting demand for a product which a business cannot supply. Whilst new products or changes to existing ones must be developed in response not just to identified market needs but also in relation to the production capacity and capability of the organisation.

43. Production levels therefore must be determined by how much can be produced and how much can be sold. The two must be considered together otherwise business will be lost through shortages of stock or money will be 'tied-up' in stock which you cannot sell.

Quality Assurance

44. It is important that quality standards are set which must then be regularly monitored to ensure that products are always produced to the required specification.

45. In a manufacturing situation, a widely used definition of quality is that of 'fitness for purpose' whilst in a service environment the 'best possible standard' is often used. But, however it is defined, quality is about the attributes of a product which are needed in order to satisfy a customer.

46. Setting and meeting quality standards usually means that customers are less likely to complain and more likely to purchase again in the future.

Time scales

47. The time taken to manufacture a product will vary considerably depending on what it is and the process used. Bread and cakes, for example, may take less than an hour to bake, a car several hours to assemble, a lift several days to produce, whilst building a house may take weeks or months.

48. Each of these requires raw materials which take time to acquire before being processed and may need to be held in stock which requires finance. Whilst finished products must be checked for quality before despatch. The important point is that production planning must allow time for all the stages involved and this must be recognised when drawing up the business plan.

Task 9

8.2.3 (C3.2)

For your chosen business idea, whether it be a good or service, outline the production plan.

1. Consider all the issues which you feel are appropriate in paragraphs 24–48.

2. Consider the costs involved and how each of these will be financed.

Resource Requirements

49. The production plan is concerned with identifying the **physical** resources needed for a business in terms of premises, equipment, and raw materials. To bring these together, however, also requires **financial** and **human resources** which have been discussed in detail elsewhere in this text. In Element 8.1 we referred to the resource requirements in respect of business planning including the very important aspect of the substantial **time** commitment involved for anyone who runs their own business. Two other important issues to consider in presenting the plan are those of obtaining finance and employing people.

Obtaining Finance

50. Once you have estimated your business's financial requirements you can begin to explore sources of funding. For the new and expanding business, getting enough money at the right time is often the biggest problem. There are many ways to raise business finance but all routes benefit from a properly presented business plan.

Potential sources of finance include:

❑ own funds

❑ Venture capital

❑ Government grants, for example a DTI Regional Selective Assistance grant; Business-Start-Up Scheme run by TECs.

❑ local authorities

❑ equity capital

❑ business development loans are usually available for new and small businesses from banks and other sources

❑ overdrafts

❑ credit from suppliers

51. There is also a Small Firms Loan Guarantee Scheme. In return for a quarterly 'insurance' premium the Government will guarantee a proportion of a loan up to £250,000 over 2 to 7 years and allow capital repayments to be deferred for two years in certain circumstances. This is used where a loan is justified but not supported by a track record or sufficient security.

Task 10   **8.2.4 (C3.2)**

Identify and describe 2 sources of short-term, medium-term and long-term finance and state how each might assist your business idea.

Employing People

52. Initially, it may be possible to run your business by yourself or with limited family help, but if not, or as it expands, it may be necessary to employ staff. Before doing this, it may be worthwhile considering sub-contracting some work which may be more cost effective, especially to iron out short-term trading peaks and troughs.

53. If you do employ staff, it is important to be aware of the legal responsibilities involved, including the payment of wages, tax and national insurance contributions and protection such as unfair dismissal, statutory sick pay, trade unions, health and safety and redundancy.

54. Other issues to address include:

   ❏ determining the exact skills required and wage to be offered.

   ❏ preparing a job description and contract, including terms and conditions of employment.

   ❏ recruitment using an advertisement, Job Centre, Careers Office or private Employment Agency.

   ❏ devising an application form, interviewing and checking references.

   ❏ personnel record-keeping, including a system of review or appraisal.

55. Once staff are appointed, it is important to keep them happy and motivated so that they give of their best.

   ❏ Treat people as you would wish to be treated and set an example of the standards you expect such as punctuality, good manners and commitment.

   ❏ Involve them as much as possible in the business and ask for their ideas and suggestions.

   ❏ Delegate where possible, praise them for work well done and

   ❏ express care and consideration by showing an interest in their domestic circumstances and personal well-being which may have an important effect on their performance at work.

   ❏ Always try to sort any problems quickly and establish a 'grievance procedure' so that an employee knows what to do if they have a complaint.

   ❏ Training is necessary to ensure that staff know why and how a job has to be done. It can also make them more efficient and help to increase productivity.

   ❏ Targets and bonuses are also useful for motivation, leading to greater purpose and productivity.

Task 11   **8.1.3, 8.2.4 (C3.2, C3.4)**

1. Determine the staffing needs of your proposed business. Discuss the role which each employee would undertake.

2. Prepare at least one job description and a draft advertisement and outline how you would undertake recruitment.

3. Discuss the main legislation which would influence your recruitment strategy and conditions of employment.

Financial Data

56. It is estimated that at least 80% of **all** business failures are caused by inadequate record-keeping. Unfortunately, it is often neglected in small businesses where other tasks often take priority. A methodical approach to financial record-keeping is, however, essential. An effective book-keeping system is needed not just to meet tax requirements but also to have vital information readily available about the business, including its:

   ❑ Liquidity
   ❑ Profitability
   ❑ Fixed costs
   ❑ Variable costs
   ❑ Debtors
   ❑ Creditors
   ❑ Working capital
   ❑ Stock levels

Task 12   **8.2.4, 8.2.5 (C3.2)**

Define each of the terms listed in paragraph 56 and state why they are important in a business.

Simple Accounting Systems

57. There are various systems available on the market ranging from simple manual record-keeping to computerised based systems which may be needed as the business grows. The essential records which are required include:

   ❑ Cash Book
   ❑ Sales Day Book
   ❑ Purchases Day Book
   ❑ Ledger
   ❑ Petty Cash Book

Task 13   **8.2.6 (C3.2)**

Define each of the above terms and briefly explain why they are needed in a business.

58. The books described above will provide the necessary information from which an accountant can prepare the annual Trading and Profit and Loss Account and Balance Sheet.

Task 14   **8.2.5., 8.2.6 (C3.2)**

Identify and explain the main information which a Trading and Profit and Loss Account and Balance Sheet gives about a business.

Budgeting and Cash Flow

59. 'Cash Flow' refers to the money which flows into and out of a business over a period (see Element 7.2, Chapter 23). It is important to understand the difference between this and profit. A business may be operating profitably but still unable to meet its day-to-day expenses because its resources are tied up in stock, or even worse, equipment.

60. Part of this problem comes about because for many businesses sales and payments are not made by cash but instead involve credit. For example, an invoice for a sale made in July may not be paid until August or even September. These delays in making and receiving payments can have a significant effect on a business's cashflow. Therefore it is important to plan the cash requirements in a business by preparing a cash-flow budget, revising it at three or six-monthly intervals and checking back against what actually happened. It should be possible to explain any variances and take remedial action if necessary.

61. Certain regular **expenses** can be readily identified such as wages, rent, PAYE, National Insurance Contributions, telephone, insurance and repayments for loans or leasing arrangements. All other expenses should also be included.

62. In order to meet these commitments, you will then need to identify a **sales target** for the business (see paragraph 19). Whether based on firm orders or just expectations, it is important that the target is realistic. Having calculated the cost of materials and additional overheads to achieve your sales target, all these figures can then be included in your forecast. It should also be remembered that there may be a cash flow time lag between actually completing work and being paid for it. Hence, you may well have to meet the costs of materials and wages in advance.

63. Cash flow forecasting can help you to identify potential difficulties in advance, particularly deficient months and thus take appropriate action. During trading, actual and projected performance can be compared and if different, help can be sought from your bank or financial adviser. This is important because they may spot a basic error which can be put right or recommend practical measures to help overcome the problem. An example might be, reducing the time you allow customers to pay and/or asking suppliers for longer credit time, whilst a short-term overdraft may be needed to get through a difficult period or to provide additional working capital if the business is expanding.

64. Thus, the essential points about a cashflow forecast are that:

    ❏ it identifies cash shortfalls before they happen.

    ❏ it enables potential surplus cash to be identified and used efficiently, for example, invested.

    ❏ it emphasises the importance of getting maximum credit and allowing the minimum.

    ❏ it encourages more efficient use of resources and control of costs.

    ❏ it helps to determine decisions about when to buy stock and materials.

    ❏ it helps to determine priorities between spending time obtaining work and actually doing it.

    ❏ it ensures sufficient cash is available for any necessary capital expenditure.

Profit and Loss Forecast

65. Finally, it is important to distinguish between a cash flow and an **operating budget**. Cash flow is about when money which comes into or out of a business and when it is likely to occur whilst an operating budget is concerned with profit and loss. A budget is used to plan the use of resources to achieve objectives. It is important for helping to control costs. Thus, for example, if you allocate £2,000 per month for wages and £100 for advertising, it is important to compare the actual against the budget to ensure that you do not overspend.

66. The operating budget therefore provides a profit and loss forecast as the example paragraph 69 illustrates.

67.   **Example of a cash flow forecast form**

Cashflow forecast

Enter Month		Budget	Actual	Budget	Actual	Budget	Actual	Budget	Actual	Budget	Actual	Budget	Actual
Figures rounded to £'s													
1	Receipts Sales (inc VAT) – Cash												
2	– Debtors												
3	Other Trading Income												
4	Loans Received												
5	Capital Introduced												
6	Disposal of Assets												
7	Other Receipts												
a	Total Receipts												
8	Payment Cash Purchases												
9	Payments to Creditors												
10	Principals Remuneration												
11	Wages/Salaries (net)												
12	PAYE/NI												
13	Capital Items												
14	Transport/Packaging												
15	Rent/Rates												
16	Services												
17	Loan Repayments												
18	HP/Leasing Repayments												
19	Interest												
20	Bank/Finance Charges												
21	Professional Fees												
22	Advertising												
23	Insurance												
24													
25													
26	VAT												
27	Corporation Tax etc												
28	Dividends												
b	Total Payments												
c	Net Cashflow (a-b)												
29	Opening Bank Balance												
d	Closing Bank Balance (c ± Line 29)												

Basic Assumptions – Please specify the following assumptions in completing this form and list any other relevant ones overleaf:
Credit Taken – the average period taken from creditors   Days
Credit Given – the average period given to debtors   Days

68.   **Example of acompleted cash flow forecast for a new business**

Year 1 – Cashflow forecast for Year One

	July	Aug	Sept	Oct	Nov	Dec	Jan	Feb	Mar	April	May	June	TOTAL
	£	£	£	£	£	£	£	£	£	£	£	£	£
Income													
Sales	375	875	1,125	1,325	1,625	2,050	2,375	2,625	2,525	2,150	1,900	1,700	20,650
Outgoings													
Cost of Materials	150	200	250	–	280	370	450	500	550	460	400	360	3,970
Telephone	100	–	100	–	–	150	–	–	200	–	–	150	700
Bank charges	100	–	50	–	–	50	–	–	50	–	–	50	300
Advertising	150	50	50	50	50	50	50	50	50	50	50	50	700
Printing, postage and stationery	50	110	10	20	20	20	30	30	20	20	20	20	370
Motor expenses	450	50	50	50	150	75	100	100	75	75	75	200	1,450
Accountancy fees	–	–	–	–	–	–	–	–	–	–	–	300	300
Insurances	35	35	35	35	35	35	35	35	35	35	35	35	420
Sundry expenses	30	20	20	20	20	20	20	20	20	20	20	20	250
Purchase of equipment	1,000	–	–	–	–	–	–	–	–	–	–	–	1,000
Hire purchase repayment	175	175	175	175	175	175	175	175	175	175	175	175	2,100
Class 2 National Insurance	20	20	20	20	20	20	20	20	20	20	20	20	240
Income tax/Class 4 National Insurance	–	–	–	–	–	1,000	–	–	–	–	–	1,000	2,000
Drawings	700	700	700	700	700	700	700	700	700	700	700	700	8,400
Total outgoings	**2,960**	**1,360**	**1,460**	**1,070**	**1,450**	**2,665**	**1,580**	**1,630**	**1,895**	**1,555**	**1,495**	**3,080**	**22,200**
Net income less outgoings	(2,585)	(485)	(335)	255	175	(615)	795	995	630	595	405	(1,380)	(1,550)
Bank balance b/f	–	(2,585)	(3,070)	(3,541)	(3,286)	(3,111)	(3,878)	(3,083)	(2,088)	(1,557)	(962)	(557)	–
	(2,585)	(3,070)	(3,405)	(3,286)	(3,111)	(3,726)	(3,083)	(2,088)	(1,458)	(962)	(557)	(1,937)	(1,550)
Overdraft interest	–	–	(136)	–	–	(152)	–	–	(99)	–	–	(52)	(439)
Bank balance c/f	**(2,585)**	**(3,070)**	**(3,541)**	**(3,286)**	**(3,111)**	**(3,878)**	**(3,083)**	**(2,088)**	**(1,557)**	**(962)**	**(557)**	**(1,989)**	**(1,989)**

Reproduced by kind permission of Barclays Bank Plc

69.   **Example of an operating budget form**

Operating budget

Enter Month		Budget	Actual	Budget	Actual	Budget	Actual	Budget	Actual	Budget	Actual	Budget	Actual
Figures rounded to £'s													
1	Sales Home												
2	Export												
a	Total Sales												
3	Direct Costs Materials – purchases												
4	Wages and Salaries												
5	Stock Change (Increase)/Decrease												
b	Cost of Goods Sold												
c	Gross Profit [a-b=c]												
d	Gross Profit as % of Sales [c÷a×100=d]												
6	Overheads Production												
7													
8													
9													
10													
11													
12	Selling & Distribution												
13													
14													
15													
16													
17													
18	Administration												
19													
20													
21													
22													
23													
24	Other Expenses												
25													
26													
27													
28													
29													
30	Finance Charges												
31	Depreciation												
e	Total Overheads												
f	Net Profit before Tax [c-e=f]												
g	Sales required to break-even [c÷d×100=g]												

Task 15   8.2.5 (N3.3, T3.3)

For your chosen business idea, prepare a potential cash flow forecast and operating statement for a 12 month period. Use a spreadsheet is possible.

70.   **Example of a profit and loss forecast for a new business**

Year 1 – Profit and loss forecast for Year One												
	July	Aug	Sept	Oct	Nov	Dec	Jan	Feb	Mar	April	May	June	TOTAL
	£	£	£	£	£	£	£	£	£	£	£	£	£
Sales	750	1,000	1,250	1,400	1,850	2,250	2,500	2,750	2,300	2,000	1,800	1,600	21,450
Cost of materials	150	200	250	280	370	450	500	550	460	400	360	320	4,290
Gross profit	**600**	**800**	**1,000**	**1,120**	**1,480**	**1,800**	**2,000**	**2,200**	**1,840**	**1,600**	**1,440**	**1,280**	**17,160**
Administrative expenses													
Telephone	100	–	100	–	–	150	–	–	200	–	–	150	700
Bank charges	100	–	50	–	–	50	–	–	50	–	–	50	300
Overdraft interest	–	–	136	–	–	152	–	–	99	–	–	52	439
H.P. interest	50	50	50	50	50	50	50	50	50	50	50	50	600
Advertising	150	50	50	50	50	50	50	50	50	50	50	50	700
Printing, postage and stationery	150	10	10	20	20	20	30	30	20	20	20	20	370
Motor expenses	450	50	50	150	50	75	100	100	75	75	75	200	1,450
Accountancy fees	–	–	–	–	–	–	–	–	–	–	–	300	300
Insurances	35	35	35	35	35	35	35	35	35	35	35	35	420
Sundry expenses	30	20	20	20	20	20	20	20	20	20	20	20	250
Depreciation of equipment	–	–	–	–	–	–	–	–	–	–	–	200	200
Depreciation of motor vehicles	–	–	–	–	–	–	–	–	–	–	–	1,500	1,500
Drawings	700	700	700	700	700	700	700	700	700	700	700	700	8,400
Total expenses	**1,765**	**915**	**1,201**	**1,025**	**925**	**1,302**	**985**	**985**	**1,299**	**950**	**950**	**3,327**	**15,629**
Net profit (loss)	**(1,165)**	**(115)**	**(201)**	**95**	**555**	**498**	**1,015**	**1,215**	**541**	**650**	**490**	**(2,047)**	**1,531**

Reproduced by kind permission of Barclays Bank Plc

Start-Up Balance Sheet

71. In addition to the cashflow and profit and loss forecasts a bank or other financial backer will want to know not only the amount you wish to borrow and the security available but also:

❏ the total capital requirements of the business
❏ how much you personally are putting into it – usually at least half would be expected and
❏ how the balance is being found.

One way of showing this is to draw up a simple balance sheet.

72. The following example illustrates how the first two balance sheets of a new retail business might look. As explained in Element 7.3 this shows the assets and liabilities of a business at a particular time and can be used to analyse its financial performance and efficiency.

73.

Balance Sheet of J Lawrence as at

1st June 199-	Start-up		30th June 199-	End of Year 1	
Fixed Assets					
Equipment	4,000		4,000 (less 10% depreciation) 3,600		
Vehicles	5,000	9,000	5,000 (less 10% depreciation) 4,500	8,100	
Current Assets					
Debtors	–			520	
Stock	1,600			1990	
Cash	500			800	
	2,100			3,310	
Less Current Liabilities					
Bank Overdraft	1,000			700	
Creditors	800			700	
	1,800			1,400	
Working Capital		300			1,910
Net Assets		9,300			10,010
Financed by:					
Capital	6,300			6,300	
add Net Profit	–			1,210	
Long Term Liabilities					
Bank Loan	3,000			2,500	
	9,300			10,010	

Taxation

74. In considering the financial aspects of your business it is important to understand the implications of taxation. Just about everyone pays tax on income, whether it be PAYE from employment, dividends or interest from investments or an income from self employment or other sources, or some combination of them all.

75. For business purposes, sole traders and partnerships pay income tax. A company pays corporation tax on profits, whilst employees' wages and salaries are subject to income tax. You may also be involved with capital gains tax on the disposal of capital assets.

76. If your business exceeds a turnover of £46,000 (1995–96) for the supply of certain goods and services, you are obliged to charge VAT and pay it over to the Customs and Excise Department, less any VAT on goods and services supplied to you (materials, telephone etc), in the course of business. This has to be paid every month or quarter.

Allowable Business Expenses

77. In your business you are allowed to deduct from earnings any revenue expenditure which is 'wholly and exclusively incurred' in carrying on your trade or profession.

78. This includes business expenses which principally cover:

   ❑ **Cost of raw materials or goods bought for resale.**

   ❑ **Running costs** such as light, heat, rent, rates, advertising, cleaning and insurance. If you use your home as an office, you can claim up to two thirds of the running costs as a business expense, if your tax office agrees. But this may mean having to pay capital gains tax on the 'business' part if the house is sold.

- ❏ **Packing, delivery and carriage costs.**

- ❏ **Wages and salaries.** You cannot count anything taken out by a proprietor but it is possible to reduce tax by paying a salary to your spouse.

- ❏ **Entertaining.** Costs of entertaining staff or overseas visitors are allowed.

- ❏ **Travel.** Costs of business travel and a proportion of the costs of running a car can be claimed.

- ❏ **Interest.** This is allowed on loans and overdrafts for the business, as are any hire purchase or leasing charges.

- ❏ **Business Insurance,** including any taken out on behalf of employees, is allowable.

- ❏ The **VAT element** in allowable business expenses, such as VAT on petrol can also be claimed.

- ❏ **Professional fees** such as legal or audit fees.

- ❏ **Subscriptions to professional or trade bodies.**

- ❏ **Bad Debts** actually incurred are also allowable.

- ❏ **Business gifts** to employees may also be allowable.

Tax and National Insurance Contributions

79. If you employ full or part-time staff on a regular basis, you are legally obliged to deduct tax and National Insurance Contributions (NIC) from their wages. You are also liable to pay employer's NIC. The local tax office will notify you of the amount of tax to deduct for each employee and where to send the money. You are also required to keep a record of each employee's earnings and deductions and to inform your tax office annually of the amounts.

> **Task 16**   **8.1.3, 8.2.5 (C3.2)**
>
> 1. Outline the ways in which taxation and national insurance can affect a business.
>
> 2. Find out what would be the current rates of each payable by a small business?

Monitoring and Reviewing Performance

80. Most businesses, from the largest conglomerate to the smallest, one-man-concern, have one thing in common. The overall objective of making profits, without which no business can survive.

81. As you know, the 2 key elements involved in producing profits are:

- ❏ **generation of sales**, thus marketing is vital to success.
- ❏ **keeping costs down**, and within budget is essential

82. It is necessary therefore to monitor the actual performance of the business against the Business Plan, cash flow and operating budget forecasts. This should take place on a regular basis, at least monthly, so that problems can be identified and remedial action taken where necessary.

83. If, for example, sales are not meeting targets, then it will be necessary both to try and obtain more business and also to look for ways of reducing costs such as overheads or possibly cutting back on staff.

84. If, on the other hand, problems are being caused by slow paying creditors, then tougher credit control measures may be needed. This is vital if cash is tight because later payment makes you late in paying your own debts. This might not only damage your reputation but is also likely to increase your overdraft which in turn costs more in interest, thus reducing the overall profitability of the

business. Therefore, it is important to monitor the **aged debtors** list, analysing it to identify the slow payers on the basis of how much they owe and how long the debts have been outstanding. **Aged creditors** are also important to ensure they are paid on time thus avoiding breach of contract and the risk of legal action and/or loss of future credit.

85. You may find the use of computers helpful for monitoring and controlling your business. The use of new technology is now widespread in businesses of all sizes and ranges from record-keeping to word processing to robots and other forms of computer aided manufacturing.

86. Technology can help to save time and money and increase efficiency and productivity as well as giving a competitive edge. Technology, of course, costs money both for installation and maintenance but should be seen as an investment which is worthwhile it is offers an appropriate profit return to the business.

Task 17 8.1.8, 8.2.1, 8.2.6, 8.3.2, 8.3.3, 8.3.6 (C3.2)

As a final task in this chapter you are asked:

1. To write a **summary** of the key factors to consider in starting your own business.

2. To list the 20 key questions/factors which you feel should be considered before making a decision to start up.

3. To put these in order of priority and explain what would be needed to develop them into an action plan.

4. To discuss the importance of monitoring performance and how this could be done with your chosen business idea.

Summary

93. a) Business objectives are the starting point of a business plan.

b) All aspects of a business are concerned with marketing.

c) A marketing plan should cover the key elements of the marketing mix – product, price promotion and place.

d) The particular mix used will vary with the type of goods and services and circumstances at the time.

e) Marketing activities and sales targets must be planned against an appropriate budget and the objectives to be achieved.

f) A production plan will include premises, equipment, raw materials, labour requirements, the production process, product design and development, production levels, quality assurance and time-scales.

g) Finding suitable premises at the right price is seldom easy but can be critical for business success.

h) Human and financial resources are needed in addition to physical resources for production.

i) Some 80% of all business failures are caused by inadequate record-keeping and accounts.

j) Cash flow, profit and loss forecasts and a start-up balance sheet are all used to evaluate the financial viability of a business.

k) Taxation and national insurance are important financial considerations.

l) Performance should be monitored and reviewed to ensure that targets are met and/or to enable remedial action to be taken.

Review questions *(Answers can be found in the paragraphs indicated)*

1. Identify the key components of a business plan. (1–2)

2. In what sense is marketing concerned with all aspects of a business? (3–5)

3. Outline the importance of the marketing mix in a business planning. (5–15)

4. What factors would a business need to consider when choosing its selling methods and setting its sales targets? (16–21)

5. Why does a business need a marketing budget? (22–23)

6. Identify the main components of a production plan. (24)

7. Why is it so difficult for a business to find the 'right' premises? (28–36)

8. Explain the difference between product design and product development. (37–40)

9. Briefly explain why quality assurance is of importance to a business. (44–46)

10. Identify some potential sources of funding for a new business. (50–51)

11. What issues does a business need to consider when employing staff? (52–55)

12. Explain the significance of cash flow in a business. (59–65)

13. Why might a financial backer want to see a new business's operating budget, profit and loss forecast and start-up balance sheet? (65–73)

14. How is a business affected by tax and national insurance? (74–79)

15. Why does a business need to monitor and review its performance? (80–86)

Assignment – The Business Plan **Elements 8.1, 8.2**

Having completed all the tasks in this chapter you are now asked:

1. To prepare and present a Five Part Business Plan for your business idea. Include clear aims, objectives and targets plus a marketing plan, production plan, resource requirements and financial support data. You may find it helpful to ask a bank for a specimen form to complete.

2. Include all the necessary documentation to support your plan. This, for example, may include some actual market research findings, location or layout plan (if appropriate) and a prototype of your idea.

3. Outline when and how you would monitor and review the plan.

4. Identify at least 5 factors which may cause you to make changes to your plan and describe the action you would take or need to take.

5. Calculate your break-even point.

6. If possible, present your plan to a bank manager and write a report on their reaction to it. If this is not possible, present it to a group of colleagues, teacher(s) or other appropriate person(s). Use visual aids, as appropriate, in your presentation.

7. Identify other possible sources of funding for small businesses. You may need to contact your local TEC, Enterprise Agency or library for this information.

8. Finally, an issue for anyone starting their own business is that of a future pension. Discuss why this is important and how you would go about securing your finances beyond retirement.

28 Planning for Employment or Self-Employment

This chapter is about planning for employment or self-employment. It includes:

- ❏ Types of employment
- ❏ Paid employment
- ❏ Self-employment
- ❏ Voluntary work
- ❏ Statutory requirements
- ❏ Remuneration
- ❏ Statutory deductions
- ❏ Voluntary deductions
- ❏ National Insurance
- ❏ Income tax
- ❏ Tax and the self-employed

- ❏ Self assessment of tax
- ❏ National Insurance and the self employed
- ❏ State benefits
- ❏ VAT
- ❏ Pensions
- ❏ Company registration
- ❏ Working Abroad
- ❏ Sources of information
- ❏ Employment opportunities
- ❏ Employment skills
- ❏ Personal planning

Types of Employment

1. In this text we have discussed a range of different types of organisations each of which offers opportunities for employment. In Element 2.1 we investigated business organisations in both the public and private sector some of which offered paid employment whilst others involved self-employment or voluntary work. Some key points about these types of employment are discussed below and considered in more detail in Element 5.2

Paid Employment

2. Most people still work for someone else and in return they receive a wage or salary. Paid work is available in both public and private sector organisations. In the public sector this could include working for a public corporation, government department or agency or local authority.

3. In the **private** sector you could perhaps work for a small local **sole proprietor** in a shop, office or factory. Alternatively you could work for a **partnership** such as a solicitor, dentist, doctor, accountant or estate agent or a franchise such as MacDonalds, Pronto-Print or Swinton insurance. Many people, however, work for **limited companies** which again could range from relatively small local **private** concerns to large **public companies** with locations not just in the UK but possibly in Europe or even world-wide.

4. In Element 4.2 we considered the types of job roles and working conditions which you might experience in different types of employment, whilst in Element 4.3 we looked at the recruitment procedures which you might have to go through to get such a job.

Task 1	**8.3.1 (C3.4)**

Using local and national newspapers or magazines, identify 3 examples of each of the types of employment outlined in Paragraphs 2 and 3. Wherever possible try to

- ❏ use local examples;
- ❏ choose employment which might interest you and
- ❏ include copies of advertisements.

Self Employment

5. This type of employment could also take many forms. For example, you could **work in the family business** (where one exists) possibly receiving a wage in the form of drawings but also a share of the profit. You could perhaps be a partner or a shareholder if it is a limited company.

6. If there is no family business but you want to work for yourself there are several other types of self-employment which you could consider. These include:

   ❏ **starting-up from scratch** either by yourself or in a partnership with a friend or friends with whom you could pool your ideas, capital and skills.

   ❏ **purchasing an existing business** where someone has done the work needed to get it established as a going concern. This may be more expensive and you will probably need professional advice to help assess its price and potential.

   ❏ **purchasing a franchise** which provides a lot of help and support to help you get started plus the use of an established name.

   ❏ **joining the Government Business Start-Up Scheme**, operated via the TECs which provides help to get you started, details of which are given below.

7. **Business Start-Up Scheme (BSUS)**

   The BSUS (formerly the Enterprise Allowance Scheme) helps unemployed people to start their own business. A weekly allowance is paid for between 22-66 weeks of the new enterprise as well as business training and counselling.

   To qualify:

   ❏ individuals must be over 18 and unemployed for at least 8 weeks

   ❏ have £1000 to invest in the business, although this can be a loan or overdraft

   ❏ the business must be considered suitable for the scheme and should not have started training until accepted.

Self-Assessment

8. Before getting started it is also important to assess your own personal characteristics against those required to succeed in business. By assessing your strengths and weaknesses, it will help you to decide if you have got what it takes. Weaknesses may not necessarily hold you back but you may need help or advice to compensate.

9. The following is a list of 20 factors to help you to assess your suitability for running your own business.

   ☐ I am self disciplined, able to keep control and not let things drift.

   ☐ I have the full support of my family

   ☐ I am ready to work 7 days a week, if necessary

   ☐ I can get on with and communicate well with people

   ☐ I can make considered decisions

   ☐ I can cope under stress

   ☐ I do not give in when the going gets tough

   ☐ I can learn from mistakes and take advice

   ☐ I have the skills and knowledge needed for my business idea

   ☐ I am patient and prepared to work for success

   ☐ I can motivate people

   ☐ I am in good health

   ☐ I am enthusiastic, determined and committed

   ☐ I am aware of the risks involved

☐ I have specific personal and business aims

☐ I am innovative and resourceful

☐ I am good at planning

☐ I would enjoy doing bookwork

☐ I am good at controlling my finances

☐ I am prepared to risk everything if necessary

Task 2　　　　　　　　　　　　　　　　　　　**8.3.1 (C3.1, C3.2)**

1.　Try the above self-assessment, first for yourself and then ask someone who knows you well to carry out the same assessment on you.

2.　Compare the results and comment on any differences.

3.　Identify which you feel are the most important factors and why.

10.　If you are now seriously considering starting your own business then Element 8.1 and 8.2 will guide you through the essential steps to help you on your way. It is important that you consider in detail what it entails, have a clear idea of what you want to do and can support this with a thoroughly researched and carefully prepared business plan.

Voluntary Work

11.　A further type of employment which many people undertake is that of voluntary or charity work. Essentially this means working without any form of payment, although sometimes a subsistence allowance or expenses may be paid. Voluntary workers may either be part-time, perhaps for just a few hours a week, or much longer involving perhaps a 6 or 12 month commitment.

12.　For example, charity shops are usually run by volunteers, the WRVS provides meals on wheels for the elderly, 'specials' are 'employed' to help the police force, primary schools often have 'assistants' to help children with reading, many hospitals have radio stations and country parks are run with the help of volunteer wardens. Government schemes such as Community Action also provide opportunities to do voluntary work (see Element 5.2)

Further afield organisations such as Voluntary Service Overseas (VSO), Oxfam and the Red Cross provide the opportunity to work abroad helping people, particularly in developing nations.

13.　It is important to recognise that people may want to do voluntary work for many different reasons, for example:

❒　some do it to gain experience because they cannot get paid employment

❒　others already in work want to spend a few hours helping people

❒　whilst increasingly many young people like to 'take a year out' to do something completely different after leaving school, college or university.

Task 3　　　　　　　　　　　　　　　　　　　　　**8.3.1 (C3.2)**

1.　Identify 10 examples of voluntary work in the area where you live.

2.　State, with reasons, whether or not you personally would be interested in carrying out voluntary work and if so what it might be.

14.　**Statutory Requirements**

In Element 8.1, we outlined the wide range of legislation which impacts on businesses and you were asked to consider this in relation to a proposed business of your own. When planning for work, whether employment or self-employment you should also be aware of some of the main statutory requirements which will affect you.

15. For example, there are legal requirements covering remuneration, national insurance, income tax and pensions which affect all employees, whilst the self-employed may also need to consider VAT, company registration and state benefits. Whilst anyone seeking employment outside the UK will also need to ensure that they have a passport and any necessary work visas.

Remuneration

16. With the exception of perhaps some charity and voluntary workers most people work for money. An employee has a right to be paid on the basis of their contract of employment. This determines for example their rate of pay, how it is paid, any arrangements for overtime and any holiday and sick pay entitlements. When they are paid employees by law are entitled to receive an itemised pay slip detailing pay and any deductions.

Gross and Net Pay

17. The gross pay of an employee is the total amount earned before any deductions are made. Net pay (or take home pay) is what is actually received after deductions have been made by the employer. There are two types of deductions – statutory and voluntary.

Statutory Deductions

18. These are compulsory and must be deducted by law.

- ❏ **Income Tax** which is collected under Pay as You Earn (PAYE). The amount an employee pays in income tax depends upon their personal circumstances (which determines their allowances) and the rates of tax fixed by the Government. (see paragraph 31.)

- ❏ **National Insurance** which everyone earning over a certain amount has to pay. This money is then used to help finance the National Health Service, provide a range of benefits including unemployment benefit, sickness benefit, state pensions and maternity sick pay. The rate paid varies with the size of a person's income. The higher the income, the bigger the deduction (see paragraph 20).

Voluntary Deductions

19. Many employees choose to have other deductions made straight from their wages, for example:

- ❏ **Superannuation** which is a contribution to an employers private pension scheme. When an employee retires this pension is paid in addition to the state pension
- ❏ **Trade Union subscriptions**
- ❏ **Private medical schemes** for example BUPA
- ❏ **Company social club**
- ❏ **Savings schemes** for example the government Save As You Earn (SAYE) scheme.

National Insurance

20. This is a form of direct taxation collected specifically to help finance the National Health Service and to contribute to the funds needed to provide unemployment and sickness benefits. There are four classes of National Insurance contribution:

- ❏ Class 1 – paid by employees and their employers;
- ❏ Class 2 – paid by the self-employed;
- ❏ Class 3 – paid voluntarily for pension purposes; and
- ❏ Class 4 – paid by the self-employed on their taxable profits between certain upper and lower limits. This is in addition to their Class 2 contribution.

The Class 1 rate paid varies with the size of a person's income, the higher the income the bigger the deduction Employers must also pay National Insurance for ever person employed and they contribute over 50% of the total amount.

21. For example, the amounts payable in 1995/6 for an employee are as follows:

   ❏ Earnings under £58 per week – nil.

   ❏ £58-£440 per week – 10% of the amount over £58 plus £1.16.

   ❏ Contracted out of SERPS (see paragraph 50) – 8.2% of amount over £58 plus £1.16.

   ❏ Married woman's stamp – 3.85% of total earnings.

22. Employees earning less than £58 per week do not pay National Insurance. Employees earning more than £440 per week only pay up to that limit. Employers, however, pay National Insurance on the total earnings of all employees.

Task 4

8.3.2 (N3.2)

Calculate your National Insurance contribution under SERPS if you earned (1) £200 per week; (2) £900 per month; (3) £450 per week.

Income Tax

23. For tax purposes income includes pay, bonuses, tips, pensions and benefits in kind (e.g. company car, cheap loan, mobile phone, health insurance), some state benefits and income from investments (e.g. dividends from shares, interest on savings.)

24. The method used to collect income tax from employers is called **Pay As You Earn (PAYE)**. Under this system employers deduct tax each week or month directly from employees wages before they are paid. The employer then pays the tax to the Inland Revenue. How much tax a person pays depends upon how much they earn, what allowances they can claim and the current rate of tax.

25.

TAX ALLOWANCES 1995/96	
	£
Personal	3,525
Married Couple	1,720
Additional personal and widow's bereavement	1,720
Personal (65–74)	4,630
Married Couple (65–74)	2,995
Personal (75 plus)	4,800
Married Couple (75 plus)	3,035
Age allowance income limit	14,600

26. Everyone who works completes a **tax return (P1)** which the Department of Inland Revenue uses to calculate a **Tax Code**. This code number indicates how much 'Free Pay' an employee can earn before they start to pay tax, for example, a single man with allowances of £4,600 would have a code of 460L. This means he would only pay tax on earnings above this amount.

27. Each week or month the employer uses the Tax Code to calculate the amount of tax to be deducted. This is based on special tax tables provided by the Inland Revenue. This code number will change when someone's personal circumstances change. For example, when a single man gets married he will be given a higher code. The higher the code the more one can earn before being taxed.

28. Notice of Coding

Inland **Revenue**

Issued by
H.M. Inspector of Taxes

**TAX OFFICE NAME AND
ADDRESS PRINTED HERE**

PAYE - Notice to employer of employee's tax
code (or amended code) and previous
pay and tax

BLUE BOTTLES LTD
15 LEWIS ROAD
LONDON NW8 4TR

Date
17/9/95

Employer's PAYE reference
123/B1234

Employee's name   *T P MURPHY*

National Insurance number
*(To be entered on the Deductions
Working Sheet and to be quoted
in any communication)*   *YB 12 3456C*

Works/Payroll no., Branch etc.

Code:
The code of this employee is amended to   *525 H*

for the year to 5 April   **1996**

*Please use this code from the next pay day after you receive
this form and follow the instructions in Part A overleaf.*

Previous Pay and Tax

*Where there is an entry here
please follow the instructions in
both Parts A and B overleaf.*

Previous pay

Previous tax

P6 (T)

29. If someone does not have a Tax Code an employer will deduct tax at what is called 'emergency code'. This means paying a higher rate of tax because the code does not include any allowances. Any tax overpaid will be refunded when the correct code number is known.

30. The tax year runs from 6 April to 5 April the following year. The rate of income tax is set at so much in the £by the Chancellor of the Exchequer. Any changes are announced in the Budget which usually takes place in November each year. The rates of tax for 1995-6 are as follows:

31.

INCOME TAX 1995/96	
Taxable Income*	RATE
£1–3,200	20%
£3,201–24,300	25%
Over £24,300	40%

* Taxable income is income after deducting allowances and outgoings such as mortgage interest and pension contributions.

Tax Forms

The most important tax forms are as follows:

32. P45 which is given to an employee when they leave a job. This gives details of their Tax Code, gross pay to date and the tax deducted. The P45 is in three parts. Part 1 is sent by the employer to the tax office so that they know that the employee has left. Parts 2 and 3 are given to the employee to hand to their new employer. The employer keeps Part 2 and sends Part 3 to the new tax office.

33.

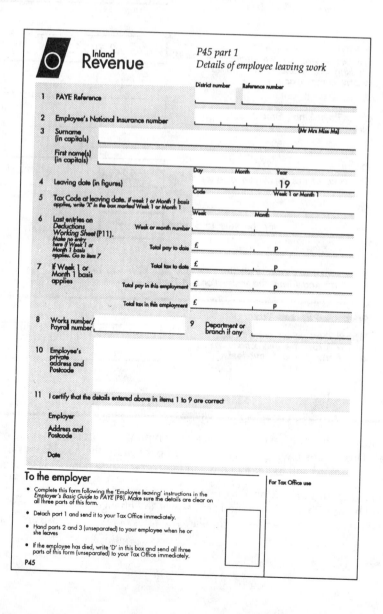

34.

End of Year Summary

				To Inspector of Taxes

Employee's National Insurance number | **Employee's date of birth in figures** *if known* DAY MONTH YEAR | **Enter here 'M' if male 'F' if female**

Tax District and Reference | **Year to 5 April 19**

Employee's Surname in *CAPITALS* | **First two forenames**

Employer's full name and address

National Insurance Contributions in this employment

Contri-bution Table letter	Earnings on which employees contributions payable *Whole £s only* 1a	Total of Employee's and Employer's contributions payable 1b	Employee's contributions payable 1c	Earnings on which employee's contributions at Contracted-out rate payable included in 1a *Whole £s only* 1d	Employee's contributions at Contracted-out rate included in 1c 1e
	£	£	£	£	£
	£	£	£	£	£
	£	£	£	£	£
	£	£	£	£	£

Employee's works/payroll number etc

Employee's private address *if known*

Complete only for occupational pension schemes newly contracted-out since 1 January 1986
Scheme contracted-out number
S 4

Amounts included in the 'Pay' section of the 'This employment' box below ▶	Statutory Sick Pay £	Statutory Maternity Pay £

Date of leaving if before 5 April *in figures* DAY MONTH YEAR	Total for year		Previous employment		This employment	
	Pay	Tax deducted	Pay	Tax deducted	Pay	Net tax deducted or refunded *if net refund mark 'R'*
	£	£	£	£	£	£

For official use

Directors and certain employees:
You need to make a return on form P11D if there were any expenses payments or benefits

Other employees:
You need to make a return on form P9D only if you have made any of the payments shown on that form.

Final tax code	Employee's Widows & Orphan's/life insurance contributions in this employment £	Payment in Week 53. Include pay and tax in totals above and enter 'X', '54' or '56' in this box. See *Employer's Further Guide to PAYE.*

DSS COPY

35. P11 An employer records PAYE on this form which is sent each month the the Department of Inland Revenue.

Task 5   **8.3.2 (N3.2, C3.4)**

> ### RATCLIFF ELECTRICAL COMPANY LTD
>
> School Leaver required for
> **GENERAL OFFICE WORK**
>
> Starting wage £130 pw gross + profit sharing
> Flexitime scheme in operation
> LV's, 40 hour week, annual increments
> Apply giving details of personal interests
> and examinations (to be) taken.
>
> Mr K Shields
> Personnel Manager
> Ratcliff Electrical Co Ltd
> 4 Grant Street
> SKIPTON

Study the advertisement above and answer the following:

Task 5 continued

1. What do you understand by the following?

   a) gross

   b) profit sharing

   c) annual increments

   d) LV's

2. a) Explain how flexitime works

   b) Give one advantage to Ratcliffe Electrical and one advantage to its employees of operating flexitime.

3. Assume that you are successful in getting this job, how much per hour will you be paid?

4. At the end of the first week you receive the following pay slip:

Name	Gross Pay	Tax	NI	Other Deductions	Total Deductions	Net Pay
	£160.00	£27.25	£6.00	£6.50	£ ?	£ ?

   a) What do the letters NI stand for?

   b) Is the NI calculation correct? Give reasons for your answer.

   c) Give two examples of 'other deductions.'

5. Calculate the following from the information given in the pay slip.

   a) Total deductions

   b) Net pay.

Tax and the Self-Employed

36. Although the tax paid by employees is spread out throughout the year if you are self-employed it is paid in a lump sum in arrears. You must keep full and accurate records and accounts for all your transactions and provide the details on your annual tax return. Your profits are then assessed to work out how much tax your must pay.

37. The rules about tax are quite complicated and you must tell your local tax offices as soon as you start in business. The best way to do this is to complete form 41G. This is available from any tax office along with helpful leaflets.

38. If the turnover in your business, before expenses, is less than £15,000 p.a. you only need to send a summary of takings, total purchases, total expenses and profits. For turnover in excess of £15,000 however you must submit detailed business accounts showing the

   ❏ Profit and Loss Account and

   ❏ Balance Sheet.

39. Normally tax will only be assessed after you have completed 12 months trading. But you will then receive two assessments together covering the first two income tax years. If actual figures are not available estimated figures will be used.

40. For example, if you started in business in say January '95 no assessment will be made until some time after January '96. Assessments for both 1995-6 and 1996-7 would then be made. The tax due for 1995-6 would have to be paid in full within 30 days of the assessment (tax bill). The tax for 1996-7 would have to be paid in two equal instalments on 1st January and 1st July 1997.

41. After the initial start-up period tax on the profits of a business is usually paid on these 2 dates each year. If your business makes a loss you can normally claim tax relief for it.

Task 6 **8.3.2 (C3.4)**

The following leaflets are examples of those available from your local Tax Office, Enquiry Centre, or Department of Social Security Office.

1R 28 Starting a business
1R 24 Class 4 National Insurance Contributions
1R 90 Tax allowances and reliefs
1R 105 How your business profits are taxed.

Obtain copies and use them to

1. Find out how business losses are dealt with for tax purposes.

2. Prepare a simple example showing how business tax is assessed.

3. Explain what you can do if you disagree with a tax assessment on your business.

42. **Self assessment of tax**

In an attempt to produce a simpler, cheaper system of tax from April 1997 a new system of assessing and paying tax is being introduced. Under Self Assessment anyone who completes an annual tax return will be able to calculate their own tax liability. A clear timetable of what to will be issued with interest and penalties payable if people fail to comply with the new rules.

National insurance and the self employed

43. As well as informing the Tax Office when you start in business you should also tell your local Department of Social Security (DSS) Office which needs to know for national insurance contribution purposes.

44. The DSS will arrange to collect the flat rate class 2 contributions either by direct debit or quarterly bill. Earnings-related Class 4 contributions, however, are normally calculated, assessed and collected by the Inland Revenue at the same time as income tax or the business profits.

Task 7 **8.3.2 (C3.4)**

Using the leaflets obtained from the Tax Office (or DSS) for Task 6 answer the following:

1. Who pays Class 4 National Insurance contributions?

2. The current rate of Class 4 contributions.

3. How contributions are dealt with if a business makes a trading loss.

State Benefits

45. If you are employed, but on a low wage you may be eligible to receive benefits which will help to supplement your income. For example, **income support, housing benefit,** or a **rebate on your council tax.** Other forms of benefit for which you might be eligible could include **family credit, disability working allowance** and **child benefit** in addition to **unemployment benefit.** Some of these benefits may also apply if you are unemployed and most represent income which you would need to include on a tax return. You may also be entitled to receive extra help in the form of, for example, free prescriptions, free school meals for children, free eye tests and dental treatment.

46. If you are self-employed you may also receive 'benefit' help, particularly to assist you to get started in business, e.g. the Business Start-up scheme, local authority grants, DTI grants or local TEC support.

Task 8

1. With the help of a library, DSS office, Citizens Advice Bureau or other local advice centre, write brief notes on each of the benefits highlighted in paragraph 45.

2. Comment on the role of the Benefits Agency and whether or not you think that state benefits are a good idea. Say in what ways, if any, they might influence your choice of employment.

3. From April 1996 unemployment benefit and income support is being replace by a Jobseekers' Allowance. Write brief notes to explain what it is and why it is expected to help people to find jobs.

Value Added Tax (VAT)

47. This is another consideration for anyone planning to become self-employed. VAT is discussed more fully in Elements 1.3, 6.2 and 7.2. However, it is important to note here that businesses with a turnover of more than £46,000 (1995-6) must register for VAT and submit quarterly returns and payments to the Customs and Excise Department.

48. The VAT on supplies (input tax) can be claimed back but VAT on sales (output tax) must be collected. The business must then either pay the difference or claim VAT back if the input tax is greater than the output tax. Therefore you need to recognise that VAT will need to be added to your prices and that time must be set aside to ensure that accurate VAT records are kept.

Pensions

49. When employees retire from work they are usually entitled to receive a pension. This is a regular payment in consideration of past service which they receive until they die. In the UK a person's pension is paid either by the State, an employer or from a personal pension scheme.

50. **State pensions** involve a flat rate payment to women from the age of 60 and men from 65. This is often topped up by SERPS (State Earnings Related Pension Scheme) under which an additional amount is paid based on the employee's former earnings and how much National Insurance he or she has paid. Self-employed people are not eligible for SERPS. Since 1988, employees in SERPS have been able to 'contract out', that is leave it and take out a personal pension plan instead if they prefer. The retirement age for women is being raised to 65 from 2020.

51. Employers may also pay a separate work-related pension to employees. Such **occupational pension schemes** are often an important fringe benefit when attracting staff. Additionally employers can claim tax relief on contributions.

    Employees can top-up occupational pension schemes by taking out a Free Standing Additional Contribution Scheme (FSACS) on which they receive tax relief.

52. **Personal pension plans** are operated by financial institutions such as banks and insurance companies. Contributions are invested and the resultant pension is therefore dependent upon the amount paid in and the rate of return on the investment.

53. Whatever the type of pension they all require considerable administration, both for the employer and other organisations concerned. Larger organisations which operate an occupational scheme often have a separate pensions department for this work.

54. If you are self-employed, you will need to consider the future and how you can provide income and protect your family when you retire. Therefore it is advisable to take out a personal pension plan. Even though to you retirement may seem a long way off it is nonetheless important to plan for it as soon as possible to ensure that you have adequate provision when it is needed.

Task 9

PENSIONS PROTECTION

New legislation is being introduced following the recommendations of the Goode Report conducted in 1993 which looked at ways in which pension scheme members could be protected. This followed the Robert Maxwell Mirror Group scandal when the funds went missing and and concerns about mis-selling due to bad advice.

Company pension schemes were worth a massive £427 billion at the end of 1994, but until 1995 there were no laws designed specifically to make sure that money is safe, although there is a Pensions Ombudsman to deal with complaints,

Personal Pension Plans (PPPs) were introduced in 1988 as part of a government campaign to extend individual pension choice and privatise part of the state scheme by allowing people to opt out. More than 5 million people have now got PPPs but their apparent success has been marred by a series of scandals.

These were partly brought about because in its eagerness to transfer part of the burden of state pensions to the private sector the government paid little attention to the level of competence of those selling the product (many of whom it was subsequently found had received little or no training) nor did it question the level of charges deducted by pension companies to cover administration costs and sales commission.

In December 1993 the Securities and Investment Board which regulates the investment industry reported that only one in ten PPPs had been sold on the basis of good advice. This triggered a national enquiry to find victims of mis-selling, who were mainly employees wrongly advised to transfer from occupational pension scheme benefit to PPPs. By mid-1995 the enquiry was widened to include sales of PPPs to older employees and low-earners, advised to opt out of SERPs when the state scheme would have provided better benefits.

The main points of the new Pensions Act, following consultation with pressure groups are

❏ A compensation scheme in case of theft or fraud from the pension scheme.

❏ A minimum funding requirement to make sure the fund can pay the pensions.

❏ Up to one-third of a pension scheme trustees can by appointed by its members.

❏ The Occupational Pensions Regulatory Authority (OPRA) set up to police pension schemes.

❏ On divorce, part of a pension will be ear-marked to be paid out as maintenance after retirement.

❏ The State pension age to be equalised at 65 by 2020.

❏ Abolishing the guaranteed minimum pension.

❏ War widows will continue to get their pension if they remarry.

---

1. Explain the following terms which are used in the above article.
   'Occupational schemes.'
   'Personal pensions'
   'SERPS'
   'Compensation Scheme'

2. Why was pensions legislation needed?

3. Identify the key features of the legislation and comment on the impact which you feel it will have on the pensions industry.

Company Registration

55. If you decide to go into business by forming a company then under the various Companies Acts certain legal requirements must be met. (see Element 2.1) Essentially before being allowed to begin trading you will need to draw up the Memorandum of Association and the Articles of Association and send them to the Registrar of Companies at Companies House. If the legal requirements have been met a Certificate of Incorporation will be issued which allows trading to begin.

56. **Example – Certificate of Incorporation**

CERTIFICATE OF INCORPORATION

OF A PRIVATE LIMITED COMPANY

No. 2150456

I hereby certify that

BUSINESS COMPUTER MANAGEMENT SERVICES LIMITED

is this day incorporated under the Companies Act 1985

as a private company and that the Company is limited.

Given under my hand at the Companies Registration Office,

Cardiff the 27 JULY 1987

P. A. Rowley

MRS P.A. ROWLEY

an authorised officer

HCDC7A

Working Abroad

57. If you are seeking employment outside the UK then you will need to ensure that you have a valid 10-year passport. You can get full details and an application form from main Post Offices. Depending on where you live you must return the form, plus 2 photographs and the appropriate fee to the regional office address given. By post processing can take up to two months although personal callers can usually get one the same day.

58. You are also likely to need a visa and/or work permit to enter the country. For **EU countries** this is relatively easy because you can enter the country with a valid passport and stay up to 3 months without any formalities after which a residence permit is compulsory. You should apply for this at a local town hall or police station within 8 days of arrival and for which you will need to prove that you have a means of support.

59. **Outside the EU**, however, work permits and visas can be very difficult to obtain. In virtually all countries you must find an employer willing to apply to the immigration authorities on your behalf, months in advance of the job's starting date, whilst you are still in the UK. Official visa information should be requested from the Embassy or Consulate address in London of the country concerned. It is important to apply in good time because it may take several months for your application to be processed. Travel agents keep copies of the monthly Travel Information Manual (TIM) which contains all visa, customs and other essential information.

Task 10   **8.3.2 8.3.3 (C3.4)**

Your local library will almost certainly contain books about working abroad, either long-term or as a short-term job possibly during the summer.

Find out what you would need to do to work in the following countries:

1. USA.

2. Germany

3. Israel

4. Japan

5. Australia.

Sources of Information

60. Information and advice about all types of employment is available from a wide range of sources. some of the main places include:

□ **Job Centres** which are located in most towns to help people to find jobs. Many employers notify vacancies and use them for recruitment. They can also offer advice on a range of government training programmes.

□ **Employment/Recruitment agencies** are often referred to as 'temp' agencies (see Element 4.3) but many employers also use them to help shortlist and select candidates for jobs. Many people successfully find permanent employment after working for an agency.

□ **Media** including newspapers, television and radio. These are extensively used to advertise job vacancies and also run features on both employment and self-employment opportunities and developments.

□ **TECs** are responsible for organising a range of training programmes to meet local skill needs. They also offer help and advice to people seeking employment or self-employment.

□ **DTI**. This is the government department mainly responsible for developing relations with industry. For example, it offers advice and support to foster the creation and development of small and medium sized businesses and encourage jobs through regional development, inward investment and assistance to exporters.

□ **Local Councils** may provide help for small businesses, for example by setting up enterprise workshops which provide low cost premises for new or developing businesses.

□ **Careers Service** which you probably have already had some contact with whilst at school or college.

61. Depending upon the type of employment you are seeking other sources of information, particularly if you are seeking self-employment, include:

□ **Banks** which produce helpful publications for small businesses. Many also have a small business advisor who provides free advice to people thinking about going into business.

□ **Chambers of Commerce** can provide information and advice, training opportunities and possibly contacts with local businesses or organisations.

□ **Federation of Small Businesses** a nationwide organisation with local branches which provide help for small businesses.

□ **Prince's Youth Business Trust (PYBT)** is a charity which provides professional and financial support to help young people (aged 18-29) in England, Wales and Northern Ireland to set up and continue to run their own business.

Task 11 8.3.3 (C3.2, 3.4)

Libraries are also an invaluable source of information about employment and self-employment opportunities. In addition to information about some of the sources identified in paragraphs 60–61 they also keep books and other publications which may help you.

Visit a local library and identify at least ten specific sources of information which will help you to pursue an employment or self-employment opportunity or idea, including addresses and telephone numbers where appropriate. Comment on how each could be useful to you.

Business Link

62. We have identified a large number of different organisations which can provide information on employment. To make things easier for people seeking self-employment in 1993 the DTI introduced Business Link and a network of 200 is planned by the end of 1995.

63. A Business Link is a partnership usually including TECs, Local Authorities, enterprise agencies, Chamber of Commerce and often banks, accountants, and other local business agencies.

They provide a **'one-stop-shop'** for local small to medium-sized firms based on nationally agreed standards.

64. Personal Business Advisors are expected to maintain regular pro-active contact with a portfolio of firms and provide a link between the client and person with the expertise to assist them with identified problems.

Task 12 8.3.3 (C3.4)

The following is a summary of what a Business Link is seeking to provide.

> To become a Business Link, a local partnership must be committed to a genuine and substantial integration of services to business.
>
> At the heart of the service are three simple resources for business:
>
> 1. A fast and reliable business information service.
>
> 2. Personal advice from commercially experienced business advisers.
>
> 3. Specially tailored services on subjects including:
>
>   ❐ exporting
>
>   ❐ innovation
>
>   ❐ training
>
>   ❐ business health checks
>
>   ❐ events, promotions, conferences and networking opportunities to meet other local business-people.

1. Identify and make contact with your local Business Link. Find out where it is located and when it was established.

2. Comment on its partners, the range of advice they can offer and how the 'Link' can help local businesses.

3. If you are interested in self-employment suggest at least 3 ways in which Business Link could help you.

Alternatively **if you are seeking some other form of employment**, state, with reasons, whether or not you feel that Business Link could have an impact on your potential employment prospects.

Employment Opportunities

65. In Element 5.2 we discussed the changing trends in employment which have and are affecting us all. For example

☐ the continuing decline in manufacturing and growth in service industries

☐ increasing numbers of women in the work-force

☐ more part-time jobs

☐ Sunday trading

☐ short-term contracts

☐ periods of unemployment

☐ rapid developments in communications

and

☐ other technology

in turn leading to

☐ need to constantly update skills

☐ possibility of working from home

☐ computerised 'neighbourhood' work base, rather than travelling to an employer's premises

☐ inter-active links to almost anywhere in the world.

66. Just these few examples help to make us realise that the employment opportunities of the future are likely to be very different and much wider than ever before, and could range from working at home to virtually anywhere in the UK, Europe or even the world.

67. Improvements in transport and communications also assist this process. Examples include the growing motorway network (although the UK has less miles than most other industrial nations), Channel Tunnel, high speed Advanced Passenger Trains, and the development of London's third airport at Stansted and a second terminus at Manchester airport.

68. The point about all this is that when considering what type of employment you would like it is important to examine the full range of opportunities which are available to you. The sources of information identified in paragraphs 60-64 will help you in this as will consideration of the statutory requirements for any particular type of work.

In the next part of this chapter we look at the employment skills needed to match these opportunities, followed by the personal planning which will help you to secure your future employment.

Task 13   8.3.4 (C3.4)

1. Using the sources of information discussed earlier, identify and give brief details of up to ten employment opportunities which might be suitable for you in the UK, the EU and if appropriate anywhere in the world.

2. Comment on how easy, or otherwise, it was to produce your list.

3. Finally state what particular feature(s) attract you to each employment opportunity selected.

---

69. The main differences between an employee and a self-employed person are shown in the table.

	Employee	Self-employed person
Tax	PAYE ('pay as you earn' tax) deducted by employer	Responsible for own tax returns. More deductible expenses. Allowed to pay tax in arrears
National Insurance	Paid partly by the employer and partly by the employee	Responsible for paying own NI contributions
Occupational pension	May be entitled to pension financed by employer	Must pay own pension contributions
Sick pay	Usually receives pay for a certain length of time when unable to work due to illness	No paid sick leave
Holiday pay	Usually receives holiday pay	No paid holidays
Contract of employment	Entitled to one	Not entitled to one
Notice	Statutory minimum	Depends on contract (if there is one)
Unfair dismissal	Allowed to claim	Not allowed to claim
Maternity pay	Entitled	Not entitled
Health and safety	It is the employer's duty to provide for the safety and welfare of the employees	The employer has a lower common duty of care towards a self-employed person
Employer's control	The employer has more control over the way the employee does the job	The employer has less control over the way a self-employed worker does the job

Task 14

8.3.2 8.3.3 8.3.4 (C3.2 C3.4)

Comment with reasons on how, if at all, the above table would help you in preparing a personal plan for employment.

Employment Skills

70. Whether you want to become self-employed or prefer to seek paid or voluntary employment you will need to possess a range of skills. It is important therefore to identify what particular skills you possess and try to match these with your preferred choice of employment. Where there are gaps you may need to consider undertaking training or some other form(s) of help in order to improve those skills. A good way to start may be to evaluate your own **strengths and weaknesses**.

71. For example, some **strengths** could include:

❒ Good at English, French and Maths – qualified to GCSE Grade B.

❒ Physically fit and helpful – only missed 2 days study in the past 3 years.

❒ Conscientious – able to stick at things and get them done.

❒ Neat and tidy worker – good at presentation.

72. On the other hand, some **weaknesses** might include:

❒ Lack of confidence – find it difficult to mix with others.

❒ Impatient – easily get irritated by people.

❒ Poor information technology skills – some knowledge from GNVQ core skills but still not very competent.

❒ Poor timekeeper – have trouble getting out of bed in the morning.

8.3.5 (C3.1)

Task 15

1. Make a list of your ten main strengths and ten main weaknesses. Use your National Record of Achievement to help you with this list.

2. Share and discuss your list with a colleague, preferably someone who knows you well. Comment on whether or not you agree or disagree with their observations.

3. Many people find this Task very difficult to do, particularly when it comes to identifying their weaknesses. In fact, being able to identify strengths and weaknesses is a skill in itself. Comment, if possible with reasons, whether or not this was the case for you.

4. Briefly state how you feel each of your weaknesses could be overcome.

5. Repeat 2 with a colleague, reversing roles, and make a note of your own observations.

73. In considering your strengths and weaknesses you will have already begun to realise that you possess or lack certain skills needed for employment. By developing your skills of self-analysis and evaluation you will be better able to assess your own suitability for particular types of employment.

74. Some of the key skills required for any type of employment are likely to include:

- ❑ **Working with others.** Very few people work alone and therefore the ability to co-operate well and get on with people is important. Team working is usual in most organisations. (See Element 4.1)

- ❑ **Planning.** The ability to organise work activities and the methods to be used to achieve objectives.

- ❑ **Time-management.** Planning your use of time to ensure that you use it effectively and can prioritise work which needs to be completed first.

- ❑ **Setting targets.** This is necessary to ensure that tasks are completed on time and to the required standard.

- ❑ **Reviewing progress.** To ensure that targets are being met and/or to take remedial action if necessary.

- ❑ **Decision-making.** The ability to make judgments and choose between the alternatives available.

- ❑ **Problem solving** to overcome obstacles or difficulties which can restrict progress towards completing tasks and achieving your objectives.

- ❑ **Information receiving and handling.** In most work you will need to use a range of sources of information to complete tasks. It is important therefore to know where and how to find what you need and be able to handle it appropriately.

- ❑ **Communicating.** The ability to communicate both internally within the organisation and externally with customers, suppliers and other contacts is vitally important whether by telephone, letter, personal meeting or whatever. (See Element 2.3)

- ❑ **Applying number.** Another important core skill which employers frequently find that young people leaving schools and colleges are not very competent at doing.

- ❑ **Using information technology.** From the experience of your GNVQ course you will doubtless have realised just how critical this skill is in today's business world. e.g. the ability to input and access data, use spreadsheets and other packages such as Desk Top Publishing and word processing.

Task 16 **8.3.5 (C3.1, C3.2)**

1. Having considered the employment skills identified in paragraph 74 would you wish to amend the list of your own main strengths and weaknesses prepared for Task 15. Give reasons for any changes made **or** say why you feel that no changes are needed.

2. Rate yourself in terms of what you feel your basic level of ability is in each of the skills in paragraph 74 compared with colleagues with whom you work and/or study.

   Use a scale of 1–5 where 1 = excellent, 2 = good, 3 = average, 4 = fair, 5 = poor and comment briefly on each rating given.

3. Share your ratings with a colleague and make notes on the outcome of your discussion.

Personal Planning

75. To increase your chances of success in either finding employment, suitable voluntary work or being involved in your own business it is important to take account of the many factors discussed in this and other chapters and plan accordingly.

76. Your plan will need to include the

   ❏ **Statutory considerations** discussed in paragraphs 14–59.
   ❏ **Sources of help, support and information needed** discussed in paragraphs 60–63.
   ❏ **Actions to be taken** in terms of who, what, why, how, where and when. For example who to contact; where, how and when to contact them; what to request or say and so on.

76. Your plan will also need to be considered against the **time-scales** involved. In the **short-term,** the first 1–12 months, your main concern will be what needs to be done either to set about getting work or making plans to start your own business. In the **longer term** covering the first 1–5 years, you will perhaps need to plan your first career moves and/or the training and experience needed in order to work towards your ultimate goal. If self-employed initially survival and break-even are important but if successful profit growth, market share and expansion may be part of your plan.

77. Finally then, having completed your Advanced GNVQ Business, armed with the skill and knowledge which you have gained, your action plan will take you forward on the road to what will hopefully be a very happy and successful future. Good luck!

Summary

78. a) Employment opportunities are available in both the public and private sector and may be paid, or voluntary or involve self-employment.

   b) All types of employment have statutory requirements which could include national insurance, income tax, pensions, VAT, company registration and state benefits.

   c) Working abroad requires a passport and a visa/work permit.

   d) Everyone in employment or self-employment pays national insurance which is used to fund the NHS and unemployment and sickness benefit.

   e) Everyone is liable to pay tax on income received although the amount paid depends on their allowances and the rate of tax.

   f) The self-employed pay tax on trading profit details of which are submitted annually to the Inland Revenue.

   g) The unemployed and those on low incomes may receive state benefits such as income support, housing benefit, or Council Tax relief.

   h) Sources of information about types of employment include Job Centres, recruitment agencies, the media, TECs, DTI, local councils, Careers Service, banks, Chambers of Commerce, Federation of Small Businesses, the Prince's Youth Business Trust and Business Link.

i) Employment opportunities could range from working at home to virtually anywhere in the UK, Europe or even the world.

j) We all have strengths, weaknesses and specific skills which may influence employment opportunities.

k) Some of the key skills required for employment include working with others, planning, time management, setting targets, reviewing progress, decision-making, problem solving, information seeking and handling, communication, applying number, and using information technology.

l) A personal plan which includes the statutory considerations, sources of information and actions to be taken considered against the time-scales involved will increase your chances of employment success.

Review questions *(Answers can be found in the paragraph indicated)*

1. What types of public and private sector organisations offer opportunities for employment? (2–4)

2. If you were or are planning to become self-employed how might you go about this? (5–10)

3. Give 4 examples of possible full-time or part-time voluntary work. (11–13)

4. Outline the main statutory requirements which affect the remuneration of employees. (16–19)

5. What is National Insurance, who pays it and why is it needed? (20–22, 43–44)

6. Explain what is meant by taxable income and the factors which determine how much tax people pay. (23–31)

7. How are self-employed persons taxed? (36–41)

8. Who is most likely to receive state benefits and why? (45–46)

9. Why is VAT an important consideration for anyone thinking about self-employment? (47)

10. Briefly describe why pensions are important and the types of pension available in the UK. (49–54)

11. What factors would you need to consider if planning to work abroad? (57–59)

12. Outline some of the main sources of advice available about different types of employment. (60–64)

13. Identify some potential employment opportunities and comment on how these are being affected by change. (65–68)

14. Discuss the main skills needed for employment and how you might assess your own level of skills. (70–74, 8–9)

15. What is involved in personal planning for employment and how might it assist you in finding work? (75–77)

Assignment – Planning for Employment or Self-Employment

Element 8.3

1. Select at least three types of employment in which you would be interested (one of which could be self-employment) and prepare a summary, with examples, of the main features of each.

2. Choose **one** type of employment and prepare a list of opportunities in the UK, European Union and/or other international location. Identify the relevant sources of information and statutory requirements relating to it.

3. Record a discussion with colleagues, career/business counsellors or advisers which analyses your personal strengths and weaknesses in relation to the skills needed for the employment opportunity chosen in 2.

4. Finally use the above information to help you to prepare a personal plan for your chosen employment. This should be in four sections covering the:

    ❏ **time** needed to realise your employment or self-employment intentions

    ❏ **information** needed and sources available

    ❏ **actions** to be taken to enable you to become employed or self-employed in either business or voluntary work

    ❏ **statutory requirements** for your selected employment or self-employment opportunity.

Index

Index of names